Dance with the music

Dance with the music

Dance with the music

The world of the ballet musician

ELIZABETH SAWYER

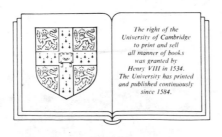

The right of the
University of Cambridge
to print and sell
all manner of books
was granted by
Henry VIII in 1534.
The University has printed
and published continuously
since 1584.

CAMBRIDGE UNIVERSITY PRESS

Cambridge
London   New York   New Rochelle
Melbourne   Sydney

Published by the Press Syndicate of the University of Cambridge
The Pitt Building, Trumpington Street, Cambridge CB2 1RP
32 East 57th Street, New York, NY 10022, USA
10 Stamford Road, Oakleigh, Melbourne 3166, Australia

First published 1985

Printed in Great Britain at the University Press, Cambridge

British Library Cataloguing in Publication Data
Sawyer, Elizabeth
Dance with the music: the world of the ballet musician.
1. Ballet dance music
I. Title
782.9′5   ML3460

Library of Congress Cataloging in Publication Data
Sawyer, Elizabeth
Dance with the music.
Includes index.
1. Musical accompaniment.   2. Ballet dance music.   I. Title.
MT 950.S3   1985   782.9′5   85-10964

ISBN 0 521 26502 9 hard covers
ISBN 0 521 31925 0 paperback

SE

The artist is not a person endowed with free will who seeks his own ends, but one who allows art to realize its purposes through him. As a human being he may have moods and a will and personal aims, but as an artist he is 'man' in a higher sense – he is 'collective man' – one who carries and shapes the unconscious, psychic life of mankind.

Carl Jung, *Modern Man in Search of a Soul*

The future of music may not lie entirely with music itself, but rather in the way it encourages and extends, rather than limits, the aspirations and ideas of the people, in the way it makes itself a part with the finer things that humanity does and dreams of. Charles Ives

Contents

Illustrations

All photographs are by the author, except No.5 (by unknown student).

Acknowledgments

A BOOK can be written in two ways: from the author's personal views, research and theories, or from a wide experience of and interchange with many people. The two, of course, are not mutually exclusive, and this book – like many – is a blend. But the emphasis is strongly on the latter here – so much so that my book is, above all else, a passionate tribute to all of the people who in one way or another are part of it. Because of this, I must cite an unusually large number of names in my acknowledgments.

It is customary to thank those 'without whom this book would not have been possible'. I must go further and say that *this* book could not have reached even the point of conception, let alone realization, without my fortuitous and boundlessly stimulating association with Antony Tudor, in which I was exposed for many years to his ideas, wit, acuity, artistry, imagination, whimsicality, musicality and wily tyranny. (He is *not* to be held responsible for any theories which the reader may consider ill-advised or eccentric.) Thus, Tudor comes first, to be followed by the many others who have enriched, stimulated and helped me: certain focal dance and music associates and friends, members of my music and dance classes – in which the dancers have taught me at least as much as I have them – and remarkable relations.

To: Antony Tudor, who endured, then indirectly and subtly transformed, an embryonic accompanist with fingers of steel and an almost total lack of suitable repertoire into a dedicated collaborator in an enthralling new world. Martha Hill, from whom I have had, through the years, warm friendship and every possible encouragement and assistance in her role of tireless, dedicated and matchless director of the Dance Department of the Juilliard School, New York (aided by the inimitable Mary Chudick). Kazuko Hirabayashi, indomitable and many-faceted, who helped so much at the critical point of a new chapter in my life. Margaret Black and Alfredo Corvino, with whom a long-term, felicitous association vastly increased my knowledge and appreciation of ballet, as well as being deeply rewarding personally. And I owe them much for their practical help in Chapter 8. Margaret Craske and Benjamin Harkarvy, working for whom was also of inestimable value to me, with each – in different ways – adding to my balletic awareness and perception.

To: Maro Ajemian, that so-excellent pianist, teacher and dear friend, who somehow bore my maddening rhythmic deficiencies and rebellious musical tastes.

ix

Vincent Persichetti, whose early musical impact upon me is incalculable, his singular personal magnetism unforgettable, and his huge catalog of works full of 'wonderful stuff'. Dorothy Ann Sarnataro and Helene Carol Lewis, two delightful companions with whom I frequently, if deplorably, played truant to go and glory in the forties' big-band sound from Broadway stages when we should have been in high-school classes. John Nicolas Boyle, my droll and affectionate 'coz', whose untimely death has left a permanent void. His supremely good nature, generosity and merry passion for living will be missed by the many who loved him. He rescued me from my teenage wasteland of high-school musical conventionality, reinforced my belief that music did not end – or begin – with the Three B's, and through the years continually inspired me with the intensity and persistence of his wide-ranging love for music – whether as rapt listener or ardent amateur performer. Robert Dennis, an infinitely good-humored and imaginative fellow-traveller down the more irreverent paths of music. Stanley Wolfe, the most impassioned musician I have ever known, who influenced my musical thinking more than he realizes. Faz Fazakas, who discovered with me, on a momentous day in 1964, the New World of Beatle-harmony. Mildred and John Loftus, in honor of their staunch friendship and help – with special memories of our Yorkshire idylls and Manhattan evenings. Jim Campbell, another lover of the Yorkshire Dales, whose aid, affection and understanding have made many a rough moment smooth, and who, to my joy, shares my love of Britten's music. My dear 'family' at the Windmill: Jim Lias, with his unflappable optimism and infectious passion for music-making as creator and leader of the M6 Breakdown Band, and his wife Audrey, my 'adopted' sister, for her intelligent sympathy, merry company and endless typing. Betty Hargreaves and Marjorie Haggas, two fine friends, who with characteristic Yorkshire forthrightness and hospitality, have brightened my life for so many years. Patricia Townsend, whose leonine bravery, common sense and tenacious, delightful friendship throughout a two-year crisis helped me through the final stages of writing this book. Peter Crowsley, the quintessential Englishman, who has all the winning eccentricities and charm of this breed, in memory of our happy chance meeting at the Aldeburgh Festival, 1970. Michael Brozen, with his keen ear, penetrating mind and beautiful musical creations, who has shared with me and enhanced countless listening-hours, introducing me to treasures ranging from Carissimi's *Jeptha* to Led Zeppelin's 'Gallows Pole'. Edward Pollard, another rock-comrade of longstanding, who helped me out of a very tight spot by his uncannily timed generosity and kindness.

To the dancers. Compelled to be selective, and subject to imperfect memory, I can only hope that the many other dancers who have inspirited me during my teaching and accompanying, or in leisure hours, and whom I would wish to include will sense who they are and forgive my omissions. Regarding all, listed or not, I here record my appreciation for their interest and friendship, and for my students' tolerance (patient or otherwise) of my foibles or pedagogic biases and hobby-horses:

Ahuva Anbary, Airi Hynninen, Anna Rodriguez, Anthony Salatino, Audrey Keane, Beatrice Lamb, Ben Harney, Betty Jones, Blake Brown, Bruce Marks, Bunty

Kelly, Carol Levitt, Carolyn Brown, Catherine Sullivan, Christopher Pilafian, Colette Yglesias, Cynthia Stone, Dalienne Majors, Daniel Lewis, David Blair, David Briggs, David Vaughan, Dian Dong, Diane Grey, Diana Byer, Dianne McPherson, Donya Feuer, Doris Rudko, Elizabeth McCarthy, Elizabeth Sung, Eric Hampton, Ethel Winter, Eugene Harris, Evelyn Thomas, Francia Roxin, Fritz Ludin, Gail Spear, Gayle Young, Gerri Houlihan, Gretchen Langstaff, Hannah Kahn, Harry Bernstein, Helen McGehee, James Waring, Jan Mickens, Jane Hedal, Jane Lowe, Jean Anderson, Jennifer Muller, Jerry Bywaters Cochran, Jerry Weiss, Joyce Herring, Joyce Trisler, Kathy Gosschalk, Lance Westergard, Lar Lubovitch, Laura Glenn, Leslie Brown, Libby Nye, Linda Spriggs, Lisan Kaye Nimura, Lucia, Lynne Wimmer, Margaretha Asberg, Marilyn Banks, Martha Clarke, Martina Ebey, Mary Margaret Giannone, Mercedes Ellington, Michael Uthoff, Micki Goodman, Muriel Topaz, Nancy Mapother, Nanette Hassall, Nina Feinberg, Nurit Cohen, Oshra Ronen, Pamela Kniesel, Patricia Birsh, Paul Sanasardo, Paul Taylor, Peter Sparling, Pina Bausch, Remy Charlip, Revel Paul, Richard Caceres, Robert Lupone, Robert Swinston, Robyn Cutler, Rosanna Seravalli, Saeko Ichinohe, Sallie Wilson, Sally Brayley Bliss, Shebnem Aksem, Sheldon Schwartz, Shirley Brown, Sirpa Joraasma Salatino, Sue Knapp Steen. Susan Osberg, Susan Sindall, Susan Theobald, Susie, Suzanne Smith, Sylvia Yamada Brown, Viola Farber, Virginia Carmany, Virginia Klein, Whitney Rau, William Belle, William Louther, Yaeko Sasaki, Ze'eva Cohen.

And the Transcendent Seven: Chieko Kikuchi, Eleanor McCoy, Emiko Tokunaga, Jennifer Masley Linnell, Sandy Brown, Sarah Stackhouse and Yasuko Tokunaga.

Finally, the profoundest tributes of all, with immense love and gratitude:

To the memory of my mother, Lilian Sawyer, who beyond the most exacting standards of maternal duty, lovingly and gallantly struggled to obtain for me the best possible musical training. Even more important was her unconsciously feminist example for me: that women could go out into the world to work, to enjoy this, and to consider it as important and natural as domesticity.

To the memory of my grandmother, Nan Moore Sawyer, a wise, proud, independent woman, who began my piano lessons when I was but three, developed in me a remarkably early literacy, and instilled a rigorous Yankee realism in a basically romantic spirit. But her greatest gift to me was an infinite curiosity about all of life's marvels. For her, the eighth deadly sin was boredom. The absence of this despised quality in an otherwise sadly flawed granddaughter is a tribute to the talent she had for conveying the joys of learning.

To Martha Jane Wills, technically an aunt, but spiritually a remarkable blend of mother, sister and boon companion. For the five decades since she inexplicably became captivated by an undersized and not particularly prepossessing infant, there has been a tenacious empathy and love between us. And how odd that her great passion, dance, turned out to be so important in my work and life.

To John Francis Brady, who bore, with varying degrees of stoicism but persistent faith, the mental torment and domestic inconveniences of living with a wife who is writing a book. I am deeply indebted to him. My gratitude for his help and loving support – even when he must have felt on many a cold Yorkshire evening like burning my manuscript to get at least some practical value from it – is utterly inexpressible and ineradicable.

Preface

The autonomy of special departments of human activity is a disastrous phenomenon of modern times, and to extend the dividing lines backward into former ages is a falsifying interpretation of history.　　Erich Kahler, *Man the Measure*, 1943

THIS BOOK has several aims, but each is part of one all-encompassing goal: a search for unity – an attempt to amalgamate seemingly diverse elements. Music and movement in ballet are the specific subjects here, and I hope that their treatment will prove to be of value in utilitarian and esthetic ways to musicians, dancers and teachers. But they are also my particular access to the seminal problem of our time: disjunction – or, to use the academic phrase, the dualism of Western civilization; that is, the idea that the world can be split into oppositions: the conflicts of physical *vs.* spiritual, matter *vs.* mind, good *vs.* evil, World *vs.* Self, animal *vs.* man, 'art' *vs.* 'life'. This dualism, as countless thinkers have observed, has led to alienation and perpetual frustration. These, and the related disruptive forces of separatism, elitism and escapism, are increasing, and they underlie every area of our lives, from the mundane to the threateningly apocalyptic. My work has been in the area of the relationship of music and movement – one of the earliest and most fundamental examples of unity in human experience. And, for me, the damage that Western dualism has caused in recent centuries to this ancient relationship offers a microcosm of the general crisis of late twentieth-century society everywhere.

The original impetus for this book came from my growing awareness of how isolated the average musician and dancer are from one another – this in sorry contrast to their earlier harmony. My initial idea was to provide an informative manual for the accompanist such as I would have welcomed when I was a struggling novice. I soon realized, however, that this was not only inadequate and circumscribed, but symptomatic of the disunity itself. How could I isolate and address only one member of an enterprise which involves so many? Thus my potential audience inevitably had to include dancers, teachers and choreographers; musicians who love dance, dancers who love music and all those, professional or amateur, who love both. This resulted in a far more challenging, and often daunting, project, but one about which I cared passionately, particularly when I went on to realize the relevance of the music and dance relationship, with its problems and strengths, to important issues in everyday life outside the studio. Once I perceived this link between 'inside' and 'outside' this book became not only an inquiry into the nature – and possibility – of harmony within the framework of ballet, but also into the meaning of this harmony for the world at large. That world is characterized by the modern mania for categorizing, isolating and narrowly exploiting areas of human knowledge and endeavor. To achieve work of even modest value, the ballet world depends upon synthesis and cooperation. I believe,

xiii

therefore, that it also possesses in microcosm an important *example* for the everyday world. I also believe that we cannot counteract, significantly and enduringly, the disunity which often damages the music–dance relationship without at least some awareness of the larger crisis and how it affects music and dance.

These two arts will be examined from many vantage points, some analytical and practical, others generalized, or, if you like, philosophical. Philosophical, because – in accord with the definition of philosophy as 'that which deals with the most general causes and principles of things' – I feel that solutions lie in a return to integrative principles, for to continue the modern impulse to put the arts in tidy compartments separate both from one another and from 'real life' is simultaneously to degrade 'art' and to deprive society of a profound and healthy force which is desperately needed.

I must, however, leave these larger issues until later, and return now to the original point of departure for the book.

Oddly, considering my goal of 'unity', I at first found myself in a dilemma: on the one hand, I felt that it was worthwhile, and possible, to communicate my experiences as a ballet-musician and the conclusions derived from these; on the other, I recognized the possibility that this would be what Margaret Craske considers the intellectualization of something which is intrinsically not mental at all. An even more serious problem soon materialized; because rhythm is crucial in both dance and music, it figures importantly in this book – yet Antony Tudor has maintained on several occasions that a good rhythmic sense cannot be taught or acquired; it is inherent and intuitive.

Tudor's assertion is somewhat easier for me to challenge than Craske's for I have personal experience here. 'Rhythm' is, essentially, phrasing – and there can have been few young piano students so unable to comprehend or manifest this in their playing as myself. Yet, after playing for ballet long enough to understand movement-phrases, the mystery was finally penetrated. Perhaps the explanation is that I had a (very latent) potential in this area which was only developed by exposure to certain principles of the rhythmic movement of the body – a dramatic, immediate experience in comparison with movement of notes, fingers and piano keys. Ironically, the mystery was solved through the spectacle of Tudor's teaching.

Similarly, I have observed dancers who had hitherto never considered the nature and function of phrasing in dancing make something new and vivid out of a previously flaccid or inflexible movement-phrase when corrected by the teacher. Sometimes the change was slow and infinitesimal, sometimes quick and dramatic. But always it demanded analysis of some sort, and conscious effort, for it involved the breaking of sometimes years-old kinetic habit patterns. What is desirable, of course, is to grow as soon as possible through this stage to a more spontaneous, intuitive approach to rhythmic movement, yet some analysis certainly seems necessary in the early stages of correcting faulty body-rhythm, and, in particular, this within a phrase or sequence of steps.

There are those, however, so opposed to this view that they actually advocate learning-through-mimicking (not Tudor or Craske!). This is perhaps even more common in dance than in music. The teacher shows and the student copies. But even a cursory reading of what has been affirmed by the greatest ballet teachers will show strong rejection of this method. Fine music teachers, likewise, do not want carbon copies of themselves. They encourage thinking and exploration.

So, fortified by these and other reflections, I pressed on with the book in the hope of stimulating thoughts about and reactions to various aspects of the movement–music relationship, many of which have not to my knowledge received much attention in print.

Running throughout the book is my belief that dance and music are connected at their very roots and can be most fully understood and experienced when this is realized. I am not ignoring their differences, but these are comparatively obvious and do not really require attention here. They were born in a unity of impulse and unity of function. Music has its base, to a large degree, in vocal utterance and expression, and dance likewise – only more circuitously: it is gestural, unspoken utterance. Both can be produced by the body alone – without need of external instruments or raw materials. Both, furthermore, move in a special form of *time* – that is, rhythm. This rhythm is different from that of, say, painting or architecture, for it exists within a continuum of elapsed time and must proceed through this in a successional way, whether for 3 minutes or one hour, in order to communicate. There are other similarities also, in which the broader unity may be understood as a primordial impulse to relate and integrate individual experience to the communal.

My views and conclusions developed from my daily experiences, over a long period, of the mutual functioning of movement and music and the special nature of the association of dancer and musician. These experiences took two forms: one, my ballet accompanying in class and rehearsal, and, two, the gradual extension of what I had learned there when I taught music history and theory, and principles of rhythm to dancers in my Literature and Materials of Music, and Musical Coaching classes at the Juilliard School in New York.

I was amazed by the dance students' reaction to musical concepts and even theoretical matters. From my own experience as a former L and M student, I can say that the dancers generally exceeded, in receptivity, involvement and sheer aliveness, most of my fellow-musicians during our own four years of L and M.

How could this be? Why were dancers, training in an art which was already taking 101% (see Appendix A) of their energies able to extend their curiosity and love to include music? Instead of the often bored groups of music students putting in required time but actually existing only for their major lessons in which they would finally practice their art, I saw students who looked upon the classes as places of discovery (albeit of hard work and occasional perplexity, even irritation). And the students' aliveness did not stop there. They were responsive to the *relation* of music to other things – to dance, society, the past, and, simply, existence – in a questing manner which few student (or professional) musicians of my acquaintance had ever shown. As Hugo Cole observes, 'music students involve themselves less in politics, the sister arts, or sociability for its own sake than art students or acting students. The problem for their teachers is often not to encourage them to concentrate on their work but to encourage them to take a look at the world around them.'[1] Instead, they submit to 'the bondage of academic training which lays so much emphasis on the specialist techniques appropriate to nineteenth- and twentieth-century standard classics'.[2]

There is certainly growing resistance to this within the ranks – due in large part to the new climate created by ever-increasing enthusiasm for the more 'primitive' minimalist composers. But, by and large, the average musician's preoccupation with the technical mastery of instruments (the word signifying both sources of sound and means to future stardom) and, often, his blinkered acceptance of a sanctuary consisting of what Cole describes as 'belief in absolute musical truth; in masterpieces without blemish, in god-like master-composers',[3] severs his relation to real live. Cole stresses the dangers of the attitudes of purists, concerned 'only with the ideal ways of performing and understanding music', and analysts who, 'blinded by staring too long at the sun, retreat into the inner recesses of their minds'.[4]

In general, dancers are more irreverent regarding the stuff of their art. Their motley, communal lifestyle militates against the psychological isolation of what Cole calls 'would-be soloists who live perpetually in a land of unrealistic hopes',[5] and the physical dangers that eternally threaten their so-vulnerable bodies tend to reduce sharply absolutism in any form (although rampant egotism can intrude in the ballet studio as elsewhere).

While teaching, I at first simply luxuriated in the chance to draw on a vast spectrum to illustrate my musical points and get those vivid reactions that contrasted so sharply with my own experience of music classes, both as student and, later, observer.

As I got to know the dancers better, I came to see that the difference was due to a combination of their comparative irreverence and their musical orientation. Often untrained in music, or trained to a different end, they were free to respond in ways which musicians, still trapped in their inherited assumptions, could not. *But* in their own field, they often displayed the musicians' absorption in technical problems and unrealistic hopes for a career. With dancers, however, two prime realities militate against technomania, egocentrism, and insularity. First, any sensible dancer (or teacher) knows and accepts that aspirants will go into various branches of dance. Baryshnikov embodied this attitude most endearingly when he simultaneously enthused about the great gamut of exciting dance thriving in New York – from classical ballet, through musicals to small experimental groups – and bemoaned not being able to participate in all these riches at once.[6] Second, and more important, unlike musicians with their concrete scores, dancers depend on *one another*. As in the early bard-tradition, dance has been passed on *orally* from teacher to student (in a communal setting), and elder dancer to neophyte, with choreographers often altering their dances. Despite the modern use of dance notation (which is both more complicated and less comprehensive than music notation) this personal, alive, unfixed approach remains strong, and helps to undermine doctrinaire, egotistical attitudes. Dancers *have* to be generally more receptive and flexible for they need each other as musicians do not. These qualities came across in class. I did find a problem, however. My students were often inhibited at the beginning of the course; many, after perhaps years of being told (by musicians) that they were tone-deaf and 'unmusical', were unable to forget their real or supposed deficiencies and concentrate on study of the music. Yet, by the end of each year, a remarkable proportion had conquered their defensiveness and often presented questions and comments which caused *me* to look at music differently. And, most gratifying of all, their attitude towards 'technique' in dancing had often altered as a result of their musical discoveries.

But all this felicity is by no means a norm, and it heightened my awareness of the more common situation. Compared to my earlier experience within the ballet studio circuit, I inhabited a musician's paradise. These were dancers studying in one of the comparatively few establishments which comprehensively try to reinstitute the bond between dancer and musician, movement and music. And if the institutional possibilities are sparse in this respect, the situation in the studio world is, all too often, dire.

Rare it is for dancers in large, mass-production studios to be encouraged even to think – let alone to approach music in an organic way. This problem is, of course, related to another, more general one: the separation of music from dance, with an attendant 'higher development', as musical partisans view it. To most studio dancers, there is 'ballet-music', and there is, vaguely, the 'masterpiece' category, which does not usually concern them. This is, naturally, the converse of the musician's position. The problem lies in the common conception of 'masterpiece'. To the dancer, a musical masterpiece can be a source of intimidation in one form or another; to the musician it is a cause of a peculiar sort of superiority. For both it is a problem and a source of alienation.

During my research for this book, I came time and again upon references to 'pure music' and 'pure dance'. I saw clearly that such concepts were instrumental in my impulse to write the book. Most of the problems with which the book is concerned would not have arisen if the idea of 'pure' music or dance did not exist. Nothing is more natural than the impulse to move when hearing music which stirs us. What is *un*natural is to sit respectfully (or bored) with composed hands in order not to distract the concert-goer seated next to us (equally respectfully or bored). The epidemics of coughing and rustling which often distract and depress concert artists are, needless to say, manifestations of thwarted kinetic responses which stem from unrealistic ideas of how one is supposed to listen to music. We cannot, of course, get up and dance in the aisles – except at rock concerts – but we can at least try to understand and resist the pressures which would make music a cerebral experience rather than a bodily one *into which the mind is integrated*.

Children are free from such inhibitions and misplaced respect. They throw themselves around their living rooms with the abandon of barbarians when music they love is played. It is in subsequent years that training in music or dance systematically kills their intuitive perception of the affinity between musical sounds and physical movement. This progressive deadening of children's spontaneous reaction to music, against their assumption that it has a physical basis, shows us in speeded-up fashion what happened over three centuries as music became categorized as 'head-music', i.e. 'classical', 'intellectual', 'self-sufficient', etc., and 'body-music', i.e. 'popular', 'emotional', 'second-rate', etc.

The channeling of music into a category within which it began to develop and function separately, 'according to its own laws', has indeed produced much wonderful music, but it has also paved the way for two of the curses of our time: specialization and abstraction. It leads to the arts becoming ends in themselves, removed from daily life and the 'underlying harmony and unity of all things'. [7] George Steiner, discussing this problem, referred to it as 'distancing'.[8]

With music, however, the problem of 'art for art's sake' is most acute, for it lends itself more than any other art to the pursuit of abstraction. 'There is nothing but the notes'; 'It is about nothing but itself'; 'architecture is frozen music' (Is music melted architecture?) – these and similar fancies attempt to reduce music to a technical, structural fabrication, and the more it is interpreted as achieving these dubious goals the more it is lauded as 'pure'.

Dance is far more resistant to such efforts, but it too has been affected by this esthetic. Pure dance, like pure music, is now an ideal to some – as if they had both previously been degenerate or contaminated. And it is curious that the word 'autonomy' is so often used when advocating the desirability of pure dance or music, and that it is assumed to be something desirable, or even attainable. In social life the concept of autonomy leads to the idea of total 'freedom' and individualism of the self at any cost to the group. In music it can lead to, among other things, specialization, acute malnutrition and hermeticism; in dance mainly to boredom and artifice.

There are, of course, many clever arguments for defending the idea of art for art's sake. Those who prefer to consider it in relation to its setting and the people who were or are involved with it are often called romantics. It would seem, however, that those who wish to separate art from life and put it in a golden cage are the true romantics in the sense of the dictionary definitions, 'remote from experience', or 'removed from everyday life'.

A comparatively recent manifestation of interdependency of the arts and their function within the daily round is the Gothic cathedral. Here religious ritual – a recurrent necessity in people's lives – was served and illuminated not only by architecture, but also by sculpture, painting, pictures in stained-glass, literature (in the form of the liturgy) and even dance, not only in the vestigial choreography of the movement-patterns throughout the Mass, but within the medieval liturgical dramas. And, of course, by music. Each of these might be splendid 'in its own right', but it was not thought of as a separate 'art-form'. Rather, each was a fine craft, which contributed to a totality within ordinary, everyday existence. Now they are extracted for special admiration and appreciation. We 'take in' each, in isolation at museums and concert halls, forgetting that they once existed in a functional and expressive symbiosis.

Many are content with this state of affairs. For my part, however, I have grown increasingly dissatisfied with the concept of pure music in which I was educated. The longer I worked with dancers, the more natural it seemed for music to be associated with other things. I had always, like Adrian Stokes, experienced intense associations of music to a time, place and scene (this is, in fact, an extremely common if largely unexplored phenomenon).[9] But I did not realize for some time how deeply this must be linked to man's experience of music in the past when it *was* a part of his daily place and scene. Only an instant of history has seen music as a thing set apart to be 'gone to' in the form of concerts, and I believe that the innate impulse toward integrality survives under our cultured veneer (it is certainly interesting that audiences for that artistic pot-pourri, dance, according to attendance records in the US, far exceed those for musical concerts, and are continually and exuberantly growing).

Certainly some have tried to challenge this separatism. In rock music there seems to be a strong rebirth of the essentiality which once characterized all music. And, despite the comparative artificiality of ballet (although this is much less pervasive than in pre-Fokine times), it still contains the seed of the original relatedness of music, movement and milieu. Here one can experience music as an integral part of a group activity and vision.

Too many musicians, unfortunately, scorn music for dance as betraying its (recent) enviable autonomy and architectural destiny. But such badly aimed disdain rejects one of music's most essential elements: the human body in its daily context. This element, however, is more powerful than disdain; it flourishes in every vital, enduring passage of music, no matter how hard the intellect tries to interpret the music as abstract or spiritual or disembodied (an exception is found in the wonderful sacred polyphonic literature of the Middle Ages and Renaissance – but this, of course, was *intended* to be disembodied and other-worldly. Yet to the seeker after abstraction it too is 'impure', being inextricably linked to words). Much of the time, to be sure, particularly in certain periods, the physical element is overshadowed by the mental or constructional (although even such technical masters as Bach, Mozart and Beethoven never intended that this should occupy the forefront of the listener's consciousness). The art-music of the past few centuries has achieved much of its glory through elaboration of form and techniques. An Elizabethan galliard, or even a Josquin motet, is a minor achievement when measured against the craft, intricacy and scope of, say, twentieth-century serialism, Mahler's apocalyptic symphonies, Beethoven's *Eroica* or Bach's *The Art of Fugue*. But such glories were not achieved without cost, and the cost was specialization and isolation, both musical and cultural. Specialization and isolation are, naturally, related. Highly developed musical techniques for the musician, both composer and performer, and removal of music from the everyday world of the common herd, these create the problem: a problem which is, of course, hardly limited to music; it is ubiquitous in the twentieth century.

Yet even in our splintered, technological euphoria, we still hear admiring (and wistful?) references to 'the Renaissance man' – a creature who was not imprisoned within the category of a 'field'. Cultured men and women of the sixteenth century took for granted that they would dance, sing, play, compose, write poetry, speak other languages and comprehend mathematics and politics. They spent, in fact, an astonishing amount of time in these and other activities. They may not have reached the specialist's cold perfection, but they did *do* them, with passion and interaction.

We say, 'Oh, this is not possible now. We know too much about each to be able to cope properly with more than one.' The question here, I think, is *why* we have allowed ourselves to develop in such a way, to the point where, as the cliché goes, we know more and more about less and less – the logical conclusion being to know everything about nothing. But worst of all is the trend of *receiving* art from others – specialists – rather than making it oneself. In our particular area of inquiry, is it admirable to know everything about music but nothing about dance? Or not even to be able to dance rhythmically? Is it of real value to be able to do 64 *fouettés* or a perfect *arabesque* yet understand nothing of the music which is accompanying these, or not even be able to play or sing its tune recognizably? Are dance and music audiences obtaining the fullest rewards of these arts immobilized in front of a stage or the TV and hi-fi at home? And do they realize their acute deprivation in not dancing or making music with *others* – two of life's most deeply satisfying experiences?

I have foreshadowed certain important issues of this book. There are many loose ends and unresolved arguments, but they will recur as we venture into various areas of dance and music, becoming, I hope, satisfactorily sorted out as we proceed. In the last chapter many of these issues will receive a final look and summation during which I hope the seemingly outrageous nature of some of my assertions will be tempered by a new and broader perspective on matters which the reader may never before have thought much about.

I have presented my basic views (or major biases) and goals at the outset. This is not a short-cut, How-To-Do-It book for the ballet musician or a capsule Guide-To-The-Ballet for the dancer. Certainly, I have tried to clarify and illuminate as many aspects as possible of our complex subject which I consider of potential value to those who work in ballet, or who love it from the audience. But my main concern is that larger unity which I stressed at the beginning, both in its own right and as it powerfully affects the apparently separate elements of ballet, whether overtly or subtly.

PART I

The art: perspectives

1   Introduction: the situation

> The experiencing of a work of art is indivisible; hence any thinking about, any
> focusing upon a partial aspect of the whole can take place only within our analytic
> heads.   Stanley Burnshaw, *The Seamless Web*, 1970

MUSIC AND DANCE are deeply intertwined, yet a chasm separates many musicians and dancers today. Unfortunate as this may be as a general condition, it becomes catastrophic in the functional situation of the ballet studio. The daily ballet class too often finds musician and dancer associated through necessity but sundered by mutual ignorance and lack of communication and sympathy.

How is this possible? We are no longer obsessed by virtuosity as were the ballerina-dominated audiences – and choreographers – during the nineteenth century. In that period, which saw a long, inexorable decline into spectacle and artistic decadence, almost no serious composer subjected his talents to the choreographic tyranny which reduced staff composers like Minkus, Pugni and Drigo to the status and function of a circus cymbal. The few exceptions, Tchaikovsky, Glazunov and Delibes, only emphasize the musical poverty of the status quo. The average ballet score was almost completely lacking in the color, personality and lyrical vitality of the music for *Coppélia* or *Sleeping Beauty* – but none, choreographers, dancers, or audiences, seemed to care, or even to notice. They were concerned with other matters.

In contrast, we live in a century which has seen choreographers of the stature of Fokine, Massine, Tudor and Robbins, among others, create a tradition of ballet in which the most poetic feelings and deep psychology of human nature and experience are communicated to perceptive, responsive audiences, thus restoring a balance between dancer and dance, dance and music. For these choreographers' scores came not from musical hacks but from Chopin, the young Stravinsky, Bizet, Berlioz, Liszt, Mahler, Koechlin, Bach, Bernstein, Glass, etc., and were an integral part of their choreographic visions. Ballets of this sort are forming a twentieth-century tradition which Ruth Page compared to the 'synthetic theatre' of the Greeks, 'in which all of the theatrical arts . . . were freely and interchangeably used to heighten the intensity of the drama'.[1]

And, within a different esthetic, we have Balanchine. 'I do not believe', he said early in his career, 'in the permanence of anything in ballet save the purely classical. Classicism is enduring because it is impersonal.'[2] And throughout his career – like his close associate, Stravinsky, regarding music's inherent qualities – he disallowed the idea of 'expressivity' in dance. This, as manifested in his striking preoccupation with spatial patterns and stylistic devices, and, perhaps most of all, his skilful but idiosyncratic use of music, places him within a sharply contrasted tradition. 'Music

3

is, by its very nature, essentially powerless to *express* anything at all, whether a feeling, an attitude of mind, a psychological mood . . . its indispensable and single requirement is construction',[3] asserted Stravinsky. Selma Jeanne Cohen, in effect, paraphrased Balanchine's views on expressivity when she wrote,

For Balanchine, emotion in dancing, as in music, is a disruptive factor, something better gotten rid of as soon as possible. Let the audience . . . admire the dancing – its rhythm and its linear design – that's enough to absorb anyone's attention. The relation of movement to music may be extremely complex, but not for any dramatic reasons . . . The effect is reason enough, there is no need for emotional motivation.[4]

Written twenty years ago, this remains essentially apt. Despite what some now describe as the 'romanticism' of certain dances created during his last period, that does not constitute Balanchine's paramount contribution to ballet, nor is it likely to be what he is most remembered for. But the point here is that, in his own way, he also furthered this century's awareness of music as an important element in choreography.

It is not only choreographers who have changed in attitude: many contemporary composers recognize music's altered status, actually preferring the companionable collaboration of a ballet score to the more esoteric, segregated world of twentieth-century concert music. Countless articles, too, by famous choreographers, dancers, and critics reiterate the magical function of music in ballet. Symposia and teachers' conferences include discussions of musicality in the dancer and choreographer, and are conscientiously attended by dancers and teachers. Courses in music are offered at more and more dance schools and university dance departments. Everyone, it seems, agrees that music is important in ballet.

Yet, curiously, this preoccupation is not reflected consistently in the technique classes which proliferate all over the country. For whatever reasons, all too many are permeated by a nineteenth-century balletic attitude towards the music – an attitude accepted (sometimes reluctantly) by teacher, student and pianist – which regards music as at best a stimulus and a showcase for technical display, at worst a necessary evil to be dominated and even ignored whenever possible. The pianist often commits the parochial sin of splitting all music into two categories, forever different: 'ballet music' (i.e. lowbrow, shallow, hack) and 'serious' (i.e. highbrow, profound, professional). This leads to accompanists passively supplying a narrow repertoire of mediocre (if comfortably predictable to some teachers) Trivia, or, in a misguided attempt to escape such frustration, intruding the 'serious' music they revere, leaving the class to flounder or sink in a balletic limbo of Bach fugues, Beethoven sonatas and Mozart fantasias. This music does have a limited value in class; occasional tastes can provide stimulation and variety, but a steady diet is unthinkable. It could only result in kinesthetic malnutrition of an art which is physical, not intellectual–theatrical, not contemplative. The first extreme at least has theatrical associations.

I am fully aware that these generalizations are not absolute. I know teachers who are wonderfully musical, or who have the desire and potential to become so; there are sensitive and receptive musicians who would like to make the transition from good pianist to valuable accompanist. Yet, how many of those whose life is spent in the ballet studio can say that they are satisfied and fulfilled in an environment which permits them to use their skills, talent and artistry without impediment? Are the dancers satisfied, who daily have to cope with numbing, quasi-musical or hyper-virtuoso sounds which annihilate their rhythmic responses and lead them to dwell ever more confiningly on the technical aspects of steps in isolated sterility? Hardly a day goes by that I do not hear plaintive voices of students expressing a distress which is the result of a struggle against music which, rather than easing and aiding them in their physical efforts, assaults their ears and bodies and diminishes their *ballon* and their sense of joy in movement.

Are the teachers, hordes of whom are denied a setting in which any innate musicality or stylistic sensitivity might flourish and communicate itself to the students, any better off, being faced instead with the distraction of a continual battle to obtain suitable music from a seemingly uncooperative or even unqualified accompanist? I have seldom spoken with a ballet teacher who did not express some measure of dissatisfaction in this area; sometimes it approaches a feeling of near-desperation regarding the search for a pianist with whom they could work well. These teachers range from the narrow sort, obsessed with turnout and technique, who simply do not want the dead weight of a pianist who needs constant surveillance, to the musically imaginative, creative masters who want support and inspiration. Many teachers have, as a last resort, turned to the use of recorded music for class. This is a measure, of course, which sacrifices spontaneity and interaction for security.

We are left with the accompanists, who so far seem to be the scapegoats. Are they any happier, in what often seems to them outright torture, expending their skills in an environment made up of teachers and dancers who are not sensitive to or even interested in their music? Again, it would seem not. My memory seethes with laments from pianists who have felt, in various classroom situations, ignored, exploited, resented and unconnected to the dancers; in short, miserable. Clearly, something is wrong. Despite exceptions, the prevailing conditions in the average ballet studio are not, to say the least, what they should be.

But now we must turn from general observations to a brief survey of specific problems which will be investigated at greater length in this book. The dearth of good accompanists is due to many things. First, consider the accompanist herself. To be valuable in the ballet studio, the pianist must be blessed with or acquire many attributes. A minimal facility at the keyboard is to be taken for granted; far more is required. She must have some knowledge – the more the better – of the basic principles of ballet and what differentiates it from modern dance, in which she may also have some experience. Furthermore, she must understand the French vocabulary of ballet which is used internationally, be familiar with the many ballet steps and combinations used daily in class, and, not least, have an awareness of the dancers' physical strengths and weaknesses.

On the musical side, she must have a good memory, a large repertoire of suitable music (including excerpts from the most popular and enduring ballets), some facility in improvisation, ability to sight-read and – above all – she must possess a strong, flexible rhythmic sense. It would be a paragon indeed who enjoyed all of these in equal measure. Each one can, however, be acquired and expanded if the desire is there; a large part of this book is devoted to showing the way.

I have left the most important requirement until last, and it is one without which the preceding ones are weakened or even negated. The accompanist must have a temperament which allows her to forego the featured role of a soloist with its more dazzling, somewhat self-centered rewards, and see accompanying as a rich partnership, rather than as a demeaning loss of status or a contest between piano and bodies. (In fact, the accompanist who commands the skills listed above runs the pleasurable risk of having her head quite turned by the intensity and fervor of appreciation which grateful teachers and dancers may lavish upon her. She may even find this a more meaningful experience than the rarefied isolation of the concert soloist.

The teacher presents us with another aspect of our predicament. Certainly a highly qualified accompanist is an asset – in fact, a necessity; who would really dispute it? But she needs encouragement, appreciation and respect from the teacher (and consequently from the dancers, who are quick to sense the teacher's attitude toward the pianist). Furthermore, these must be expressed in the concrete form of a decent, realistic wage. Many teachers do not seem to realize that this is a job which is extremely demanding, both physically and mentally. A reasonable wage is a simple acknowledgment of this fact. It is also necessary for dispelling the unfortunate but undeniable 'hack' aura which permeates the ballet studio in many musicians' minds. This will persist as long as the average accompanist's wage stays at its present inadequate level. Raising it would go far towards providing an incentive which could lure more good-to-excellent musicians into the alien world of ballet. Many pianists have expressed an interest in ballet work to me, but have quickly lost it when they found what the pay amounted to.

We are faced with an inescapable fact: skimping in this area is the most false economy possible. A teacher who refuses to see that the necessity for paying a good wage to the pianist is equal to the necessity of spending more for the rental of a studio with a floor free from splinters and holes can only be described as lacking in perspective, and dense to the point of impenetrability. Such teachers are, moreover, encouraging a situation which affects not only themselves; teachers who are happy to pay a good wage must often settle for mediocrity because of the scarcity of good accompanists due to the lack of adequate pay. How do we break this vicious circle?

To begin with, immediate pressure should be applied to raise the average level of pay, at every opportunity, by teachers and dancers who are weary of making do with poor music, and by the pianists themselves – who should refuse, militantly whenever possible, to accept any job which offers an unrealistic and insulting wage. (I must stress, however, that the teacher is often an unwilling participant in this problem. If he is subject to the policy of a ballet company or a school administration, his only recourse is protest or even resignation.) Every idea presented in this book is directed in part towards increasing the skills and awareness of the accompanist; she in turn must be given an incentive to do so.

I now turn to the objectives of this book. My original idea was to write a manual in which analysis of the practicalities and problems of accompanying could provide a guide and a reference for the pianist. I soon realized that such a book would fall short of my basic goal, which was to help to raise the level of ballet by encouraging pianists to become involved in the totality, as educated participants, rather than alien and detached sources of regulatory tempos or mood-music who have only a limited idea of what the class is for in the first place.

I have personal knowledge of the difference. During my early accompanying days I came across several collections of pieces for ballet class. Some were better than others (although there was a striking number of duplications of pieces). Two or three even included a few comments, but these were tantalizingly and frustratingly brief. All of the collections I saw, helpful as they were to one who had almost no suitable repertoire at all, were treatments of a symptom, and they failed to attack the basic problem – comprehensive understanding by the pianist. They partially filled a need, but did not analyze the source and nature of this need. Learning a number of 'pieces for class', to be played by rote, merely perpetuates the vacuum occupied by so many ballet accompanists. Such an approach only reinforces the role of pianist-as-outsider. And thus I remained for an uncomfortably long time.

It seems to me unarguable that knowledgable and sensitive accompanists will have a profound effect all the way along the chain of pianist–dancer–teacher–choreographer. If, for example, a choreographer finds that the dancers he is to work with possess musicality, sensitivity to phrasing and a wide dynamic range, reflecting consistently imaginative training by teachers who are stimulated by alert, involved accompanists, he will be affected by this in his approach to the dancers and the choreography. We will, therefore, be all the closer to a widespread fulfilment of ballet's potential as fervently described or achieved by figures like Noverre, Massine, Fokine, Tudor and their inheritors. Partial, sporadic achievement will no longer be acceptable to artists and audiences (Massine felt that dancers of the future might be more effective than those of his time simply because they may have a more profound knowledge of music).

Another thought struck me forcibly. Since the vital point I want to establish is the necessity for interaction and communication between the four members of the chain mentioned above, I felt I should not address only musicians, but also try to reach the teachers and dancers and choreographers themselves. The lack of communication between musician and dancer on matters ranging from terminology and the difference between musicians' and dancers' perception of quality and rhythm, all the way to esthetics, reaches sometimes appalling proportions. Valuable time is wasted in the classroom or rehearsal studio because of this; tempers fray and the separateness is reinforced. To speak to only one member of the chain would encourage the continuation of the barriers.

Regarding gender, since I am female, I refer throughout to the accompanist as 'she'. For teacher and choreographer, I use 'he', although there are obviously many women working in each capacity. As for form of address, certain contexts seemed to demand the direct use of 'you, the accompanist', but this is in no way intended to exclude other sorts of readers or to discourage them from trying to look at such passages through the accompanist's eyes and thus gain a new perspective. Another important point: although my work-experience has been mainly in the world of ballet, I believe that this book contains much of interest and relevance for modern dancers also – especially since, despite certain essential differences, ballet and modern dance have increasingly interacted and cross-fertilized.

I write primarily from the musician's viewpoint, not only because I *am* one, but because, despite my belief that dance movement is the most important element in the hybrid art of ballet, I consider the music to be the most important element in the studio. Without some support of sensitive phrasing, musical style, dynamics and animated rhythm, even the finest teacher is unable to transmit the full value of his knowledge and experience, and the finest dancers cannot fully explore their stylistic and expressive (or even technical) potential.

The music determines, to a surprising degree, whether the class is a daily drill permeated by the almost inevitable obsession with technique which rushes in to fill the vacuum left by the departure of quality and musicality, or a varied and enlarging experience in which the teacher functions at his optimum and the dancers' bodies and minds are stretched and stimulated. This latter transcending of the dismal step-by-step, count-by-count, struggle to acquire 'a technique' will create the foundation for the transformation of ballet steps into a moving communication in the theater. (Outstanding, exceptionally gifted dancers, of course, manage to surmount the difficulties caused by poor accompanists, but few of them would not eagerly welcome musical classes. And what of the remaining 95% of dancers among whom many potential, if lesser, talents may realize their abilities only partially or not at all because of unrhythmical, stultifying music throughout class?)

As the scope of the book widened, the difficulties multiplied. Despite this, however, I felt committed to making the attempt. I realize that it may seem rash to address musicians and dancers in the same breath, but this only underscores the need for such an effort. Composers such as Monteverdi, Lully, Gluck (and even Mozart), worked closely with dancers, and themselves danced; choreographers and teachers – *maîtres de ballet* – learned music as a matter of course, and played the violin for rehearsals and classes. They inhabited a musical dance-world in a way which subsequently vanished. My central problem has been to illuminate elements of both arts which are of equal importance for dancer and musician while coping with the different technical (and esthetic) worlds within which each functions – and to show that these are not, perhaps, so different after all.

To accomplish this, I have felt it necessary to introduce aspects of dance which on the surface might not seem of interest to the musician, and aspects of music which the dancer might consider abstruse and irrelevant to her goals. I can only answer that in my view all such material is essential to my arguments throughout this book, and that I hope it will prove of interest and value – if not always in an immediate and practical way, then at least as a catalyst for long-range investigation.

Three points need to be stressed. First, I have not attempted a full historical survey and analysis of ballet or its musical scores. To be even minimally adequate such surveys demand their own books, and many already exist. Some are ordinary, some good, and a few outstanding. (Although ballet music in its own right has been the subject of only a few books compared to the seemingly endless torrent of chronological or analytical studies of the choreography, I felt that these were informative enough to relieve me of the impossible task of treating it properly in a book of this sort.) Rather than giving an inadequate sketchy version of what already has been done fully, I considered it best to refer the reader to some of the most comprehensive books on ballet and its scores. This would leave me free to concentrate on the special aims of the present book.

Secondly, as is probably already evident, this is not an objective book. Being based on my experience first as an accompanist and then as a teacher, the formation of my balletic esthetic through fruitful contact with or reaction against the teachers for whom I played, plus my personal views on the relationship of art to 'real life', the book could not be anything *but* subjective and opinionated to a large degree. To counteract this I have, however, tried to weigh the value of each argument for the reader who shares neither my particular background nor my principal views, and to provide clear points for contention. I consider argument preferable to apathy, and if I lead readers to think on subjects which they had never seriously concerned themselves with before, then I shall be satisfied. I should add that this book has presented a formidable challenge, and I do not feel that I have fully solved the problems inherent in such a project. It is the vision of one person, offered as a stimulus to reactions and actions.

Thirdly, the fundamental message – the necessity of a continuing interchange between dancer and musician, a productive mutuality and cross-fertilization – is hardly original. I hope, in fact, that the quotations which appear during the course of my arguments will confirm its widespread acceptance, uniting so many otherwise diverse dancers, teachers, choreographers, musicians and critics. The persons quoted may not fully agree with me (or each other) on every point, but we are in harmony in regarding the desirability of a true marriage of movement and music.

The book is divided into two parts, the first of which attempts to provide a broad perspective for the details of the second. In Part I we are concerned, in Chapters 2 and 3, with ballet in the theater; Part II leads us to the studio wherein the theatrical experience is made possible – finding eventually that we must re-enter the theater and, finally, emerge into the world at large.

Chapter 2 is concerned with the relationship of movement and music, approaching this through the special nature of each, the qualities they share, and what takes place when they are combined (which is often more subtle than one might think).

Since, as every ballet-goer knows, not all music functions happily within the hybrid art of ballet, Chapter 3 attempts to categorize the different types of music to which the late twentieth century has access in live performance and on records. Our time is unique in the wealth of music available. Never before has it been possible to hear pieces from every century of Western music – not to mention the 'ethnic' music of other cultures. This is a mixed blessing; the majority of choreographers, ballet teachers, dancers and even musicians have been conditioned by a narrow band in that wide musical spectrum. Because of this they can bring prejudices and preconceptions to music which lies outside the comfortably familiar area. But whether the amazing variety of available music confronts the choreographer with the need for perception, selectivity and unusual inventiveness, or requires of everyone concerned a more open, catholic view of music, the growing use of pieces outside the 'normal' tradition of ballet music makes it necessary to look closely at the nature of 'ballet music', potential music for ballet, and music which, if not impossible to use, is certainly problematical and hazardous.

With Chapter 4, which opens the second part, we begin an investigation into the practicalities of ballet and its music in the studio. It examines the role of the accompanist, and what precisely is demanded of her. There are many serious problems which beset the ballet pianist today, but there are also profound rewards. My observations stem not only from my own twenty-odd years as accompanist and teacher, but from the experience of many accompanists whom I have known – as, of course, does much else in this book.

Chapter 5 proceeds to one of the most important parts of studio life for the accompanist – the teacher. It is impossible to ignore this focal figure, for he determines directly or indirectly whether the accompanist's lot is a happy, or even a bearable, one.

Having observed the ballet accompanist as a person and as an important element in the class, and the teacher for whom she plays, we must look in great detail at the skills and talents which are essential for good accompanying. The first – the ability to select a large repertoire which is both varied and suitable for the exercises and combinations of ballet class – has three chapters devoted to it. Chapter 6 is mainly theoretical, concerned with what determines whether a piece will help or hinder ballet movement. Since rhythm is the core, heart, or soul of dancing, an investigation into what rhythm actually consists of will form the core of this chapter. Chapter 7 looks at what may be called the esthetic side of the selection of music – its style and quality. These are elusive attributes, often defying precise analysis, but certain elements can be identified and described, and I have tried to show their importance for movement. Chapter 8, using the principles of the preceding two chapters, applies the theoretical and the esthetic to the practical task of selecting music for specific combinations. At the same time I attempt to establish the *dance* principles behind the selections so that the information directed to the combinations under consideration can be applied in a general way at other times. The chapter ends with a survey of sources – where and how to look for music.

The selection and amassing of enough music to serve for ballet classes day after day, month after month, year after year, is a challenge in itself. But the other side of the coin is the performance of this repertoire. The most wonderful pieces are worthless if played badly, with no sense of rhythm or style. Chapter 9 is devoted to analysis of what constitutes good performance and how the act of performing is affected by the simultaneous perception of dance movement. Many of the observations apply also to dance performance, if from an unfamiliar vantage point. The crucial element shared by musicians and dancers is rhythm, and although their mediums are different, and the execution calls different mechanisms into action, the organic principles are the same.

An aspect of accompanying which lies between repertoire and performance is the art of improvisation. Although improvisations augment one's learned repertoire and are thus another facet of it, improvising is and always has been intimately linked with the *playing* of music. I felt, therefore, that it was best to establish the basic principles of good performance in ballet class before tackling the more complex act of simultaneous playing and creating. No matter how large the accompanist's repertoire may be, it is an enormous advantage to be able to create music on the spot – to improvise for a particular combination. Chapter 10 examines the history and nature of improvisation, with analyses of the materials with which the improviser works as they appear in various types of music. This is followed, in Chapter 11, by a closer look at two periods in which improvisation was a key agent – the sixteenth century as embodied in its dance-music and the Age of Rock. Not only do I find these enormously interesting and exciting, with their mutual wedding of the physical body and the musical ear – the kinetic force of the dance being integral to both – but I consider them to be valuable in providing in simple, exposed ways many facets of and clues to imaginative improvisation. Although this chapter is, in a way, a diversion from the main path of the book, it is on the other hand a statement and reinforcement of the basic themes with which I am concerned throughout.

Finally, in Chapter 12, I return to the setting of Part I – ballet in the theater – by way of the rehearsal situation and the special skills needed by the pianist. Although class and rehearsal draw upon certain similar talents, others are peculiar to the latter or greatly emphasized. But, going beyond ballet *per se*, I expand ideas originally stated in the Preface, for while the ballet world is valuable in itself, it also provides a microcosm of wider, vital concerns and a key to these.

As I have said, I hope that there will be something of interest in each chapter whether the reader is a musician, dancer, teacher or choreographer, but some chapters are more directly pertinent for each than others. Chapters 2 and 3 are the most uniformly aimed at everyone who is involved in ballet.

The accompanist is, of course, the main figure I speak to in Chapter 4, yet the teacher and dancer may learn much about their partner in the studio, and be stimulated to think about certain matters.

Teachers can suffer from an inability to see themselves as their accompanists see them. Chapter 5, therefore, should not only inform accompanists of what may lie in wait for them in the form of the teachers for whom they will play, it can also demonstrate to teachers the problems which they may embody at some time or other. I hope, in any case, that this chapter will help to remove some of the prevailing barriers between teachers and accompanists.

The function of Chapters 6, 7 and 8 for the accompanist should be clear, but the teacher and dancer can also benefit from them. Many teachers, particularly inexperienced ones, are limited in – and at worst incapable of – communication of their musical wishes to the accompanist or musical corrections to the dancers, and dancers of understanding them. After reading these three chapters this should be less of a problem than before.

Similarly, although Chapter 9 is obviously directed primarily to the accompanist, teachers and dancers who are unable to analyze what disturbs them about the performance of their accompanists should be in a stronger position regarding their wants and needs after reading it, and also can apply it to *dance* performance.

Chapters 10 and 11 are the two which are aimed most exclusively at the accompanist, yet budding choreographers may find the principles of improvisation discussed here to have some application to their work. Dancers, in addition, may find that these principles have some bearing on their approach to movement.

Although the final chapter concerns the rehearsal pianist most intimately, dancers and choreographers can benefit from the pianist's perspective on snags which arise during rehearsal. Much time is wasted because of misconceptions and misunderstandings, whether created by the pianist or the dancers and choreographer. Empathy – that valuable ingredient in the making of a ballet – is eroded by the musician, dancers or choreographer working at cross-purposes. Tempers rise, spirits sink, and the rehearsal goes badly. Chapter 12 attempts to show why this happens and how it can be avoided, and, at the end, to review the wider implications of all that we have been examining – which concern everyone.

Thus we begin in the theater and end in the world outside, via the studio and theater, for technique and talent cannot be viewed as ends in themselves. They are essential to ballet in the theater but meaningless when severed from communication.

2　The relationship of movement and music

The rhythm of ballet is not either the rhythm of the music or the rhythm of the movements of the dancers, but the relation of each to each.

Anthony Asquith, in *Footnotes to the Ballet*, 1936

. . . the eye is not satisfied with seeing, nor the ear filled with hearing . . .

Ecclesiastes, I

BALLET is but one of the many forms which dance has taken, and it has existed for only a moment in history. This moment, despite its briefness, has seen a variety of emphases. Often the adored ballerina ruled. Sometimes story or spectacle overwhelmed and devitalized the movement. And on occasion even music has been allowed to dominate – perhaps the oddest imbalance of all.

This uneven, capricious development – from ballet's origins in royal entertainments of the Renaissance and seventeenth-century opera, through the vagaries of Romantic and Classical ballet in the nineteenth century – was suddenly arrested by a stunning event. The Diaghilev Ballet exploded into the midst of one of ballet's most degenerate periods, transforming an arid landscape into one of dazzling color, passion, and new heights of choreographic expression. And it was not only a theatrical landmark; its impact actually led to intellectuals and artists taking ballet seriously as a major art-form.

In Paris, 'the evening of May 1, 1909, saw the birth of a new art',[1] and this view has continued, from the amazed reactions of those who saw that première to re-evaluations of the event written only yesterday. This explosion released – in the focal figure of Michel Fokine – a vision whose time had come. It had only been sought in the past by a handful of choreographers. Fokine reaffirmed and expanded the ideals of such men as Noverre, Vigano and Ivanov, who had in their times tried to rescue ballet from sterility and technical excesses. In his translation of ideals into reality and his sensitivity to the early twentieth century's broadening perspective – its emergence from the parochial nineteenth century illusion of stability – he altered ballet for all time.

But not alone. Under the dynamic guidance of Diaghilev, an extraordinary collection of talents contributed to the idea of ballet as a totally integrated experience. Leonid Massine, Igor Stravinsky, Leon Bakst, Alexander Benois, Vaslav Nijinsky, Tamara Karsavina, Anna Pavlova – these and many others brought their gifts. Sometimes there was a prevailing harmony. At other times, temperament and artistic conflict marred the final product. Yet the collaborations, strong or weak, altered the future of ballet with such works as *Prince Igor*, *The Firebird*, *La Boutique fantasque*, *The Three-Cornered Hat*, *The Rite of Spring*, *Les Sylphides*, *Carnaval*, *Le Spectre de la rose* and *Petrushka* – the last of which is often

13

lauded as Fokine's masterpiece. 'It is difficult to believe from seeing and hearing *Petrouchka* that this ballet was the result of a collective creative enterprise. Rather does it seem as if a single super-genius, equally gifted in music, art, painting and choreography, had conceived, devised and staged this ballet. It is, of course, the greatest achievement of the *Ballets-Russes*, their admitted masterpiece.'[2]

Rejecting the dead-ends of ballerina-worship, gaudy spectacle, preoccupation with story, or musical tyranny, Fokine and his colleagues visualized a complex creation which could utilize movement, music, story or dramatic mood, sets and costumes to achieve a totality which is, mysteriously, far more than the mere sum of all these. Think what this aim requires: 'Unity, or wholeness . . . is essential to any work of art but in ballet it has a special significance and is difficult of attainment. A picture, a symphony, a poem – each of these springs from the mind of one man, and its wholeness is a reflection of his own integrity of thought and vision. But ballet is a composite art to which many make a contribution. Because it is so difficult to achieve, unity in ballet induces an emotion of utter satisfaction such as is provided by few other artistic experiences.'[3]

Each time this happens one marvels anew at the victory over all the possible difficulties, for, 'if the initial collaboration of scenarist, composer, designer and choreographer fails, everything fails'.[4] If it succeeds, the reactions of viewers are in proportion to the potential hazards of such an endeavor, leading to such statements as, 'Noverre's magnificent dream of a dance drama in which the poetic idea, in which music, costume, and decoration should unite in inspired naturalness with a technically finished but not self-sufficient dance – this great and beautiful dream is realized at the beginning of the twentieth century in the Russian ballet.'[5] Much of the written reaction to the achievement of Fokine and his collaborators is so deeply felt and so inspired that it borders on poetry. This is hardly surprising, for successful collaboration in the arts is not common – particularly when so many elements are involved. Some argue that Fokine's ideal surpassed his achievement, and his emphasis on dance-drama is irrelevant to our more 'abstract' period. But even now, when dance-drama occupies a more balanced position within a general picture that includes 'mood' and 'classical' ballets in which dance *per se* is primary, the latter types have been profoundly affected by Fokine's essential, timeless esthetic: that ballet should be expressive rather than exhibitionistic, with music integral to its organic unity. And, of utmost importance, although Diaghilev for twenty years attracted an elite 'balletomane', and intellectual following, he at the same time stirred the enthusiasm of many who would normally never have had the slightest taste for ballet. Now they formed an eager new audience.

Yet there remains a paradox. This unified endeavor, with its goal of equality among the collaborators, contains an apparent contradiction, for two of the components have a special affinity – movement and music. This is true, moreover, not only of the ballets in the Noverre–Fokine tradition, but of all. In the most decadent of ballets or the most abstract, plotless, scenically stark, one thing remains constant – the presence of music, whether it is vulgar, bland or enriching. Despite the occasional ballet that dispenses with music, totally or in sections, dancing-time is inextricably linked to music-time through their mutual impulse.

Origins

Dance and music are allied, not only because they both move in time, but because they spring from a common human source, related to time – the rhythm of daily life. From the first lullaby, work-chant and invocation to nature, they have been closely associated, although authorities disagree over the exact nature of their early relationship. Some hold that music served in dance merely as a rhythmic accompaniment – a regulator; others maintain that it was equally expressive, a spontaneous simultaneous impulse, provoking strong feelings in the dancers and reinforcing their movement-qualities – a primitive form of feedback. A growing majority does seem to favor the latter theory, which is more convincing in the light of our increasing anthropological knowledge. A provocative theory is offered by Sachs when he writes, 'Time beating and melody are not the first sound accompaniments of the dance. Imitation and the involuntary expression of emotion precede all conscious sound formation . . . Ecstasy in the broadest meaning of the word dominates the throat as well as the limbs.'[6] This stresses both the expressive origin of music and the primal affinity of singing and dancing. Sachs says of this essential unity of dance and song, 'whether we speak of individuals or of entire tribes, peoples, and races, their melodies and dances must always be closely related. For both are determined by the same impulse to motion.'[7] If these statements by Sachs – and similar ones by other authorities – are true, they strongly challenge any idea of music originating as a separate, deliberately differentiated, component or as a subservient one. The weight of the evidence is on the side of a mutal intensity and a close expressive bond between music and dance; furthermore, both were used within the larger framework of ritual in which dance was not the focal element – to be admired and estheticized – but rather part of an experienced totality.

As human life became more intricate so also did dance and music evolve into complex, sophisticated, highly controlled organisms, yet the same physiological rhythms govern our bodies today as governed those of our primitive ancestors. Rhythm remains the generating force. It underlies every other aspect of these two arts. In music we can be stirred by the bare bones of rhythm unaccompanied by melody or harmony. Melody, in fact, cannot be created without rhythmic organization; harmonies cannot function until the static blocks of sound are motivated by some temporal impulse. Similarly, movement can exist without the five ballet positions, story, stars, sets or, even at times music, but the one essential which transforms it from disjunct motor activity to a form of expression is rhythm.

Aural *vs.* visual perception

Throughout the integrated, unified experience of a ballet in the Noverre–Fokine tradition runs the thread of sound-rhythm combined with movement-rhythm, and their unique affinity and power to reinforce each other. This power does not come from a mirroring; rather, aural and visual responses combine in our minds to create an illusion of oneness. 'The eye and the ear complement one another', writes John Dewey,[8] and the power of an illusion of oneness stems in part from certain peculiarities of each. In an analysis of the difference between seeing and hearing, Dewey has much to say which is relevant here. He deserves quoting at length both for his intrinsic interest and for the light he casts on our own inquiry:

The eye is the sense of distance – not just that light comes from afar, but that through vision we are connected with what is distant and thus forewarned of what is to come. Vision gives the spread out scene – that *in* and *on* which . . . change takes place . . . The material to which the ear relates us through sound is opposite at every point. Sounds *come* from outside the body, but sound itself is near, intimate; it is an excitation of the organism; we feel the clash of vibrations throughout our whole body. Sound stimulates directly to immediate change because it reports a change . . . Its import is measured by the care animal and savage take to make no noise as they move. Sound is the conveyor of what impends, of what is happening as an indication of what is likely to happen . . . Vision arouses emotion in the form of interest – curiosity solicits further examination, but it attracts; or it institutes a balance between withdrawal and forward exploring action. It is sounds that make us jump.

Generically speaking, what is *seen* stirs emotion indirectly, through interpretation and allied idea. Sound agitates directly, as a commotion of the organism itself.[9]

Despite the eye's complexity, this is surpassed by the ear. 'The human ear is an extraordinary instrument . . . its sensitivity is so great that, to use the analogy of the noted physicist Alexander Wood, it will respond to a level of energy comparable to a 50-watt light bulb viewed at a distance of 3000 miles.'[10]

Duration is also a factor. We can listen reasonably attentively to, say, a long symphony – but would find it very taxing to be compelled to look for forty minutes at one painting. This is because the *concentration* of the ear is, normally, more intense and longer-lasting than that of the eye.

A thought-provoking aspect of the difference between seeing and hearing is discussed by Zuckerkandl, who contrasts the behavior of blind and deaf people – the quietness, equanimity and trust so often found in the blind, and the irritability and suspicion encountered among the deaf, who show 'the typical reaction of the prisoner, the man spied upon, who must always be upon his guard'.[11] Contrary to what one would think, those who cannot hear tend to feel more shut off from the world than those who cannot see. Why is this, when we are so visually oriented? Zuckerkandl makes an illuminating observation: 'When we open our eyes on the world we see objects; things that confront us, are directed toward us, close in on us. Tones carry outward; lead us away with them. That music is a window opening in the world of objects that closes in on us, a window through which we can look out from our world, men have always felt.'[12] Hearing lets us *participate*.

Few would disagree with the opinion that music is the most immediate of the arts in emotional effect (this is given alternately as the reason for its superiority or its inferiority, depending on the argument). Again, differences between the perceptions of eye and ear are involved. 'Immediate' meaning 'direct, not separated by any intervening medium', the hearing of music is obviously the ultimate in immediate artistic experience. The seeing of dance, on the other hand, is not an immediate experience but an intermediate one. 'Only living motion', writes Zuckerkandl, can perceive living motion: self-motion can only be self-perceived . . . Perception of living motions of others, seeing them – the flight of a swallow, for example, which I see as animate motion – is mediated, is not perception in the proper sense: interposed between the motion perceived and the perceiving agent is another body whose motion is 'its own'. What I see is the trajectory of an animate motion, not the motion itself.[13]

There are, of course, the involuntary muscular responses – sympathetic vibrations, so to speak – which take place in the ballet audience, but not only are these minute in comparison with the fully realized (and self-perceived) movements of each dancer, they are experienced second-hand.

'There is, however', continues Zuckerkandl,

such a thing as music, tonal motion, *audible* living motion. In music I experience an animate motion which is neither my own nor someone else's and which I perceive directly, rather than through the intermediary of a body whose motion it would be – pure self-motion, bound to no body, no 'self'. The act of perceiving this motion must itself be a motion. What the eye cannot achieve – namely, direct perception of animate motion – can be achieved by the ear. In the act of hearing, living realities come into direct contact; hearing tones, I move with them; I experience their motion as my own motion. To hear tones in motion is to move together with them.[14]

Such considerations as these are clearly relevant to the affinity of dance and music, and have a strong bearing on the drastic impoverishment of dance by a choreographer's thoughtless or inept choice and use of music. The combination of these two senses results in a unique and compound affective force. And, among other virtues, it helps to correct the imbalance of our sensory response. We have become increasingly visual, sacrificing the acuteness of our other senses in favor of sight (it is well-known how deficient we are compared to animals or our ancestors in hearing, touch, smell and taste). Decadent ballet always stems primarily from an over-emphasis on the visual – whether of spectacle and decor or of the technician–gymnast.

Even when treated in an integrated manner, dance-movement, sets, costumes, lighting – all the elements, that is, but music – are visual; thus, in the present context, they are sensorially redundant and uniform in their ability to stimulate. 'The appeal of ballet being primarily to the eye', writes Audrey Williamson, 'there is a constant danger of the art degenerating into spectacle for its own sake, and of the audience contenting itself with looking and ceasing to think. "It is shameful", wrote Noverre, "that dancing should renounce the empire it might assert over the mind and only endeavour to please the sight."'[15] This quote within a quote forms a double-barreled attack on what can be called 'visuomania'. By adding the aural element we leave orgies of the eye and move into a new dimension, one created by a union of outward and inward reactions. The visual elements are separate, outside us; the musical tones, with their 'clash of vibrations', become part of us, immediately, and also help to stimulate the thinking mind sought by Noverre and Williamson.

Art *vs.* acrobatics

Even the most cursory glance at ballet's past shows that the aural–visual phenomenon could be ignored only at great cost. In every period which disregarded the music and stressed visual elements, ballet became a sterile art, narrow and elite, and, as Sachs claimed, 'the legs become more important than the spirit'.[16] Balletophobes, of course, are usually aware of only this distortion and seldom seek the exceptions in every style and period. 'The history of ballet as an art', writes Williamson, 'is a history of its struggle for dramatic expression as apart from mere display and technical virtuosity. It is imperative that this is realized if ballet is to maintain any intellectual hold on the imagination and the high rank as an art of the theater which many educated people, unaware of its dramatic and poetic range of expression, still deny to it.'[17] In her discussion of the reforms of Noverre and Fokine, and throughout the book, Williamson clearly assumes that music is an integral part of this dramatic and poetic range of expression.

After describing the marked similarity of Fokine's beliefs to those of Noverre, she cautions,

The warning note here is obvious. The fact that Noverre's basic principles had to be reasserted little more than a century after his death emphasized the constant liability of ballet to degenerate as an art. This degeneracy invariably occurs under the same conditions, excessive concentration on the executant and the virtuosity of dance steps and arrangements, and its seed is inherent in the material of ballet itself.[18]

Fokine's efforts to counteract this tendency to degeneration were consistently strengthened by a particular emphasis on music's role in this task. Innumerable quotes are to be found in the writings of artists who were associated with him which vividly depict his belief that an aural poverty will weaken the visual aspect, even when the visual is being accentuated by every other means possible.

Similarly, the Danish teacher and choreographer, Auguste Bournonville wrote,

The aim of art in general and of the theatre in particular, is to uplift the soul and to invigorate the spirit. Dancing, then, should be on guard particularly against the too emphatic preference of a spoiled public for effects which are as contrary to good manners and good taste as they are to the real interests of art . . . Noble simplicity will always be beautiful. Display, on the other hand, ultimately becomes boring. Dancing can, with the help of music, rise to the heights of poetry. Equally it can sink to circus tricks through excess of acrobatics.[19]

This is a thought which every dancer (and choreographer) could profitably meditate upon frequently as an antidote to visuomania.

'Musicality'

You rarely hear anyone involved with ballet state baldly that music is of no importance to it – in fact, there seems to be a reassuring theoretical agreement with those idealistic views quoted above. But a practical understanding of musicality in ballet and how to go about developing it is another matter. A disconcerting vagueness or insufficiency is often the predominant note.

If pressed for a definition of music's role in ballet, the average dancer or musician usually first replies to the effect that music is an 'accompaniment' which sets the meter and tempo. There sometimes seems, in fact, to be a universal obsession in the dance studio with the concept of music as successions of 3/4 or 4/4 *bars*, and as a timekeeper (strict and inhibiting). Edwin Denby observes: 'I often notice how dancers who are keeping time become dull and unrhythmic, keeping time at all costs destroys the instinctive variability of emphasis, it destroys the sense of breathing in dancing, the buoyancy and the rhythmic shape of a dance phrase.'[20] A preoccupation with 'beats' is the main feature of this view. 'Keep in time . . . stay on the beat . . . you're not counting . . . don't lag behind', teachers drone monotonously. ('If I count', Margot Fonteyn once said, in contrast, 'I can't hear the music, and if I get nervous I forget to count! Then I'm really lost.') If music is degraded to the role of a metronome, trouble quickly ensues. While everyone is frantically 'counting', the accompanist pounds out beats and measures with all of the expressivity and flow of a pile-driver and the dancers thud onto the shattered concrete.

This shambles is directly linked to the semantic problem of the words 'accompanist' and 'accompaniment'. The Oxford Dictionary defines accompaniment thus: '1. *Appendage*, thing that attends another. 2. (Mus.) *Subsidiary* part, usually instrumental, *supporting* solo instrument or voice' [Italics E.S.]. This, of course, is precisely the meaning that prevails in the general balletic usage of the term, and it automatically makes nonsense of the integrated ideal discussed above. One is left with only the bare bones of the equivalent of a drumbeat for gymnastics, and, more important still, the idea of *separateness*. A definition from another source is helpful here: 'Accompany – to perform with another performer, but in a subordinate capacity; so *accompanist*, accompaniment – a piano being usually understood unless another is specified. When the performers are thought of as equal partners, e.g. in a violin and piano sonata, then *accompany* and its derivatives are to be avoided.'[21]

Obviously, to be consistent with the idea of ballet as a unified effort 'accompanist' should be replaced by a word implying collaboration. (This might have an interesting psychological effect on members of the species who feel down-trodden and low in status.) The term 'ballet pianist' is more neutral, but not adequate for the partnership.

We are left, meanwhile, with that problem of the metrical pile-driver, and this leads to a contrasting problem: repelled by this approach, some teachers and choreographers swing to the opposite extreme. They do not try to force disjointed dance steps onto a metronomic beat, but rather sink into a passive state which is just as much of an obstacle to a dance–music partnership. Now the idea is to respond to and interpret the music. Instead of 'you're not counting . . . keep in time', we hear, 'you're not feeling the music . . . express the feeling . . . feeling . . . feeling'. This is perhaps even worse than the metronomic approach as a preparation for performing.

For a dancer to go onstage with the idea of responding to the orchestra and feeling the music is to invite various forms of disaster. Mishap if the conductor or musicians err while she is totally dependent on the sounds they are making, dramatic tastelessness in the form of intrusion of her personality and 'feelings', dramatic vagueness stemming from her fluctuating reactions to the music as opposed to having a prior conception of the role based on its phrasing and attack as embodied in the music; if these are not bad enough, we can continue. Detachment from her fellow performers – how are *they* 'responding to' and 'feeling' the music? Certainly not, being different people, in quite the same way. The executant and interpretative hazards for an ensemble of dancers should be obvious. And what about her reactions? She cannot simultaneously hear and respond to the music. There will be a time-lag between what she (and the audience) hears and her resulting movement, and this is uncomfortably evident to the audience.

The time for 'response' to the music is not on stage, but beforehand, when conceiving the performance and rehearsing to the music. Reacting to music has nothing to do with the act of performing; it is the perception and use of it in conjunction with its movement phrase – both of which are determined by the larger dramatic vision that unites them – that results in an experience in which others can share. As Suzanne Langer writes,

we can *use* music to work off our subjective experiences and restore our personal balance, but this is not its primary function. Were it so, it would be utterly impossible for an artist to announce a program in advance, and expect to play it well; or even, having announced it on the spot, to *express himself* successively in allegro, adagio, presto and allegretto, as the changing moods of a single sonata are apt to dictate . . . Music is not the cause or the cure of feelings, but their *logical expression* . . .[22]

One may object that the dancer was told to feel the music, not to 'express herself', but what else is the dancer doing but expressing what *she* 'feels' about the music's 'feeling'? As I have seen repeatedly in my teaching, ten people will have ten different feelings about one piece of music. When asked to discuss these, they invariably tell more about themselves than about the music. So, all in all, personal response on the spot to the music would not seem to be a productive approach (I am not denying the spontaneous response which can heighten a prior conception on those magical occasions when everything seems reborn. I am decrying reliance on *luck* on stage).

In the classroom, the problem is different in one respect. There it is not a matter of dancing to known music. The dancers must quickly pick up the quality of the music – which they may never have heard before. This is indeed a challenge. Even if the teacher has the accompanist play while he demonstrates (by no means the rule), their attention tends to be focused on the mechanics of the steps rather than the relationship of what they hear to what they do. The very nature of the ballet class – its structure – make this all too likely. Time is limited, there are many technical faults to be corrected; how can the teacher attempt to deal adequately with the music? A really good teacher, of course, can by some sort of legerdemain manage this, but only if the will and the ability are there. Meanwhile, the difficulty does not warrant despair, for if the dancers have the determination to cope, it is amazing how rapidly they can develop the knack of perceiving and using their music on the spot. To balance the difficulty, there is the immense value this has in training their musical ear and muscular responses. What has no value at all is the command to feel the music; this leads to vagueness of phrasing and attack, and sluggish reactions.

More serious, perhaps, than the 'feeling' of the music by the dancers are the repercussions this attitude has on choreography. A surprising number of choreographers, critics and esthetes have subscribed to this theory. Music is not beats and measures onto which the dance is superimposed; it is 'the controlling model' of dance, and 'the efficient and supporting cause of it'.[23] Dance movement is but a leaf caught up in a musical stream. A favorite phrase within this camp is 'dancing the music', and Isadora Duncan's choreography is the prototype of – and judging from most accounts, warning against – this approach. (She scorned ballet, but influenced its development considerably, and one should distinguish between her rich impact on dance *movement* within ballet and her structural use of music.) 'Isadora Duncan', wrote Lieven, 'was the first to bring out in her dancing the meaning of the music. She altered the whole direction of the dance from pure movement to movement expressing sound.'[24]

Not only is this not true in the sense in which it was intended – the best moments in ballet, from *Giselle* to Ivanov's work, incorporated this idea – but Fokine had already been developing his new concepts in Russia, before he saw Duncan dance. Contrary to the popular notion, Duncan did not directly 'influence' Fokine. Their affinity was more a parallel to the coincidences of discovery that occur in scientific research. But the real danger lies in such phrases as 'The meaning of the music', and 'movement expressing'. Dance would indeed have to be a form of magic, as our ancestors believed, to capture a 'meaning' which has eluded musicians, philosophers and scientists despite ceaseless attempts to discover it. Worse – how does one 'express sound'? No, Duncan was dancing the meaning of the music to *herself*, and she was expressing her *reaction* to the sound, not the sound itself. She herself said, 'My art is just an effort to express my being.' And by allowing the music to command her 'effort', she evaded the choreographer's primary responsibility which is to control and shape many elements into an entity. (Said Adrian Stokes, 'Such a dancer as Isadora Duncan was really a most unconventional kind of conductor. In less inspired moments she followed the music as a bear might pursue a mouse.')[25]

Now, *dancing* the music is closer to our ideal than dancing *to* (i.e. alongside) the music, but what gets lost in this subjective orgy of personal response is the choreographer's vision as perceived by an audience: self-expression vs. universal art, in brief. The major difference between Fokine and Duncan is not that he retained classical ballet technique and she rejected it, but rather that Fokine insisted that the performers 'dance the music' as a means, not an egocentric end. Music or dance *per se* are not, as I have stressed all along, what make ballets. Each must be integrated with other elements, into an organism which partakes of these different elements but is not any one of them, overwhelming the others. (Easily said: 'The fact is', Tudor once observed, 'the general audience sitting out front doesn't realize that it's the music that's sending them most of the time, and not the choreography.')

This concept necessarily excludes both music-as-metronome, and music-as-motivator. True, the choreographer hears and is stimulated by certain musical works, but artists such as Ivanov, Fokine, Tudor, Ashton, Robbins, MacMillan and Tetley are stimulated by the assistance the music *can give* them towards their choreographic goal, not by what it will *make* them do. Within the sometimes precarious balance of ballet's several components, we are faced with another paradox; in one sense the partnership *is* unequal: music gives assistance to the dance; the dance does not give assistance to the music.

Dance: autonomy *vs.* collaboration

So what is 'dance'? As Langer says, 'No art suffers more misunderstanding, sentimental judgment, and mystical interpretation than the art of dancing. Its critical literature, or worse yet its uncritical literature, pseudo-ethnological and pseudo-esthetic, makes weary reading.'[26] Because of this, I must attempt a partial definition within the context of our inquiry – partial because a comprehensive and adequate one is impossible within the scope of this book. I shall draw heavily on Langer's ideas for, frankly, in clarity, consistency, and broadness of perspective I have not read her equal. Dance, according to Langer, is first of all an independent art with its own 'primary illusion' brought about through gesture which creates 'vital forces' or 'powers'.[27] The relation and interaction of these forces, conveyed through rhythmicized gesture, create what we call dance. Gesture is the raw material to be shaped.

All dance motion is gesture, or an element in the exhibition of gesture – perhaps its mechanical contrast and foil, but always motivated by the *semblance* [italics, E.S.] of an expressive movement . . . oddly enough, artists who hold the most fantastically diverse theories as to what dancing is – a visible music, a succession of pictures, an unspoken play – all recognize its gestic character. *Gesture* is the basic abstraction whereby the dance illusion is made and organized.[28]

In defining 'gesture' she writes, 'Gesture is defined in the dictionary as "expressive movement." But "expressive" has two alternative meanings . . . it means either "self-expressive", (i.e. symptomatic or actual) or "logically expressive", (i.e. symbolic or virtual).'[29] Later in this passage, she continues,

In the dance, the actual and virtual aspects of gesture are mingled in complex ways. The movements, of course, are actual; they spring from an intention, and are in this sense actual gestures; but they are not the gestures they seem to be, because they seem to spring from feeling, as indeed they do not. The dancers' actual gestures are used to create a semblance of self-expression, and are thereby transformed into virtual spontaneous movement, or virtual gesture . . .

But what controls the performance of the actual movement? An actual body-feeling, akin to that which controls the production of tones in musical performance – the final articulation of *imagined* feeling in its appropriate physical form. The conception of a feeling disposes the dancer's body to symbolize it.[30]

Or, as she writes elsewhere, '[Dancers] give the illusion of response, not the image.'[31] In the light of this analysis of dance, the discussion above of music as motivator may perhaps now be clearer. Yet to Langer also, music is an integral factor:

The play of virtual power manifests itself in the motions of illusory personages, whose passionate gestures fill the world they create – a remote, rationally indescribable world in which forces seem to become visible. But what makes them visible is not itself always visual; hearing and kinesthesia support the rhythmic moving image, to such an extent that the dance illusion exists for the dancer as well as for the spectators.[32]

Although Langer refers to dance as an 'independent art', and deplores the interpretative view of dance as response to music through personal feeling, she qualifies this 'independence' continually. She does so, vividly, in a passage describing the intense body-feeling, the muscular readiness which pervades innate dancers, and which gives them a sense of freedom from gravity: 'The dancer's body is *ready for rhythm*', and 'the rhythm that is to turn every movement into gesture, and the dancer himself into a creature liberated from the usual bonds of gravitation and muscular inertia, is most readily established by music'.[33]

Those who attempt, as Langer does, to counteract the subjective fantasies which infect so many writers on the dance, understandably stress the independent nature of dance – that unequal partner – yet at the most basic level it is obviously not independent or autonomous in the manner of painting, say, or literature. Andrew Wyeth's intensely American paintings do not need a simultaneous performance of patriotic music while being viewed to make their point; *Wuthering Heights* can be read without external reminders of the Yorkshire moors by means of sets. These complete, self-sufficient worlds are transmitted directly from the creator to us via the tangible medium of canvas or printed paper. A hybrid form like ballet or opera involves several minds creating together *and* intermediary performers, and this gives George Borodin's statement (see p. 14) an added significance. What he says relates not only to the problem of collaboration but the problem of transmission to the receiver.

This leads us to a further consideration: movement and music have been linked since primitive times, but a distinction must be made between primitive, ecstatic dance in which all are participants and later dance which is performed for a separate group, or what Langer calls 'activity' and 'spectacle'.[34] Regarding the latter, she writes,

This [development] dictates all sorts of new techniques, because bodily experiences, muscular tensions, momentum, the feelings of precarious balance or the impulsions of unbalance can no longer be counted on to give form and continuity to the dance. Every such kinesthetic element must be replaced by visual, audible or histrionic elements to create a comparable ecstatic illusion for the audience.[35]

The music, which in primitive ritual was – in part – a direct emotional stimulus, now has a different function; it becomes an agent which helps to connect dancer and spectator. The gulf symbolized by the proscenium in the theatre is spanned through the music which both hear simultaneously.

Fernau Hall writes,

The spectator sees the movement of the dancer's body, hears the music, and translates the two into a kinesthetic image, i.e. a sensation of the muscular effort which accompanies the corresponding motions of his own body to the rhythm of the music. This kinesthetic image carries with it a wealth of associated emotions, actions and ideas . . . Since the music is common to both dancer and spectator it assists greatly in the transference of this image from one to the other . . . the dancing predisposes the audience to hear the music in a certain manner in the same way that the rhythm, melody and atmosphere of the music gives the dancing an emotional significance it would lose if performed in silence.[36]

Hall obviously thinks of the dance neither as caused by the music nor as self-sufficient, able to exist fully without its musical score. Dance and music are complementary, linked by and functioning within the unified theatrical experience, just as the dancer and the spectator are linked and, in a sense, functioning together.

This is perhaps one of the few ways left to us, in our civilized fragmentation, to regain some feeling of the harmony which was lost when the integrated use of dancing–singing–playing–emoting which belonged to everyday life became transformed into separate, specialized, and frequently mechanistic forms of art for consumption by passive 'appreciators', or for intellectual analysis. We have gained much by the compartmentalization of art, but possibly we have lost more. Since we can in no way return to that state of innocence, yet many of us obviously feel its loss deeply, we are peculiarly sensitive to the shadow of it which exists in the hybrid arts of ballet and opera. And perhaps it is this awareness, conscious or not, which separates the spectators who lack it – who need to applaud wildly pyrotechnics and display – from those others who hope, even for only a moment, to recover that harmonious state of grace.

The harmony which results from music and movement complementing each other does not depend on any one approach. There is no infallible 'method'. What we find is a variety of possibilities which can be assembled into three main types, but each must be used discerningly to be wholly convincing. Adrian Stokes gives us an important clue here: 'The connection between music and action', he writes, 'should be one of harmony rather than identity.'[37] Identity implies one 'correct' way; harmony suggests options. I hope that the following analysis will show not only that a great many possibilities exist within the three categories, but also that total commitment to either of the first two is inviting disastrous effects of paralyzing boredom, inadvertent amusement or acute irritation, and to the third – unless the choreographer is unusually talented and clear-sighted – vagueness and confusion, and a sense of his having over-reached himself.

Synchronization – opposition – assimilation

Classifying the following techniques proved difficult at times; it was a bit vexing to assign one to x. only to find it slithering towards z. This should, therefore, be regarded as an informal tally in which clearcut distinctions as listed may not be absolute. Nor do I try to list every possibility!

1. Synchronization

a. Meter, or grouping of beats; tempo; quality; general style and mood – all dictated by the music.

b. Rise and fall of dance phrase coincides with that of the musical phrase; dance follows musical rhythms closely; uses same accents and dynamics: the phrase goes up, the ballerina is lifted by her partner; it goes down, she does a *penché*; the music has a dotted rhythm, the dancer does *pas de chats*; it is sustained quarter notes, she walks in time; to quick running notes, we see *pas de bourrées*; the fourth beat is stressed, the dancer follows suit with a sudden change of direction.

c. Attempts to mirror musical form and technical structure: if one group of dancers enters to the theme, another group is bound to enter from the opposite side when the theme is repeated in a musical sequence; if the music is ABACABA, the dance will have identical sections inserted where musically appropriate; with a fugue, we will see the statement of the dance theme while the fugue subject is stated, and again to each subsequent entry of the fugue subject. The dance is, in effect, imprisoned by the music.

d. Corresponds in texture: in lightly scored musical passages there is only a soloist or a small group of dancers; in huge climaxes or powerful finales, the whole cast strives to project comparable excitement, or a male ensemble performs *grands jetés, entrechats* or perhaps the music is matched by thirty-odd bodies spinning about in triple *pirouettes*.

e. Similar to a. except that the music has little or nothing to do with any intrinsic stylistic or mood quality the dance may have. It is neutral – or as much so as music can be – supplying a metrical framework only. The dance may be executed by a Spanish grandee or a choreographic Carmen, but apart from an occasional 'Spanish' harmony or rhythm, the music is nondescript, pseudo-Romantic nineteenth-century 'ballet music'. This is wallpaper music, written to order, cut and pasted at the ballerina's whim, and interchangeable in sound and application. Since the general practice was to choreograph and compose separately any true harmony was a matter of luck. Here is synchronization at its nadir.

In general, the surface, regulatory aspects of the music are followed, but inner relationships on deeper levels are bypassed. At its best, this category contains ballets that are good solid work, comfortable, reliable, more-or-less predictable and often theatrically exciting. At its worst, it contains two extremes: one is the 'performing seal' esthetic so rampant in the nineteenth century when choreographers staged what were primarily showcases for virtuosos. Neither the dancer nor the choreographer – let alone the audience – understood or cared about the effects of the musical poverty which were inevitable given the working situation. At the other extreme we find what Constant Lambert described as the turning of the stage into a vast lecturer's blackboard. This is most frequent in 'abstract' ballets which find their mechanics in the music. There may be genuine invention and interest where the movement is concerned, but the music is continually swallowing it up and distracting us. The dancers become puppets who are moved about to illustrate the choreographer's lecture as we passively receive a lesson rather than actively participate in a theatrical experience. Between these two extremes we find the dancing-the-music approach, through subjective reactions on the part of the choreographer. This is neither careless, as in the 'performing seal' esthetic, nor is it intellectual and analytical in the way of the 'lecturer's blackboard' efforts. These two are essentially impersonal and non-expressive, while dancing-the-music is, above all, personally 'expressive'. None of these three in unrelieved form can be wholly satisfying in the theater, although they can have many moments of interest or beauty.

2. Opposition

a. Tempos and qualities are contrasted: slow, sustained movement against quick, staccato music; sharp, percussive movement against slow, flowing music.

b. Movement changes accents: by using syncopation it stresses weak musical beats and ignores strong ones; similarly, it ignores or challenges musical dynamics; thus dance and music phrases do not coincide, producing asymmetry and tension.

c. Deliberate dramatic antithesis: sets bright, happy steps to a funeral march or slow dragging movements to a jig, etc. This can be used either to exploit, in an abstract ballet, music's ambiguity or, in a dramatic one, to aid psychological development or to depict temporal change in the manner of the film flashback, i.e. an originally quick, joyful movement-phrase repeated later, in tragic circumstances, to mournful music – or done half-time to the original joyful music.

d. Music's formal organization ignored, or contravened for purposes of design or drama.

e. Stylistic disparity: richly expressive, complex movement is set to, say, a formal Baroque theme and variations; stylized eighteenth-century dance steps to Schoenbergian expressionism.

f. Textures are contrasted: one dancer carries a full orchestral sound; a large ensemble of dancers is finely honed by solo flute.

When used imaginatively, opposition can produce kinetic and dramatic electricity not achievable by synchronization. It fascinates or moves one by its balancing of risk and artistic conception. This choreographer is saying, 'I know I am taking chances, but my conceptions compel me to search for unusual means.'

When only the intellect is at work this category of techniques invites disaster far surpassing that which lurks in the other categories. Above all, it can expose the choreographer as egotist. Now he is saying, 'Look how musical I am – observe my cleverness in knowing how to resist the musical directions, my endlessly fascinating distortions of classical ballet technique.' He is, of course, quite unaware that he is the most fettered of all. In his obsession to defy the music he can never forget it for a moment; spontaneity is crushed when intellect dominates.

While the choreographer is being gratified by his inventiveness, the dancers are often faced with arbitrary, discontinuous movement which is hard for the body to remember, and a weariness of spirit resulting from the contrived aura of the proceedings; and the audience is suffering perplexity, irritation and frustration – sometimes to the point of their leaving the auditorium. When a choreographer is primarily concerned with presenting an image of himself as an inspired computer there is not much for the dancers or the audience to participate in unless they are fascinated by machines which can defy the 'limitations' of normality.

3. Assimilation

Here we enter a complex world, which, while using techniques from the first two categories, transcends their limitations through use in a different context. They are what might be called specific; assimilation is blended. Many ballets generally considered to be outstanding fall into this category.

In addition to transmuted techniques from the other categories, we find:

a. The movements are often not even tied to obvious musical events, either in a positive (1) or a negative (2) way (the choreographer, as one critic put it, sensing the hidden emotional core of the music); they may use the basic metric scheme but pull it into their own rhythmic flow within the larger musical phrase, or draw upon subtler elements, say, an instrumental timbre or interplay underlying a prominent melody.

b. The dance does not consistently rely on any one relationship to the music. It proceeds with a constant awareness of how the two will interact, but in a subtle and flexible manner blends various techniques seamlessly. In the other categories a switching from one technique to another will be much more apparent. And, the dancer may be running to quick music, as in 1b, but she is doing so for a different reason.

c. Part of its strength lies in the many combinations available: Tudor's *Jardin aux lilas* has the stylistic similarity of 1a (e.g. Romantic movement to 'romantic' music), with some textural correspondences of 1d and contrasts of 2f, the contrasted tempos, accents and phrases of 2a and b, the dramatic opposition of 2c – at an extreme – when the dancers are immobile within a deluge of sound at the music's climax, the varied rhythmical approach of 3a, with a continual over-riding of 1c's formal demands as the narrative's unfolding sweeps the music's somewhat obvious technical devices into its own dramatic logic. These are but a few of the various choices which Tudor integrates into one of the most consistent, deeply moving ballets of all time.

Permutations of all the techniques from the three categories seem endless, and it takes wisdom and artistic discipline to view them not as possible elements in a choreographic juggling act but as potential agents within an over-all conception. Tudor remains unparalleled in his creation, over a lifetime, of ballet after ballet showing musical perception of a quality and range that is, simply, astounding. One may or may not be in sympathy with Tudor's esthetic goals, but his insight into music's 'hidden emotional core', his attention to its most infinitesimal detail while retaining awareness of the sweep of a phrase and large-scale inter-relationships, his uncannily apt choice of (sometimes most unlikely) scores, his genius for expanding the musical 'meaning' and dimensions of a piece, and, above – or underlying – all, his wedding of craft and heart deserve the greatest respect and admiration.

Tudor may be unparalleled, but many other choreographers try to go beyond the obvious in their use of music, and show signs of impressive, unusual musicality. Yet attempts at assimilation are often unsuccessful (although one may have greater admiration here for the failure than for the success of a ballet within the more circumscribed categories); lack of skill or controlled vision will produce a kinesthetic muddle for dancer and audience. But, when achieved, assimilation can give us what is possibly the most acutely revealing, multi-dimensional experience to be found in any of the theater's many forms. This is not to decry the other categories; many distinguished, satisfying ballets use the simpler techniques of synchronization and opposition in which the music guides them more literally.

The point here is that the *type* of ballet will determine what techniques will be used. To cite some examples, the multi-act fairytale *à la Sleeping Beauty* is composed of conventional sections within a relatively simple structure: set-pieces like *grand adage*–variations–coda interspersed with story-telling passages. Here the first category usually suits best. Complex psychological narratives like *Pillar of Fire* and *The Invitation* will demand the intricacies of the third. In ballets which do not tell a story, yet evoke strongly some mood, e.g. *Les Sylphides*, *Dark Elegies*, *Dances at a Gathering*, the emphasis will again be on the third, towards the goal of conveying an abstraction of some aspect of the human condition: a timeless evocation of Romanticism (*Sylphides*), communal grief (*Elegies*), the evanescence of youth and relationships (*Dances*).

At an extreme are ballets which are in effect abstractions of an abstraction – the 'pure' relationship of music and dance as *design*. *Agon* is a particularly exciting and effective example. Because these exclude emotion as far as is possible in an art in which human bodies are the medium, and, as Katherine Sorley Walker writes, 'Where audiences are concerned, the appeal of the pure-dance [i.e. wholly abstract, in her context] is largely visual or at best aural-visual',[38] the choreographer tends to rely on the more unsubtle techniques from the first two categories. Unfortunately, story or mood being absent, music can rush in to fill the vacuum and little remains for the audience to watch and experience but the translation of musical patterns, albeit often with *élan* and artistic skill, and dazzling dancing. This is not, by the way, 'dancing for dance's sake' as so many claim, but dancing for *music*'s sake. It is within the equipoise of movement and music found in ballets like Ashton's radiant *Symphonic Variations*, Balanchine's lyrical *Serenade* and Tudor's limpid *The Leaves are Fading* that dance for dance's sake truly exists (dance here not being viewed as autonomous but as a distillation of some facet of 'life') – which raises a point I would like to mention in passing.

These ballets are usually identified as *abstract* ballets. Why do I make a point of this unremarkable fact? Because the term is too casually used, producing confusion. Certain critics make the (illogical) equation, 'dance for dance's sake' + 'pure'-music-as-master = 'abstract ballet'. Others use the term as a catch-all for every plotless ballet from *Les Sylphides* to the latest exercise in musico-gymnastics. Neither is very helpful or illuminating. If one agrees with Langer's definition of dance as *semblance* of expression rather than depiction of it, then *all* types of ballet are 'abstract' (and one begins to wish that the term had never started to be used in connection with dance).

In any case, the important thing here is to remember that however a ballet is classified, each type must achieve, in its own way, the essential fusion of dance and music which contributes toward a fully realized ballet. And whether synchronization, opposition or assimilation are employed to this end, the choreographer is continually beset by problems stemming from aural *vs.* visual perception.

Problems and impossibilities

All choreographers have in common the problems which arise in an art which uses two mediums – the visual one of embodied space, and the aural one of sonorous space. These are radically different, and each is subject to laws peculiar to itself, some being non-transposable except through illusion. One could say that dance makes space visible through gesture, pattern and grouping, and gives an illusion of sound through dancers' rhythm and movement quality; music makes sound-relationships audible through melodic and harmonic progressions, and gives an illusion of space and movement through the use of 'low' and 'high' registers, alone or in combination, and rhythmic patterns. The visible dancer can mimic the heard running eighth-notes, but try as she may, it is impossible for her to depict literally musical key-relationships and modulations or the musical effect of a fugue (four dancers imitating the fugal entrances and subsequent contrapuntal combinations cannot combine to form the resultant changing harmonies between the four voices; they remain four separate bodies whereas the four separate musical voices combine to form a totality).

Even simple musical harmonies cannot be paralleled by bodies. Several notes forming a chord all seem to be occupying the same space as a single tone. The spatial effect on the hearer is different in each case, but a four-note harmony does not take up more 'room' than one note alone. Four bodies, however, obviously need more space than one body, and even if they stood on each other's shoulders in the manner of acrobats, the visual effect would not remotely resemble the entity of a chord.

Another peculiarity is that musical 'movement' is discontinuous while a dancer's movement – apart from poses – is continuous. Each tone is disconnected – a static entity. In going 'up' from tone-entity A to B to C, change takes place as each tone ceases and *is replaced* by the next (no matter how legato the musical performer's effect). The dancer's body, on the other hand, always *remains itself* while moving up or down, left or right (and, conversely, is incapable of true staccato action). The only possible approximation to the dancer's movement, where tones are concerned, would be the continuity of a siren or a slide whistle, which fills in the gaps between the different tones.

Similarly, no direct analogy is possible between movement and music regarding the dancers' spatial *patterns* and direction. 'Music cannot divide space and arrange it methodically; this is left to the dance, the art of mobile sculpture.'[39] Music cannot provide a literal equivalent to swirling circular formations, or a strong unvarying diagonal entry by a soloist, let alone the intricate elaborations which are possible with these and other types of patterns. It cannot even go literally up and down with the dancer, although the natural reaction seems to be usually to follow the musical line's apparent direction. An ascending scale is not the same as an ascending body; the scale has not 'gone' from one place to another, for a tone 'is not an object, to be found in the outer world'.[40] The music gives the *illusion* that it is getting 'higher', but the dancer has *traveled* up through space. This seeming correspondence of direction is a pitfall for choreographers who stick too closely to it; a continual mimicking approach results, unfortunately, in often unwanted humorous effects.

What is the reason for the apparent direction of notes? It has to do with *tension*. This can most simply be illustrated by the action of a singer's vocal cords, although it applies in principle to all musical instruments. The vocal cords consist of a pair of muscles in the larynx, and a stream of air sent against them from the lungs results in their vibration. The higher the note sung, the thinner and more stretched they become; the lower the note, the thicker and more relaxed.[41] (This natural process exists 'mechanically' in all instruments, in varying ways.) The singer's muscles tense more to produce a higher note, and a dancer's muscles are more tense in a leap than in the descent into *plié*. Yet, here lurks an anomaly. A dancer moving downward in, say, a *penché* is not relaxing her muscles as is a singer going 'down' a scale; the *penché* might require more tension than many upward movements. There is also the complication of the counter-action of one leg's elevation. Despite this, a descending scale accompanying a *penché*'s downward shape may *seem* more suitable than an ascending one – at first thought. But it, and many other downward movements in ballet indicate heightened dramatic or expressive moments, i.e. heightened tension – thus theoretically calling for 'rising' music. Another, somewhat bizarre, example: picture a mountaineer tensely descending a sheer rock face, then contrast with it a girl rising effortlessly in a balloon. 'Logically', in a film-score, which one would the ascending music suit, with its inherent tension of performance? Which the descending? However confusing all this may seem, it should at least be apparent that too close an adherence to the illusion of movement in music can be misguided or even idiotic. It is, of course, an effective technique in cartoons, but risky in choreography. It is more complex and subtle than it seems.

Many other such examples of the non-correspondence of the aural and visual mediums could be given, such as *scale*, which has at most only the merest approximation in movement:

An orchestral fortissimo is over a million times louder than a pianissimo, the highest musical note is roughly ten times the lowest, and the fastest tempo has roughly two and a half times as many beats per minute as the slowest. The best human dancer, on the other hand, cannot leap more than about four feet in the air and fifteen feet across the stage, and human limbs can never keep up with the fastest antics of human fingers.[42]

Clearly, identity, rather than harmony, of dance and music is not only undesirable, it is impossible beyond a minimal point. All else is illusion of one kind or another. Realization of this would help to prevent choreographers from pursuing a comic phantom.

Wordlessness: corporeal and intangible communication

We have examined several elements of the dance–music relationship. Now we must scrutinize another – one of great consequence. This is the non-verbal nature of our otherwise dramatic–theatrical ballet. Opera and legitimate plays communicate through words. Dancing must project its message mutely.

Here again music offers one of its unique strengths, which is disputed only in certain rarefied spheres: that is, by means of a wordless language to be able to convey and stimulate, in a non-literal way, feelings and experience of the greatest intensity, which are impossible to isolate and name. All the arts pose ultimately insuperable problems in discussing their nature and meaning, but music does so in a different way from all the other arts; music seems to depict feelings, but a painting, say, depicts both the artist's 'feelings' and the rose or landscape or face which are the form or object he has chosen as the means of expressing those feelings. Music's non-material, objectless power of expression is indeed strange, and no other art possesses it.

Although using 'material' (the body), dance, like music, is wordless. 'A step', writes Noverre, 'a gesture, a movement express what no word can say; the more violent the sentiments it is required to depict, the less able is one to find words to express them. Exclamations, which are the apex to which the language of the passions can reach, become insufficient and have to be replaced by gesture.' They differ, however, in their communication of feeling or states of being in that dance is corporeal, music intangible. But both express, within a time-continuum, unnameable qualities which are nevertheless capable of communicating character or mood to an audience. In this shared ability, again the underlying common power is rhythm. The quote from Fernau Hall regarding kinesthesia (p. 23) was a precursor of what now follows.

The audience participates dramatically and kinesthetically in – it comprehends without words – the joyful ebullience of the young Aurora, the evocative poetry of the sylphs in *Les Sylphides*, or the anguish and need of Hagar in *Pillar of Fire*. How? In a bad performance, very likely from a super-imposition of 'acting', i.e. posturing and grimacing; this approach, unfortunately, reduces the 'participation' to nearly zero for the audience, *or* the dancers, and creates a split between dancer and dance, and dance and audience. You will find that communication of a role in an integrated and dramatically convincing manner comes in another way entirely:

When our dancers act a character they are likely to show what they mean; but they seem to be explaining him to you instead of turning into someone else. Impersonation in dance comes less from explaining the 'psychology' of the character than from sensing who he is from the dance rhythm of the part. For only the effects of dance rhythm can touch the heart in ballet. They are the only ones that look unself-conscious and innocent and therefore really serious . . . [Dancers who 'act'] stress oddity of pantomime rather than expression through undistorted rhythm.[43]

Edwin Denby is writing here about dancers in story ballets, but the principle applies to mood-plotless and abstract ballets as well. Elsewhere he writes,

The dance phrase is formed by variation in speed and variation in stress. Its total length is determined by the length of the musical phrase; its total dynamic range by the nature of the steps and leaps that are used, by the amplitude that is given them in this particular musical setting. And from these different elements the visual reality of dance phrase emerges; and in the course of a piece, the special dramatic characterization of a dance role.[44]

(Oddly, even an actor – despite his seeming advantage of words – must function rhythmically, not only in his speech-phrasing, but bodily. Those who have suffered

while watching a mediocre actor destroy his text, and thus the character he is
portraying, through unrhythmical, unconvincing movement, will appreciate this.
'A great actor must be a great dancer', writes Walter Sorell, and one could add that
a great dancer *is* a great actor.)[45]

The expert choreographer is always, of course, leading the audience to hear the
music in a bodily, physical way and see the dance in an aural disembodied manner,
while combining the two within the larger kinesthetic experience, described by
Fernau Hall. The dance rhythms are already familiar to the audience in their most
basic forms. An angry man moves with different dynamics and rhythm than a
fearful man. In ballet, the Black Swan moves with different ones than the White; the
Giselle of the first act with different ones than the same character in the second act,
and so on. These various universal rhythms of the emotions clothe the bare frame of
classical ballet technique and enable it to be expressive, despite its wordlessness.

The technique alone cannot be expressive any more than the letters of the
alphabet can; the basic steps must be combined within the dimension of carriage, or
bearing, and rhythm. The carriage is a precondition for rhythmic movement. It is
not possible to catch the proper rhythm without some conception, which is then
translated into an appropriate bodily feeling leading to a readiness for action. In a
good dancer this preliminary process need take only an instant. (Or, as Adrian
Stokes writes about the dancer's arrival on stage from the wings, '. . . see how he
leaps into the glare in time with the music: he has taken the plunge without
semblance of hesitation: he arrives as if he has never begun to dance because he has
never stopped dancing'![46]) And at this point, after rehearsal of the rhythmic
movements in the studio, no further thought should be necessary. The body and
muscles take over. In the separate 'acting' described above, continual thinking is
necessary for knowing what to 'do' at a given moment. In one, the dance phrases
persuade; in the other, the dancer imposes his will. In some ballets, for instance
those in the Petipa tradition, it is possible (though not desirable) to get away with
the latter. In those following the Fokine tradition it is difficult-to-impossible to do
so. It is certainly hopeless to approach a Tudor ballet in this way. A dancer who fails
to grasp Tudor's inherent – and often extremely subtle – dance rhythms and their
indissolubility from the mood or character of the role will simply disintegrate
Tudor's unity of rhythmic characterization. The choreographic totality fragments
into steps *and* poses *and* acting, all tainted with a detachment stemming from the
resultant sense of strain and technical preoccupation which is inevitable given
Tudor's movement-phrases – so formidable when approached arhythmically.
Without rhythm, his characters cease to exist; with it, they form themselves.
'Tudor', says Lucia Chase, 'does not explain the feeling he wants; he shows emotion
by motion, by demonstrating the movement. You have to sense the meaning from
him; to find out what he is after, you have to keep doing the movement until you feel
it.'[47] Similarly, says Margaret Black, 'In Tudor's choreography, you never have to
superimpose feeling. *You* don't have to make the movement speak; *it* does'[48]
[italics E.S.].

Regarding a quite different type of ballet, Sara Leland says, 'Mr. B. [Balanchine]
depends on the movement itself to bring out the quality he wants in a ballet, he does

1   Antony Tudor at rehearsal, 1967

2 Antony Tudor rehearsing *Little Improvisations* with Mercedes Ellington and William Louther. Juilliard 1960

3 Class with Antony Tudor. Metropolitan Opera Ballet School 1960.
(Students include Remy Charlip, Pina Bausch, James Waring and Bruce Marks)

not try to develop "expression" in the dancers. It is there, he tells us, in the choreography – we have only to dance the choreography to express it.'[49] An odd similarity of viewpoint in two men whose goals are so different (although, semantically, Leland's term 'quality' is more apt for Balanchine's esthetic, whereas with Tudor we move into the area where the connotation of 'express' as conveying emotion applies more strongly).

To each of them, of course, music is of surpassing importance, and both are habitually described as extraordinarily musical. But rather differently! 'For Tudor, the development of character and emotional tensions, reflected in the music, determine the movements of the dancers. For Balanchine . . . the relation of movement to music may be extremely complex, but not for any dramatic reasons'[50] (you might re-read, here, Cohen's remarks quoted in Chapter 1; this quote forms part of the original passage). For both, however, a phenomenon exists that affects how audiences will react to their so-divergent aims – to, in fact, the work of all choreographers.

Ambivalence, ambiguity and expressivity

Think back, now, to Fernau Hall's description of the mutual effect dance and music can have on one another, predisposing the audience to see and hear in a certain manner. In all sorts of ways, the choreographer can create and organize recognizable emotional rhythms and the music can aurally reinforce, counterpoint, and project these. This variety of ways – harmony rather than identity – is due primarily to a striking characteristic of music (and of dance also, to a lesser degree), even the seemingly most expressive and eloquent: that is, its unspecific, unconnotative nature.

Every listener knows that the same piece of music can affect him differently on different occasions. What at one moment may seem genial and lyrical can, at another, become deeply poignant and even depressing; at still another time, both of these reactions can happen with baffling simultaneity.

There are two reasons for this. First, the musical experience can be colored by the listener's accompanying state of mind at that moment, and also by associations carried over from past hearings. Secondly, no specific, unmistakable 'meaning' can be assigned to any work. Musical tones are in no way the equivalent of a verbal vocabulary. At most they are an alphabet. A *vocabulary* consists of assigned meanings which are learned and later recognized. But the progression C–G–F, say, in music has 'meant' a thousand things in a thousand different pieces. (Unquestionably, metaphor and subtlety stretch literal word-usage until, in fine poetry, it can *approach* music; yet, no matter how far poetry can transcend prosaic meanings, it can never actually become wordless. Music is wordless, *per se*.) Thus music has, as Langer, Leonard Bernstein and others have said, an ambivalence, 'Having either or both of two contrary values or qualities.'[51] It could also be described as ambiguous, 'Obscure, of doubtful classification, capable of more than one meaning.'[52] It is because of this capacity that the choreographer has so many options among the variety of techniques listed in the three categories earlier, depending on his artistic purpose. 'What music expresses', wrote Wagner, 'is eternal, infinite and ideal; it does not express the passion, love or longing of such-and-such an individual on such-and-such an occasion, but passion, love or longing in itself, and this it presents in that unlimited variety of motivations which is the exclusive and particular characteristic of music, foreign and inexpressible to any other language.'[53]

Four choreographers could take Ravel's *Le Tombeau de Couperin* and arrive at four totally different treatments of the rhythm, mood, form and 'message' of this piece – each convincing in its own way. For, as Hans Mersmann has observed, 'The possibility of expressing opposites simultaneously gives the most intricate reaches of expressiveness to music as such, and carries it, in this respect, far beyond the limits of the other arts.'[54] Langer quotes this, adding: 'the real power of music lies in the fact that it can be "true" to the life of feeling in a way that language cannot; for its significant forms have that *ambivalence* of content which words cannot have . . . Music is revealing, where words are obscuring, because it can have not only a content, but a transient play of contents.'[55] Hermann Keller is in accord with Wagner, Mersmann and Langer when he writes, 'Such violent emotion as tragedy can evoke in us is not given to music, but music touches areas into which words cannot reach.'[56] And it can do this because of its ambivalence and ambiguity, touching several areas simultaneously and indefinably.

These give music and dance a limitless expressive scope, powerful but elusive. How does one, for example, extract and identify the quality of the opening section of Beethoven's Fifth Symphony? Is it assertive, aggressive, defiant, bullying, optimistic, stern, confident, affirmative or yet something else? Depending on the performance, I have heard it sound each of these, and, on occasion, several ways at once. Similarly, how does one describe that most joyful of dances – Graham's *Diversion of Angels*? Is it ecstatic, invigorating, gay, cheerful, sunny, athletic, touching, poignant? Again, I have seen it be each, or many, and on one occasion I wept for joy – a most ambivalent reaction. Why was I weeping? I could never *say* why, and the laboriousness of the attempt would destroy the spontaneity and complexity of my reaction (although I am compelled here to *attempt* the capturing of qualities by words).

To convey the many layers of my feeling I would have to resort to a string of descriptive terms; while seeing the dance they existed all at one moment. *One* quality, in any case, cannot exist in isolation within music and dance any more than it can in everyday human experience.

Music goes even beyond movement in this respect because of its immateriality. Despite the unconnotative, wordless nature of dance, one still cannot mistake, say, a female lover's tender gesture for that of a male lover in the same *pas de deux*. There are limits to ambiguity. This aspect alone would prevent dance from achieving the degree of 'abstraction' possible in music. Dance's corporeal nature introduces the sexes, with their structural and physiological differences and our ineradicable associations to these.

Despite this inescapable difference, however, music and dance are alike in the enormous flexibility and variability which their wordlessness allows the choreographer. At no moment is he pinned down to one 'correct' use of gesture or space, musical notes or their quality. He creates his own truth through a magic play of light and shade between the music and the movement, their relation to the theme or idea, and the design of the production, and he does this differently in different ballets.

Perhaps we can see more clearly now why ballet can go so far beyond the idea of music as 'accompaniment', or dance as only reflection of or 'response' to music. Bright *allegro* steps to bright *allegro* music, with the dance mirroring the apparent musical mood and its accents, dynamics and ups-and-downs – this is one valid (if limited) approach. When, however, the choreographer is not satisfied with just pretty or clever steps that suit the music, or an incoherent outpouring of his emotional reactions to the music's surface impressions, he widens both his artistic range and the audience to whom he can speak. The more he frees himself from subservience, the more layers of experience he can explore and the more people he will therefore touch.

All good music and dance has these layers, and it takes time and familiarity for the layers to be completely revealed. They are not set out for you on a glittering surface. During your first contact with such works you may sense that there is much more than you perceive, rewarding as this first impression may be. It is this which makes one return over and over to see or hear a particular work – as opposed to trotting about here and there to compare virtuoso performances of a balletic or musical show-piece. But, not only do these layers stimulate the desire on our part for greater knowledge and perception of a work which has them, they are the main reason why dance and music can affect one another in the first place and why the choreographer has the choice between bringing out some expressive aspects and underplaying others.

This is why many choreographers could use Ravel's *Le Tombeau de Couperin*, to arrive at totally different, yet convincing and 'truthful' ballets. One could emphasize the work's obvious crystalline classicism and symmetry, one its piquancy and subtle asymmetry, the third could focus on its deceptively childlike simplicity and ingenuousness, and a fourth might respond most to its profound tenderness and poignance. It has all these qualities and more, and no *one* choreographer could express them all in a ballet; each of the four will select according to his personality, taste, and artistic theme and vision. Compare with this four choreographers choosing to use the music of the *pas de deux* from *Don Quixote*. In place of layers of feeling or meaning (which are not dependent on thickness of musical texture; Ravel's *Tombeau* is lean and spare in this respect) we have one dimension. Often, indeed, the 'ballet music' of Minkus, Pugni, *et al.* seems to lack any dimension of feeling at all. There is but a top layer of bravura *allegro* music or sentimental tunes for *adage*. And, when you add to this the choreographic esthetic of 'dancer as performing seal', you face the danger of complete superficiality. Uses of the *fouetté* in ballet gives us a clear example of the differences. 'Perfected by the Italian dancer Legnani and used by her in The Swan Lake, it caused a sensation, the audience counting aloud as she performed her famous 32.'[57] Despite this, and the later use of it in many ballets, Legnani's feat was viewed warily

by many. 'It was considered by the best writers an unworthy acrobatic trick . . .
Valerian Svetloff, writing around 1910, said: "If 32 fouettés, why not 42, 52 and 80,
on to infinity, resulting in the complete mechanization of the dance. Technique
must go no further."'[58] But then Massine saw the *fouettés*' expressive potential
and, 'choreography caught up and began to use them, not as acrobatics, but to
express some definite emotion, with dramatic justification; gaiety in *Le Beau
Danube*, the spinning of the top in *Jeux d'enfants*.'[59] Adrian Stokes provides a
vivid description of the latter:

> . . . Bizet had called this piece of music "La Toupie", the top. No interpretation could be happier
> than these *fouettés*, literally whipped steps. Baronova's revolving point and body is the spun top,
> while the other leg by which she gives impulsion is the whip.
>
> At the same time, this movement is not a mere 'following-out' of the music: such is never the
> case in ballet [an optimistic statement, E.S.]: it is more the other way round. The music itself seems
> to become visible, to become a shape *that is complementary to the dancer's shape*.[60]

If, however, the dancer makes us conscious of the difficulty of the *fouetté per se*
rather than leading us to see her – through the spinning-whipping rhythm – as a
living top, this moment will be spiritless and disconnected. We will see merely a
body minus rhythm plus effort, not a dancer-who-is-the-music-which-is-a-top-
which-is-the-music-which-is-the-dancer-who-is-a-top . . . Such unity is what
Stokes describes as '. . . the deftness which is so large a part of the grace in ballet
movement and which, in turn, is an outcome of the ease in execution. This deftness,
this economy or neatness of expression, is a primary characteristic of ballet
dancing . . .'[61] and it should be clear by now that this deftness depends on carriage
and rhythm.

Rhythm and musicality

Stokes, Denby and Haskell emphasize repeatedly in their books the necessity for
effortless rhythm in the dancer – the connection between rhythm and a dramatic,
theatrical projection by the dancer. In all perceptive books on ballet, in fact, the
words 'rhythm' and 'musicality' make their own little entrances and exits and re-
appearances in different contexts, very much like the shifting patterns and
emphases within ballet itself. And to speak of one is to speak of the other, for music
is above all rhythm (see Chapters 3 and 6 for a fuller analysis of this). But, as I
observed very early in this book, 'musicality' is too often applied in a fragmented
narrow way to dancing. A dancer's musicality is even more complicated than the
musician's (which is complex and subtle enough!). A musical dancer is not a
musical musician; her musicality is a blend of two different – but related – things.

Her performance must combine muscular impulses and extremely subtle
shadings of body-timing with the framework of musical phrasing, rhythms and
quality – as used by the choreographer – and the two are by no means the same. This
is why 'dancing on the beat' is so devastating a concept; most of the crucial
preparatory and connecting movements are outside, or even contrary to (*contretemps*) the tick-tock of the beat and meter. They are, as a result, executed (in more

than one sense) in a kind of coma which lifts only when the beat + pose is reached, only to descend again on the way to the next beat + pose. Thus, since all 'high' moments are utterly dependent on the preparations and connections, they remain forever unfulfilled. One could say that the important moments for the audience are the peaks – the fullness of the arabesque, the top of the jump, the spin of the pirouette – and they should not be aware of the preparations and connections *in themselves*, but for the dancer it is the opposite. Most important for her are the goings-into and the comings-out; if these are sensitively and rhythmically done, she will not focus on the peaks for they will achieve themselves *through* the preparations. A flower does not force itself to bloom; the bloom is the result of an integrated process.

No music possesses the *specific* rhythms of the *glissade*, the *pas de bourrée*, the breath before the *chassé*; the dancer finds and creates these through the musicality of her body, aided by the musicality of her ear.

As I have said, in connection with Tudor's ballets, the dancer without this all-encompassing musicality can detract from or even demolish the choreographer's handiwork. No matter how successful he has been in his rhythmic characterization and dramatic interplay between the dancers, these can only come to life through the medium of the dancers themselves. The dancer is the weakest link in the chain and her most vulnerable point is her musicality.

It is when ballet is understood in the Noverre–Fokine sense that the dancer needs true musicality. During the degeneracy of ballet, when music is merely an accompaniment, the dancer requires but a good ear and a dramatic sense that is something apart. In the musical ballet, as distinct from the ballet with music, the ability to act and the ability to understand music are very closely linked together.[62]

Even in ballets outside this tradition, moreover, a truly musical dancer can perform miracles. To see a Fracci, Bruhn, Verdy, Nureyev, Fonteyn, Park, Seymour, Makarova, Baryshnikov, Kirkland, *et al.* in a moth-eaten showpiece can be an unforgettable experience as they bring qualities to it hardly dreamt of at the time of its inception.

When, however, the dancer has musically sensitive choreography to work with, and the choreographer musical dancers, the transcendental moments in ballet are given to us. Certain dancers have been singled out, time and again, for their extraordinary musicality; to me, Fonteyn, Seymour, Makarova and Baryshnikov are supreme among this glorious few. When we read about Fonteyn's 'most vital quality – her sensitive musicality',[63] we are reading about a flesh-and-blood translation of the ideal which this chapter has examined from so many viewpoints.

By so phrasing her movements that each step or pose in an *enchaînement* is given its proper accent, timing and emphasis she brings out their inherent physical qualities as well as the style, character and expression of the dance which a choreographer demands from his interpreter . . . she fills the space between the beats with movement . . . she draws her line and falls into each cadence so naturally and harmoniously that dance and music become one.[64]

A book could be assembled by simply quoting observations of this sort from those writers who perceive the inseparability of musicality and fine dancing (and projection of a dramatic quality or character). Note, in the observations which follow, the striking similarity in conception of ballet, and imagery. I did not, I may add, have any difficulty in finding them; the problem lay in limiting myself to the number quoted.

In a discussion of the second-act *pas de deux* from *Swan Lake*, van Praagh and Brinson say, 'Earlier *pas de deux* by Petipa required mime to say "I love you" because the dance which followed usually expressed little but the virtuoso qualities of the dancers. Ivanov's *pas de deux* required no mime to convey its message. Its movements were visual music so expressive in themselves that even today this dance remains one of the greater choreographic love-poems.'[65] Agnes de Mille says to the young dancer, 'Watch any fine orchestral conductor and you will see how his hands define the shape and dynamics of what he wants to establish audibly. His hands are visual music. Your whole body should be just this . . .'[66] Similarly, '. . . throughout her work [Fonteyn] is made memorable by her musical sense. In performance Fonteyn appears to take the music into her feet; and watching her one sometimes feels – so easily and naturally does she phrase her dancing with the sounds of the orchestra – that she herself is making the music with her own movements.'[67] Regarding Fokine and Fokina's last performance – at the ages of 53 and 45 – the reviewer wrote, '. . . to watch Fokine and Fokina in the simplest movement is to feel the music that is sounding somewhere, and, when the dance is over and the music gone silent, to remember its phrases is to see the dancers again.'[68]

Austin writes of 'this new element which the ballerina has created by the fusion of music and movement [when] the music has been made visible, painted on the air as if by the fine brush-strokes of her limbs. She will, in the truest sense, have made music with her dancing.'[69] Makarova has 'a response to music so sensitive that the music is like the song of her own body when she dances'.[70] We read of 'the dancers whose movements are music made visible . . . rather than obeying the prescription of composer and choreographer, they seem to be inventing the music as they go along,'[71] and '[Seymour's] exquisite floating arms that seem to drift on the slow tides of the music . . .'[72] One can hardly read a dance article these days without finding similar tributes to Baryshnikov.

All describe in some way what Marie Rambert called 'the interpenetration of movement and music, so that you almost hear with your eyes and see with your ears'. An intriguing parallel is found in Eisenstein's *Film Form*, where he writes about the, to him, surprising similarities between the Japanese Kabuki theater and sound-films. He says, 'In experiencing Kabuki, one involuntarily recalls an American novel about a man in whom are transposed the hearing and seeing nerves, so that he perceives light vibrations as sounds, and tremors of the air – as colors: he *hears* light and *sees* sound [italics in original]. This is what happens in Kabuki! We actually "hear movement" and "see sound".'[73] Thus, in dance, these senses can be extended and transfigured so that, in addition to their normal functioning, they seem to change places. This happens, of course, in direct proportion to the successful integration of eye and ear, and the Kabuki theater is possibly the ultimate example. 'The Japanese', writes Eisenstein, 'have shown us another extremely interesting form of ensemble – the *monistic ensemble*. Sound-movement-space-voice here *do not accompany* (nor even parallel) each other, but function *as elements of equal significance*.'[74] Certainly, no form of theater could be further from the star-vehicle ballet.

Paradox of the indispensable dancer

I began this chapter by affirming the value of the truly integrated ballet and, touching on many things which make this possible, I tried to show why music is essential to this vision, and why musicality in the dancer is needed – even in ballets not in the Noverre–Fokine tradition. Proceeding from the general, the collaboration of ballet, to the specific, the dancer who is its instrument, seemed to me the best way to present my argument. This is due to another paradox – the fact that the dancer is in a sense the focal aspect of ballet. She is indispensable for without her there *is* no ballet. All of ballet's other elements can be integrated without her, but this is not ballet. One such way is within the abstract cartoon. The section of *Fantasia* which uses Bach's Toccata and Fugue in d, used music, mood, design and movement to form a whole. Many years ago I saw a fascinating abstract cartoon with a magical score by Matyas Seiber, in which the music was complementary in every way to the visual beauties and patterns. The whole work was a marvel of imagination and integration, but it was not ballet nor did it provide the experience which comes from watching such integration achieved through the human body.

As in all things human, the dancer is a mixture of frailty and strength (which is one reason for the excitement and exhilaration peculiar to good ballet dancing – its defiance and conquest of normal physical human limitations). She is both the weakest link in ballet's chain and the means of the chain. The choreographer cannot exist without her. Despite my continual stress on music and musicality, I must emphasize that the music assists the dancer – the dancer does not assist the music (although she can enrich and expand it).

It is the function of ballet music to provide the best possible foundation – both in the theater and in the studio – and the choreographer, teacher, and dancer are successful to a large degree according to how well they use this foundation. Fine music, however, cannot rescue poor dance. It will simply inundate it. Monk Gibbon describes the situation perceptively:

Ballet is not adorned from music. It starts from it, and before the curtain goes up at all the overture is focussing our attention. Respect for music, respect for the art of ballet itself, and respect – in a profound degree – for the talent of the dancer, these are the qualities which are going to add enormously to our enjoyment as spectators. For though everything may start from the music everything unquestionably ends with the dancer, and it is our delight in his or her skill and gift for interpretation that brings us into theater. Ballet exists only by virtue of the dancers, and what others can do with and for them.[75]

Conclusion: interdependency

As is probably evident by now, the subject of totality is an extraordinarily complex and elusive one, which does not lend itself easily to a linear approach. Ballet is like a

kaleidoscope, in which the crystals fall into ever-changing patterns and relationships; now one or two colors and forms being emphasized, then others. To select
one aspect of ballet and say '*This* is the most important', is no more sensible than to
select one's favorite color or pattern in the kaleidoscope and say 'I only like that
part', and attempt to extract it from the mutable totality. True, while the choice of
basic elements determines both the kaleidoscope's myriad effects and a ballet's
import, viewers will react differently, some preferring or focusing on one element
over another. Yet, the elements all exist in a context and cannot, ultimately, be
separated; a fragment of red glass is quite different from slashes of red in a gold,
black and white kaleidoscopic pattern.

Writers like Gibbon are, consciously or not, aware of this interdependency, and
struggle continually with the difficulties of presenting a coherent written analysis of
our elusive subject. After writing, for instance, the passage quoted above, he later
cautions us:

Ballet does not exist merely to display the prowess of individual dancers. If that were so it would
be simple to see them in a concert programme, just as, if verse-speaking were *all* that counted in
Shakespeare, one might as well stage a concert recital of all the best speeches. It is the dancers who
have made ballet possible. It is their devotion to a great art and their strenuous efforts that have
enriched and enlarged its borders; but *they* in themselves are not ballet.[76]

Austin sagely refers to the dancer as 'the arbiter in [the] age-long argument between
music and the dance . . . It is through her judgment that the music is phrased,
stressed or lingered over. The choreography is not her creation, but the *dance* is
hers . . .'[77] (italics E.S.).

This necessity for continual qualification makes demands on both writer and
reader. The easiest books to write and read are those which state, in effect, 'Music is
the guiding light of dance and possesses all of the necessary impetus for it', or,
'Dance for dance's sake, without the distractions of story, music, costumes, sets, is
what is needed to save ballet from modern impurity and restore to dance its lost
autonomy.' Hall, Gibbon and others quoted herein reject such simplistic attitudes,
and attempt to perform a literary juggling act, showing us now one aspect, now
another, while inter-relating them all.

While emphasizing the importance of the dancer, Gibbon, like Austin, affirms
the equal importance of what is done *with* her and her capacity *for* interpretation.
And both make it clear that ballet's 'starting from music' does not mean musical
tyranny. Although some choreographers allow the music to browbeat them, there
is no inherent power in music which makes this inevitable. We have seen that one of
the most valuable contributions of music to movement is its lack of precise meaning
– its ambiguity and ambivalence. This characteristic gives the choreographer great
flexibility within the more restrictive aspects of phrase-lengths, sections and the
practicalities of meter and rhythms.

There is one constraint, however. Not all music is suitable for ballet. The
problem is to recognize the various pitfalls.

We have looked at the relationship between music and dance; now it is time to
look more closely at the music itself – while bearing in mind Antony Tudor's words
of wisdom:

In ballet the music and the dance are partners, taking in turn the places of junior or senior partners, perhaps not always seeming to get along compatibly, but nevertheless there to complement each other successfully. I do not feel that the composer should have to be burdened with the choreographer as a parasite, living off the blood of the musical creative genius.[78]

3   Music for ballet: stepchild, despot or helpmeet?

Adolphe Adam wrote tunes to dance to, nice for the feet . . . This is music to which one dances. With Tchaikovsky, it is a matter of music in which . . . or beyond which one dances.   Natalia Makarova, *A Dance Autobiography*, 1980

B
ALLET MUSIC, in the truest sense, is not just concert music with movement added to it. Nor should it be music which is worthless away from the dance for which it was composed – although this is often the case. The banal, stereotyped scores which exist are exposed as failures rather than prototypes by the many other ballet scores which have character and musical imagination.

It is easy enough to say what ballet music is not. To say, concisely and indisputably, what it *is* cannot be done. This chapter, therefore, is primarily an attempt to raise questions by looking at characteristics of concert and ballet scores and to challenge certain criteria which often mislead or beguile. Sometimes, as with the 'Germanic' tradition of eighteenth- and nineteenth-century music, my views are somewhat iconoclastic. I offer them, however, because they are shared by quite a few other musicians (and listeners) and because the criteria challenged are so deeply entrenched and unquestioningly accepted in some circles that I believe they could do with more scepticism than they tend to receive.

I do not, however, intend such opinions to be regarded as absolute, nor do I wish to imply that the suitability of music for ballet is determined by comfortable, clearcut rules. A hundred persuasive arguments against the use of certain types of music will not prevent the delightful shock of Jerome Robbins using Bach's *Goldberg Variations*, Antony Tudor and Kenneth MacMillan using Mahler's *Das Lied von der Erde* or Twyla Tharp Haydn's Symphony No. 82 for *Push Comes to Shove*. Nor that these ballets are flawless masterpieces; they suffer from problems, as one would expect given the nature of their scores. Yet each offers something of great value, with results that are unique.

Perhaps, however, this uniqueness is an indication of the difficulties involved, for such achievement is rare indeed; the failure of ballets to similarly 'unballetic' choices of music is *not* rare, and acts – if not as a complete preventive – as a restriction and caution. Still, tomorrow a choreographer may use Brahms' First Symphony, or Beethoven's last string quartets (as Paul Taylor has done in modern dance, with *Orbs*) to wonderful effect, no matter how remote the possibility of success might seem before the event. So, keeping in mind the absolutely non-absolute nature of the subject, let us see in what ways music is conceived and heard – and how these affect its use as a partner of movement.

I shall begin with a few observations on the nature of music for the theater, followed by a look at the two antagonists, 'music for ballet' and 'ballet music'. Then I approach the central issue – what actually happens in a piece of music – from four

44

vantage points: self-sufficient music *vs.* music as a collaborator, 'structural' *vs.* 'episodic' forms, the battle between form and content, and, finally, the different ways in which music can use time, and the related problems of how we *listen* to each type of 'musical time' and how well each suits *choreography*.

Since these are all untidily entangled there is bound to be some overlapping, although I tried my best to separate the strands for discussion. Also, I must mention that my comments are not directed towards the wilder shores of 'modernism'; it is too early to attempt distillation of general principles from such work.

I. The nature of music for the theater

Glamour

One matter on which most writers seem to agree is that music for the theater must have the quality of *glamour*. This being defined as 'magic, enchantment; delusive or alluring beauty or charm', that view seems reasonable. The theater originated in ritual magic, and even today, magic or enchantment is a part of the delusion or illusion which is common to all convincing theater. It can be degraded to sheer escapism but, at its best, theater involves and transforms.

A related attribute is that indefinable something called 'atmosphere' or 'presence'. Every successful piece of theater music has this also, and no other qualities can compensate for its lack. One problem which besets the theatrical composer is that, while every well-conceived piece has a definite style, quality or mood, it does not necessarily have atmosphere in the theatrical sense. While I cannot dissect and analyze this quality, I can say which composers – for me, at any rate – *in general* have or do not have theatrical atmosphere. Purcell has it, Corelli does not. Similarly, Schütz but not Bach; Monteverdi but not Palestrina; Weber but not Beethoven; Tchaikovsky but not Brahms; Bartók but not Babbitt, Copland but not William Schuman. The difference lies in the composer's intent, his selection of materials, and the manner in which he composes them (needless to say, the presence or absence of glamour does not, in itself, determine the worth of a piece of music).

Oddly, the music of the nineteenth-century hack ballet composers often has glamour. It is difficult to say, however, whether this is inherent or due to the association with their glamorous ballets (what is *not* difficult to say is that this music represents some of the worst music ever written, in any time or place). But whether the score is the made-to-order music of Minkus and Co., or the inventive *Sleeping Beauty*, it must have, in whatever way, an aura which contributes to that brief spell that a successful theatrical experience casts over us.

Effectiveness

Good theatrical music can be characterized in another, simple, way: it loses its effectiveness away from its accompanying action. Opera holds an analogy. The music and words – and dramatic action – work as partners. No matter how much you may enjoy an opera aria in isolation, it is artificial and incomplete – one-dimensional – when heard out of context with little or no idea of its function within the dramatic development. Similarly, the music for the Bluebird *pas de deux* from *Sleeping Beauty* is charming, vivid and exciting in a concert performance – but only a fraction as much as when heard in conjunction with the movement. Pre-existing music, used by the choreographer without face-to-face collaboration, will also take on this quality if it is of the sort which makes a good partner. Once you are familiar with *Le Spectre de la rose* (Fokine–Weber), *Theme and Variations* (Balanchine–Tchaikovsky), *Jardin aux lilas* (Tudor–Chausson), *Enigma Variations* (Ashton–Elgar), *Ziggurat* (Tetley–Stockhausen) or *Configurations* (Choo San Goh–Barber), their scores are ever after permeated with dance-images and it is, happily, impossible to hear them completely 'in their own right' – as the pianist John Browning observed of the Barber score during the British ITV program on Baryshnikov (23 December 1983). Never again, he said eloquently, could he play it without seeing various movements and patterns throughout: a welcome tribute from a famous virtuoso.

Timing

Timing is a crucial element in theatrical music – timing being the way in which the composer uses melody, harmony and rhythm to create different, illusory, perceptions of time-spans. For music to contribute towards theater it must, in general, make its effect hand in hand with the action, neither dragging on the action through the necessity of the listener's remembering past events in the piece in order to make present ones meaningful from a structural point of view, nor impeding progress of the action by a need for a deep absorption in the musical present in order to comprehend future musical developments.

II. Music for ballet *vs.* 'ballet music'

For most people who are interested or involved in ballet there are two categories of music. For anyone who detests ballet there are also, to an even greater degree, these two categories. The first category is 'good' ('serious music'); the second is 'inferior' ('ballet music'). The dichotomy was most acute during the nineteenth century, although we have inherited it and it still haunts us. Fokine challenged the distinction between serious music and ballet music, but he did not end it. As long as the showcase ballets of the nineteenth century remain in the repertoire, and as long as composers approach the composing of a ballet score with less love and respect than a concert piece, it will continue. It is partly due to a particular historical development – the detachment of ballet from its original connection with opera (and, earlier, masques).

Purcell, Monteverdi, Lully (who began as a dancer), Handel, Rameau, Gluck and Mozart all wrote the music for the dances which formed part of their operas. It was taken for granted that the 'serious' composer would provide music for the dance-sequences which was of the same high standard as the vocal music. (Sometimes the composers even helped to arrange the dance-sequences.)

These composers, in other words, wrote for dance, as well as for voice, orchestra, a consort of viols, string quartet, or glass harmonica – and they did so with equal craft and love. Their nineteenth-century successors, however, separated into two worlds, one high, the other low. Serious composers, as we shall see in a moment, deserted ballet – or at least the 'great' composers did so. The low world of composers, however, became more and more enmeshed in it – to the detriment of dance, its spectators, and themselves. Their closest counterparts today are not, as some have said, film composers, but rather the suppliers of 'music' for TV commercials. The number of composers who have combined first-rate film work with other outlets is too great to list here, except to cite Benjamin Britten, Vaughan Williams, Aaron Copland and Serge Prokofiev. The number of TV-commercial composers who have done the same is, to say the least, small.

So, in the nineteenth century you had composers of music and makers of jingles. Of course, composers continued to write dance music within opera. Some of these are Auber, Mehul, Boieldieu, Weber, Rossini, Donizetti, Verdi, Bizet, Berlioz, Massenet, Saint-Saëns, Gounod and Wagner. Note, however, that of all these, only Wagner, Berlioz and Verdi (the latter usually on the strength of his later operas, *Otello* and *Falstaff*) are considered first-rank composers. But even the worst of this lot shines in comparison with the composers who wrote only, or primarily, for ballet.

Why? How could a tradition, which goes back, in Western music, to the captivating and vigorous medieval ballads or dance-songs, and the brilliant, often poignantly beautiful Renaissance and Elizabethan court masques and ballets, be so corrupted and perverted?

'Serious' composers and ballet

Two different but simultaneous trends can be blamed for this schism between 'good' music and 'dance-music'. The first trend is a musical one. The remarkable group of composers born during the ten-year period, 1803–13, had personal and professional aims which were antithetical to the new, Romantic ballet – which was born around 1830, wildly applauded during its period of glory, and exhausted by mid-century. Berlioz, Chopin, Schumann, Liszt and Wagner: none of them wrote scores for this concurrent phenomenon. Even Berlioz and Wagner with all their important work in the theater did not grant ballet more than a minor role. While including the traditional dance-sequences in their operas, these were comparatively negligible within the context of the two composers' somewhat grandiose dramatic schemes. The emphasis in the Romantic music of these five, and other, lesser, talents, was on the two extremes of intimate, personal – sometimes almost obsessively so – solo expression through piano or voice; and grandiosity of length, size of performing group, and concept. Neither of these extremes was particularly suitable for the sort of ballet which was being developed at this time.

Such antipathy between music and ballet was, in a way, ironic, for both were attempting a new type of expressivity. They were rejecting the formalism and clichés which had suffocated each by the late eighteenth century when Classicism had deteriorated into cold pretentiousness, and were entering expressive areas never before exploited.

As in music, the greatest significance of the Romantic ballet was not technical, but expressive. Reflecting the neo-Gothic flavor of art and literature in this period, it sought to move the emotions more directly than Classicism could – evoking echoes of the early seventeenth century Venetian school's sensitivity and passion – and to create heightened, sometimes almost hallucinatory, poetic effects. In so doing, it repudiated the escapism of the stereotyped gods and goddesses and sterile forms of expression of opera and ballet in the previous era – the preoccupation with virtuosity and machinery which had been ardently challenged by Noverre, Gluck and Viganò, a brilliant musician as well as dancer–choreographer, who often composed his own scores (and with whom Beethoven collaborated, not too happily, to write his only ballet, *The Creatures of Prometheus* (1801)). These men achieved much, between about 1750 and 1820, but not enough to stem the growing decadence.

While rejecting the sterile escapism of the past, the new music and ballet were, paradoxically, creating at the same time one of the most extreme forms of escapism ever known in the arts. The Industrial Revolution was well entrenched by the 1830s, and people were already bemoaning, in anticipation of our century, the despoliation of the environment and the machine-like quality of modern life. For both composer and choreographer, the escape-routes were the supernatural, the 'poetic' beauties of nature, a glamorized peasantry far from the grim realities of everyday life, and exotic excursions to lands which bore little resemblance to their true-life counterparts. While these all embodied flights from the socio-political implications of the greed, mercantilism and appalling exploitation surrounding the artists, they were admirably suited to the rejection of classical formalism and the exploration of new modes of feeling and communication.

Yet, despite the intense preoccupation of composers and choreographers with these themes, the major figures of each did not come together. The intimate or grandiose self-expression of the composer could not co-exist happily with the relative impersonality of ballet production in which other figures besides the composer must be reckoned with. This was true also, of course, of opera production, but to a lesser degree; most important was the absence in opera of the figure of the choreographer who could and would challenge the composer at every turn. Even within opera, the composers had continually to assert themselves and establish their 'supremacy'. Berlioz and Wagner, both semi-megalomaniacs, drove their operatic associates mad with excessive criticism and a deficiency in the art of compromise. Picture the battleground if an equally dominant choreographer were involved in an extended ballet-form.

An extension of the composers' strongly personalized goals was the importance which performance-stardom had in their careers. Berlioz was unable to capitalize on the demand for 'romantic' solo artists, having learned to play – moderately well

– only the guitar; but Chopin and Liszt achieved renown as concert pianists, and Wagner was a conductor. With the emphasis on self-expression, there was just no psychical room left for the collaboration necessary in even mediocre ballets.

But perhaps it was just as well, for the second important trend of this period would have brought disaster in one form or another to such a project. No longer enjoying the (mixed) benefits of the earlier royal and noble patronage, choreographers and dancers were cast into the cash world of the market-place. Composers, naturally, were also affected by this, but could and did retreat into private worlds to write music for 'posterity' if public circumstances became too difficult. Ballet, however, being a public, theatrical art, obviously could not do the same. It became, more than any other art except opera, a blatant commercial enterprise, and the rivalries for favor and money which had always existed, under any system, were now cruelly intensified by the full flowering of the star-system.

The result was a fierce competitiveness and tyranny. Ballerinas became super-beings who could indulge every whim and command obedience and adulation. They would interpolate completely foreign music into a ballet score in order that they could show off their latest variation-triumph; they refused to dance to certain sections in the music because these either overshadowed them or were too 'difficult' to dance to (They also, of course, were the media through which the exquisite and ethereal evocation of the Romantic spirit soared).

The choreographers, also competitive, alternated between humoring these demands and exercising their own dictatorship. Above dancer and choreographer, the director often ruled all, exploiting both ballerina and choreographer. He could be richly rewarded, and his main concern was the prospect of huge profits (Véron, who became director of the Paris Opera in 1831, when it was changed into a private enterprise, managed to retire in five years with a fortune).

But, because of the ballerinas' immediate, direct relationship to the public, they were, in one sense, supreme: Grahn, Taglioni, Grisi, Elssler, Cerrito, magical, powerful names. Speaking of the preoccupation with the virtuoso, and other negative elements of Romantic ballet, Peggy Van Praagh and Peter Brinson wrote: 'None of these elements was so damaging as the emphasis placed upon the ballerina. By elevating the ballerina at the expense of her partner romanticism in the end drained away the drama and emotion it once gave to choreography. Form dominated content so that display became the principal end of dancing.'[1]

This situation was not likely to entice the composer from his own intense dedication to musical innovation and self-expression. In an art-form which elevated the ballerina so absolutely, composer and ballerina would be antagonists. One or the other would have to yield, and composers of the stature and mentality of Chopin, Liszt, Berlioz, Schumann and Wagner would not do so. But was this inevitable? Even if the 'great' men were unenticeable, other, good composers existed.

How frustrating that the Romantic ballet, which began in a spirit of poetry and expressivity, could first largely ignore then make hostile the very agents who could have expanded and extended its importance, and that as a result, it soon deteriorated into circus and cliché. So the sterile formalism of the eighteenth century was replaced by virtuoso claptrap. But, perhaps this *was* inevitable because of the inherent conflicts which beset mid-nineteenth-century art and society. Poetic and expressive aspirations were confronted by the inescapable realities of the commercial ethos within which they were struggling to develop. 'For the first time in the history of mankind the artist became a "free" artist, a "free" personality, free to the point of absurdity, of icy loneliness. Art became an occupation that was half-romantic, half-commercial.'[2] And none more so than ballet. Being cast into the market-place, as I observed earlier, ballet adopted the 'survival of the fittest' rules of commerce to an extreme. As a result, it soon lapsed into the trappings of Romantic art, leaving the deeper essence to music and literature.

Because of this concern with outward values rather than inner ones, 'The necessity of really good music for ballet only began to be understood when the romantic ballet was nine-tenths dead.'[3] But then it was too late.

The initial potential was only partially realized, short-circuited by commercial circumstance, yet it managed to achieve a new type of ballet, one which left a mark on dance history. One figure who profited from the short circuit was – the ballet composer.

'Ballet music'

Very few of the dozens of ballets popular in the mid-nineteenth century are still performed. One of the reasons often given for the survival of *Giselle* (1841) is its score, which was far superior to those for the other ballets of the period. This alone should demonstrate the appalling quality of Romantic ballet music; Adam's score, while undoubtedly written with care and imagination and having lovely moments, cannot stand serious comparison with the later ones of Tchaikovsky, Delibes and Glazunov. But, it is at least musical and, in its limited way, inventive, with effective use of leitmotifs, and even a four-voiced fugue which has a dramatic purpose. Adam is known to non-balletomanes by his anthem, 'O Holy Night'; the following composers are known to very few, for *any* works. Here is a partial list of popular ballets of the time, with their choreographers and composers:

1832 *La Sylphide* (F. Taglioni – Schneitzhoeffer (1832)/Løvenskjold (1836)
1836 *Le Diable boiteux* (Coralli – Casimir Gide)
1839 *La Tarentule* (Coralli – Casimir Gide)

1842 *Napoli* (Bournonville – Paulli)
1843 *La Péri* (Coralli – Burgmueller)
1844 *La Esmeralda* (Perrot – Pugni)
1845 *Pas de quatre* (Perrot – Pugni)
1846 *Paquita* (Mazilier – Deldevez)

Just as the names of Berlioz, Chopin, Schumann, Liszt and Wagner do not exist as far as Romantic ballet is concerned the names of the above-listed ballet composers do not appear on the roster of significant Romantic composers. They inhabit two, forever separate, worlds.

These ballet composers were kept busy. Since their 'type' of music was considered suitable for choreography, they wrote for production after production – unchallenged by competition from outside their closed musical world. Benjamin Lumley, the greatest impresario of the time, wrote of Pugni's music for *La Esmeralda*, 'for this style of composition his talents seem to have been peculiarly fitted'. In fact, they were not even up to the mark as 'ballet music'. For the somewhat melodramatic, hyper-romantic scenario of *Esmeralda* – which was loosely based on Hugo's *Notre-Dame de Paris* – the score is, in Fernau Hall's words, 'quite inadequate'.[4]

Here, actually, is the most serious deficiency of the Romantic ballet music. No reasonable person expects a ballet score to be a masterpiece, but these ballet composers did not even have the craft and imagination to serve melodrama or supernatural fancies effectively. And they certainly were incapable of matching the poetic mood, emotionalism and exoticism of the better ballets. *Giselle* and *La Sylphide* survive, but others, perhaps equally effective, did not. Cyril Beaumont calls *La Esmeralda* one of the great dramatic ballets, yet it fell from the repertoire, except in Russia. If not the *only* reason for this, its score is sure to be an important one, burdensome to the dramatic action and trivial musically.

This is an extremely sobering thought, for the history of nineteenth-century ballet could have been changed radically if the great imaginative composers of the time had been collaborators. The themes of this choreography cried out for the visionary and original musical minds of men like Berlioz, Chopin and Liszt.

What these themes got, however, was music with no originality and but little craft. The inadequacy of dramatic imagination was in fact the expressive result of mediocre musicianship. The ballet music was merely (apart from sporadic, naive attempts at 'atmosphere') a metronome to keep the dancers 'in time'. It gave only guiding meters and simple rhythms. Thus, the many scores of this period were, in general, indeterminate, interchangeable, and of varying degrees of inanity. Specifically, as Joan Lawson observes of what she calls the nineteenth-century purveyors of Special Ballet Music, 'the rhythmic flow of melody suggests a regularly spaced set of poses with only sufficient time between each to allow the dancer to move from position into pose and out again into another position or pose'.[5]

An interesting side-issue of this flat pose-rhythm is the approach of these ballet composers to their scores for ballets with a nationalistic flavor. This can be seen clearly in the music for *La Esmeralda*, *Paquita* or *La Sylphide*, each of which almost totally lacks any true feeling of France, Spain or Scotland – their respective settings.

Rhythm is of all musical elements the most important; in fact, it underlies harmony and melody, which could not exist without it. It is particularly essential to musical evocation of a country. Each country has characteristic, highly individual verbal rhythms which the composer absorbs, consciously or not. A composer born in Spain will create markedly different rhythms from one born in England or Russia (assuming that their native rhythmic stresses are not obliterated by training in International-Academese). And a composer, born elsewhere, who wishes to evoke France, Italy, Spain, Russia, Germany or any other country, must employ their indigenous rhythms, or he will fail. Perhaps the most strikingly successful musical-travelling was done by Debussy and Ravel in their many imaginative trips to Spain. Close examination of these scores will show how important a part rhythm played (see also Chapter 7).

Anyone with a good ear will be aware of the different inflections, patterns and rhythmic continuity of various languages, even if they are incomprehensible grammatically. The incisive rapidity of Spanish, the fluid grace of Italian, the guttural, assertive pace of German, the somewhat percussive yet monotone cadence of American English, the powerful but curiously liquid nature of Russian – none of these could be mistaken for another.

We find even a national difference in carriage – physical bearing – and movement. Perhaps the most obvious is the electric, proud carriage of the Spaniard which is intensified in the flamenco dancer. But within the musical Esperanto of the ballet music purveyors, the national rhythms are translated into an international sameness. A few 'Spanish', or 'Russian' harmonies or melodic clichés, accompanied by equally clichéd rhythmic mottos, are dotted here and there, but the native rhythmic *cadence* never has a chance to prevail. A generally neutral landscape is sprinkled with bits of local color.

As a result, the carriage of dancers who are performing, say, *Paquita* or the *pas de deux* from *Don Quixote*, is something which is superimposed on mainly neutral music which could have been (and often was) interpolated from another ballet, one set in a different country altogether, equally indeterminate. Instead of having music which could stimulate, through its rhythms, appropriate bodily-response, the dancers must create a dramatic nationality out of musical anonymity. The national dances, on the other hand, in *Coppélia* and similar examples of imagination and quality, illustrate vividly the missed opportunities of the pseudo-nationalistic ballet music.

Not only nationalistic or exotic scenarios suffered; those of a poetic or Gothic-supernatural character were equally marred by the music. Such qualities could not be evoked by the banal, similar melodies, the limited, flaccid harmonies or the academic rhythms which prevailed.

In this way, a vicious circle was established, composed of the dominant ballerina who never hesitated to shuffle bits and pieces of ballet scores in order to show herself off to best advantage, or generally to ignore the music except for its meter and tempo, and the composer who mechanically ground out characterless scores to order – scores in which such mutilation did not matter. The resultant imbalance, in which the music was a liability rather than a strength, continued as a legacy for the rest of the century and well into the next. The handful of composers who, in contrast to this dreary tradition, illuminated ballet, was not enough to shake such a firmly entrenched nullity.

Writers do not seem to be able to agree whether the schism between serious music and ballet music originated from the musical camp or the balletic one. Probably no one answer is adequate. Certainly serious composers did not give ballet the benefit of the doubt, and choreographers did not wish to have competition from men of equal or greater stature.

The temperamental qualities which made the Romantic composers unlikely partners for ballet creation do not necessarily prevent their music from being, in many cases, highly suitable. *Les Sylphides* (Fokine–Chopin) *Carnaval* (Fokine–Schumann) *Dark Elegies* (Tudor–Mahler) *Dante Sonata* (Ashton–Liszt) and *Dances at a Gathering* (Robbins–Chopin) are some of the best posthumous musical 'collaborations'.

I have dwelt on the nineteenth century here not only because this is the decisive point in the ordination of art-music *vs.* dance-music, but because a message of great significance lies in the musical folly perpetrated by composers, choreographers and directors of the time. Yet perhaps the danger now lies more in the opposite camp; choreographers today all too frequently are impelled to use music which either fights the movement or swallows it. This will be one of our main preoccupations in the following sections.

III. Self-sufficiency *vs.* collaboration

Ballet music was too weak to be a true collaborator; at the other extreme lies the music which is, in certain ways, too strong to permit the co-existence of another art. If collaborative music could be compared to a tent, which is flexible and adaptive, a 'self-sufficient' musical work is a fortified castle. Or, to put it another way, we have just seen music as a servant, deprived of the benefits and responsibilities of an equal partner. Now, in contrast, we shall be concerned with music as a master.

This might seem a straightforward problem, but in fact it is deceptive and subtle. For one thing, although the ideal is considered to be music composed in conjunction with the choreographer's creation of the movements, many such direct collaborations have produced musical scores just as dominating and unsuitable as already existing ones. The determining factor is, actually, the essential nature of the music – its intent and compositional procedures. Many composers for ballet permit themselves to indulge in the same absorption in technical devices and formal games as they do in their concert music. *One* such section is enough to disrupt a ballet. An existing score can be a partner as well as, or sometimes better than, a live composer can.

Since choreographers everywhere are ransacking even the most unlikely areas of music, we should look closely at the properties which make music (whether existing or commissioned) suitable or hazardous for the choreographer. To begin, a comparison of the self-sufficient, or autonomous, score and the collaborative, or marriageable, one.

Automatic greatness and assumed inferiority

'If the composer gives of his best in the ruthlessly self-centered way which produces great music, then the odds are that he will produce bad ballet music. Music of the highest quality of inspiration and architecture must necessarily be complete in itself.'[6] This statement by Antony Hopkins provides two examples of traditional attitudes and values. First, it presents blatantly the elitist, ivory tower view – narrow in the extreme – which continues to afflict musical criticism and pedagogy. It fairly bristles with pre-conceptions, value-judgments and academic prejudice. Note the words, 'his best', 'great' and 'the highest quality of inspiration' – not to mention the idea that the latter is present only in music which is 'complete in itself'. This nineteenth-century Superman propaganda has harmed composers no end, from those who were obsessed by and tried to emulate Beethoven's 'greatness', to the student composer today who can feel a pressure to produce 'important' or 'significant' music every time he writes a measure or a phrase.

In addition, Hopkins has given us a valuable phrase in 'the ruthlessly self-centered way'. To have ruth is to have compassion, and compassion not only means the sharing of feeling, but implies an inclination to help. The 'great' composer, in his ruthless self-absorption, obviously not inclined to do anything of the sort, *cannot* approach composing in the co-operative spirit of a partner. *He* must have full control over his musical materials and their 'significant' development.

As for Hopkins' 'great' music, 'of the highest quality of inspiration', many other writers have implied or stated pointblank that ballet can only be successful when it uses 'second-rate' music. This is unhelpful, being again but a value-judgment. What such writers almost always turn out to mean is that 'great' music = 'masterpieces' = 'pure' or 'absolute' music. This cannot be challenged too strongly; a work which is not 'self-sufficient' or 'pure' is *not* automatically inferior or second-rate. A true criterion should be whether the work in question is good in its own terms. If the score is good, i.e. musical, inventive, invocative, compelling, convincing, technically adequate for realization of its musical materials, etc., then it is not only good *ballet* music but good *music*.

Some musicians, fortunately, dismiss such pre-conceptions. One of the most anti-elitist musicians I've known, Norman Lloyd, wrote,

Dance, opera, a play with incidental music, and vocal music with a text are forms in which music is combined with movement, words, lighting, sets and/or costumes. These forms have ancient roots – many of them are traceable to primitive religious rituals. To relegate such music to a secondary position in a hierarchy, behind so-called 'pure' or instrumental music is a bit naive. Such an attempt to rank different types of music shows a lack of understanding of the many natures of music, which exists for many different purposes and in many different ways.[7]

Self-sufficiency, invariance and purity

Antony Hopkins conventionally associated 'great' music with the architectural principle. The pieces acclaimed (in the Western world, that is) as masterpieces turn out, with boring predictability, to be those in which formal procedures, and structural tensions and balances are paramount. And these are, without a doubt, the most uncompromising of masters for the choreographer.

Such music is the most 'abstract' of forms of art. And yet, paradoxically, the same kind of 'self-sufficiency' can exist in the much more concrete medium of words. As Constant Lambert observes, '. . . a Beethoven symphony, like a speech in Hamlet or an ode by Keats, satisfies us completely in its present form. Any action which might accompany it would either be an irritating distraction or a superfluous echo'.[8] As a contrast, he asks us to transport mentally Tchaikovsky's Blue Bird music to the concert hall referring to 'the flat effect',[9] which could only satisfy us incompletely. Elsewhere he speaks of the *concentration* of a Hamlet speech, an intellectual poem by Donne or a Keats ode. The word concentration gives us a major clue.

Being abstract, music lends itself to a peculiar sort of concentration of ideas and craft which are perhaps comparable to philosophy and mathematics. Even good composers are tempted to pursue the intricacies of technique for its own sake – the 'working-out' of material – because such concentration and refinement of their materials are intellectually challenging, and somehow more elevated than the aim of swaying a listener's emotions.

The fugal exercises produced by students are the most extreme form of this concentration, in which almost all content and expressivity are squeezed out by the mental joys of fabrication – although Bruckner, Reger and Busoni are not too far behind on occasion. Such music goes *beyond* self-sufficiency, because no other art would care to, or could, associate with it. It is a meaningless self-sufficiency which can be compared to a factory product, for it shares with this the concentration – that is, the elimination of non-essential, unproductive elements – which is necessary for successful and profitable manufacture. Stravinsky (himself something of a cultural factory on occasion) actually used this term when he wrote, 'The Germans manufactured, and manufactured music with themes and leitmotive, which they substituted for melodies.'[10]

Taking into account his natural bias, this still raises an interesting point. It is undeniable that musical self-sufficiency has been the province of German composers, or those trained in a prevailingly Germanic academicism which could be found in music schools from Russia to America throughout the nineteenth and early twentieth centuries. (A necessary distinction is made by Paul Henry Lang between 'German' and 'Austrian' symphonists in an illuminating discussion of this complex and often misunderstood area.)[11] But even composers like Haydn, Mozart and Beethoven, who are considered part of the Austrian tradition, obviously belong to the 'architectural' mode in their symphonic works, which are masterpieces, not of free-form or theatrical imagination but of imagination controlled by established structural principles.

Stravinsky's curt appraisal has no doubt raised eyebrows and caused irritation among masterpiece-worshippers since it first appeared in print. The following comments by Lucia Dlugoszewski – a musician who has worked for some time with Erick Hawkins – may stir even more unfriendly, probably violent, reactions in certain quarters. Yet, is she so far off the mark when she writes:

Invariance extends our control over the natural world to staggering dimensions and defines the realm of the senses as impermanent, contingent, subjective, untrustworthy, and finally evil. It is thus responsible for the distinction of sacred as against profane and for the problem of art versus life. It is responsible for the German tradition of music, which is demonstrably still the essence of American music, and which considers itself abstract, theoretical, disembodied, spiritual, and absolute . . .

In this German tradition, music is defined as sacred and theater is profane . . .

With such a tradition music would inevitably dominate dance unless it involved a second-rate composer badly performed. Dance could never make such impressive claims to invariance nor successfully hide its contingence. It is obviously trivial. Actually to join such music to dance is impossible and it is a failure of long standing.[12]

Whether one is a foe or a partisan of the Germanic tradition, it incontestably occupies a unique niche. And Dlugoszewski not only points out the sacred-seriousness of this tradition, but, in referring to its 'spiritual', or metaphysical, character, she helps to explain why even the Germanic music which departs from the pure, instrumental, medium to use words is often equally self-enclosing, at least where use for dance is concerned.

I would like to assert at this point that, in fact, once one begins to question the automatic superiority of works in this tradition a new world opens. A fully realized argument on this subject is simply beyond the scope of the present book, although it appears as a thread which runs throughout it.

I am well aware that the music world at large does not agree with my views on this subject, or those of Stravinsky and Dlugoszewski. To many, in fact, they appear heretical. But whether they believe that this tradition is but one – sometimes oppressive – of many valid forms of expression, or that it is the culmination of centuries of musical creation, both camps agree, for the most part, that such music is not for dance, or is at best extremely chancy.

In case there is any misunderstanding, I must make it clear that I am not for one moment denying the expressivity and humanity of the best of Bach, Haydn, Mozart, Beethoven or Brahms. I am, however, denying that the use of all such works, bad or good, as a criterion by which to judge the treasures of the thirteenth to twentieth centuries which lie outside this tradition is reasonable. It is at once foolish and an exercise in sophistry. It is to say that even the dullest symphony is tacitly granted first prize.[13]

And I must remind the reader that the concept of a musical 'masterpiece' is the merest newcomer in history, or the idea that pure music is the best. Before the eighteenth century it was taken for granted that music must serve words, dance or social functions. Rather than being an end in itself, it belongs to the everyday world and the many activities of man – of which singing and dancing are two of the most important – as it did spontaneously, until the advent of the self-conscious conception of the composer–creator.

Music which so emphasizes the abstract and spiritual, demands, because of its often remarkable concentration, the listener's full attention. And underneath all the arguments against the use of such music for ballet lies a most basic one – the interplay between eye and ear.

Seeing and hearing

The aspect of these two modes of perception which concerns us here is their respective powers of concentration – and also how their concentration is affected by music which is too 'concentrated' to leave room for dance. While it is pure snobbery to reject the use of a great symphony or fugue for ballet because it is 'too good' for it, awareness of the perceptual conflict caused by the combination of movement and a 'masterpiece' is only common sense. A fully realized work in this category is most exacting.

During works, however, like Debussy's *La Mer*, Mussorgsky's *Night on Bald Mountain*, Schumann's *Carnaval* or a Chopin Nocturne, the concentration of ear might be described as relatively relaxed or diffuse. The listener, in fact, is almost invited in varying ways to suspend concentration or thinking, and even to visualize scenes, moods or events. This visualization is a radically different activity from the cognition necessary for full understanding of a symphony or fugue.

Self-sufficient works such as a Bach fugue or a Beethoven symphony or quartet require so much aural effort and processing of musical information that the mind cannot cope with – or often even perceive – any additional stimulus. Either what one is hearing blots out what one is seeing, or each activity becomes superficial and incomplete. One of my most vivid theatrical memories is a performance of José Limón's *Musical Offering*, to Bach's score of the same name. The music became a radio performance which someone was perpetually tuning in and out, and the choreography became a film in which, over and over, the screen went blank only to pick up again at some later point in the action. As a result, neither the music nor the choreography made any sense overall; I had gathered bits and pieces, mutually exclusive high points, along the way in each, but I had no idea at all of the submerged form. One thing which all self-sufficient works have in common is that this submerged form must be part of the listener's experience *throughout*. Although it is preferable, obviously, that the listener give consistent attention no matter what type of piece is being heard, self-sufficient and programmatic or evocative music actually call for two different *sorts* of attention. With the first, the attention must be *ex*clusive; with the second it is *in*clusive, permitting another sense, the eye, to co-exist with and contribute towards a mutual effect. Otherwise, a battleground is created – as with the *Musical Offering*.

Concentration *vs.* spontaneity

'The merit of a ballet score', writes Fernau Hall, 'cannot be judged in isolation from the content of a ballet for which it is composed. The best score is not necessarily the one most suitable for concert performance, what matters is the impression the music makes on the audience *while the ballet is being performed* [Italics in original]. The audience do not listen to the music with the same concentration with which they listen to a concert.'[14]

So, there are two types of listening involved. The first is the peculiarly exclusive sort demanded by a self-sufficient work; the second is the sensitive awareness suitable for program, mood and theatrical music. The self-sufficient master does everything to command attention from the audience–spectators. (An unusual departure for Tudor was the use of Beethoven's *Leonore* Overtures for *La Gloire*. The composer seemed not to appreciate this; in Denby's words, 'Beethoven kept trampling madly on the bits of it.')[15] And this master possesses many powerful and intricate means for such command – all precluding a quality which dance-music requires almost above any other: spontaneity.

No truly self-sufficient musical work has overall spontaneity. Controversial as this may seem, I must say that you will look in vain for it in a symphony or a fugue (although fine performers can given an illusion of it). Actually, it is their various *excellences* which bar it. The very nature, intention, construction and economy of such works call upon its opposite – *will*. Will must be employed to write such works and to comprehend them fully as a listener.

Let us consider in this light some dictionary definitions: spontaneous – 'acting, done, occurring without external cause . . . involuntary, not due to conscious volition; growing naturally without cultivation'. I believe that many people confuse musical inspiration with spontaneity. No matter how 'inspired' themes or possible developments of them which occur to the composer may be, they are ordinarily subjected to continual rigorous – conscious or subconscious – thought and shaping.

'External cause': the deliberate shaping of themes and motives suitable for symphonic or fugal development; 'involuntary, not due to conscious volition': it is impossible to expand and fulfil such themes and motives without a great *deal* of conscious volition; 'growing naturally without cultivation': leaving aside the semantic problems of 'natural', it can at least be hazarded that a symphony or a fugue is one of the most *un*natural things in all art – at least in the sense of 'natural' as 'instinctive', or 'physically existing, not spiritual or intellectual' (although a fine composer of course merges inspiration with intellectualization during their creation).

It does not seem far-fetched to say that the usual aversion of those of Latin temperament to the fugue and the sonata-allegro principle is directly related to the above observations. This would be due both to the mental concentration demanded of composer and listener, and the unspontaneity in the physical sense. The Latin peoples have always been a bit contemptuous of what they view as the northern teutonic–Anglo-Saxon physical repressiveness and intellectuality.

If you are immersed in a perceptual process, you are not free to move. The mind has precedence over the body. But good dance music must aid precedence of the body over the mind not only in the dancer, but also in the audience. To dance is, among other things, to *abandon* yourself, to, in the words of Victor Zuckerkandl, enlarge and enhance the self. And, most important to this present argument, it is a means of breaking down the barrier between what is being contemplated and those who contemplate it. To intrude inappropriate, 'self-sufficient' music is to *erect* a barrier between dance and audience, and to enervate the physical abandon and kinesthetic, interacting experience of both.

Since this is not so much a linear examination as a circling one, let us move round to our next vantage point and look at self-sufficient and collaborative music in their more specific roles of what may be called *structural* music and *episodic* music.

IV. Structural obduracy *vs.* episodic adaptability

In this section, what we have been calling 'self-sufficient' music will be termed 'structural', and 'collaborative' music 'episodic'. If the structural category contains music in which the composer is *primarily* concerned with logical, formally balanced edifices created through the imaginative yet always controlled manipulation of material deliberately fashioned, then the episodic can be described as being that in which the composer is working in looser, more flexible, or extremely free forms which consist, again *primarily*, of emotive, poetic or evocative materials. These are, as a rule, neither intended nor suitable for the extended development and architectural balance of structural music.

Although a fugue is, in a way, the Parnassus of the structural principle, a Beethoven sonata, symphony or quartet offers the most dramatic illustration of the structural mind at work. In his remarkable musical sketchbooks we see the methodical, painstaking, almost obsessive molding and altering and hacking away of basic themes and motives until they attain a form which is appropriate to his structural and expressive vision.

Of course, a good symphonist does not concoct a theme, and then proceed to develop it: the theme and the future developmental and structural possibilities must be conceived, to at least a minimal degree, in tandem. Episodic music, in contrast, seems more to evolve – in the case of narrative or emotive works like Mozart's *Magic Flute*, Liszt's *Totentanz* or Chausson's *Poème*, or to spontaneously change scene or mood – as in poetic or illustrative ones like Telemann's *Don Quichotte*, Debussy's *Préludes*, Schumann's *Papillons*, Mendelssohn's music for *A Midsummer Night's Dream* or Tchaikovsky's for *Sleeping Beauty*.

One of the most strict, uncompromising, 'logical' pieces ever written is the Prelude and Fugue in B flat minor, from Bach's *Well-Tempered Clavier*, Book 1, yet the expressive effect is shattering. I can think of few works which equal it in conveying a dark sense of the inevitable, while at the same time overwhelming the listener with an affirmative passion. Conversely, the strikingly evocative and emotive score of Britten's *The Turn of the Screw*, which so magnificently illuminates the drama and ambiguity of Henry James' ghostly tale, is a remarkable technical achievement. All too many operas – in all periods – are episodic in the extreme, being inorganic strings of solos, duets, ensembles and recitatives – collections of short, separate 'numbers'. Not so with this triumph of craft. There is, however, an important difference between these two works, one rigorous almost to the degree of a mathematical formula, yet deeply moving; the other impassioned, stirring and ominous, yet controlled by an ingenious and omnipresent technical substructure. The difference was brought home sharply to me while teaching. Several years running I played each for my sophisticated third- and fourth-year dance students in the Literature and Materials of Music Course. At the end of the Bach Prelude and Fugue I would wait, year after year, for that gratifying confirmation of one's own taste, the group response to a piece much loved – and what I got instead was mainly a mixture of blank faces and pained expressions. Then, as usual after playing a work, I spent some time in an analysis of it – the material, how Bach expanded it from beginning to end, the resultant shapes and curves, uses of tonality and dissonance, motivic relationships of the Prelude to the Fugue, the inexorable build-up of dramatic tension, the ways in which he approached the final phrase and cadence of each, and more.

Every year, I *then* saw a growing interest in this piece – initially perceived as 'harsh', 'dry', 'boring', 'depressing', 'sterile', 'too technical', to repeat only a few typical comments – with several students interrupting my analyses to offer their own observations. Almost always, the mood of the entire class had changed. It of course was different each year, for no two class-groups react identically. But, although a few might still find it ugly, the remainder of each class would range from extremely interested (in this 'boring' piece) to emotionally stirred.

The Turn of the Screw was quite another matter. The first hearing produced the mixed results one would expect from listeners with different tastes. Then, my analysis was followed dutifully or with moderate interest. The second playing produced, unlike the Bach, more-or-less similar reactions to the first – and when I tried to stimulate the students' interest by reminding them of particularly inventive technical aspects, they were polite but unmoved. Each, almost without exception, retained the original response – bored, curious, fascinated or stirred.

After several years of this, I was forced to conclude that the emotional import of the Bach Prelude and Fugue could only be released for the listener through some prior conscious perception of the note-by-note techniques, the craft from section to section, and the resulting over-all structure. And, in contrast, the technical substructure of *The Turn of the Screw* simply did not seem to matter. The students who liked it responded to its emotional import with or without technical knowledge, and those who didn't like it were not won over by its infinite marvels of craft.

I realize that this illustration only scrapes the surface of the perceptual differences in listening to different types of music, but it serves as an introduction to the arguments of the following sections.

Thematic character

Of all the differences between structural and episodic music, perhaps their respective thematic material is the most obvious. Speaking in the most general way, one could say that in the former the theme or motive is less important *in itself* than what it leads to, being more or less impersonal, whereas in the latter the thematic material has immediate presence. More precisely, the generating material of a structural work seems import-laden, pregnant, reaching out, while that of an episodic work is already born and existing now. It retains this feeling of entity, moreover, no matter what thematic transformations may take place, whether the entity consists of a singing melodic line like the *grand adage* love-theme in Act Two of *Swan Lake*, a series of dramatically thrusting harmonies as in the opening of Liszt's *Les Funérailles*, or strong, brief rhythmic motive of the sort which appears throughout Stravinsky's *Rite of Spring*. In each case, the material is so strongly of the moment that the listener is unlikely to project ahead, being absorbed by the *now*. A structural theme, however, is not what might be called a *fait accompli*, but a potential – sometimes the merest shadow of a potential, considering the relative duration of some motives and what subsequently happens to them. The motive may consist of three or four notes, which the composer then shapes, molds and fulfils throughout a fugue, a symphonic movement (or even an entire symphony).

The generating material or theme of episodic music, in contrast, strongly resists this sort of treatment. Being so much itself and of the moment, the atomizing, expanding, or disguising processes which are used to construct structural pieces tend to destroy its entity or integrity. Polyphonic procedure, of course, most lends itself to 'abstract' realization of thematic potential, with, as we shall see, the symphony (or sonata-principle) occupying a hybrid position.

Deryck Cooke writes of the polyphonic masterpieces:

the themes are sometimes scarcely more emotionally expressive than brick or blocks of stone and are used simply as raw material capable of being built up into large-scale sound-constructions by means of interwoven lines, various sections being balanced one against another in size, until their combined mass makes possible a final climax, setting a seal on the whole like a tower or a dome . . . The experience derived from a piece of polyphony, like that derived from a piece of architecture, consists mainly of a perception and admiration of its form . . .

On the other hand,

. . . in most cases, the experience derived from a piece of non-polyphonic music, like that derived from a painting or a literary work, is only partly referable to an appreciation of its form: much of it derives from our emotional response to its actual material . . . a theme in a sonata, like a hand in a painting or a line in a poem, is already of absorbing interest in itself, even if its full significance is only appreciated when its integration into the overall form is understood.[16]

All quite true, but in need of qualification. The symphony could be said to stand between, to partake of both structural and episodic-literary qualities. It is difficult to categorize, for it encompasses both architectural and emotive features, the latter becoming more and more important during its later development. On the emotive side, the symphony originated in the spirit of drama – statement, action and *dénouement* determining the three-part sonata-form of its first movement (although not in the degree or manner of the histrionic symphonies of the mid and late-nineteenth century). The related idea of conflict continued to grow and intensify through the symphonic work of Haydn, Mozart, Beethoven, Schubert, Brahms and, most extreme of all, Mahler. Themes and motives could be highly significant and expressive, unlike those of the originators of the symphony. But, to keep this in perspective, remember that all symphonies in which no dramatic program challenges the logical thought and balance which is the main attribute of the symphony, possessed one essential feature. This feature, in fact, was the very seed of the symphony – that is, a particular use of tonality. The prime *raison d'être* and excitement for the composers who introduced the sonata principle – C.P.E. Bach, Stamitz, Monn, Richter, and others – was *the relationship, conflict, and resolution of tonal centers.*

This is not limited, of course, to the earliest symphonists, but it is most nakedly clear in their work. Their 'themes', or subjects, often are no more than sky-rocketing arpeggios or scale-patterns – anything which will clearly establish the *key*, which was the real hero of their symphonies. This becomes more masked as one progresses through Haydn, Mozart and Beethoven because of the greater emotive content of their themes and subsequent developments of them. One need, however, only scan these works, noting the tonalities in each section, to see how carefully plotted and balanced they are. As one musician has put it, the themes are the costumes which are worn by the real protagonists – the tonal centers or keys.

Now, a key is hardly the stuff of emotive drama; of tonal drama, certainly, but here we are back in the world of self-sufficient, abstract music. And, whether or not the reader disagrees with any of the previous observations, I think that few would deny that a theme from a symphony by Berlioz, Liszt, Tchaikovsky or Mahler – all excluded from the hallowed world of 'pure' symphonists – is different from a theme from the symphonies of Haydn, Mozart, Beethoven or Brahms, and also plays a different part throughout the work.

Beethoven offers a particularly interesting illustration for, because of the dramatic nature of his symphonic themes and development-sections, many listeners believe that he 'burst' the formal bonds of the symphony. Nothing could be further from the actuality. His themes and their treatment were *dramatic*; the themes of the composers who broke through symphonic form to create the symphonic poem and the dramatic-symphony, were *histrionic*, with an emotive directness. Beethoven's thematic drama and expressivity are, in comparison, somehow once-removed; they are impersonal in the sense that the power of Fate is impersonal. His themes do not speak to us with the direct, revealing intimacy of Chopin's, Tchaikovsky's or the other Romantics' themes.

Beethoven was uncompromising, never sacrificing balance and control as achieved through tonal tensions and releases for expressivity (although his contemporaries often thought he had taken leave of his compositional senses). Emotive composers, in contrast, while often working with symphonic principles, relinquish repeatedly the structural ideal to self-expression, or, often, themselves as embodied in the various protagonists of their 'program'-music. The theme is indeed the hero here, not the tonality – which has either become subsidiary or, particularly in Berlioz, Liszt and Mahler, begun to disintegrate. With Rachmaninov and Tchaikovsky, in fact, the themes are such entities that they can serve as the bases of twentieth-century popular ballads.

So, in the final analysis, the themes of the great symphonists – Haydn, Mozart and Beethoven – no matter how expressive they may seem, still belong more to the realm of raw materials than to that of fully realized expressive statements. To Constant Lambert, this is a matter of 'physique'.[17] He offers an interesting argument through examples of two composers, Mozart and Tchaikovsky, who divided their time more or less equally between the concert hall and the theater, observing that while the *essentials* of their music exist in either setting, there is a different *physical* expression of these in the concert piece and the theatrical. He then compares the tunes in Mozart's operas with the first and second subjects of his symphonies, concluding that these are in no way interchangeable. One could say that they move and breathe differently.

Tchaikovsky, too, although his symphonies are 'impure' and diffuse by Mozartian standards, shows different physiques. His ballet themes, with their kinetic anatomy and small-scale, sectional organization, relate to dance-impulses and events; those of his symphonies relate in their disembodied expressive way to the spacious evolution of a large-scale, self-justifying form.

V. Form *vs.* content

Crouched beneath all this is the age-old dilemma of form *vs.* content. To those who indulge in this depressing debate, Form is associated with, among other things, the 'objectivity' of self-sufficient or structural music, whereas content is relegated to 'subjective' music dependent on pictorialism or dramatic emotiveness, which is either formally weak, or, at best, of less significant form because of its smaller scale or looser organization. This categorization indicates both an artificial separation and, on the other hand, one peculiar difference.

'Form' here *should* mean 'form of expression' but it tends to be used in the sense of form = mold or scheme. It is also commonly believed that 'technique' creates form. Content is viewed as an antithesis, a mysterious blob of expressivity which awaits the discipline of form and technical manipulation. Form involves technique; Content consists of emotion.

These distinctions are not only foolish, they are verbal and conceptual gymnastics and a perversion of analytic method. To produce what we call music, 'form' must shape some sort of expression, and content cannot be amorphous and formless. Or, to use a verbal analogy, a diagram of sentence structure has no literary meaning, or content, whatsoever; conversely, a collection of attractive words: opalescent, luminous, evocative, poesy, illuminate, alliterative, etc., is equally meaningless, for the words are not shaped to form a communication any more than a collection of random notes or harmonies will form a musical thought. Separation is a futile exercise, much like the attempt to separate 'mind' and 'body'.

It is, however, equally foolish to maintain that form does not play a larger part and a different role in some works than in others. Form, moreover, can exist in one very particular sense. Just as a body can be seen without its inherent mind, and a sentence-diagram can exist independent of its actual word-content, so can musical 'form' be visualized and diagrammed, abstracted from its actual note-content. In this sense alone can form be divorced from content, and it has no musical value whatsoever, except to puzzle-fanatics. 'In the work of any composer, "form" and "content" are not separate, nor even fused, but ultimately two aspects of a single entity: "form" is, in fact, as the word implies, the form-into-which-the-composer's-emotion-has-been-converted, and "content" is a word to indicate the fact that this form can be converted "back" into some kind of equivalent of that emotion.'[18]

This concept clearly has nothing to do with the unendurable 'analyses' of symphonies and fugues which academic music professors substitute for integrated comprehension of Mozart or Beethoven. It also transcends the cold, calculated constructions turned out by musical mechanics of the eighteenth and nineteenth centuries (or the twentieth-century mathematician-composer Milton Babbitt and his followers). Cooke's concept of form is a living, dynamic one.

Another difficulty exists in our artificially separated subject. This is that only a tiny minority of listeners respond primarily to the formal aspect of the musical entity. I know that I, a life-long musician, become interested enough to explore deeply the formal aspect of a work *only* if it has moved or excited me. This is why the many assignments to analyze works of no expressive interest to me form the most dreary memories of my entire life as a student. Much of the music I most loved, moreover (and still do), is considered so formless by some academicians as either to resist 'proper' analysis or to be unworthy of it. Mussorgsky and Debussy are two examples both of whom were militant rejectors of institutionalized form and technique – Mussorgsky, especially, for political, idealistic reasons; his identification with the serfs' struggles forced him to eschew Western music's rhetorical principles and return (with great future impact on composers) to the roots of primitive and Oriental Russia. As a result, he was misunderstood and considered clumsy.[19]

Cooke considers that '. . . in music, as to a greater degree in literature, a work can be outstanding in spite of being cast into a most unsatisfying form: we listen to works like *Boris Godunov* and Delius' Violin Concerto, as we read books like *Tristram Shandy* and *Moby Dick*, not for their formal beauty but for the fascination of their material'.[20] This may seem to suggest the separate existence of form-as-diagram referred to above, but it does not. *Boris Godunov* may not have traditional 'beauty of form', yet, understanding form as organization and coherent expression, this opera, or *Pictures at an Exhibition* – to name another work considered 'primitive' by form-purists – do not and *cannot* lack it or they would not have such a powerful dramatic effect. The organization of their expressive materials is suited to the rough, 'chaotic' essence of these materials.

Out of these related problems of self-sufficiency *vs.* collaboration, structural conception *vs.* episodic and form *vs.* content, one fact emerges which has a particular bearing on music for choreography: namely that self-sufficient music appeals *indirectly* to the listeners' emotions through particularly rigorous and extended modes of formal organization of materials, while emotive or episodic music – suitable for collaborative existence – appeals to the emotions *directly* through more apparently spontaneous expressive procedures, or, as in Mussorgsky and Debussy, no traditional procedures at all.

I have tried to show why self-sufficient music is peculiarly unsuitable for choreographic movement in ballet, but will add Constant Lambert's view before ending this section. According to him, symphonic form, 'the most concentrated, intellectual, and withdrawn from present action (as opposed to emotional retrospect)',[21] exceeds any other type of music in its unsuitability for physical and dramatic expression.

My only quibble with this statement is that he omits mention of the fugue, which is even more concentrated and 'intellectual' than the symphony. But his reference to emotional retrospect is valuable for our inquiry because it focuses on a key element – the use of time. Every piece of music fills a given span of time, but not all do so in the same way.

VI. Time

Music exists in the medium of time, but this is never a 'real' time. It can fill its allotted span in various ways, none of which correspond to the passage of time in everyday life as marked off by a clock. This peculiarity is one of the greatest powers of music. Real time is suspended by perceptual time. But, since this can take several forms, which affect the listener – and the dance – differently, we must describe each one in some detail.

Constant Lambert approaches this problem when he compares two possible compositional approaches to time: one, the dramatic succession of themes as found in, say, Liszt or Strauss, and, two, the temporal dictations of formal balance, as in Mozart's symphonies. The first resembles acts of a play or appearances of characters; the second embodies architectural-tonal principles. Thus, the first involves the gradual unfolding of character or event, leading to a final catharsis, while in the second, a theme's recapitulation cannot provide this dramatic release of emotion. Instead, it 'balances' the exposition in the way that trees on either side of a picture balance one another.

Lambert refers here to two ways in which composers use time. Actually there are four recognizable ways, and I shall call them static, immediate, narrative and 'becoming'. The first has not, up till now, been examined closely; like the second and third it belongs to the categories of collaborative or episodic music, discussed in previous sections, and the last is the self-sufficient, structural type (the narrative and 'becoming' categories are the two referred to by Lambert). I will then consider the additional question of variation-time.

Static, non-progressing music

This is seemingly the simplest of all, yet it is perhaps the most difficult to work within. Usually employing few or none of the forms and technical devices which the average listener takes for granted as the 'normal' methods of writing music, it exists in a curious dimension – a timeless one. One of the most extreme examples, for Western ears, can be found in the apparently formless, endless Indian ragas – which to nine out of ten Western listeners are simply 'monotonous'. Other examples are the music which forms part of the Japanese Kabuki Theater, equally suspended and immobile, the hypnotic Tibetan chants, and the glittering, jewel-like music of the Balinese gamelan orchestra. Most music, in fact, outside the Western tradition seems to us similar in that it does not 'progress'.

What, then, of Western music? Despite the infliction upon Western society of progress, some composers declined the pursuit of such a goal: to write music which 'advances'. With these composers, in fact, the rejection of the techniques and forms which create a feeling of striving towards goals was often a deliberate rejection of the philosophy behind the musical means, and an attempt to return to the non-striving, timeless philosophies of the East. This is, perhaps, most clear in the pantheistic music which Debussy wrote under the influences of Balinese gamelan music and medieval organum (which was more Eastern in concept than Western).

Mussorgsky also, as I have said, rejected Western techniques, responding to the Eastern elements of Russian music and culture rather than the Westernized academicism of the Moscow Conservatory. As a result, his music was considered 'interesting' but regrettably primitive, with Rimsky-Korsakov going so far as to attempt to pull it together and give it shape by, among other things, altering harmonies in order that Mussorgsky's chordal 'aberrations' would become *progressions* with comfortable destinations.

Other composers who suspended time in many of their works are Satie, Delius, Koechlin, Stravinsky, Vaughan Williams, Messiaen and Chávez – whose *Antígona* and *India* Symphonies do so in two almost opposite ways, as we shall see in a moment. Sometimes a composer may write a static section within a work which proceeds more traditionally elsewhere. The opening of Holst's *Hymn of Jesus* and the slow, 'night-music' movement of Bartók's *Music for Strings, Percussion and Celeste* both seem to be in a state of trance. More recently, we have the minimalists – Riley, Reich and Glass, among others.

Earlier non-progressive music exists in the ethereal, bodiless Gregorian chant, the medieval organum already mentioned, the complex sacred polyphonic motets of the fifteenth and sixteenth centuries and the organ fantasias and toccatas of the seventeenth. All of these, in fact, in addition to Eastern sources, figure importantly as influences in the later composers I have cited. All such music, to a greater or lesser degree, is pervaded by a feeling of suspension, of contentment in a moment out of time. This music simply *is*. It has no past or future.

This state of being can be induced either through rhythm or harmony – or a combination of the two. In Gregorian chant, which has no harmony, it is created by the pulseless rise and fall of the melody. In Palestrina, or other polyphonic composers of his type, it comes from the pulseless interweaving and asymmetrical phrasing of the various contrapuntal lines, each of which comes to rest or soars at different moments than the others. The motion of each is different in actuality even though all are moving theoretically in conjunction.

In such music, rhythm produces a static quality because it lacks a 'beat', but it can also operate in the opposite way – through the most energetic, stirring kineticism. much of Chávez's *Sinfonía de Antígona* uses the former: a beat-less, disjunct motion; his *Sinfonía India* is a *tour de force* of the latter approach. Here we are confronted, almost physically assaulted, by small kernels of rhythmic patterns repeated over and over and over with the force of a 'primitive' ritual. The amount of energy produced throughout is formidable, yet in a strange way it is not a *pro*gression of energy but a *com*pression. One might say that the timelessness of the former, non-metrical, sort is macrocosmic and that of the hyper-metric latter, microcosmic.

Stravinsky's *Rite of Spring*, of course, has this latter quality in the extreme, as does much of Bartók's fast music. Many sections of Mussorgsky's *Pictures at an Exhibition* are made up of these typical microscopic rhythmic patterns sometimes prolonged almost to the point of frenzy. Even the Promenade theme consists of recurrent small patterns which seem to make the one promenading to be going round in circles rather than from picture to picture.

The static feeling produced by *harmonic* usage can be found in most of Stravinsky's works, and also throughout Debussy, Messiaen and the more 'impressionistic' pages of Delius and Vaughan Williams. In pieces like 'Nuages', from Debussy's *Three Nocturnes* for orchestra, *La Cathédrale engloutie* and *La Terrasse des audiences au clair de lune*, from his piano preludes, or throughout the opening section of Vaughan Williams' Third Symphony, we are far from the convention of harmonic agents moving through time towards a future goal. Rather the chords seem to vibrate in a haze, each one existing only for itself, only for that instant. Every succeeding chord is more or less unpredictable, thus directionless in the conventional sense of to and fro.

All such music is, as I have said, non-striving music – markedly un-Western in concept. Our tonal harmonic system was devised to assist the depiction of contrast, progress and resolution; the works I have mentioned have no contrast in the Western tonal sense, little feeling of progression, and certainly equally little feeling of being 'resolved'. Often, in fact, they either stop dead, as if they had been cut off, or drift away, seeming to be continuing somewhere out of earshot. Much of it could even be described as seeming to exist in space rather than in time.

On the simplest harmonic level, it is the difference between a. and b.:

    a. I–V–I–V–I$_7$–IV–V$_7$–I
    b. I–II–VI–III–II–IV–III–V–VI

The first progression pulls us through time from the first chord to the last, even though it lacks meter. The second progression – or rather succession – seems to float hither and thither, without a set course or feeling of time passing. During the first we have a sense of moving somewhere, but during the second we may need reassurance that we are not about to disappear into a timeless void. The latter music, in fact, is often disconcerting to traditionalists, who counteract their uneasiness by dismissing it as 'primitive' or 'uncraftsmanlike' – just as they label the static music which is arhythmical as 'boring' and 'uneventful', and that which is rhythmically repetitious, hypnotic and excitingly relentless as 'noisy' or 'monotonous'.

I should mention here one particularly odd type of musical non-movement, never found before the twentieth century. This is the non-repetitious, unsymmetrical rhythms used in twelve-tone and much *avant-garde* music. Here we have perhaps the most curious sort of immobility of all, for the rhythms themselves are jagged and electric, full of nervous tension, yet the overall effect is arhythmical. Not only do the complex, varied rhythmic patterns within the ensemble tend to cancel one another out, containing almost no sense of pulse, but the underlying harmonies also tend to de-rhythmicize these patterns even further. As complex as the rhythms, dissonant, so fast-changing that they perversely seem to stand still, the general effect of such chords is almost totally unphysical – except in the sense of a feeling of paralysis which often results from the hyper-tension of both the rhythms and the harmonies. This is the immobility and timelessness of anxiety, and differs from the suspended or the kinetic sort.

Immediate

In music which makes an immediate effect, the present is all-important. The listener *exists* in a continuing present and the music has continual *presence*. It is the theme, the phrase or the section which matters, not where each came from or where it may go. This music, however, is not static, seeming to come from nowhere and go nowhere; it is more a case of our being so caught up in the momentary event that we are not concerned with origins and destinations. And within its continuous present it very definitely *moves*. Here we are neither suspended, nor are we taking a prolonged, often complicated journey as is the case with music which narrates or is in a process of becoming. Rather we are making a series of short excursions. These excursions may take the form of alternating themes or sections of equal interest, or of successive pieces in simple, short A–B, A–B–A, or rondo-forms. Well-known examples abound: Prokofiev's *Visions fugitives*, Stravinsky's *L'Histoire du soldat*, Ravel's *Ma mère l'oye* and *Le Tombeau de Couperin*, Saint-Saëns' *Carnival of the Animals*, Bizet's *L'Arlésienne* suites, Chopin's preludes, mazurkas, waltzes and nocturnes, Schumann's *Carnaval* and *Papillons*, Schubert's songs, Telemann's *Don Quichotte Suite*, Handel's *Water Music* and *Royal Fireworks Music*, Purcell's incidental music for *The Gordian Knot* and *Abdelazar* – and, of course, ballet scores like *Coppélia*, *Sleeping Beauty*, *Nutcracker*, *Gaîté Parisienne*, *La Boutique fantasque* and *Cinderella*.

The first thing which leaps to mind is that these works are almost exclusively homophonic. Involved counterpoint plays little part in such music. This is partly due to the time-scale; contrapuntal writing requires a certain amount of time in which to spin out its lines convincingly (and the somewhat absurd effect of a little *fugato* section stuck in between two homophonic ones – which appears in more than one reputable composer's work – is partly due to the abrupt juxtaposition of two modes of musical time). With music of an immediate nature, this time is not available; it makes its thematic or sectional point clearly and moves on to the next moment.

These short forms are particularly suited to poetic or pictorial sketches and impressions. (In this sense, a Chopin prelude is as 'impressionistic' as one by Debussy.) They easily contain the quick brush-strokes of an evocative picture or idea. These evocations, moreover, are not obtainable through polyphonic means. A work with interweaving contrapuntal lines can gradually create a strong feeling of mood, but not only is this usually limited to one mood for its duration, unlike the sharp mood-contrasts possible in homophonic music, it does not have that pointed, instantaneous impact which is essential to immediate music.

Some composers, notably Schumann, use movement of inner voices to create 'false' counterpoint. This device effectively enriches and enlivens the main lines – giving an added feeling of movement – but these inner voices are not autonomous in the manner of long contrapuntal lines. They are, rather, intermittent and dependent.

Immediate music, therefore, is usually homophonic and composed of short time-spans, each of which is relatively complete in itself, although there may be hidden links throughout. One outstanding example of disguised thematic relationships occurs in Schumann's *Kinderscenen*, in which the opening theme appears either overtly or subtly from movement to movement. This is not the thematic transformation of a large-scale symphonic poem, nor the thematic evolution of a symphony. It resembles instead an actor donning different costumes to play several roles. (Interestingly, this is the way in which Tudor fashioned his *Little*

Improvisations to the Schumann; as usual, he perceived a deeper musicality – theatrically so effective.)

The effect of music in this category can be, despite its comparatively limited means, surprisingly rich and varied, but no matter how much so, its use of time is always simple and direct. Immediate music consists of a captivating succession of moments, similar or contrasted.

Nationalistic music has a particular immediacy. Being generated by folk-songs, it shares with them an existence in the here and now. Utterly unsuited to long subtle development and 'architectural' structures, the works based on or incorporating the spirit of folk-song need to be constructed sectionally. These sections may be separate, as in Dvořák's Slavonic Dances and Liszt's Hungarian Dances, or contained within one continuous but contrasted movement as in Tchaikovsky's *Capriccio Italien* and Rimsky-Korsakov's *Russian Easter* Overture. Many composers have made the mistake of using a folk-song as the basis for a symphony; not only does the immediately perceived entity of the folk-song defy the breaking down into parts which is necessary for symphonic treatment, but its minute time-scale is dwarfed within the immensity of a symphonic movement.

The folk-song could be viewed as the prototype of all immediate music, possessing its characteristics – brevity, instant evocation of mood or scene, and absorption in the moment – in the most concentrated degree.

Narrative unfolding

Music which adheres to, or develops and embellishes a dramatic theme, occupies time quite differently from static or immediate music. This is so whether it tries to depict literally the adventures of a protagonist – as in Berlioz's *Harold in Italy*, Strauss's *Till Eulenspiegel* and Tchaikovsky's *Romeo and Juliet* – or uses the themes themselves as symbolic heroes – as in Chausson's *Poème* and Liszt's *Funérailles*. Both types are designed to convey a sense of dramatic progression through time and experience, with a conflict leading to eventual resolution (as in a play), or even transformation (as in Strauss's *Death and Transfiguration*).

This is a peculiarly nineteenth-century approach, histrionic and emotional, cast not in the form of dramatic opera, with its scenes and numbers, but in the unfolding form of the tone-poem or the symphonic poem. The latter term is more apt, for it points up the contradiction and the problem which beset composers of such music. Borrowing large-scale, extended concepts and procedures from the 'absolute' symphony, they at the same time had to bend, distort and inflate these in order to accommodate the poetic, emotive or dramatic time-sequence.

Using musical time to depict character, events, or development and interplay of states of mind, such music is continually faced with the factors of balance and structure which are the major features of the symphonic procedure which so influenced these narrative works. A very successful narrative work is Richard Strauss's *Till Eulenspiegel* (used by, among others, Nijinsky and Balanchine). Here, despite the underlying rondo-form, we proceed through Till's various adventures, the two main themes conjuring up Till's world and his character. These themes sweep us along by means of alteration and orchestra coloring, through what seems to almost be real time. In a freer form, and without a story, we have Chausson's *Poème*. Here a dramatic main theme, with expressive subsidiary ones, conveys a sense of theatrical unfolding in time, even though there are no characters and events. The melodies themselves are the characters, and the evolution of the music consists of what the passage of time, and their interaction within this, does to them. Other examples of narrative form include Liszt's *Les Préludes*, Rachmaninov's *Isle of the Dead*, Sibelius's *Tapiola*, Schoenberg's *Transfigured Night*, and Rimsky-Korsakov's *Sheherazade*. The emphasis in all these works is on contrast of mood and character within a flux of musical time more seemingly realistic than in any of the other categories.

The process of 'becoming'

From what has been said about structural, or self-sufficient, music thus far, it should be clear that such music is from first note to last becoming itself – realizing its ultimate *gestalt*. It does not do this in the narrative-dramatic manner of music which creates a simulacrum of real time; there, although the music might also be said, in one sense, to be becoming something, this is not a fully realized *form* but a quasi-theatrical or an emotive experience.

Music which 'becomes' in an architectural sense does so either mono-thematically, as in a fugue, or through the use of two or more themes or subjects, as in a symphony or quartet movement, or a sonata-allegro type of overture. The main characteristic of either is that the music cannot be pinned down and savored at any one moment, for itself. No portion offers itself to us for immediate, involved enjoyment in the present, like, say, a Chopin prelude or a section from *Sheherazade*. The concluding stretto of a fugue is not an event; it is simply the most intense, concentrated experiencing of time within the overall flow of the fugue. In itself, it has no more organic meaning than the last instant of a gesture. Similarly, the recapitulation of a theme in a symphony, or its coda, is but a part of a cumulative perception. But, as I have stressed, this cumulative effect, using past, present and future, differs from that in narrative or mood music. The finale of Mozart's Fortieth Symphony or Beethoven's Fifth leaves us with the feeling of a disembodied (though powerful and affecting) ideal – an apotheosis – whereas works like *Tapiola* or *Transfigured Night* (or Chopin's Prelude in D minor, op. 28, no. 24, which is almost a miniature 'tone poem') produce the personal catharsis experienced at the end of *Hamlet* or *A Doll's House*, achieved through a sense of temporal 'advance'.

The question of variation-time

I have left the problem of variations until the last, for they offer a curious example of music which can utilize time in any of the four ways discussed above. *Variations*, moreover, must be distinguished from the *variation-principle*, which has been part of the musical experience since the very beginning. Variations, as a set form, were simply the structural materialization and codification of an age-old process. Since the subject of variation looms large in the chapters on improvisation, I shall only make a few comments which are pertinent here.

It was in the seventeenth century that the structure which we call Theme and Variations was solidified. One of the most famous examples is the Corelli sonata, 'La Folia', which is both exciting music and illustrative of certain problems. Here we have the essential formula: theme plus x number of varying treatments of it. These treatments were, however, extremely repetitious and formalized compared to later developments in variation-technique. Although such sets of variations were tonal, and thus had the feeling of motion which accompanies the use of keys, the over-all feeling is a *static* one. The inexorable succession of variations, usually beginning and ending in the home key, plus the thematic and harmonic repetitiousness, creates the feeling that one is simply not getting anywhere at all. Often, in fact, there is no way of telling, in an unfamiliar set, which will be the last variation. Whether good, like 'La Folia', or mediocre, like so many, they seem to just go on and on – and then the last one stops, and that is that – often not a very satisfying end. But this was a matter of circumstance, and partly due to the large role which improvisation could play in the performance of such works.

Now, not only might variations differ from performance to performance but some actually be left out on occasion, or others added. Thus it is an *open* form. It has, moreover, a thematic continuity but not a temporal one. In many cases, we could shuffle such variations about with the total effect hardly altered. This is not to say that all variations of the period were lacking in complexity or growth. Couperin's *Passacaille* combines, most dramatically, rondo-form with theme-and-variation procedure, Purcell's arias over ground-basses are masterpieces of ingenuity, and other composers also avoided the static repetitiousness characteristic of the simplest variation-sets.

Later, Mozart, then Beethoven, used structural principles within variation-forms to create miracles of invention and imagination while conforming to the restrictions of the Classical ideal and its time-orientation.

Romantic composers, of course, brought their characteristic qualities to variations, using time in immediate or narrative-dramatic ways – sometimes deftly combining these. Schumann's *Carnaval* and *Kinderscenen* seem immediate, but actually are subtle examples of a variation procedure which was one of Schumann's most striking contributions to music. They are immediate in that each separate section can be fully enjoyed in itself, but on a deeper level, they are dependent on the basic thematic material which assumes different guises, and at times even approaches the narrative-dramatic use of time. Tchaikovsky's Theme and Variations from the Suite No. 3 for strings also is primarily immediate in its effect. Each variation is enjoyable as a set piece, like one of the *Sleeping Beauty* or *Nutcracker* dance-variations, although there is also a larger cumulative effect through the work as a whole.

D'Indy's *Istar* variations are a full-blown narrative use of time, in which the theme – for programmatic reasons – is not fully revealed until the very end. This work is a lush example of the variation-form as symphonic poem.

The variation-form has thrived up to the present, with, among many others, Brahms, Schoenberg, Webern, Stravinsky, Britten and Elliott Carter adapting it to their particular needs. And its monothematic nature, involving continual transformation and metamorphosis, has increasingly affected music at large, with the rhetorical symphonic concept of development and restatement of contrasting themes being challenged by the gestural dynamic of the latter-day variation-principle with its innate theatricality – of which Britten's *Turn of the Screw*, constructed as a theme and fifteen variations, is a brilliant example.

VII. Ways of listening (and looking)

Each category, static, immediate, narrative and 'becoming', requires a different listening approach. It is not a matter of conscious choice; the composer can lead us in different ways, and to respond appropriately we must follow his pace. A failure to do so can interfere disastrously with the listener's perception of a musical work. If, for instance, one listens to music of the static or immediate sort expecting the long, drawn-out, cumulative development of a symphony, the former will seem simple-minded, sketchy and frustrating. If, however, the listener is seeking vivid dramatic or poetic depiction, a sense of action and event such as it obtained from narrative music, he will be bored and depressed during the extended development of a symphony. The listener who looks for the pointed, instantaneous effect of immediate music, or the timelessness of static, will find the processes of both narrative and 'becoming' tedious.

Within any audience, moreover, there will be three types of listening taking place. These may be described as sensuous, emotional and intellectual-esthetic. Sensuous listening consists of response to instrumental tone-colors, a generalized perception of light and shade without awareness of detail, and often the weaving of fantasies to the music which have little to do with its actual content. It is hedonistic and diffuse. Emotional listening is more focused, consisting of a direct, if ambivalent (see Chapter 2), response to what is actually going on musically. It can, however, be very spotty, with the listener reacting to one section which sweeps him away, and then going blank in another which does not touch him at all. The emotional listener is somewhat more aware of detail than the sensuous listener, although not for its own sake.

The intellectual-esthetic listener differs from the other two in that he is above all preoccupied with detail. Techniques engross him, developmental procedures are followed with the greatest care, and overall form and balance are his main criteria for a successful piece. Music which does not approach technical perfection is considered weak and deficient, and thus it gives him minimal pleasure.

I have presented these types in an extreme form partly as a warning against the dangers of each. I have also separated them, although in the truly musical listener *elements of all three are blended* and different pieces will call for different *proportions* of each within the whole. As with the perception of time, an inappropriate orientation will interfere with the composer's message; it will also produce discomfort in the listener. If the passive sensuous element predominates and the work being heard is a fugue, the listener will probably go to sleep halfway through in self-defence. But abortive as such an experience may be, it at least avoids the aridity of a 100% intellectual-listening, with detachment and contempt, to the glorious sounds and emotion of works like Monteverdi's *Orfeo*, Vivaldi's *The Seasons*, Tchaikovsky's *Swan Lake*, Debussy's *La Mer*, Kodály's *Háry János* or Messiaen's *Turangalîla* Symphony.

The sensuous, emotional and intellectual-esthetic listeners have their counter-parts in spectators of ballet. The sensuous spectator responds primarily to the impact of sets, costumes and brilliant dancing – existing within a blur of titillation. The emotional spectator is carried along by dramatic action, or stimulated by mood in a plotless ballet. The esthetic-intellectual spectator picks apart the fabric of the choreography; he knows all of the steps and their relative difficulty, he can identify the technical devices used by the choreographer and perceive clearly the structure of the ballet as a whole. The same dangers of extremism in any one of these apply as strongly as with musical listening. A blending of the three exists in the ideal spectator.

The question of response also arises with regard to the *simultaneous* perception of music and movement. It is, for example, quite possible to find a sensuous listener and an intellectual-esthetic spectator occupying the same body – and, of course, the converse. Or the emotional listener may operate only on the sensuous level of viewing. Such disparities prevent one from perceiving a ballet as a whole.

VIII. Suitability of music for ballet

Now we must return for a moment to the issue of time. Western dance, except for branches of avant-garde modern dance and ballet, approaches movement in a progressive kinetic manner. It goes somewhere and so does any underlying plot, unlike the static, symbolic timelessness and infinite subtleties of the Japanese or Indian dance. It moves through time whereas they seem to exist within it. Western dance, that is, shares the predominating characteristics of Western music.

How well, however, do the four different categories of musical time found in Western music serve ballet? We have the *static*, in which time seems suspended – the least characteristic of Western music; the *immediate*, in which every moment has an instant impact; the *narrative*, in which the listener is swept emotively through time, a time in which not only momentary events are important but their histrionic implications for the future *dénouement*; and music in the process of *becoming*, in which structural or tonal proportions are paramount.

Strict lines of demarcation do not always apply. The scores for, say, *Swan Lake* and *Coppélia* blend elements of narrative and immediate time. Berlioz's *Romeo and Juliet Symphony* attempts to be both narrative and 'becoming'. Stravinsky's *Rite of Spring* combines, in a curious way, the static, immediate and narrative.

Let us look briefly, however, at each type in its pure form from the point of view of the choreographer. *Static* music of the floating, non-tonal sort, i.e. Debussy's

Prélude à l'après-midi d'un faune, Vaughan Williams' predominantly modal-impressionistic works, much of Delius's music or practically all of Messiaen's is dangerous for the choreographer (and dancers) because it lacks a strong sense of pulse and kinetic rhythm. Thus it can lead to vague, listless movement which is both trying to watch and difficult for the dancers to remember, and can also produce a generally formless and unsatisfying dance (although Jerome Robbins cleverly side-stepped the problem in his subtly humorous *Afternoon of a Faun*). In the hands of a fine choreographer, however, it can – if the piece is not over-long – help to create an exquisite, unworldly type of ballet which is impossible to achieve with the other musical time-orders. Static music of the intensely rhythmical sort, with a relentless sense of pulse and hypnotic, 'primitive' repetition of patterns, i.e. Stravinsky's *Rite of Spring*, Chávez's *Sinfonia India* or Orff's *Carmina Burana* can mesmerize the choreographer into believing that he is matching the power of the music in his movements. Also, the enormous drive characteristic of such music, resulting from incessant repetition, can lead the choreographer to become bogged down and directionless. The dancers, too, bound by the drive and intensity of the patterns may execute all of the movements of a section on one dynamic level, without the light and shade of attack so necessary for rhythm and phrasing. The exciting rhythm of the music can beget dull unrhythmical dancing. Used well, however, it is likely to produce a stunning, electrifying ballet – a true *tour de force*, exciting for the dancers and overwhelming to the audience.

The expressionistic, twelve-tone or serial branch of static music contains the obvious difficulties of arhythmical, tensely dissonant sounds. To sustain and illuminate a long piece of this sort is exceedingly difficult (although Schoenberg's high-tension *Pierrot lunaire* stimulated Glen Tetley to great effect), but if it is on a small scale, it can be used to produce an unusual, piercing – or even witty – ballet.

Music in the *immediate* category is by far the easiest for the choreographer. Being conceived on a small scale, with frequent stops and changes of mood, it does not demand great sustaining powers from him, and if one section is relatively weak choreographically, the next may be so effective as to make this relatively unimportant to the ballet as a whole. If, however, the choreographer is unable to see the entire ballet as more than a collection of parts, it will become a jumble of disconnected, momentary effects. Any reasonably good choreographer can fashion a series of pretty, effective dances to such pieces as *Carnaval*, *Kinderscenen*, a group of short Chopin works, Bizet's *Petite Suite for orchestra* or Tchaikovsky's Serenade for String Orchestra. It takes a master of the theater, on the other hand, to create ballets like *Carnaval*, *Little Improvisations*, *Les Sylphides*, *Jeux d'enfants* and *Serenade*. Each of the choreographers used an immediate, decidedly sectional score to produce not a string of disconnected dances, but movements within a controlling, overall concept.

Narrative music may be constructed sectionally or in one continuous movement. Any sectional writing, however, is unified by the narrative thread running through the piece, and thematic relationships. The scale is, of course, larger than that of immediate music, demanding greater sustaining powers of the choreographer. This music also requires a keen sense of dramatic timing and thematic interplay from the choreographer, which can often be sorely tried by the music going in one expressive direction when he needs to go in another. To cut the music at such points would, of course, weaken its dramatic thrust and shape as conceived by the composer.

One great strength of narrative music is the frequent presence of leitmotifs. These are recurrent themes or motifs which are assigned to dramatic characters, events or ideas. If the choreographer refrains from using these too literally, they can be helpful as integrating elements, and also can be used to illuminate the dramatic development, particularly if the choreography relates present action to past and future events. Taking two well-known works constructed around leitmotifs – Strauss's *Till Eulenspiegel* and Prokofiev's *Peter and the Wolf* – both of these simple and direct examples of this technique, it should be obvious how clumsy it would seem if the choreographer assigned the same movements and choreographic content to each appearance of the different leitmotifs. Subtlety is necessary here – and the reward can be a ballet of unusual depth and penetration of character (of the several choreographers who have used *Till Eulenspiegel*, critical comment seems to indicate that Nijinsky's version realized the music's tragi-comedy the most profoundly).

If narrative music occasionally contains a snag, a point at which the musical and choreographic intentions diverge, then music which is in a structural state of 'becoming' confronts the choreographer with a large field bristling with barbed wire. I have said enough in the previous sections, I think, to indicate the formidable task facing the choreographer who wants to use music of this sort, so I shall limit myself to two points here. First, think back to what Lambert calls 'emotional retrospect', that response to music which supplants a tendency to 'present action' (see p. 64); this present action, or kinetic force, which is sucked into the totality of a fugue or symphony and, so to speak, defused by intense aural concentration needs further comment. We have not yet looked at the kinetic force in its balletic guise of *ballon*, and will begin to do so in the last part of this section.

My second point is that many choreographers are seduced into using structured, 'becoming' works because certain portions or movements seem so very 'danceable'. This is particularly true with Vivaldi concertos and Mozart symphonies. I remember at least ten budding choreographers who selected such music and set to work. In each case one or more of the following three things took place: one, the deletion of a movement or 'repetitious' sections; two, large patches of choreographic stagnancy while the music happily pursued its logical course in ways which defied translation into movement; three, tiresome (and unfruitful) revisions after the first dampening showing, which often resulted in even weaker choreography than the original efforts. One practical result was that several of these choreographers turned to the music of Bartók, Stravinsky, Ravel, Purcell, Britten and Terry Riley. The outcome in each case was a far happier one for choreographer, dancer and spectator. No longer faced with obvious structural details and technical devices in the music which they felt compelled to honor, and no longer subject to frequent collisions with the composer's tonal schemes, these choreographers were able to put aside deference and to function with somewhat more spontaneity.

I have been speaking of student choreographers, but the situation is no different with more experienced ones – except that in having more craft they can carry the project through, not abandoning it after a third revision. The result, of course, is usually a polished, sterile, boring ballet, although there is always the possibility that a unique piece of choreography will emerge.

Three types of ballets

Choreography is usually assigned to one of three categories: narrative, mood or abstract (as in van Praagh and Brinson's enlightening analysis).[22]

Narrative has recognizable characters, usually identified by name; like opera, it has a plot with dramatic development and resolution (whether of the Classical genre – with story interrupted by set-pieces as in *Nutcracker* – or the seamless dramatic flow of *Pillar of Fire*) to convey character and action through the classical vocabulary of dance steps, although mime may be included. The inspiration can be the supernatural (*Giselle*), a fairy-tale (*Sleeping Beauty*), 'real life' (*The Invitation*) or the subconscious mind (*Undertow*).

Mood – although this type of ballet does not have a plot, it can evoke a strong sense of situation (*Dark Elegies*) or it can be but the merest essence of a situation, an atmosphere (*Les Sylphides*) – but in either case great expressivity is required from the dancers. There is emotion, but it is, in effect, symbolic or abstracted from individual experience to become generalized. It is, as van Praagh and Brinson write, 'as if the outer shell of personality had been removed to reveal what takes place in the heart and mind'[23] – except that it is not a specific character's heart and mind.

Abstract – here the dancing *per se* replaces dramatic characterization and the evocation of mood. It goes further than the mood ballet, 'peel[ing] away the emotions as well as character, leaving only bodies with a technique of dancing . . . Dancing becomes a thing in itself; its movements stem only from the music as if all the symbols on the musical stave had come to life on stage.'[24]

The narrative ballet could be called fleshy, the mood-ballet etherealized, and the abstract ballet skeletonized (although the bones can be most attractive). Each category provides a different visual experience. While the response by a spectator is primarily a matter of personal taste, where the musical score is concerned it cannot be only taste. The choreographer must use this music in such a way as to convince the audience that these sounds are essential to the realization of his ballet, whether they love or hate the music in itself. And he can only do this if the music is compatible with the type of ballet.

Many ballets do not, of course, fall tidily into one type. *Les Sylphides* is often referred to as the first abstract ballet, yet it is at the same time one of the finest evocations of mood in all dance. Certainly it is not abstract in the manner of *Agon*, in which movement is as removed from emotion and poetic atmosphere as seems possible. *Jardin aux lilas*, while partaking of the mood-approach, also conveys a ghost of a story, with a highly dramatic *dénouement*.

Ballets and their scores

Now let us take a quick look at some ballets which continue to flourish in the international repertoire or are considered noteworthy even if not produced regularly now. The only selectivity I have exercised is to omit ballets with scores by Minkus and Co. Since we are concerned here with music as a partner rather than a servant, I have only cited ballets in which this goal is generally considered to be at least partially achieved.

Each ballet is identified as narrative, mood or abstract – or a blend – and each score as *structural*, i.e. 'architectural', 'becoming' (in which thematic development, formal proportions, key-relationships, contrapuntal complexity, etc. are paramount), or *episodic*, i.e. 'static', 'immediate' or 'narrative' (which use time in a pictorial, mood-poetic or histrionic manner), with combinations of any of these three possible within one piece.

Ballet	Choreography	Score
Afternoon of a Faun (Robbins–Debussy)	Narrative	Episodic
Agon (Balanchine–Stravinsky)	Abstract	Episodic
Choreartium (Massine–Brahms)	Abstract	Structural
Cinderella (Ashton–Prokofiev)	Narrative	Episodic
Concerto Barocco (Balanchine–Bach)	Abstract	Structural
Coppélia (Saint-Léon–Delibes)	Narrative	Episodic
Dances at a Gathering (Robbins–Chopin)	Mood–Abstract	Episodic
Dark Elegies (Tudor–Mahler)	Mood–Abstract	Episodic
Enigma Variations (Ashton–Elgar)	Narrative	Episodic
Giselle (Coralli–Perrot–Adam)	Narrative	Episodic
Goldberg Variations (Robbins–Bach)	Abstract	Structural
Invitation Narrative (MacMillan–Seiber)		Episodic
Jeux d'enfants (Massine–Bizet)	Narrative	Episodic
Jardin aux lilas (Tudor–Chausson)	Narrative–Mood	Episodic
Orpheus (Balanchine–Stravinsky)	Narrative	Episodic
Petrushka (Fokine–Stravinsky)	Narrative	Episodic
Pillar of Fire (Tudor–Schoenberg)	Narrative	Episodic
Le Sacre du printemps (Nijinsky–Stravinsky)	Narrative	Episodic
Serenade (Balanchine–Tchaikovsky)	Abstract	Episodic

Ballet	Choreography	Score
Shadowplay (Tudor–Koechlin)	Narrative–Mood	Episodic
Swan Lake (Petipa–Ivanov–Tchaikovsky)	Narrative	Episodic
Sylphides, Les (Fokine–Chopin)	Mood–Abstract	Episodic
Symphonic Variations (Ashton–Franck)	Mood–Abstract	Structural
Symphony in C (Balanchine–Bizet)	Abstract	Structural

This list is, of course, only a fraction of the ballets produced during the nineteenth and twentieth centuries, but other equally successful or noteworthy ballets will be seen to adhere closely to this pattern. The exceptions may be said to prove (in its original sense), more or less successfully, the rule. By far the largest proportion of this list have scores which consist of episodic music, less exacting than structural on both the choreographer and the audience, and, of course, the dancers. It is episodic music – mainly narrative or sectional – which has played the largest part in choreography. This is because of the nature of its use of time and the comparatively small part which intellect plays in its aural perception. No matter what other aspects may differentiate such scores they have these two attributes in common.

A review of major ballets of more recent years will show the same preponderance of narrative and sectional scores; despite many new developments in ballet and the incorporation of 'unballetic' elements of Eastern dance, modern dance, jazz and rock, successful ballets still largely require music which – unless the choreographer, through skill and genius, transcends the norm – is not too intellectual or philosophical. On the whole, despite extremist examples here and there of abstract dance-as-musical-notes and ponderous dance-dramas with stories that need lengthy program notes, the ballet scene seems to me to be in a healthy state of growth, variety and amalgamation. And this is inextricably linked with the recent choreographers' perception and choice of music, whose rhythms can effectively combine with various movement rhythms to produce Asquith's higher rhythm which is created by their interaction.

Rhythm

Rhythm is so basic, yet so complex, that it is given a chapter to itself (Chapter 6), but a few comments are necessary here. One extremely important consideration was recognized by John Martin when he wrote:

It is wise when considering rhythm in the dance to put aside all preconceptions deriving from musical rhythm. The latter, it is true, originates at the same source, namely, the natural rhythm of the body, but as music has been developed as an absolute art, its relation to bodily experience has become increasingly attenuated until in many instances it approaches the point of disappearance.[25]

All music, of course, is 'rhythmical' in the sense that the notes must be grouped and phrased. The difference is obvious, however, between the rhythm of a fugue and that of a waltz, or the rhythm of Schoenberg's Fourth String Quartet and that of *Petrushka*. Both the fugue and Schoenberg's quartet are physically dense and 'breathless', whereas the waltz and *Petrushka* are open and breathy. Other rhythmical considerations exist, and we shall look at these closely later on.

It is by no means a simple matter; pulse alone, for instance – that aspect which is most obviously lacking in a fugue or the Schoenberg quartet – is by no means the *only* element in ballet music although it is certainly one of the most important. Pulse provides 'the source of energy and character because it represents the natural human reaction to the rhythmic qualities in music. Audiences react to it as instinctively as dancers. Hence pulse is an expression of the primitive link between the community, music and dance. In this way, ballet, however sophisticated, remains a communal activity.'[26]

Communal activities are not normally centered around intensive use of the brain; they are, above all, physical manifestations of energy and power. The perception of pulse has little to do with concentrated thinking processes. And since pulse is a major factor in the development of *ballon* – that essential element of the balletic experience – it almost becomes a clear-cut contest between brain and *ballon*. They do not co-exist happily, and, as I have tried to show, the intense mental effort necessary to the perception of complex, large-scale music has the effect of partially or completely channeling the more direct kinetic impulse into the indirect or cognitive area for dancer and audience.

Ballon is a rhythmic release from the body's earth-bound existence. Unfortunately, much beautiful music is inimical to it, whether functionally for the dancer, or kinesthetically for the spectator.

Nietzsche said that there is a music in which the spirit dances as opposed to a music in which the spirit swims. I would like to paraphrase this, to say that there is a music in which the body dances as opposed to a music in which the dance drowns. The first is kinetic and open, the second contemplative and dense, i.e. physicality vs. mentality.

This chapter is, inevitably, insufficient for the subjects discussed; I have had to compress subjects which cry out for full-length treatment. But I hope that I have at least shown the need for thorough questioning of certain assumptions.

My wish is to lead musicians, dancers, and audiences to as comprehensive an appreciation as possible of the power and subtlety of the music–dance relationship. This aim pervades the book, in various guises, but the nature of the material covered in this first section makes it the most liable to misinterpretation. With this caution regarding our examination of the end, or goal, let us now go on to look at the means.

PART II

The practice: in the studio

4   The contribution of the accompanist

I don't like the word *accompanist*. The person I work with is a collaborator. We have fun together. There has to be rapport more than anything else.

Beverly Sills, Interview in *New York Times*, 1975

I. Function

A GOOD BALLET ACCOMPANIST is as necessary for the training of dancers as is the floor which supports them, although dancers and teachers vary somewhat in their appreciation of this fact. Arnold Haskell makes a distinction between dancers and acrobats when he says that it is in her approach to the music that a dancer identifies herself as one or the other. The acrobat listens to the music for tempo and guidance, aspiring to technical perfection alone; the dancer listens for tempo, content and interpretation. The music in class should provide ample opportunity for the development of dancers rather than acrobats, because ears and minds deadened by music which is trivial, lacking in style and carelessly performed cannot help but be equally unresponsive when the time comes for the dancer to rehearse and perform on stage.

The development of a strong dance technique is, of course, such a demanding process that it is understandable, if unfortunate, that the average dancer and teacher thinks of little else in class. Every day, in cities and towns throughout the country, hordes of dance students run through their gymnastic routines, committing what to Fokine was almost the worst artistic sin – that of ignoring the music. In so doing, they are dwarfing their potential and misunderstanding the meaning of dancing. They resemble pianists who practice, say, a Chopin étude or the 'Emperor' Concerto for months in order to be able to play all the notes 'correctly' and to develop strength and co-ordination – and who then decide the time has come to 'add' the phrasing and expression, the dynamics and style. The 'correctness' of a performance and the use of expression and style are not different stages of a process; they are inseparable from the very beginning of one's practice, whether of musical notes or of dance steps. Even the most basic technical exercises as scales and arpeggios, pliés and frappés, are more beneficial if approached with a sense of dynamics and phrasing rather than an unremitting attack on the keyboard or the body muscles in a mechanical manner.

Combine a failure on the part of the accompanist to provide music with scope and character, sensitively performed, with the dancer's frequent tendency to 'work out' gymnastically and her habit of dissecting phrases into static clumps of unrelated steps, and you are well on the way to producing the characterless automatons who throng to auditions and frustrate imaginative choreographers. It is very likely, however, that the average dancer's lack of a musical sense is partly a

83

defense gradually developed against years of musical mediocrity to which they have been exposed. The teachers compound the problem by tolerating this mediocrity which has, in turn, dulled their own response. A vicious cycle is thus established; many dance students will eventually become teachers and perpetuate it, unintentionally.

You, however, can break this cycle. And if you play for classes of children just beginning their training you are in a particularly strategic position. Children do not, as a rule, suffer from musical deafness; the kinetic response of a young child to music is something nearly everyone has seen. There is an immediacy of muscular reaction which is precious, and it should be encouraged and channeled. In my experience of playing for children, I have been delighted by their aliveness to 'pretty pieces' which make them 'want to dance'. They have favorites, which they are not shy in demanding, and they show great pleasure in class when they recognize a piece they love. This is a wonderful opportunity for the accompanist to encourage their interest and to stimulate a musical curiosity. It could be crucial in preventing the usual withering of the child's intuitive relating of movement to music and the gradual emergence of the adult monomaniac who sees nothing but technique and steps as a path to 'success'.

But even the jaded adult dancers are often potentially receptive to your music. A dancer with years of professional experience said to me, 'most of the time we don't even notice the music, unless it intrudes because it's so awful. But if the pianist is really alive and plays inspiring music, suddenly the movement becomes a wonderful thing, and so much *easier*'.

This 'inspiring' music is a problem in itself. What is inspiring at one moment can be catastrophic at another (see Chapters 6–8, on selection of music). The greatest gift an accompanist can possess is a kinesthetic imagination – a muscular empathy with the dancers (see also Chapter 9, on performance). Clear phrasing and a reliable tempo are mandatory; impassioned outpourings with no discernible shape may be stirring and impressive, but they are of little practical value in class. The problem is to play music which will stimulate the dancers and circumvent their tendency to use you only as a metronome, while also exercising discipline. And, as we shall see later, there are ways to achieve variety in your daily efforts – to titillate the dancers' ears, not anesthetize them. Through your choice of music, also, aspects of the movement can be clarified for the dancers. Best of all, you can bridge the gulf between the piano and the dancers' bodies, and become so involved with the movement that you are nearly dancing yourself. This is, of course, the interpenetration of music and movement discussed in Chapter 2; the dancer's body becomes visual music while your music dances.

I have already stressed in the Introduction that you, the accompanist, are, in effect, as important as the teacher. (Most ballet teachers I have spoken with agree with this vigorously – and in their next breath ask where accompanists who merit this importance are to be found.) You are not a mere accessory – an ambulatory phonograph. You must be a participant. There are many records on the market designed for use in ballet class, but even the very best are not adequate for daily use. The selection of music and the performance are frozen. A record, moreover, is

4   Between classes: Antony Tudor and Alfredo Corvino. Juilliard 1962

5   Between classes: Sarah Stackhouse, Eric Hampton, the author and Antony Tudor. Juilliard 1966

inanimate; no interplay is possible. A human accompanist, on the other hand, is conscious and can respond to circumstances.

The daily class can vary considerably within its traditional pattern, and the pianist can be most valuable in her perception of this. The temperature of the studio can determine the tempo of the beginning *pliés*: the dancer's muscles are more difficult to warm up in a drafty, mid-winter studio than in a hot, humid summer one. The teacher's mood is a major factor; despite a prevailing harmony between you and him, even the most equable teacher is subject to fluctuations of mood (as are you), and your rapport can vary. The dancers' moods also must be considered. There are days when, for mysterious reasons, the whole class seems down and dispirited. You can help to enliven it. But only an alert and participating accompanist can cope with such variables.

It would, of course, be absurd to maintain that a good accompanist could make up for a poor teacher in every respect. The dancers must be intelligently guided in the training of their bodies in the rigorous discipline of ballet. Still, the pianist can, to a surprising degree, make or break a class. She can contribute atmosphere, excitement and a sense of direction to a dull or mediocre class. For combinations which are rhythmically confusing to the dancers she can inject zest and help to clarify the rhythmic impulse.

The greatest teacher is, on the other hand, hampered and devitalized by a poor accompanist who cannot follow and illuminate the teacher's inventiveness, and who creates a miasma of boredom. A poor accompanist can, in fact, demolish a potentially fine class. In addition to the teacher losing valuable time when he must repeatedly stop to correct or guide a struggling pianist, the atmosphere is tainted by a feeling of uncertainty. This cannot help but be less rewarding for the dancers than a class which is pervaded by a musical reliability – a security in which the dancers can direct their attention to more profitable concerns than apprehensiveness about the pianist's ability.

The teacher, unfortunately, often does not know how to utilize his pianist to the fullest; on the other hand, a poor pianist cannot fulfil and enrich the teacher's intentions. The relatively infrequent combination of a musical teacher and a good accompanist is an event which should make every dancer in the class *jeté* for joy.

To review now what you can contribute, we have seen that you can:

1. Help to counteract the dancer's tendency to concentrate solely on technique by stimulating her ear with appropriate, varied and muscularly inspiring music.
2. Keep the class running smoothly by being knowledgable and reliable.
3. Help to alleviate the dullness of a mediocre teacher, and also help to clarify the rhythm of combinations.
4. Enhance the contribution of a good teacher through empathy and involvement.
5. Perhaps most important of all, be alert to the possibilities of making contact with the dancers, both children and adults, and contribute to their knowledge of music; above all, to stimulate their curiosity about it.

The accompanist, however, often has trouble in functioning consistently and reliably. I do not think that there are many accompanists who could not improve at least one aspect of their work whether it be their selection of music or their performance of it, not to mention their balletic knowledge. These and other problems will be dealt with in other chapters, but we should confront, at this point, a problem which is perhaps more responsible for the generally low level of ballet accompanying than is any technical or musical deficiency. This, is simply, how the accompanist feels about her work.

II. Attitude

Most ballet accompanists – apart from the hopeless hack, who is unlikely to be reading this book – will fall into one of three categories. Within each there will be individual differences, but for purposes of general identification we have:

1. The naturally qualified musician, who has a good memory, a feeling for rhythm, imagination, and pianistic skill, but who, unfortunately, suffers from lack of interest in or even a marked dislike of ballet work.
2. The poor or more modestly equipped musician, who has, however, a strong desire to improve her skills while increasing her knowledge of ballet, yet is for some reason or other having problems.
3. The naturally qualified musician who combines the attributes of the first type with the zest of the second.

We do not have to worry about accompanists of the third type. They will almost certainly have a gratifying abundance of work and appreciation, plus a feeling of satisfaction in their daily classes. It is those in the second and first categories that we must concern ourselves with here, for they are usually inadequate or uninterested because they hamper themselves by certain beliefs and attitudes.

The main problem is that of *status*. A dismayingly large percentage of musicians tend to feel that playing for ballet classes gives them a low status in the world of music – rather like being a grimy manual worker in a white collar society.

Granting that there are, in some circumstances, grounds for feeling a bit debased artistically (playing, for instance, in a grubby back-street studio for an inept teacher and third-rate dancers), I must still protest that any sweeping condemnation of ballet work is unfair and biased. It has always puzzled me, for instance, that the same musicians who scorn ballet work will turn round and play for fifth-rate vocal coaches, or teach in an inferior music school under the illusion that this has more prestige than accompanying for ballet. Yes, there are all too many travesties of ballet schools everywhere (usually advertised 'Toe, tap, acrobatics'), but these are only a part of the scene, and any good accompanist should be able to give them a miss (except in very small towns, where there may be only one such studio). She will, in fact, often find that she can be choosy; the need for good accompanists is usually so acute that she often cannot fit all the available work into her schedule.

This is, of course, the prime practical reason for increasing your qualifications as much as possible. The atmosphere of the mediocre ballet studio is so deadly that you would need an extraordinary sense of your own worth to not feel demeaned and defeated by association with such a place. Aim for the best, and implement this aim with every means at hand. Your rewards will be a very definite prestige in ballet circles, the enrichment which meaningful work can give to you and an expansion of your horizon through intimate contact with another art. You may find yourself in some unsatisfactory studios along the way, but they are still *experience*, and you can try to make your stay as short as possible.

As you become more proficient, you will be able to play for advanced and professional classes. These are, naturally, more exhilarating – and more difficult – than beginners' classes; you will often see well-known, even famous, performers who are most interesting to watch (such sights may give your failing sense of status and prestige a vicarious lift). Even in schools outside the large cities there is a chance of playing for such performers when they are passing through on tour.

Other possibilities, moreover, await. You might compose the score for a ballet, become the musical director of a small company, teach classes in music for interested dancers or even take up ballet conducting. Accompanists have done all of these. And such work, in addition to a good accompanying job, is a far cry from the stereotype of the ballet musician as a 'failure', banging away in a disreputable studio.

Such achievements, however, are not possible if you look on your daily accompanying as a chore. This is the second serious handicap for the ballet pianist (and it is of course related to the concern with status and prestige). Anyone – in any field – who looks on his work as a chore is doomed to a work-life of boredom and sterility. I realize, needless to say, that everyone, no matter how great their devotion to their work, is capable of only so much uninterrupted concentration. Some teachers, also, are more stimulating to play for than others, and their idiosyncrasies mesh better with one's own. The daily class, furthermore, cannot help but vary somewhat in interest depending on how well the teacher is teaching that day, how well the students are responding or even how well *you* are feeling. Whether any of these circumstances inevitably lead to your work being a chore is largely, however, up to you.

When the accompanist is bored, everyone suffers. Often this boredom is based on a superficial acquaintance with ballet, one which is partly responsible for her dismissal of ballet as an inferior art and her resultant feelings about her work.

Many musicians dismiss ballet work as non-prestigious or a chore mainly because of their view of dancers. Despite the exacting requirements of the dancer's training, musicians are prone to think of them as exhibitionistic and undisciplined. The truth is that there are two distinct species of dancers. In any field, of course, we find those whose egos are conspicuously larger than their talents – thus, the egomaniacal dancer species, which is notable for its limited awareness of anything but its dazzling *pirouettes*, flashy beats or ear-high extensions. A large proportion of dancers, however, belong to the other, so different species – the dedicated, self-critical one (there are, of course, many gradations within these two extremes). They are dedicated, moreover, in a way which revivifies this somewhat tired word. Their effort, application and perseverance can be awesome. In their zeal, they sometimes drive themselves beyond wise limits and they are, generally speaking, more painfully aware of their inadequacies than artists in any other field.

Despite any cries of outrage which this statement may be evoking from musicians, I stand firm. Bear in mind the extreme fragility and vulnerability of the dancer's medium – her body – and the mandatory daily regimen. No matter what the circumstances, no matter how afflicted she may be by the aches, pains and mental frets to which we are all subject, she must drag herself to daily class and somehow make a rebellious or exhausted body – every inch of it – spin, flow, leap, and emerge from class in one piece. If she skips class she pays for it with an immediately perceptible lessening of agility and limberness. Add to this the potential horrors of splintery, uneven stages encountered on tour, studios which seem to be either freezing or airless, generally low salary levels combined with expensive practice gear and, worst of all, seemingly continual injuries, vague disabilities and the poor diet encouraged by peculiar and overloaded schedules: I, for one, marvel at and respect the dedicated dancer as I do no other artist. Some say that to be a truly conscientious, fine dancer you must be a little mad. If so, it is a beautiful form of insanity.

In your role as accompanist, you will come into contact with both species. You may as well resign yourself to the probability that the egotist-dancer, in extreme form, is generally a lost cause. As far as she is concerned, you and your music hardly exist. This is inevitable when she works so hard at proving that she could dance just as well without music – better, perhaps; it usually gets annoyingly in the way of her gymnastics, rushing her past that fourth pirouette she would so like to crowd in. Of course she is the first to complain about the music, but her concern with it is a rather different one than that of the intelligent, sensitive dancer's awareness of and response to what she hears.

Some may question my reference to the 'intelligent' dancer. Do banish the myth that all dancers border on the mentally defective. This may, like other myths, be based on a partial truth, but many of today's dancers would put to shame the narrowness and simple-mindedness of a considerable number of artists in other fields. One still finds the dancer who eats, sleeps, breathes, and gossips nothing but ballet (usually in its most superficial aspects), and the dancer-robot who is a unique product of a particular contemporary ballet esthetic, but they are simply not the whole story. As I affirmed in the Preface, many of the most stimulating and inquisitive people I know are dancers, and part of this inquisitiveness is directed toward increasing their musicality. It is in these alive, seeking dancers that your efforts will find a response.

If, however, you remain uninspired by the idea of reaching and affecting the musically receptive dancers in class it is quite possible that you are akin – consciously or not – to the dancer whose aim is to dazzle with technique or to outshine others. To overwhelm an audience by pyrotechnics and the force of one's concert personality is the goal of a depressingly large number of musical performers today. Permeating a ballet class with musical vitality and penetrating the concentration of hard-working dancers may seem mundane compared with holding an audience spellbound from the concert stage, but your work in class can be far more meaningful than the sterile barrage of notes which constitutes the average piano recital.

Before you protest about your experiences with dancers who are insensitive to the music, remember what I have already stressed in regard to *their* experience and expectations of music in class. This book was written with the hope of altering this situation, and to replace what Agnes de Mille has called 'musical hacks, who provide cheap tunes, banged or dribbled out mercilessly,'[1] with musical *partners*.

III. Requirements and benefits

Now that we have examined various aspects of the accompanist's function in the ballet studio, considered possible attitudes toward playing for classes and looked at the dancer's point of view, we can progress to certain practical requirements of the accompanist and also to what the benefits and drawbacks of ballet work may be.

Requirements

Beginning with the need for involvement which I have already mentioned, I must now emphasize that this involvement needs to be reinforced and enriched by knowledge of the art of ballet. Without specific familiarity with its vocabulary, technique and theatrical fruition, you will – unless you are that rare being who has an intuitive feeling for ballet work – be unable to become an equal partner. You could even, at worst, be an acute liability; no one can do her best work in a vacuum.

You would not, surely, approach the sonatas of Beethoven or the preludes of Chopin without a perspective based on knowledge of their historical context, techniques peculiar to the composer, or his general esthetic. Nor would you be wise to enter a first-rate singing teacher's studio prepared only to play the day's required opera arias and lieder mechanically, with no conception of their texts and contexts. If you failed to recognize and recreate the different worlds of a Verdi aria and a Schubert song, viewing your contribution as a mere underpinning to a technical effort on the part of the singer to sing as loud and high as possible, you would not only be operating in a vacuum: you would find that your services would probably not be much in demand. The same applies, of course, to the accompanying of violinists or other instrumental soloists. Why, therefore, do so many musicians seem to feel that ballet accompanying is different, requiring but a bodily presence and a detached, unconcerned performance?

But knowledge and perspective must be underlaid by good musicianship. The more facility you have at the keyboard the greater the range of what you can provide. You must above all be able to keep a steady tempo, and not be limited to a narrow selection of music because of technical weakness in scale-passages, arpeggios and the like. You must also possess a feeling for tone-color and dynamics. None of this means that you must be a virtuoso, but simply that you need enough facility to be able more or less to forget about technical hazards and devote yourself to the important, and demanding, task of daily providing valuable stimulation and variety for the dancers (these points will be amplified in the appropriate places within the chapters on selection of music and performance).

Personality plays an important part in accompanying, also. If, for instance, you tend to be a domineering sort, who does not respond easily to correction or suggestion, life will be very difficult for you, the teacher and the dancers. On the other hand, accompanying is not suitable work for the acutely insecure, easily intimidated person (although I must add that if you can stick it out during the early difficult days, a gradual increase in knowledge and ability can have an extremely therapeutic effect on your general self-esteem).

These, then, are the three major practical qualifications required of the accompanist: knowledge of the different aspects of ballet, reliable facility at the keyboard and the sort of personality which will allow adventurousness combined with dependability and co-operativeness.

Benefits: the pianist–accompanist

Now, what are the practical benefits of accompanying? Are there any disadvantages? How does ballet work fit in with the pianist's life? Accompanying can mean different things to different people. It depends on the pianist's situation and ultimate goals. She may be a struggling student, intent upon but quite a way from a concert career. She may be launched, modestly as yet, upon one, and need a supplementary income. Or she may have given up earlier dreams of this form of 'success' entirely, but wish to continue using her musical skills and training. In the first two situations, the pianist may be subject to conflict between her career-oriented, vocational efforts and her economic, avocational ones. If she is dedicated solely to the goal of a concert career, resentment can arise at the demands of ballet work. If, however, she finds she is being drawn more and more into the world of ballet, she will have to re-appraise her goals, and may even happily transfer her passion for a solo career to permanent, full-time work with dancers.

Those in the third situation, who have renounced for one reason or another, a concert career, have in ballet work a splendid opportunity to continue their musical life, in a situation which needs their talents desperately. They can devote themselves wholeheartedly to another form of music-making.

Certain practical difficulties may arise. In addition to the common drawback of low rates of pay which I have already raged against in the Introduction, the accompanist is sometimes unlucky, being burdened by a time-wasting schedule with useless pockets of 'free' hours. I know that even the most vigorous, demanding class never fatigued me in the way which these hours of waiting for the next one did.

Again, if unlucky, you may have to play for classes which are dotted all over town, and have to spend much time (and energy) rushing to and fro. One friend of mine played at the Graham Studio in the morning, proceeded to dance classes at Juilliard, and then returned to the Graham Studio for evening classes. This sort of thing can be extremely debilitating and also create a serious problem, as almost no time is left for anything else.

Even if you are not beset by such extremes, there is the omnipresent problem of practice-time *vs.* accompanying-time. Those who spend many hours practicing for a concert career may find it difficult to play several hours a day for class. This is an individual matter; some pianists have more endurance than others, and some will be more in need of whatever extra money they can make. My own – somewhat unorthodox – view is that playing-hours in the ballet studio can equal or surpass in value hours spent in concentrated isolation at your own keyboard. This is not to infer that accompanying should supplant intelligent practice in private, but it certainly can supplement it, enriching and stretching your performing skill in ways which might surprise you (see also Chapter 9).

Whether this might be considered an artistic or a practical benefit, there are others which are more clearly practical. We have looked at the possible disadvantages; now let us see the advantages – which I believe far outweigh the negative aspects.

I will say immediately that I consider the prime practical advantage of accompanying to be its convenience. Despite the possible fate of an unsatisfactory schedule or having to dash all over town, I would say that easily 80% of *my* accompanying life has been characterized by convenient, manageable and endurable schedules – particularly when I compare my ballet schedules with certain brief jobs I had as a student, in a bakery, a candy shop and an insurance office. I had, somehow, to endure these episodes, but the memory of those eight- and nine-hour workdays of enervation and frustration at being so removed from music during their long hours has never faded. The contrast, needless to say, made my subsequent accompanying life all the more enjoyable and rewarding.

Even teaching, privately or in a school, can be generally less desirable and convenient than accompanying as a way of supporting yourself. This view is, of course invalid and irrelevant if you have an unshakeable passion for teaching and the good fortune to function in an outstanding establishment, within a reasonable schedule, under a department head who is intelligent, imaginative and supportive, with students who are models of curiosity, involvement, open-mindedness, intelligence and talent – and lovable as well – plus a reasonably — good salary (such schools *do* exist, and I taught for many years in one).

Many teachers, unfortunately, do not enjoy these pleasures. Quite a few of my friends teach music, in one form or another, all over the US, and the picture I often get is one of unsatisfactory schools or dictatorial superiors or bored and boring, detached and dull students or insufficient salary – not to mention outrageous schedules and crushing amounts of paper-work. Not all of these apply in any one job (one hopes), but each is all too common, especially if one is on a student fellowship.

Private teachers of my acquaintance have differed widely in their views, some finding it deeply gratifying, but others considering it to be boring, tiring, or unsatisfactory financially unless they accept so many pupils that their day is overloaded (assuming, of course, that they can *get* enough pupils to make an adequate living). Some, also, find it disturbing if they themselves are attempting a concert career. Ballet work utilizes a pianist's talents but does not touch directly upon the insecurities and special ambitions which attend solo performance.

And here I must expand a rather delicate point, touched upon earlier. With regret, I say that only a fraction of aspiring concert pianists will achieve the success which motivates them. Listen to Paul Hindemith: 'we are teaching each pianist . . . as if he had a chance to become a Horowitz . . . although we know that the entire concert life of the civilized world can hardly absorb more than ten or twelve great soloists in each field.'[2] Or Peter Cooper: 'To judge from the fate of the hundreds of aspiring pianists who present themselves before the public each year, in emulation of their seniors, many are "called" but few "chosen".'[3] Why not 'choose' for yourself, and use your talent to achieve success of another sort? Regarding the sometimes frantically misguided efforts of pianists to attain stardom, I can only say that it is a natural thing to want to succeed in one's field, but unfortunately success is often viewed in narrow, exclusive stereotypes.

Still, if you are determined at this point to aim for the top of your profession, or a more modest performing career, you should remember that your performing skills can benefit immensely from the process of becoming a first-rate ballet accompanist. *Everything* which goes into excellence in the ballet studio increases your range as a performer. I am, possibly, a poor illustration of this assertion as I was an unwilling piano student from the very beginning – but perhaps this might prove my point all the more vividly. Because of a precocious facility at the keyboard, and the gift of perfect pitch certain adult figures decided when I was five that I should be groomed for future stardom. Since *I* knew all along that underneath those deceptive flying fingers I was *not* virtuoso-material, my childhood was a prolonged charade. Practice-torture was relieved only by my frequent re-composition of the Mozart, Beethoven, Chopin, etc., I was supposed to be mastering.

Little did I know that the day would come when all those deplored hours at the keyboard would prove to have laid the foundation for a radically different existence as a pianist (and, later, teacher). No longer an agent of lonely hours and misguided goals, the piano now became the gateway to a universe of ever-increasing interest, communality and expansion.

However, my entry into this universe was painful, for at the beginning I had no conception at all of *the* essential element of music – phrasing. My long-suffering (and excellent) piano teacher had labored for years to develop it but, through no fault of hers, I continued to play from note to note. As an *accompanist*, the process of osmosis began. By simply watching Tudor demonstrate his ballet combinations hour after hour in class, suddenly one memorable day everything fell into place and I at last understood what a 'phrase' was and what went into shaping it. I continued to learn by watching the dancers and comparing their varying success in achieving the teacher's impeccable phrasing and timing. Poorly phrased music is bad enough; poorly phrased dance movement is calamitous. Not only do the consecutive steps lose continuity, it is nearly impossible to execute the steps themselves properly. Thus, poor phrasing in dance has a particular immediacy.

You can, in addition, strengthen various facets of your playing. Without conscious effort to do so, in the three to five hours spent playing daily for classes, I developed a technical facility which would have astounded my teacher. Simply by being forced to manage various technical hazards in order to not lose the pace (much as in playing four-hand music with an expert), I found that they were becoming less and less problematical. And the fact that this was done in conjunction with my newly born sense of phrasing is no coincidence. My skill increased at a reasonably steady pace – and *without* supplementary practicing at home. There are two basic schools of thought. The first insists on the necessity of daily scales, arpeggios, parallel thirds and the like, preparatory to embarking upon pieces containing these. The second maintains that one learns the technique while practicing the actual pieces rather than isolated studies for them. From my experience in acquiring a strong technique during class-hours, I cannot help but incline to the second view.

At the same time, I developed to a surprising degree something of which no pianist can ever have enough – physical endurance. This is, of course, another attribute which is considered to be best developed through the aforementioned exercises. However, I believe that endurance can be equally, if not better, developed by simply being compelled to press on. It can be a formidable task to play stimulating music for the last big jumps of a five-hour ballet day, especially if the class is crowded. (The average dancer or teacher is not aware of this; if they think about it at all, they are probably comparing your easy, comfortable job seated at the piano with their efforts to keep from collapsing.) You find yourself wondering if you can possibly keep going without a breather; sometimes you can't, indeed, but it is *not* a good idea to make a habit of stopping in the midst of a lively combination just because you feel overtaxed. I usually saved my dramatic recuperative pauses for times when I felt that the dancers were being somewhat solipsistic in their efforts to go across the floor for the fourth time. For the most part, however, I just kept playing, and found that my point of desperation receded ever further, and that it actually became rare for me to feel that I could not continue. Here I had my most striking illustration of the power of phrasing, for without total immersion in the phrase – my own and that of the movement – this development of endurance would have been unlikely. When tired, one tends to tense one's muscles; finger, wrist, arm, shoulder and back muscles become, unconsciously, stiff and gripped. This increases the very thing you want to avoid – diminishing resilience and spontaneity of muscular reaction. Shaping the musical phrase and dancing the movement through your music distracts you most beneficially from the tiresome concern of whether you can continue to function. (This is so important that I shall go into it more fully in Chapter 9.)

Last, you gain experience in playing before groups, and for anyone who suffers in the least from performance-nerves, this is extremely valuable. If it is true that some of the dancers would only notice you if the piano suddenly caved in, then this can encourage you to stop fretting over the possibility of a few wrong notes here and there. If you know the dancers to be mainly interested in and appreciative of their music, you can also relax, for their concern is primarily with the meshing of your music and their movement. You do not have that feeling of being under a microscope which exists when you play for fellow musicians and critical audiences who are holding their breath, awaiting your next wrong note or deviation from 'tradition'.

Since there is a significant difference between practicing in your room, solitary and at your own pace, and playing before fellow creatures with whom you feel functional contact and cannot stop and start as you would while practicing, you should look upon ballet accompanying as a singularly beneficial arena to develop self-possession and powers of musical projection. If you can get occasional work playing for ballet performances, that is even better, for you are getting experience in a public hall, but you are not entirely exposed; the focus is on the dancing, not the pianist.

When one views the possible negative points of ballet accompanying against the backdrop of these important benefits, they do not seem very troublesome and I hope that if my remarks have encouraged any pianists who have viewed accompanying with mixed feelings to see it in a different light and to wish to become involved with it in a more committed manner. The day I first entered a ballet studio was (though it didn't seem so at the time) one of the luckiest of my life.

Benefits: the composer–accompanist

Composers who work with dancers are, in some ways, in a more felicitous position than are pianists. Since the composer is usually by nature not interested in the world of 'concertizing' (except when playing his own music), he avoids the potential conflicts which can beset the pianist, both psychological and practical. Furthermore, apart from the essentially nineteenth-century Romantic, ivory-tower concept of music which still infects too many composers, his experience of music is more likely to let him view it as a collaborator, as in opera and song, incidental music for plays and, of course, ballet. Instrumentalists are more prone to seduction by the idea of 'absolute' music and the enclosed, exclusive world of sonatas, quintets, fugues and concertos.

A composer who is in sympathy with the theater can benefit from an intimate knowledge of ballet and its dramatic principles and mechanisms. He can gain an understanding of dramatic timing and the atmospheric use of music in the theater, which will be most helpful when he writes *both* theatrical and non-theatrical music. A composer who tends to approach his writing academically, who is more concerned with how notes are worked out on paper than with aural and dramatic effect on the listener, can receive a salutary shock if he works with a choreographer. A great deal, also, can be learned about economy of means, both compositional and instrumental. Since few ballet companies can afford a large orchestra, he will be forced to work with small ensembles and to get the very most from each instrument.

The composer may not, of course, have great pianistic skill. But he has the same opportunity to increase his technical equipment and endurance as does the modestly equipped pianist. To balance the possible disparity in technique, the composer is more likely to visualize music (other than the piano repertoire) in its original instrumental colors, and thus perform it more vividly and convincingly than the average pianist.

The most probable drawback to accompanying for the composer, apart from the ones already mentioned of pay, schedules and travel, is that he may find it difficult at times to go from accompanying to composing. One's mind and inner ear can become so saturated by the music one has been playing that no room is left for one's own sounds. Concentration and freshness suffer. Some composers of my acquaintance solved this problem by arranging their schedule so that they composed in the morning, before going to the ballet studio.

IV. Summary

If, then, you accept the challenge of becoming a fine and valued ballet accompanist, we should briefly review the situation:

1. General musicianship – whether this is not too striking at present or whether it is already well-developed, your musical abilities can be increased significantly in several ways through your work in class.
2. Practical convenience – you have the probability of being able to arrange – sooner or later, depending on your professional status – a schedule which fits well into your other activities and which pays a reasonable rate, as opposed to the drudgery of an 8-hour job outside your field or the inadequate pay and boredom of the typical part-time job.
3. Transference of affection   for those who cannot achieve a concert career, accompanying provides an outlet for their musical drive, and the rewards of contributing something important and deeply appreciated.

For my own part, I can state without hesitation that an involvement with dance on a meaningful level can enrich your life and expand your artistic universe. You will have intimate contact with another art, but one which has been intertwined with yours since the beginning of human experience, the pleasure and interest of working with stimulating, unusual people, the perspective on your own art to be gotten from understanding the dancers' point of view, and the satisfaction of knowing that many of them look upon you as a support and an inspiration.

Then, too, your close association with the teacher can bring out capabilities, which you never suspected you possessed, as you explore ways in which to reinforce and illuminate his teaching. This brings us to the next important part of your ballet-life: what are the different types of ballet teacher which you may encounter, and how will they vary in what they ask of you?

5   Teachers and schools

Tudor choreographed phrases in his class which were so exquisite to dance that the
whole sense of dancing them was, in itself, having mastered the technique. Just being
in his class was a glorious dance.

Lar Lubovitch, in *The Private World of Ballet*, 1975

THE FOCAL POINT of life in the ballet studio is the teacher. He affects,
continually, the attitude, achievement and felicity of the dancers and the
accompanist. Every dance class is a creation, good or bad, which reveals the
imagination, character and mood of the teacher. As accompanist, your relationship with him, moreover, is a peculiarly intimate one – more so than with most
employers. This is true whether you are in harmony with one another or at odds.
You are in direct contact with him throughout the class, and since you are also, in
your own way, a focal figure, you may become heroine or scapegoat.

Teachers range from exhilarating and inspiring to debilitating and obnoxious,
with many possible gradations between these extremes. At best, you and he will be
like a single functioning organism; at worst, your communication will end with
'good morning'. You will also find differences in quality: excellent teachers – the
elite; good, well-rounded ones; knowledgable but uninspired ones; and some who
should be forcibly prevented from ever entering a ballet studio. In the Preface I
mentioned dancers' unrealistic goals and absorption in technical problems amid a
comparison of musicians' and dancers' attitudes. Despite my generally more
sanguine view of the dancers, one very troubling aspect of their world needs
exposure here. That is the tendency of all too many teachers to focus on flashy
technique – partly because of their wish for a reputation as the producers of 'stars'.
As Robbins observes, their classes are 'drills' in spectacular jumps and turns
designed to excite audiences.[1] Kerensky, too, is worried by this emphasis,
attributing it to the dancer's 'desire to make a quick impression on a new,
unsophisticated mass audience . . . and reap a quick reward'.[2] Quantities of such
dancers throng to the city, encouraged and mal-formed by glorified gym-teachers
(who also exist, in more prestigious forms, in the sophisticated cities).

Teachers who succumb, for whatever reason, to this meretricious esthetic are
harming both their charges and the work of choreographers. They must be resisted
and counteracted in any ways possible. Although the ever-growing popularity of
dance is welcome, it would be dreadful if this acted as a force to undermine its
integrity and maturity, traceable back to Diaghilev and contributed to by so many
since.

98

The imperfect teacher

The perfect teacher does not exist, needless to say, for each excels and lacks in different ways, and I recommend playing for at least two teachers in order to experience varying approaches and personalities. Not only is this more interesting and informative, but it will develop more versatility in your work than if you were conditioned by only one teacher. During one period, early in my accompanying career, I played regularly for three teachers, all male, and intermittently for another, who was female. This provided a fascinating (if at times a trifle confusing) study in contrasts. The woman was an interesting combination of disciplinarian and visionary, and the three men were, in turn, a fledgling choreographer who was demanding and musically imaginative; a volatile performer, with a Russian fire and physicality – who seldom specified any music; and a famous choreographer who possessed the most encyclopedic and subtle mind I have ever known. This was, of course, Tudor.

I could not have had a more fortunate apprenticeship. If I had been restricted to playing for only one of these four teachers, I might have had a more tranquil work-life, but I would have been deprived of much valuable experience and the development of various capabilities in myself as I struggled to cope with all of the so-different demands. Each complemented the others, although they varied in excellence.

The imperfect accompanist

The perfect accompanist is also an impossibility. No matter how good you may be, and how well-suited to some teachers, there remains the elusive matter of taste, and what may be inspiring to one teacher may displease another. The less elusive matter of temperament is also a decisive element, and can be unpredictable, for on one occasion a teacher may be a lamb and on another somewhat less docile. Fokine, despite his admirable qualities, was reputedly prone to hysterical outbursts during the tension of final rehearsals, and used his pianist (among others) as an outlet. Shrieking 'throw out that pianist' on several occasions, at his amazingly good pianist, Pomerantz, he eventually was deserted by 'that pianist', who was replaced by a very even-tempered gentleman![3] Although these scenes occurred during rehearsals, Fokine was not free from temperament of this sort in class either. Still, although I would not care to have been 'that pianist', it is hard not to forgive a man of his stature and musicality for being difficult in this area; unlike many teachers' outbursts, his stemmed from deep concern for the work at hand.

Tudor, similarly, has throughout his career been notorious for his demands upon hapless accompanists. Unlike Fokine, however, he seldom loses his temper (although the infrequent occasions when he did do so in class were memorable). He is also musically self-reliant when necessary: 'Tudor had to have exactly the right music, and if he didn't get it, he simply asked the pianist to leave, and we did the rest of the class to Tudor's singing "Onward Christian Soldiers".'[4] Yet the pianists who failed to satisfy Tudor may have got on very well with other teachers of different temperaments. Since Tudor is, by nature and design, subtly intimidating, his reputation would lead new accompanists to enter the studio paralyzed with apprehension – not the most favorable state in which to function well.

Other situational hazards abound. I briefly played for a woman who, though sensitive and nervous, was considered by many to be easy to work for. During my encounter with her, she vacillated between outrageous fits of temper and sudden fits of weeping. The students and I suffered together, but I, unfortunately, received the main force of her ailing disposition. Later I discovered that during this time her husband – also a ballet teacher – had been having an affair with another dancer. After this, I viewed any fluctuations of temperament on the part of the teacher in a different light. Although it would be best if one could leave behind one's extra-balletic problems upon entering the studio, it is often not possible. (The same fluctuations can, of course, affect the accompanist, but I found that, in direct proportion to my growing involvement with what went on in the studio, my problems faded for at least the duration of the class.)

You should not, therefore, be surprised or hurt if you and a certain teacher are not suited for one another, either because of his musical taste or his temperament. In the first case, you may simply choose to go elsewhere, and in the second, you may tolerate occasional outbursts, or flee at the first opportunity a temperament which clashes with your own.

The first few classes with any teacher are a mutual testing-period, but the time required to arrive at a solid working relationship can vary considerably. You and he may work harmoniously from the beginning *pliés*, but more usually a pattern of trial and error is necessary before things go smoothly.

Communication

A major problem for accompanists who are not experienced is that of communication between you and the teacher. You will seldom find that you talk about music similarly. A dancer just does not perceive and view it in the same way as a musician (even when specially trained in music theory or history; the dance-factor inevitably colors her understanding and perspective). This does *not* mean that the dancer's understanding of music is inferior to the musician's (Tudor, during our twenty-year association, showed consistently a deeper and more intuitive perception of music than most of the musicians I have known). Often, however, the dancer is so intimidated by musicians with whom she has come into contact that she defensively avoids learning even the basic rudiments and terminology of music. She discusses it, instead, in ways which the musician tends to find vague, confusing and ignorant. Thus the gulf widens.

Two hazards

The two most common hazards are the different approach to counting of dancers and musicians, and the different conceptions of tempo of each. On innumerable occasions I have seen dancers baffled and musicians scornful over a problem of 'counting-out' a phrase. The musician's scorn is misplaced. It is *foolish*, because one should always remember that the entire system of measuring note-values and assigning meters is a convention, and although by now highly developed after several centuries of adaptation to different needs and circumstances, it is still imperfect. It is not Holy Writ, or precise in the sense of $E = MC^2$. (This subject is so important that I shall return to it in Chapter 6.)

The musical dancer, interestingly, tends to count in relation to the *phrase*, going over the bar-line; musicians are often conditioned and imprisoned by the beats *within* the measure. As a result, dancers can contrive some counting-out which makes no sense at all to the academically bent musician, but which is still true to the inner rhythm of the phrase. Ballet teachers often make a mistake involving the imprecise nature of notation referred to above. I have been asked time after time for a '3/4' before I knew what the combination would be. Since I can think quickly of at least eight different types of 3/4s, this request is impractical (see Chapter 6). To the teacher, a 3/4 often means something specific: a mazurka or a waltz; to the musician it is highly variable. Your task, with such a teacher, is gently but firmly to reveal to him the large family of 3/4s. Your approach depends on the teacher, of course. If he has a sense of humor you may play a 3/4 chosen at random – which will almost certainly not be what he had in mind, except by great coincidence. If he is humorless, try tact. If you get nowhere, make it a habit to ask him to demonstrate the combination – which he should of course have done, by some means, in the first place instead of presenting you with the riddle of the three-fours (or two-fours or four-fours).

The other serious hazard is that of tempo. It arises for semantic reasons, and because the musician does not understand tempo in the body as opposed to the head and fingers. The first involves differences in *meaning*, and the second involves *scale*. The semantic confusion can be upsetting. You are playing along happily, and suddenly the teacher says, 'Slower, slow-er . . .' You then reduce the tempo – only to be admonished that you are 'dragging the beat'. Who is at fault, you or the teacher? Neither, and both. Neither, because you are each reacting according to your particular application to the word to your art. Both, because you are each failing to project yourself into the other's world. As a result, the teacher may be somewhat irritated at your lack of comprehension, and you – if insecure and inexperienced – will suffer mild paranoia, or – if self-confident – will be affronted.

All this is unfortunate. Granted that there *are* occasions when the tempo is blatantly unsuitable (either because the teacher has misled the pianist by demonstrating out of tempo or not at all, or the pianist *is* inept or a bit dim that day), the larger proportion of challenged tempos tend to lie in a more subtle area.

The teacher gives the accompanist misinformation and the accompanist accepts it at face value. What really is wanted is not a metronomically slower pace but rather a slightly heavier feeling and texture, and possibly a lower register. The pianist may have been playing a tinkling little bagatelle, thin of texture and in the middle-to-high register, *at a correct tempo*, but the *effect* will have been one of excessive speed. And, perhaps, the over-all thinness of quality, texture and register may have led the pianist to rush, ever so slightly, from time to time, within the generally correct tempo. In this case, the solution is not to reduce the tempo, but to select another piece or to transpose the tinkling bagatelle down a 5th or an octave, and also to play with more weight in the forearm, or even the upper arm (see Chapter 9).

The problem of *scale* is related to the different performance-mediums of dancer and musician. The dancer must move her entire body; the pianist actively utilizes only a relatively small proportion of hers – and is supported by a chair. Owing to factors of gravity, inertia and available energy, this comparative employment of the body inescapably makes tempo a different matter for the dancer than for the musician. The musician's fingers can move with a speed unattainable by the swiftest-moving dancer. Similarly, the musician can, with no problem, save those of phrasing and interpretation, perform music at a pace slower than any dancer could possibly sustain (or any male partner could endure while having to elevate and manipulate a hundred-odd pounds of sylph for any length of time). Both musician and dancer are conditioned by and oriented to scale in radically different ways. Thus, if the teacher says, after a combination has been performed in a moderate *allegro* tempo, 'Let's take it faster now', the dancers will visualize a modest quickening of the previous tempo and the musician will visualize 'The Flight of the Bumblebee' or Paganini's 'Moto Perpetuo'.

In order to avoid such demoniacal choices, it would be helpful if the accompanist attempted to execute even the simplest *allegro* exercises from the *barre*, such as *dégajés* or *frappés*, while singing either of the above selections or playing them on the hi-fi. Then try the same exercises to slightly slower music, and continue going down the tempo scale with your musical choices (remaining within the *allegro* range). You will begin to understand that what you may consider unremarkably fast could seem paralyzing to a dancer, especially if you mentally substitute a complicated *allegro* combination (see extensive discussion of dance-tempos in Chapter 9).

Solutions

To correct such problems of communication as the ones discussed above is not impossible, although a certain amount of effort is needed. This effort can be directed in three ways – through reading about ballet technique, referring to the several excellent books available from libraries; through close, continual observation of the dancers during class (combined, of course, with genuine interest, and empathy with them in their struggle to do their best); and fraternization with them outside class. Talk with them about their problems in class and how they feel about music – this can help them as well as you; and, finally, encourage informal talks with the teacher before, after or outside class. One friendly chat can accomplish more than a month of confrontation or trial and error in class, where time is precious. Such chats, accompanied by close attention to the teacher's comments and corrections during class, can eventually result in your knowing more about ballet than the average dancer in the class. (The above suggestions apply of course in reverse, for investigation by dancers and teachers into musical mysteries.)

Particulars

Since the foregoing comments are, for the most part, general, it is time to be more specific. I will, therefore, provide the following:

1. Three basic categories of musical preference in teachers.
2. Three methods employed by them in obtaining music from their accompanists.
3. Statements from teachers for whom I have worked, describing what each looks for in an accompanist.
4. A Rogues' Gallery of my most memorable pedagogical afflictions.
5. Brief portraits of my three favorites.

1. Three basic categories of musical taste

Teachers will differ in taste, as I have already mentioned. In particular, they will tend to prefer music from one of the three following categories as a steady diet, although some teachers – by far the most enjoyable to work with – may combine the three in varying proportions.

a. The standard, familiar ballet repertoire, which is the most restricted of the three categories, using as it does only mid-nineteenth- to very early twentieth-century music. Since, also, much of it is grossly over-used by unenterprising accompanists (and teachers) familiarity can breed nausea. Fortunately, there is at least a large selection from which to choose, so that one does not have to play the music from *Les Sylphides*, *Giselle* and *Swan Lake* without respite. The teacher who, in extreme form, insists on only music which everyone enters the ballet theater humming, is usually musically undeveloped, insecure, or pathologically nostalgic, attempting to relive, vicariously, past glories. In milder form, selective preference of familiar ballet music indicates a teacher who knows what he likes and likes what he knows.

b. Unconventional, even esoteric preferences for music in class indicate two different types of teacher. The first type is negative; the idea of appearing to be a musical intellectual, 'different' and daring, leads him out of his depth, for he seldom knows what to do with the novel sounds he calls forth from the accompanist. The second type, in contrast, is usually intelligent, imaginative and inventive in his teaching. Rejecting a dependency on the standard repertoire, he welcomes an accompanist who can provide unusual pieces. A teacher in this category is to be treasured, and even problems of temperament can be overlooked or endured as a small price to pay for such a stimulating opportunity for the accompanist. You must, of course, be prepared to play (and continually to seek out) the most extraordinary and obscure novelties, in addition to less startling but still untypical fare. If you like a comfortable, predictable existence, this teacher is not recommended; if you enjoy a challenging, uncircumscribed one, he is a stimulus and a delight.

c. Between these two extremes we find the teacher who is jaded with the balletic warhorses but is either unfamiliar with or uninterested in the esoterica. This type is pleased by music from the late eighteenth century and the Romantic repertoire, including less well-known music by the composers of *Giselle*, *Les Sylphides* and *Swan Lake*. All he asks is that the music be melodious, unproblematical and suitable for the combinations. This teacher is neither so humdrum to play for as a., nor as exhilarating and satisfying as the positive form of b.

As I have said, the ideal teacher, to me, would happily accept music from all of the categories, depending on his needs at a particular moment, although, if it is necessary to work with the pure form of one of the three, b., obviously is greatly to be preferred, simply because so much beautiful, breath-taking music exists outside the standard ballet repertoire and the pieces which can be heard in every concert hall every week of the year. Still, the 'ideal teacher' wisely uses all of these, without prejudice, for the dancers should become familiar with as much music, from various sources and periods, as possible. The accompanist and the teacher also benefit from the general atmosphere of freshness and breadth. I have put ideal teacher in quotes, but – despite his comparative rareness – I have played for at least five teachers who, although of varying musicality, never rejected a piece which was suitable for the combination at hand because of bias and stubborn preference. Such a teacher is the gateway to one of the happiest, most rewarding work-lives imaginable.

2. Three methods of evocation

In addition to having personal preferences, teachers will vary in the method by which they obtain the music from the accompanist. Again, although many teachers fall exclusively into one of these three categories, there are also those who use now one, now another of them.

a. The first type will talk or demonstrate the combination, leaving you to cogitate (quickly) and – on the basis of what you are expected to know of his preferences – to select the music without consultation. The teacher can function in this way for several reasons – ignorance, musical apathy, admirable flexibility or a heart-warming trust in your ability. In any case, this method will present you with few problems if the teacher is the type who gives more or less the same sort of class every day; if he is imaginative or erratic, things can get a trifle difficult for you unless you are reasonably experienced. One variation of this approach will, however, drive you mad if it happens consistently. This is the tendency of some teachers to talk every combination – whether *adagio* or *allegro* – in a bland *moderato* tempo (or to demonstrate it in a markedly different tempo from the one which they actually wish). I have never understood why teachers practice something which wastes as much class time as does this foible.

A teacher who habitually demonstrates combinations with a clear indication of tempo, attack and style or quality is precious at any time, but never more so than when he belongs to this first category.

b. Quite a different sort is the teacher who asks for a particular piece or type of music and is not content until he gets it. Two variations on this are the teacher who merely *informs* you what he wants and then turns to the class to demonstrate, leaving you to sort things out, and the teacher who *requests* a piece or a mood and proceeds dreamily (or alertly) to stand in front of the class, allowing inspiration to flow while you play. The first, of course, usually has come to class with the exercises worked out and already set; the second employs spontaneity, altering here and there while he extemporizes. The first approach produces a more efficient use of class time, but the second can be more imaginative and intuitive to the special needs of a particular class.

c. Last, and a rare delight for the musician, is the teacher who *sings* – expressively and accurately – the piece of music he wants *while demonstrating* the combination. He may only sing a reasonable approximation, but still with feeling for the phrasing and quality (teachers who emit la-la-las in a heavy monotone do not qualify for this select category). Even if his vocal quality leaves much to be desired, his conviction of delivery more than makes up for any slightly out-of-tune passages. And this approach creates in the studio the balletic ideal of interpenetration of movement and music, for the teacher is, of course, in the best position to know just what is suitable for a particular combination.

This is definitely not to say, however, that an experienced accompanist who is intimately acquainted with the teacher's method and working-philosophy cannot achieve miracles of perception and bring out qualities in an exercise which surprise and delight the teacher. Obviously, a balance between the determining of the music by the teacher and the selection of it by the accompanist is infinitely preferable to one or the other exclusively. If the music is *always* stipulated – verbally or melodiously – by the teacher, the accompanist becomes passive, and a source rather than an active participant. If, however, the teacher *habitually* leaves the choice to the pianist, he is both evading a musical responsibility and remaining detached; in this case, it is he who is the non-participant. The intelligent blending of the two extremes results in flexibility on the part of both teacher and accompanist, and an aura of spontaneity for the entire class.

3. In their own words

I have drawn on my own experience and that of friends in order to describe what you may encounter temperamentally and musically among teachers. I think that personal statements now by teachers themselves will prove illuminating and add another dimension. When this idea occurred to me, I realized that such statements would be of value not only because of factual, practical content but because the very phrasing, the philosophy underneath the practicalities would reveal much. They would be of value, also, because each statement would help to demonstrate the variety of types which may be encountered, and how a dance teacher can differ from a musician when talking about music. I must add that although – with a few exceptions – these are all teachers for whom I played regularly, over a long period (in several cases with great mutual empathy), I do not necessarily agree with every sentence. Since, however, the purpose of including such statements is to introduce points of view other than my own, total agreement would be undesirable and redundant.

Here, then, in alphabetical order, are statements from teachers of strongly varied backgrounds, temperaments and approaches to teaching. They range from extremely experienced, even legendary figures, all the way to one who is just beginning her teaching career. Some of the statements are very precise views on the accompanist's contribution, others offer a more generalized evaluation of the place of music in ballet class.

Margaret Black

I have come to the following conclusions about the relationship between rhythm at the *barre* in training and the ability of this to place energy in correct value to muscle tone in the center. All of the following is related to a specific *body placement*, however, and doesn't function without it. I firmly work on the principle of energy and correct muscle tone, through correct rhythmical usage in training, producing movement and not tension, which goes very much against musicality and prohibits movement in ballet.

Barre is not only to warm the dancer but to improve the aforementioned areas. As it is necessary for the dancer to be rounded so as to respond in different forms of movement in the muscles – as well as different tempi – these principles must be employed from the very beginning of class. This is contrary to what many accompanists believe. Viewing *barre* as just a warm-up, they do not see that musicality is as important – if not more so – at *barre* as it is in center work. All *barre* exercises have specific value and develop muscular responses for the center. It seems to me that the daily *barre* should be worked out accordingly, and I've found rhythmical changes and variety in tempo work very successfully in helping the center combinations which follow.

All vocabulary in ballet has a basic rhythmic co-ordination, which is necessary to produce each individual step technically. This never alters, but the tempos certainly do, and the dancer has to learn the inherent rhythmical control of each movement and, then, understand how to produce that in various movement-speeds while still retaining the basic rhythmical co-ordination of the step.

All vocabulary, both *barre* and center, springs from this; it is very important. But without an accompanist who is knowledgable and sensitive to the foregoing principles, work in class becomes difficult or even impossible. The accompanist must understand the basic movements and also what happens to them at various speeds.

Alfredo Corvino

The music which the dance accompanist provides for class work is the spiritual breath on which the dancers draw for their movement. The accompanist must have the sensitivity to relate the quality of the music which he plays to the quality of the dance steps to be executed.

With this kind of sensitivity the accompanist gives the dancer the level for his *ballon*, the breath for his *élan*, and the pulse for his movement motivation. All this is done with a modesty which serves the dancer and does not impose upon him.

Such accompanists are greatly appreciated. Their respect for dancing is implicit in the tender care with which they select their classroom repertoire and lovingly afford the dancer an extra support for his art.

Margaret Craske

I do find it extremely difficult to intellectualize something that for me is definitely a thing of growth. Growth between the union of the music and the dance. It is a matter of time. Between, for

6 Antony Tudor rehearsing *Dance Studies (Less Orthodox)*. Juilliard 1962

7 Antony Tudor at rehearsal with Margaret Black, assistant. Juilliard 1963

8 Antony Tudor rehearsing *Little Improvisations*, with Margaret Black. Juilliard 1963

9 Antony Tudor rehearsing *A Choreographer's Comments*, with Pina Bausch and Koert Stuyf. Juilliard 1960

10 Class with Antony Tudor. Metropolitan Opera Ballet School 1960

11   Antony Tudor rehearsing *Jardin aux lilas*. Juilliard 1967

instance, a pianist and a teacher there must be an understanding, mostly not formulated in words, but as the result of working together.

This must sound elementary; I am sorry I cannot help more, but this is the way I have always worked, and at 84 years of age I do not feel it is possible to make a more mental approach to something that has usually worked out by simply tackling it.

Kathleen Crofton

To fulfill his function competently, as an integral part of a lesson in classical ballet, the pianist must immediately catch the rhythmic pattern of each exercise and *enchaînement*. If a suitable piece of music does not readily come to mind, he must be able to improvise adequately. It is necessary for him to have a large repertoire committed to memory, from which he can draw on the spur of the moment. He must never hold a lesson up while searching through piles of music for a particular piece which might be suitable; he must know it by heart. And he must remain alert throughout the session.

Nina Fonaroff

The accompanist should be an excellent musician – i.e. technically strong, rhythmically infallible, a rich tonal quality, and a natural sense of phrasing.

My preference in music for ballet is (not in order): Chopin, Schumann, Schubert, Mendelssohn, Tchaikovsky, Stravinsky, Prokofiev, Czerny – and music that is melodically and rhythmically enticing.

Benjamin Harkarvy

I look for:

1. Genuine musical feeling which makes anything sound logical no matter how it is broken up rhythmically.

2. *Energy*!

3. The ability to keep strict time.

4. Involvement in the teaching process, the kind of focus that supports the teacher in his cultivation of the professional attitude that one must always *be* there, totally committed, concentrated.

5. If the accompanist does not improvise, the repertory played should be a big one so that many qualities and responses could be asked for.

6. Control of dynamics and shading, coloring – whatever the piece calls for. Too many pianists play *f* to *ffff*! all the time, feeling that this is energy. On a long-term basis this inhibits the teacher's process of making a dancer aware of nuance, etc.

7. Musical culture. I find this facilitates my relationship with the pianist in terms of being a 'team'.

I like an accompanist to be a collaborator. We can feed each other and in doing so enrich the whole process.

Fiorella Keane

An accompanist should wholly empathize with the teacher to the point of almost predicting the mood of the class. The accompanist should, if possible, be very familiar with the teacher with respect to the form the class takes as well as knowing the usual type of movement that is particular to that teacher.

Personally, I don't mind if the music is a well-known or a little-known piece, or even if it is an improvisation; my own concern is that it fits the movements to perfection and also the mood of the class.

Monotonous sprawlings over the keyboard, or single repetitive chords and notes should be avoided at all cost. The ideal music is that which helps the dancer *dance*. Much to my students' joy – and mine – not long ago an accompanist played a Beatle composition as a rousing waltz. It was positively inspiring for that particular movement and class.

An accompanist who has succeeded wholly in a given class is the one that is ignored by the teacher, but whose work and music has made the class exciting to the student and inspiring for the teacher.

Rosanna Seravalli

The accompanist in dance class is as important as the teacher. Music provides the rhythm and dynamics for the steps, and it is absolutely essential that the accompanist understand the quality of the combination in order to choose appropriate music so that the students will dance with the right accents.

If the accompanist doesn't know much about dancing, the teacher can be very helpful by asking for a specific music (3/4, 4/4, 6/8, etc.) until familiarity sits between them. It is important to explain to the pianist *why* certain music is good for certain steps. Example: an *adage* consists of slow and stretched movements, so the music also should have a slow and stretched quality. Jumping needs a feeling of *ballon*, so it demands a musical 'push' to make the jumps higher and free. I think it is a good idea for accompanists to come to the teacher to discuss anything that is unclear, and I am always happy to try to explain.

Emiko and Yasuko Tokunaga

What do we look for in a ballet (dance) accompanist? A good dance accompanist must have not only a good command of his/her instrument (good technique, artistic expression, etc.) but also an extensive repertoire of classical and contemporary music, as well as improvisational skills. He/she must have a good feeling and understanding of movement (quality, timing and phrasing) coupled with patience and a desire to be an extension, not an imposition.

What do we think the value of music in dance class to be? To us 'dance' is a way of life, and music helps us reflect this 'life' through all its different phases. Music helps us to organize and stabilize our movements, underscoring a rhythm, a phrase, thus enabling us to execute an efficient melodic, muscular flow which goes beyond technique. We train as dancers in a class to achieve the necessary technique required for us to build a more efficient, economical movement vocabulary which will help us last longer in our profession/life. Whenever music is in a class, it is our obligation to develop a sensitivity to musical sounds, so we dance *with* the music not just to the music. Good music in a dance class is essential in building not only a dancer but in turning that dancer into an artist.

Antony Tudor

A rehearsal or class pianist who is really good needs most of all some of the qualities that the conductor of the orchestra should have – the abilities to see with two eyes not only the score but simultaneously the movements of the dancers, and also to be able to relate them to each other. My favorite accompanists are seen to echo in their bodies while perched on their piano seat most of what the performers on the dance floor are doing. Then, of course, this accompanist needs enormous patience, which is perhaps a quality associated with the *chefs d'orchestres*, and also a memory for scores.

Colette Yglesias

As a young teacher of beginning students of all ages my requirements for an accompanist are few, but essential.

One of the basic needs is that the pianist should not take class time in search for the perfect piece. Since a beginner class consists of relatively simple combinations it is much better for the pianist to be very well acquainted with two or three pieces for each exercise rather than have ten or twelve from which to choose. The time spent on the choice of a perfectly matching piece of music to an exercise is of value only on an intermediate or advanced level. The music should be interesting but simple. One purpose of the use of music is as an aid to development of an instinctive feel for musical phrasing. If the pupil must concentrate on counting the music, his movements quickly became static and mechanical. He must be able to feel the beginning and end of a musical phrase and thus shift his attention to matching the flow of the music. Music with complicated or unusual phrasing should be reserved to challenge the intermediate and advanced student.

A common problem for beginning accompanists is in maintaining the tempo set by the teacher. Too often he will watch the students and give in to their desire to speed up an adagio or slow down a jump. A steady tempo must be accurately set and maintained.

I have also found that a pianist who can improvise is invaluable. It is inevitable that occasionally one's mind will draw a blank. Rather than spend valuable class time searching through stacks of music a pianist should be able to take a theme from another piece of music, or a theme of his own, and adapt it quickly and appropriately to the given exercise.

Gayle Young

Of first importance is the meter, or is it rhythm? I'll let you decide. The accompanist must have the interest to watch the teacher demonstrating in order to decipher the meter (rhythm) appropriate to the combination – whether it is 6/8, 3/4, 4/4, 2/4, etc. A combination can, of course, be done to several meters – with various results; some, alas, disastrous if the pianist is not attuned to the teacher's needs – some beneficial.

After the meter, I should think the mood of the piece is next in importance, the atmosphere it creates for the dancer's muscles. For the meter alone is not enough. Does the music soothe for the stretching of the thighs and achilles in *pliés*? Does it electrify for *frappés*? Does it indicate the lushness of a slow *fondu*? Does it, in short, lead the student along the path toward a fuller technique through a sensual response to the music?

Finally, I think that the most important quality an accompanist should have is this – to have in his arms the sense of the dancer's thighs – a curious image, I admit, but there it is.

Anything less than what I have cited is an irritating disaster, anything more is a gratefully welcomed bonus.

As to choice of music, *Les Sylphides* (Chopin) is forbidden. Improvisation is welcomed.

Each of these statements reflects a different preoccupation, sometimes very pointedly. Because of this, the statements as a group present a good cross-section of what accompanists may encounter in other teachers. Some, of course, overlap on one or more points. An involvement with the dancers and the progress of the class is expressed or implicit in nearly every statement, as is a concern for what music will be played. Other points are unique, appearing in only one statement; the relation of *barre* to center work, the concept of spiritual breath and the virtue of modesty, growth between pianist and teacher, the pleasure of an accompanist who is musically highly literate or cultured, the attributes of being ignorable and a kinesthetic link with the dancers and having the general qualities of an orchestra conductor. (I myself would agree with every one of these but that of ignorability –

but, since this is a not uncommon viewpoint, it is valid, if arguable, and warrants inclusion.) Since the statements needed to be short and distilled, several of the unique assertions might, of course, be echoed by other teachers represented here.

I should add that one omission exists in this collection of viewpoints; none of the teachers is a musical illiterate, the species which creates so many problems and bad feelings for accompanists.

4. Rogues' Gallery

Now that some teachers have had their say, I shall return to my own vantage point and offer a personal rogue's gallery of certain idiosyncrasies which I had to endure at various times during my accompanying career. While representative of a general type, each is based on a specific teacher. Other species no doubt exist, but I thought it best to limit myself to those I have worked with.

In addition to providing an outlet for past grievances, in a mellow spirit of forgiveness, the purposes of this gallery are to put other accompanists on their guard, or to comfort those who are already suffering from similar (or worse) afflictions. Some of these contacts occurred when I was inexperienced, and more than once I thought of retiring from the battlefield; only the rewards of playing for more congenial teachers during the same periods of trial prevented total flight. I was, however, glad later that I had stuck it out and added to my knowledge (and, in retrospect, amusement). I have described these characters in order of my own degree of tolerance, beginning with the most fiendish and ending with the least repellent.

a. The illiterate

Many well-known, successful dancers turn to teaching when they have passed their prime as performers, or do a certain amount while they are still active on stage. In this category lies, perhaps, the greatest potential for trouble. By illiterate, I mean that with many their careers were pursued and realized either on a mainly intuitive level, or achieved through the Svengali–Trilby manner of coaching and guidance from wiser heads. In either case, they – at their worst – do not understand the principles of ballet beyond what was required specifically for their own achievement. They especially cannot bridge the gulf between dancer and musician and explain or, often, even perceive what they want or need musically. They often have no conception of phrase-structure, even within the traditional four-, eight- or sixteen-bar organization of the dance-phrase. The steps within their combinations have little direction or continuity, and because of this, the dance-phrase frequently ends before or after the musical one. The class is a study in imagination as each dance-student attempts to solve for herself the conflicting data.

My most memorable contact with this type came at a time when, fortunately, I had several years of experience to bolster my morale. A venerable Russian ballerina came to teach a special course at the school where I regularly played. Her name was magical but her class was chaotic. From the beginning it was obvious that it would be an obstacle course for both dancers and accompanist. Few exercises survived in their first 'form', which of course confused the dancers (and me). By the time we reached the *grand adage*, everyone had been scolded frequently for 'inattention'.

The demonstration of the *adage* was fascinating. She performed it with fire, theatricality and obvious relish six times, in silence, except for her own (adjustable) counts. Each version was noticeably different. I noticed the dancers looking, somewhat desperately, at one another and shared their feelings. Because she had reacted violently to previous questions I kept my own counsel and chose the last materialization of her ghostly basic idea because it was nearest in time and also seemed the least problematical.

We began. Things went well enough until we approached the mid-point of the combination. No two dancers seemed to be at the same point in the phrase. Some already had oozed into the second half of the *adage*; others were floundering in the first. Since I could not possibly accommodate both the tardy and the premature, I had to make a quick choice. Going by the majority, I extended the music slightly by a *ritard*, hoping that a miracle would occur and the dancers would manage to recollect themselves at the clear beginning of the next musical phrase. Of course, any sensible teacher would have called a halt long before this, but perhaps she, too, was weary of the search for the lost combination. Certainly by the end of her sixth demonstration she had begun to show signs of ennui.

At this mid-point, however, she did finally stop the dancers – indirectly – by screaming at me, 'What are you *doing*? The dancers, they are not *horses*!' Since I had been attempting, in impossible circumstances, to do something helpful, this seemed to me a trifle unreasonable. After venting her wrath (and, possibly, embarrassment over the elusive *adage*), she set the combination once again. This time, despite further confusion, I merely played metronomically to the end and, as the dancers straggled into the finish-line (like race-horses), I had a respite while I listened to her castigate the dancers for the fiasco.

At the end of class I informed the office that they could look elsewhere for an accompanist for this special course. (In such a situation, do *not* – as do some touchy accompanists – stalk self-righteously out of class before it is over. The teacher may deserve this, but it is unfair to the dancers.)

b. The tyrant

This type is related to a., but is more tolerable because underneath the bullying is usually at least skill and a clear conception. Another difference is that a. is essentially a performer, and although b. may have been as famous, he is also a teacher and understands basic principles and can communicate them – however boorishly. Your problem is that you function in a strait-jacket and can never relax. The class is conducted with a military control; the dancers are drilled like soldiers and spontaneity is snuffed out.

My tyrant combined this rigidity with an expectation of clairvoyance from me. The *barre* work was no problem after the first few days because it never varied. The mind-reading problem began with the exercises in the center. Standing before the class, poised to demonstrate, he would command sternly, 'Play, maestro'. The first time this happened I naturally asked what the combination was to be. '*Play*', he repeated. Since I was in acute need of work at the time, I played – although the result has faded from memory. Soon, through sheer tension, I managed to develop a split-second perception of what his first movement heralded, and I just managed to survive until I found another job. The general strain – accentuated by his invariable command to 'Play, maestro' being delivered in an intimidatingly heavy Russian accent – would have been unbearable for long, but I was later glad to have had this experience for it certainly promoted quickness of perception and response.

c. The shouter

The maddening effect of this type varies with your powers of aural tolerance and your mood.

Shouters usually are galvanized into action by the first note they hear. Until the final beat, all is pandemonium. The majority count loudly over the music, with occasional bellowed corrections to the dancers. An increase in noise level is sometimes achieved by explosive hand-clapping (not always in rhythm). A dramatic refinement is the stamping of the floor with foot or stick. The music is, of course, obliterated, and you get a headache.

I must admit that this type can be enjoyable, in an odd way, for the vitality necessary to maintain such a barrage of sound, if accompanied by balletic interest and a (subterranean) musicality, may prove highly exciting. If the temperament of this type is malevolent or simply unpleasant, his shouting is the last straw; my shouter however, was quite unobjectionable in other areas, and so I found myself able to revel in the percussive accompaniment to my accompaniment – his hand-clapping, stamping and cane-thumping – especially since he often exuberantly clapped, etc. in syncopated rhythms.

d. The ignorer

A type bordering on the offensive. His only possible 'virtue' is that often he leaves you undisturbed, to daydream or to read the newspaper – whatever catches your fancy instead of playing a rewarding ballet class. If you prefer to be involved in what you are doing, he will drive you mad with frustration and boredom. To him, you are, at best, a musical machine; at worst, invisible. You may receive warm greetings and farewells, but during class you do not seem to exist. In fact, you sometimes get the distinct impression that your music does not exist either. This type of teacher is conducting a course in gymnastics, not dance. He does not give rhythmical or musical corrections to the dancers; in fact, he manages somehow never to mention anything even vaguely related to music.

The studio is a limbo of pointed feet, stretched legs, 'correct' positions, competitive leaps, bravura pirouettes and mannerism rather than artistry.

A woman for whom I played occasionally was so extreme in her disregard for music that sometimes half of the class-time was spent with the dancers executing the steps in musical silence, to her (arhythmical) counts. It was obvious that she was far more comfortable when she was counting for them, evading competition, and the possible exposure of her musical obtuseness. Her efforts were divided between the technical problems of the dancers and exhibition of her own dancing prowess. A student once called her a 'frustrated ballerina', but she was not unique, for quite a few teachers have a weakness in this area. (She also, like many such teachers, prided herself in conversation on her musicality.) The worst examples of a., b. and c. may have given me the most torment but they never paralyzed me with such dullness.

e. The infant

Here we have an adult in need of pacifiers. Like a baby, he seeks security in a frightening world. Familiarity is the keyword; a handful of pieces serves: comfortingly well known and unthreatening, preferably associated with past successes on the stage. Any new sounds produce in him nervousness and even bad temper. I played, during one period, for a man bearing one of the most famous family names in ballet. He was, actually, quite sweet and completely without temperament, except of an amusing sort, but his classes were about as stimulating from a musical point of view as the sole ownership of a record of Chopin's Greatest Hits. In fact, Chopin was the keynote of his classes, although some Tchaikovsky and Delibes was also requested, plus a few other odds and ends, mostly Offenbach.

Almost all *adagios* were demonstrated while he hummed, in an unforgettable, abrasive voice, Chopin's Nocturne, op. 15, no. 2. When he tired of this, the Prelude from *Les Sylphides* was substituted. Most *allegros* were done to an obscure piece which I was never able to identify, but of which I managed to concoct a version acceptable to him. Waltz combinations called forth his vocalization of an Offenbach favorite. *Allegros* across the floor invariably led him to sing, with the merriest expression, the first theme from the Act IV *Entr'acte* of *La Vie parisienne*.

Perhaps if he had been less droll and even-tempered I would have reacted differently, but these undemanding classes, coming as they did at the end of a very long accompanying-day, were mildly boring but bearable. If, however, most of my daily classes had been with him, I would have learned little about ballet and become lazy and unenterprising, for he was, although not a poor teacher, easygoing and predictable with the students also.

f. The intellectual

I have put this rogue last because even in his worst manifestation, you can usually console yourself by playing music which is interesting and unusual, unlike most of the other types.

Since I have already commented on the intellectual in the discussions of teachers' musical preferences, I will limit myself here to saying that the pseudo-intellectual makes class a musical competition. Basically insecure, under his hairsbreadth veneer of musicology, he is forever challenging the pianist in some way. He will gleefully hurl *Rite of Spring*-like metric changes at the accompanist – and be delighted if any problem arises in finding such music. As a rule, his fabulous mathematical concoctions make no movement-sense, and lack any discernible phrasing. This is movement from the head, not the body. (Needless to say, the dancers have counting-problems, and he can transfer his condescension from you to them, although you, as a musician, are preferred.) He is capable of proudly firing at you a request for a sarabande – and then demonstrating a combination which turns out to be a 4/4 (more or less). He is enamored of the *idea* of a sarabande but not too clear what it actually is. Or he will (he thinks) impress you with his excellent musical vocabulary. 'Play this one with lots of *allargando*', he says – and no one would be more annoyed than he if you slowed down frequently during the exercise.

The teacher I particularly remember of this type was all the more irritating because he alternated between feverish attacks of pretentiousness and total musical apathy. I never knew, therefore, when I went in to class whether Dr. Jekyll would ignore me or Mr. Hyde would be thrusting his musical rapier recklessly throughout the lesson.

The bona fide intellectual can, on the other hand, be stimulating and interesting, for he usually approaches the dancing in an intellectual way, in addition to the music. I would not want to play exclusively for such a teacher, but it can balance very nicely playing for the infant or the ignorer, and, often, unusual and controversial ideas can be absorbed from him.

Both the pseudo and the bona fide intellectual tend to reject anything bearing the faintest resemblance to Ballet Music. To play Tchaikovsky is to produce a look of nausea. The dreariest, least kinetic Bach, a trifle from Mozart's infancy, a Palestrina motet, a piece which should have ended up in Schoenberg's wastebasket – such things can send the intellectual into raptures (whether they send the dancers' bodies into movement is another matter). He may, however (particularly the bona fide), ask for perfectly suitable music – music which possibly has never before been heard in a ballet studio.

Since my first experience with this type came early in my career, such musical demands only confused and hindered me, particularly since he was of the pseudo-species. I couldn't possibly come up to his esoteric standards, and it was at this time that I went gratefully into my last class of the day, with the predictable infant.

5. Galaxy of delights

To balance the preceding 'rogues', I must now describe briefly three teachers who counteracted – superbly – any dissatisfactions or damage caused by even the worst of the lot. Although I accompanied for several teachers who were, for various reasons, rewarding to work with, these three represent both my longest associations and my greatest joys.

Margaret Black

Zealous; dedicated; trail-blazing; methodical; sensitive; excitable; merry; kind; musically receptive and inquiring; endearing.

Alfredo Corvino

Buoyant; kinetic; invigorating; intuitively, unerringly musical; courteous; serious; playful; inspiring; thorough; lovable.

Antony Tudor

Absorbing; demanding; unpredictable; subtle; witty; superbly and astonishingly musical; amusing; maddening; capricious; endlessly enlightening and stimulating; unfathomable; unparalleled.

From the foregoing, it will be obvious that I have endured or delighted in many different types of teachers, who varied temperamentally and in their degree of musicality to an enormous extent. Recollecting them for this chapter I found that I did not regret accompanying for any (although I was glad that contact in some cases was brief), for the diversity of experience was fascinating and invaluable. And, curiously, while time has erased the upsets caused by the rogues, the memory of my classes with the outstanding guardians of creative ballet whom I was fortunate enough to work with remains as fresh as ever. This memory will continue to color and enrich my life – which would have been so different and so diminished if I had never met them.

My earnest hope is that accompanists who read this will have similar good fortune – at which point we come to the brink of a long discussion of the elements which determine your choice of music for class. For without a solid, reliable, imaginative repertoire, your chances of a rewarding, long-term association with a good teacher are rather slim. A handful of pieces, delivered with numbing predictability, will almost inevitably doom you to the gypsy life of so many accompanists – who flit from job to job, never seeming to settle anywhere. Or, if there are only one or two studios in your town, it may doom you to no work at all.

Let us, therefore, begin our inquiry into the complex matter of building a repertoire which can make you treasured and sought after: and who would not wish for this?

6   Selection of music 1 – Theoretical: rhythm

Many feel that the dance movements must exactly correspond with the movements
in the music. I call this 'rhythmomania'.

Michel Fokine, *Memoirs of a Ballet Master*, 1961

A LARGE AND VARIED REPERTOIRE is the accompanist's greatest practical
asset, and vital, imaginative performance of it the most important artistic
one. In this, and the following two chapters, we will discuss the acquisition
of repertoire, and, in the ninth chapter, how to bring it to life in connection with the
dance.

Two problems face us in the search for music: *what* to look for and *where* to find
it. Many accompanists begin with the latter, pursuing the where before they
understand the what. Countless hours of conscientious searching, therefore, result
in little that is usable. I knew one accompanist who collected sections of over 200
eighteenth-century sonatinas, pasting them neatly into a notebook which he
carried to classes – a great deal of effort, but with little balletic value. Not only were
many of them designed primarily to develop piano technique, thus being narrow in
expressive content, but a steady diet of any one style in class would daunt even the
most enthusiastic dancer.

In selecting music which so over-emphasized this restricted area of musical
literature, the pianist demonstrated an ignorance of the *why* which underlies the
what and where. Why is one piece suitable for class and another not? And why
should one not concentrate on only one or two styles of music? I shall try to offer
answers to these questions and help the accompanist to amass a usable repertoire
based on understanding of the dancers' needs.

The crux of the matter is whether the accompanist functions passively or actively.
To make do with a meager, ossified collection of tunes, used with numbing
regularity, is to be passive and detached. I have stressed the desirability of an
interchange between teacher and accompanist. This is active. Ideally, he gives you,
in some way, a clear idea of what music is needed; you in return must be equipped
with music – or rather knowledge transmuted into music – in order to respond. This
establishes a cyclical relationship in which both of you continue to expand through
interaction. Through ideas suggested to him by your music, in its liberating variety,
his classes will not stagnate, but rather grow. In turn, the variety and continuing
interest of the teacher's ideas will inspire you to greater efforts and a desire to
discover yet more stimulating music: a most fruitful and mutually beneficial
association.

120

I. Determining factors

An imaginative repertoire might include, say, a thirteenth-century song, an Elizabethan dance-suite, a Purcell air, a Mozart rondo, some Chopin waltzes and mazurkas, a Puccini aria, sections from *Sleeping Beauty*, a Vivaldi Adagio, a Berlioz march, parts of *Tosca* and *Petrushka*, a Bartok folk-dance, a Beatles song. But no matter how danceable any of these may be in their own right, each must encompass five requirements:

1. A kinetic quality; strong sense of pulse
2. The appropriate meter
3. Phrases which are harmonious with the dance phrases
4. A functional tempo
5. A definite, recognizable quality and style which enhances the movement.

The rather rare musician who fits quickly and easily into the ballet world may never have to think consciously about these; her sensitivity to movement may be intuitive. For the rest of us, however, some analysis is necessary. But before plunging into what is one of the more technical sections of this book, I should make some preliminary comments.

1. Kinetic quality

This can be described as the ingredient in music which makes us want to move rhythmically – to get up and dance. No strict guidelines can be given. It may be found in many different types of music: an African drum-pattern, a Strauss waltz, an Indian raga, a Mozart aria or a Beatles song. 'Primitive' is the word most often used to describe the kinetic reaction, and appropriately so, for it is the basic ingredient in the dance-impulse. Much of the time it involves a strong pulse but this alone does not produce kinetic feeling. The surface tick-tock of the beat can even prove deadening. Pulse may be present, but in itself is not rhythm – as we shall see in Section II.1.

2. Appropriate meter

If the teacher does not specify it, the choice is yours, and this is not always as easy as it might seem. There are many pitfalls where meter is concerned, which can confuse even musicians. True, all meter falls into either a duple or a triple grouping, or combinations of these – but what does this mean in practice, and which type will prove to be best for a particular combination? Section II.2. is devoted to an examination of what meter is, and, perhaps more important, what it is not.

3. Phrases

The sensitive accompanist will select the music with *phrase* as the main guide rather than measure or meter. Every well-made dance and music phrase has a clear structure, as does a verbal phrase, or statement, but many teachers and musicians who are quite capable of speaking in coherent phrases never think to apply the same principles to dance or music. Yet a feeling for phrase is essential in the ballet studio, for without it all we have is a succession of counts rather than a progression of movement. Phrases give scope to pulse and meter and create *rhythm*. They also make possible the two important aspects of ballet: breath and *ballon*. Sensitivity to phrase can never be faked, but it *can* be developed and encouraged. Section II.3 looks into this.

4. Tempo

Until *tempo* – the speed of performance – is brought into play, pulse, meter and phrasing remain more or less abstract concepts. As Deryck Cooke writes, 'the rhythm itself, independent of tempo, is nothing more than an ebb and flow of rhythmic tension. Obviously, everything depends on the speed at which this ebb and flow occur . . .'[1]

The tempo of a piece played for dance certainly cannot be ignored; the discomfort of steps taken too fast or too slow makes this impossible. It is, however, often neglected in a curious way. That is to say, tempo is a twofold problem in the studio. Whether or not the pianist is playing a piece in the proper tempo for the movement can hardly be mistaken; what is not so obvious is whether the piece has been employed at a proper tempo for *itself*, and can be played sensibly. Every piece has limits of speed, fast and slow, which cannot be exceeded without demolishing the spirit of the music. Section II.4. is comprised of such concerns.

5. Quality and style

A fully realized piece of music has an immediately recognizable quality and style. Contrast a symphony by Mozart with one by Mahler, a song by the Rolling Stones with one by Cole Porter. Or, compare the Germanic profundity of a Bach organ fugue with the lyrical Italianate grace of Vivaldi's *The Four Seasons* or the French elegance and precision in Ravel's *Le Tombeau de Couperin*. And how different each of these is from Mussorgsky's *Pictures at an Exhibition*.

Dance, similarly, has different qualities and styles. Is it conceivable that a dancer could perform a brilliant variation from *Sleeping Beauty*, the *Valse Brillante* from *Les Sylphides* and the Scotch Dance from *Coppélia*, all with the same quality and style? Yes, just as pianists can play a Bach toccata, a Beethoven sonata, a Liszt rhapsody, and a Debussy prelude with equal bombast and total lack of comprehension for anything but technical tricks. No, it is not conceivable if the dancer has any awareness of the different qualities and styles inherent in the choreography.

Quality and style are inseparable from the so-called technical elements of music and dance: the raw materials of notes and steps, rhythm, dynamics and attack, but these are, so to speak, the bones and muscle, whereas the quality and style are the face and personality. What actually happens with our bravura dancer and our bombastic pianist is that they alter the rhythm, dynamics and attack (and sometimes the steps and notes!) of the original, using an egocentric approach which *replaces* (rather than illuminates) the composer's or choreographer's face and personality. Chapter 7 is devoted to the elements of style, and its role in performance is analyzed in Chapter 9.

Each of the five factors discussed above is related to 'rhythm' in some way, but the meaning of this statement will not really be clear unless we define adequately this term which is used in so many ways.

II. Rhythm

Each aspect of dance movement and music which we choose to discuss involves rhythm, directly or indirectly. It is the generative and unifying force in dance and music as it is in life itself, and, indeed, it can seem as difficult to define rhythm as to define life.

The problems include difference of terminology. The all-encompassing term 'rhythm' is often used when writers are actually referring to the specific components, pulse or meter ('the rhythm of this section is 3/4'); differences exist also in emphasis, with one aspect being cited as more important, when they are all part of an integrated totality, and there are even differences in basic conception. An additional difficulty here stems from the difference between *dance* rhythm and *musical* rhythm.

But let us look at some definitions, beginning with the most typical, in order to see the difficulties more clearly.

i. According to George A. Wedge, 'rhythm in music is the arrangement of notes differing in mathematical value upon the pulses of the meter, a definite note value having been assigned to the pulse.'[2] This is a common academic view, which manages to devitalize the most vibrant aspect of existence – rhythmic motion.

ii. George Balanchine, in an interview: '"Rhythm is a bar", he said, framing a rectangle with his hands . . . "It's the structure of time within the bar" . . .'[3] Here vitality and vibrancy are confined in a cage.

iii. Rhythm, in the *Oxford Companion to Music*, 'covers the ensemble of everything pertaining to what may be called the *time* side of music (as distinct from the *pitch* side), i.e. it takes in beats, accents, measures or bars, grouping of notes into beats, grouping of beats into measures, grouping of measures into phrases and so forth.'[4] And so forth – through a most unrhythmical prose into a wasteland of bits and pieces.

Notice that all of these are essentially mechanistic and quantitative, and, somehow, separating and isolating. (The third at least mentions phrases, but, in effect, as an afterthought rather than what it really is – a guiding principle from the very beginning.) A significant change is made by Cooper and Meyer:

iv. 'Rhythm may be defined as the way in which one or more unaccented beats are related to an accented one.' But, as they go on to say, 'Rhythm is independent of meter . . . bar lines, which serve to mark off metric units, do not indicate what the rhythmic organization is. Rhythmic groups are not respecters of bar lines. They cross them more often than not . . .'[5]

It cannot be stressed too heavily that measures and their rigid bar lines are a *convention* – a visual aid for the performer, who would find a long continuum confusing, and for the participants in ensemble music, where they help to prevent chaos. Much of the world's music has, furthermore, never felt the need for the despotic rule of the bar line; it is a Western invention. Rhythm can exist with meter or without, but meter does not create true rhythm.

v. Going even beyond this broader concept, however, we turn to two illuminating statements. Langer, in a typically perceptive and wide-ranging passage, refers to the doctrines of Heinrich Schenker concerning meter and rhythm, 'namely that rhythm is a function of tonal motion, not of time division; such motion depends as much on melodic and harmonic tension and direction as on tempo.'[6] Cooper and Meyer add: 'Just as a melody is more than simply a series of pitches, so rhythm is more than a mere sequence of durational proportions. To experience rhythm is to group separate sounds into structured patterns. Such grouping is the result of the interaction among the various aspects of the materials of music: pitch, intensity, timbre, texture and harmony – as well as duration.'[7]

Thus, rhythm in music may be said to be an organizer, functioning on many different levels at once, from the simple pulse to the most subtle tonal tensions. It is dynamic and expansive. Meter, in itself, is but a regulator, a device which is restrictive and closed in. Or, as Ludwig Klages observes, 'Meter . . . draws boundary lines, interrupts and separates. Rhythm is the unbroken continuity of a flux, such a continuity as the wave most graphically represents . . . Meter is repetition of the identical; rhythm is return of the similar. The machine runs metrically; man walks rhythmically.'[8] This passage applies, of course, to rhythm in dance as well as music.

A comparison of these more all-embracing definitions with the first three is all the more pointed when one reflects that the Greek word *rhythmos*, from which comes our 'rhythm', means *flow*.

More questions may by now have been raised than answered, so we will proceed to examine in detail the time-elements of rhythm: pulse, meter, phrasing and tempo.

1. Pulse

Pulse is the most basic element of rhythm; it can exist in isolation, but is also necessary for the creation of meter. It is described by Cooper and Meyer as 'one of a series of regularly recurring, precisely equivalent stimuli . . . pulses mark off equal units in the temporal continuum'.[9] Curiously, although music is notated metrically, and pulse is part of the organization of a measure, the *feeling* of pulse can be absent, as in a polyphonic Palestrina motet, the almost immobile opening of the Prelude to *Tristan and Isolde*, or much of Debussy's music. Without seeing a conductor beating the successive and regular pulses, we would be hard-pressed to discover either the simple pulses or their metrical distribution in such music.

Although a feeling of pulse is characteristic of dance music it must be organized to be effective. Human beings try to impose order on their environment, and the steady dripping from a water tap or the clackety-clack of train wheels will, almost unconsciously, be grouped in our minds into patterns of twos or threes. This creates meter.

2. Meter

A first step toward rhythm, meter is the organization of regular pulses into units of time called measures. These are normally marked by a recurrent accent on the first beat (or pulse) of each measure, the 'downbeat'. Meter differentiates; pulse does not. Meter is a specific, even at times arbitrary, part of rhythm, and if taken too literally, may prevent the perception of rhythm in its larger sense, and impede its flow in time. 'Keeping in time' and 'beating time' refer to pulse and its metrical restriction. And, as Zuckerkandl writes, '"Time" and rhythm here appear even to exclude each other; rhythm resists regular time; "time" appears to suffocate rhythm.'[10] But, 'meter and rhythm can meet on other terms than those of enmity and opposition . . . out of the regular succession of measured beat rises the wave; the prototype of rhythm grows from the seed of meter',[11] and '. . . it is not rhythm despite meter, but, on the contrary, rhythm from meter, rhythm fed by forces dammed up in meter'.[12]

A major limitation of meter is its neutral quality. Meter, or 'time', is not the same as rhythm simply because '3/4 time' is not the same as a waltz-rhythm, and '2/4 time' is not the same as a polka-rhythm; 3/4 time includes, among others, waltz, ländler, mazurka, polonaise, minuet and sarabande. 'What is fixed about metric organization is the number of beats (per measure) not their disposition.'[13] Meter, in other words, is inexpressive and characterless. A '2/4' is to a polka what 'a man' is to Fred Bloggs; a '3/4' is the mathematical mind at work; 'a waltz' is human experience in action. What this means in practice is that duple and triple metrical organization and notation are not necessarily the same as duple and triple rhythmical feeling.

First, let us examine the basic difference between duple and triple meter, which is that the physical effect of one strong beat followed by one weak beat (Ex. 1) contrasts vividly with that of one strong beat followed by two weak ones (Ex. 2):

Ex. 1

Ex. 2

Duple rhythm has been described as forceful, strict, rigid, confining, or down to earth. Triple, on the other hand, is graceful, free, lilting, or buoyant. They could also be contrasted as angular vs. circular, or controlled vs. spontaneous, as with a march vs. a waltz or a polka vs. a jig.

When selecting music in class, the pianist is much of the time faced with a choice between a duple and a triple feeling. One of the most common instances of this is the choice between a 'flowing, *moderato* 4/4' and a waltz. We are, however, already in trouble. I have said, irresistibly, duple *rhythm* and duple *feeling*, as opposed to a duple *meter*. Now, Exx. 1 and 2 show meter on what Meyer calls the primary level – the one designated in the time-signature. But what happens when we move to a different level – that of subdivision?

Ex. 3

Ex. 4

In Ex. 3 the feeling of the duple subdivision is consistent with the primary duple meter of Ex. 1 but in Ex. 4 the duple subdivision seems to alter the rounded feeling of the triple meter as experienced in Ex. 2. This is what is implied, partly, in the statement that triple meter is not the same as triple rhythm or a triple feeling. And, to make things worse, when we look at the meter of 6/8 (Ex. 5) in which there are two beats per measure we find that the inherent subdivision of 6/8 – three eighth notes to a beat – gives a triple feeling which is profoundly different from the primary duple meter of the 2/4 reinforced by the duple subdivision (Ex. 6):

Ex. 5

Ex. 6

Postponing the problem of Ex. 4 for a moment, let us see if we can climb out of this morass of theory by means of a combination: *glissade, brisé, glissade, brisé, brisé, brisé, brisé, entrechat quatre*. Obviously a bright 2/4 – yes? no? Yes, if you are feeling it on the primary level of the duple 2/4 meter; no, if you remember the triple subdivision of the compound 6/8 meter. But what actually determines your choice, when either one is theoretically acceptable? Apart from simple personal preference (and assuming that the teacher has not indicated one or the other) your guide will often be the context. If, for instance, the class has become rather bogged down in a period of intense concentration on technical problems – which happens in the best of classes – a lilting 6/8, with its triple feeling, can go far in restoring a sense of direction and vivacity. A 2/4 at this point, no matter how delightful, could reinforce feelings of restriction and confinement.

The opposite may be true; the more controlled duple rhythm is often preferable. The teacher may, for instance want to introduce a feeling of concentration, even severity, after a grand free-for-all of big jumps, or perhaps, after such a combination, wish to end the class on a tranquil, pulled-together note with a simple *port de bras*. In either case a duple rhythm would convey the appropriate subdued and sustained feeling.

Now to the rather involved problem of Ex. 4. Compare the following examples of 3/4 meter:

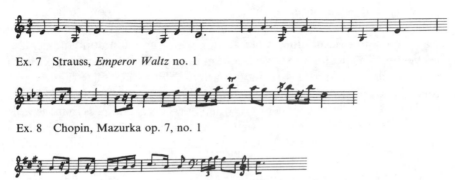

Ex. 7   Strauss, *Emperor Waltz* no. 1

Ex. 8   Chopin, Mazurka op. 7, no. 1

Ex. 9   Chopin, Polonaise op. 40, no. 1

Each of these is reasonably typical of its kind, and each will produce a different approach to the counting-out of the basic three beats. The waltz will lead one to count *measures*: *1*-and-a, *2*-and-a, *3*-and-a, *4*-and-a – absorbing each of these four measure's three beats into one larger rhythmic unit. The mazurka and polonaise, however, seem to mark off *beats*, with four measures of the mazurka counted *1*-**2**-3, *1*-**2**-3, *1*-**2**-3, *1*-**2**-3, and the polonaise **1**-*2-3*, **1**-*2-3*, **1**-*2-3*, **1**-*2-3*.

These differences are partly due to the general factor of tempo, but, more specifically, they arise from each type's inner rhythms and dynamic impulses. These include characteristic stresses (closely related, of course, to the dance-movements associated with each): in the waltz, as we see, the accent falls, or is felt, on the first beat; in the mazurka, sharply on the second; while in the polonaise, all three beats feel relatively emphatic. These stresses interact in each case with the other elements of subdivision, rhythmic patterns and phrasing to create the special flavor and personality of each '3/4'. Thus, a waltz has the rounded feeling of a triple rhythm, with the beats and any subdivisions of these being swept into a higher level of flow; a mazurka is edging away from 'roundness', its syncopation and occasional marked subdivisions altering and challenging the theoretically round three; and a polonaise carries this resistance to the point where the overall triplicity has been transformed into the 'forceful' quality of the frequent, emphatic duple subdivisions that are so typical of this proud music-dance form.

I have dwelt on this aspect of meter *vs.* rhythm, not to madden the reader with musical mathematics, but to illustrate the assertion that duple or triple meter does not necessarily indicate duple or triple rhythmic feeling, and to attempt a description of the potential expressive differences between duple and triple rhythms. This is an important factor in the choice of music for class. In addition, duple or triple rhythm affects steps technically. Joan Lawson states that steps with three changes of weight, i.e. *pas de bourrée* or *pas de basque*, 'are best performed to a 3/4 [sic] if each movement is to be given equality of spacing'.[14] Of course, teachers or accompanists often choose a duple rhythm for these, producing an equally effective, if different, sense of phrasing.

One important matter which I must mention here is what might be called the mathematical *relativity* of meter. As long as the note-values, phrasing and tempo markings retain a given relationship, there is actually no one 'correct' meter. This makes the composer's choice of meter often a personal matter or a reflection of current fashion. Sometimes, in fact, the choice can seem quite illogical, as in slow movements of Beethoven where it results in pages black with sixteenth, thirty-second and even sixty-fourth-note patterns. In earlier ages there was a certain theoretical relationship of meter to tempo, but this ceased after the Baroque period. One offshoot of the subsequent 'freedom' of metrical choice is that the waltz, which we notate in 3/4, often was notated in the nineteenth century in 6/8. When it later became fashionable to use 3/4, editors altered the original notation of the earlier waltzes. This, partially at least, accounts for the tendency mentioned above to count waltzes as 1-and-a, 2-and-a – as with a 6/8 – rather than 1-2-3 as with a mazurka: an instance in which one meter, the 6/8, seems more suitable than another.

Yet, with countless pieces, various choices would appear to serve equally well. Take, for example, the *adagio* in Act II of *Swan Lake*. Tchaikovsky chose to notate this in 6/8. Look, however, at some other ways which are possible:

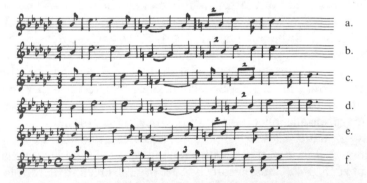

Ex. 10a–f   Tchaikovsky, *Swan Lake*, Act II, *pas de deux*: varying time signatures, same durational relationships

With a sensitive conductor, who is aware of the overall phrasing and the music's inner rhythm, the listener could not tell, if his eyes were closed, which notation was being used. The notation is not the music; it is merely a visual scheme for transmitting it. As long as the durational relationships of each remain the same, the changed physique of the musical symbols usually makes little difference in performance.

One qualification is necessary, however; composers often, though not always, choose meters for practical reasons. One meter may require more sixteenth or thirty-second notes, or groupings like triplets which are outside the normal metric scheme. Since copying music is laborious, at best, any effort saved is welcome. Thus, of these six versions, the 4/4 is least desirable, for the triplet-groupings are automatically provided by the other meters, and do not require the extra indication. (In these others, the duple grouping lies outside *their* metric scheme, but there is only one of these compared to four of the triple.)

The 12/8, on the other hand, conveys the long line of the phrase best of all, being broken up by bar-lines less often – yet Tchaikovsky preferred the 6/8 version. My main point here is that metrical notation is a choice, not an absolute, and as such has varied considerably during its history. Composers have even re-notated pieces (Stravinsky in particular), so that the visual physique of the music is radically different in each, yet the original aural effect remains.

We have examined meter at some length, and I hope that I have at least demonstrated that (1) meter, in itself, tends to divide and confine rhythm in its larger sense, and (2) it can seem to be something which it is not, and thus mislead all concerned. I have, for instance, mentioned the tendency of teachers to ask for a '3/4' which could mean, depending on the teacher's association, a waltz, mazurka, polonaise, or other such fixed identity; never, on the other hand, have I been asked for a '6/8' when an *adagio* like the Tchaikovsky example was wanted.

This sort of misrepresentation and circumscription does neither teacher nor accompanist any good. When the subject of meter arises, both should amplify numerals with nouns or adjectives – a polonaise, a sarabande or 'a 3/4 like the Snow King and Queen's *pas de deux* from *Nutcracker*'; a quick 6/8, a solemn 4/4, a folk-like, strong 2/4 or a Tyrolean 3/4. These all convey recognizable qualities, saving time.

I have already touched on phrasing apropos the notation of the *Swan Lake pas de deux*, and we should now turn our full attention to the elements which contribute to it.

3. Phrasing

My introductory comments will figure importantly in the chapter on performance, but it is necessary to present briefly these issues here.

Meter divides, phrasing connects; meter measures time, phrasing enriches it. In phrasing we release the confines of metrical counts. We do not 'beat' against the imprisoning bar-lines; we soar over them. The dancer should certainly appreciate this for no one can achieve much in the way of soaring – either literal or figurative – with a focus on beats and without the use of breath throughout the phrase. Similarly, the wind-player or singer always depends upon a breathing through and over the regular counts. Since pianists can (or often seem to) play without breathing, they can too easily evade the whole matter. If one single word could be used to describe the pianistic quality of the pyrotechnomaniac, it would be 'dense', with torrents of notes and counts suffocating one another. This also applies to the music of those avant-garde composers who are so preoccupied with the number of complexities which they can cram into each measure that they seem to have completely forgotten music's origin in human utterance and song.

Song, from the simplest folk-tune to the most subtle *Lied* of Mahler, Debussy or Webern, consists above all of melody. What is melody but a succession of phrases? And phrases, as William E. Brandt points out, have an important function:

. . . all melody is organized into sections, called *phrases*, which measure it off into understandable units. This kind of division probably first resulted from the limitations of the human breath capacity in singing; certainly the convenient pause at the end of a phrase allows time for a breath to be taken in order to go on with the following phrase. Instead of interrupting a continuous line of melody to gasp for breath, the artistic creators of melody in all ages have turned the melodic line at these points so that it comes to rest momentarily upon a tone of some stability before continuing. Such a cadence satisfies the musical requirement for a logical rest point as well as the physical one for breath.[15]

Although a musical phrase is by no means always created by melody alone, it is melody which is the main strand, for as Brandt writes, '. . . the harmony, rhythm and form of the entire composition depend upon [melody]. These other factors support, clarify, modify and intensify the melodic element, and while it may exist without them, they cannot go on for long without it.'[16]

Phrasing and melody are certainly, for most people, closely associated. This is the case in ballet, melody providing the most obvious thread and guide to phrasing for the dancer. Writers on dance rely over and over again on melody to help them to make points regarding phrasing of steps. 'An *enchaînement*, like the line of a song, must be so phrased that the climax appears to be the logical outcome of what has gone before and arises out of the careful weaving of the movements.'[17] Criticizing the complexity of some contemporary scores which chop up the sense of phrase, van Praagh and Brinson write, 'frequently it becomes impossible for dancers to do more than remember the steps which go with the music because each is equally intricate. Inner feeling and character have become lost, so we need a new simplicity in ballet music because ballet needs and always will need a clear melodic line'[18] (although people vary widely in what they consider to be one).

When, furthermore, they say 'clear melodic line', it could as easily be 'clear musical phrase'; the terms 'melody', 'line' and 'phrase' are habitually used interchangeably. If a critic pays tribute to a singer's musicality by referring to her 'exquisite shaping of the musical phrase', he is obviously not referring to the music's harmonies; the reader will know that he means the melodic line. 'Line' in dance has a different meaning, referring to physical harmony or 'the ability of the dancer to dispose limbs, head and body so that they not only harmonise with each other but also appear to fill the space within which the dance is set.'[19] The dancer's interchangeable term for 'phrasing' is 'flow of line', which is, again, used as an analogy for melody, with Lawson, among others, stating explicitly that 'flow of line can be likened to the melody'.[20]

Despite the linking, however, of 'phrase' to 'melody' and 'line', it is not quite this simple; for example, the singer's – and dancer's – shaping of the phrase actually will be due in part to a sensitivity to the underlying harmonic structure and its continual effect on the melody. Chord progressions exert a strong gravitational and expressive force on the melodic line; what might seem a weak or awkward melody-tone, upon reading or singing only the tune, could actually be the focal moment in the entire phrase through its conjunction with the harmonies before, during and after its sounding.

Even more important than harmonic structure is rhythm, for melodic phrases can only exist through some sort of rhythmic organization. A folk-song or the unaccompanied melody which begins *L'Après-midi d'un faune* can exist without harmony, but without rhythm they would be merely incomprehensible series of tones. Even tones which incorporate a clear harmonic structure remain inanimate non-phrases without rhythm. Take, for example, this series of notes:

Ex. 11

Not overwhelmingly expressive, it seems to most resemble a rather tricky vocal exercise, ending with an awkward little twist. Let us see, however, what some rhythmic organization may achieve, beginning with a pedestrian approach:

Ex. 12

This at least conveys something, if only that the mind which conceived it is a bit stodgy.

See, however, what happens when two master composers use these same notes (I have transposed the Mozart example from its original G minor to make the comparison easier to follow):

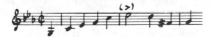

Ex. 13   Mozart, Symphony No. 40 in G minor, fourth movement

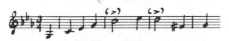

Ex. 14   Beethoven, Symphony No. 5 in C minor, third movement

No one could mistake one for the other; in fact, many musicians never realize that they both use the same nine notes. Their effect is totally different, not only because of their meters, but in the alternation of long and short notes with their differing groupings and phrasings. And, most important, each melody has a different goal or stress point. If it occurred to you to put Ex. 11 in the form of regularly recurring beats in 3/4 or 4/4, you would still be little further towards a melody. The results would be characterless, dull, even senseless, for they would lack that ebb and flow of stress and dynamics which give phrases in music and dance shape and personality. In Ex. 11 or a steady 3/4 or 4/4, the flux of phrasing is absent leaving only components which take us nowhere.

Mozart and Beethoven, however, have with these notes led us clearly, each in his own way. Notice each composer's choice of the note which receives the most stress. Mozart makes the high E flat the arrival point. This is achieved both through the E flat being the longest note-value and by its falling on the down-beat (in addition, he underscores this stress point with a tense and dissonant harmony). The Beethoven is more problematical; much controversy surrounds the proper phrasing of this line. Some conductors emphasize the C of the second measure, others the D of the third. But never would the E♭ (sixth note) be the most stressed – yet in the Mozart it is the most important of all.

So, from nine notes, seemingly meaningless in Ex. 11, we obtain two entirely different melodic phrases (and many others exist potentially), through the use of meter, stress and grouping.

Phrasing is flow and grouping. In music and dance, as in language, 'understanding is not a matter of perceiving single stimuli [our nine notes] or simple sound [and movement] combinations in isolation, but is rather a matter of grouping stimuli into patterns and relating these patterns to one another'.[21] Without grouping or shaping there is no comprehensibility; without comprehensibility there is no communication – because without grouping, the isolated notes and steps are only a potential. The created meaning lies in how they are patterned and linked. In all well-shaped phrases – music, dance or verbal – we find interaction, continuity, pattern and rhythm as they move through time to their completion.

Despite the similarity of principle between the dance phrase and the musical one, there is, however, a significant difference. This is true not only of performance (see Chapter 9), but of the intrinsic design of the individual elements of phrase, and one must be careful not to mistake an illusion of similarity between the two for the reality. When choosing music, remember that there are musical rhythms which are neither possible nor sensible in movement, and, of course, the reverse is true. To provide the actual dance-rhythm of an *enchaînement* musically is to create a musical joke. Take, for example, a dance-phrase which begins with small *jetés*. To achieve *ballon*, the dancer will spend the minimum functional time necessary in the preparatory *plié*, and the maximum fulfilling time in the air. The rhythm could be notated thus:

Ex. 15

or even, in extremely buoyant dancers:

Ex. 16

These eccentric-looking rhythms need explanation. Jumps usually land on the downbeat, but – and this is a crucial point where *ballon* is concerned – the landing in *plié* should flow so quickly into the next ascent that the dancer seems almost to have gone into the air on the downbeat. In reality she is passing as swiftly and smoothly through the *plié* as possible; the illusion is that she is already in the air. The superlative dancer will approximate the rhythm of Ex. 16. This is, of course the true *frappé* rhythm, as opposed to the equalized kicking out and in of a moribund foot which is the norm in many classes. Dancers deficient in *ballon* time their *jetés* thus (and they are usually counted or marked by the teacher in the same deceptively even manner):

Ex. 17

Not only is this unutterably dull to watch (or to perform), it is devilishly tiring for the dancer. But the pianist cannot help the situation by trying to mirror the dancer's correct rhythm. Although this facilitates continuity and phrasing in dance, in the accompanying music such a rhythm would become obtrusive and irritating. All that a literal musical equivalent would accomplish is a chopping up of the overall phrasing of the steps; paradoxically, rather than the musical syncopation combining with that of the dance to produce lightness and flexibility, the two would fight each other, and the dancers' muscular responses would become constricted and choppy – just what we want to avoid.

Such over-zealousness from the misguided pianist is what Margaret Craske disparagingly calls 'playing the movement'. This literal approach is always a hindrance, and it invariably destroys the overall phrase.

The *jeté* example is an extremely simple type of dance phrase; many are diabolically complicated where attack, continuity and overall timing are concerned. Scrutiny of a slow-motion film of ballet phrases would prove that it is never possible to mirror musically the perpetual subtle adjustments of timing and physical balance which go into the fashioning of a dance phrase. You might ask a teacher to demonstrate slowly (but in rhythm) an exercise such as *chassé, pas de bourrée*, double *pirouette*. Clearly no music ever written contains precisely the rhythm of the entry into the turn, the turn itself or its completion, or even more subtle, the *contretemps* rhythm which generates the *chassé* or the linking of the *pas de bourrée* to the *pirouette* preparation. Add to this the variations in timing and attack from dancer to dancer – a key factor in dance-personality – and you should see the futility of a pursuit of the wild goose of musical identity.

Give the dancer, in other words, a musical phrase to dance *through* – to use in shaping their own phrases – not a tonal cage. A mirrored rhythm confines and isolates each one of their steps; a flexible harmonious one liberates them. You cannot play the 'up' for the dancers, but you can give them a musical reason for going up. As Edwin Denby writes, 'the dance accents frequently do not reproduce the accents of a musical phrase, and . . . even when they correspond, their time length is rarely identical with musical time units (a leap, for instance, that fills two counts may end a shade before, and the next movement begin a shade after the third count). The variations of energy in dancing around which a dance phrase is built are what make the dance interesting and alive; and they correspond to a muscular sense, not an auditory one.'[22]

In *effect*, dance and music are together; in *reality*, the dancer is using, throughout his phrase, *rubato*. This is a 'free' way of phrasing in which the performer accentuates or minimizes the components, *without losing the basic flow of rhythm*. Because of the importance of *rubato* we shall return to it toward the end of this chapter and in Chapter 9.

I have stressed that a major fault in dancers is to reduce *enchaînements* to their separate components, and have tried to show how accompanists will contribute towards this by mistakenly seeking to translate dance rhythms into musical ones, thus splintering the overall phrase. Another problematical aspect of phrases which, despite its importance, is all too often overlooked is what might be called concord of design. The dance phrase and its accompanying musical one, should, in other words – unlike the dance and musical rhythms *within* the phrase – share a particular sort of identity.

Most ballet exercises and *enchaînements* within Romantic, Classical, and many modern ballets are based on multiples of 2, 4, 6, 8 or 16 count segments – usually in a symmetrical fashion (although the principle under discussion applies also to asymmetrical phrases). For example, here is the beginning of a simple *adagio* combination:

Développé to front *grand rond de jambe* into *arabesque* back
1 – 2 – 3 – 4 – 5 – 6 – 7 – 8

Ex. 18

You may think that any slow, eight-count phrase could do for this, as long as it is attractive and melodious. If, however, you play for this dance phrase, which unfolds without a break from counts one to eight, a phrase consisting of four plus four rather than a continuous eight, several forms of ruination will occur.

(1) The (potentially) beautiful transition and *expansion* into the *grand rond de jambe* will be severed aurally, producing a jarring esthetic discrepancy between what is heard and the inherent design of this movement. At the very moment of expansion, the music will drop, and – in conjunction with the movement design – almost seem to begin again. (2) The pianist (if he is watching, and playing *with* the dancers rather than *at* them) will feel uncomfortable, both mentally and physically, because of the conflict of designs. (3) Any dancers who are listening to the music, rather than concentrating on pulse counts (in which case they will feel uncomfortable and unrhythmical throughout) will experience a jolt as they enter upon the *grand rond de jambe* rather than a connection. (4) As a result, the breath which is essential at that moment, that simultaneous link *with* the foregoing *développé* and the expansion *from* it into the arc of the *grand rond de jambe* will be choked in the body, and the moving leg will become that of a mechanical doll with no sense of flow and space.

Finally, the arrival point of the phrase – the flowering – will in effect cease to exist for the spectator and the dancer (except for those whose main interest in an *arabesque* consists of how high the human leg can be jabbed into the air). This is because the flow of energy needed to produce a meaningful, alive *arabesque* – alive because it is the culmination of the unfolding which began with the very first count of the *développé* – will have been baulked by the misdirection of sound, which is following a path all its own. Musically, it is the difference between:

Ex. 19   Chopin, Prelude op. 28, no. 20

Ex. 20   Tchaikovsky, *Swan Lake*, Act II, *pas de deux*

Now, not only does Tchaikovsky's music circumvent every one of the above-mentioned disasters, it continues the kinetic quality and flow of energy to whatever may come next in the dance phrase. Like the *développé–grand fond de jambe*, it simultaneously flowers to a peak moment – a point of gravity – and sustains the level of energy beyond itself, like a wave.

The Chopin, with its short-breathed and repetitive phrases, while moving and successful in its own terms, is at odds with the design of this dance phrase. Instead of expanding and flowering, it seems to obsessively go back and feed on itself. It would take a dancer with artistry to surmount the difficulties of phrasing to this music. (This does not mean, of course, that a break of phrase is never acceptable. Continuity and flow of energy can be created in many other ways than the obvious and intensely sustained one which I chose. As always this is determined by the particular context. Furthermore, even the most flowing of movements are not always danced to a continuous, thick stream of honey. If this were so, all *adagios* should be performed to only the more glutinous passages of Delius.)

Two more observations may be of interest here. In the Tchaikovsky, the phrase is not actually complete at the point of the *arabesque* back. This is only half-way in the progress of the sustained singing line, which gives the feeling that it will continue spinning itself out into infinity. Secondly, if the teacher or choreographer ignores this, trouble will ensue. For example, to fashion an *adagio* in which, at count nine, the opening phrase was repeated on the other side, would be most unfortunate. With the music surging forward but the movement beginning again, not only would it look incongruous, but, for opposite reasons, it would feel just as uncomfortable as our long dance phrase which was cut up by the music. In that, the music halved the dance phrase; in the other, the dance halves the musical phrase.

The point, which I am continuing to emphasize, is that your first consideration when selecting music – apart from style and quality, which will be examined presently – must be the dance phrase as a whole, not individual steps and counts. I must, however, remind you that our subject defies the strict rules and precision of a driving manual, being perhaps more like a cookbook or sex manual in which certain basic methods and ingredients are used in endless combination, and usually altered intuitively by the practitioners. In addition to basic guides and principles there must be flexibility, intuition and spontaneity. In many cases, short musical phrases might be preferable, or a combination of short and long. Consistently good judgment of which to choose can only come with experience.

To sum up: the accompanist or dancer is perpetually juggling two facets of phrase – the separate components of notes and steps as they exist in small time-units and the overall phrase design which organizes and gives meaning and focus to them. In music and dance, as contrasted with theory-books, they cannot be separated for they are interdependent. Since, furthermore, they are the foundation of music and dance, we must elaborate upon the comments in this section when we reach the three practical analyses in Chapter 8. But we should consider now the aspect of rhythm which animates pulse, meter and phrase.

4. Tempo

Tempo is a modifier, and it is usually assumed that it specifically modifies pulse. Certainly the speed with which each beat is marked off is of prime importance, but what actually determines this? Every good musician knows that the composer's message becomes distorted or even senseless if the music is taken too far from the 'right' tempo. (Except in the case of a composer who repeats a theme or section at a markedly different tempo for dramatic effect.) True, a certain amount of flexibility exists, but fundamental restrictions seem to operate in some way or another. How, then, does one recognize the restrictions and interpret the musical information in order to choose a good pace?

The painfully obvious answer would of course be through reference to the metronome markings, or the verbal directions such as *adagio* or *allegro*, helpfully supplied by the composers. But the obvious is inadequate. For one thing, metronome directions only identify tempo in what may be called the *velocity* sense; important, to be sure, but, oddly, often fallible (composers being notoriously capricious and unreliable when the time comes to set them down before the score goes off to the printer).

But worse – metronome markings were not even used until relatively recently. With Maelzel's patenting of the metronome in 1816, composers could indicate exact tempos, but despite the nineteenth century's increasing use of it, the almost pathological desire for absolute precision which can be served by this grown-up toy did not become fully developed until the twentieth century, in which Bartok could specify, down to the second, how long a movement should last. (Many composers, of course, resisted rigidity, and began to qualify metronomic speeds with *circa*, i.e. 'approximately'.)

As for the verbal directions, they are so imprecise and so often stretched beyond their bounds, that they give only the vaguest help, i.e. *adagio* is, literally 'at ease', *allegro* is 'happy', *andante* 'walking', and so on, and these can mean very different things to different composers. And while they appear from time to time in the music of, among others, Purcell, Handel and Bach, often they do not mean the same thing as in nineteenth- and twentieth-century music, for all tempo directions in music not of the past century and a half are highly suspect, usually being added to modern editions by inspired or foolish divination on the part of editors, aided on occasion by theoretical writings from the period in question. These theoretical writings, plus such specialized exceptions as dance-pieces, do, of course, give valuable information. Such dances as the galliard, courante and menuet were taken at tempos corresponding to the speed in fashion for the dance movements (although this raises another problem, for as Curt Sachs has written, dances tend to become slower as time passes, and the menuet, for one, metamorphosed into a tempo in the nineteenth century which would have astonished the earlier less genteel performers). The tempos of madrigals were strongly affected by their words, as this quotation makes clear: 'Do not keep strict time throughout, but, as in modern madrigals, use here a slow tempo, here a fast one, and here one that, as it were, hangs in the air, always in accordance with the expression and meaning of the words' (Frescobaldi, Preface to First Book of Toccatas, 1614).

In the Renaissance and Baroque periods another indication was that of metric signatures: '3/1 = *adagio*; 3/2 = faster; 3/4 = faster still; 6/4 = *allegro*', according to Frescobaldi, but, as Praetorius admonished, 'C is slow and ₵ is fast, but look at the music to discover exactly how slow or how fast it should be.'

All undoubtedly helpful – up to a point – but we are still left with the problems of metronome markings and verbal indications in more recent music, which comprises the bulk of what will be used for ballet class.

The problems surrounding the 'right' tempo have, moreover, not yet ended. We cannot examine them until later, but I must mention the fact that the same piece may be played at very different tempos depending on the acoustics of the particular auditorium, whether it is played indoors or at an outdoor concert, and whether a dance score is played for a ballet or as a concert piece. In addition, very few pieces do not deviate within themselves; it is the exception to have one unchanging tempo from first to last, or even throughout a section.

It should by now be evident that tempo in music is a far from simple matter, and that to examine it fully, one must go beyond mere pulse-speed. We are still without an answer to our original question, and in order to provide one, we must ask two other questions, which take us out of the temporal realm into what might be called the 'psychological'.

When Praetorius advised musicians of the early seventeenth century to look at the music to discover exactly how slow or how fast it should be, he anticipated Wagner's statement, made over two centuries later: 'The whole duty of a conductor is comprised in his ability to indicate the right tempo.' On the surface merely one of Wagner's outrageous witticisms, it in turn leads us to our two new questions, for it implies, through its seeming absurdity, the deeper answers. How does the composer who uses metronome markings and verbal directions which are as precise as possible, bearing in mind his frequent fallibility, arrive at such markings? And how is tempo determined by the performer if they are absent, or if they are vague? Cooper and Meyer write, 'it is important to recognize that tempo is a psychological fact as well as a physical one. Thus eighth-notes in two pieces of music may move at the same absolute speed, but one of the pieces may seem faster than the other. This is possible because the psychological tempo, which we shall call 'pace', depends on how time is filled – upon how many patterns arise in a given span of time.'[23]

Here we have a beginning for our answer to the above questions, which are essentially one question posed from two different vantage points. It is, however, only a beginning since there are at least four characteristics of music which are involved in psychological tempo, or 'pace'. Each affects the choice of tempo:

a. The number of rhythmical patterns
b. Harmonic rhythm, or the speed at which the underlying harmonies change
c. The type of rhythmic patterns; dotted vs. smooth
d. Volume, or the loudness or softness, within the phrase.

All of these, normally, are interactive, although an unaccompanied melody or instrumental unison will not bring the harmonic rhythm into action, except by inference.

a. The number of rhythmical patterns

The amount of notes per beat can have a marked effect on the feeling of pace. A 4/4 section proceeding in even quarter notes tends to seem slower than one with subdivisions of the basic pulse. An illustration may make this clearer:

a.

b.

Ex. 21   Mendelssohn, Symphony No. 4 'Italian', fourth movement
          a. altered, b. original

Ex. 21a is a skeletal version, retaining, in addition to the basic pulse, the harmonic scheme and the melody in sketch form. Ex. 21b gives the music as written, with the quarter notes subdivided into triplet eighth-notes much of the time, and the triplet feeling spilling over, into even the notes which are not sped up by subdivision. Singing the top line of each while beating the quarter note pulse or playing the whole on the piano will convey decisively the difference in apparent speed (being careful, of course, to use the same tempo for both).

Here is another comparison, with an even greater laceration of the original than in the Mendelssohn example:

a.

b.

Ex. 22   Mozart, Symphony No. 40 in G minor, first movement
a. altered, b. original

Ex. 22a resembles the tick-tock of a rather harassed clock, whereas in Ex. 22b the original melodic subdivisions combined with the eight-note ostinato-pattern in the accompaniment create the feeling of restlessness and tension which permeate the entire movement. In Ex. 22a the fluid restlessness has disappeared, to be replaced by rigidity, which somehow seems to slow down the tempo, even if it is played metronomically the same as Ex. 22b.

Our third comparison increases the subdivision, with sixteenth-notes intensifying the speed and energy of the composer's vision. (Again, the melody is given first in skeletal form – in quarter notes, with a subdivision into eighth-notes. The harmonic accompaniment is the same in both versions).

a.

b.

Ex. 23   Beethoven, Symphony No. 7 in A major, fourth movement
a. altered, b. original

This movement has often been called 'bacchanalian'. Certainly it is one of the most amazing manifestations of energy in the entire musical literature. And to achieve this force Beethoven needed the momentum of the rushing sixteenth-note subdivisions. In no other way could he have established such power and velocity. The skeletal version sounds like a nursery song, even though it retains the original harmonies, accompaniment, and the basic shape of the melody (note, however, the increase of interest when the eighth-notes enter).

A musical sleuth may have noticed a similarity among these three examples – which foreshadows our second modifier of psychological tempo. That is, the harmonic rhythm. Now, I did not select these pieces deliberately. They were random choices, and upon reviewing others which I could have used instead, I realized that most of those also resembled each other in the same way. The link was the speed with which the harmonies changed. In our three examples, the harmonic rhythm is on the slow side. In Ex. 21 the underlying harmonies change only twice in a measure – on the first and third beats. In Ex. 22 the changes are even slower, the original G minor harmony lasting through three measures and only changing on the downbeat of the fourth (the harmonies change a bit more quickly in the next phrase, but are still comparatively slow-moving). In Ex. 23 they change from measure to measure, always on the downbeat.

Let us, then, take a closer look at harmonic rhythm, and how it affects the apparent, or psychological, tempo.

b. Harmonic rhythm

The faster harmonies change, the more seems to be happening within a measure, but this creates a different *feeling* of event and movement than does subdivision. This can be illustrated by altering the skeletal version of the Mozart:

Ex. 24   Mozart, Symphony No. 40 in G minor

This shows a decided picking-up of the apparent pace of Ex. 22a. Instead of the static ticking, we now seem at least to be going somewhere. The kinetic movement of the original accompaniment-pattern is now replaced by the tonal movement of the quicker harmonic changes. For some combinations, or at particular times in the dance studio, pieces with such a harmonic rhythm might be preferable to the slower, more static one of the Mozart – which he of course used deliberately, in order to achieve an emotional pace and quality essential to this movement. His expressive intent would have been nullified by the use of quicker-changing harmonies, and cluttered by *combination* of them with the restless accompaniment-pattern.

The Beethoven, being more extreme where subdivision and feelings of momentum are concerned, would suffer even more, perhaps, than the Mozart by a speeding up of the harmonic changes. The velocity generated by the rushing sixteenth-notes *plus* quicker harmonic progressions would result not in added excitement, but in an uncomfortable feeling of excess and mania. The measures and phrase would be crammed to overflowing, and the psychological tempo would be adversely affected. (This is, incidentally, one of the main causes of the discomfort which many listeners experience with avant-garde music; the complexity of rhythmic pattern combined with the often formidable speed of harmonic rhythm is simply too far beyond their powers of aural comprehension.)

Our examples have been of fast music; now let us see how harmonic rhythm functions in a slow tempo. Oddly, despite the slower pulse-beat, there can be a similar feeling of overcrowding if the harmonic rhythm is quickened.

a.

b.

Ex. 25 Gounod, 'Avant de quitter' (*Faust*)
a. original, b. altered

The serene quality of the original – achieved largely through its slow harmonic changes – alters drastically when the harmonies are speeded up. The soaring melody then seems to be impeded and chopped into bits and pieces, resulting in a curious staggering psychological tempo. The accompaniment gives quite enough movement and flow to the melody; the added harmonies merely distract, changing the spaciousness to a crowded and uncomfortably fast sense of pace.

Thus, it seems – when one looks at a great number of pieces from the seventeenth to the early twentieth century – that composers work either with fast subdivided note values or quick movement of harmonies, but not both at once – except for particular effects. This is true whether the piece is in a slow or a fast tempo, although there is obviously more leeway, generally speaking, in slow music.

While looking for examples to illustrate my points, I was particularly struck by one characteristic. In a significantly large number of pieces with either fast-moving subdivisions or quick harmonic changes, these were operating over a pedal point, i.e. a sustained or repeated note which remains constant no matter what happens above it, like the drone-note of a bagpipe. (It can also appear in an *inner* voice, rather than in the bass.) Sometimes this continued for a large portion of the phrase, sometimes for almost a whole section with perhaps one or two chord-changes during it. Pedal-points can be seen in every one of the examples; Mendelssohn, Mozart, Beethoven and others all used this device, in varying ways. Once you begin to look for pedal-points, it is surprising how often they seem to crop up in both fast and slow music – and they seem especially prevalent in ballet music. If I had gone only to Tchaikovsky for these examples, I would indeed have had to be selective to avoid them.

Harmonic rhythm provides a valuable guide to tempo. The composer has disposed the chord-changes with a certain effect in mind. If one plays some music too fast, they will be crowded together, making the sense of the phrase too concentrated; in other cases, if taken too slowly, the phrase will tend to fall apart, to lose continuity.

c. Even and dotted rhythms

Even or smooth, and dotted or jerky rhythms affect the apparent pace and thus the actual metronomic speed of music. We can, perhaps, best see the different effects of each through an extreme example. With the original dotted rhythms smoothed out, one gets a feeling of unimpeded speed; when the dotted rhythms are restored, this quicksilver pace is replaced by an amazing electricity. The notes now seem to be tumbling over each other:

Ex. 26   Delibes, Scotch Dance from *Coppélia*
a. altered, b. original

Curiously, although the original does not have the fluid rapidity of the smoothed-out version, it seems faster. The stretching-out of some notes and the speeding-up of others result in the sort of tension one associates with extreme speed. The original jerky rhythms produce an intensification of the inherently fast pace. This provides, moreover, a particularly clear example of an inner guide to tempo for the performer. Even without any metronomic or verbal direction, the dotted rhythms impede any attempt to take this piece too fast.

With music in a slow metronomic tempo, dotted rhythms can intensify and alter the apparent speed in an opposite manner, this time making it seem somehow slower:

Ex. 27   Beethoven, Symphony No. 3 in E flat major, second movement
a. altered, b. original

The 'extra' slowness of the dotted original is emphasized when the uneven rhythm is in the form of a syncopation (third measure). This creates a laborious, stumbling pace, which is, of course, particularly effective for a funereal mood.

Slow or fast, the inner tempo of music which employs dotted rhythms seems exaggerated beyond its metronomic speed. Just how much this is so depends on the proportion of dotted rhythms to even ones; the intensification in the Delibes example is, as I have said, extreme, for the dotted rhythms are almost unremitting, but they can also be used more sparingly. But whether they are used with abandon or moderation, the apparent or qualitative speed is different than the metronomic or quantitative speed. A favorite device of Romantic composers was, in the final glorious movements of a coda, to transform themes with smooth rhythms of quarter or eighth-notes into dotted-note versions, applying the whip to the (sometimes faltering) musical steed without wishing to pick up the actual tempo. (Note also that dotted rhythms contribute to and intensify *qualities* in music: joyful can become hysterical, poignant can become depressing, and triumphant can become chaotic. This connection between tempo and quality is demonstrated by such terms as *allegro* which means literally 'happy', but came to indicate 'fast', and *adagio*, 'at ease' literally, transformed into 'slow' temporally.)

The problem of apparent tempo as contrasted with metronomic tempo is an important one in ballet class. A teacher, for instance, who requests a certain tempo for an *allegro* combination can receive a shock if his ears are assaulted by a piece filled with hectic dotted rhythms when he was expecting a smooth or a moderately lilting one. And invariably he will complain that it is 'too fast', or, in the case of an *adagio* with too many dotted rhythms, 'too slow' or 'dragging'.

d. Volume

Tempo, both metronomic or temporal, and apparent or psychological, is strongly affected by loudness or softness. Metronomic tempo, for instance, is almost always affected by a *crescendo*; the performer seems compelled to speed up even though he has only been directed to get louder. Some composers have, in fact, resorted to the use of such directions as *non accelerando* or *tempo giusto* to counteract this tendency. The same occurs in reverse with music which gets softer, the performer adding a ritardando to a decrescendo. It works in an opposite way, of course; an accelerando is almost inevitably productive of a marked increase in volume even when the composer has clearly indicated that the soft dynamic should be maintained throughout the section. When the music maintains a steady tempo, without accelerandos or ritardandos, it is still affected by dynamic levels; a passage seems faster when played loudly and slower if played softly. (Although other factors can affect this, it can serve as a general rule; a quick passage played softly may take on a breathless quality and thus seem to be quite fast, yet if it is played loudly, a driving force results and it seems even faster.)

A variant exists in the sudden introduction of a different dynamic level. In the Scotch Dance (Ex. 26b), the abrupt *forte* on the last chord of the phrase has a galvanic effect on the pace, adding an extra thrust to the forward motion. A similar effect occurs in the *Volante* from Sleeping Beauty, also at the end of the phrase. Take away, in either case, this surprise, and the overall feeling of speed is reduced. These interactions of speed and volume are related to expenditure of energy. For one thing, although soft playing demands more control, loud playing requires a greater amount of energy, which tends to spill over into the tempo-area.

A few general comments on tempo as it operates in dance should be included here, including a look at rubato – that tempo-phenomenon which functions so differently in dance and in music. I will then conclude with a glance at tempo in the *interaction* between dancer and musician.

III. Tempo in dance

The tempo of dance movement in the theater is determined by the music, and, on a deeper level, by the dramatic content and mood created by the choreographer in conjunction with the music. The conductor, of course, can wreak havoc by speeds which differ from those of rehearsal, and also through a lack of response to the dancers' tempo-needs of the moment (a cold theatre, a problematical stage, etc.). He can, on the other hand, often utilize tempo to infuse spirit and coherence into a flagging dance ensemble.

In the studio, the dance tempo is determined either by the teacher while marking the combination, or by the judgment of the pianist, who takes the place of the theater conductor – and who can be equally erratic or supportive through tempos.

The teacher in the studio differs from the choreographer with respect to flexibility of speeds. Unlike steps within choreographic phrases, the classroom steps ordinarily function within a narrow tempo-range, for, 'in pure classical ballet, where emotion and characterisation are not taken into account, certain steps have always been associated with definite speeds because they require particular timing if they are to be developed according to the academic rulings'.[24]

These traditional timings in the studio allow the dancer to attain proficiency and a clear mental and muscular image of the pure steps. Having achieved this, she is ready for all of the variations and transformations of the basic vocabulary of dance which give ballet its wide range of expression.

Because of the restricted tempo-range of classroom steps, the choice of music takes on a particular importance. It should not be difficult to visualize the difference in atmosphere and achievement in a class which is stimulated by variety of musical mood and style from one which is deadened by repetition of only one or two safe but overworked pieces, day after day, for the same steps at the same speed.

The development of ballet technique requires a narrow range of speeds, but the development of *dancing* and dance-*intelligence* demands, as a counteracting force, the widest possible range of styles and moods within these tempos. This will help to prevent the pupils from becoming robots and to prepare them for choreographic deviations from the comfortable predictability of classroom timing (see Chapter 7).

Rubato in the timing of steps

Speed as it varies within the phrase – that is, *rubato* – is a major problem for dancers, and is often a source of confusion for accompanists. (*Rubato* is linked with performance, and will be discussed in Chapter 9, but some mention should be made of it in these general comments on tempo.) It is essential in the shaping of a phrase, although it is wildly misused and over-used by many musicians (particularly Chopin specialists). The word means, literally, 'robbed', and is generally used in place of the precise form, which is *tempo rubato*, i.e. robbed or stolen time.

Although it is applied to both dance and music, we shall see a significant difference in its use in each, but in one respect they are similar. Used properly, as in a Strauss waltz or throughout Chopin's works (Chopin made it clear that correct use of *tempo rubato* in his music required the pianist to maintain the pulse in the bass and apply *rubato* to the melodic line), the robbing is a beneficent one; the time which is taken away being put back, so to speak. Understanding of this would prevent the maudlin wallowing in sentiment which self-indulgent Chopin 'experts' inflict on their audiences as each wave of 'feeling' on the pianist's part attenuates the phrases and prolongs them to the point of bathos. A dancer, similarly, should not languish and droop in a poignant moment so that phrase-endings and beginnings become misshapen and blurred, nor should she demoniacally attack a favorite pose, marking time before and after, only to dart similarly into the next unrhythmic pose. This is not *rubato*, for *rubato* can only function within a framework. The entire phrase should occupy roughly the same time-span with or without *rubato*; the robbing occurs *within* the measure or phrase and must be balanced so as to not shorten or elongate the larger time-span. Thus, both dancer and musician employ flexibility within restriction to obtain an appropriate flow or attack.

Dancers differ from musicians, however, where *quantity* of *rubato* is concerned. The dancer must alternate and balance speeds within the phrase to a degree almost inconceivable for the musician. (The example of *jeté* rhythm in the section on phrasing has already introduced this peculiarity of dance.) To shape a dance phrase can be to fluctuate in speed *continually*. When describing a ballet class made up of some of the best young male dancers in the country, Edwin Denby compared, unfavorably, their equally divided rhythmic stresses – their 'metronomic regularity' – with the flexibility of Danilova and Markova, 'who can vary the time values of steps – or, more exactly, of the component phases of a step – so as to create in a sequence the sense of a homogeneous dance phrase with a rise, a climax and a finish',[25] or, in other words, their 'quickening or retarding of motion'.[26] (This is a different matter entirely from the dancer who jabs at a stress and then drags momentarily until the music catches up.)

Such fluctuation in speed is, as I said earlier, the decisive reason why an attempt by the accompanist to mirror the movement is so futile. Dance and music proceed in different ways through their shared time-span. In music (in varying degree, depending upon its style and context), *rubato* is used to heighten expression at certain moments and to bring some elasticity generally to the rigidity of pulse and meter; in either case a little *rubato* goes a long way. In dance, however, *rubato* is intrinsic to the proper realization of steps and phrases – not to mention the greater intricacies of dramatic conception in the theater. Both academic studio dancing and theatrical dancing require it continually for merely correct *technical* execution. But in both dance and music, *rubato* is a matter of flexibility, not license; it must be used for communication, not self-expression or display.

Interaction of dance and musical tempos

One problem which I have seen arise over and over again is created when the dance-tempo is right but not the musical one. It usually stems from a determination on the part of teacher or accompanist to use a piece of music too far out of its natural tempo-range. And whether it is the teacher or the accompanist who is overwhelmed by an inopportune compulsion to hear a certain piece, it is the dancers who will suffer most.

Take, for example, the Gavotte from Prokofiev's *Classical Symphony*. I once played for a teacher who was so enamored of it that she attempted to use it in almost every class. Unfortunately, the combinations of the day were frequently unsuitable for this music and she would end up trying to fit it to the last across-the-floor *allegro*. The studied pace of this Gavotte being well out of the range of flashing *piqué* turns or quick *brisés*, she would desperately demand that I play faster. The result was that the measured formality of the music metamorphosed into a chaotic polka. With the note-patterns and the harmonic rhythm taken so far out of their normal tempo-range, the inner rhythm was blurred and the quality of the music completely altered. Since this created a feeling of demented compression, similar to that experienced while watching a speeded-up film, the dancers' kinetic reactions were distorted even though they were moving in a reasonable *dance*-tempo.

With music taken too slowly the opposite will happen. Any vitality or continuity in the original version will be dissipated or attenuated, and again, despite the technically correct pace of the dance-movement, the music will exert an unwelcome force on it. The movements will feel sluggish and laborious, and the dancers will have to use considerably more energy than if the dance and musical tempos were psychologically harmonious.

I have known teachers, usually inexperienced, who reversed the process, speeding up or slowing down the dance-tempo and sacrificing it to the correct musical pace. This is even worse, for in so doing they are ignoring the pedagogical reasons for giving the combinations in the first place. The accompanist can help by trying to substitute an equally favored piece which suits the tempo of the combination as it *should* be performed.

Whether the inner pace is right in the dance but not in the music, or vice versa, it is wrong in the *interaction* of dance and music. The physical tempo tells you the *amount* of time being used; the psychological, or inner, *how* it is used. They must not be viewed as separable for they depend critically on each other.

The subjects of this chapter could be considered theoretical, each an element to be extracted and analyzed. In fact they both defy complete analysis and contribute to those most synthesized properties – style and quality. Now let us see what can be said about these elusive yet essential attributes, and how they affect the accompanist's selection of music.

7   Selection of music 2 – Esthetic: style and quality

> Style takes its final shape more from attitudes of mind than from principles of composition.   Otto Strunk, *The Elements of Style*, 1965

STYLE AND QUALITY are the flowering of a creative effort. They are a consequence rather than a point of departure, for neither property can be consciously and deliberately sought. No composer, choreographer or performer can don style or quality like a costume; the ways in which they have employed the 'mechanics' of their art will involuntarily produce these seemingly distinct traits. That is, it would be impossible to say, 'I adored the composer's style in that piece – but I didn't much care for his melodies (harmonies, rhythms).' The 'style' can only be formed by the composer's overall aim and his personality as these are expressed through his choice and treatment of his raw materials. And, as Bennett wrote of literature, 'Style cannot be distinguished from matter . . . You cannot say exactly the same thing in two ways.'[1]

Despite this attempt to show that style is inseparable from materials, I have given it a section of its own because certain points can then be made which do not fit conveniently elsewhere in this book. Always bear in mind, therefore, the preceding cautions.

I. Style and quality in movement

Since we are concerned with style and quality in music as an aid to the *dancer*, let us review quickly how these apply to the dancer's material – her movement. There are three main considerations: 1. carriage, 2. response of different parts of the body, 3. attack and timing.

1. Carriage

Carriage in a dancer takes three forms: potential, actual or arrested motion. She must have mastered the traditional deportment of classical ballet, but standing or moving within a perfect academic alignment is not in itself carriage in *dancing*. It is merely a basis from which to work.

The theme or mood of a ballet, the choreographer's directions, costume – these will help to determine the dancer's carriage. But the strongest clue of all lies in the music. Musical sound has a powerful effect on deportment and gesture. It is no accident that soldiers are propelled into battle with the sounds of trumpet, drum or

147

bagpipe rather than those of harp or violin. A lover, on the other hand, does not attempt to seduce his beloved through the sound of a tuba; a guitar or flute is more likely to produce the desired response. And, of course, the music played by the martial trumpet or bagpipe will be consistent in quality with the sound of the instruments, as will the music played on the lover's guitar. A brisk, invigorating fanfare performed on the celeste might be disappointingly ineffectual as an agent for moving unwilling bodies into battle.

A dancer, similarly, will carry herself differently to the romantic sounds of *Swan Lake* than she would to the lean, astringent sounds of Stravinsky's *Symphony of Psalms* or the grandiose thrust of Berlioz's *Symphonie fantastique*. José Limón once said that he had to substitute the restrained elegance of Purcell for the more descriptive, emotive music of the contemporary score to which he had begun choreographing *The Moor's Pavane* because the latter score had made the dancers 'droop and languish'. The tension between Purcell's contained beauty and Limón's seething passions makes this dance a unique, remarkable experience.

In the studio, the theatrical factors are absent, leaving two guides for the dancers: the quality with which the teacher may demonstrate the combination, and the music. Since many teachers merely set the dance phrase by talking it in a characterless manner, the music becomes a life-line for the dancers. It can help to mitigate the deadly uniformity which prevails in so many studios as dancers wend their blinkered, anonymous way in pursuit of a 'perfect technique'. Of course, to be lacking in response to musical style as translated into carriage of the body is, automatically, to be deficient in rhythm, characterization, expressivity – in short, dancing itself.

And this is when affectation and mannerism rush in to fill the vacuum. These probably create more balletophobes than anything else in ballet (and they will hate ballet as long as performers are mesmerized into the competitive race for success rather than encouraged to love the endeavor of dancing for its own sake). As Kay Ambrose observes, 'mannerisms result from the mechanical appliction of the same formulas to all dance movements'.[2] Style, in contrast, is achieved through a continual perception and response *in different contexts*.

Exposure and reaction to musical styles in class are an essential part of a dancer's training. She cannot be a characterless robot in class and then suddenly transform herself into a responsive participant on stage, with the capacity for the varieties of carriage demanded by today's ballet repertoire.

2. Response of different parts of the body

Different parts of the body are affected by musical style and quality. Despite the generative nature of the back and spine, common to all ballet movement, a particular emphasis can go to the hands and feet, wrists and ankles or thighs and upper arms. In, for example, a combination comprised of small jumps and beats, which is executed to a sparkling, light Mozart *allegro* the energy should be directed to the dancer's wrists and ankles. This response, aided by the music, not only fulfils and enhances a particular style which is called for at that time, it aids the dancer's *technical* training. If she brings the thighs wildly and wastefully into action she is, in addition to being deaf to the muscular and stylistic boundaries set by the tempo and the music, defeating herself technically. Excessive emphasis upon the thighs works against the speed and dexterity which it is so important for her to develop for brilliant small-*allegro* work.

Or perhaps she is dancing an *adagio* for which the teacher has chosen a lyrical, sustained Chopin nocturne, and 'feels' the music by means of fluttery wrists and disconnected legs shredding the air. Here she is ignoring the message of the music to her back and spine, concentrating (weakeningly, in this case) on the extremities.

3. Attack

We viewed earlier the use of *rubato*, which the dancer achieves through variations in speed and the distribution of attack. This process is, in fact, one of the major forces in the creation of style. A dancer, of course, might perform with admirable *rubato* – her timing impeccable as she enters and leaves her jumps, *pirouettes*, *arabesques*; now fast, now slow, now staccato, now legato. This alone, however, would not preclude the possibility that she is limited in style and quality, for she could be using formulas in each case, relied upon for every occasion. The result would be not a dancer without any style, but a one-style dancer valuable only in choreography which shared this style with her. This, needless to say, is true of many dancers. They resemble film 'personalities', possibly expert in their craft and attractive to many, but who never permit their audiences or themselves to forget who they are. The same gestures, timing, emphasis, idiosyncrasies – all of these appear in every role.

In the section on phrasing I remarked that the accompanist cannot play the 'up' for the dancer, but only give her a *reason* for going up. You must, in fact, give her many reasons for going up or down or around, for speeding up or slowing down within the phrase, and these reasons relate, among other things, to style. A variety of musical styles in class offers at least the possibility of appropriate responses from the dancers; a stylistic monotony will discourage it.

II. Style and quality in music

Having focused briefly on style in dancing, we can now proceed to look at certain facets of musical style. We are concerned here with syncopation, tone color, texture, register, keys, musical nationality, and period. Each of these affects style in a special way (although tone color, texture and register are closely linked).

1. Syncopation

This is a relatively simple means by which the composer varies and alters the regularity of metrical organization, but it is not merely a technical device, for it can radically affect style and quality. Syncopation can produce excitement, vivacity, piquancy, tension, apprehension – in fact, innumerable qualities. To syncopate is to defy the regular pulses by a displacement of stress. This results in a feeling of instability. The no longer predictable rhythms frustrate normal expectations, but in a positive way. At its simplest, the underlying beats continue to be felt as a reference point and the jagged rhythms which relate to yet challenge them sweep the listener along, generating a unique dynamic quality.

Certain types of music, moreover, *depend* on syncopation; it is intrinsic, for instance, to jazz and blues (in powerful alliance with *rubato* performance). Here is a typical syncopated jazz rhythm:

Ex. 1

The sinuous and suggestive feeling of this passage evaporates completely if the tied-over rhythms are replaced by the normal accent pattern:

Ex. 2

Tchaikovsky's music abounds in exciting syncopation, and his ballet scores owe much of their extraordinary kineticism to the virtuoso or poetic use of it. These scores deserve close scrutiny for the seemingly limitless number of effects which he achieved by this means.

It should, of course, be used in the studio, although many teachers and accompanists tend to shy away from it, relying on solid, predictable, square rhythms. It can exist not only in the music or dance-patterns, but in the juxtaposition of the two. An attractive use of accent displacement occurs in this *barre* exercise of Tudor's for which he required a bolero:

E = extension   T = point tendu   C = close in 5th position

Ex. 3 *Grand battement* exercise

By pitting a duple rhythm against the established triple one, thus shifting the accents, the movements (and the music) are given an added excitement very simply. Ex. 4 uses the hemiola – that is, the introduction of groupings in twos within the basic one of three (or vice versa):

Ex. 4

This device is typical of much Latin-American music and dance, and José Limón was particularly attracted to it in both his choreography and exercises in the studio. An outstanding musical use of it can be found in the second movement of Ravel's String Quartet, which bounds back and forth between 6/8 and 3/4.

Through the various forms which syncopation can take, the accompanist can stimulate the kinetic impulse – and the mind – of the dancer. It will give bite and vivacity to fast movement, breadth and passion to *port de bras* and *adagio* combinations. It should be used with sense and discretion, however, for too much of the wrong sort can lead to a choppy, distracting feeling in class. As I said, not all teachers will like it. The more conservative ones avoid it, even though they may find it perfectly acceptable in a ballet score. It is, in any case, best used as a spice – to enrich the flavor but not to dominate.

2. Tone color

This poses a special problem in selection of music for class. In certain ways, the piano is the worst possible instrument in the studio, both for class and for rehearsal (see further comments in Chapter 9). Combining a limited spectrum of tone-color, an intrinsic percussive quality, and the potential of a debilitating inundation of sound, it actually *challenges* the accompanist to provide helpful sounds rather than fully aiding her. The piano is a recent choice for dance classes; originally, and up till the early twentieth century, the *maître de ballet* conducted classes and rehearsals while providing his own music on the violin. This is far superior for the purpose. It is often compared to the human voice, possessing a similar flexibility, marked differences of attack and tone color, not to mention its sinewy, long-breathed *legato*. All this is of course featured in the music written for it.

The piano repertoire, on the other hand, naturally relies strongly on powerful sonorities, sharp percussive effects and dazzling virtuoso figurations which can cover the entire keyboard. Small doses of these heady sounds can be wonderfully invigorating, but too much reliance on the piano repertoire in class is unwise. The good accompanist will make her audience forget that they are listening to a solo piano during an entire class. She will evoke singing or pizzicato strings, an oboe, a brass band, a full orchestra and sometimes even a piano.

3. Texture

The thinness, density and spacing of harmonies and accompaniment patterns very much affect the illusion of varied tone color on the piano (Debussy and Ravel were masters in this respect). A harmonic passage, for instance, using closely spaced voicings contrasts strikingly with one using the same notes with air between them:

a.

b.

Ex. 5   Beethoven, Sonata No. 23 'Appassionata', second movement
        a. original, b. altered

Melodies played in octaves (Ex. 6b), without the usual pianistic accompaniment-patterns of Ex. 6a, can produce a remarkably string-like quality, approximating an ensemble of violins and cellos.

a.

b.

Ex. 6

The following melody could be accompanied by typically thick, heavy chords, loaded with that lovely pianistic sonority (Ex. 7a), but see how attractive the light-textured, agile accompaniment of Ex. 7b can also be, and how much more effective for a quick *allegro*:

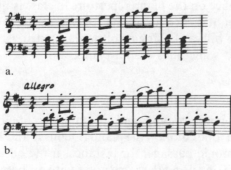

a.

b.

Ex. 7

Many lovely moments in music have simple harmonies in the treble with the melody in the bass, reversing the 'normal' scheme. This gives a different textural sound.

These are only a few of the possible variations in texture; there are many – too many to rely on piece after piece with the same thick texture, full chords in both hands, or melody accompanied only by sonorous chords or turbulent arpeggios (transcriptions of ballet scores often offend in this respect, making little apparent attempt at least to approximate the composer's original orchestration). Not that the fuller sounds cannot be suitable and exciting, but too much sonority, without relief and variety, tends to dull the ear and the kinetic response.

Textures, in fact, play a large part in *all* kinetic responses. Not only do thick chords and arpeggios tend to make the body feel heavier and slower-moving, but widely spaced octaves or simple intervals will have the opposite effect, and give lightness and speed. No one has as yet accounted satisfactorily for the illusion that dense harmonies seem to be 'heavier' and to occupy more space than do intervals or single tones, but listeners undoubtedly hear and respond kinetically to different densities. The accompanist must always keep this in mind when choosing music.

4. Register

The highness or lowness of notes works with texture to influence tone color. And, as with texture, the variety of possible effects is often overlooked by accompanists. (One can be left with the impression after visiting many classes that our musical heritage was conceived only in the middle of the piano keyboard.)

Take, for instance, music written in the higher octaves. In combination with other factors, it has even greater impact.

Ex. 8

Here we see, in addition to high register, a spare texture, unusual spacing and alternation of staccato and legato working together to seem surprisingly like a woodwind duet.

Another sound, this one appropriate for the weighty and strong movement in men's class, comes from the use of the lower register. A magnificent example of its characteristically rich sonorities is found in the 'Appassionata' Sonata (Ex. 5a).

Awareness of the potential of texture and register in class gives the accompanist flexibility and a wide range of sound-worlds from which to choose. One caution, however; when using those which depart noticeably from the middle-of-the-keyboard rut, a danger lurks. Avoid incongruity. That is, if one played Ex. 8 for a vigorous muscular combination in men's class, one should expect to receive quizzical glances. (I *have* seen this happen, more than once.)

An illusion similar to that of 'heavy' and 'light' textural densities exists with register; a note or chord in the higher registers always seem 'lighter' than one in the lower registers. Notes moving up or down, similarly, seem to be getting lighter or heavier as they progress. Again, the effect of this on the dancer's kinetic response should always be considered by the accompanist.

Close examination of orchestral music is invaluable for developing awareness of the many ways of evoking various qualities through texture and register. It will open up new worlds of sound for those who are too strongly conditioned by the more limited use of those in the traditional piano repertoire.

5. Keys and modulation

Modulating or shifting key-centers is not only an effective structural and expressive musical device, it is of concern to the accompanist in a more utilitarian way. I will never forget one class which I watched, during which the accompanist used the key of A minor almost entirely. The effect was marked. I became vaguely depressed, with an inexplicable feeling of fatigue – and the dancers obviously felt much the same.

A little bit of A minor goes a long way in class, but even the brightest of keys will pall if used consecutively. Choice of key is important not only for variety of sound, but to the shape and pace of the class. If the dancers have just performed, say, a modest little *allegro* combination to a bright G major sound and the teacher then gives them a dynamic combination which develops and extends movements from the previous *allegro*, how does this affect the choice of key in the accompanying music?

To follow the quality of G major with, for instance, that of E flat minor might be dramatic, but it could also diminish energy and intensity just when the teacher hopes to increase these. But to choose an even brighter key than G major – D or A major, for instance – would be consistent with the teacher's aim. Keys are powerful elements in musical expression, and many composers are famous for repeatedly choosing certain keys for certain moods, thus indicating the significance and power which they can hold for the composer. Unfortunately for any consistent theory of key-quality, different people hear different qualities in keys, not to mention the fact that Beethoven's Fifth Symphony in C minor sounded almost a semi-tone higher or lower in 1803.

This is due to the lack of standardization in instrumental tuning then. (Even today, despite the theoretical norm of the 440-A, orchestras diverge widely in tuning-practice, usually because of the esthetic and expressive biases of their conductors.) Whether each key contains an inherent significance and quality is one of the most vexing and inexplicable questions in music. Much has been written, pro and con, with sometimes violent disagreement between authors. But, controversial and subjective as key-quality may be in theory, in actuality it exists as an obvious force. The simplest difference to perceive is that between major and minor keys. Even if listeners disagree about the comparative 'brightness' of B major and D major, they generally perceive the minor keys as 'darker' or 'sadder' than the major ones. Many factors can qualify the brightness or sadness — rhythm, dynamics, instrumental color, among others — but an intrinsic difference between major and minor seems indisputable.

The effect of unvaried key, or minor where major is best, will be felt by everyone in class (including the accompanist) even if they cannot analyze the reasons for the monotony or anti-climax which they are experiencing. The choice of keys in class is an art, just as it is within a piece, an album made up of several songs, or a concert program. The alternation and juxtaposition of keys has much to do with the listener's cumulative feeling of satisfaction or unease.

6. Nationality

Few qualities in music are as dramatically apparent as national flavor. Think of the Russian temperament as expressed by Tchaikovsky or Rachmaninov, the Italian of Verdi or Puccini, the French of Berlioz or Debussy, the English of Purcell or Elgar, the American of Copland or Bernstein, In each case, if the composer had been born into another national tradition, despite his personality and innate talents, his music would have taken a different path. Some composers, of course, are more outwardly expressive of their country's flavor, but all are shaped to some degree by the countless factors which form national character.

This flavor comes, in music, from melody, harmony or rhythmic patterns. First, a Rachmaninov melody, typical of many to be found in his music:

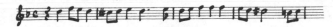

Ex. 9   Rachmaninov, Piano Concerto No. 3 in D minor, first movement

This contains the three most striking aspects of Russian liturgical chant (from which, like many Russian composers' melodies, it is derived) — the very limited compass, a sinuous weaving back and forth, and the somewhat obsessive repetition of certain tones. This obsessive quality, indeed, permeates much of Russian music. For sheer crushing (yet beautiful) gloom, few composers have outdone the slow movements of Rachmaninov, Tchaikovsky or Mussorgsky. (Even the comparatively livelier, brighter melodic moments in Russian music often have more than a tinge of melancholy, never achieving, say, the light-hearted buoyancy of Italian *allegros*, or the near-manic assurance typical of the more extrovert American fast music.) Russian harmonies also have an obsessive quality — brooding, pessimistic or even tragic. These harmonies, needless to say, were not invented by the Russians, being common to music of many countries, but here, their relentless reappearance and often unusual juxtaposition produce uniquely somber and powerful results.

Rhythm can play either an obvious or a subtle part in musical nationality. Certain patterns are associated with certain countries; the Scotch snap is a familiar pattern to lovers of Scottish folk-song or bagpipe music, and the typical Italian rhythm obtained by ending a phrase on the off-beat is equally recognizable. A more subtle rhythmic aspect is the link between everyday speech and musical rhythm.

Many writers have explored the relationship of language to national temperament and how this affects music. In the Italian language, the emphasis on the penultimate syllable (signōra, vivāce, giocōso, lasāgna, arrivadērci, etc.) is the verbal equivalent of the rhythm cited above.

One of the songwriter's greatest concerns is the observance of the natural word-rhythm so that the text is not obscured through distortion of this (except for special effects), but rather clarified. But, even in non-vocal music, the rhythms relate to language. Most writers agree that the influence of one's native tongue is so strong that even when instrumental music was developed, challenging the previous ubiquity of vocal music, the traditions and characteristics of the now silent words persisted. Although strings, winds or brass carried the music, unspoken language directed their patterns.

Nationality in music is certainly not always undiluted. Some composers combine features from several countries. Mozart can be Austrian, German, Italian – sometimes within a single work. Chopin wedded Polish accents with those of the Parisian salon, and Stravinsky combines the Russian obsessive repetition of small mosaic patterns with the elegant diction of French. And one school of American composers has superimposed the motor-rhythms of German or Italian Baroque music on to the strident optimistic assertiveness of Horatio Alger. Such combinations of musical accent (some odd indeed) could only take place if the accents were clearly audible. (They do not, interestingly, cancel one another out, but instead tend to interact, to form a new sort of nationality.)

In the ballet studio, national styles can be used with delightful results. Nothing can so pick up the spirits of a class as the sound of a tarantella, a jig or a czardas. A good selection will automatically provide interest and variety, not to mention that definiteness of quality which is so preferable to the faceless music heard in some studios which sounds as though it could have been written by anyone, anywhere, at any time. A good choice of music in different national styles is, of course, essential for character classes.

7. Period

Every factor mentioned above, plus many others, combines to form what we call style – but they do so *in a particular setting*. Composers have unique musical styles, but so do periods in history. Human emotions and impulses are said to be the same in every era, but their expression and emphasis unquestionably varies. Sadness, in the eighteenth-century world into which Haydn and Mozart were born, is expressed differently than in the nineteenth-century world of Chopin and Wagner, or the twentieth-century one of Britten and Bartók, so much so as to often seem a different emotion. Each member of the pairs cited above differed, of course, in personal expression of sadness, but beyond this is the spirit of the period in which they lived. Think of the different attitudes toward sadness which have prevailed in each of these three centuries: the nineteenth century gloried, almost wallowed, in it to a degree which would have been incomprehensible to Haydn and Mozart, while the twentieth century is tinged with a poignancy born of nihilistic, and now nuclear, horror and the attendant despair or cynicism.

The means, also, differ from period to period, and certain qualities are more difficult to achieve in some styles. I find it interesting also that not until the mid-twentieth century could terror and the supernatural, or a sense of extra-terrestrial existence be adequately evoked by music. Not that many composers had not attempted this throughout the centuries, but the means were simply not there. Now we have highly charged, tense dissonances, inhumanly complicated melodies and rhythms, and the medium of the electronic synthesizer.

Similarly, the possibility of expressing joy as we find it in Mozart – conveyed through the stability and dependability of the tonal system (which reflects so well the *belief* in rationality and order characteristic of that period, even if it was not such an Age of Reason as the myth leads us to accept) – is dim indeed within, say, the style of the early twelve-tone composers. Joy, in fact, is conspicuously absent in this music, for the sounds, in their disjunct complexity and prevailingly high level of tension, simply do not seem to correspond with the joyful impulse as felt by man.

Since the quality and expressive content of music is so affected by its time of conception, stylistic periods are of direct concern to the accompanist. Awareness of them can save much time. An *allegro* combination, for instance, designed for precision of attack and elegance of body does not deserve to be drowned in a torrent of sound from one of Romanticism's impassioned outpourings. And a florid, sweeping *adage* will dwindle pitifully when done to a restrained air from an eighteenth-century suite.

But what causes this disharmony? Why the discrepancy between movement and accompanying music? We approached this issue earlier; now we should pursue it further in the present context of period.

Reverse the two examples cited above, giving a Romantic outpouring to the *adage*, and a crystalline eighteenth-century *morceau* to the elegant dance-*allegro*. Why are these more apt? A major clue exists in the feeling in different parts of the body while performing each piece. The Romantic *adage* music will demand the strong use of the upper arms, shoulders and even pelvis. But the eighteenth-century *morceau* definitely will not, for, consistent with the generally more contained, fastidious essence of this music, the *physical* means are also more contained, just as with the dancer's performance. Music which brings into play the pianist's shoulders and pelvis is almost invariably wrong for movement which primarily stimulates the dancer's wrists and ankles – and vice versa. (I am, of course, speaking of music in the dance studio, for in the theater many odd but effective juxtapositions have been created for dramatic reasons.)

Even orchestral music transcribed for the piano will be consistent in this respect. Although not written originally for the piano, its intrinsic kinetic qualities remain the same and the pianist will be experiencing at the keyboard the same sensations as those of the conductor and instrumentalists (assuming that *their* kinetic responses have not been crushed by one-sided teaching). To watch a good conductor, in fact, is illuminating; many have been accused by academic critics of being 'too choreographic'. (Some conductors have even fallen off the podium in their exuberance, necessitating the use of guard rails.) Unless their choreography stems from egotistic display, that is nonsense. The conductor's use of his body brings him closest of all musicians to the dancer. Watch him – his stance, gestures of his hands, the comparative scope of his movements in Mozart, Beethoven, Wagner, Stravinsky, Bartók and Boulez. I have watched conductors play orchestral scores on the piano, and their kinetic reactions were identical – apart from their seated position – to the ones I had seen when they conducted the same scores from the podium.

To perceive more fully the kinetic qualities of different style-periods, I strongly recommend listening to several examples from each of the following. This can be done even if you are stationary, but, if possible, try simple movements or steps to various pieces in order to feel bodily which music seems to suit a certain step best, and what the different styles do to the movement. See if your conclusions are consistent with observations I have made. If not, analyze for yourself the causes of your different reactions. You will not be at fault if you disagree, only if you feel *no* kinetic variations among the styles.

Medieval	{	1. 13th century	Popular dance music; sacred music
		2. 14th century	Machaut: secular and sacred vocal music
Renaissance	{	3. 15th century	Burgundian Court: Dufay; Binchois chansons
		4. 16th century	Polyphony: Josquin, Lassus; Palestrina motets
		5. 16th century	Elizabethan madrigals and dance suites
Baroque	{	6. 17th century	Venetian School: Gabrieli; Monteverdi
		7. 18th century	Bach; Handel; Scarlatti; Couperin (Rococo)
Classical		8. 18th century	C.P.E. Bach; Haydn; Mozart (minor works as well as 'masterworks')
Romantic	{	9. 19th century	*German*: Beethoven; Wagner; Mahler *Italian*: Verdi; Puccini *French*: Chausson; Bizet; Delibes *Russian*: Glinka; Mussorgsky; Tchaikovsky
Impressionistic		10. Late 19th to early 20th century	Debussy; Ravel; Delius
Contemporary	{	11. Early to mid-20th century	Schoenberg; Stravinsky; Webern; Bartók; Copland; Gershwin; Kern; Porter
		12. Mid- to later 20th century	Stockhausen; Boulez; Terry Riley; Charlie Parker; Miles Davis; The Beatles; The Who; Led Zeppelin; Kraftwerk

This list is, of course, highly selective. As the centuries proceed, more and more styles and types of music exist within each stereotyped division. It does serve, however, as a guide for exploration. Most musicians have little awareness of music which lies outside their own narrow segment of the Western musical heritage – not to mention ballet students, whose acquaintance with music often seems to begin with Adam and end with Tchaikovsky. An even casual acquaintance with as much as possible of the repertoire listed above will be a good start towards awareness of the amazing kinetic and stylistic variety possible in music.

Above all, dancers and musicians should interchange ideas on style and quality. Ask one another questions, and demonstrate points. This could be particularly interesting to the musician, for dancers have an engaging way of conveying information. The Juilliard cafeteria contains students from the percussion, string, wind, brass, piano, dance and drama departments; the dancers' enclaves can easily be identified by the sight of bodies which suddenly leap to their feet and erupt into movement. Rather than being a burst of exhibitionism, this is merely the dancer's way of making a point.

Ask them to compare their muscular sensations while performing to different musical styles and qualities. Watch closely, and stimulate controversy among them. Try to evaluate their comparative successes in achieving what seems to you the best stylistic results. Since a certain amount of room is needed, before or after class, in the studio, will be the best time, also providing a piano. If the studio is not free, use a hallway and sing for them. And, of course, you could invite a few dancers for coffee and information. If, meanwhile, your persistence has made the dancers think, possibly for the first time, about style and quality as related to the kinetic impulse, you will have been a valuable catalyst and an instrument for bringing dancer and musician closer, while yourself learning much.

I have attempted to describe, as fully as possible, what seem to me to be the most important aspects of rhythm and style, both as they relate to the choice of music in ballet class, and as they affect the ballet student. In order to present these ideas in what I felt to be a necessarily broad perspective, I have frequently ventured beyond the merely practical or theoretical. The next chapter, in contrast, will concentrate on more utilitarian matters, and we will examine in detail three very basic classroom exercises, and the thought processes which go – whether intuitively or consciously – into the selection of music for each. In doing so, I hope to make certain general principles clear enough that they can be applied in many situations, for many combinations, no matter how advanced the steps or complicated the dance phrases may be.

8 Selection of music 3 – Practical: three combinations

> The significance of an event is inseparable from the means employed in reaching it.
> Leonard B. Meyer, *Music, the Arts and Ideas*, 1967

WE HAVE EXAMINED the selection of music from theoretical and esthetic points of view. Now we are about to view it from the keyboard and translate the foregoing ideas into practical action. A quick review of certain factors which affect your choices will be followed by detailed analysis of three simple combinations, and, finally, we will evaluate the possible sources of your repertoire.

But first I must remind you that when you seat yourself at the studio piano you cease to be an autonomous individual in that your personal likes and dislikes in music become subsidiary, and also that you are not now a performer who plays *for* an audience, but rather a participant who plays *with* them. And you play with them not only artistically but also, so to speak, playfully. A ballet class is not only a serious, earnest, dedicated endeavor; a good class will include the element of fun for teacher, dancers and pianist: no human being, from a mathematician or philosopher to a woodcarver or plumber, can function at his optimum without a sense of humor and play.

Where the accompanist is concerned, the playfulness will not only be part of her performance, but also part of her selection of music. A light note introduced at a low ebb in the class can work wonders. This could take many forms: a bit of jazz, a current rock number, an absurdly sentimental nineteenth-century trifle, a patter song by Gilbert and Sullivan, 'Turkey In the Straw' or 'The Battle Hymn of the Republic' – any such departure, as long as it seems suitable to the time and the combination. Dedication does not mean perpetual solemnity. This is not to say that you should turn the entire class into one long musical joke – as I have seen some accompanists do – but unleavened seriousness definitely can pall.

I. Practical factors

Many factors determine your choice of music. We have analyzed the musical ones – kinetic feeling, meter, phrasing, melody, harmony, style and quality. It should be helpful here, poised as we are at the keyboard ready to begin work, to review briefly the practical factors which determine your choices – ones over which the accompanist has little control. An understanding of each of these points is part of your basic equipment. In every class they exist as active and dynamic factors which affect what music you play.

160

1. Differences among teachers

Since, as I mentioned in Chapter 5, you may play for more than one teacher, and each may differ radically in taste, you will find that you are both extended and limited, needing a large repertoire to be used selectively. If teacher A thrives on a diet of eighteenth-century sonatinas, B may loathe them, preferring moments from obscure French and Italian operas, while C feels happiest with the standard repertoire, and D despises this, reveling in sixteenth-century madrigals, Bach suites and the latest rock hit. You cannot argue with the teacher's taste; you must be able to function happily within it – or leave.

2. Pace of class

Teachers work differently, and their classes vary in pace. If it is unusually quick, with few pauses for corrections and discussion, you need many more pieces ready at hand than if the pace is leisurely, allowing time for reflection. It is amazing how blank one's mind can become under the pressure of an unremitting volley of combinations. The more pieces one has on tap for each sort of combination, the more likely that one or two will stay with you, and prove at least adequate. If, on the other hand, the pace is very slow, with frequent and seemingly endless individual corrections by the teacher (which I once heard students of a certain teacher refer to as seances), it would be wise to have a ready assortment of absolute gems. When playing for such a teacher, any musical mediocrity will intensify the feeling of kinetic attenuation and slow progress which results no matter how interesting or valuable the teacher's comments may be.

3. Design

Classes, in general, are either varied or cumulative. In the former, the teacher gives a daily selection of the basic movements and steps, to no particular scheme other than the traditional academic one. The accompanist has only the 'normal' problems to face in this case. With the cumulative approach, however, you need unusual concentration and familiarity with the ballet vocabulary. Some teachers develop particular movements throughout a class, beginning even during *barre*. To match the creativity and ingenuity of such a teacher, you must select the music carefully indeed. (Although only the experienced accompanist could be expected to cope fully with this approach, it does not hurt to be aware of it from the start.) You must be careful to avoid anti-climaxes. The teacher will not be happy if you have played *the* musical sensation of the class early on, and then subside into ordinary, over-familiar pieces for the later moments which are the culmination of his grand design for the day.

4. Varied meters

If you are lucky, you will play for teachers who habitually use more than one meter for an exercise. The greater demands placed on your repertoire are offset by the added interest and experience offered as you see how the same steps are affected by different rhythms. It can, however, seem a burden to you since it is much less effort to provide one piece per combination, rather than two or three. You will be better prepared and more relaxed if you always think ahead. Anticipate the other possibilities which the teacher may be visualizing. Even if he does not do so in that particular instance your efforts are not wasted, for every exercise of your memory and your deductive powers increases your skills.

5. Attentiveness

Although it is not mandatory, you would be well-advised to follow the course of the class as attentively as do the dancers. I know accompanists who, between exercises, bury their heads in stacks of music, read newspapers, chat with dancers, look out of the window, work out their budget – in short, who do anything but follow the progress of the class. This is about as rewarding (or tolerable) as popping in and out of an auditorium throughout a concert. But if you absorb the teacher's criticism and corrections and watch the results, you will develop not only a sense of community, but also a keen eye, ever-increasing knowledge, and, very likely, a richer love for ballet. One could say, in any case, that inattentiveness makes everything I have written irrelevant.

6. Size of class

Last of all, a rather prosaic consideration – one of numbers. If every dancer in town seems to have come to class, put away your more exuberant virtuoso pieces. If you don't, you will suffer, especially during the across-the-floor segment of class. Long lines of students queuing up to fly across the floor for the second or even the third time (depending on the indulgence of the teacher) will make your arms ache, your fingers cramp and your mind boggle. As you lose muscular control your tempos will fluctuate and your sense of dynamics will narrow to a pounding *forte*, neither of which is beneficial to the class or to you. Pianists vary in muscular endurance, of course. If you choose music with your own level of endurance in mind, you can develop it gradually while sparing yourself and others needless pain.

II. Three practical examples

We now examine our subject in relation to specific combinations – small *allegro*, *pirouettes* and *adagio* – and to provide a concrete application of material from preceding sections. It should be remembered throughout that the relevance of a comment is not necessarily confined to the example it refers to. Many could apply to each of the three, and also, of course, to steps and combinations which I have not included.

I have chosen these three combinations for their functional value in demonstrating to the accompanist the processes of evaluating movement and selecting appropriate music for it. My main concern was to use combinations which were simple enough not to confuse the novice-accompanist, yet which had interesting shape and a sense of continuity. (All accompanists should collar a dancer to demonstrate the exercises and show the dancer's essential practical details of possible opening and closing positions, co-ordination of arms, etc., which space prevents my including.) I needed clear examples of some of the most common technical snags so that the accompanist might see how the music can exaggerate or alleviate these.

I must emphasize two general points. First, the musical solutions I have offered are in no way intended as definitive. They are on the same simple, forthright level as the combinations, and are selected for analytical purposes. I believe that, just as the dancer must begin with basic principles – mastering, for instance, the action of the *demi-plié* and body-placement, before attempting a *cabriole* or a *grand jeté* – so must the accompanist. After the basic principles of musical selection are understood and absorbed, then the flights of imagination can begin.

Secondly, few pieces will be uniformly suitable throughout all of their phrases, or even in the details of one phrase. Thus, the challenge is to find music which is as helpful as possible for the main elements of the dance-phrase, and which has also a quality and flow that will spill over into and color the remainder.

Each combination will be examined from the vantage point of the movement and that of the music, the movement being first since the accompanist cannot very well choose suitable music until she understands what it must suit. This is analogous to the situation in the studio: the accompanist sees (or is told) the combination and arrives at her choice through an evaluation of the elements of the movement. The difference here, of course, is that we are doing all this at leisure, and separating the various factors; in the studio the evaluation and decision must be quick and the factors are not so artificially disunited.

I have settled upon a certain economical scheme for the following analyses; obviously I cannot refer continually to every relevant factor and repeat *ad nauseum* all the details contained in former sections. The reader, therefore, must consider these to be implicit, and must contribute some efforts of memory and application. I have, however, tried to incorporate as many as possible in the following scheme:

The movement: what to watch for
1. Structure of phrase
2. Overall curve; high point(s) of phrase
3. Details and potential technical problems

The music: what the accompanist must provide
1. Meter; duple or triple rhythm?
2. A harmonious phrase-structure and curve
3. A harmonious melodic line
4. Appropriate harmonic rhythms
5. Helpful rhythmic patterns
6. Quality and style which are compatible
7. Breath and space; textural room for movement

1. Small *allegro*

Our first example is very simple. It is also the sort which is massacred daily throughout the world. Despite its ordinary appearance, however, it can be shaped into a convincing, even exciting dance-event. The music will have a great deal to do with whether it is approached as a routine ordeal or an occasion for the perfecting of technique through enjoyable dancing.

a. The movement

Glissade jeté, glissade jeté, jeté jeté jeté assemblé

1. First, the structure of this phrase. It consists of 8 counts (which may or may not be the same as the metrical beats of the music), and these are grouped into two main parts with a subdivision of the first. The latter is indicated by a dotted line and the former by a light, continuous one. (These diagrams can only be careful approximations. It is just not possible to delineate precisely the relation of counts to moments during steps, or exact phrasing and attack.)

Glissade jeté, glissade jeté, jeté jeté jeté assemblé

and 1   and 2   and 3   and 4   and 5   and 6 and 7   and   8

Ex. 1

Keeping this structure in mind, and leaving the punctuation for comment a bit later on, let us look at the overall curve which makes this a phrase rather than a succession of small segments.

2. Already, at this early stage, the average dancer (and accompanist) will have misconceived the combination and thus made it more difficult. That is, she will have considered it on only the first level – that indicated by the dotted line. Every true phrase draws together the smaller portions such as these into a larger characteristic curve with an inner flow. This produces one long statement with contributory fluctuations:

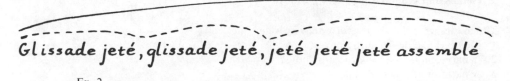

Glissade jeté, glissade jeté, jeté jeté jeté assemblé

Ex. 2

Notice that even in such a simple combination there are subtleties. The phrase-curve shows, for example, a slight difference between the first *glissade jeté* and the second. There is a subtle intensification of the 'repeat'. If it is approached as merely a restatement it becomes superfluous or redundant (which is, of course, usually the case). The same is true of the three *jetés*. If they are considered as three identical events they cannot contribute towards the growth and flow of the phrase; sameness destroys rhythms and phrasing. If, however, they are treated as stages within a larger event, they can play their proper part in the shaping of this event (as can the *glissade jetés*). But this brings us to the details which exist within the smaller segments of the overall phrase.

3. Look now at the punctuation of the diagrammed combination. This could be said to indicate the short clauses within the sentence-phrase. If, however, I had written it as it is usually executed in class it would have taken either of these two forms:

Glissade jeté glissade jeté jeté jeté jeté assemblé

Ex. 3

Glissade, jeté; glissade, jeté. Jeté, jeté, jeté, assemblé.

Ex. 4

Let us see what each of these does to the structure of the phrase, the overall shape and the inner continuity. In Ex. 3 there is no fluctuation at all – thus no phrase. A peculiar continuity exists, it is true, but without a focus; it is but a continuously trickling stream. In Ex. 4 the original phrase has become two phrases, with a disturbing pause between the two *glissade jetés*. Here we have a splintered phrase with no continuity at all, and the final blows are administered by the misplaced stresses ($>$, $-$), the significance of which will emerge in a moment. Instead of the trickle of Ex. 3 we have a stream intermittently dammed up. The problem here is, therefore, how to utilize continuity within a sensibly shaped phrase.

Neither effective continuity nor shapely phrases can be achieved without continual attention to detail – not in an obsessive manner but in an organic one. Details must always be viewed as part of a process. A 'perfect' *glissade* or a 'brilliant' *jeté* may be academically admirable, but they can at the same time be kinetically meaningless if they are not related to what comes before and after, and appropriately and organically linked to these surrounding movements (admirable *glissades* or *jetés*, moreover, are far less likely to occur if performed in isolation).

Consider, now, the break between the two *glissade jeté* segments. This could be viewed as the result of a technical fault, i.e. produced by a failure to link the end of the first *jeté* with the second *glissade* through a supple, functional *demi-plié* (thus the ($-$) of the diagram, indicating the downward emphasis which breaks the flow). But, turning it round, any dancer who was aware of the function of this moment *within the phrase* would be most unlikely to short-circuit the *demi-plié*. Our dilemma is, does the technique determine the overall conception or does this conception encourage the necessary technique? I think a reasonable answer would be that not only is each dependent on the other, but that both technique and conception will be capable of far greater development when they are viewed as partners. With this inter-dependency in mind, let us look briefly at some other details.

Ninety-nine out of every hundred dance students will execute the *glissade* incorrectly. Often, instead of a quick, neat, economical, *terre à terre* movement, we see a great galumphing assault on space – although *glissade* means *glide*. Here the timing is distorted both through the stressing of the *up* and the failure to close the second foot quickly – leaving it dangling too long in second position; thus there is no available means for pressing swiftly off the floor into the *jeté*. This distorted, 'up' impulse was indicated on the diagram by (>). It has two results; (1) the functional or technical value of the *glissade* as a preparatory movement is now demolished, and (2) it detracts rhythmically and kinetically from the following movement. Here is the effect:

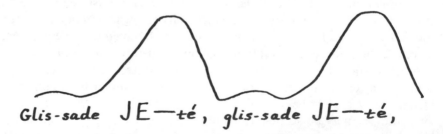

Glis - sade, je -té; glis - sade, je - té

AND   1   AND   2   AND   3   AND   4

Ex. 5

At best, the arc of the *glissade* is equal to that of the *jeté*; at worst it may even exceed it so that the *jeté* becomes a pathetic anti-climax, a mere afterthought. But watch a rhythmical dancer and these are transformed:

Glis-sade   JE—té,   glis-sade   JE—té,

Ex. 6

Note the difference in timing here. The *glissade* is much quicker, the *jeté* elongated yet sharper at its outset. The extra time gained from the swift *glissade* and the immediate entry into the *jeté* is employed in staying in the air longer – a lovely example of intelligent *rubato*. In Ex. 5 careless evenness produces dull non-rhythm; in Ex. 6 functional 'unevenness' creates vital rhythm, and the possibility of utilizing these segments towards the shaping of a phrase (this being what Denby was referring to in his remarks on Danilova and Markova quoted on p. 145).

Now, remembering that the second *glissade jeté* should be slightly intensified, what is our next concern? It is the link between the final *jeté* of the first half (count 4) and the initial one of the second half (count 5). This is the point which is so commonly punctuated with a semi-colon or even a period (the result, of course, of the disjunct *glissades jetés*). And if the dancer does this, she has, in effect, to begin all over again regarding the generation of kinetic energy. Instead of initiating a flow of energy which can spill over from the *glissades jetés*, she has stopped any potential growth. The phrase is already shattered, with the dancer stuck in *demi-plié* after a thudding *jeté*.

So, let us turn to our rhythmical dancer. Now despite the obvious value of a continuity of energy at this moment and a sense of direction, i.e. a moving through the entire phrase, the ideal solution here is not an inexorable crescendo to the end (although it could be in another, different, combination). A little light and shade will be more effective. This means that, while counts 4 and 5 will be linked, a small fluctuation is in order:

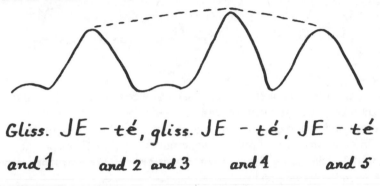

Gliss. JE -té, gliss. JE - té, JE - té
and 1   and 2 and 3   and 4   and 5

Ex. 7

Here we have not a *diminution* of energy but a *conservation*, directed towards the end of the phrase. It resembles the gradation of dynamics often employed before a musical crescendo.

But now that we have effected this little conservation of energy, what is its purpose? The answer to this lies in the overall curve of the phrase; to indicate the phrase as a whole, I originally diagrammed it as an arc, but, in fact, it has a different shape. Every phrase has a highest point, what Robert Schumann called its central point of gravity, which can occur at the very beginning, during its course, or at the very end. In this case it is at the end, in the *assemblé*. Thus the little conservation of energy at count 5 – the first of the three *jetés* – is going to expand through the *jetés* to culminate in the *assemblé*. So, rather than the dull and even succession of *jetés* which is so common, followed by an equally dull *assemblé*:

je-té , je-té , je -té , assem-blé

Ex. 8

or a forced and spuriously brilliant one:

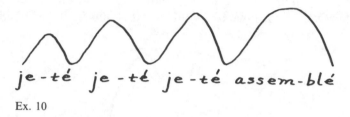

je - té, je - té, je - té, assem-blé

Ex. 9

we will have an organic and exciting one:

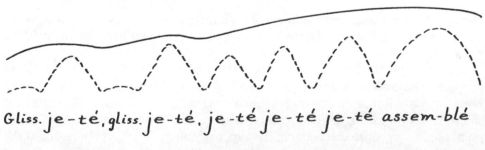

je-té   je - té   je-té   assem-blé

Ex. 10

Such a diagram is, of course, only a frustrating compromise, but anyone who has seen a dancer with an even rhythm moving beside one with a dynamically apportioned one will understand my point. The first dancer, with the even heaving up and down of her body (and not very far up at that) is *dispersing* energy; the second, with her fleet, functional use of transitional and preparatory movements, is *conserving* and *releasing* energy.

Let us look at the entire phrase as it would be danced by one who perceived both its overall curve and the continual details which shape this:

Gliss. je - té, gliss. je-té, je-té je-té je-té assem-blé

Ex. 11

As I have said, this can only be an approximation. Dancers will differ for instance, in the timing of the *demi-pliés*, and certain subtleties cannot be diagrammed. I hope, however, that the main points are clear regarding the shaping of a phrase as opposed to a disconnected succession of steps. (I must point out that the *jetés* do not necessarily increase in *elevation*; rather it is a matter of an increase in intensity or aliveness, a feeling of expansion in the dancer's body.)

I have referred to *energy*. It is the use of energy which differentiates the rhythmical from the non-rhythmical dancer. *Frappés* were cited as one of the most obvious and common examples of non-rhythm, thus of misuse of energy. This can be compared to the unrhythmical even *jetés* described above. The incorrect evenness of the split-up *frappés*: in-out-in-out, corresponds to the lifeless pauses in the *jetés*: down-up-down-up. Rhythmical timing, in contrast, would consist of: in-out - - -, in-out - - -, or plié-up - - -, plié-up - - -. This may *look* oddly disjointed, but in action it is the very source of rhythm (assuming, of course, that the elongated moments are alive and growing, not held statically).

'There is no rhythm', writes John Dewey, 'save where there is alternation of compressions and releases. Resistance prevents immediate discharge and accumulates tension that renders energy intense.'[1] In our example, the galumphing *glissade* which shoots away from the floor, thus detaching itself from any subsequent step, is *scattering* energy. But since this *glissade* is a preparatory movement, it should be *compressing*, or *gathering*, energy (thus the neatness and economy of a well-executed *glissade*), producing momentary resistance. This will quickly be discharged into, in this case, the *jeté*: compression leading to expansion.

Furthermore, 'there is, at the moment of reversal, an interval, a pause, a rest, by which the interaction of opposed energies is defined and rendered perceptible. The pause is a balance or symmetry of opposed forces.'[2] This pause occurs at both the crest (the top of the *jeté* or the *assemblé*) and the trough (the depth of the *demi-plié*). These moments correspond to the action of a lively rubber ball, but they can be seen more dramatically in the action of waves. And the fascination and awe with which we watch waves breaking and swelling correspond to that with which we watch rhythmical dancing. It is not the dancer who emulates the even, continuously-running or the halting, blocked-up, stream who excites and inspires us; it is the one who manifests, in human form, the compressions and releases of energy of the surf.

The bewildered or impatient accompanist may be wondering by now what all this has to do with her. Although I would hope that earlier chapters have made this clear, I shall state briefly my reasons for this long analysis of a dance-phrase.

1. The compression and release of energy also applies to performance on the piano, even though in a different and less dramatically apparent way.

2. This action is the manifestation of *rubato*. As I have said, *rubato* is less continual and marked for the pianist than for the dancer, yet the basic principles apply to each. I found, and hope that the reader will find, a deeper understanding of *rubato* in music from seeing it applied to dance-movement.

3. On the other hand, the alternations of energies, and thus rhythms, that shape a dance-phrase, which I have analyzed in such detail, should show why the attempt to provide literal dance-rhythms is so undesirable, or even futile.

4. I believe, obviously, that the more the musician knows about the art and technique of dancing the better able she will be to achieve the transformation from pianist into valuable and valued ballet-partner.

5. Since the principles of phrasing and rhythm in movement remain the same – although *specific* application will vary – whether the dance-phrase is *allegro*, *moderato* or *adagio*, brilliant and marked or lyric and sustained, I can avoid much repetition in the following three analyses.

Now let us try to select a piece for our little *allegro*.

b. The music

1. Meter and rhythmic subdivision should pose no problem here. The obvious first choice, for both teacher and pianist, will be a suitable straightforward duple rhythm.

2. The dance-phrase consisting of eight counts, which is then repeated to the other side, the musical one can either be the same or it can form half of a 16-count phrase. This will affect the dancer. My view is that a repeat is often quite acceptable but a continuation may be preferable, if only for variety. It will also prevent the feeling of beginning again on the second side: this is good, for a longer phrase can help the dancers to develop the capacity to sustain interest and psychological (and physical) endurance throughout the larger-scale *enchaînements* of ballets. I have seen many dancers fall apart half-way through one of these in an evening rehearsal even though they had done well that morning in the brief combinations of class. I suspect that this lack of sustaining power is at least partially due to their (and the pianist's) habitually thinking and moving on a small-scale, broken-up manner in class. Thus, I would suggest that the pianist frequently should play music which continues rather than mirroring the repeat to the second side. The varied music to which this repeat is danced will both color the movement, replacing a possible feeling of mere repetitiousness with one of growth, and help the dancers to experience the sensation of a larger breath.

What should usually be avoided is the splitting of this 8-count dance-phrase into a musical one which consists of four counts plus an exact repetition of these. This would exaggerate every problem I have discussed, particularly the break between the second *glissade jeté* and the first of the consecutive *jetés*.

3. You have many melodic options for a combination like this one. The main restrictions are the avoidance of one which chops up the flow of the movement or which is flaccid and lacking in the vitality which this combination needs. The melody should, as a rule, share the same 'point of gravity' as the dance.

4. The pace at which the harmonies change will naturally be determined by the composer in conjunction with the melody. Yet a harmonic rhythm which changes, say, every two beats might be acceptable with one melody but not with another *for this particular combination*. Thus, it is not the harmonic rhythm in conjunction with the melody which is important so much as it is the conjunction of both of these with the movement-phrase. Although harmonic rhythm is very important, it must be approached in this integrated manner, excepting such obvious points as the undesirability here of a hectic fast-changing succession of chords.

5. The next question is what sort of rhythmic patterns will suit this movement. Should they be even or dotted, running or detached, repetitious or varied, and so on. Clearly, too many dotted patterns would tend to chop up the movement, and a torrent of running sixteenth-notes might blur it and detract from the necessary clarity of line and incisiveness of attack.

6. If the teacher does not clearly indicate the style and quality, the accompanist must do so. This combination allows several possibilities, but certain ones are obviously at odds with it. Impressionistic, hazy music would dampen its vitality;

dense, serious late-Romanticism would pull it to earth; and trivial, joyless banalities would destroy its potential. Many choices, however, remain; it could be given a driving and clean-cut Baroque sound, an elegant Classical one, a fanciful Mendelssohnian or Schumannesque one, or a light, crisp bit of Soviet wit, not to mention one of the many sparkling Tchaikovsky Allegros.

The choice will depend partly on the point at which this combination is given in class – how warmed-up the dancer's muscles are (thus affecting the tempo), what combinations were given already, and which styles and qualities have predominated so far (it may, that is, be time for a change).

Let us examine two pieces, measuring them against what has been said about the movement-phrase and the general musical considerations only the opening phrases are given in the musical examples).

Ex. 12

Ex. 13

Ex. 12 is the sort of thing we have all heard wafting out of an open studio door at one time or another. It is so dreadful, and unsuitable in almost every way for our combination, that it hardly needs comment. Still, a few brief observations may be helpful.

Its phrase-structure is a stark $2 + 2 + 2 + 2$. This will inevitably lead the dancers to approach their movement on the small-scale, broken-up level rather than to generate a flow which carries them through the first-level breaks to produce a higher-level continuity. The predominantly downward shape of the melodic line is not in itself bad; it is the interaction of this with the dull, predictable harmonies, the repetitious patterns in both treble and bass, and the resultant start-stop feeling which is negative.

Whatever style and quality this music has can only be said to be *not* what we want. One can view it as a dismal example of 'ballet music', or as a first-grade piano study called 'Hesitation' or 'Hippety-Hop'. Neither quality is likely to invigorate the dancers. As for breath and space, the music's perpetual turning in on itself prevents any feeling of buoyancy or openness; it is an enemy of *ballon*. From every point of view, this piece seems designed to defeat the dancers' aims, to reinforce any problems they may have with this combination. Where there should be resilience there will be sag; where there should be continuity there will be gasps.

Although the second piece also falls, more or less, into the 'ballet music' category, it is significantly different from the first. Its phrase-structure should certainly help the dancers to bridge those lower-level, potential breaks. Here we replace the musical $2 + 2 + 2 + 2$ with an almost seamless 8-count phrase; even the slight pause of the semi-cadence is bridged by the impetus generated by the first three beats (among other things). Let us look at the various elements in action, as they contribute to the over-all shape of the dance phrase.

The melody takes off immediately and does not flag; it thrusts forward to its moment of fulfillment in much the same way as should the dance-phrase. It has the same general drive, with a slight fluctuation in energy (just before the beginning of the three consecutive *jetés*). This is not a mimicking of the movement's ups and downs, but harmony of energy-distribution. These properties of the melody are aided by the chords and the rhythmic patterns. Although the chords are simple, there are some things worth noting. The slight, passing dissonances between the melody and the harmony on the 2nd and 3rd counts, the first inversions on these counts, the pedal point – with a resultant spicy little dissonance on the 6th count, and an inversion on the 5th count, also resulting from the pedal point – all of these contribute modestly to an undramatic but lively interplay between melody and harmony. The second 8-count phrase will continue in the same melodic and harmonic vein, of course, with more inversions to assist the harmonic flow, but deviating somewhat, thus giving variety to the repeat of the combination on the other side. Not only does Ex. 12 repeat a somewhat dull motive but it has no touches of interest, in the form of effective inversions or dissonances.

The rhythmic patterns of Ex. 13 are also more interesting. Note that the bass has patterns which are similar to those of the first piece. But the interplay of this bass with the treble in the second one makes the difference. Although the bass rhythm firmly establishes a clear pulse, the treble flies away from its predictability and frees it. In the first piece, the treble echoed it and weighed it down. In addition, the energy implied in the early sixteenth-notes of the second piece is released into the continuous sixteenth-notes which drive towards the crest of the first phrase. Thus you find both similarity and variety – a principle of good rhythm (see Chapter 10).

The difference in the feeling of breath or space between Ex. 12 and Ex. 13 is marked. Ex. 12 is closed in and airless, Ex. 13 opens out and leaves room in which the dancers can expand. This is due, as is the style and quality – cheerful, playful, effervescent, and slightly mannered – to the nature and interplay of the melody, harmony and rhythm.

We are still not quite finished with this combination; many teachers will want to give it at a quicker tempo, with a different quality. What this usually means, after the usual '2/4' or '4/4', is a triple rhythm, a '3/8' or a '6/8'. Let us see what a light, sparkling 6/8 can contribute; the second theme of the Forlane from Ravel's *Tombeau de Couperin* may be just what is needed. Listen to a good recording of it, while visualizing the combination. You may find yourself impelled to try to dance it.

The phrases of the Forlane are not so continuous as those of Ex. 13, but the half-way mark of the first 8-count phrase does not present us with an awkward break as in Ex. 12. Although Ravel's 8-count phrase might seem at first to be two of 4 counts each, the restless quality of the cadence on the 4th count and the path of the second 4 counts colors the partial repetition, and prevents the phrase from being divided into two separate parts. This is a good example of the principle of repetition leading to intensification (it is also an illustration of the impossibility of establishing rigid rules). This particular repetition intensifies through the interest and liveliness of the other elements, whereas in Ex. 12 the uniform dullness of all the elements underscored the monotony of the repetitious phrase-structure.

The Ravel melody is in itself delightful. Without being startling, it yet has a feeling of unpredictability as it darts here and there. This is accentuated in the first 8-count phrase by those characteristic Ravelian harmonies, particularly on counts 3 and 4, and 7 and 8, with their modal cadences. In the second phrase, the melody and harmony continue in a pleasingly consistent yet even more unpredictable manner – again with a fresh-sounding modal cadence. The interest of the melody and harmony never flags and continually helps the dancer over the awkward moments which we have discussed.

Ravel's rhythmic patterns may seem to be repetitious, but they are enlivened by their interaction with the melody and harmony. A subtle touch occurs in the second phrase, on counts 4 and 5. The unexpected arrival on a strong harmony on the off-beat, plus its being tied over to count 5, gives a strong lift at this moment, a thrust to the rest of the phrase, and colors in retrospect the first phrase (which will, of course, be heard again in this light when the combination is repeated by the second group and then again by both groups).

Its style could be termed neo-Rococo. Being Ravel's tribute to Couperin, it combines in an interesting way Ravel's 'modern' clarity and incisiveness with the earlier elegance of Couperin's similar qualities. It evokes a radically different world from those of Exx. 12 and 13. Although it could also be described as playful, this is a very different sort of play from that of Ex. 13, and should evoke a different response from the dancers – what is sometimes called a 'throwaway', in which nothing is lingered over or too obviously pointed out. The impulses throughout are more subtle with, for instance, the build-up of the *jetés* to the *assemblé* comparatively underplayed. Here it is a matter more of a continuously sparkling movement-phrase, delicately shaped, rather than the obvious use of light and shade in Ex. 13.

If played with the fastidious strength (if I may juxtapose two such seemingly contradictory qualities) which will bring out the wonderful clarity of the Forlane, it will seem light and airy and buoyant; if played with a heavy hand (and pedal-foot) punching out the rhythms, all of its charm and *élan* will be lost. No pianist who is sensitive to its transparent texture, however, should fall into such error.

There are, needless to say, countless other harmonious pieces for this combination; each will fulfill in its own way the requirements I have analyzed. Now it is time to look at a very different sort of combination to see how these requirements apply to other qualities and phrases of movement.

2. Pirouettes

a. The movement

Chassé pas de bourrée, to 4th position, double pirouette (en dehors) close in 5th position.

1. The structure of this phrase is even simpler than that of the small *allegro*, with the exercise composed of four renditions of it to alternating sides. Its simplicity is, however, somewhat deceptive.

2. Done properly, each 4-count phrase has a continuous crescendo to the very end, although there will be, of course, fluctuations in detail:

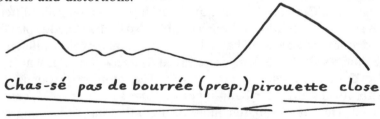

Chassé pas de bourrée pirouette close in 5ᵗʰ position

and 1   and   a   2   and a 3   and   a   4

Ex. 14

The curve, however, which this phrase all too often gets is the result of misconceptions and distortions:

Chas-sé pas de bourrée (prep.) pirouette close

Ex. 15

This will give us a particularly vivid illustration of the way in which the dancer's technique suffers when she does not comprehend the kinetic flow and the curve of a phrase.

3. Many dancers begin with a disproportionately large *chassé*, followed by a disconnected *pas de bourrée*. This is unhelpful, to say the least. The *chassé* is an instigator, not a moment of glory; if overemphasized, it both distorts the overall phrase and disperses energy, preventing the *pas de bourrée* from being a smooth, continuous gathering of energy for release – through the preparation – into the *pirouette*. The result, in other words, is a bumptious and unfunctional *chassé*, a spread-out *pas de bourrée* (usually done with stilted or sloppy feet), i.e. a non-beginning.

These produce, in turn, the coarsest distortion of all – a squatting in the preparation and the complete cessation of flow with which so many dancers signal that (1) they are about to do a *pirouette* and (2) they do not understand turning either in itself or in relation to a phrase. And, in fact, the next event – the turn – leads one to wonder whether the preceding miscalculations are causes or symptoms, for what happens now is usually that the *pirouette* becomes an ascent rather than a spinning or whirling about. Many teachers actually shout 'up' at this point. So up the dancers hop, teetering on an ill-prepared *relevé*, throwing themselves off balance, and invariably making what should be a continuous and *expanding* double turn two separate, jerky revolutions – or even general disintegration.

Now, regarding cause vs. symptom, this hectic scramble can be viewed as being caused by the disassociation of the preliminary *chassé, pas de bourrée* and preparation from the turn. But, if one views the faulty turn not as being *caused by* but as the *cause of* the distorted preliminary movements, they will be seen as the symptoms which they are. The *pirouette* is the cause of the ruination of this phrase in the sense that it is often all that the average dancer and teacher seem to think about. Apart from the natural turner, dancers tend to approach *pirouettes* with apprehension. They focus on them so exclusively that everything else in the phrase fades away. Thus, instead of the turn being a part of the culmination of the phrase it becomes an isolated feat; from the opening *chassé* they are projecting ahead to that dreaded, revealing moment. And because of the ensuing kinetic and rhythmic paralysis of the preliminaries, they make almost certain that they will turn erratically. Furthermore, it is not only that the *pirouette* receives all of the dancer's focus but that a particular portion of it – the entry into it – is the prime goal. This produces impact followed by dissipation and loss of clarity and direction, or

'The significance of an event is inseparable from the means employed in reaching it';[3] this is true of every event in music and dance, but never more so than with *pirouettes*. And, one might add, the means alter the end – the turn – at the same time that the end alters the means or the preliminary movements. Thus the end cannot 'justify' the means because the means will be affected by it.

Always in this vicious circle potential catastrophe looms: the ungraceful/disgraceful falling out of the misbegotten *pirouette* – that awful stagger down from *relevé*. If the turn fizzles out, it then subverts the loveliest moment of all – that heart-catching suspension at the finish of a well-executed *pirouette*. Result: the sudden, sharp decrescendo, and anti-climax, of Ex. 15 rather than a following-through and final flowering of the turn. A neat, precise, controlled yet expansive arrival and closing makes a *pirouette* ten times more exciting in retrospect, just as a loss of shape, direction and flow of energy will make even an (undeservedly) lucky turn meaningless, or even jarring.

I have seen dancers perform this combination with only a single *pirouette* – not the most dazzling of feats – yet the connection of the one turn to what preceded it and the perfection of suspension and then resolution into the final closing position produced something of great beauty: the greatest feat of all.

How can the accompanist encourage the dancers to view the *pirouette* as a flowering rather than as an isolated source of fear? Speaking generally, by the scrupulous avoidance of any piece which is dull or choppy. But, although on the surface it might seem the easiest thing in the world to find suitable music for this combination, it is not, and much more than the avoidance of dull and choppy music is involved. Many seemingly complicated combinations present a far lesser challenge to the accompanist.

b. *The music*

1. A combination of this sort usually introduces the first *pirouettes* of center-work; its purpose is to provide a simple framework within which the dancers can concentrate on problems of placing, elements of the turning action, etc. without distraction. Therefore, it will be done in a *moderato* rather than an *allegro* tempo. The bravura turns come later. The most obvious choice, then, is a waltz: not too quick and brilliant, not too slow and lush.

2. Since it consists of a short, 4-count phrase, which is done four times, it can easily become a repetitious study in endurance, much like the simple *barre* exercises. The music can help to prevent this by being sustained in interest throughout, by not dwindling after an early high point. It is not unusual for a composer either to deliberately place his peak towards the beginning or to taper off inadvertently through lack of sustaining power. Since the dancer obviously will benefit from approaching the four phrases as parts of a whole rather than four consecutive but separate ordeals, you should avoid pieces which decline or peter out.

In addition to the large-scale structure of the combination viewed as a whole, there is that problem within each small phrase of the potential break between the preparation and the turn. Any music which tends toward a 2 + 2 feeling rather than a continuous 4 or 8 should not even be considered.

3. Although the melodic line should carry the dancer happily towards the *pirouette*, the last thing you want is a tune which leaps up to punch out the third count. Since the dancer should already have entered her spin by then (another example of *rubato*), accenting it harshly is not only silly, it will interfere with the flow of the turn. Yet many accompanists do just this in the belief that it is 'helping' the dancer. Such false accents, moreover, are often followed by a blank feeling for the '4-and-a'; this chokes off the desired culmination and feeling of breath or aplomb at the very end. The *pirouette* is not the end of the phrase and the melody should not dwindle at that point.

4. Although, as I have said, the harmonic rhythm of a piece is strongly affected by the other musical elements, one could say generally that for this combination it should be neither quick and abrupt nor slow and lazy. Too many chord-changes within the phrase would break its flow; the same harmony continuing for too long would devitalize the kinetic impulse. An extreme example of this occurs in the following piece; not only is the harmonic rhythm very slow, this is reinforced by the melodic outlining of the chords:

Ex. 16   Johann Strauss, 'Sphaerenklange' Waltz No. 1

5. The rhythmic patterns are somewhat circumscribed by the nature of a waltz, yet some waltzes are almost excessively flowing, others will contain unsuitable patterns for this combination, and still others may have such accented or syncopated patterns as to veer towards a mazurka rhythm. Each of these will have its time in class; in this case, rhythms which are mainly smooth but with a propelling impulse would seem to be the most suitable.

6. Since our combination is moderate in tempo and use of energy, i.e. non-bravura, the music should not venture into extreme areas. It would, for instance, be a bit soon to introduce the brilliant, satirical sound of a big waltz by Prokofiev. A languorous, sensual waltz, on the other hand, with the quality of Debussy's *La Plus que lente*, would be unlikely to strike the right tone at a time when the center-work is just beginning to move along.

7. For such a simple, exposed combination, it is especially important to avoid density, to provide instead a rich yet transparent texture. There must be a feeling of breath throughout so that what might be called the dancer's density of concentration on the *pirouette* is counteracted.

Now a brief look at a waltz which I have heard more than one accompanist use for this or similar combinations:

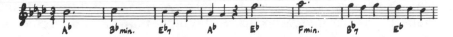

Ex. 17   Chopin, Waltz op. 34, no. 1

Although this waltz is lovely, it has little to contribute, in my view, to our combination. Its melting, drooping quality is wonderfully Romantic, but the feeling of lassitude fights the purpose of the exercise. Examination of the details of phrasing, melody, harmony and rhythm would show that at almost every point these accentuate the dancer's technical and interpretive problems. To take two instances: first, the over-all curve of this musical phrase is opposed to that of the dance. Whereas the short dance-phrase is a gradual, continual crescendo, each corresponding musical one tends towards a decrescendo. And at the end, just when the dancer should be expanding into her moment of poise or aplomb, the music is expiring with a delicate sigh. This is true of all four of the opening phrases.

Secondly, the music has very little kinetic impulse during the moments of the preparation and the turn. Instead it seems to float, then waft gently down. In short, the necessary guides to attack and timing are just not there.

A sharp contrast is offered by the following:

Ex. 18   Schumann, *Valse Allemande*

This is equally unsuitable, if for different reasons. Here, instead of lassitude and gentle expirings, we have a jagged, syncopated series of sharp exhalations. These interfere constantly with the dance-phrase. The preparation for the *pirouette* is made almost absurd, and there is a great hole between the two where there should be continuity and growth. The jagged rhythmic patterns persist throughout the following three phrases (and the second section, although less abrupt in feeling, is not much better).

Now, leaving these two extremes, let us approach a middle ground, which can be found in the clear, graceful flow of an Offenbach waltz:

Ex. 19   Offenbach, *Orpheus in Hades*, Act I, duo

Bearing in mind that few pieces can meet each movement problem with equal success, or be uniformly harmonious throughout every phrase, this one clearly avoids most of the snags discussed above. The structure of the phrases and their overall curves are far more suitable than those of the previous two pieces. Most important, the break between the preparation and the *pirouette* is avoided, there being a strong kinetic flow between the second and third counts of each phrase. The phrase-curves also produce a feeling of suspension for the *pirouette* rather than a wavering or a jagged one. The curves, moreover, differ slightly; that of the first phrase emphasizes *directly* the finish of the *pirouette*, while the second one does so indirectly through the syncopation-energy of the third count. This gives the dancer an opportunity to play a bit with the movement, and to explore different timings and sensations.

The melody is not only tuneful and continuous, it contains a flow of energy similar to that desirable for the combination. Its distribution of impulses is harmonious with the movement's ebb and flow, and it encourages a smooth yet purposeful *pas de bourrée*. The harmonies move at a moderate pace, and frequent inversions add interest and, at important moments such as the preparation and the *pirouette*, they contribute to the forward impetus which is so necessary for this dance-phrase.

Amidst the general rhythmic regularity (which is modified by the melody and harmony), the little syncopations referred to above are just enough to give a lift to the whole. The regularly recurring syncopations of the *Valse allemande* (Ex. 18), on the other hand, are too much for this dance-phrase; they keep pulling it down and interrupting it. The style and quality of the Offenbach (Ex. 19) are obvious – simple, straightforward, lyrical and romantic, but not lush. There is, too, all the breath and space that the dancer could wish. This music has the buoyancy of a wave.

Another, quite different, choice of music could serve: the waltz-theme from Berlioz's *Symphonie fantastique*. This is marked *allegro non troppo* in the score, and if it is taken too fast, it will sound notey and dense. Thus, it shines best with a combination such as this – of an unextreme nature, both in quality and tempo. It is delightful in this context. The surge of the phrase, the way in which it sweeps past potential breaks and brings out the full values of the *pirouette* and its completion, not to mention its soaring quality and its elasticity – all these are, of course, the result of the smaller details of melody, harmony and rhythmic patterns, and, in turn, result in music which is not only extremely danceable, but also helps to solve the troublesome movement problems we have been examining.

3. Adagio

One of the most important moments in class is the *grand adage*, or *adagio*. Less flashy, and more treacherous as an exhibition of a dancer's ability than *allegro* exercises, *adagios* are in a sense the basis of all balletic work. They reveal, in their remorseless, slow unfolding, all the faults which can be at least partially masked in the quicker *allegros*. Although 'adagio' is translated literally as 'at leisure' or 'at ease', any leisurely ease you see is an illusion created by the dancer's skill in disguising the effort and strength which an *adagio* requires. It is designed to develop, among other things, balance and an ingrained sense of the various classical positions of the body. The value of the former should be apparent. Regarding the latter, there is no time, when moving quickly, for the mind to direct the body; the achievement of positions and orientation in space must be instantaneous. *Adagio*-work provides the basis for this, and must, therefore, be done at a slow tempo, with strong emphasis on fluidity, continuity and co-ordination of all parts of the body.

Phrasing might be said to be more important in *adagio* than in any other exercise, not only because the dancer cannot draw upon the more obvious excitements of glittering *allegro* steps or bravura leaps to help cover lapses in technique, but also because the habits developed during the slow-motion *adagios* will inevitably be carried over to movement in other tempos. *Adagio*-work in this sense is the fountainhead of phrasing in ballet at every tempo.

Dancers, unfortunately, often approach *adagio*-work in class either as a form of torture and grim survival, or as a study in how to pose prettily (or, if male, dramatically). 'Line' is an essential attribute in *adagio* – as elsewhere – but when misconceived as applying only to a static *arabesque* or *attitude*, rather than to a continuous flow of movement *incorporating* various positions, 'line' becomes pointless design.

Positions in ballet resemble harmonies in music. No matter how pretty or dramatic they may seem in themselves, they come alive and have dramatic, expressive potential only when they exist in a context, as part of a sequence. If isolated and disconnected, they are merely one-dimensional. Balletic poses, however, are tempting in a way that particular, separate, chords cannot be. An *attitude*, say, or an *arabesque*, both undeniably pleasing shapes, seem to have a meaning of their own to many dancers, that meaning being an opportunity to show off 'technique'. This is perhaps an understandable temptation, for 'technique' is a relatively concrete goal – at least in comparison with the more elusive ones of personality, style and quality.

The accompanist should do everything in her power to circumvent the temptation to ignore the *flow* of line, the less dramatic yet essential connecting movements, for the sake of disjointed moments of display. The *adagio* should be the focal point of the class musically just as it is the key point balletically – or the central point of gravity in Robert Schumann's meaning. Not only must the dancers be given, as always, a piece with clear, musical phrasing which suits the movement-phrases, they will thrive on music which is particularly beautiful, well-loved or out of the ordinary. An occasional pedestrian or nondescript *allegro* during class is not a catastrophe, but the *adagio* must be at the very least *good*, and, preferably, it should be superb.

Providing outstanding *adagios* day after day is no easy task. In addition to the necessity for an excellent repertoire or expert improvising (to be discussed in Chapters 10 and 11), it demands the most careful and sympathetic evaluation of the construction and quality of the combination. To offer habitually one of a handful of all-purpose old reliables is both to cheat the dancers and to deprive yourself of much pleasure – musical and kinesthetic.

Until, however, you feel confident and reasonably experienced, it is best to use only music which is relatively simple, with very clear phrasing (which does not mean that you are limited to Everybody's Favorite Piano Gems or Ballet's Golden *Pas de Deux*). Nothing is worse than shapeless cascades of arpeggios, thick and sluggish harmonies or meandering melodies – particularly when these are, as is often the case, sloppily performed. But when the basic principles are understood, many unusual and somewhat complicated pieces may prove valuable, and illuminate the entire lesson with their beauty.

a. The movement

I. *Grand plié, chassé* forward into *attitude croisée*
    1–2–3– 4–5   –   6   –   7   –   8

    Promenade en dedans to *attitude effacée*, into 1st *arabesque, relevé*
    1   –   2   –   3   –   4   –   5   –   6   7 – 8
                                       5   –   6 – 7 –8

II. (flat) *Passé développé croisée devant* (close in 5th pos.), *développé croisée derrière*
    1   –   2   –   3   –   4   –   5 – 6 – 7 – 8

    (5th pos.) *Développé ecarté devant, rond de jambe en dehors* into *attitude croisée derrière* to *attitude grecque.*
    1   –   2 – 3   –   4 – 5   –   6   –   7   –   8

1. Here we have a combination which most teachers would count out in four 8-count phrases. These are clearly grouped into two sections of equal length, I and II. Although this structure may seem uncomplicated, several problems of phrasing on a higher level exist for the sensitive dancer.

2. The dotted lines indicate the first, mundane, level of conception. If the dancer is satisfied with this, she will fail to achieve the more subtle curves which are integral to this *adagio*:

$$\overparen{1-2-3-4} \overparen{-5-6-7-8} \quad \overparen{1-2-3-4} \overparen{-5-6-7-8}$$

$$\overparen{1-2-3-4} \overparen{-5-6-7-8} \quad \overparen{1-2-3-4} \overparen{-5-6-7-8}$$

Ex. 20

These short spans add up to little more than gymnastics. The dotted lines clearly show a start-and-stop direction of energy, a predictable and boring progression, which destroys the innate quality and energy-flow of the *adagio*. The continuous lines, in contrast, show the basic phrase curves, and create a different pattern. They equal what we can call the second level of conception, and are necessary for the generation of the gradual crescendo of energy in the first section and the crescendo of energy in the second section which reaches its point of gravity just before the concluding *attitude greque*. This will be discussed in detail in a moment, so I shall merely say here that we have two sections of 16 counts each, the second one consisting of a slightly different curve than the first – *not*, as on the first level, a collection of eight 4-count gasps.

3. These curves, and their total effect within the combination, depend on a great deal of detail along the way, detail which contains many of the most common faults in the execution of *adagio* phrases. The first fault occurs almost immediately, with the completion of the *grand plié* on count 4. Innumerable dancers break the flow of energy here rather than carrying it onward to the next movement – in this *adagio*, the beginning of the *chassé*-glide. This in turn will diminish the flowering of the *attitude croisée*. But, even worse, the average dancer will, almost absent-mindedly, drop the energy level at the onset of the *promenade*, just when it should be increasing. The *promenade* should be the logical kinetic result of the previous movements rather than, as is so often the case, an event in isolation. The latter is bad enough, but it leads to what is perhaps the worst fault of this entire section: the conception of the *attitude effacée* as a pose. Not only will such silliness mar any lucky moments of grace possibly achieved earlier, it will shatter the potential beauty of the stretch from *attitude* into 1st *arabesque* and its wonderful spilling over into the *relevé*.

The fragmentation of this section – shown in dotted lines in Ex. 20 – into separate moments and poses makes impossible the subtle rises, falls and continuity of energy which are needed for the shaping of these 16 counts into a coherent span of dancing. And the resultant disaster is twofold. Not only will the section be of little visual beauty as a continuous event, but the dancer is very likely to have technical problems throughout because of her sporadic directions of energy.

A forced, shaky *attitude croisée* is but one of the many hazards awaiting her. The *promenade* will challenge her powers of balance and line, the *attitude effacée* will as a result tend to feel awkward, and so will the stretch into 1st *arabesque*. As for the *relevé* in *arabesque*, this will be a matter for prayer or sheer grit, neither of which can help much at this point. The awkward *arabesque* plus the erratic phrasing will almost inevitably result in a forced *relevé* which is quickly fallen out of by the unwilling dancer: always embarrassing and irritating for the victim.

Now let us see how easy it is to destroy the overall curve of the second section. Unlike the first, this is a succession of waves. The main problem is to make these connect within the larger curve while also giving each its full value. Again, the average dancer will hack the section to pieces. The conclusions of the *développé croisée devant* and *derrière* will most likely be accompanied by deadening thuds of the foot into position instead of live contacts with the floor, ready to generate the next wave. This is usually due to the point of view that the leg stuck up in the air is the *end* of each *développé* rather than its *peak*, or crest.

The effect is rather like that of a wave which crashes against an obstacle rather than freely completing its natural cycle. By the end of the second *développé*, moreover, the dancer will be so accustomed to these truncated events that she will approach the *développé* into *écarté devant* similarly. Unfortunately, this is not followed by another *développé*, but spills into a *grand rond de jambe* – a potentially magical moment which, in this case, becomes disjunct and pointless (it will probably, as it should never do, drop at some point, the extended leg and foot failing to describe a continuous line throughout space). The *attitude croisée derrière* consequently becomes pointless also, and diminishes the lovely concluding curve into *attitude grecque* into an afterthought rather than a rich after-curve.

The esthetic result of all this anti-phrasing is boredom or distaste in the viewer, and the practical result a distortion of the structure of this *adagio* and the exaggeration of technical problems.

For the dancer with a sense of flow and direction of energy (that is, general dance-intelligence), this *adagio* is quite another matter. Instead of the forced bits and pieces we have seen, she will approach it as an apparently effortless progression of interacting shapes and events, the basic curves being achieved through continual awareness of the detail within them. Ex. 20 showed, by the solid line, the general curves of the two sections; Ex. 21 depicts the more specific rises and falls that create the large-scale design. Again, phrasing and continuity are not analogous to a monotonous run-on sentence, but rather to the fluctuations within the larger unity of eloquent prose or poetry. Thus, for instance, the antidote for the alternation of legs brandished *en l'air* with directionless thuds into position is not a steady oozing – a sameness of flow and attack – from beginning to end, but a sensible and kinetic disposition of energy within an overall conception of phrasing. Approached thus, the *attitudes*, *arabesques* and other 'poses' will become luminous flowers supported and made meaningful by the flow of energy modulated appropriately through the various preliminary and connecting moments.

What can music do to encourage the dancer to conceive of this *adagio* as a series of phrases within an entity, during which energy must be employed suitably, in conjunction with beautiful line, co-ordination and style – all of this fully yet economically?

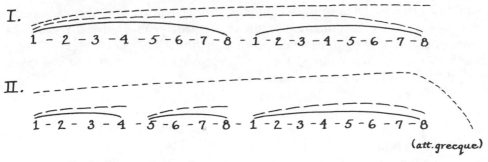

Ex. 21

b. The music

1. As always, a duple rhythm will tend to evoke a strong and forthright feeling, and a triple rhythm a rounded and fluid quality (these are not, of course, absolutes; they can be affected by variables. Compare, for instance, the duple rhythm of the *grand pas de deux* from *Nutcracker*, Act 2, with that of *Giselle*, Act 2, or the triple rhythm of Coppélia's *andante* solo in Scene 1, Act 2 of *Coppélia* with that of the Rose *adagio* in *Sleeping Beauty*). The choice of one or the other, if not stipulated by the teacher, will depend partly, as usual, on the preceding center-work. If, however, the majority of the class habitually has trouble with phrasing, the choice of a rounded triple rhythm is usually better.

2. Since one of the major faults of the dancer is to break down an *adagio* into disconnected poses, the primary concern for the accompanist is a piece of music which forcefully (or gently) carries the dancer's impulses through the phrase and the section – and, ultimately, the entire *adagio*. In this one, our main sources of trouble are the *attitude croisée* into *promenade*, the three *développés* of 4 counts each and the link between the third *développé* and the *rond de jambe*. In addition, there is the large-scale curve of the combination, which reaches its peak, or point of gravity, just before the end. A piece of music which dwindles away from an early climax thus would not be suitable.

The following three elements interact continually:

3. The melodic line, obviously, must be constructed so that it does not fight the details of phrasing which we have considered. It does not have to follow literally either the over-all curves or the inner waves; the harmonic rhythm and direction and the rhythmic patterns affect the melodic line strongly.

4. For this *adagio*, neither a harmonic rhythm which changes quickly and dramatically nor one which moves extremely slowly will do. There should be a feeling of pace, certainly, but not one of crowding or choppiness (such harmonic rhythms might be perfectly fine in the *music*, but it is the effect in combination with the movement which is relevant here).

5. Although the actual rhythmic patterns are affected by the melodic and harmonic characteristics, it is safe to say that sharp, dotted rhythms are likely to fight the flow and sweep of this *adagio*. Markedly even rhythms on the other hand,

would also tend to fight a sense of continuity, and to constrict the various waves – especially in a duple rhythm. Many of the famous *adagios* have musical ostinatos or continuous running-patterns underneath a rhythmically varied melody. Such basses provide an inner thread for the different melodic patterns above them, dotted, syncopated or heavily marked and even.

Highly complicated rhythms or over-florid arpeggiated patterns usually tend to blur the inner sense of pulse which is so necessary for the dancer in class. The exception to this general rule is music which has an outstandingly clear melodic line with a strong sense of direction.

6. The range of musical styles and qualities for an *adagio* of this sort is, happily, wide. Different styles, and qualities will naturally affect the dancer's conception of the *adagio*. Take, for instance, a lush late-Romantic aria by Puccini, an elegant but simple miniature by Ravel, an intense section from a late Beethoven sonata, a nostalgic, gentle Chopin nocturne, a serious andante from a Mozart symphony or concerto, or a clean-cut, harmonically forthright, yet lyrical, slow movement by Vivaldi. In each case, for the dancer, everything from basic carriage to the lavish or controlled use of space will be influenced differently.

7. The range of choices listed above contains various sorts of musical breath and space. The densest texture will probably be found in the Beethoven or the Puccini, the most open and airy in the elegant Ravel or the Chopin nocturne. Musical breath and space are extremely important in *adagio* work. Even the lushest piece must leave room for the dancer's flow of line, not enveloping it in a dense mass of sound (see also item 5, above). But, at the same time, the music should not be too thin or lacking in a feeling of flesh and muscle. If the over-all quality is bony or attenuated, the kinetic effect will be flimsy or disjointed and will create problems for the dancers.

Breath and space in music are, as I have said, closely linked to melody in certain ways. And it is essential for *adagio* work in class that the concept of breath in singing – that quality of expansiveness and measured energy which good singers possess – be embodied in the accompanist's selection of music. Tudor was fond of startling the dancers in class by requesting that one unfortunate victim sing the melodic line of the music while performing the *adagio*. Almost invariably those who were able to overcome their embarrassment and sing loudly enough to be heard more than a foot away moved more fluidly, with an increased sense of phrasing and projection. 'I always want the body to sing', says Tudor. 'Therefore, nearly all my phrases are as though they would be sung. That's why I'm against counting. No one can count if they're singing. Also, a singer has a breath for a certain phrase.'[4]

Makarova agrees: 'I divide Tchaikovsky's music into phrases, not measures, trying to sing them . . . with my dancing . . . I do not count them, and neither do I worry about exactly fixing each position against the music or "freezing" the arabesques and attitudes. . . . I feel that such sensationalism is all but fatal, tearing, as it does, the continuity of the choreographic texture to the detriment of its meaning.'[5] (Her innate musicality of course is not confined to Tchaikovsky, but sings across a wide spectrum, according to the nature of each score and ballet.)

The accompanist can encourage the dancers to sing with their bodies by providing music with melodic shapes which are so singable that, even though the dancers are not actually vocalizing, they experience the same openness and expansion as a fine singer – who, even when singing full out, gives the impression that much lies in reserve and that there is power to project twice as far.

Harmony and rhythm strongly affect musical breath and space, but melody is – at least in the studio – the first consideration in selecting *adagio* music. A melody which truly breathes is a life-line for the struggling dancer; that is, if it breathes in conjunction with the movement-phrases. For our *adagio*, the melody must, among other things, have a long line; short repetitions will not do at all. This *adagio* is spacious, and the melody must enhance and augment that quality – although it can do so in different ways.

I have chosen three pieces to illustrate what is involved in selecting music for an *adagio*, each of which I have heard accompanists try to use for an *adagio* similar to ours. No trite ballet music; all are beautiful and excellent in their own right. Whether they are suitable for this *adagio* is another matter.

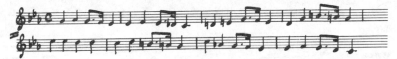

Ex. 22   Chopin, Prelude C minor op. 28, no. 20 (see also Ex. 19, Chapter 6)

This Chopin prelude is a magnificent miniature, laden with mood and feeling. It is also disastrous for our *adagio*. It has a clear melodic line, rich and expressive harmonies, and an unmistakable quality, yet its texture is somewhat dense for our purpose. And, more serious, the rhythm and phrase-structure fight the *adagio* continually.

First of all, the phrases are grouped clearly in fours throughout. A good pianist can, it is true, gather the problematical, small-scale phrases into a larger continuity, but at best there is a somewhat dragging, interrupted feeling (Chopin's aim, of course), the opposite of what this *adagio* needs. The prelude exaggerates nearly all of the dancer's problems described above. It encourages her to make a gap between the completion of the *plié* and the *chassé*, to ignore the kinetic link between the *attitude croisée* and the *promenade*, to lack flow from the *attitude effacée* into the stretch to first *arabesque*, to make a sharp demarcation from one *développé* to the next, and to break the swell from the *écarté devant* into the *rond de jambe*.

All of these are due mainly to the fact that each grouping of fours droops or falls back on itself. This is, musically, highly expressive, but at odds with the curves of the dance-phrases. It is true of every phrase, but is almost ludicrous during the first *arabesque–relevé*. Here, if the dancer followed the energy-flow of the music, she could hardly *relevé* before she was descending.

The overall rhythmic progression, finally, consists of marked and regular quarter-notes (with a dotted pattern on the third beat of each grouping). Effective as this may be musically, in conjunction with the *adagio* it would challenge the finest dancer's sense of flow, co-ordination and projection, for the tempo would have to be funereal, to allow time for the dancer to feel fully each position, causing the steady, non-subdivided quarter-notes to fall apart. Taking it in hectic double-time, as I have seen some attempt, is *not* the answer. This only creates new, worse phrasing-problems.

All of these discrepancies between movement and music stem essentially from differences in the disposition of energy in each. These can be diagrammed, comparatively, as crescendos and diminuendos of energy. Viewing these as shapes may make my point clearer:

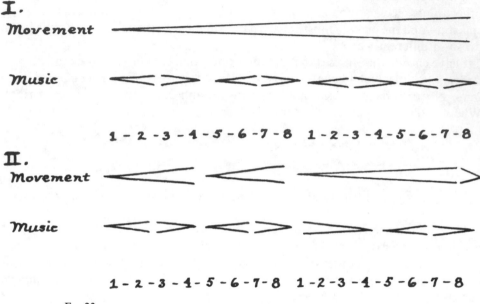

Ex. 23

The only point where the energy-flows are harmonious is at the very end, and this is a bit late to repair the damage.

Music of a very different nature should be examined now: the slow movement from Beethoven's 'Pathétique' Sonata. On the surface, this seems far superior for our purpose to the Chopin, which it is (certainly a teacher who has just spent several minutes trying to get something sensible from his accompanist would accept it with relief). Going deeper, however, we can see several things which will present problems for the dancers.

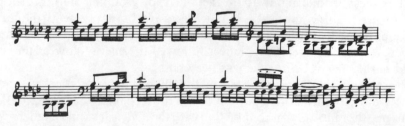

Ex. 24   Beethoven, Sonata No. 8 'Pathétique', second movement (Section II)

Its *quality* is obviously suitable. There is a flowing, *espressivo* feeling, with a singing melodic line and touching harmonies. The texture, although closely woven, is not as dense as in certain other piano works of Beethoven. All of this is fine, but let us see what happens when it accompanies the movement-phrases of our *adagio*.

Things begin well enough. The music suits the *grand plié* (being, in fact, a good choice for the series of *pliés*, *demi* or *grand*, which begins *barre*), and leads the dancer gently into the *chassé* forward. The first problem arises with the *attitude croisée*; here the desired flowering is accompanied by a musical falling-away to a cadential resting point. But much worse is what this does to the *promenade*, which must, as it were, generate itself after the musical cadence rather than be generated by the flow from the *attitude croisée*, which in this case was short-circuited by the inopportune semi-expiration of the music.

The ungenerated *promenade* is problem enough, but here the troubles really begin. The second phrase of the music consists of a melodic see-sawing followed by a touching but, in the circumstances, kinetically dampening step-wise descent to another cadence – this time a full one. While the dancer will be trying to pivot smoothly in *attitude croisée*, the melody is rocking back and forth, and just when she should be stretching impressively and securely into first *arabesque*, then ascending buoyantly into *relevé*, the music is telling her that she probably will not make it. The downward rocking of the first half of this phrase has already intimated that this section is gravitating towards its closure; the last 4 counts confirm this. And, as with the Chopin, it is just when the dancer's body will want to stretch to the fullest, in *relevé*, that the musical line draws in.

The second section of the *adagio*, the third 8-count phrase, has for its music an almost literal repeat, although it seems expanded in scope and has a different accompaniment-pattern. Still, since Section II of the *adagio* initiates fresh movement-shapes and phrase-structures rather than growing without a break from Section I, this is not too dismaying. The music, in fact, is quite harmonious with the first two *développés*, but the problem of the musical see-sawing arises again, this time even more acutely, for it diminishes the dancer's energy-flow into what should be a rich and climactic *développé* into *écarté devant*. Only if this is achieved with the full loveliness one expects at such a moment, and the technical concerns of co-ordination and continuity, will the movement-curve of the last 4 counts be effective. And, of course, one of the dancer's perennial battles will probably be lost here. That is, the dropping of the leg during the *ronde de jambe*. The common tendency is to start high and then swoop round in an ever-dropping line. The music, with its feeling of drawing in, will tend to encourage this misconception, but the damage was actually done earlier, during the *développé écarté devant*. A dancer who achieves a full, alive extension here is far less likely to drop the leg in *rond de jambe*. Music, therefore, is needed which inspires her to a crescendo of energy from counts 1 through 6 rather than a diminishing. The *attitude croisée derrière* will, of course, profit enormously from such a crescendo, and achieve a fruition which irradiates the entire *adagio* up to this point and gives meaning to the tapering-off of the *attitude grecque*. All of this will be difficult to achieve with the Beethoven music.

Here we should again compare the crescendos and diminuendos of energy within the phrases of the movement and the music:

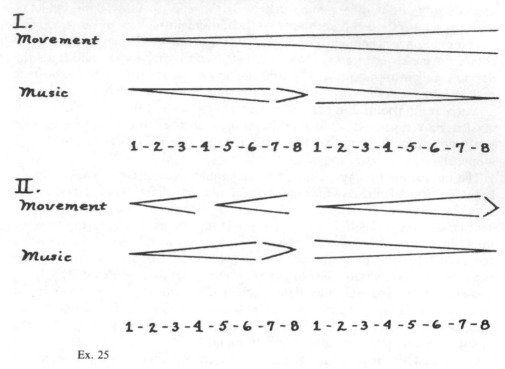

Ex. 25

Despite the satisfactory over-all quality of this music, the dancers will find that, though they may not analyze the details, the performance of the *adagio* to this music will be, somehow, *un*satisfactory. The very things which they are working for technically will be made more difficult, and the desired flow of line and energy will be foiled continually. An *adagio* is never easy, but it should not be made unnecessarily hard and awkward by the music. Much of the bafflement and frustration which dancers often feel after the *adagio* is caused by music which is not right – but is not wrong enough to be obvious and lead the teacher to stop proceedings and request another piece.

The reader may be wondering if *anything* will prove suitable. Let us now try the *grand adage* from Act 2 of *Swan Lake*.

Ex. 26   Tchaikovsky, *Swan Lake*, Act II, *pas de deux* (see also Ex. 20 Chaper 6)

I should mention here that this music illustrates one of the compromises which can bedevil the accompanist. As I have said, only in ballet choreography can the music and the movement be perfectly harmonious. The choreographer has time to shape and alter the movement where he wishes. In class, excepting very lucky or expert choices of music, somewhere in the combination a problem or a discrepancy is bound to occur. Here the moment of compromise is at the very end. Since, however, the rest of the music is, as we shall see, so suited to the *adagio* and so helpful in aiding the technical and interpretative problems of the dancers, it seems to me to be a good subject for analysis despite its one weak area. We will, therefore, accept this just as we might have to in the studio.

The melodic line is outstandingly long and sustained (played by the violin in the orchestral original), but, even better, it is particularly harmonious with the movement-phrases. The chords underlying it move neither sluggishly nor too quickly, but in a manner which aids the flow of line throughout. The harmonic tensions and releases and arrival-points assist the gentle fluctuations of the melody, giving an added sense of motion, one of Tchaikovsky's greatest attributes as a ballet composer. Note, for instance, the conjunction of mild dissonances and active inversions with important moments in the first two dance phrases. These contribute to the forward impulse necessary for a proper kinetic flow.

The rhythm of this music differs from that of our first two choices, both of which were duple. Here, the rounded triple subdivision creates another sort of quality, and is more likely to induce a flow and use of space in refractory muscles and to minimize muscular tension. The texture is, in addition, exceptionally transparent and airy.

As a result of these musical qualities, the dancer who is responsive and uses them as a guide to style, phrasing and attack will find that she needs roughly 50% less energy and force than with the Chopin, and considerably less than with the Beethoven. This is not because the Tchaikovsky music mimics each movement, going up or down as the leg and body do, but because it parallels the ebb and flow of energy consistently.

From the opening *plié* onwards, it encourages a continuity and growth. The end of the *plié* and the *chassé* are bridged smoothly and a musical expansion accompanies the dancer's expansion into the *attitude croisée* and fosters a link between this and the beginning of the *promenade*. Then, the feeling of suspension at counts 3 and 4 of the second phrase leads to a smooth transition and flowering into the stretch to first *arabesque*. The melodic curve which follows, moreover, discourages a forced, hard *relevé* detached from the previous movement – a common transgression – and instead suggests a smooth supple pressing away from the floor. The latter, of course, assuming good placement and alignment, is far more likely to lead to a successful and fully realized *relevé*.

At this point, count 8 of the second phrase, the music reaches a breath – a momentary arrival from its sustained, forward-moving journey. But at the same time there is a feeling of expectancy, which is just what we want for the coming series of *développés*. Thus, at the same time that the overall curve of this section is fulfilled, it links smoothly with the next 16-count section. The first *développé* will, therefore, have quite a different sense of direction with this music than with the Chopin or Beethoven pieces, each of which projects other sensations of motion altogether. And, not only does this music contain the 4-count waves of the first two *développés*, but with the third *développé*, into *écarté devant*, it continues on past the fourth count into a longer phrase, just as the movement does. In this way, the music bridges the potential gap or static moment between the completion of this *développé* and the *rond de jambe*.

In addition, as the music reaches its climactic point – the high B flat towards which it has been spinning out since the very beginning – it has the capacity to carry the dancer's extended leg through space into a strong and beautiful position from which it will seem almost to float without conscious effort into the *rond de jambe*. Such fluidity of phrasing is a far cry from the thoughtless puncturing of the air which often passes for a *développé*, or the coma which afflicts so many legs at moments like the one between the extension and the *rond de jambe* (the blame for these peculiarities is usually shared by the dancer and the music she is hearing).

At this point we reach the musical compromise. The last phrase does not contain the 8 counts of the others. With a differently designed *adagio* this might render the entire piece unusable. Fortunately, in our *adagio*, the *rond de jambe* will not suffer, coinciding as it does with the high B flat, and the final 3 counts of the movement proceed continuously from this in a concluding curve. The *attitude grecque*, moreover, is an inward-drawing curve which tapers off gracefully, rather than a final blaze of glory. In such a case, many teachers, happy with the over-all excellence of the music, might accept a skillful extension of the short musical phrase. (It ends on an imperfect cadence while, ideally, a piece should close with a full tonal cadence at a combination's end – but a good musician can make other types reasonably convincing.)

A glance now at the increase and decrease of energy throughout the *Swan Lake* excerpt will reveal how much better it is suited to the energy-flow of our *adagio* than are the first two choices:

I.

Movement

Music

1 - 2 - 3 - 4 - 5 - 6 - 7 - 8   1 - 2 - 3 - 4 - 5 - 6 - 7 - 8

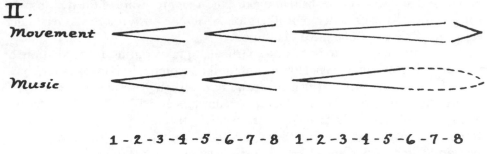

1 - 2 - 3 - 4 - 5 - 6 - 7 - 8   1 - 2 - 3 - 4 - 5 - 6 - 7 - 8

Ex. 27

Subtle fluctuations, naturally, occur within these. Counts 1–4 of the second musical phrase, for instance, have a melodic down-curve – but the underlying expansion and forward-moving energy are maintained by the harmonies and the descending bass-line. The three 4-count crescendos (the third being extended into an 8-count phrase), also, are not undeviating; the second 4-count wave is slightly more intense than the first, and the third wave – which is elongated – is more intense than the second (this should be true also of the dance-phrases).

This matter of energy-flow and fluctuation is the rebuttal to those who can think only of 'ups and downs'. It is the disposition of musical energy in a phrase or section, including harmonies and rhythmic patterns – rather than the rise and fall of melodic line alone – which determines whether or not a piece is suitable for a combination (or for choreography). And, as I have said, for particular reasons this is perhaps more important during *adagio* work than at any other time in class.

I have tried to show clearly the factors which determine the selection of music for a combination. To do so, I needed to analyze many aspects of music and movement in detail. Obviously no one's brain could – or should – function in this way throughout class. (Some combinations, however, especially complex *adagios* and bravura jumping combinations across the floor, demand as much thought as time permits). But whether conscious analysis is applied or not, important questions must be answered. In the experienced accompanists this process can be intuitive, almost instantaneous, but it is not so simple for the novice, who certainly will have to consider these questions during class (as quickly as possible) and through some homework.

At this point I must stress yet again that there is never just one 'correct' choice. It is always a good sign for the accompanist not to feel, somewhat desperately, that her selection is the sole possibility but to know that she can immediately produce another piece if the teacher rejects her first choice.

For this and other reasons, therefore, I say again that the foregoing evaluations are in no way intended as definitive. Their purpose was to show what goes into making choices of music in class, in a way which could be applied in diverse circumstances, by accompanists very different in background and temperament from myself. But, ultimately, my own judgement and conditioning by various teachers are bound to affect my approach and views. My hope is that these analyses will save other accompanists much of my own early insecurity and floundering about, and at the same time help to make dancers more aware of the reasons why some music is so much better than others for an exercise – why it seems so very much easier to perform to one piece than another.

The teacher may wish to bring out a particular quality during a combination, or do something 'different'. What this means for the accompanist is that she *must* have a varied repertoire upon which to draw. For, although several pieces may be theoretically possible, the *immediate* circumstances which I have described elsewhere will narrow the field. The narrower it is, the more pieces she must know. If the accompanist can muster only types A and B, the teacher will invariably – and perhaps irritably – demand C or D. What a relief for everyone if she also has C and D, plus E, F, G, H and I on tap.

The question, of course, is *how*.

III. Categories

A vast repertoire awaits discovery. As I have said, in my early accompanying days I floundered about, not knowing where to look, for I knew nothing whatsoever about ballet. Whatever suitable pieces I did happen to play were a matter of pure luck. Gradually, as my appalling ignorance diminished, more and more sources occurred to me, until I found I was dipping into everything from the standard piano literature to obscure chamber music. Some categories were more productive than others, but every one contained some treasures.

I have put them into what I found to be their increasing order of value. Other accompanists may, of course, differ, depending partly on the types of teachers for whom they play.

1. Band music
2. 'Early' music
3. Popular music
4. Chamber music
5. Lieder
6. Piano literature
7. Opera arias
8. Ballet music
9. Orchestral repertoire

1. Band music

Restricted as this category may seem, it is a source of good, strong 2/4s and 4/4s, which are particularly suitable for men's class, but can also be used sparingly for mixed class. Marches have drive and vigor, which can be welcome when energy and spirits flag. They also, for some reason, often seem to amuse the class. One source which I found useful is the collection of recordings by the Scots Guard Regimental Band and Massed Pipers (some of the bagpipe selections are delightful for combinations with small beats, and for point class). As with some of the other categories, the accompanist needs transcriptions or a good ear and memory (see specific comments in relevant items below, and Section IV).

2. 'Early' music

Until recently this music, which covers about six centuries, was the grab-bag known as 'pre-Bach music'. Since it ranges from Medieval, through Renaissance, to early Baroque styles, it contains a great variety of sounds: simple, lilting Medieval and Renaissance songs and dances; powerful and lyrical Renaissance and Elizabethan, and Early Baroque dance suites; and excerpts from Early Baroque oratorios – all these offer marvelous music, although a certain amount of skill is needed to transcribe it gracefully for the piano. Definitely not an all-purpose type of music for class, it still provides fresh and lively moments to sprinkle here and there with discretion.

3. Popular Music; Rock; Folk

Not all teachers care for this sort of thing; some consider it too trivial for such a lofty art as ballet. But remember that originally all dance music was 'popular' music, and the segregation into popular and serious (i.e. 'classical') music is an extremely recent development, only becoming fully crystallized in the eighteenth century when such composers as Haydn and Mozart made the use of popular, or folk tunes and dances 'respectable' in symphonic works, despite their now lowly status. From then on, even though composers continued to incorporate popular tunes into large-scale masterworks, they remained something separate. Now, composers such as Reich, Riley and Glass are attempting to demolish the barriers which divide serious and popular music.

Since dancers generally tend to be less snobbish and doctrinaire about the origins and status of music, not only have some exciting, successful ballets been created to the various branches of popular music, but many dancers welcome its use in class. One qualification, however; when it is played with the square, dead rhythm characteristic of many 'classical' musicians who attempt popular music, the effect is disastrous. In no music is a strong rhythmic sense and flexible *rubato* more necessary. I might add that I have never known a pianist who played popular music well not have a rhythmic aliveness far above average when playing the 'serious' repertoire.

Popular music of the nineteenth and early twentieth centuries is, of course, a bit more respectable than that of our own time. Stephen Foster, Louis Gottschalk and others of this breed provide sweet sentimental tunes with strong melodic lines or jazzy, syncopated rhythms not usually found in their more hallowed contemporaries.

Here again, as with the first and second categories, do not over-use; a little can be delectable, but too much can be tiresome. Another qualification: popular music of the Kern Porter variety seems less successful than other types. It is, indeed, sometimes relied upon – in desperation? – by inexperienced accompanists. Traditional folk music, rock and some jazz, on the other hand, have a strength and muscularity which much show-music, for a number of reasons, lacks.

4. Chamber music

This is a wonderful but vexing area of music to investigate. The string quartets of Haydn, Mozart, Schubert, Beethoven, Debussy, Ravel and others, contain lovely, usable music. There is a wealth of music, also, for mixed chamber groups: quintets, septets, sextets, octets, etc. The main problem is that much chamber music tends to be highly contrapuntal. Chamber ensembles cannot produce the gorgeous sonorities and weight of a full orchestra, and must rely instead on other means for sustaining interest. The intimate interplay between different voices, or what is often called the dialogue – so much a part of this music – is essentially linear, or polyphonic, rather than harmonic. This results in asymmetrical phrases, overlapping voices, strict canons and fugues – all problematical for ballet class. This interplay of voices is also often difficult to encompass within two hands on the keyboard. Despite these frequent hurdles, however, there are often sections which are homophonic and more symmetrical. Learning this music from the printed page requires some skill in score-reading, which will be discussed in Chapter 12.

5. Song

The collections of art-songs, called lieder when they are of German origin, contain an amazing variety of moods and styles. Hundreds of songs exist by Schubert, Hugo Wolf, Schumann, Brahms, Debussy and Vaughan Williams, to name only a few composers. Some are from song-cycles; others are individual miniatures. Here you will find strong, or infectious and melodious *allegros*, delicate *allegrettos*, lyrical and poignant *andantes* and *adagios*.

A strong melodic line is this category's strongest asset, but songs are also frequently distinguished by a highly dramatic theatrical quality. Many of the finest have, in fact, been termed operas in miniature. (Be sure to bring out the melodies clearly amid what can at times be rather complex accompaniments.)

The snag here, which unfortunately makes many songs unusable for class, is the irregular phrasing which so often results from the extension or echoing of the symmetrical vocal line by the piano accompaniment (this is, of course, one of the prime beauties of this music – the use of the accompaniment to comment upon or intensify the singer's melodic line and to develop the dramatic content of the words). But a little ingenuity will often enable you to round off phrases gracefully to conform to the symmetrical ones characteristic of most ballet exercises. Some teachers may even be interested in creating dance phrases to match the musical ones if they are not too far from the norm.

6. Piano literature

This is unquestionably a valuable source of music for class, and a seemingly endless one, yet it is unwise to rely too heavily on it. While much is excellent for our purpose, the fact remains that, in addition to the general problems of piano in connection with dance, a large proportion of the piano literature was designed to exploit the special features of the piano as much as possible: its power, density, sonority – all the thunderous harmonies and dazzling figurations which are so overpowering, and such a large part of the piano's popularity with concert audiences.

You must, therefore, pick and choose from the available music, avoiding its more densely figured and harmonically turgid moments. Schumann, Chopin and Ravel wrote for the piano with marvelous clarity. Many sections from the Beethoven sonatas are good – if chosen with care – and some Brahms pieces, including the Handel and Paganini Variations can be used. Large-scale suites such as *Pictures at an Exhibition* and *Carnival of the Animals* contain much variety, suitable for many sorts of combinations.

One tricky area of the literature is, as I have mentioned, the rarefied world of eighteenth-century sonatas and sonatinas. Unlike the piano music of the Romantic period, which was aimed at thrilling large audiences, or moving small, intimate ones, the large proportion of passage-work – the cascades of scales and arpeggios – produces the over-all feeling of preoccupation with the fingers which makes this music, charming as it may be, seem curiously lightweight for much ballet movement. Moments from these pieces can be delightful in class, but only moments – not hours.

Used indiscriminately and to excess, the piano literature can result in a numbing and decidedly unkinetic feeling in the dancers (and you); used with selectivity and care it can bring inspiration and excitement.

7. Opera arias

A rich category, ranging from Monteverdi's theatrical works, through Mozart, Gluck and Berlioz, and all the familiar nineteenth-century favorites, plus lesser-known delights like Bizet's *Pearl Fishers*, to parts of twentieth-century operas. Not only does opera possess beautiful melodies, it has a physicality and scope. Opera and ballet, were, from their earliest history, intimately associated, and despite their separation in the mid-nineteenth century – resulting in more specialized development of each – they share an aura.

Opera's lighter side exists in the operettas of Offenbach and Gilbert and Sullivan. While the former is inextricably linked to ballet through frequent use of his music by choreographers, the latter are often overlooked by ballet accompanists. This is a pity, for this music has a vivacity and gaiety, bubbling over with good spirits. The patter songs are excellent for *allegro* work, and there are many charming *allegrettos* which serve well for point class. Rossini, in his comic operas, has a similar ebullience (his more serious operatic efforts are also worth investigating).

The piano vocal score of an opera will present the same problem as do songs, perhaps even more so. The orchestral reduction is often fuller than a song accompaniment, so that there are more notes and patterns to cope with while bringing out the melodic line clearly.

8. Ballet music

It often seems that this is what is heard 99% of the time in ballet studios everywhere, but perhaps that is only because so much of it is so maddeningly familiar. I have repeatedly cited the weaknesses of nineteenth-century 'ballet music'; yet another shortcoming of this music, used for class, is the greyness of sound which results from its being played on the piano. The lack of intrinsic musical value is not quite so apparent when these scores are heard orchestrated. The instrumental colors and power of a full orchestra lend a certain amount of vitality and interest, whereas on the piano the bare bones of their triteness and one-dimensionality are cruelly exposed. This music demands a great deal of pianistic imagination and rhythmic skill from the accompanist.

Still, its strength lies in the fact that many ballets (or excerpts) from this tradition continue to give pleasure to audiences and in the viewer's or dancer's mind they are gratifyingly linked to their music. Even though the waltz from the popular *Don Quixote pas de deux*, for instance, closely resembles at least two other equally banal waltzes by its composer, Minkus, it conjures up excitement and glamor, and revives memories of past performances. Because of this associative power, even the most offensive (to the musician) ballet music can be welcome in the studio. Many dancers, and teachers, get a strong lift from the sound of a familiar old chestnut.

Also, despite their general mediocrity, some do possess moments which are genuinely attractive or exciting in which the composer comes to life, however briefly.

In another realm entirely, far removed from the rut of Minkus, Pugni, Drigo *et al.*, lies the inventiveness, charm and beauty found in ballet scores by Delibes, Glazunov and, above all, Tchaikovsky. These are bursting with music for class. Tchaikovsky, in fact, challenges the restriction of not playing too many pieces of the same type for class; his ballet scores possess such exuberance, vitality, poetry and variety that even over-reliance on them evades monotony. One of the miracles of music is the success with which he transcended an intense morbidity and negativity to produce what many consider the finest ballet music ever written. The *allegros*, waltzes, *adagios*, character variations – each is the balletic epitome of its type, and has never been surpassed. All contain a miraculous kinetic feeling which defies analysis. Adrian Stokes gives clues to this when he writes, 'Tchaikovsky's ballet music seems firm yet crisp. It is the opposite of music that seems moist. A romantic haze hovers near, but it is a haze that obscures nothing'.[6] Or, put as succinctly as possible, 'ballon is forever enshrined in this music'.[7] Its great value for class, where we wish to encourage the dancers to develop style and phrasing within the daily routine, lies in the fact that, as Haskell once said, not only is his music an inspiration to the dancer and his melodies of great beauty in themselves, they are also a complete guide to style and attack. Working within the rather moribund rhythmic conventions of the nineteenth century, when rhythmic inventiveness was largely sacrificed to melodic and harmonic lushness, Tchaikovsky uses syncopation and unusual phrasing in a fresh and galvanizing way.

Of twentieth century ballet composers, Prokofiev, perhaps, comes closest in approach to Tchaikovsky, although he lacks Tchaikovsky's consistency and all-pervading sense of *ballon*. Still, *Cinderella* and *Romeo and Juliet* contain excellent music for class, which is more symmetrical in phrasing than most contemporary ballet music. Excerpts from Stravinsky's early ballet scores, with their Slavic impressionism, are good (although they may need a bit of imaginative adjustment of irregular phrases).

On days when you are not at your most alert or creative, you will be safe if you rely on the category of ballet music, but otherwise, it is preferable to balance it with music from the other categories discussed here.

9. Orchestral repertoire

Here we have a huge treasurehouse with almost inexhaustible riches. These range from Bach's orchestral suites and Brandenburg Concertos, Handel's *Water Music* and *Royal . Fireworks Music*, countless short excerpts from eighteenth- and nineteenth-century symphonies by Haydn, Mozart, Beethoven, Schubert, Schumann, Berlioz and Brahms, to snippets from orchestral music of the first half of the twentieth century by Bartók, Hindemith, Copland, Shostakovitch, Leonard Bernstein and others. (Even though most successful symphonies are unsuitable in their entirety for ballets, many excerpts from them work well in class, containing quite danceable sections.)

In addition to symphonies and other works which emphasize form, the orchestral repertoire abounds in the looser-structured symphonic poems: Liszt, Chausson, Franck, Berlioz, Tchaikovsky, Mussorgsky and Rimsky-Korsakov are particularly good sources. There is exciting fast music and melodically florid, slow music, permeated by the drama and color which is so suitable for dance movement.

Most of the standard orchestral repertoire is available in transcription for piano solo or duet, but here again, one should enrich the printed page through frequent listening to the original scoring. This will help you to absorb the music in all its rich instrumental variety rather than to view it only in the pianistic (dis)guise of the transcription. Any transcription is, at best, an approximation or sketch, which inevitably must distort the original to some degree. A piano reduction *reduces*; certain aspects of the music dwindle and disappear at the same time as the music is made manageable for two or four hands at the piano. Familiarity with the orchestral version will give your performance flexibility and imagination (see also Chapter 12).

These nine categories of music are the ones which I have found fruitful. An ever-shifting balance of them has, in my experience, been the best solution to the challenge of providing music day after day, hour after hour, for classes. The dancers benefit in many ways from the variety, and the accompanist avoids the occupational hazard of becoming a musical automaton through habitual reliance on a limited, familiar repertoire.

IV. Sources

How does one gain access to all this music? I have used four main sources:

1. Music shops and libraries
2. Radio programs and recordings
3. Concert and ballet performances
4. Visits to other ballet classes

1. Music shops and libraries

Since no one wishes to spend most of her salary on expensive music, which may prove unusable, the music library is a boon. Those in large towns and cities will offer more scope, but many smaller libraries will try to obtain material for you if they do not have it. Since, however, you have at least nine categories of music to investigate, you may be surprised at what awaits you in even modest libraries.

For those with a little spending money, the second-hand bins of music shops are helpful, but the wisest course is to buy only music which you already know, from the following three sources, to be good for class use.

2. Radio programs and recordings

Here are my favorite and most reliable sources for an ever-growing repertoire. Having heard a piece which might be useful for class you can either buy it, or borrow it from a library or a fellow musician. Some of you may be sufficiently skilled at memorizing music that you can pick up a piece at one hearing on the radio. Records allow you to repeat it as many times as necessary (see Chapter 9 for techniques of memorization). Even if you have difficulty in doing this, radio and records are valuable, both for discovering possibilities without tedious searches through stacks of music and for acquainting you with the original sounds of music not written for solo piano.

3. Concert and ballet performances

Preferable in one way to radio and records is exposure to live music. The best modern reproduction cannot give you the excitement of hearing music in a concert hall or theater. There is a physicality that no recording will ever achieve, which comes from the presence of the performers, the sight of bow upon strings and fingers upon valves, and that sense of participation and feedback which affects both musicians and audience.

An added dimension in the ballet theater is, of course, the choreography. You will see the basic vocabulary of ballet steps to many different types of music. This will increase your knowledge and scope for choosing music for class, and, most important, it will transform your performance of the standard ballet excerpts in class. You may have played music from *Coppélia*, *Sleeping Beauty* or *Giselle* from piano transcriptions (or music originally written for piano, like the score for *Les Sylphides*), but after hearing it in conjunction with movement you should never again play it in quite the same way. Not only will the orchestral colors alter your view of the music, the magic and glamor of its theatrical setting will color your attitude toward even the most familiar ballet music which you may have been mechanically thumping out in class. To know ballet and its music only in the context of the studio is like reading only the introduction to a book.

4. Visits to other ballet classes

Watching other accompanists in action can be most illuminating. Since we are all, to some degree, bounded by our temperaments, imagination and knowledge, it is good to see what someone else brings to a shared endeavor. You may be astonished by music that another accompanist chooses for certain steps – music which never occurred to you as remotely suitable. Intriguing, also, are the possible variations in performance by other pianists of music which you use. You may discover new aspects to a piece, which had formerly eluded you. You may also, on the negative side, see weaknesses both in selection of music and in performance; faults which might turn out to be ones you share. Observing the accompanist working with the class gives you a perspective and objectivity which is not attainable when you yourself are at the keyboard. (Be careful, however, not to indulge in an orgy of comparison, whether in your favor or to your detriment.)

Ask yourself what it is that makes her choices good or bad. Far more can be learned in this way than by playing blindly through a dozen classes. You can develop analytical and artistic powers which might otherwise remain dormant. If you think the choices good, ask the pianist after class to identify unfamiliar ones for you – an easy way to add to your repertoire.

These, then, are the categories of music and the means of access to them which gradually enabled me to escape my early prison of a pathetically limited balletic repertoire. Different accompanists will favor and emphasize different music. Temperament and teachers, as I have said, play a large part in musical choices. The main thing is to be adventurous. Taking some chances, rather than falling comfortably into a predictable pattern, will keep you ever-expanding. Always try out one or two new pieces during a class, if possible. This will prevent you from falling into a state of inertia. Occasional disasters will not matter if the teacher and dancers know from experience that you are alert and involved, and the successful fresh sounds that you introduce will make up for lapses.

V. Memorization

You may amass the largest repertoire in the annals of ballet accompanying, but if you are forced to carry piles of music to class in order to utilize it, our main purpose is defeated. You would be better off playing a handful of memorized pieces over and over. No teacher can spare time for the pianist to hunt frantically through mountains of pieces for an elusive page. No dancer enjoys standing around while her muscles grow cold. The accompanist, moreover, cannot continually divert her attention in this way and, at the same time, be a participant. Everyone's concentration will suffer, the pace of the class will fall apart, and you will be an outsider. A panicky, disorganized feeling is created by a pianist who turns into a burrowing mole every few minutes. One who, in contrast, always has *something* – no matter if it is occasionally a bit ordinary – at her fingertips helps to knit the class together and to furnish a musical floor free from splinters and holes.

Thus, memorization is as much a part of your equipment as a varied repertoire and lively performance of it. Since memorizing is intimately linked to performance (in both music and dance), being more a kinetic process than a mental one, I shall discuss the approaches which I have found most helpful in the next chapter.

We have now, in fact, reached the point at which the most crucial and exciting aspect of accompanying thrusts itself upon us – how to bring music to life in connection with movement.

9   Performance: musician and dancer

I am no great games player, but I feel a kinship with tennis champions. Perhaps I ought to feel more kinship with ballet dancers, for there is a powerful and important element of gesture, mime, and acting in piano playing.

Sidney Harrison, *The Young Person's Guide to Playing the Piano*, 1966

AFTER CLASS ONE DAY, during a discussion of music, a ballet student who intended to teach complained about the repertoire of the average ballet accompanist. In answer, Antony Tudor said, 'It is not so much *what* is played as *how* it is played.' Unquestionably true, for the most inspired choice of music played without a sense of rhythm and style will be enervating, while the tritest Old Favorite played with spirit and conviction can be electrifying. Tudor's statement should, of course, be taken with a grain of salt. He is notorious for his demands on accompanists' repertoires. But certainly the performance is the final link in the chain composed of interest, knowledge, involvement, empathy with the dancers and perceptive choice of music.

Performance in class is a threefold activity. The pianist must cope with the nature of the piano – its potential drawbacks and its splendid yet dangerous sonority; she must play the music well; and she must approach the music in the spirit of the dance. The class pianist is not a solo performer but a member of an ensemble. Just as a violinist in a string quartet or an oboeist in an orchestra is not autonomous, so the accompanist is not. Despite the common phrase, 'play for class', she actually plays *with* the class – or within, in the sense of being part of an ensemble of performers. The solo artist, furthermore, who plays 'for' an audience, manifests individuality within the frame of the music, but the ballet pianist must *in addition* manifest it within the meaning of the movement. I believe that the understanding of playing for movement – the solution of such problems as attack, density, rhythm, among others, as part of a ballet ensemble – will spill over into other areas of performance and benefit the pianist in any performing situation, whether on, say, the recital stage, as a soloist in a concerto, or when playing for an amateur opera group.

I. The piano as an instrument for class

The piano is by far the most popular solo instrument with audiences, despite certain inherent defects as a tonal medium (or perhaps, in many cases, because of them). I struggled with these, unsuccessfully, as a student, and only learned to cope with them during years of ballet accompanying.

As I have stated, the violin was for long the traditional instrument in ballet class, played by the *maître de ballet*. By the early twentieth century the piano had become

201

predominant. It can, of course, encompass a far wider range of *notes* than the violin, but unfortunately its *expressive* range is all too limited compared to this and other popular solo instruments such as flute, oboe, clarinet, cello and guitar which I have heard played in dance classes to great effect.

But what *are* the defects of the piano, and why is it so problematical as an accompanying instrument for dance?

One writer, who loves the piano enough to have devoted an entire book to performance on it, writes, 'Its chief deficiency is in tone, it has a lack of expressiveness which sometimes makes it an exasperating instrument to play . . . In the second half of this century, a new type of piano, and, consequently, pianist, has emerged. No longer is there respect for quality of touch, because on this new piano it cannot be cultivated.' This passage is part of a general lamentation over the decline of sensitivity and tonal expressiveness of the piano which was accompanied by an increase of power and sonority – as Cooper says, 'quantity rather than quality'.[1] Taylor warns against 'that kind of athleticism which the modern grand piano encourages'.[2] I know many dedicated pianists who admit the often vexing nature of their chosen medium. As several writers have noted, the phenomenal Glenn Gould considered the piano an extremely limited instrument, and his habitual humming and singing – and conducting, if one hand was free – vividly demonstrated his frustration. George Bernard Shaw damned it as 'this triumph of ironmongery'. Of course, countless others can find no fault with the piano and consider it supreme.

But whether pianists wish to admit it or not, their careers involve a continuing struggle against the intractability of the piano. It is hardly surprising, therefore, that so many try to turn inherent pitfalls into strengths by exaggerating them. Sonority, power, and a large note-compass are the potential glories of the piano at the same time as proving destructive of musical values. Used sensitively and appropriately they are magnificent; mis- or over-used they make one's head ache.

Density

The main problem could be called over-crowded aural space. This is, unfortunately, most often the case just when the pianist is most enjoying (expressing) herself. Those mountains of sound, those avalanches of notes! Wonderful as exhibition or catharsis, but overwhelming to the more musical in the audience – and certainly a bit daunting for dancers.

We have, of course, the other extreme, in which the pianist recoils tastefully from all that vulgar power and concentrates instead on producing sonorities which are dainty tinkles, little icicles of sound. The piano can be very effective played in this manner, but more often than not the result is lifeless – a peculiar sort of density. To play well (and certainly to play well for dance) you want instead an openness, which dancers call 'breath'. This musical breath not only improves the musical performance, it also helps the dancer to develop that essential: *ballon*. And herein lies another problem.

Ballon and breath

A basic conflict exists: the piano's mechanism involves striking rather than breathing yet every ballet teacher hopes for a sense of *ballon* from his pianist. Since ballet's very soul *is* – more than elegance of line, technical facility or histrionic ability – the quality of *ballon*, the accompanist who lacks it will suffocate the movement. It depends on *breath*, and breath is smothered by density: the main characteristic of the pianist without *ballon*.

The literal translation of *ballon* is 'balloon'; thus it should be clear why this term is associated by dancers with buoyancy, elasticity, resilience and a defiance of gravity. Not the same thing as elevation, it contributes importantly to it, for they are interdependent, and 'one is not much good without the other'.[3] *Ballon* is a physical necessity, for without it the dancer's muscles become shortened and cramped, the legs and feet do not develop properly and the body is continually subjected to jars and thuds from the inelastic use of the muscles. It should be evident why the accompanist needs to encourage *ballon* in the dancer, and also needs it herself, in the sense that she should play with elasticity rather than rigidity, buoyancy rather than pedantry, breath rather than density. This breath is linked with *ballon* both figuratively and literally.

Now, in order to avoid the monotonous droning of the hack-accompanist, many teachers ask their pianists to 'play like a concert pianist'. This can be disastrous. What they *want* is to avoid lack-luster or heavy-handed unmusical playing. What they probably will *get* is the *density* of the average recitalist. Dense playing means playing which leaves no room for anything else, but, apart from the physical density of notes crowded together, there is another kind of density. This is related to the peculiar isolation of the narrower concert artist, and could be described as *mental* or psychological density, a density of concentration. In a sense, this type of performer is communing with herself and with the music and, almost incidentally, with the audience. The ballet accompanist does not commune; she communicates and participates, functionally, in a group activity.

When psychological density manifests itself in the ballet pianist, it certainly excludes the dancers, at times almost to the point of obliterating them. A change is obviously necessary, not only in attitude (see Chapter 4), but in approach to playing. Breath and *ballon*, in musical as in dance performance, require air, or room in which the music and movement can *breathe*. The pianist's physical approach to playing may, however, make this impossible to achieve. For one thing, the notes produced by the fingers cannot be effective if they are aimed into the depths of the piano. They must, in various ways, project – go outward into the surrounding space. Since the mechanism of the piano actually encourages the former, you must find ways in which to circumvent this dive-bomber approach. Many accompanists, dimly aware of the need for *ballon* and the antithetical nature of the piano, resort to futile attempts to achieve it. They, instead, end up trying to get the dancers into the air through brute force.

One of the most common, and gruesome, resorts is the striking of a heavy arpeggio in the bass, on the first beat of each measure. Not only does this disorganize the overall phrasing, it leads to irregularities in the pulse and confusion in the dancers. Worse, however; this sound is utterly inimical to *ballon* because of its appalling density. Yet the unrhythmical pianist habitually resorts to it, or other musical eccentricities. In such cases, the result is more destructive to movement (not to mention music) than if the pianist were to play with a total lack of dynamism.

We must, therefore, proceed from the piano *per se* to the problems of attack, tone color and tone production by the pianist. These, in a sense, underlie the broader aspects of performance such as phrasing, dynamics and style.

II. Tone production, tone color and attack

The pianist, unlike the performer on a wind or string instrument, or the singer, cannot control tone quality and production beyond a minimal point. This is because the pianist's contact with the actual means of tone-production is indirect. 'In order', writes Abby Whiteside, 'to influence tone quality in an instrument the performer's tone-producing energy must contact the vibrator which produces the pitch. In the case of the piano, a felt hammer hits a string – the vibrator. The performer applies his power to a key. The key action trips the hammer which strikes the string. The performer can only make the hammer hit with greater or less force.'[4] Thus, the *illusion* of tone control conveyed by a good pianist comes in reality from rhythm and dynamics. Wind and string instrumental playing combines these with an inherently greater range of tone production and, thus, color. It is for this reason that they are more 'expressive' than the piano. This is not a subjective judgment but an acoustical one.

Pianists and audiences alike are besotted with the idea of 'touch'. 'He has such a beautiful touch' – the ultimate praise. But this concept is both inaccurate and confusing, for

Is the pianist correct who thinks that he can vary the timbre of a single tone by his 'touch'? He is wrong. All he can do is depress the key at a certain speed, thereby regulating the loudness. No pressing or wriggling can possibly influence the overtone constellation, because, even at the moment of impact, the player is totally out of touch with the string. The only variable at his disposal is the speed of his finger, hence the velocity of the hammer, hence the loudness of the tone. Any lingering illusions have been removed by experiments at the University of Pennsylvania in which single tones were first played by a famous pianist and then duplicated by a cushioned weight falling on a key. No difference could be heard.[5]

The *seeming* control over tone-color through touch actually begins when consecutive notes are played. As Levarie and Levy state, 'the "singing *legato*" melody is the result of the performer's carefully holding over one tone to the next while sensitively diversifying the successive dynamic levels'.[6] They cite what they term tangential qualifications such as the use of pedals, but consider these minor points. Like Miss Whiteside, they consider rhythm and dynamics to be the originators of what is thought of as touch, tone-color or timbre. Now, rhythm and dynamics are dependent upon the attack: the different ways in which the keys are activated. This attack is partly a matter of speed, as Levarie and Levy point out, but it could also be described as a kinetic event.

Attack (a problematical term)

Although the pianist's fingers descend, in a vertical action, the muscular *feeling* should not be onto the keyboard or into the interior of the piano. Playing onto or into the piano denies space and creates a cramped, bounded world; playing out or away from it enlarges the apparent space and creates buoyancy and rhythmic aliveness. The difference can, perhaps, be seen particularly clearly in dance – for what I am pointing to is in many ways related to the dancer's *plié* action. All dance movements are connected, in varying ways and degrees, by the *plié*. *Plier* means, literally, to bend, but it is its functional meaning which concerns us here. Joan Lawson describes the *plié* as a mainspring, and writes, 'when correctly used in relation to the action of the foot help[s] to control, amongst other things, the take-off, height and landing of a jump, the speed of a *pirouette*, and the staccato or legato quality of many different movements'.[7] Is the connection between *plié* in the dancer and the muscular activity of the pianist clear?

With both dancer and pianist, the muscular activity in relation to their respective performance-surfaces is either one involving *impact* or one involving *resilience*. Everything depends on which it is. The pianist wants, for instance, powerful resonance. What the average player produces, however, is ferocity, a literal attack on the keyboard – what Cooper describes as 'slaughtering the piano as though they hated its inside', their big playing 'smashing down from above the keys'.[8] This is the impact of a collision. (My own attack, during our early days, led Tudor to inquire pointedly whether my fingers were made of steel or flesh and bone.)

Similarly, the misguided dancer behaves as if she hated the floor – or were afraid of it. Never utilizing it as a source of action, she teeters across it or thuds onto it. Again, we have impact as opposed to resilience. And if, in class, the dancer and the pianist hear and see each other performing in this manner, they will reinforce and magnify one another's faults.

I have used the terms 'resonance' and 'resilience'. Perhaps it would be illuminating if I transposed their normal usage. One conceives of a good dancer as a master of resilience, or, as the dictionary defines it: 'resile (of elastic bodies) rebound, resume shape and size after stretching or compression; have or show elasticity or buoyancy or recuperative power. Hence *resilience*'. A good pianist commands, on the other hand, varieties of *resonance* from her instrument. Resonant is defined as 'echoing, resounding, continuing to sound, reinforced or prolonged by vibration . . .' Now, good dancing could be said, metaphorically, to possess resonance – to echo within the visual space, to resound, rather than to give the effect of ceasing from moment to moment. In the same way, good playing could be described as rebounding or showing elasticity – to be a muscular, bodily experience rather than the more common digital one. And both dancer and musician might ponder the implications of Antoinette Sibley's admiring observation: 'Baryshnikov uses the air just like most of us use the floor' – applying it to the pianist by substituting *aural space* for 'air' and *keyboard* for 'floor'.

Attack and personality

Just as pianists have characteristic ways of playing, each dancer has an innate approach to movement. The two most basic categories could be described as sustained and lyrical, or sharp and dynamic. Dancers, like musicians, must be encouraged to broaden their scope, and not rely on their most comfortable, habitual way of moving. The use of attack, as manifested in rhythm and dynamics, is the means for both dancer and pianist.

A fascinating offshoot of this exists in the work in movement-therapy of recent years. Approaching feeling externally, rather than internally as in psychoanalysis, workers in this field have discovered that the *action* of a movement – hostile, gentle, flirtatious, optimistic – can encourage the experiencing of its emotion. This has implications for the performer; even if she is by nature phlegmatic, if she 'unnaturally' executes the *rhythm* of a fiery temperament, she will both add variety to her performing and begin to understand the nature of fieriness.

Certainly it is important that the accompanist not be limited in this area, too comfortable and habitual in her playing. The dancer needs to have new approaches to movement made clear, and a pianist with a narrow range of attack can be of no help to her.

I have been examining attack and touch, thus far, largely in an isolated manner, but in performance they are determined by a more all-encompassing factor – the entire body. I will call this the physiological factor, although this in turn is absorbed into attitudes and feelings.

III. The physiology of performance

The average pianist plays from her hands and fingers, as if there were no body attached to them. This is the application of energy from the wrong direction; in a sense it is like trying to make the arrow activate the bowstring. The very nature of the piano encourages this absurdity; unlike almost all other instruments it does not demand that a significant area of the body generates the production of tones. Watch other instrumentalists. The good ones always move, in ways consistent with the nature and mechanism of their instruments. The string player sways and bends, the wind player moves in accordance with the breath-requirements of his instrument and the music he is playing, and the percussionist approaches dancing as he beats out his rhythms and sonorities. The good singer, also, like the wind player, moves in conjunction with her breathing of the phrases and the expressive content of the music.

In contrast, the pianist glues her bottom to the seat, with two arms extended, which propel hands and fingers up and down a stationary keyboard. What these fingers are able to do, mechanically, can seem so fascinating that all else is forgotten. Herein lie nearly all of the physical, and many of the musical, problems of playing the piano. (I know that some pianists go to the other extreme and sway and weave almost to the point of seasickness. Despite their apparent bodily sensitivity, they are not much more alive than the first type. Their movement stems from self-expression or emotionalism and, as such, is sucked *into* the music; an alive body, on the other hand, is always generating the music.)

Abby Whiteside tirelessly points out the drawbacks to this arrow-activated bowstring. Although there are other piano teachers, a minority, who recognize the immense importance of the whole body in performance, I have never known any go so clearly to the heart of the matter as Abby Whiteside. She states, very early, her major premise:

The body is the *center* of [pianistic skills], even though . . . there is a necessary periphery . . . this periphery is, of course, the actual contact of fingers against the keys. But . . . the center controls the periphery; it can never be the other way around . . . The fingers in themselves have no power of coordination. The *body* must be taught, and the fingers will find their way under the guidance of this central control.[9]

Further on she restates her premise: '. . . any skilled coordination takes place from the center to periphery – not from periphery to center. The hand is the periphery of the playing mechanism.'[10] She then adds, 'If it is trained to act independently, habits are established which definitely interfere with any balance of activity throughout the arm.'[11]

Needless to say, many dancers also operate from a periphery – feet, hands, or head and neck – while the body itself is static. This is one of the chief sources of mannerism and of the 'feeling' of the music, discussed in Chapter 2. One teacher was particularly enraged by these two peripheral evidences. She had two stock attacks; for the first offense she would shout, 'Oh look at the little baller-*in*-a', and for the second, 'Why do you express with your wrists (neck, head?)'

Thus, the physiological element in performance is a matter of synchronization and integration through a central control. Quantities of methods and manuals for developing 'technique' in piano-playing (not to mention dancing) seem to forget the body, concentrating on appendages. These methods are, as a result, ignoring rhythm, the absolute source of good performance, for rhythm cannot *originate* in the peripheries. These can only give voice to an impulse which emanates from a nuclear source. (This concept, of course, is Martha Graham's greatest gift to ballet. The many contemporary ballet dancers who also studied Graham technique, and the modern dancers who infiltrated the ballet sanctum, have helped to transform ballet and provide an antidote for tendencies to slip back into its unattractive, sterile, manneristic form.)

Abby Whiteside relates her central-control theory to performance in other fields: 'Like the dancer's leg movements, like the baseball player's bat or the golfer's club, the pianist's fingers are the outermost parts of a mechanism which cannot function to the best advantage without a central control.' She then defines just what she means by 'central control': 'A fundamental rhythm is this control.'[12]

Baryshnikov is a perfect example in dance of this fundamental rhythm. Jack Anderson painted a delightful word-picture when he wrote (in the March 1976 *Dancing Times*, of *Spectre de la Rose*): 'All lightness, he was a creature of the air, and the repeated curlings of his hands above his head became the culmination of upward impulses ascending from his feet through his entire body.' No peripheral distractions here; a highly developed central control obviously reigns.

IV. Shared physiology of pianist and dancer

The pianist who plays for dance has a unique opportunity to replace a peripheral approach to performance with one in which the whole body participates. A kinetic link to the dancer's movements will almost automatically correct the faults which stem from overemphasis on the hands and fingers. But how does the pianist achieve this rapport with the dancers? What, in fact, is it? The concept of interpenetration of music and movement, musician and dancer, has come up repeatedly, in various ways, but now I must try to describe as clearly as possible how it operates in the accompanist's performance.

I mentioned, in Chapter 2, the kinesthetic participation by the spectator in the dancer's muscular activity by means of the music which is shared by dancer and spectator. The accompanist is in an even more intimate relationship to the movement than the spectator because it is she who is making the music.

The kinesthetic link is, of course, weakened by unrhythmical performance by either dancer or musician. Both contribute equally to the interpenetration. The dancer must be, so to speak, inside the music and the musician inside the movement. What, however, do these somewhat vague ideas mean? Like so many other facets of our subject this becomes remarkably elusive when one tries to be specific.

For instance, the phrase 'dancing the music' is frequently applied to the rhythmically alive dancer. If taken in a general, symbolic manner (not, more literally, in a Duncan-esque way), it does somehow seems to convey the kinesthetic experience. Oddly, however, its converse, 'playing the movement', does not. It instead conjures up visions of Margaret Craske's *bête noire*: the pianist's imitating the separate steps. 'Dancing the music', in fact, serves equally well for both dancer and musician. The accompanist who produces a rhythmical response in the dancers will always prove to be one who is herself dancing. One does not have to move around on two legs to dance.

Such an accompanist will experience breath and space in much the same manner as the dancers, but sympathetically rather than literally. Because of the heightened awareness in her body she will sense the dancers' needs in a way which the inert pianist cannot. She will be sensitive to changes in balance and direction, responding to them in her own body, and give the dancers aural room in which to make these changes effectively.

Our dancing pianist will share another important activity with the dancers. I have said that every good dancer begins to dance *before* she perceptibly moves. Similarly, the accompanist will hear and feel in her body the quality and rhythm of the music and the combination about to be performed. This essential prelude to action may take only an instant, but this instant contains the birth of the impulse which will generate and sustain the entire phrase or section. One cannot begin to perform in the middle of a phrase, any more than a horse can soar over a fence with its front feet already dangling halfway over it.

The musician and dancer who, on the other hand, begin before the 'beginning', will usually find that the momentum and flow which have been generated in that preliminary instant will carry them happily over such fences as wrong notes, erratic *pirouettes*, or even momentary lapses of memory (these are, incidentally, much less likely in a rhythmical, centrally controlled performance).

Now, proceeding to a further interaction, we have what is to me a fascinating correspondence – one which I had not realized until Tudor alluded to it one day during class. Afterwards I wondered why I had never (nor had anyone else, apparently) thought of something so obvious.

Areas of the body

I have spoken of correspondences of rhythm and feeling between pianist and dancer, but there is an actual physical link between the two. While correcting a dancer's *battements dégajés*, Tudor asked her to come over to the piano and watch me play the music I had just used for the exercise. He then asked her which areas of my body were most directly involved in the performing of the music. The answer, which she supplied, correctly, was the wrists and fingers. He then pointed out that she had not performed her *dégajés* consistently with this fact. They had been forced, overlarge and sloppy. Why? First of all, for *dégajés* to be of any functional value at all they must be done with great economy of movement. Secondly, and closely related to this, they are specifically designed to develop agility and velocity in the foot and ankle joint. As a result, any concentration of effort on leg, knee, thigh, or hip defeats the purpose of this movement. What has this got to do with my fingers and wrists?

The connection is, simply, that for me to play that light, quick *allegro* convincingly and rhythmically at the proper speed I could *only* play with the emphasis on fingers and wrists. Any effort which brought the forearms, upper arms or shoulders into action would have dragged at the tempo and also resulted in jerky unsupple playing. The impulse – originating, needless to say, in the back and torso of *both* the dancer and myself – bypasses (or passes through) the hip and shoulder, thigh and upper arm, leg and forearm; traveling directly to a flexible ankle or wrist; instep and toes, or fingers.

If, however, the exercise had consisted of *grands battements* it would have been a different matter. In both dancer and musician, the extremities would have been caught up in the larger, more powerful action of the entire leg and arm, and the main area of sensitivity would be the hip-joint in the dancer and its corresponding point in the body for the pianist: the shoulder, or the area where the upper arm meets the back. The accompanist, in addition, would be sitting on her torso differently for *dégajés* than for *grands battements*. For the former she would be lightly poised – almost to the point of levitation; for the latter she would be conscious of the strength and support of the trunk. This would, of course, tend to prevent the excruciating tension which clutches the back, shoulders and arms of so many pianists in forceful passages. The centrally generated energy would flow out as one impulse, culminating in the hand, just as it must flow directly to a highly sensitive, stretched foot in the dancer's *grand battement*, bypassing the dangerous tension-areas of thigh and knee.

To test these assertions, try transposing the muscular effort and the type of music appropriate to *dégajés* to that for *grands battements*, and vice versa. Confronted by powerhouse *dégajés* and dainty, finicky *grands battements* – for these distortions will accompany the transposition – the logic is clear.

All this should not be surprising if one reflects that physiologically there is a correspondence between arms and legs. Artists can project the proportions and shape of one from the other. This anatomical connection persists into the functional area of performance. (I must stress, once again, however, that all localized impulses and sensitivity originate in the back. If, for instance, the sensations and carriage of the back during the *dégajé* exercise were either inappropriate or missing altogether, neither the dancer nor I could achieve the necessary sensations and rhythm in our extremities.)

In practice, this anatomical connection means, generally speaking, that:

i. Large movements such as *grands jetés*, *tours jetés*, *adagio ronds de jambe*, etc., require arm weight and resilience from the pianist, and a supple resistance in the shoulders and spine. By the latter I do not mean tension, but – in the pianist as in the dancer – a lengthening or pressing away from neck and head. This is extremely important, for, as I have said, performers tend to transform power into tension, which should never be present in its static, paralyzing form.

ii. Small, very quick movements such as rapid *batterie*, a succession of *glissades*, twinkling *bourrées*, or swift, small *jetés* require supple yet brilliant action in the limited area of the pianist's hand, particularly the wrists and fingers.

iii. Intermediate movements, all those which lie somewhere between these two poles, will call forth sensitivity in forearm or upper arm, as the case may be. This will depend upon the speed at which the movements are taken.

I have already ventured the opinion that tempo and physiological areas of sensitivity are directly related. The upper arms and shoulder, for instance, are activated by dance movements which need a certain amount of time to be properly executed – large, commanding movements which fill space generously. This spatial area contracts in proportion to the time allowed for the movement until, as with *dégajés* or quick beats, it seems to be gathered into the area immediately surrounding the dancer. There is, in other words, simply no time for the dancer to pump her thighs in and out, or for the pianist to fling her arms into the air continually (an emotive gesture beloved of many pianists). The quicker and lighter the movement, the further the sensitivity and focus of action move to the extremities; the slower and more sustained or forceful, the nearer it travels toward the back and torso.

Impact *vs.* resilience, and phrasing

Now I must return to ideas introduced in Section II and enlarge upon them from another perspective – one of great importance to both dancer and pianist. We have been concerned with physiology; now we should consider how the physiological mechanisms affect phrasing and the direction of energy.

I have described the pianist as 'dancing the music', and emphasized the necessity of emulating the dancer's use of *plié* action. This is necessary for the avoidance of bad physiological habits and the ability to direct the flow of energy into an appropriate continuity throughout a phrase. Pursuing the problem of impact, we must remember that the pianist should never *strike* the keys. Such an action produces a succession of separate impulses which cannot be used to shape a continuous phrase. With many accompanists, the quicker the movement that they see, the more they seem driven to hit or puncture the keys. What they actually need for effective quick playing which carries them effortlessly throughout the phrase is a resilient, lightly bouncing impulse, i.e. *détaché*; in the sense not of sharply separated, but rather of buoyant. In other words softly crisp and rounded, not sharp and angular or brittle. Just as the dancer needs above all to avoid a harsh, discontinuous striking of the floor, so does the pianist need to set up impulses which will carry her forward, not act as continual impediments.

Most people have been exasperated at some time by an old rubber ball which has lost its spring. If one tries to bounce it, the ball will smack against the ground and only rise a short distance with an effort. This action is one of impact rather than release. With a live ball, one good bounce will generate another bounce, and yet others (until inertia takes over). This resembles the generation of energy which a good preparatory *plié* gives the dancer and, in a somewhat different way, the elasticity needed by the pianist. What is actually happening with the live ball, which can be seen in a slow-motion film, is that the time spent in contact with the ground is only a fraction of that spent in the air. This is true, of course, of the dancer with rhythm and *ballon*.

Although the pianist is not bounding off the floor, or pressing and releasing from it in slower movements and tempos, she does need to achieve similar sensations in her playing, both for the sake of the playing itself, and to convey this buoyant release of energy to the dancer no matter what form it may be taking: fast or slow, brilliant or lyrical. Only thus can she set up the impulses which will carry her through the inertia of each separate, hammer-activated note of the piano to achieve a continuous phrase. And here we can pick up threads from pp. 133 and 168–9.

If the pianist wants a visual demonstration of the damage done by a harsh striking action, she should watch closely a *battement frappé* exercise given by a teacher who understands neither the body nor rhythmic phrasing. He will be saying, 'and-HIT-and-HIT-and-HIT-and-HIT', and the dancer will be alternately banging the floor and jerking the leg in to the closed position. All this in an inexorably even 'rhythm'. What they are both missing is that the ball of the foot only *incidentally* touches the floor as the foot continues to its fullest stretch (this can be seen if the *frappé* action is performed *en relevé* or within the many steps which utilize it). Although *frappé* does mean, literally, 'struck', in misdirecting the energy and direction of the *frappé* the dancer is misconceiving the point of the exercise to be the striking of the floor rather than the development of a fleet, fluid action: that lightning-quick muscular response which is essential to the many forms of *jeté*. As a result of her evenly distributed time between the in and the out movements, the dancer negates the function and rhythm of this important exercise. What should be (as in the *demi-plié* before a jump) one continuous movement becomes two separate ones. In the mis-struck *frappé*, the action is that of the old rubber ball: thunk-up-thunk-up; in the *frappé* which is executed through a rhythmical release of energy, the in position – which corresponds to the descent into the *demi-plié* – sets up the impulse of the movement, but is quickly passed through. This quick transition approximates the flattening (*demi-plié*) of the ball as it contacts the ground and the rebound (*frappé* or jump) as it regains its shape and speeds into the air.

I have described this matter of the *frappé* at such length for three reasons. First, because an incorrect *frappé* is one of the easiest misdirections of energy in dance to spot; secondly, because I wished to give a specific illustration of the interaction of physiological, muscular action and its use in achieving rhythm, and thirdly, because I hope that it will lead the reader to a recognition of the similar damage which non-functional, static impact inflicts on dance performance and piano performance. There are, to be sure, certain physiological differences between the two, and impact in dance may be more drastic because it often involves the weight of the entire body against the floor. Still, the principles are the same for each.

V. Tension

It should hardly need mentioning that a striking or hitting action is produced through a high level of tension. I do not mean here the supple tension of a cat about to pounce or a drawn bowstring, but the sort which clutches and clenches. *Tension is the arch-enemy of a free flow of energy*, and it is by far the most destructive of all the kinetic impediments shared by pianist and dancer.

From a merely practical point of view, it must be removed. Since dancing and playing the piano, if continued for any length of time, can become extremely tiring, it is obviously of the greatest importance not to divert or choke off one iota of energy. The strain and stress which accompany tension do just this, and can, in fact, immobilize parts of the body, often the very areas which should be generating the flow of activity. That is, the torso and back become dead, and the energy is harmfully deflected to neck, shoulders, wrists, hands, and, in dancers, ankles and feet also.

At the same time, far more energy is needed in this state than if one were letting energy flow rather than forcing it. Desperately seeking energy, the pianist or dancer is impelled to increase the level of tension which in turn demands even *more* energy if one is to keep active. All this frenzy makes one of the performer's most valuable attributes impossible to attain: that is, economy. One should draw upon just as much power as is necessary for the music or movement being performed. There should be, always, a sense of reserve power, no matter how brilliant or forceful the passage.

From a functional point of view, tension destroys flexible, buoyant execution in the pianist, the *plié* action in the dancer. Many teachers realize this and try to counteract it by telling the pupil to relax. To them, Abby Whiteside would reply, '[Action] certainly does not mean relaxation. It is the cat ready to spring – not the cat sleeping in the sun.'[13]

Relaxation is passive; readiness for action is dynamic. And the activity is both physiological and psychological. One antidote to tension is the action and the aliveness of the torso and back already discussed. Impulses which originate there and flow into the more distant parts of the body are outgoing impulses, whereas activity which originates in one of the distant areas is static. Outgoing activity liberates energy; inturning activity confines and constricts it.

But this is not the whole of the matter. The generation of activity and energy from a center is itself generated by a deeper force, that is, a psychological one. I referred to the 'clutching' of energy. It can reasonably be said that clutching and grasping do not ordinarily produce desirable results. Not only do they produce physical tension, they are also self-defeating. To pursue something through force or compulsion is usually either to drive it away or to ruin it. To do so is, moreover, to brace or gird oneself – often for defeat – when what you really want to do is to free yourself for activity.

This can only be achieved under certain psychological circumstances, the most important of which is the valuing of what you are doing for its own sake rather than as a means. I repeat this here because it is one of the main premises of this book, but also because it is impossible to realize fully any potential for performance if one's psychology imprisons one in a grasping after the mechanics of technical display. To do so is frustrating in the extreme, for without a free, spontaneous love of *what* you are doing rather than a concern for *how* you are doing it, all is lost – all but a possibility of a surface facility and flashiness which can never grow.

If I seem to belabor this point, here and elsewhere, it is because I am repelled by the emphasis which our society places upon 'success' (which leads to a chronic sense of 'failure') rather than upon endeavor from involvement (which brings feelings of strength and expansion). I will not pursue here the philosophical implications of this, but only say yet again that, functionally, psychological straining after excellence leads to physiological tension. This, in turn, directs the blocked energy in the wrong direction – to the extremities, which then suffer from a localized tension. This constriction produces a disjunct, jerky performance which is rapped out rather than shaped into phrases. This, in turn, destroys esthetic and kinetic pleasure for the audience and performer. The performer is thus denied the benefits of feedback, for in giving little out, there is no response to regenerate momentum and renewal.

The removal of tension, therefore, depends on a chain composed of love of the activity itself, a growing freedom and spontaneity as one corrects 'technical' faults through a forgetting of oneself, the flow of energy into phrasing which breathes and pulses, and the resultant feedback which occurs as one achieves a progressive lessening of tension and an increase in skill and artistry. This experience, I might add, resembles a never-ending spiral rather than a straight line with a beginning and an end, or goal.

One simple way of breaking out of a tense goal-orientation is available to all. This is the directing of one's gaze.

VI. Gaze and space

Dancers must possess at least *some* visual and spatial awareness, but many accompanists gaze as intently at the keyboard while playing as does a medium at her crystal ball. The kinetic force is not, however, to be found in the keys, nor is the freedom from tension which absorption in the dancers' movements can provide. This absorption is partly visual and partly sensual. The sight, however dazzling, of fingers on piano keys is irrelevant. It is also an interference; you cannot inter-relate with dancers you do not watch.

I should mention, however, that I have known accompanists who were perhaps *too* involved with the dancers. One in particular depended so much upon the presence of one or two favorites that he invariably played badly when they were not in class. True, you will function best if you watch the most rhythmical dancers. There can be an unsettling variety of rhythms in class, and you certainly do not want to interact with the worst of the lot. Just do not get carried away by personalities.

But looking at even the run-of-the-mill dancers in class is preferable to looking at the keyboard. By looking, I mean of course *seeing* them – not just glancing at them. Your visual relationship to them will stimulate mental and physical responses. As dancers know well, it is quite a different experience on stage to look at and respond to fellow dancers than to glance at them as though they were part of the scenery. Seeing them radically alters physical sensations and interpretation. This, in fact, is another source of feedback, and it is available to the pianist also, if in a somewhat different manner. Since feedback is a process of integrating old knowledge with new information, thereby producing a revision or augmentation to create future possibilities, it could actually be said to be essential for the accompanist and dancer. At the very least, looking in class, or utilizing feedback, will help the accompanist to avoid certain embarrassing situations: in one I saw the pianist continue to bang away into the keyboard, unaware that a dancer had fallen and broken his leg.

But even on a less disastrous level, you must use your eyes to the fullest. This means developing that invaluable sense of distance and space on the keyboard which both frees one's gaze for the dancing and increases one's musicianship. The more you can minimize having to look for notes, the better. If you have seen little dancing between walking into class and leaving it, you obviously cannot take in new information and will thus remain static throughout your work-life.

Feedback is valuable in another way, which relates not so much to particular dancers or details, but to the act of gazing at the scene as a whole in class – to feel space. Your sense of your body and your playing is markedly different when your head is raised and you are looking outwards. This more erect carriage will do much to relieve the tension caused by hunching over the keyboard, looking for notes.

The sense of space which comes back to you, moreover, will affect your playing as nothing else can, giving it the expansive and open quality so necessary for dance work. But here we come to a serious problem. Ballet classes are often held in cramped and dim studios which are anything but spacious. The dancers, obviously, will suffer greatly from such constriction, but accompanists also do. Some of my worst headaches and general physical and mental tension were the result of playing while shoved into a tiny corner, with dancers passing within an inch of the piano or queuing up to go across the floor and surrounding me in the process so that I could barely see the dance floor. In such a situation, it is essential for both your sanity and that of the dancers that you somehow create the illusion of space, visual and aural. Your phrasing must be impeccable, with a pervasive sense of breath. And above all you must use dynamics sensitively. You should avoid playing too loudly, not only because in a small space a high decibel-level hurts the ears, but because it fills and constricts the space even further. Even though you cannot supply more room for the dancers to move within, you can at least give them as much aural space as possible. And, at the same time, you must somehow, no matter how ridiculous this may seem, direct your gaze *beyond* the constricting boundary, even if this is a dancer's bottom only two feet away.

Most experience, no matter how dismal it may seem at the time, can usually be turned to advantage. My ordeals in tiny studios helped me to find ways in which to play with more breath, less tension and greater awareness of phrasing, and, especially, they led me to a heightened appreciation and utilization of the more spacious studios in which I played.

VII. Rhythm in performance: phrasing

There are many ways in which to examine rhythm in performance. I find it best for my purpose to take three vantage points: phrasing, dynamics and tempo. These, of course, interact; phrasing depends upon and affects dynamics, and a wrong tempo can ruin the most theoretically admirable phrasing.

The unrhythmical dancer who has no sense of phrasing, who negates it by isolated feats of skill or endurance, is usually described as an 'acrobat'. The comparison misses a vital point: for an acrobat to perform well, let alone avoid premature death, he must have an *acute* sense of phrasing. It is actually the gymnast who is closest to the dancer who moves discontinuously, for her calisthenics are comprised of segments, each of which can be added or subtracted or interchanged without interfering with the function or the execution of the separate movements.

The average pianist today is also a gymnast, absorbed in notes and patterns, the more difficult and impressive the better. Many modern pianists can toss off the notes of the 'Hammerklavier' Sonata, but few can fulfill the poetry in Chopin's Prelude in A op. 28 no. 7. Similarly, many dancers are capable of executing, through sheer determination, the requisite thirty-two *fouettés*, but how many can phrase effectively the non-bravura movements of Fokine's choreography to Chopin's A major Prelude in *Les Sylphides*?

I have already analyzed phrasing at some length in 'theory' (Chapter 6), and in choice of music (Chapter 8). Now we want to see how it functions in performance. Some overlapping and repetition is inevitable, but I shall try to keep this to a minimum.

To phrase, that is, to group into comprehensible units, means that the performer must achieve a feeling of continuity, and, at the same time, emphasize certain events within the overall continuity.

Continuity

This is the opposite of playing from note to note. It is achieved only when the performer views the phrase as a journey through a continuum. Then, the separate notes – and they are, on the piano, particularly separate – are absorbed into and creative of a total environment. They do not stick out awkwardly or recede mysteriously, for this destroys comprehensibility. The *notes* of the Chopin Prelude in A, for example, played mechanically and separately, soon seem downright inane. These same notes as part of a continuum, however, form an exquisite listening, and performing, experience. Continuity in phrasing, on the other hand, must not be misunderstood; it does not mean monotony or sameness. Continuity depends on a certain type of fluctuation, and this is achieved through a sense of breath or space.

Breath and space

I have referred to the close connection between breathing and phrasing in singing, dancing and playing. To Abby Whiteside, phrasing 'which spins an unbroken thread throughout the relationship of parts' [14] is unimaginable without a sense of breath. Roger Sessions asks, 'What . . . is a so-called musical phrase if not the portion of music that must be performed, so to speak, without letting go, or, figuratively, in a single breath?' [15]

Many writers relate breath in performance to speech: as in language, so in music, 'to phrase' means equally 'to breathe'; to phrase well means to breathe intelligently. Everyone knows intuitively that, if they wish to communicate in speech, their phrases must be shaped. Even the seemingly breathless, formless outpouring of a declaration of love has its own phrase and breath logic, a rendition appropriate to the meaning of the words. Why, then, do performers who can phrase convincingly when speaking, play and dance as if they are saying, 'oh MY dar-LING will . . . you COME away with . . . ME WILL you stay with me . . . forev-ER we . . . COULD . . . be . . . so hap-PY togeth . . . er . . .?' Not only could no one who *means* these words utter them thus, no one who is breathing appropriately could so ignore the four phrases within the declaration as to deliver only a succession of absurd halts and stresses. The opposite extreme is, however, just as meaningless: an all-too-connected, 'ohmydarlingwillyoucomeawaywithmewillyoustaywithmeforeverwe-couldbesoetc?' Two forms of gibberish. Every phrase, however short, has a beginning, middle and end, and within the one breath which unites them, there are various possible fluctuations, stresses and spaces. One breath does not mean one intonation and inflection. The monotonous pianist or dancer who is unconscious of the interaction between a phrase-breath and the spatial details within it 'never quite comes to rest; so that the dynamic scale is a bit blurred and the movement does not lift to its flower, shine and subside completely, leaving a completed image in the mind'.[16] Edwin Denby is speaking here of the inexperienced dancer, and states that this 'flowering' specifically indicates rhythm in dance as opposed to rhythm in music. Yet, if one substitutes 'music' for 'movement', the statement makes perfect musical sense.

The connection of phrases

Even though the performer may be aware that each phrase has a shape, this is but the beginning. Well-shaped phrases in isolation do not add up to a musical work. They must be connected parts of a cumulative experience. The lover's speech above consists of several short phrases, and could be diagrammed thus:

Oh, my *darling* – will you *come away* with me; will you *stay* with me *forever*? We could be *so happy* together.

Within the long thread of the whole, there are two main phrases, with subdivisions of the second. If these phrases are not shaped with an overall concept, the unfortunate lover may sound as if he is addressing four different people: 'Oh, my *darling* (Emily)'; 'Will *you* (Charlotte) come away with me?'; 'will *you* stay with me forever (Anne)?' '*We* could be so happy together (Branwell)'. As you can see, it is partly the stress within each phrase and its context and shaping, partly how this carries one phrase into the next, and, finally, how these thread into an overall conception of the large-scale phrase.

We can pursue this a bit further with a musical example which, conveniently, is associated with choreography: the Chopin Prelude in A. Although (or because) this is 'technically' very simple, it shows particularly clearly the problems of shaping and connecting phrases.

The music consists, visually, of eight phrases altogether. Each one seems remarkably similar, both in note-values and general impulse (and can produce a Chinese water-torture effect when played by an unmusical student). They look, in fact, choppy and disconnected on the page, and present a serious challenge for the performer.

The first step is to group the apparent phrases in twos. The semi-cadence, in other words, becomes a midway point in a larger phrase so that we now view the piece as composed of four phrases of four measures each rather than eight phrases of two measures. This will go a long way towards the avoidance of the pianistic expirations which usually emphasize the two-measure segments. The music contains two strong forces which the performer must respond to, one melodic, the other harmonic. At the end of each short two-measure phrase you find either a harmonic instability pulling towards the next phrase, or, when the music arrives on the tonic chord, an expectant twist to the melody, and sometimes both.

One is thus always being pulled forward at the same time that the striking similarity of rhythmic pattern is tending to halt the progress. Herein lies the subtlety of this little piece, and the challenge to the performer; there is a quiet tension (of a good sort) set up between the predictable, almost plodding, rhythm, and the gentle questioning of the melody and its delicately suspended harmonies.

Another impulse which can aid one's phrasing is that of the upbeat to each phrase. Many performers treat each one as another beginning rather than as expansions of what has gone before. What does the score, diagrammed, have to tell us?

Ex. 1   Chopin, Prelude in A major op. 28, no. 7

(The (//) and (<) are merely illustrative here, and are not in the original)

As can be clearly seen, despite the *apparent* repetitiousness of this piece, it is really an unbroken tonal journey from the first note to the last.

The further details of phrasing would, unfortunately take far too much space here but I hope that I have managed to clarify some of the general principles of continuity from phrase to phrase. Fokine's choreography to this music, in *Les Sylphides*, is particularly instructive. A less sensitive choreographer would be strongly tempted to follow the apparent stops and starts of the phrases. Fokine, in contrast, used what he called an 'echoing' impulse in his choreography. Since echoes consist of reverberations, this immediately acts as a force which bridges what seem superficially to be points of diminishing energy throughout the music. The dancer must move *through* the cadences, not come to rest. In this way, each dance phrase builds toward the next to form one continuous statement. In many performances, however, Fokine's continuity is replaced by a series of gasps in which the dancer uses each cadence as an opportunity to show off a 'beautiful' pose. The ballet usually being performed to an orchestral transcription (of the original piano versions of the seven pieces used), this tendency to pose is all the more disturbing. The strings which carry the melody are sustaining instruments; they can easily maintain the thread linking the half-note cadences to the following up-beats, whereas on the piano these moments are the hardest of all to sustain and keep moving. The dying-away impulse of the struck half-note harmony demands a strong rhythmic feeling indeed in the pianist's body to prevent a sense of dwindling.

A comparison of a performance of the Prelude by a fine artist with one by a dancer striving for effect will demonstrate the above points far more clearly than any words can do. Every pianist who has struggled unhappily to realize Chopin's ethereal vision could learn much from seeing this Prelude performed by a dancer with a sense of phrasing and continuity. It involves, of course, only one facet of phrasing. Quick or staccato music requires other sorts of articulation and continuity, but the principle, on the most basic level, remains the same. 'Always connect', said E.M. Forster, even though the connection may be achieved in different ways than Forster was visualizing.

Isolation *vs.* context

The performer who habitually has trouble with shaping a phrase and linking phrases to form a whole usually turns out to be one who views each phrase as a thing in itself, composed of various technical or interpretive problems. But many of these could be surmounted through an overall conception (as I observed of the Prelude). Often, pianists develop the habit of practicing certain phrases, the most troublesome, in isolation. Over and over they retrace their steps, as if they were sorting out pieces of a jigsaw puzzle. Since music is neither composed nor performed in this way, such an approach seems misdirected.

Particular, acute problems are posed in the 'simple' Chopin prelude because of the shortness of the phrases; let us look now at a longer, more complex illustration: the opening eight bars of our Chapter 8 *adagio* from Act II of *Swan Lake*. Play or sing this compound phrase, stopping just before the upbeat E^b in the eighth bar. Lovely as it is, this long spun-out line, it pulses with *latent* energy. Not just because of the incomplete cadence, but also because the implications, the expectations aroused by the music, demand a continuation of some sort. Even if you alter the last three beats to form a perfect cadence – which can be done easily, if somewhat abruptly, by re-harmonizing the original melody (with the dominant 7th), then changing the last note (to a G^b, with its tonic chord) – the phrase seems arbitrarily stopped. There is too much life in it to be contained so soon. At the end of this phrase you are obviously on the brink of a larger experience.

Ask someone to play a similarly pregnant opening phrase of a work that you have never heard. Your first reaction may be eagerness to hear what follows or utter boredom, but neither of these is necessarily significant in itself. As with the beginning phrases of a novel, you may be gripped immediately, only to be let down by what comes afterwards; or you may find that a seemingly unpromising opening leads to total involvement. The first phrases do not stand on their own. Their deeper meaning may only become fully apparent after you have heard or read the concluding phrases.

If an opening phrase is incomplete in itself, one extracted from the middle of a work is even more problematical – for this is dependent on both what comes after it and what has gone before. We can see this clearly in a poem. Poetry resembles music in the way that both build upon and interrelate phrases, but since poetry's medium is words and ideas the dependency of phrases upon one another is easier to appreciate.

One of the most vivid phrases in all poetry occurs in the middle of Yeats' 'The Second Coming':

> The blood-dimmed tide is loosed, and everywhere
> The ceremony of innocence is drowned;[17]

Magnificent as this may be in isolation, one sees but a glimmer of the power it holds when the preceding and succeeding phrases combine with it to form Yeats' vision of disaster and rebirth. The words and images are in themselves beautiful, just as the phrase which follows our opening of the *Swan Lake adagio* is beautiful, but it is their relationship to what surrounds them which changes them from a fragment to a force.

My first acquaintance with this phrase was its partial use in Britten's *The Turn of the Screw* as an isolated quotation, or commentary upon the action. When I learned that it was from a poem, I could not rest until I learned what came before and after. In the same way, I do not listen to certain phrases within a piece of music out of context by putting the phonograph needle back to repeat them. Everyone has phrases which they particularly love, but they are totally dependent on their context. (Britten's fragmentary use of the poem's phrase is a deliberate, dramatic device, functioning within a *new* context.) One could, conceivably, make a tape on which a favorite phrase or two was repeated forty times. The result would not, however, be forty times as much pleasure as one hearing of it, but almost no pleasure at all. An equally destructive act is the rending of phrases out of context by subjective performance. We have all seen the intense concentration and the meaningfully inclined body-position with which the performer indicates that she has come to a phrase which she particularly 'feels'. To emphasize it in this way is to lift it out of context as surely as if it were played in isolation. Many pianists will begin a piece in what seems almost an absent-minded way, only apparently coming to life some moments into it, and then subsiding into indifference until the next spark strikes. What is the listener supposed to make of this as music? Spectators at a circus wait for such sporadic high moments, but a pianist is not a clown or a monkey on horseback. And, of course, dancers do the same thing; they will throw away three-quarters of a section as mere preparation in their mania to get to the nice juicy phrase at the end. Even if they manage, somehow, to execute this final phrase well (a feat even less likely in dance than in music performance) it will be forced and unpleasant to watch.

A work as a whole is meaningful only if the parts are connected and integrated. The phrase is the crucial factor, standing as it does between the microcosm of the details which form it and the macrocosm of the entity which it helps to create.

VIII. Rhythm in performance: dynamics

Dynamics, or the means by which certain moments are brought forward or made to recede, are not separate from phrasing, but one of its shaping forces. A dynamic is not a static *thing* but rather part of a flow. That is to say, it is this in a good performance; in a poor one, accents bristle and protrude and soft moments become melodramatic instants – histrionics rather than expressivity. Certainly, in one sense dynamics set apart, or differentiate. This is not, however, a matter of emphasis of notes for their own sake any more than differentiation of words within a phrase is intended to extract these at the expense of the others. The purpose of dynamics, or fluctuations in volume, is to convey as clearly as possible the meaning of a phrase. The monotone version of the lover's speech, above, completely lacked dynamics; the jagged version misplaced them. Thus, both versions were, in different ways, unphrased.

The use of dynamics takes three forms. In one, they designate a general level of volume to be used throughout a phrase or section, although there are bound to be deviations within it. In the second, they are used for brief, dramatic stress or heightening of particular tonal events, perhaps only one chord or note. Then there is the intermediate function of dynamics as used to increase or decrease, gradually, the level of sound: the crescendo or diminuendo. With all of these, the levels of sound, or tonal gradations, must be in an organic relationship to their surroundings.

The pianist, even when there are no specific accents or crescendos and diminuendos indicated, is continually making certain gradations in volume, often quite subtle. If a composer has indicated *pp*, this does not mean that he intended the entire passage to be played with scientific exactitude. The rise and fall of the melody, harmonic progressions and shifts, rhythmic patterns – all of these lead the responsive performer to stress certain moments and mute others, but it is a matter of degree. The period and style of the music are a guide. No sensible performer could approach dynamics when playing Scarlatti in the same way that she would when playing Rachmaninov or Debussy. Each of these composers demands a different dynamic orientation in order to make rhythmic and expressive sense of their music.

Dynamics, like other facets of rhythm, are related to what Sessions calls 'emotional energy'. And I have heard him describe music as 'not so much sound as movement'. This concept should help to counteract the tendency to superimpose dynamics rather than to use them as part of the flow of a phrase. Viewed just as sound, as dramatic effect, a dynamic can be treated in isolation; perceived as an impulse within the music's movement, it strongly resists such separation. With the latter, moreover, dynamics are produced through kinetic energy, not by an application of greater or lesser force and effort. In this connection, one misunderstanding of dynamics is particularly common. To many performers a soft dynamic indicates a drooping or relaxed rendition, and a loud one indicates tension and force. Neither of these is, in fact, so. And they both indicate a view of dynamics as sound rather than as an expressive direction of energy. Soft tones actually require a greater intensity than loud ones, and loud tones, conversely, are most effective and able to be used as part of a rhythmic progress when produced through a loosened sensation in the body. Not that the soft tones require tension and the loud ones relaxation, but rather that soft tones must bring forth a heightened concentration of the muscular activity and loud ones a liberation of energy. Otherwise, the former will not project and the latter will become harsh and strident. In both cases the inappropriate muscular sensations will hamper the phrasing of the music as a whole.

IX. Rhythm in performance: tempo

To the musician, tempo all too often represents the means by which she can make an impression, whether by playing faster (she hopes) than human ear has ever heard; or slower – to the majestic and awesome (she fancies) brink of immobility. In either case, tempo mocks what it should be enhancing: rhythm.

For the dancer, also, tempo tends to override other aspects of performance, but for a different reason. There are, of course, many dancers who view tempo as a virtuoso weapon, but, unlike musicians, dancers are dependent upon and vulnerable to tempo in a bodily way. With all dancers it is an ever present preoccupation, for it dictates how quickly or slowly (and often uncomfortably or hazardously) she must move an entire body, equipped with awkward appendages to be harmoniously disposed and co-ordinated, and prone to problems of balance and continuity.

The accompanist in contrast, seated securely on her piano stool, has little comprehension of the formidable problems which beset the dancers as she and they proceed together through a phrase. The accompanist often chafes at the restrictions which playing for dance imposes, but the pianist who has a feeling for tempo as it functions within movement will be a better performer in general. Each step or movement of the dance-phrase requires a certain amount of time to function properly and to make its point – which, in turn, allows the phrase to make its larger effect. There must also be an inter-relation of tempos from phrase to phrase, and so the dancer cannot speed up and slow down at will.

Pianists are commonly tempted both to crowd notes within the phrase, or attenuate them for expressivity, and also to fluctuate wildly from phrase to phrase for the same reason. These tendencies, of course, bring us back once again to the all-important building-element, the phrase. Tempo and phrasing are, in fact, inseparable.

Tempo presents several problems for the dance-pianist. Some are peculiar to the rehearsal situation – although they may exist in lesser degree in class – and will be examined in Chapter 12. What concerns us now are those which arise continually in class, so I will turn to these and also make some general observations which seemed to me to be more pertinent here than in the section on tempo in Chapter 6.

Effective rhythm and tempo

Many pianists work harder than they need to. They feel, consciously or unconsciously, that fast passages must go as fast as possible. This is due to an uncertainty regarding both rhythmic detail as it relates to a sense of pulse, and rhythmic continuity on a larger scale. It is, however, unnecessary and in fact undesirable to take a piece too quickly. This will not only make the music itself less effective, but it automatically adds to the rhythmic problems of the pianist and makes them even less likely to be solved. Good rhythm, according to Kurt Adler, 'will make a piece seem to flow faster; the tempo, therefore, may be more deliberate. Weak rhythm tends to slow down music. This is the reason why so many interpreters take a composition at top speed. They do not have a strong rhythmic feeling and try to compensate for this by hurrying the music.'[18]

So, you have the pianist, tense and unrhythmical, jumbling notes together but making the music actually sound slower. And because of the tension, this problem is self-perpetuating, for the pianist is unable to stem the rushing torrent of notes in order to attain a strong, secure rhythmic sensation in her body. She is, actually, being *driven* through the phrase out of fear that it will not be effective unless taken at top speed, rather than controlling its elements to produce a flow. Sometimes, on the other hand, pianists speed up slow passages because they cannot find in their body the rhythmic thread which pulls the phrase together and must resort to speed to keep the flow going.

When, during solo performances, you are impelled to take a piece too quickly or to rush certain passages, you fail only yourself; when you do it in ballet class, you interfere with the activity of a group of people. Since dancers *cannot* train their bodies properly if they are being hurried through a phrase, let alone develop any sense of muscular rhythm, erratic tempos from the accompanist could be said to be the most inacceptable weakness of all. And if you find that the teacher and you are in frequent conflict over tempos, that he must repeatedly tell you to go faster or slower, you can be reasonably sure that the problem lies in your weak sense of rhythm (allowing, of course, for the possibility that it is the teacher who is deficient, so mark whether he is the only one who takes you to task).

I said faster or slower because rhythmic weakness also takes the form of dragging the tempo. There can be so little sense of continuity that the music simply falls apart. This is particularly true of slow music (although it can also arise when the pianist cannot solve certain 'technical' problems in an *allegro* or *vivace* tempo).

Two factors in particular can cause inappropriate or fluctuating tempos. These are inorganic emphases and erratic volume-levels.

Accents, dynamic levels and tempo

One of my greatest irritants when teaching piano was the tendency of many pupils to rush the notes which preceded a strong accent or arrival-point. All that mattered was the destination; the path to it was, in effect, non-existent. The notes which made the accent or the arrival meaningful had in themselves no meaning at all, and as a result the moment to which they led came as an unwelcome surprise. This, of course, resembles the dancer's continual blurring of preparatory or connecting movements such as *demi-plié, glissade, pas de bourrée* or *chassé*. All she is concerned with is getting through them as quickly as possible *en route* to an accent or arrival.

In both dancer and pianist, this rushing indicates a lack of breath. Now, breath is partly dependent upon a strong feeling of pulse plus disposition of accents appropriate to the patterns and rhythms of the phrase. To help my pupils gain these I had them sing the melodic line of the phrase, first in the breathless gasp which characterized their playing of it, then in strict metronomic tempo with as many variations in *rubato* within this as possible. Then I asked them to select the version which seemed most convincing and play the phrase thus on the piano. Interestingly, when again actually playing, most pupils tended to rush as before, even if they had managed to *sing* the phrase rhythmically. This showed that the physical rhythm which they had achieved when breathing during the sung phrase was, for some reason, not taken into the body when it became an activity of hands upon a keyboard. Here again, we have a manifestation of peripheral performance rather than energy spreading outward from an alive, breathing center. Unwanted deviations in tempo, the hurrying (or dragging) of notes before an arrival, in fact, are a clear indication of a peripheral approach. After I remorselessly continued to turn part of each piano lesson into a vocal adventure, most of the pupils more or less grasped the point and this was reflected in their more relaxed yet dynamic and tactile shaping of phrases at the keyboard. Flow replaced gasps.

With my ballet students I tried a similar approach. Since most of them, laughingly rebellious, refused to try to sing, I asked them to use their feet upon the floor as if they were functioning within a singer's breath during the phrase, and to treat the feet and floor as the same indissoluble whole as the singer must view breath and notes. In other words, instead of approaching the preliminary or connecting steps as so much dead wood to be hurried over on the way to the arrival, I asked the dancers to give each movement adequate value in time, appropriate to the situation, with full sensitivity to the floor.

With both pianists and dancers, the increased awareness of the *path* to the goal relieved the compulsion to rush, and it led to a far greater effectiveness of the focal moment itself, and thus the phrase as a whole. This was achieved through a sense of heightened functional *contact* with keyboard or floor; misguided force was replaced by sensitively directed rhythmic energy. Also, they said that they *enjoyed* performing the phrase, whereas it had originally been either a chore or a source of fear and tension.

The other common type of fluctuation is a more subtle and problematical matter, for it may originate in instinctive physiological reactions. This is the compulsion to speed up during a crescendo or slow down during a diminuendo or, conversely, to increase in volume when the tempo accelerates or decrease when it slows down. It is a rare pianist who does not do one of these, even when the composer has, being aware of this tendency, specifically indicated, say, '*non accelerando*' or '*sempre f*'.

Possibly in our primitive past loud music did produce faster movement and fast movement an increase in volume. This seems, in fact, to be our natural physical reaction since loudness and speed are both expressions of heightened states. One does not normally 'whisper for joy', or to warn of an impending catastrophe, and abrupt gestures do not, as a rule, indicate serenity but rather disturbances and excitations.

In our less visceral, more 'sophisticated' music, however, composers skilfully use the interplay of what seem to be expressive opposites: prevailing softness and increase of speed, prevailing loudness and decrease of speed; or they demand steady tempos or dynamic levels. The performer must cope with these perhaps 'unnatural' techniques, and never more so than when playing for dance.

There are pieces which combine tempo and dynamics in unusual ways. One of the most striking of these is Ravel's *Bolero*. This much-maligned piece is a fascinating study of the gradual development of tension which results from an increase in volume set against an undeviating tempo. Ravel wished to demonstrate the power of a crescendo, and to do so, he excluded another important musical feature – gradation of speed. Using simple tonality and materials throughout, he employed a variety of instrumental tone-color and an increasing level of sound to sustain interest.

Ravel foresaw that 99 out of 100 conductors (and instrumentalists) would be impelled to quicken the tempo as the dynamic level increased, and came into bitter conflict with conductors on this point. He was adamant that the tempo should remain constant from the first beat to the last. Most conductors, needless to say, deliberately or inadvertently, get faster as the music progresses. And, even if the rare one resists this in order to fufill Ravel's intention, he will almost always jump to a disruptingly quicker pace at the end, where the music unexpectedly modulates from its eternal C pedal-point to E major.

Having heard Ravel's performance on an old recording, I can attest to the extraordinary impact of both the piece as a whole and the shift to E major at its climactic point when there is not even a hint of an *accelerando*. What frequently becomes a forcing of excitement through acceleration and a melodramatic jumble of notes at the very end is in Ravel's version a masterly and inexorable, and subtle, study in contrast.

The *Bolero* is an extreme – a trick, if you like – but it is a useful demonstration of the power of tempo, and of the decreased effectiveness which results when the performer ignores the composer's purposeful use of it. Most pieces, however, go through a variety of speeds and deviations in tempo during their course, and this complicates matters for the performer. It would not do so, or not to such a degree, if tempo were the only consideration, but the performer must balance tempo *and* phrasing. These are, as I have said, interactive, but they are at the same time antithetical.

Time *vs.* rhythm: tempo against phrasing

Tempo, or the constant speed of the underlying pulse, and phrasing, or the rhythmic shaping of patterns, continually oppose one another. (I speak here of measured or metrical music; Gregorian chant, vocal *recitativo* and other non-metrical music obviously achieve rhythm only through phrasing.) The performer's main problem could be said to be the achieving of a balance between staying 'in tempo' *and* bringing to life the varied rhythmic patterns which almost always require at least a small amount of *rubato* or flexibility (see Chapter 6). The musical performer, in other words, somewhat mysteriously, employs strictness and suppleness at the same time.

This inherent conflict becomes all the more acute when playing for dance. A ballet teacher once said to me, on my first day in his class, 'I must have a good, reliable tempo – no speeding-up and slowing-down! But it needs to have a little give and take.' We looked at each other for a moment, and then began to laugh. He then added, 'Well, what I mean is that the pulse must be predictable but it can't be confining.'

Certainly the beginning accompanist is confused by these conflicting requirements. During her piano training her teacher will have commanded her to 'play in time', *or* she will have pleaded for some sense of phrasing and expressivity, but not, as a rule, for both at once. The average piano teacher will tend to focus on one or the other, depending on her concept of performance. Even when a teacher is aware of both problems, she will often treat them in isolation: one section was 'erratic in tempo', the next, 'deficient in phrasing'.

Now in dance class, the pianist, thus conditioned, suddenly finds that either one alone is inadequate – unless, of course, she plays for a teacher who is only concerned with dancing in strict tempo, or one who is preoccupied with free 'expressivity'. And, if the pianist is accustomed to emoting all over the piano, the command to keep a steady tempo will offend her; she will protest (inwardly, at least) that she is not a metronome. If, on the other hand, she is accustomed to playing like a machine, she will be at a loss, unable to give the dancers the supple phrasing and breath which they so need.

Unquestionably the ballet pianist must play with more regularity of tempo than the soloist. Deviations of speed which are acceptable in a recital performance are impractical when dancers are involved. This will be particularly problematical in the playing of the Romantic repertoire, not necessarily because the composers themselves indicated wild fluctuations, but because (generally speaking) the nature of the music causes performers to react more subjectively to it than to Baroque, Classical or contemporary music.

The misunderstanding arises over the conception of a steady pulse as necessarily metronomic and static. While it is often in danger of becoming so, it also offers the strongest possible point of departure to lively playing. When the pulse takes hold of the entire body so that one need not fear 'losing time', then the performer is free to play around *within* it. Jazz and blues represent a very special form of this approach, but careful listening to the best performers in this field can lead to a greater understanding of flexibility within regularity, and the basic principles can be applied to other types of music. Jazz and blues merely take an ingredient of all music, *rubato*, to its greatest extreme. I shall not repeat my comments on *rubato* here, so perhaps a re-reading of the relevant sections in Chapter 6 would be helpful. I will simply say that a steady pulse throughout the body supplies a reliable basis for the larger rhythmic sense.

Practicalities in class

It is essential that the dancers have both a steady tempo and rhythmical phrasing from their accompanist, but the former is necessary for two specific, practical reasons. First, the dancers not being clairvoyant, they have no way at all of knowing when you may change the speed. Many dancers have described to me their perpetual apprehension regarding this when certain accompanists play for class. Never knowing when the tempo may vary, sometimes radically, the dancers cannot concentrate properly on their own business when they should actually be able to take a reliable tempo for granted and devote themselves to performing the steps rhythmically, i.e. to phrase.

Secondly, because of the different approaches to dancing – the varying attacks – which, as I have said, can be found in any class, there will always be some students who lag behind the beat, some who anticipate it and others who are squarely on it (plus the ones who are *within* it if the music and the performance of it allow them to be). If you do as some accompanists do, and alternately speed up and slow down as your gaze travels around the studio, you will drive everyone mad and be of help to no one. Watch instead the dancers who are working within the tempo originally set by you or the teacher.

Two main exceptions exist regarding a constant tempo. In center work, the teacher will often put the most advanced and alert students in the first group, to do the combination faster than the second group can (and you must retain these alternates in your body). The other situation – also involving levels of dancing ability – arises in across-the-floor work. In this case, the most advanced dancers may wait at the end of the line in order that they can do the combination at a faster or slower tempo than it was taken by the other dancers. You will get some black looks if you continue in the original tempo; here is their chance to jump higher and move more grandly, to do *piqué* turns more fleetly. Everything, in short, will be *more*. And you must anticipate this and recognize when the first members of this advanced group is about to embark. The original tempo, of course, must flow gracefully into the new one so that a sudden change does not jolt the dancers of that first group.

Oddly, the moment when the advanced dancers begin is often the very time when the accompanist speeds up (when she should be slowing down for, say, big jumps) or drags (when she should quicken for brilliant *piqués* or beating-combinations). I suspect that, in certain cases I have known, this is partly psychological – sometimes a form of rebellion, other times insecurity. In addition, it can be due to the tense fatigue which overtakes the unrhythmical pianist as class progresses. She cannot control the tempo because she is forcing the notes. Above all, the accompanist should be reliable in the concluding combinations, for these can be the most demanding of all for the dancers.

One other form of tempo alteration of this sort is the practice of putting the male dancers in a separate group, or at the end of the across-the-floor queue with the teacher requesting different music for the men, demanding a correspondingly different muscular feeling in the pianist.

I have been speaking in a general way about tempo-changes, but actually three definite categories of speed will be found: those appropriate to the beginner's class, to the advanced or professional class, and to the intermediate class, which has neither very brilliant dancers nor very weak ones.

Since the beginners do not have the skill or co-ordination to be found, in varying degrees, within the other two levels, they must take *allegro* movements somewhat slower, and sustained or *adagio* movements faster. All tempos will, in other words, gravitate toward a mid-point, neither very slow nor very fast. The advanced class will, on the other hand, often work at the outer speeds, not *moderato*, but *molto allegro*; not *andante*, but *adagio* to *largo*, to the limits of the power of the body to sustain. Whereas the big jumps will be, in the beginners' class, lower and not so grand, in the advanced class they will be in virtuoso style, and thus slower. Intermediate class, of course, is not so extreme, although there can be a surprising range of proficiency in a class composed of neither beginning nor advanced students.

In any case, whatever general tempo-range you are working within, it must be consistent and the tempos must be clearly established. Again, and always, you *do not follow* the dancers; you *establish* a workable tempo to which they must adhere. I have known accompanists who habitually followed all the variations in speed which they saw from dancer to dancer, in the mistaken notion that they were 'helping' the dancers. Which ones? In continually altering tempos according to who seems in need at the moment, you will confuse and impede the other, unfavored dancers. Most detest this sort of thing. The only exceptions I have known are those devils, of both sexes, who crave special attention, sidling over to the piano to wheedle, 'Play slower (faster, livelier, etc.) when *my* turn comes.' But we will ignore these poor creatures, who live in a world bounded by their needs and wishes. Most of the dancers I have known would not dream of making such demands.

I have described the aspects of tempo which I consider of greatest importance for our purposes, but, since in a book of this sort only a small proportion of space can be devoted to such a complex subject, I have necessarily had to limit myself. I hope that this section, in conjunction with the observations in Chapters 6 and 12 on tempo, will at least indicate some of the major problems and lead to further inquiry.

X. Orchestral music on the piano

This aspect of performance for dance is so particularly important in rehearsal that I shall postpone the bulk of my examination of it until Chapter 12, but some notice should be made of the playing of music outside the piano repertoire for class. This is necessary because, as I have already stressed, the accompanist who relies only on music written for the piano will be painfully limited. This is true regarding not only repertoire but also performance, for the effective rendition of orchestral music on the piano will add another dimension to the pianist's playing. If, however, you cannot find the means necessary for bringing orchestral music to life on the piano, you would be better off in limiting yourself to the piano repertoire. But since this would, for several reasons, be a pity, let us see what some of the problems are.

The first, of course, is the radically different nature and mechanism of the piano compared with those of orchestral instruments. This could be termed the acoustical problem. It is particularly acute when the music has been learned only from a piano transcription, which is unavoidably monochromatic and homogeneous compared with the original many-hued instrumental version. I cited earlier the vexing instances of transcriptions of the Tchaikovsky ballet scores. Performances of this music in class – which may be frequent because of its great suitability for so many combinations, and the predilection of so many teachers for it – can be depressing indeed. Based only on the transcription, they can bear as little resemblance to the original as the connect-the-dots kits sold in craft shops do to the famous paintings on which they are modeled.

This means that in order to do justice to this music, you must become familiar with the orchestral version. Only then can you have a basis upon which to contrive some approximation on the piano to its original effect. If you play it literally, going only by what you see on the page, you will be unaware of sometimes crucial details and characteristics, and will be confined to the often unimaginative spacings and undifferentiated clumps of sound offered by a run of the mill transcription. You will have neither the inherent interest of music which exploits the glories of the piano nor the advantages of the myriad effects possible in the orchestra; only a sort of instrumental no man's land.

Added to the problems of sameness of color and attack, and a grey instrumental effect, there is the dilemma of which lines to emphasize and which to let recede. In a piano transcription, all notes are equal simply because of their uniform tone color. An ostinato in the bass (which might be scored for cellos and bassoons) coalesces on the piano with the melody in the middle range (played by, say, two clarinets in parallel thirds). Add to this one of Tchaikovsky's favorite devices, a counter-melody in a contrasting timbre, say oboe, and you are faced with potential pianistic mud.

The only way to make aural, and kinesthetic, sense out of such a mess is through a highly sensitive inner ear based on *familiarity* with the original sound combined with the *tonal imagination* necessary to approximate, to give the illusion of, these sounds and textures on the piano. This is particularly necessary with ballet music because of the dancers' relationship to it in the theater. It is generally necessary with other orchestral music in order to make it bearable, let alone enlivening, on the piano.

I have introduced these problems in the context of class, and will, as promised, elaborate upon them during our look at the pianist in rehearsal in Chapter 12.

XI. Circumstances

Not all aspects of performance in class are 'artistic'. Our first concern here could be termed aural neatness, or perhaps just courtesy. Do not, for instance, turn exercises into run-on monologues. When the dance ends, the music should end, preferably on some recognizable cadence. So many accompanists dribble on, just when the teacher will want to make corrections or discuss the combination just performed. No teachers that I have known enjoy a wall of sound when they are trying to make a point, and the dancers, also, will be distracted and unable to hear the teacher's comments clearly. This applies, needless to say, to the rehearsal of music which you will be using for the *next* combination. If you do not know it at that point, or have any idea whether or not it will suit, it is a bit late for such trial and error. Better to use a piece which you are sure of and postpone the other so that you do not drown out the teacher's setting of the new combination. There are some teachers who ask that the music be played beforehand, but usually this is to guide them, after which they will repeat the exercise clearly for the dancers, or to accompany them as they demonstrate. Often a teacher will stop the class part way through a combination if it is going too badly. You should be alert to this possibility so that you do not crash on while he is attempting to clarify matters.

On the other hand, it is equally important for the accompanist *not* to stop unless required to do so: unless corrections or clarification – or catastrophe – require silence, you must go on playing. I have known quite a few pianists who suffered in ballet class because they were habitually compelled to play through a piece without stopping. Their discomfort stemmed from deeply ingrained practice-habits. Each of these pianists used their hours of practicing to correct details rather than to grasp and perform phrases. Accustomed to halting at wrong notes or other misplayed details, and either beginning again at the offending point or going back to the start of the piece, they found the need to ignore such lapses during class deeply disturbing.

In fact, a significant number of them were so conditioned by this start-stop-repeat routine that they often broke off during a combination. I need not go into the matter of their approach to a dance-phrase, but I should point out what may have already occurred to the reader. That is, they radically disrupted class, irritated the teachers – and several were eventually fired. There will, inevitably, be times when the pianist *is* forced to stop; occasional mishap, however, is quite different from habitual indulgence. The two obvious correctives are awareness of the dance phrase, and transference of this to one's practice-hours. This can only benefit the pianist for 'Actual playing involves the exact reverse of stopping. Why then practice stopping? . . . It is a matter of *which* is more important: a slip in the production of tone, or the disruption of the rhythm. A performance is not too greatly marred by a faulty tone, but it is ruined by a faulty halting rhythm.'[19] This problem, of course, is related to continuity (see above).

One circumstance beyond your control is the temperature of the studio, but you can help by adjusting your tempos to suit. On days when the studio seemed like the inside of a refrigerator, I was often asked to take the beginning *pliés* at a considerably slower tempo than usual. I have even known teachers to continue thus for much of the class when the room was particularly cold. Time will be saved if the teacher does not have continually to speak to you because you have galloped off at the more normal tempos.

XII. Memorization

A large, varied collection of pieces for class carried around in a heavy brief-case is a burden and a source of problems; the same collection transported in your head is a boon to all concerned. As I have said, frantic searches through music during class interfere with your work, not to mention that of the teacher and dancers. Thus, even though you may always have found memorization of music difficult, it is a must, and you will have to develop this important skill. By the merest coincidence, no doubt, my piano pupils who had the greatest trouble memorizing pieces were the ones who played notes rather than phrases, and stopped at every mistake rather than carrying on without breaking the flow. Those who, on the other hand, understood phrasing and played with continuity usually memorized all but the most complicated works in a short time.

I have known many piano teachers who viewed memorization as something separate. Their schedule consisted of learning the notes, 'adding the expression', and, finally, remembering all of this without the printed music. This resembles the piece-work of the assembly-line, except that one person is performing all of the detached operations. I suggest that none of them can be practiced in isolation with musical results. Certainly the process of memorization should *begin* with the first reading of the *music* (as opposed to notes). By 'reading' I mean also listening, whether the first acquaintance with the music is through the inner ear while studying the score or while actually playing it. For, as Sidney Harrison says, 'too many people play with their eyes, as though deaf'.[20]

The same considerations apply to the memorizing of music as do to performance. 'Muscular habits in production of tone', writes Abby Whiteside (dancers take note):

will determine the habits of listening and thus have a very definite bearing on memorizing. Notewise procedure (single initiations of power, as with a finger technique) will develop notewise listening, and that will hamper facility and security in memorizing. Muscular habits which correspond to a continuous flowing rhythm are a constructive assistance to memorizing. They keep attention on the statement as a whole, and parts are assimilated because they contribute to the meaning of the whole statement.[21]

Three types of memorization

The accompanist will, naturally, memorize many pieces from the printed music. But, if she limits herself to this, a great deal of extremely valuable and beautiful music for class will remain largely unused. Even if she has, as recommended, augmented her repertoire with pieces not originally written for piano, these are not practical for use in class unless they are memorized. It is unthinkable to carry heavy orchestral or opera scores around. The best road to memory for this music is through records or radio performances. But, I found a third way to memorize. This gradually developed while I was playing the music in class, and proved to be the most valuable of all. The three approaches vary in difficulty, and some will find one easier than another. I believe, however, that all should be used. The different activity involved in each will reinforce the others and strengthen one's memory-processes.

a. From the printed page

Some pianists have photographic memories. While this retention of detail is impressive, and useful up to a point, it does not in itself solve the problem of memorizing music as a flow. A photographed page is static; it cannot move, and what you want is the translation of separate marks on a page into movement. Music travels through time, whereas printed notes, whether on the page or fixed photographically in the mind, stay put until given continuity by the performer. Thus, the dynamics of memorizing music are absent despite the fixing of detail in the mind. A photographic memory, in fact, should be viewed as the mixed blessing which the wise musician knows perfect pitch to be: a source of help when used in conjunction with other skills, but a potential trap which leads to over-reliance and the consequent dulling of other, possibly more important skills.

When memorizing as you play from the score, the most important thing is the scanning of phrases: that is, reading over and beyond the separating bar lines, using your peripheral vision to the utmost. As you practice this, you should gradually be able to encompass more and more while you are playing. *Never* try to memorize within the confines of one measure, and another measure, and then another. Your memorization depends upon continuity – the relating of many events to one another. The details within the measure should become absorbed into melodic contours, harmonic and rhythmic patterns, and their direction through a phrase.

Recall Harrison's wry comment on 'deaf' pianists. While you are proceeding from phrase to phrase, always scanning ahead, you must also be *listening* to what you are playing, *remembering* it, and *hearing* what is coming. Since you cannot literally hear future music at the same instant as present and past music, you must develop a musical sixth sense. I will refer to this as 'projection'. Projection is musical prediction based on retention of the information which you have been gathering. Not only is this essential for expert sight-reading, it helps the memory-process. When you project, you are actively involved in the making of the music – somewhat like the composer himself; when you only read from note to note, being faced continually with surprises, you are trying (unsuccessfully) to live in an eternal present. Attempt projection every time you read through a piece. You will be surprised at the difference it can make in the speed and tenacity of your memorizing.

Performing through the fingers, without the aid of both the inner and outer ear, impedes memorization more than any other factor. An important aid to aural memory is the careful observance of dynamics. Dynamics, of course, present yet more details with which to cope, yet they make the process of memorizing easier. Music being the movement of sounds, rather than sounds *per se*, and this movement of sounds consisting of a dynamic flow, or alterations in intensity, the performer who approaches memorizing while bearing this in mind is in a strong position. Movement, or continuity of events, is far easier to perceive and remember than separate details (as anyone who has tried to memorize the *words* of a poem should realize).

If, furthermore, you are experiencing gradations of volume within the flow of the music as aspects of movement rather than sound you will, unless you are remarkably inhibited, almost certainly be moving sympathetically while playing. This will reinforce your efforts to memorize, for the body remembers much more deeply and reliably than the mind.

The forgetful performer is said to have 'lost her place'. Again, this has to do with movement. Music does not consist of a series of 'places'; it is *activity*. It is, therefore, imperative that the pianist who is attempting to memorize from a printed page begin with movement as the basis of her effort – both physical, kinetic movement and aural perception of musical phrases. Dynamics are an inextricable part of these directings of energy. The physical movement must, needless to say, be appropriate to the musical motion of the phrases or they will fight one another. Incompatible physical movement will produce distorted dynamic motion. The music will then be harder than ever to remember, for it cannot be taken spontaneously into the body.

Other aids exist for the pianist who is memorizing from the page. The first is to be aware of the muscular sensation in the hands peculiar to each key. Playing in D major, for instance, is quite different from playing in, say, E^b major, and radically different from B^b minor. This is partly due to the varying distributions of black and white notes in each key. Even so close a key as A major feels different from D major.

The second aid is both more far-reaching and more difficult. It incorporates *two* activities, both practiced away from the keyboard. After several attempts at memorizing a section, move away from the piano and try to sing through what you have just played (without the score, of course). The melody will usually tend to be the easiest element to recall, but try also to reproduce in your mind the accompanying harmonies, rhythmic patterns and counter-melodies. Be as precise as possible. It is just as important not to waver and lose the rhythm when singing it as when playing at the keyboard. Keep an alive pulse in your body and do not allow the more complicated rhythms to alter it. In addition, do not be careless about such matters as dotted eighth- plus sixteenth-note patterns. It is all too easy to change these into triplets consisting of a quarter and an eighth note. After reviewing as much as you can remember away from the piano, return to the keyboard and repeat your efforts, first playing from score then going across the room and singing. See, also, if you can *add* to the amount memorized each time. I know, incidentally, several pianists who say that they developed quite a reliable relative pitch by such means. This is due, no doubt, to the repeated act of singing and mentally hearing the music – at the proper pitch, of course – in this concentrated fashion. The physical and the mental–aural activities reinforce one another effectively.

A further development of this method involves the use of the body. First, describe shapes in the air with your hands and arms, and even legs, which seem appropriate to the quality and motion of the music you are singing. Then, as you gain confidence, move your entire body. If you use very simple movements – preferably balletic ones – and repeat them over and over with the music, this can prove invaluable as a mnemonic device. They must, however, be executed with the same scrupulous attention to rhythm as you gave to the playing and singing.

A third aid uses otherwise empty traveling-time. In this case, you will first read a section or two and then try to hear it in your mind without looking at the score. This, of course, demands concentration. To do it at all well you must shut out the noise and bustle around you – which is in itself a valuable exercise. An extension of this approach is the visualization of simple *barre* exercises and combinations which go well with the music you are memorizing. In order for this to be helpful, however, you must have a reasonably clear sense of the muscular feeling and attack of, say, a *dégajé* or *frappé*, a simple *pirouette* or *adagio* combination. Visualizing movements is beneficial in three ways. Not only do you aid your musical memory through association, but you also make ballet movements more familiar and natural. In addition, you are inter-relating the movement and music in your own mind. In class you must comply with the external requirements of teacher and dancers; here you are creating the inter-relationship yourself (and, incidentally, utilizing your memory regarding *movement*).

b. *From recordings and radio*

Memorizing through the ear only, without reference to a score, *should* not be difficult. It was, in fact, the only way to transmit music from one person to another until the relatively late development of musical notation. But two developments made memorization a problem instead of a part of the performer's normal equipment. One is the increased *complexity* of the technical capabilities of instruments and the simultaneous increase in musical complexity. The second, related, development is the growing reliance on *notation* in which the eye supplants the ear in the learning of music.

This shift in emphasis had far-reaching effects. Not only was the performer eventually conditioned to accept the notation as absolute, but the function of aural memory was undermined by the convenience of the printed page for reference. As a result, it was trained to a far lesser degree, being brought into action only at the *end* of the learning process instead of, as originally, from the very beginning. (See discussion of performance and notation in relation to improvisation, Chapter 10.) Because of this, a surprising number of performers never manage to develop reliably an aspect of their craft which once was taken for granted.

Certainly, many medieval and renaissance musicians used, when available, the relatively scarce scores of their times. But these were spare indeed: in effect, musical shorthand rather than the attempted precise totality of the nineteenth and twentieth centuries. Their function was not to convey all possible information, but to jog the memory and remind performers of details already absorbed through aural transmission by other performers (similar to the role of dance notation today). This was reinforced by *association*, either of music with words, or music with movement of their own bodies or of dancers whom they were accompanying.

Although by modern standards these performers were much less technically proficient, they had a common strength, lacking in the average performer today. When, through necessity, they learned the music physically and aurally rather than visually, they not only escaped the muscular inhibitions from which so many performers now suffer, but they were compelled to approach music as a manifestation of breath and phrase. It is the visual learner who reads and attempts to finger and memorize *measures*; these do not exist as such for the aural musician, being swept into the general flow of the music, just as the fingers which play the notes are gathered into a larger bodily response. For these reasons, I consider the learning and memorization of music through the ear alone to be one of the most valuable – in fact, irreplaceable – aspects of the performer's training. We cannot, obviously, dispense with notation, but we *can* prevent it from usurping the role of the ear in developing musical memory.

Moreover, aural memorization has an important practical benefit, particularly if the accompanist has only limited access to scores. No one can buy all the music necessary for a wide-ranging repertoire, and only a small proportion of libraries have a really comprehensive collection of circulating scores. Your field is, therefore, expanded to an otherwise unattainable degree if you can memorize music from recordings: your own, those of friends, or music played on the radio.

If you have never tried this, it is best to begin with quite simple pieces, for one or two instruments, with clear melodic lines and simple accompanying figures. Most folk-songs would be suitable, as would popular ballads and dance-tunes. Somewhat more complicated, but still suitable for early attempts, are pieces such as the sonatinas of Mozart, the simplest of Schubert's songs, or popular Verdi arias. The Gilbert and Sullivan operettas, also, are not too challenging.

From the very beginning you must listen for phrases and shapes, rhythm and impulse, rather than notes and details. Contours and motion can remain with you long after specifics have been forgotten (early medieval scores, in fact, were based on contour, as a simple memory-aid). If you listen only for *notes*, you will inevitably miss a large number of them during the course of the music, and the ones you did somehow catch will form only disconnected half-memories. Fragments are of little use. You need continuity (some fragmentation is, of course, unavoidable at first). It is best to begin by using records rather than radio, for the knowledge that you can repeat the music will give a sense of security.

One advantage you will find is that a great deal of music utilizes the principle of repetition. The simplest forms of this are A-B-A, A-A-B-A and A-B-A-C-A or rondo-form. Even when the forms are more complex, the composer repeats themes, if over a longer time-span. Thus, it is not a matter of now or never. You will usually have at least two or three re-hearings of the main material.

To aid your first efforts, keep a small notebook by the record player. As you listen to the first statement of the melody, try to grasp quickly its shape and direction. Does it move up in a stepwise fashion? Down with frequent leaps? Does it continue in a broad arc or does it alternate up-and-down motion? Is it a continuous, spun-out phrase (like the *Swan Lake adagio* discussed earlier) or are there little motivic repetitions? Does it begin with a dramatic leap or rhythm and then subside, or does it begin quietly and conclude in some dramatic fashion? All of these are easily transformed into shapes and patterns which you can sketch in the air and then, during repetitions, in your notebook. (This is partly a visual technique, of course, but not in the sense of static symbols on a page. Here the visual is a depiction of actual movement which you have felt in your own body).

After the first hearing, you should be able to retain at least the opening patterns, their subsequent occurrence within the section, and, above all, a sense of the section as a shape, or succession of shapes. If there is an immediate repeat, this offers an opportunity to jot down clear rhythmic patterns, and, if you have a quick ear, some of the underlying harmonic progressions: I–V–I–V–I$_7$–IV–V$_7$–I, for instance.

If the piece is in A-A-B-A form, you will now be faced with a contrasting section. Do not give in to the temptation to mark time during it, merely waiting for a return of the opening. The B section, no matter how contrasted to the A it may *seem*, usually relates to it in some way or carries its thought forward (see Chapter 10 on contrast, pp. 263–4). Otherwise it would be in a different piece. Approach this section in the same way as you did the beginning – through its shape and flow rather than particular notes. If there is a repeat, use it for reinforcement of your first impressions.

When the A returns, it should seem like a friend – if not an old one, at least a familiar one. If you have listened properly to its original statements, you should now be able to grasp even more of the patterns and details within it.

At this point, stop, and without reference to your sketch immediately try to sing the melody of what you have just heard. You may falter when you come to the B section, but at least keep the pulse and continuity in your body until the return of the A. (I need hardly add that the entire effort should include gradations of dynamics and *some* expressivity.)

Now you must repeat the entire operation – with one difference: try to sing the melody throughout while playing the record. If you simply cannot manage the B, which is quite likely, listen attentively and then pick up the return of the A. Then reflect for a moment on what you have heard (and sung) and try again to sing it through. *This* is the time to attempt the filling-in of detail. The advantage of records – repetition at will – should certainly be exploited, but only after you have an overall feeling of the piece. To begin by playing short passages over and over again is not only useless but nerve-wracking. If you can only get the melodic details, go to the piano and *sing*, do not play just yet. Try instead to *hear* the harmonies, in relation to the melody. Otherwise you will merely end up fumbling for isolated chords. Then, attempt playing the harmonies, singing meanwhile, in a slow but rhythmical tempo. As you reach each chord of the sequence, do not break the melodic line, but try to hear the harmony and then play it as soon as possible. Continue thus until the end of the phrase. All of the harmonies, incidentally, should be played in block form even if, in the music, they are broken up or arpeggiated in some way. You can pursue complications later; what you are attempting now is the quick hearing of the different harmonies as you sing through the phrase, followed as soon as possible by the playing of them, without interrupting the flow of the melody.

This may all sound like a particularly painful form of pulling yourself up by your bootstraps; the degree of pain will depend on how far you have allowed your musical ear to atrophy. But no matter what level of skill you are now at, these efforts can also be exciting and rewarding as you advance from one level to the next.

Check your progress from time to time by attempting to memorize one or two simple pieces from single hearings over the radio. Your memorizing-program should now be at level 2 of difficulty for recorded music and level 1 for radio-music. Carry on in this manner, keeping recorded music at a slightly more complex level than radio music.

No matter how little progress you may seem to be making, do not give up. The value of a highly developed ear and memory far outweighs any travail, for reasons which I *hope* I have made clear.

For years, I automatically switched on the radio for an hour each morning before leaving for class. By far the largest percentage of my repertoire was, in fact, obtained in this way. At the very beginning I listened to the radio mostly for the identification of usable pieces which I could then learn from the score. Then I found that I was retaining more and more of the music I heard, at least long enough to use in class that day. At this point, another application of memory took over – the close identification of a piece with a combination which the teacher used frequently.

c. In class

Here we come to a primarily kinesthetic approach. I recommended relating movements to music when learning from printed notes or recorded music. In class your memorization will be assisted by the actual visual experience of movement reinforced and supported by your playing.

For this to work reliably, you must feel an empathy with the dancers. More than at any other time you must have the sense of dancing yourself. This will intensify the association of music to movement and imbed both deeper in your memory. It is astonishing how tenacious this type of memorization can be. Many times in class I have been reminded of a piece, long since filed away in my mind, by the teacher giving a combination which I particularly associated with that music. Often the mere 'talking' of the combination, rhythmically, was enough to stimulate my memory. Even now, if I visualize certain teachers giving their favorite combinations, I can quickly recall the pieces they preferred for these. And this ten to twenty years after I last played for those teachers.

Dancers benefit from kinesthetic memory also. Many references to its value can be found in books on dance. 'It is . . . a fact within the experience of dancers', write van Praagh and Brinson '– attested by Tamara Karsavina and Lydia Sokolova in their memoirs – that a kind of muscle memory exists alongside conscious memory. It springs from the stimulus of music. Often when dancers seem to have forgotten a role, the playing of the music will stimulate their limbs to respond with the appropriate steps.'[22] Earlier, Bournonville recognized this: 'The principal strengthener of memory, both with regard to dance steps and mimed action, is the music whose melodies and rhythms are transplanted from the ear to the rest of the body, and in striking fashion guide these movements along the correct channels.'[23] A fascinating two-way street, for both dancer and musician.

Kinesthetic reinforcement of the memory saved me many otherwise lost treasures. I found that if I played a piece hastily assimilated from a brief radio performance for a striking combination in class an hour or so later, I rarely forgot the music. If, on the other hand, the occasion to use a newly and quickly memorized radio discovery did not arise that day, portions of it could be forgotten. Since I might never hear it again, this made it forever useless for class.

I do not mean, by the way, that one should always play the same piece for a combination which the teacher uses frequently. Quite the contrary! As I have stressed in discussing the selection of repertoire, the dancers benefit enormously from doing the same movements to different pieces, with various styles and attack. I mean simply that, within reason, the repetition of a piece to the point where you have a strong visual and muscular association to a particular combination is one of the strongest possible aids to the memory, and should be used as such – but never as a crutch for a lazy imagination regarding the selection of music.

While you are developing your musical memory, it will be helpful to carry the little notebook with your jottings and sketches. This can be quickly and unobtrusively referred to during class. Your goal, however, is that admirable state of freedom from any notes, when all of your repertoire is in your mind and body. Your notebook can be of value, of course, as a comprehensive record of all the pieces you have used through the years. You cannot play every one in your repertoire regularly. Thus some items are bound to be unused for a while, and a record of them with enough identifying notes to bring them back is recommended. Place your greatest reliance, however, on your kinesthetic memory.

XIII. The 'perfect' performance

In answer to the question, 'Does one perfect performance of a composition subsist as the ideal toward which every actual one should aspire?', Edward T. Cone answers: 'Most people would probably agree that, even if a perfect interpretation is conceivable, it is hardly possible of achievement, and that every actual performance must be at best an approximation of it.'[24]

I shall go a step further, and say that in my opinion the concept of a perfect performance is a mechanistic and grisly one. This will be gone into in relation to improvisation in Chapter 10, but one point should be made here.

When playing for dance movement, the possible variations in musical perform-ance – the valid ones, that is, as opposed to temperamental whims – are demonstrated in a unique and fascinating way. Everyone has heard the differences in 'interpretation' which various performers can bring to a familiar piece. It is even more striking to *see* the differences in conjunction with movement. The malleability or ambiguity of music (see Chapter 2) is then all the more apparent. That is to say, the dance phrases can alter, sometimes radically, the character and flow of the accompanying musical ones. One day you may play 'O mio babbino caro' from Puccini's *Gianni Schicchi* in a certain way for an *adagio*, and the next day, when using it for another, quite different, *adagio*, find that, without conscious intent, you are shaping the phrases, and inter-relating them, in a markedly altered way. The movement may lead you to stress certain moments which you glided through the previous day, and underplay other moments which then seemed the most important.

I am in no way indicating conscious deviation or distortion. It is, rather, a case of making the same journey on two occasions, but focusing on and experiencing aspects of it with a different emphasis each time. Both starting and ending points are identical, each journey equally rewarding, yet, perceived in different ways, the events within each are not quite the same. The first *adagio* may have had a dramatic moment which coincided with the octave leap at the end of the second phrase of 'O mio babbino caro', followed by a restrained sequence. The second *adagio* might, on the other hand, sail through the event of the octave leap to culminate in an expressive peak within the following musical phrase. I have heard singers automatically punch out the octave leap every time they sang this aria, and others perform it with varying degrees of emphasis from one performance to the next. When a fine performer brings such flexibility to a piece of music, you will be convinced at the time that this is the only way it could possibly be performed, even though you may have a marked preference for another interpretation, or have been equally convinced by yet a different version the week before.

Similarly, with one dance-version you may feel it to be utterly right – only to discover the next time, when you play a piece for a different combination, that you are being moved to play with quite a different approach, which feels equally right. The accompanist should be particularly sensitive to the effect which dance-movement has on the phrasing of the music. If you find that you habitually play a piece in exactly the same way, no matter how different the combinations may be, you should be suspicious. This can only happen if you are utilizing a preconception rather than responding to a situation.

In conclusion, I must say that one of the most enlightening things which the accompanist can do is to take part in a class herself. Even the usual evening class composed of rank amateurs is, if given by a good teacher, an excellent opportunity to experience ballet from the opposite side of the wall (the wall that we want to remove).

In addition to the pleasure in moving that tripping about in a leotard can give you, it may help to free you from the physical inhibitions common to so many pianists. This new sense of physical freedom can have many beneficial repercussions on your playing. And, very important: participating yourself will give you the chance to evaluate its accompanist in the most direct possible way. How does she help or hinder you in your struggles to learn the exercises and move with continuity? You can also chat with the other students to learn their reactions to the music provided for them and its performance. This will differ from talks with the dancers in the classes which you yourself accompany, for now you actually will be in their shoes.

I hope it is now firmly established that an accompanist who is sensitive and responsive to the dancers' needs is by definition an excellent pianist. Said the famous Ignaz Friedman: 'There are the notes, there is what is between the notes, there is what is behind the notes.' I will add: Here are the steps, here is what is between the steps, here is what is behind the steps. Although the medium of one is the most abstract (sound), and the other the most concrete and familiar (the human body), good performance in each depends ultimately on the same principles.

10   Improvisation 1 – Some basic principles

We all possess unsuspected talents, powers and capacities without knowing they
exist, but stored up in the subconscious mind, and which the conscious mind ignores.
E. Herbert-Caesari, *Vocal Truth*, 1978

I. The significance of improvisation

NO MATTER how large and varied your repertoire may be, and how
wonderfully you perform it, something vital will be missing from your
artistry and versatility as a ballet accompanist if you cannot improvise
well and frequently. The ability to improvise well also implies a higher level of
excellence in your other accompanying skills. Furthermore, your life in the ballet
studio will prove much easier, and far more interesting, if you can create your own
music on the spot.

Unfortunately, the art of making music as you go has suffered a sharp decline.
Since the earliest days of music, improvisation was one of its most basic aspects. As
Vincent Persichetti writes,

For many centuries performers have contributed to the process of shaping music. Improvisation,
or the spontaneous creation of music, has existed from the beginning of musical practice. Before
the era of Western music the division of creative musician, performing musician and passive
listener did not exist. Ties between the composer and performer were so close that clear
distinction between the two was impossible, composer and performer being frequently the same
person.

Even after the development of musical notation, which included alphabetical symbols,
tablatures and neumes, the impulse to create spontaneously remained. There is scarcely a
compositional technique or form that did not originate in improvisatory practice.[1]

This impulse to create spontaneously continued to thrive even as relatively
recently as the periods of Beethoven, Chopin and Liszt. Chopin, for instance,
seldom played a composition twice in the same way, but altered it according to the
mood or situation at the time. Later, for publication, he would settle on one
version, which was then frozen within the printed score, thus misleading music-
lovers of later times into the belief that this was the original 'composition'.
Actually, it was the distillation and re-working of perhaps a dozen previous
versions. Many people attended his salon recitals more out of interest in his
improvisational imagination than in specific pieces. Now, the average music lover
goes to a concert to hear 'the' Chopin *Fantaisie-Impromptu* (note the implications of
this title) or 'the' Scherzo in B flat minor.

Spontaneous public invention was gradually replaced by an adherence to the
precision notation demanded by the ever more complex – in content and in
ensemble – works of the nineteenth century. Increasingly entrapped by the

240

dictator–composer, with his barrage of musical symbols and signs, verbal directions and specific notes which must be played 'correctly', the performer ceased to be a co-creator and became essentially an interpreter (who might be accused of egocentric distortion of the composer's 'message'). Even the most undogmatic of today's artists cannot, no matter how sensitively they play, eradicate this new tradition of separation of composer and performer, and adherence to and perpetual repetition of the minutest printed detail (even though this adherence is based on a delusion, for notation in all its complexity remains imprecise, unable to convey many nuances and potentialities of performance). Says Thurston Dart: 'This progressive annihilation of the performer's share in the creation of a piece of music is an alarming phenomenon and one that has never occurred before in the whole history of music, European and non-European.'[2] A performer was once appreciated for his imaginative treatment of a basic theme or scheme; now he is appraised according to his 'faithfulness to the composer's commands,' or what Dart scornfully calls 'the Authorized Version'.[3]

Sensitivity to what Whone and others have called the play element in performance could go far to ameliorate the modern temptation to view notation as a slave-driver whom one must either labor for obediently or escape from egotistically. Whone describes Eastern improvisation wherein 'the player, opening himself to supra-personal forces becomes a vehicle for imaginative play' – which also once was the case in the West – contrasting this with the modern Western player's greatest limitation:

that he cannot let himself go because of his trained committal to the written note and to his own identity . . . Ideally a musician is said to play an instrument – he does not work an instrument. Like the painter doodling, his play at its best is near to extemporization – a state of being freed from time . . . The reconciliation of opposites is the condition of creative play – of imaginative play; and if the opposites are out of balance that play is impossible.[4]

The venerable tradition of improvisation balanced the opposites of energy and form; performers within the modern Western tradition of detailed notation tend to be pulled dangerously close to one opposite or another.

It is remarkable that the near-destruction of the composer–performer, the performer–improviser, could have taken such a short time. Only two centuries, after a tradition spanning thousands of years, and it has been achieved to a degree that the instigators could not have imagined. Some of these were 'the late eighteenth-century pedants, who turned counterpoint and harmony into "paper work" [and who] have much to answer for; they forced the ear to abdicate in favour of the eye, and they broke the links of extemporization that in all earlier times had held composer, performer, and listener in a single musical chain.'[5]

Mercifully, however, the destruction is not total. The performer–creator is not an extinct species. Some composers still improvise while composing, as Vincent Persichetti says, 'in their heads – draft after draft. Those who happen to have keyboard facility and can "think with their fingers" are able to illustrate what they are thinking. Perhaps we are at the beginning of a new era of improvisation.'[6]

Persichetti not only employs this age-old art when composing in solitude, but devotes much time to public activity. To him, improvising is a necessary, everyday part of living, and he practices it in the most diverse roles – from church organist to creator of musical 'portraits' of friends at parties. He also gives concerts made up of improvisations upon themes and motives supplied by the audience.

Other moves back to improvisation exist. The interpolated sections within electronic pieces, in which live performers are given licence to extemporize, reflect a straining against the bonds of precision, as did the controversial efforts of Cornelius Cardew's Scratch Orchestra, and the many other composers who use or evoke an improvisational style, in an amazing variety of ways.

Improvisation is also still kept alive to a degree by dance accompanists, and pianists who play for the various sorts of 'creative movement' classes which are popular today.

There are, certainly, performers here and there who seem to have been born with a feeling for improvisation. Original yet coherent music pours from their fingers, although rarely is the result as remarkable as with Persichetti, to whom improvisation is as natural as breathing. Most performers do not or cannot give it the necessary time and love that is needed for excellence. Even if a potential is there, it usually remains unstirred. Because of conditioning and training, the majority of performers tend to be so enslaved and obsessed by the printed note that the spontaneity which improvisation demands is choked off. Or, if they manage to preserve a knack for it midst the usual constrictions, this exists as part of a musical schizophrenia. One side of the personality improvises, the other 'executes' pieces. And, as Abby Whiteside writes,

the talented person who loves to improvise and does it expertly does not necessarily play the classics with the same kind of delightful rhythmic flow. The improvising uses ears and rhythm as a fused unit. The eye, reading, or habits of practice can and frequently do interfere with this fusion of ear and rhythm, and the result in playing is a lack of rhythmic progression which distorts dynamics and creates a performance without any of the charm which was a part of the improvisation.[7]

Thus, another of the many benefits which improvisation possesses eludes us. Perhaps if performers realized in how many ways improvisational skill could transform their musical life they would take action. The overused eye would be superseded by the under-used ear and inner rhythmic sense, and for the accompanist this fusion of ear and rhythm would be augmented by the element of dance movement.

To improvise well for class you need quick reactions indeed. Your eyes and ears must be as keen and alert as those of a wild creature. Now, it may seem 'easier' to rely on repertoire, but this is a negative refuge. Also, it can lead to the sacrifice of two valuable elements: freshness and flexibility. These give you welcome variety. But something else, equally important, is needed.

Consistency and variety

Two characteristics are vital: consistency and variety. To be consistent means first of all to have some sort of conception or general frame of reference. According to Abby Whiteside, 'Improvisation cannot start unless some idea is formulated. The fact that an idea takes place will mean a going forward to its conclusion. It is this starting with a definite purpose of fulfilling, completing the idea, which produces action that does not sag and fall apart.'[8] (For a certain qualification of this theory, see end of chapter.)

Improvisations which begin in a Mozartian style and metamorphose into a (vaguely) Puccinian one, or which begin in a Russian idiom and soon travel to Italy (or, more often, an odd musical no-man's land) are frustrating and incoherent for the listener. They also convey ineptness. 'Don't start what you can't finish' is a maxim peculiarly pertinent to improvisation in class. To change a Mozartian clarity into a Puccinian lushness is senseless enough musically; when this is inflicted on an elegant *allegro* combination – for which the Mozartian style may be excellent – the incongruity will produce muscular, kinetic confusion in the dancers. Involvement with the over-all spirit of the combination (or potential spirit, if the teacher gives no help in this area) should help to prevent you from changing horses in midstream. A radical stylistic switch usually indicates a lack of concern in what the dancers are doing, in addition to a poor ear.

You need, however, to avoid monotony. Your basic conception must leave room for freshness and variety, or consistency will be replaced by uniformity. There are many ways to achieve variety, the best ones being relatively simple. Since one of the precepts of all good music is variety within unity, we shall look more closely during the course of this chapter at ways in which the improviser can develop both of these.

I should point out that even when you become expert, *every* improvisation cannot possibly be first-rate, or perfect for the combination at hand. Do not fret, therefore, if you sometimes produce a mediocrity. No reasonable teacher will expect infallibility. Many accompanists are inhibited, feeling that each effort should rival Beethoven's Fifth. Resist this. If you worry too much about the creation of instant masterpieces you will be tense and self-conscious. Let the music and the movement take over, so that no room is left for competitive constraint.

Hearing, perfect pitch and relative pitch

To improvise at all, you need keyboard facility – enough to prevent technical execution from being a preoccupation – and imagination. These alone, however, are not sufficient. I hold two beliefs: one, that no one can improvise consistently well without a good ear, inner as well as outer. You must be able to perceive keenly while listening to music, but you must also have the capacity to create music in your head; two, that no musician is incapable of developing a better ear than she now possesses.

The finest ears of all, many believe, are those whose owners have what is called 'perfect' or 'absolute' pitch. Any readers who do will find it a great asset in improvising. If, however, you do not, be of good cheer. In addition to its beneficial aspects it has a negative side, being one of the most pernicious of all pawns in the game of musical one-upmanship. Perfect pitch is often used as a spurious criterion despite the fact that it can be grossly over-rated. I have known musicians fortunate enough to have it – and witless enough to allow it to seduce them into a false superiority and lazy, mechanical listening habits. I have, on the other hand, known musicians without it who, by application and exercise of dormant aptitude, have cultivated what is called 'relative' pitch. This is a highly developed, very rapid aural perception and correlation of musical sounds, whereas perfect pitch is an instantaneous identification. (No one has yet fully analyzed the nature of perfect pitch and it remains a provocative mystery that deserves more attention.) Both perfect and relative pitch are forms of aural memory, although they obviously operate in different ways. The 'perfect' improviser would combine the accuracy of perfect pitch with the acumen of excellent relative pitch. Apart from the general musical value of both types of hearing, they also represent a practical shortcut for the improviser. Whereas musicians who have neither hear a certain *effect*, without reliably being able to pick out the components, those with perfect or relative pitch can, with varying ease, identify them and tuck them away in a mental filing-case for future use. They can perceive how a composer uses certain chord progressions, inversions, melodic twists and the like, and reproduce these or use them as a point of departure when desired in class.

Musicians, of course, can have good ears who do not have perfect or relative pitch. And better hearing can always be developed. The more you listen – actively, that is – the more you will be able to hear (just as the more you use your brain the better able you are to think). Increasing the ability to hear, identify and reproduce musical events better than you now can simply requires resolve, attentiveness, and consistent application. A depressingly large number of musicians do not listen to music *attentively*. They may consider their academic score-analyses to be proof of their musicianship, but the test is in what one hears. Many music-lovers and dancers, on the other hand, lack aural attentiveness in responding on only a passive sensuous level. Full-dimensional listening to music is not the norm, as it should be, but a problem – as the stacks of books on 'What to Listen For In Music' or complex theory demonstrate.

As John Blacking writes,

I am aware that many audiences before and since the composition of Haydn's *Surprise Symphony* have not listened attentively to music, and that, in a society which has invented notation, music could be handed down by a hereditary elite without any need for listeners. But if we take a world view of music, and if we consider social situations in musical traditions that have no notation, it is clear that the creation and performance of most music is generated first and foremost by the human capacity to discover patterns of sound and to identify them on subsequent occasions.[9]

His last phrase certainly has a direct bearing on improvising and its reliance on how well we can 'discover', and reproduce, sound-patterns. It is the endless combinations and permutations of the basic scales, chords and rhythmic patterns of our culture which form the raw material for your improvisations. They, like compositions, do not come from nothingness; they are a reworking – fresh and compelling, it is to be hoped – of sounds you have already heard (which is why the goal of completely 'original' creation is so silly).

We now turn from generalities to specifics, and after a bit of psychology we will survey the four basic elements of melody, harmony, rhythm and form, from the improvisational viewpoint.

Three primal weaknesses

The weaknesses described here are saddening. They can be dubbed 'subversive' because they sabotage any potential flair on higher levels. Those who suffer from them are permitting timidity to throttle imagination, and fear to deafen both their inner and outer ear. Now, it is hard to say which is the most devastating in ballet class – improvised harmonies *always* in root position, choice of only one or two keys for all improvisations (the higher the percentage of improvisations during class, the more unbearable, of course) or the compulsive use of only the middle range of the keyboard.

To identify the first ordeal, simply try to recollect the sound of attacks upon the piano by friends who 'always regret never really learning to play the piano'. Almost invariably, their struggles to reproduce some familiar ditty will include clumps of root-position triads in the bass – and not always the correct ones – resulting in awkward parallel progressions. This is not to say that parallel, root-position chords cannot be used to exquisite effect, as in the spacious, bucolic passages of Vaughan Williams, Delius, Debussy and others. Their usage is, however, sensitively visualized, not inadvertent, while here we are concerned with a harmonic 'rootedness' caused by lack of confidence.

The second ordeal is perhaps more subtle, but no less wearing. I once observed a ballet class during which the accompanist improvised throughout, and did so, without exception, in the key of A minor – or something vaguely resembling it. This was his home base, and he clearly was too frightened to leave it. The obsessive tonality was bad enough, but its being consistently *minor* drove one to thoughts of suicide. Needless to say, the expressions and movements of the dancers reflected the general morbidity (he was an extreme case, but this malady of tonal paralysis is widespread).

Third in our list of psychological infirmities is the restricted use of register. The piano is comparatively limited in tone-color and gradation; why exaggerate this by ignoring the deep bass-sonorities and glittering, incisive high treble of its huge 88-key range? Why huddle in the middle of the keyboard like a sheep in a fold? Timid improvisers seem to find an illusory security there, overlooking the fact that if you extend your range on either side you are almost certain to get more ideas than when stuck in the middle. Your textures and spacings, also, will tend to improve.

As a postscript I should mention another fault which is not as common as the ones just described, but it *is* a temptation to certain improvisers, and leads them astray. This fault is over-complexity. The other three denote the absence of certain skills and confidence; over-complexity obviously requires a high level of skill and assurance. In its own way, however, it is just as wearing and ineffectual as the other faults. And it shows an improviser who has misconceived what she is supposed to be doing. Rather than the skill being directed toward sustaining the dancers, she often appears to be seeking melodies and harmonies known only to Martians. A little singularity in class can be marvelous – but this is usually most successfully achieved through simple means. In any case, even the courageous novice will learn much more quickly, with better results along the way, if she aims for simplicity and tonal neatness.

II. Four elements of improvisation

The following does not constitute an academic analysis of melody, harmony, rhythm, and form. Space limits me, and the excellent books devoted to these would make any necessarily sketchy attempts all the more inadequate. My purpose here is to focus on the four elements in ways which are of particular importance for the ballet-improviser, and I thus refer you to the relevant books listed in Appendix B.

1. Melody

Ballet music is, as I have said, seldom unmelodic. This does not mean that you are confined to the obvious tunefulness of 'Beautiful Dreamer', for melody can mean many things. It does mean, however, that ballet music must give a clear singing line of some sort rather than mere rhythmic patterns or percussive chords (at least primarily, for *tastes* of the latter may be quite effective).

Needless to say, it is not easy to improvise a good melody, but there are ways to the development of this knack. Every composer who has a musical personality will exhibit melodic characteristics, even marked idiosyncrasies. Study these closely. They can be quite subtle, but if you take familiar melodies by 'famous' composers and alter notes here and there, you may begin to see just how important those notes and their contexts are. Deeper study, however, comes from *singing* the melodies. The rise and fall of the line, with the guiding rhythms of the phrase, will then become a physical experience, easier to perceive and remember. Then try to change notes as you sing. With familiar melodies, the effect will be physically jarring, and even more so if you alter rhythms. You can do simple movements to the original version and then the altered one to reinforce the message.

After consistent efforts of this sort, you will gradually develop the ability to absorb characteristic melodic features of various composers into your subconscious and your muscles, ready to be drawn upon when needed.

The entanglement of melody with harmony and rhythm and style forces me to save further comments for the section on advanced improvising.

2. Harmony

The imperatives of good harmonic usage are (i) the facile employment of inversions, (ii) a strong bass-line (which is inseparable from a feeling for inversions), (iii) effective spacing of the component notes, with graceful voice-leading in the inner parts, and (iv) a sense of organic progression and consistency.

You may feel that such mastery is beyond you. It is not. Some may achieve it to a greater degree than others, and more quickly, but I believe that every pianist can go a considerable way towards the goal of apt and beautiful use of chords while improvising. This is worthy of any necessary effort, for a strong harmonic sense can support much else that may be weak.

(i) *Inversions*. Choose familiar tunes, but ones which you have not actually learned from the printed page, and try to harmonize them. If the result sounds odd or fumbling, inversions – or lack of them – may very well be the cause. Before checking the score, listen to a performance of the original and try to find what you have missed. When you finally discover, by one means or another, the correct harmonization, you may find that you have used the right chords, but in root-position. Another possibility is that you have used a first inversion instead of a second, or vice versa, producing an awkward bass-line.

Unfortunately, hearing the different positions of a chord is hard for many musicians, and much application is needed. In class, I suggest to the students that they listen for different spatial and kinetic qualities. A first inversion tends to sound sharp and active, partly because of the tension between the two bottom voices with their close 3rd, and the dynamic instability of the scale's III in the bass. The second inversion, with its lower interval of a 4th, sounds more resonant and less active, the relatively stable V in the bass contributing to this (I speak here of closed positions; open ones, with the bass note further away, or with other dispositions of the upper notes, will sound somewhat different, but the basic properties remain). Root-position chords sound, depending on context, 'rooted', solid, sturdy, decisive or final. (You may dispute the 'qualities' as described; however my point is that the positions vary in effect.)

But, a chord is not an absolute; it is part of a context, or what is sometimes called a *Gestalt*: 'chord succession of any kind is not just a series of separate root points but a harmonic relationship in which chords move forward . . . Two inseparable factors are involved with harmonic progression: what chord follows what chord, and how they are connected.'[10] Both factors draw upon inversions and bass-lines.

(ii) *Bass-line*. A strong, directional bass is as important as a clear melodic line. If I were confined to only one way of teaching this area of music, I would choose the study of Bach's four-part chorales. His bass-lines have strength, direction and inventiveness, as do the spacings and voice-leadings of the harmonies above (these frequently break academic rules – a sign of a good composer at work). When listening to these chorales, follow the score and sing the bass-line (an octave higher, if necessary) in order to realize fully the *physical* strength of its progress. Better yet, for study also of the spacings and voice-leadings, get three friends to join you in choral performance of as many chorales as possible. Change round to as many different vocal lines as your range permits.

Not being limited, however, to just the Bach chorales, you can extend your studies to bass-lines in, say, Chopin's music (particularly the Prelude in E minor op. 28, no. 4, and the Prelude in D minor op. 28, no. 24). Tchaikovsky, Brahms, Schumann, Ravel, Mozart, Beethoven and Handel are all valuable in this respect. Not all composers, however, have firm control over bass-movement. See if you can pinpoint any occasionally weak passages as being the result of momentary lack of direction in the bass, or awkwardness in conjunction with the harmonies.

I should mention one specialized form of bass-line – that of the *descending* bass. This is a boon for the improviser, in any tempo. Seemingly endless variety can be achieved through it. This may be proved by a journey through the passacaglia-chaconne, or 'ground-bass', creations from the late-Renaissance onward (start with Purcell's remarkable example in the aria, 'When I am laid to rest', from *Dido and Aeneas*). Since it *demands* use of inversions, experiments with it will reinforce efforts to develop flexibility in this area. Chopin's Prelude in E minor, mentioned above, is a beautiful Romantic example of the use of inversions with a free descending bass-line, and there are many more throughout the repertoire.

(iii) *Spacing, voicing and density.* The voicing and number of notes within a harmony are important. The various forms of one particular chord can give extremely different aural and physical effects. Compare the following versions of the same basic chord:

Ex. 1

These are just some of the possibilities, with the root, C, on the bottom, and the melodic E on top. All are inherently the same chord, yet each sounds different, and will differ even more depending on what chords come before and after. Which, over used, will produce muddiness? Which can bring clarity? Serenity? Excitement? When improvising for ballet class, you must be sensitive to the physical effect of density and spacing, but, as usual, these cannot be separated from other factors, such as the motion of the *inner* voices of your harmonies. As Persichetti says, 'Outer voices govern harmonic direction and inner voices secure the relationship of the chords. For unruffled harmonic motion inner voices are moved as little as possible and common tones are held . . .'[11] This approach would be most suitable for calm, flowing, sustained exercises such as *pliés*, *moderato pirouettes*, *port de bras*, simple *adagios*, etc. But, he writes, 'Smooth progressions are but one facet of the craft. There is a danger of their becoming overly smooth and much ingenuity is required to keep them fresh. Leaping voices, straying dissonances, escaping common tones, modulatory twists and chromatic daring are all part of harmonic technique.'[12] These are particularly effective for dynamic *allegros*, complex and dramatic *adagios*, big jumps, etc.

The number of notes in a chord can require doubling of some of the basic components. Thus one has the problem of which to select. Academic thought frowned upon the doubling of the 3rd note of the scale – yet this can be used to beautiful effect. It depends on how it is done. (It is perhaps a bit riskier if the chord is in the first inversion, with the 3rd in the bass.) Experiments at the keyboard, with various doublings, will show you the charm or the awkwardness of each – within a particular context – and their choice should eventually become automatic, not theoretical.

Variation of the number of notes in your harmonies is also important. Persistent use of five- or six-note chords can become unwieldy; continual use of three- or four-part chords can sound dull or thin. Imaginative alternation, plus passing-tones in one voice, tied notes or even momentary unisons and octaves set off the chords and add variety.

Tempo, of course, operates here. The slower the speed, the larger the chords you can employ for long stretches. At the other end of the tempo-scale, rapid *allegros* tend to demand sparser harmonies or frequent alternation of contrasting textures.

The feeling of density is also affected by the harmonic rhythm. Rapid changing of chords, as discussed in Chapter 6, leads to a crammed, chaotic feeling – again relative to tempo. On the other hand, even in the slow, spacious tempo which large, many-voiced chords require, they must *move*, and give a feeling of development, not get sidetracked into a timeless vacuum. Obviously, no rigid rules are possible here; your ear must guide you.

This section has dealt with various facets of harmonic practice; now we need to recognize a force which rules over all.

(iv) *Consistency and variety (revisited)*. We return now to an issue of surpassing importance. Even though you may have great aptitude for inversions, bass-lines, spacing and voice-leading (and the other 'mechanics' such as harmonic rhythm, described earlier), these are all vulnerable to a particular fault. I have warned against changing an initial Mozartian clarity into a Puccinian lushness within an improvisation – but what produces such a metamorphosis?

The most apparent cause for the listener will be an inconsistent harmonic sound. Chords in music can be compared with colors in painting. Despite all the other interacting elements of line, use of space, brush-techniques and so on, color is what strikes the viewer with the most immediacy – requiring, as with the listener's response to harmonic effect, little intellectual exertion. I have a minimal technical knowledge of art, but my dismay would be instantaneous if a printer's aberration combined within one print a shimmering area of Impressionist pastels with a violent eruption of dramatic Expressionist hues. Similarly, the passionately somber harmonic 'color' of Berg's *Wozzeck* would shock if interspersed into the delicate palette of Ravel's *L'Enfant et les sortilèges*. Both color and harmony are *intrinsic* to the creator's entire artistic-esthetic approach, yet *extrinsic* where the perceiver's initial reaction is concerned. (A more subtle musical comparison may prove worthwhile in this connection. Listen to Mozart's *Eine kleine Nachtmusik*, then to Prokofiev's clever, light-hearted *Classical Symphony*, a brilliant evocation of the eighteenth-century spirit, yet one which few could mistake for an actual work of that era. The perpetually surprising harmonic snags and side-slips, which inevitably affect and are affected by the melody's quirky path, create a time-tourist's jaunt to another world, not an inhabitant's expression of it.)

Now we recapitulate the principle of musical variety within unity. The *unity* is created through a consistent harmonic language during an improvisation; the *variety* stems from imaginative progressions rather than harmonic clichés, linked with deft use of inversions, bass-lines, unique melodic and rhythmic twists – all continually subject to that overall need for organic progression; i.e. harmonic coherence.

We have looked at variety as an integral part of unity, but it also functions in another capacity harmonically, to bring *relief*. If you always improvise within the confines of traditional tonality, you will make unnecessary demands upon your inventiveness, and deny everyone the stimulus and challenge of the different sounds which can help to jolt the dancers (and you) out of routine preoccupations and bring delightfully unexpected lifts to the class. These sounds can be found in the repertoire, but often the pieces contain inconvenient phrasing-irregularities.

Ways to harmonic variety

Within the spectrum of Western music familiar to us (or easily available on records) ranging from the twelfth to the twentieth century, many sound-worlds exist and have been used at different times by composers. In addition to the more familiar diatonic and chromatic idioms and practices of the eighteenth and nineteenth centuries, we have:

1. Modal
2. Pentatonic
3. Whole-tone
4. Pan-diatonic
5. Polychordal
6. Neo-classical
7. Atonal; twelve-tone, or serial
8. Unisons, octaves
9. Ostinato patterns

1. *Modal.* Since I shall discuss this at length in the next chapter, I will only remark here that modal harmonies offer one of the potentially most beautiful, even exquisite, sounds of all. In ballet class it functions also as a more than welcome respite from continual use of standard eighteenth- and nineteenth-century idioms. Lovely as these can be, they form only a part of the musical experience. The modal sound is fresh, but not so exotic that it quickly becomes cloying. Each mode produces a different expressive effect, ranging from sharp and bright (Lydian) to muted and dark (Locrian), and these qualities will often stimulate improvisational ideas.

An easy way to find the modes is to play on the piano an ascending eight-note sequence beginning on each of the white keys: C–C, Ionian (diatonic major); D–D, Dorian; E–E, Phrygian; F–F, Lydian; G–G, Mixolydian; A–A, Aeolian (natural minor); B–B, Locrian. Construct melodies and harmonies based on each of these, and you will have many new sources of variety.

Modal harmonies can be found in the music of Vaughan Williams, Hindemith, Ravel, Debussy, Bartók (who was much drawn to the Lydian), Stravinsky's early ballet scores, Rachmaninov, Mussorgsky, Sibelius, Dvořák, early-Baroque sacred and secular works, Renaissance dances, and folk-songs.

2. *Pentatonic.* This sound is rather tricky, being based on only five notes (easily identified by playing the black keys on the piano). Used carefully, chord progressions constructed from these five tones can provide diverting contrast to the more conventional harmonies usually heard in class. Used badly, they will sound like doodling or fake local color. Debussy's 'La fille aux cheveux de lin' combines a pentatonic melody with modal sounds, and Ravel's 'Laideronnette' (from *Ma mère l'oye*) is a pentatonicist's paradise.

3. *Whole-tone.* This is based on a six-note scale composed of only whole-steps. Similar to the pentatonic sound in its 'exotic' quality and the lack of harmonic tension and direction that stems from the absence of half-steps, the cautious use of this idiom will also prove useful for class. To hear it at its most pervasive and

effective, listen to Debussy's 'Voiles' from the Preludes for piano, Book I, and the 'Rondes du printemps' from the *Images* for orchestra.

4. *Pan-diatonic*. This term is used to identify an odd sort of diatonicism, one without alteration or modulation. In its pure form, it is difficult to handle, for there is little tonal direction or tension and no 'exoticism'. Although sometimes called 'white-note' music, it can quickly become a grey, featureless landscape, static and drab. At its worst, it can even approach the quasi A minor meandering cited earlier. Used well, it can have a clean, uncluttered sound, which offers a contrast to the sometimes excessively lush, chromatic harmonies of the nineteenth century.

Stravinsky is probably the most noted exponent of pan-diatonicism, and his middle period could form a guide for its clever usage. This spare sound provided Balanchine with the ideal support for his athletic, angular, dispassionate choreographic geometry. *Apollon musagète* is an elegant example of pan-diatonic 'purity' and detachment translated into movement.

In class, be careful in its use, for this sound can pall quite rapidly on the piano.

5. *Polychordal*. This consists of two, or more, tonal planes combined; that is, say, G major in conjunction with B flat major. Perhaps the most famous and historically important use occurs in Stravinsky's score for *Petrushka* (the clash of a C major triad with one in F♯ major symbolizing the puppet's conflicting human and non-human impulses).

Polychords were especially popular from the 1920s to 1940s, and can easily be located in much of Milhaud and Hindemith and polychords blaze forth in the glorious opening section of Honegger's Fifth Symphony. Listen to and analyze this sound carefully, for the important thing when improvising is to keep the different tonalities clearly defined; otherwise you will produce musical mush. Clear definition comes through the use of chord position, spacing and texture. (The terms *polychordal* and *polytonal* differ in that the former refers to harmonic writing, whereas the latter is used loosely for harmonic *and* contrapuntal styles.)

6. *Neo-classical*. At its best, neo-classicism contains spice, pungency and wit; at worst, it sounds stupid, arbitrary and clumsy. Successful examples include Poulenc's *Le Bal masqué*, Shostakovich's Polka from *The Age of Gold*, and many sections in Prokofiev's *Peter and the Wolf* and *Cinderella* (his *Classical Symphony*, mentioned above, shows neo-classical skittishness restrained by a classical discipline).

This idiom is not so easy as it might seem, for the spicy added notes should enhance and, in a way, intensify the basically tonal effect, not muddle it. Characteristically, minor 2nds, major 7ths and augmented 4ths/diminished 5ths are added to simple triads (or injected melodically), producing a sort of jazzed-up tonality. In fact, these same sounds were often called upon in attempts to translate the jazz or blues singer's 'between the notes' inflections to instrumental mediums, Gershwin's *An American in Paris* being a noteworthy instance. Bewitched by American jazz, Poulenc, Milhaud, Auric and Honegger made repeated forays into this musical underworld in their 'serious' pieces. Listen to Milhaud's *La Création du monde* for a choice illustration of this simulated jazz-through-'wrong'-notes trend.

7. *Atonal; twelve-tone, or serial*. Here we enter the world of Schoenberg, Berg and Webern, and, even more complex, that of Boulez, Stockhausen, et al. The

harmonies (and formal techniques) characteristic of this branch of the avant-garde are generally both inappropriate for ballet class and fiendishly difficult for the average improviser to work with. Complicated and tensely dissonant, they resist confinement into the square, symmetrical phrases of conventional ballet exercises. On a deeper level, moreover, it is not a sound which contains a particularly wide range of kinetic impulses. Certain choreographers have, admittedly, used scores from this category with amazing theatrical results, but it can be a treacherous partner for dance – especially in class.

This does not mean that I have not (infrequently) heard expert ballet improvisers manipulate dissonant, high-tension harmonies within a reasonably relaxed kinetic context, nor that you should not try to introduce dance students to a world of music which they will encounter on stage. But you must handle it carefully, after much effort at home equips you to employ it with grace and spontaneity.

8. *Unison; Doubling*. These are not, strictly speaking, 'harmony', for doublings or treblings at the octave do not constitute a chord. They can, however, give the illusion of harmonic movement when cleverly interspersed within chord progressions, adding life and interest to what might otherwise be a rather bulky, unkinetic sound. In a slow tempo, the occasional doublings of melodic notes within primarily harmonic passages can sound spacious and soaring; in a fast one, it can be brilliant and exciting, introducing a feeling of surprise, suspense and buoyancy.

I must stress that modulation or tonal shifts are needed to prevent monotony, especially in the long spans of across-the-floor combinations. In an eighteenth- to nineteenth-century tonal style you can modulate briefly within a phrase or section, returning to the home-key at the end, or you can transpose into another key entirely when repeating a large section. Modulation to the closely related dominant (V) or sub-dominant (IV) will follow traditional practice, but going to the mediant (III), sub-mediant (VI), or relative major or minor, while also characteristic, will help to vary the predictable sounds of V and IV. Since the non-traditional nature of categories 1–6 precludes 'normal' modulation, variety must come from unprepared shifts of tonal center, or juxtapositions of compatible categories (which requires discretion and finesse).

When modulating, shifting, or beginning another piece for the next combination, you should remember that, as a rule, going to a 'higher' key (i.e. dominant after tonic), or one based on the 2nd or 3rd tone of your original key, increases tension and tonal interest. Moving to a 'lower' key (i.e. subdominant after tonic, down to the relative minor, or to the keys of the 6th and 7th tone of your original key) tends to act as either a relaxing element or a diminution of interest (although this is sometimes counteracted by the tonal interest of the added depth and sonority of the lower key).

9. *Ostinato patterns*. These are recurrent motives or patterns repeated undeviatingly throughout a phrase, section or entire piece (Italian for *obstinate*). An *ostinato* can be formed from a short melodic kernel, full chords or arpeggiated chords (and even simple repeated notes). Not in itself necessarily harmonic, it is frequently used in connection with chords, and, of course, will combine with upper voices to form harmonies. Most often found in the lowest voice (*basso ostinato*), it

can be quite effective on top, with the melodic line moving *underneath* treble intervals or patterns, as in Prokofiev's captivating 'Troika' from *Lieutenant Kije*.

Oddly, considering their theoretically static nature, *ostinato* patterns can produce an enormous power and kinetic vitality. Or perhaps this is not so odd. Detailed study of dance music throughout its history, Western and non-Western, will show that a great proportion uses short, repetitious sections, based on *ostinato* patterns, although they may be more popular in one period than another. Contemporary composers have exploited the possibilities of *ostinati* in many ways, using the gargantuan resources of the complex modern orchestra. Stravinsky's *Rite of Spring* is certainly one of the best-known examples. Carl Orff's popular *Carmina Burana* is another, less sophisticated, *ostinato*-orgy, and when performed well is absolutely electrifying. One of Bartók's favorite devices, it can be found in much of his music and simple examples abound in his books of *Mikrokosmos*. He used it to evoke primitive folk-elements. Ostinati of a different sort, although also driving and vital, are found in Chopin and Tchaikovsky. In their music, and that of other Romantics, ostinati did much to invigorate the characteristic rhythmic stolidity of the nineteenth century which resulted from the tendency to focus more on intricate thematic development, orchestral color and texture, and lush harmonies.

An ostinato requires careful use, during improvisation, so that it does not degenerate into mindless, slipshod noise. One solution is to devise one which not only is reasonably interesting, but which has the potential of generating melodic or rhythmical ideas above it. A seemingly simple ostinato-pattern can lead to miracles of invention in the treble; it can also, of course, lead to nightmares of monotony. It depends on how it is done (reflect, for instance, on the variety of results, tedious and ebullient, within the boogie-woogie bass tradition of the 1930s and 1940s). The crux of the matter is whether the ostinato quickly becomes a self-perpetuating, kinetic force rather than a conscious effort. If it is 'inside' you, and not an isolated pattern, it can spill over freely and interact with the right hand.

Accompaniment patterns

Harmony does not always consist of clusters of simultaneously sounded notes. A common variation of block-chords is the arpeggio, or broken-chord. Another is the Alberti bass. Both will be discussed later.

Arpeggiated accompaniments are frequent in the typical opera aria or ballet *adagio* of the nineteenth century, the latter being closely modeled on the former. This link is hardly surprising, since Romantic ballets were performed in the local opera house, as *divertissements* between opera acts (the eventual development of the full-length, three-act Classical ballets helping to establish ballet in its own right). Being so closely associated with opera, ballet, and its music, absorbed many of its characteristics. Compare, for instance, the music for the *grand pas de deux* from *Giselle* with a big aria, by, say, Rossini, Meyerbeer or Berlioz. Many writers, also, have related the ballet variation, or solo, *pas de deux* and other small ensemble numbers, with the solos, duets, trios, etc. of opera.

The accompaniment patterns of Romantic ballet are, generally speaking, indistinguishable from those of operas of this period. (They continue to flourish, of course, in the ballet music of the later Romantics and the more conservative twentieth-century ballet composers.) These patterns are invaluable to the ballet improviser. They give the sonority and full texture of harmonies without the tiring of the ear which can result from an uninterrupted use of block chords.

Arpeggiated harmonies also lend continuity and a quasi-orchestral richness while not fighting the melodic line as would intricate contrapuntal patterns. They provide a wonderful setting for a soaring melody, and can be an exciting element in *allegro* music.

Do not, however, get carried away into excessive cascades of notes. Study particularly the use of arpeggios in the music of Beethoven, Chopin, Schumann and Tchaikovsky. These are almost always basically simple and uncluttered (unlike many of Liszt's or Rachmaninov's, which create a desired effect, but tend to be too elaborate or fussy for dance-movement).

Many possible arpeggio or broken-chord forms exist; those which I consider most useful for our purpose are:

i. Spread, or harp, patterns   v. Alberti bass
ii. Ascending   vi. Inner voice-patterns
iii. Descending   vii. Pedal point
iv. Mixed: alternating intervals

i. The 'harp' arpeggio is that which results when you pass your hands up and down the harp-strings. In its most common form, it simply ascends, then descends on the same notes in reverse. It is potentially the most lush of all accompaniment patterns, with its wave-like cycle. A dramatic version surges through Chopin's 'Revolutionary' Etude, a simpler one in the Fantaisie-Impromptu op. 66. The rhythmic patterns can, of course, vary. Two common ones are:

Ex. 2

ii. A variant of Ex. 2 is the ascending arpeggio. This does not turn back upon itself, but always ascends:

Ex. 3

This can be heard at its most beautiful in the popular Pachelbel *Canon*.

iii. The descending form is less common, but can also be effective – perhaps more so when combined with Ex. 2.

Ex. 4

iv. The mixed-form alternates single notes with intervals or chords. This is a favorite device of Verdi's, who used it to simulate the simple accompaniment of the street-singer:

Ex. 5

Two variants of a mixed nature are:

Ex. 6

(See also 'Blind-man's Buff' from Schumann's *Kinderscenen*.)

v. The Alberti bass is familiar to anyone who has ever played or heard:

Ex. 7

Other forms of it exist, of course. Countless eighteenth-century sonatas and sonatinas which use this sort of accompaniment were written in that era's widespread reaction against intricate contrapuntal music. It is primarily a keyboard technique, although composers have also used it in other mediums. The effect can range from paralyzing boredom to an effervescent spirit in *allegro* music, or a charmingly simple underpinning for a slow, lyrical melody.

vi. An excellent way to break up chord clumps and add motion to harmonic progressions is the use of inner voices. One of the loveliest and simplest examples of this occurs in the slow movement of Beethoven's Sonata in C minor ('Pathétique'). The rhythmic patterns can vary as they do later on in this movement. 'Pleading Child' from *Kinderscenen* is also effective.

vii. Finally, a device which can be used with any of the above, although it is more effective in some cases than in others. The pedal point, like the *ostinato*, might seem to be static because of its unchanging nature. Yet, the tension set up between this immovable, fixed element and the changing harmonic and melodic relationships above can be both gorgeous and intensely physical. To prove this, one need only turn to the ballet music of Tchaikovsky which reflects (as does much of his concert music) a deep and sensitive love affair with the pedal point.

The term itself stems from the organ, on which a note can be sustained indefinitely, with figurations woven around it. Usually the term denotes a bass (or organ-pedal) note, although it can appear in any register. The organ repertoire offers countless examples; also the Baroque, Romantic and contemporary periods, in all mediums. One of the pedal point's most ancient uses is in the drone-note of the bagpipe.

A famous use of the pedal-point (combined with *ostinato*-writing) occurs in Ravel's *Bolero*. The harmonic clashes with the immutable C-pedal are not as dramatic or dissonant as those of the Bach prelude, but the characteristic tension and suspense of this device are certainly present. Other, highly effective uses of the pedal point can be heard in the opening of Brahms' First Symphony and the Farandole from Bizet's *L'Arlésienne Suite*, No. 2.

Pedal-points are, admittedly, more hazardous on the piano than when used in, say, organ, guitar, string or orchestral music. The result can be congested and deadening if great care is not taken with what is happening above. Clear spacings and convincing harmonic relationships with the fixed bass are imperative. Repeated listening to music which successfully uses pedal-points, particularly that of Tchaikovsky, will help to develop a feeling for them as no words can.

I have devoted this considerable amount of space to certain aspects of harmony in improvisation because I consider harmony the improviser's Achilles heel. I have heard potentially good melodies ruined by inept harmonies, and workable rhythmic patterns devitalized by peculiar harmonic rhythms. On the other hand, I have been bewitched by accompanists with a flair for harmony, despite varying degrees of melodic or rhythmic weakness. This does not mean that harmony should be considered the most important element in improvising, or used craftily to cover up other deficiencies, but simply that it tends to be the most obviously bad or good ingredient of the four under discussion here.

3. Rhythm

Improvising for ballet class limits you somewhat where rhythm is concerned. I have mentioned the traditional symmetrical nature of the usual ballet exercise. The essentially simple structures of these automatically prohibit complicated, disjunct rhythms. Quintuplets, septuplets, nine against three-and-a-half, alternating meters of 5/8 9/16 2/4 7/8, etc. must be left to the avant-garde composer (since I have never known an improviser to be able to handle these for any length of time).

But, within the comparatively simple rhythmic patterns and organizations of music from the late-sixteenth to the early-twentieth centuries, certain restrictions and guidelines also operate. What has been called the law of good continuation must prevail. If it does not, your musical phrases will fall apart and the dancers will be confused.

Continuity and variety

The most basic guide perhaps is to use rhythmic parallelism and continuity, guided by a sense of simplicity. Too many rhythmic patterns in one phrase hampers the flow, and certainly interferes with musical communication. Take, for example:

Ex. 8

Utter gibberish, yet I have heard accompanists concoct rhythmic 'phrases' of this sort in the belief that they are being inventive.

A less extreme example, but still chaotic and non-communicative:

Ex. 9

This demonstrates a vacillation between a direct, forceful feeling and a rounded, more graceful one. It is somewhat analogous to a piece of prose which alternated the shotgun brevity of Hemingway with the reflective, philosophical flow of D.H. Lawrence. Such an approach makes neither musical nor literary sense.

Even the following simple example does not observe the law of good continuation:

Ex. 10

It uses simple patterns and not too many of them, yet it does not hold together. The patterns lack inner unity.

But, since we do want variety in rhythm, to sustain interest and generate kinetic feeling, there must be *some* deviation. This scheme, for instance:

Ex. 11

Unless it were used with virtuoso command of melody and harmony, I think one could safely predict that it would seem a bit bogged down. Now, ex. 10 begins with this pattern but does not know where to go from it. Ex. 11 is trapped in it. What is the result when a brilliant composer uses it as his departure-point? Note the combination of clarity and subtlety of the next example, which opens Mozart's Fortieth Symphony:

Ex. 12

The use of this dogged rhythmic scheme does much to establish a sense of what may be called the pregnant obsessiveness that colors the whole movement. Yet there is just enough deviation to prevent stasis (Note the master stroke of the attempt to break out melodically at the first rhythmic deviation only to subside with the reappearance of the initial obsessive rhythm.)

Or, to take an extremely simple example:

Ex. 13

Before this pattern ends it begins to seem, when tapping it out, as if you are afflicted with St. Vitus' Dance. Yet with only the merest differences, see how Tchaikovsky continued the opening rhythm:

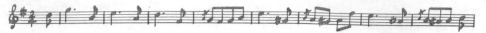

Ex. 14 Tchaikovsky, *Swan Lake*, Act III, *pas de deux*

I am, of course, showing rhythmic patterns in isolation. The accompanying melody and harmony naturally affect the rhythm in all sorts of ways. Yet even these rhythmic skeletons above convey a clear message. When tapping any of them, their monotony, incoherence or effectiveness are immediately apparent in each case.

When setting forth on an improvisation, you must be able to arrive quickly at a basic scheme (simple yet incorporating some deviation), take it into your muscles, and then forget about it, letting it become self-generating. Whether the scheme is composed of largely regular beats, dotted rhythms, triplets, juxtaposition of regular or dotted sixteenth-notes, syncopations or whatever, both consistency or continuity, and variety must be present.

Extract the bare rhythmic schemes from familiar music and reproduce them. You will find that in a good piece these rhythms will have an inner logic, will be convincing even apart from the actual tones. In a bad piece they will seem boring, jarring, discontinuous or silly, as the case may be. Then take some of the most effective examples, use the opening rhythmic kernel as a point of departure, and tap out a continuation of your own. Decide whether your treatment is as convincing as that in the original, and, if not, try to analyze why. A fellow-musician can be a helpful sounding-board.

Syncopation

A more complex way in which to add rhythmic variety is through the use of syncopation. This is the *temporary* displacement of normal accents. It can create effects which range from mildly diverting to wildly exciting, depending partly on tempo. For it to be really effective, the basic pulse must remain clear, the syncopation setting up a vital tension in conjunction with it, not obliterating it. Points of reference, in other words, are necessary so that the disruption of one's normal expectations are perceptible in a meaningful way, not merely disrupting. Syncopation does not function *against* the basic pulse, but rather *within* it. If anything, effective displacement of accent intensifies the basic pulse (see also Chapter 6).

Many types of syncopation are possible, but, at least when beginning to improvise, you had best use the simpler ones, which are in any case usually better for ballet class. These are:

  i. Simple displacement
  ii. Silent strong beat
 iii. Tying over of weak beats

i. Simple displacement is clearly illustrated in the rhythm of the cakewalk:

Ex. 15   Debussy, *Children's Corner Suite*, 'Golliwog's Cakewalk'

Other possible simple displacement-patterns include the following:

Ex. 16

Accents and dynamics are often used to create a feeling of syncopation in what might otherwise be a regular metric pattern, as in the third measure of the 3/4 example.

ii. Silent strong beats are often found in waltzes, as for instance:

Ex. 17   Tchaikovsky, *Swan Lake*, Act I, Waltz

and in the opening of Brahms's Symphony No. 3, which has a waltz-like swing:

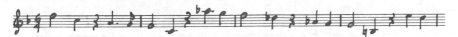

Ex. 18   Brahms, Symphony No. 3 in F, first movement

iii. The tying over of weak beats can take a momentary or a prolonged form. In the first, it acts as a variant within the meter; in the second, it alters the meter itself, sometimes for an entire section.
Momentary:

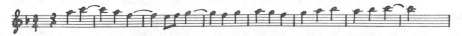

Ex. 19   Beethoven, Symphony No. 6 in F, third movement

Prolonged:

Ex. 20   Tchaikovsky, *Sleeping Beauty*, 'Panorama'

The momentary use of tying-over can provide a graceful, bumptious, or dramatic departure from the norm which, being brief, is less intense than the prolonged form.

The latter can create great tension and excitement relatively simply, which is an obvious asset when improvising in class. This form of syncopation is, of course, the hemiola (see Chapter 7, pp.150–1), and it can be used in various ways. Composers have the option of plunging in immediately, beginning the section with it, thus deceiving the listener until, with a greater or lesser shock, the basic meter is exposed (Brahms being a master of this technique). Better, perhaps, in class would be the initial establishment of the duple or triple meter, with the changed accents occurring after this is clear.

The accompanying harmonies and melodic line play a key role in the clarifying or the disguising of the syncopations. To clarify them, the harmonies can move according to the basic metric scheme underneath the syncopated deviations (Ex. 21). To disguise them, both the harmony and melody will be swept along, falling into the syncopated patterns (Ex. 22).

Ex. 21   Chausson, *Poème*

Ex. 22   Dvořák, Slavonic Dance No. 1 in C major

You must be the judge as to when the use of any of these forms of syncopation will be effective for a combination. You will learn when it is best to stick to regular accents, for syncopation in improvising is more problematical than in pieces you choose from repertoire. It is, needless to say, considerably more difficult to improvise in a syncopated rhythm than in a regular one. The more highly developed your kinetic sense, of course, the easier syncopation will be, for you will be carrying the basic pulse in your body rather than in your mind. Thus, you will be free to play about with it and not lose it in unrhythmical tempo-changes (among other things).

Irregular meters

The occasional teacher who wants music in 5/4 or 7/4 presents the improviser with certain problems. One is that of analysis. This is true also when repertoire is being used, but then the problem is merely one of analysis and choice, whereas with improvisation it is one of analysis and instant creation. If the specified meter is 5/4, you must look at the structure of the dance movements. Is the phrasing divided very obviously, or is it continuous? If divided, there are four possibilities: 2 + 3, 3 + 2, 4 + 1 or 1 + 4. If continuous, no perceptible break occurs during the 5-count segment (this is the hardest of all to manage musically). Sometimes, also, the groupings alternate as in the 'waltz' from the second movement of Tchaikovsky's Symphony No. 6:

Ex. 23   Tchaikovsky, Symphony No. 6 in B minor, second movement

The harmonic rhythm underneath, plus the melodic line, gives indications throughout the movement as to whether it is 2 + 3 or 3 + 2.

1 + 4 and 4 + 1 are much less likely divisions, but I have played for teachers who requested them. They usually work better in a twentieth-century idiom, with percussive harmonies to set off the 1. 7/4, of course, offers even more possible divisions, and is correspondingly more difficult.

If the teacher confronts you with a combination based on changing meters you have no alternative but to improvise (unless he happens to choose alternating 5/4 and 6/4, in which case you can be inspired by the Promenade theme from Mussorgsky's *Pictures at an Exhibition*).

These, then, are the musical aspects of rhythm in improvisation which will concern you in the ballet studio. Since I have discussed the relationship of dance-rhythm and musical-rhythm at length in other contexts, I need only say here that all of the points made earlier naturally also apply to improvising, perhaps more so. And to achieve good and supportive *dance*-rhythm when improvising – while also coping with the purely musical problems – requires an even greater physical sense of rhythm. You can get away with (although not flourish on) detachment when using repertoire; effective rhythm in improvising can only come from an intense involvement and kinetic empathy with the dancers.

4. Form

The problem of form is partially solved for you by the guiding structures of the ballet exercises. There are, however, certain musical points of which you should be aware. Since these two types of form, musical and dance, are equally important, it is perhaps best to try to clarify them separately.

i. Musical form. For *barre* and center exercises with the usual anatomy of 8 + 8 or 16 + 16, musical forms of A-A-B-A or A-B-A-B are made to order. As you gain experience you can be less conventional, but until you can become musically convincing in a free, unstructured form it is better to gain strength from the satisfying structure of Theme-Repeat-Contrast-Return. Theme-Contrast-Theme-Contrast is also satisfying, in a different way.

For across-the-floor exercises you can use, in addition, A-B-A, A-B-A-C-A (rondo) or a variation of this. The longer duration of across-the-floor exercises plus their open structure, allows you more scope, whereas the closed forms of *barre* and center are somewhat restricted (although sometimes the teacher may give *rond de jambe* and *port de bras* exercises at the *barre* consisting of 16 + 16 + 16. Here you have the choice of A-B-A, A-A-B or A-B-C).

ii. Dance structure. Within the forms of i. you will be faced with many possibilities from exercise to exercise. They stem from the structure, shape and flow of the dance-phrases within the basic forms. Since we have already examined this in detail (see 'Practical examples', Chapter 8, Section II), I will just say that the same considerations apply in improvising. One great boon, however, is that you are freer in this respect when improvising than when choosing from repertoire, a fact which is especially evident when you are faced with a combination which has an unusual structure. (*Barre*-work will not present this problem as frequently as center or across-the-floor work – unless the teacher is indefatigably inventive.)

An obvious point to consider is the length of your A-A-B-A, for example. As I have stressed, you do not want to chop up the dance-phrases. If they are in a structure of 16 + 16, you should avoid an A-A-B-A in which each segment is 8 + 8, totalling the 32. A 16-count A and a 16-count B would be more harmonious. Since it is easier to improvise in small segments, to repeat short phrases rather than to conceive a long-breathed line, the temptation to fall back on 4 + 4 + 4 + 4 or 8 + 8 + 8 + 8 as a norm will tend always to be lurking, causing you to ignore a possible discrepancy with the dance. Particularly so when you are tired or less involved than usual.

The coincidence of the musical phrase with the dance phrase is just as important in the simple *barre* exercises as for an elaborate *adagio* or jumping combination. If the teacher gives, say, 32 *dégajés en croix* (8 front, 8 side, 8 back, 8 side) and you play 4 + 4 + 4 + 4 + 4 + 4 + 4 + 4, you will be encouraging the dancers to commit one of their most common crimes. That is, the use of *barre* exercises as a form of self-inflicted torture. The 32 *dégajés* (or *grands battements*, *frappés*, etc.) become an endurance contest rather than a sequence of movements with a beginning, a continuation and a rounding-off. With the worst offenders, you can even see their pinched lips counting off the drops of this Chinese water-torture. This approach, needless to say, precludes *any* sense of flow or progression. It leads to clenched muscles, interrupted muscular impulses and robotism. Anything you can do musically to foil dancers who make such sequences a collection of drip-drops will be to your enduring credit. Chopping up the musical phrase will not achieve this.

For the rest, simply refer to the chapters on selection of music, applying the general principles to the act of improvising, consoling yourself for any extra effort necessary when improvising with the thought that it solves many formal problems for you.

Improvising within a form

As for how to begin, if you have never done this sort of thing, the best way is to practice creating small forms at home, and frequently. The more you absorb the principles of combining repetitions, sequences and phrases into sections, and ultimately entire pieces, the less concern you need have with this in class.

Choose a form, say, A-A-B-A, and try to experience the *feeling* of it, rather than to view it as a sort of musical coat-hanger on which to drape some (as yet unknown) notes. A statement, a repetition, a contrast and a return. A simple but effective scheme, which has been used in thousands of pieces. Yet, no matter how different the melody, harmony or rhythm in each, the scheme itself has a certain feel. Even in the abstract, with only hazy musical ideas accompanying it, this form should feel different from, say, A-B-A-B, or A-B-A-C-A-B-A.

After mulling over these various feelings for a bit, you can allow an actual fragment of music to enter your consciousness. This might be a theme, a motive or even a striking harmonic progression. Do not be timid; the results may be better than you expect. Underneath any welter of wrong or peculiar notes you at least can get some sense of a musical journey – a phrase, its reappearance, movement to a contrasting idea, and then a gratifying rounding-off with the return to your A (which should be viewed as a growing, not a mere repetition).

How, you may ask, do you make music without a previously conceived theme (at least)? But composers or improvisers by no means always begin with such a convenient entity. Often the generating force behind a piece can take the form of the merest feeling or mood, or dim perception of a melodic shape. This seems to me, actually, to have more potential for dance-improvising than the formal procedure of hacking out a full-blown theme (unless you are simply gifted in this way). You do not, in most cases, have time for this often laborious process anyway. But, in order to begin with what Abby Whiteside calls an 'idea', you can instead work with motives, which are shorter, more easily manipulated and conducive to quick association with general shapes.

Continuing your efforts now, you think primarily downward, or upward, or circularly or angularly, depending on the nature of the feeling and motive. When you have really become absorbed in the feeling of one of these, it would be unusual for *some* continuation not to occur to you: original or from music you know already, it does not matter. Play around with it, trying not to *force* its subsequent fate. (To 'try' not to force is, of course, an absurdity, but it will have to do for now.)

Matters may or may not progress nicely during your two A sections, but, upon coming to the B, you may stumble (mentally or physically). How does one concoct a contrasting B when one may barely be managing an A?

This dilemma may be solved, at least partially, if you modify your aim somewhat. True, the B section is conventionally regarded as a contrast or a shift. But if this shift is too startling the music loses coherence. You can test this for yourself by arbitrarily darting to a far-distant key for the B, changing the rhythm radically, or leaping to a totally unrelated melody. The effect of any of these eccentricities will usually be an uncomfortable one, particularly if you consider the relatively short time-spans within which you work in class. Dramatic contrasts in a large-scale piece, in which one's time-perception is different, are another matter.

Remember, also, that such forms as A-A-B-A, A-B-A-B, or A-B-A (C-A) are centuries-old dance-forms, the music following the progress of the dance. And just as a pavan would not suddenly become a sarabande or a volta in the B section, neither would the music which accompanied it abruptly change character.

Not that no change at all took place. Listen to several dances from the sixteenth-to early-seventeenth-century collections by Praetorius, Scheidt, Susato and others. A clear link between the A and B can often be heard in these. It may be inversion or alteration of melodic ideas from A, shared striking harmonic twists or key chords or, most often, perhaps, the use of rhythmic patterns from A clothed in different notes.

But it is not only in the unsophisticated, pre-Bach music that you find B-sections which transform material from the A. Continuing, through the music of Bach and his time, to the Classical and Romantic periods some surprises may await you. B themes or sections which you have always viewed in the conventional role of contrast or dissimilarity may now reveal themselves to you in their true light. Wonderful examples of kinship exist in themes (or subjects) I and II in the first movement of Mozart's Symphony No. 40 in G, and, in one of the most astounding cases of thematic transformation and kinship in all music, throughout the four movements of Beethoven's Fifth Symphony. Chopin's *Fantaisie-Impromptu* op. 66 offers an interesting example in which the moods of the A and B are sharply contrasted, but the openings of each, apart from the minor–major shift, are the same in essential notes, direction, shape and early tonal peak.

Whether these examples, and the countless others like them, were conscious or unconscious is beside the point (although this opens fascinating areas for investigation into the creative process). The point is that the seeming contrast is given coherence and intensified by the hidden unity.

We may not be functioning on the level of famous composers when we improvise for class, but the principles remain the same. If you attempt the shock of total contrast rather than the disguised relatedness which gives the *effect* of contrast, your work will be much harder. And your improvisations will certainly tend to fall apart. But if you use this aspect of the principle of variety within unity it cannot help but make your improvising easier and more satisfactory. The shock of total contrast, moreover, is effective only when the creator is in full control of the opposing elements. It demands great skill and experience, and only the accompanist who possesses these is safe in attempting it in class.

Variation-forms

Variation-form is extremely useful for class, being easily adaptable to the need of the moment. Variation-forms can be short to very long, depending on the composer's inclination or performing circumstances. Examples of large-scale variations are Bach's *Goldberg Variations*, Beethoven's *Diabelli Variations*, Brahms' *Variations on a Theme of Haydn*, for orchestra, and the two sets of variations, for piano, on themes of Handel and Paganini. In the twentieth century we have Benjamin Britten's *Variations on a Theme of Frank Bridge* and Elliott Carter's *Variations for Orchestra*.

In the short-to-medium category, which is generally less ambitious and complex, and which you would utilize for class, we find many variation-sets by Corelli, Handel, Haydn and Mozart, and others. Helpful ideas can be garnered from both these and the larger-scale type to further your efforts.

One reason that this form is so valuable for the ballet improviser is that it allows you the freedom to invent and have a bit of fun during long stretches of across-the-floor work without confusing the dancers by jumping from one sort of music to another. Such a patch-work approach is common. Either the improvising accompanist cannot follow through in the style of her opening phrases, or she becomes bored and jumps to a fresh idea from moment to moment as the long queue of dancers seems never to diminish, or she resorts to undeviating repetitions.

Close study of any good set of variations will show that the theme is *easily perceptible* and — *memorable*. To embark upon a set of variations which attempt to enhance and modify an obscure, murky theme is pointless. To do so when improvising in class is injurious to the dancers. While you are waffling about in a haze of ill-conceived melodic ideas, awkward harmonic progressions and the halting rhythms which are sure to result, the dancers will have little or no support.

Thus, when using the variation-form, make sure of a clear motive or theme, which has some singular quality. This could be fashioned beforehand, or you could investigate its possibilities at home. Do not however, try to compose a piece; let the situation of a particular class call forth on-the-spot reactions, and treatment of your theme.

Among the many techniques of variation, you have, beginning with simple ones: a change from major to minor (or vice versa), the harmonizing of originally unison melodic tones or reducing harmonic passages to a melody in octaves, and the putting of the melody or motive in the bass, with intervals, chords or a counter-melody above. Then there is the alteration of accompaniment-patterns; eighth-notes can become triplets or running sixteenth-notes. This was done so habitually in previous times that it became a cliché, but the technique is still useful if done with verve.

More sophisticated devices include the surprise-omission of important melodic notes (particularly effective in fast tempos), either in a regular manner or, if the quality of the combination allows, in a syncopated one, missing the strong beats. If you have a good harmonic sense, you can alter or substitute chords, which can create a surprisingly different feeling in a relatively simple way. Inversion – the turning upside down – of motives or themes often works well. If you keep the original rhythms at first to establish the connection you can then proceed to vary this variation.

The possibilities are almost endless, and you can easily discover many of the best, most time-honored, by listening to and reading the music of as many good composers, from as many periods and categories, as possible, then going on to enjoy experimenting, often in private, with the material you have discovered.

III. Form and style; style and quality

Improvisation, like composition, includes a formidable array of techniques and imaginative devices. I have tried to present what I consider its most basic ones – the necessities for the beginning or occasional improviser. Unfortunately, much of what I have written about is next to meaningless in the abstract. Form, for instance: that half of the ancient incendiary (and weary) debate on form vs. content. I, myself, have separated them to some degree, but I always remember, under the analytical efforts, that to refer to an A-B-A 'form' means little as far as real music is concerned; it is merely a theoretical convenience. To approach the condition of music when referring to an A-B-A presupposes that you have certain melodic patterns, harmonies or rhythmic impulses in mind, if only vaguely. This situation can, fortunately, be improved by the reader attempting to link as many of the above observations as possible to actual pieces of music. Ideally, each observation should be fully illustrated by musical quotes, but considerations of space made this impossible. Using what we do have as a foundation, we can now try to get closer to the heart of improvisation or at least put some flesh on the bones.

Style in improvising constitutes a great challenge, and is impossible without experience of a wide musical spectrum and a keen aural imagination. I shall discuss four possible points of departure, each of which goes beyond the concoction of acceptable, useful pieces which do not offend melodically, harmonically, rhythmically or formally. These are what might be called character or style-forms, historical periods, nationalism and mimicry.

Four points of departure

1. Style-forms

Here we leave the abstract world of A-B-A, A-A-B-A etc., and enter the world of waltz, mazurka, polka, polonaise, barcarolle, nocturne, elegy, funeral march, wedding march, lullaby, and so forth. These may or may not use A-A-B-A, etc. for their skeleton; what matters involves a deeper level. A waltz is 'formed' differently from a wedding march. This is because in order to express what a waltz conveys to the listener, and to express the impulse that led the composer, or improviser, to choose this as his mode of communication, the melody, harmony and rhythm must be conceived and shaped in a certain way. They must be shaped so that they are true to the nature of a waltz.

Every time someone composes or improvises a waltz (or any of the other style-forms), he is haunted, consciously or not, by the other waltzes which are part of his experience. The listener, similarly, approaches each new waltz he hears partially, at least, in the light of others he has heard. In this sense, the above-mentioned types of pieces can be called 'forms'; they embody something identifiable and repeatable. Oddly, the seemingly more precise, concrete schemes of A-B-A or A-A-B-A cannot do this. They remain textbook patterns. For this reason, it is in some ways easier to improvise a 'waltz' or a 'barcarolle' than a simple A-B-A. These represent familiar aspects of human experience; an A-B-A represents nothing by itself. Style-forms however, are, also more difficult to improvise than an A-B-A for one must be able to re-create the spirit of each through an easy command of melody, harmony and rhythm. (Obviously 'waltz' is still an abstraction compared with 'Strauss waltz' or 'Tchaikovsky waltz' although it is still a large step closer to real music. But I shall return to the adoption of a particular composer's style later on.)

Since each of these style-forms is made up of feelings (objective, not subjective) and feeling-shapes, the improviser must be able to perceive and 're-produce' them in an original, spontaneous combination of the characteristic musical elements which bring them into being or form. And while the composer–creator can mull things over for as long as he wishes in his studio, the improviser–creator does not have this luxury. The only reliable way to acquire the ability to create, convincingly from beginning to end, one of these style-forms is to soak yourself in every example of each that you can find. Listen to, study, and play many examples until they become part of you. Every nocturne is different, yet all are related. As you study them, or examples of the other style-forms, you will see the varying technical and expressive means through which each composer realizes his image of a nocturne. But you will also sense the thread which unites them all, lying deeper than the surface differences. The individual means and the generic relatedness will then act as the point of departure for your own improvised nocturnes. Identification, absorption and re-creation – these are the steps of the process. (I found it helpful when first attempting this to list every style-form I could think of with a string of adjectives describing what I felt to be the qualities and attributes of each. You may find other devices to start you off.)

Not all of your improvisations will fall into this category, of course. Often you *will* only be improvising within the impersonal A-A-B-A form, guided only by the quality of the combination. But mastery of style-forms will spill over into and color the impersonality of set-forms.

2. Historical periods

Why does one musical period sound so different from another? A naive question, perhaps, but what is it, actually, that enables one to refer to a 'Baroque style' or the 'Romantic sound' and assume that one will be understood? Certainly not the mere techniques that are particularly characteristic of one period; any technique may co-exist, if a bit unfashionably, with the favorites of the moment (as with Bach's 'old-fashioned' contrapuntal creations overlapping with the rise of homophony). Harmony offers a very strong clue, as I have tried to demonstrate. Melody – the long-breathed lines of late sixteenth-century polyphony as opposed to the comparatively jagged, flamboyant ones of the fourteenth-century Notre Dame School. Rhythm – compare, say, the artless symmetrical patterns of the early symphonists with the taut asymmetric ones of the early twentieth-century atonalists.

All of this is important, but it does not answer the questions posed, for the issue is not really one of specific details and components. Or, rather, since these are obviously significant, it is not a matter of them 'in their own terms' (that favored phrase of academics) for, as Blacking asserts, 'no musical style has "its own terms": its terms are the terms of its society and culture, and of the bodies of the human beings who listen to it, and create and perform it'.[13]

We cannot, of course, attain complete understanding of the 'terms' of the past seven or eight centuries. Never before has there been so much music, of so many eras, available, or so much 'cultural' information. It is impossible to know all about even *one* century. Yet, when choreographers are turning ever more to music outside the eighteenth- and nineteenth-century repertoire, the ballet musician can hardly continue to focus on only that period. I said this regarding selection of pieces, but it also applies to improvisation. Not all styles will be equally useful for class, but I am suggesting the need for exploration and diversity.

However, the initial questions as to what makes one period sound different from another remain incompletely answered. A step towards a fuller answer lies in limitation: no one period or culture can encompass all musical and expressive possibilities. It is said that human passions and motivations have remained the same throughout our development. But the *forms* of expression and *attitudes* toward expression and experience appear to change, often radically. Composers of each period (like artists in other fields) thus choose their materials, modes of expression, and qualities to be expressed according to the spirit, i.e. the aspirations and restrictions, of their age. Since, unfortunately, no one fully understands or agrees with others on what creates the 'spirit of an age' or the precise connection which this has to cultural expression, my question is essentially unanswerable in mere words. But, if you cannot verbalize what causes the differences among the periods, you can *hear* characteristics of each and re-generate them – in effect, transporting yourself into the feeling of an age.

To be able to provide an extemporized bit of modern, Romantic, Classical, Baroque, Renaissance and medieval gravity or joy rather than *only* Romantic or Classical expression of these and other qualities is to be of special value. Several teachers I played for were aware of the different modes of feeling, and would request, say, a 'Baroque grandness' when my own choice did not harmonize with the quality they had visualized. Being able to improvise quickly to such specifications was satisfying, and easier than trying to dredge up a piece combining the desired quality *and* a suitable phrase-design.

3. Nationalism

This is a very special category of style, which is generally associated with nineteenth- and early twentieth-century music, although 'national' traits appeared in earlier music. The German-Protestant sacred music of the seventeenth-century Schütz, Schein and Scheidt; the homophonic Venetian style of Vivaldi; the elegant French-Rococo fantasy of Couperin – these are but a few examples. (The fact that Bach could write 'French' suites or an 'Italian' concerto attests to clearly recognized national characteristics.)

This, however, differs from the later musical nationalism which consisted of a conscious, rebellious identification with the revolutionary struggles (Chopin, Liszt, Berlioz, Wagner), and a deliberate use of folk-materials to challenge the elitist control of serious music (Glinka, Mussorgsky, Verdi).

Its nature makes it dramatically recognizable even to those who know little about style in music. I have had students who midway through term could still be deceived as to whether a piece was written in the fifteenth or sixteenth, seventeenth or eighteenth, nineteenth or twentieth centuries. I have never had one, however, who mistook a clear example of Russian nationalism for Spanish, French or English. No one ever questioned that *Pictures at an Exhibition* was Russian, *Tosca* Italian, or *The three-cornered hat* Spanish.

I have already discussed characteristics of this nationalism (Chapter 7): apply this to your improvisation, remembering that nationalism is in a sense selective. That is, it attempts to exclude feelings and experience which lie outside the mother-country, for political and emotional reasons. Because of this, once you become familiar with the language of each national style, you have one of the easiest approaches of all to improvisation. Some easily achieved national characteristics will be melodic (Italian for instance), some harmonic (Spanish), some rhythmic (Hungarian, Spanish). Often two or more will be evident as with Spanish harmony and rhythm. But don't try to combine, say, a strongly Italianate melody with Spanish harmonies and Hungarian rhythms. Such a musical melting-pot would not be very convincing.

If you play for character classes, this area of improvisation, done well, can make you highly regarded by the teacher. The limited repertoire which many accompanists rely upon forces the character-teacher either to carry his own music around with him or to endure an over-used handful of suitable pieces.

4. Mimicry: sympathy and empathy

Now we come to the *ne plus ultra* of improvisation (leaving the question of developing one's *own* style for the moment): the absorption and imitation of a particular composer's style and methods (inseparable of course). This is by far the hardest of these four types of improvisation, both technically and esthetically. Particularly esthetically, for mastery of the 'technical' devices of a composer can lead to a dull reliance on formulas, thus reducing artistic value. An attempt to re-create a composer's style must go deeper than surface clichés or mannerisms.

Consistency is the main problem, and any jarring notes will tend to make the ones around them sound incongruous. You can, to some degree, get away with occasional lapses if you are only aiming for a general style, period-sound, or even nationalistic flavor. To assume, however, the mantle of Chopin and exchange it midway for that of Mahler would be nonsensical. Better to stay within a general style than to produce a case of mistaken identity.

Successful mimicry cannot, in my opinion, be taught according to a set of rules, although some guidelines may be offered.

i. Look at some pieces by composers with strong musical personalities, or what my composition teacher called 'profile'. By look, I mean *scan*; do not read the actual notes. Recognizable composers will not only sound different from each other, they tend to look different. Compare a page from Beethoven's 'Appassionata' Sonata, one from Liszt's *Les Funérailles*, 'Curious Story' from Schumann's *Kinderscenen* and Debussy's 'La Cathédrale engloutie'. All of these are characteristic of their composers. Visually, as well as aurally, they are different worlds. Each composer's rhythmic patterns are distinctive, harmonies are spaced differently and melodic shapes contrast sharply – among other idiosyncrasies (I have cited piano works for convenience; a comparison of orchestral scores would show even greater differences because of the complexities of orchestration, instrumental usage and other elements).

The visual exercise is not enough, needless to say; it is merely a useful prelude to listening. Sometimes looks can be deceptive. Still it is worth trying and ideas can be generated by this approach.

ii. The easiest way in which to begin your keyboard efforts at mimicry is, I believe, to take strong motives and themes from pieces which you know. Then, at some point, switch from the original to your own continuation. See what you can do with a simple Mozart, Chopin or Tchaikovsky melody.

iii. Take a composer's A section and improvise a B – bearing in mind the problems of contrast and unity discussed above. Try out several B's on a colleague and ask his opinion on their relative success. Have him do the same while *you* evaluate *his* results.

iv. Practice harmonizing a composer's themes by ear, seeing how close you can get to his original spacings, inversions and inner voices (you can do this in slow motion, if necessary). Here, a friend with an excellent ear buttressed by the score is essential.

v. Using the harmonic schemes of familiar pieces, ones which you can play well, try to create new melodies in conjunction with them. This must, of course, be as much in the style of the composer as possible.

vi. Finally, so that you can concentrate on sound rather than your own invention, ask your colleague to play some pieces which you do not know. They should be characteristic of the composers' styles. Listen first for an over-all impression, then as many times as necessary in order to pick out melodic, harmonic or rhythmic hallmarks of the particular composer. Throughout this guessing-game it will be helpful for you to see how much of the music you can pick up by ear and reproduce yourself.

For any of the above to produce lasting results, you must keep at it – and a half-hour a day, regularly, is far better than two hours every week or so. In addition, you can add a section to your little notebook, jotting down the most striking characteristics which you come to associate with each composer.

Your initial efforts at mimicry should perhaps be directed at composers you particularly like – although it can be quite instructive to imitate those you detest.

From my own experience, I would say unequivocally that good mimicry (as opposed to mimicry through gimmicks) comes through sympathy and empathy. Just as you cannot be a truly good ballet accompanist without kinesthetic sympathy for and empathy with the dancers, neither can you make music in a composer's unique style if you are detached (which also applies, if in lesser degree, to creation from the first three points of departure). To achieve sympathy–empathy, you do not have to construct elaborate psychodramas before each improvisation, but the closer you can get in any way to your composer, the better. Paths include a *feeling* for the general quality of his environment: the autocratic refinement which conditioned, in different ways, Haydn and Mozart; the emergent democratic ardor that so inspired the young Beethoven, and its subsequent decay which contributed to his turning inward spiritually in later years; the sparkling yet decadent atmosphere of the Parisian salons which nurtured Chopin's glamorous emotionalism while keeping within bounds his rebellious nationalism; the aura of impending catastrophe underneath the surface glitter of the pre-World War I epoch affecting the music written by, for example, Ravel, Debussy, Stravinsky, Schoenberg during that period.

You can also investigate the composer's attitude towards '*technique*'; whether, like Satie and Debussy, he viewed academic conventions as fetters to be discarded or, like Bach and Beethoven, he derived great satisfaction from the melding of free-flowing creation with rigorous formal principles.

Perhaps most fundamental, we have Blacking's idea that 'we can recall the state in which [music] was conceived by getting into the body movement of the music and so feeling it very nearly as the composer felt it'.[14] For this phenomenon inevitably permeates the other factors I have mentioned. It also helps one to challenge the view that attempting to relate music to 'real life' is romantic and sentimental, irrelevant, or sacrilegious. I consider that the belief that any art exists in a technical vacuum stems from fear, and this fear attacks creativity at its very roots. A composer writes as he does through temperament and innate gifts in an *interaction* with his environment – or perhaps those resistant to this view will argue that Beethoven would have felt and expressed the same democratic idealism and rebelliousness, through the techniques of the time, if he had been born in 1570 or 1970 rather than 1770? Colin Wilson says:

For me, no work of art can be clearly separated from the personality of the artist and his life. Academic criticism, for example, would compare the symphonies of Haydn with those of Beethoven, observing the changes in form and musical procedure brought about by Beethoven. But it would ignore the most fundamental fact: that Beethoven's whole personality and attitude to life were completely unlike those of Haydn.'[15]

I cannot prove that an attempt to develop an empathy with a composer and his environment will produce good improvisation. But I *can* say with assurance that the times when I functioned on this level were the times when my improvising most came alive, and I felt the greatest lift.

Invention

When those who have done little or no improvising actually sit at the keyboard and try to play that pregnant first motive or phrase, they may very well say, 'But *how* do I *start*?' As Eugen Herrigel put it, 'I seemed like the centipede which was unable to stir from the spot after trying to puzzle out in what order its feet ought to go.'[16]

If continuation is difficult enough, the beginning of something *worth* continuing can seem impossible. Both, however, depend on two things: a foundation and a state of mind. I am wary of adopting the fashion for Zen words-of-wisdom for every subject from sex to cooking – but, as it happens, Zen principles have much to offer the paralyzed centipede, or inhibited improviser. First, some relevant generalities. Paramount for the creator is a foundation of knowledge, expertise, skill, command, familiarity: call it what you will. Although the process of improvising is, ultimately, inexplicable, it is at the same time dependent upon specifics. Two writers have described, each in his own manner, this strange interplay.

'There is a certain mystery', writes Persichetti, 'to spontaneous creation. No improvisation can be completely explained. The quality will vary with performers, and with the same performer at different times. There is, however, a basis to improvisation of any kind. The basis *can* be explained. Intuition or talent is not enough. There must be a working knowledge of traditions and techniques of the era; one must be able to pre-hear.'[17]

In the Zen context we have the same thought, expressed somewhat differently. In reference to the art of archery, Herrigel writes '. . . the technically learnable part . . . must be practiced to the point of repletion. If everything depends on the archer's becoming purposeless and effacing himself in the event, then its outward realization must occur automatically, in no further need of the controlling intelligence.'[18]

Both of these views assume a spontaneity during the act – based on a mastery stemming from an acquired foundation. Neither, alone, is sufficient. The foundation, acquired and taken for granted, frees you from the greatest impediment – will or force. No one can force a good improvisation, or any creative act. The harder you try to improvise a 'good' piece, the less chance you have of doing so. It must, simply, happen. 'Wonderful', you say. 'Who makes it happen?' Certainly not the self-conscious You. The more you try, the worse the result. The more deeply absorbed you are in the music itself and its relation to the dancers' movement, the more likely you are to come up with something inspired. As with Herrigel's archer, 'The more he tries to make the brilliance of his swordplay dependent upon his own reflection, on the conscious utilization of his skill, on his fighting experience and tactics, the more he inhibits the free working of the heart.'[19]

Or, put simply, 'You never quite know what it is – and that's what (Tudor) wants. He wants you never to know, and be smug about it, and say, "I know how to do that". It's always some unknown thing, and that's what keeps it alive.'[20]

It is, in other words, the difference between *becoming* the process and admiring your *progress*. While improvising, you cease to exist as a detached source, an object of esteem. You may, afterwards, be filled with a sense of elation and achievement, but while making music you cannot be in the state of mind which may produce the thought, 'Oh, I *am* doing well today'. Nor can you *begin* with 'doing well' as a goal. You need to be receptive rather than calculating.

'The master no longer seeks, but finds.'[21] This captures, in a few words, the essence of the problem of ego and force in creativity.

Developing your own style

One further aspect of improvisation is the development of your own style. Composer-accompanists will be familiar with what is involved, but other readers may find these comments helpful.

Here above all the use of force is pointless. One's own improvisational style is a matter of finding, not seeking. One clue, however: it will come only through the absorption and digestion of quantities of music, not just pieces by two or three composers you particularly like, for that would keep you at the level of mimicry. A style of one's own requires an additional step. This is made up of a re-hearing, a re-experiencing, a re-integration of elements in the music of others, which mysteriously issues forth as your own voice, with its personal accents and expression.

You may feel that this lies outside your capacities. It is certainly not an essential part of dance-improvisation. But you may discover that you do indeed have a potential style of your own, and if this develops, you will then possess yet another asset and source of pleasure in your improvisational moments.

Making improvisations part of repertoire

Improvisations can be as evanescent as the dew. I think regretfully of many that are gone forever because I had not yet learned the means by which I later retained them beyond the class in which they originated.

The four processes which I found helpful are distinct from each other, but they often interacted. In what I consider their order of value – the most reliable one first – they are:

1. Kinesthetic memory
2. Muscular sensations of key
3. Key association and shapes
4. Shorthand jottings on the spot.

Except for 4. these aids to memory have been discussed in Chapter 9, but I wish to emphasize the desirability of committing the basic plan of an improvisation to memory. Not only will this increase your repertoire, but you can learn much by comparing your current work with earlier efforts. (I consider 4., by the way, to be a reinforcement of the others, not a substitute for them. A quick sketch is useful, but it should not take the place of muscular memory and mental association described in Chapter 9.)

I must anticipate Chapter 11 here, however, with a caution regarding attempts to 'freeze' improvisations, even the best ones. They are, or should be, spontaneous responses to, among other things, specific class situations, including the design of a class, emanations from the teacher, mood of the group, relative tiredness of the dancers, temperature, etc. Remember the basic plan and quality of an improvisation, by all means, but leave it flexible for the future. Circumstances change from day to day, and what may have been superb on Friday afternoon may prove ludicrous on Monday morning if you try to intrude it into a new context rather than adapting it to the fresh situation.

I have devoted a great deal of time, energy and feeling to improvisation. This is because I consider it to be the highest level on which the accompanist can function – and the most deeply satisfying. It comes closest to the wedding of music and movement in class that is part of the generative force behind this book. Few composed pieces, as I have said, can completely suit a given combination in all respects. There are bound to be discrepancies. Quick, intuitive selection from repertoire can minimize these – and no one can or should expect perfection – but improvisation beckons you into an entirely new dimension.

'Why Improvise?' asks the title of an article by Tom Johnson.[22] After paying tribute to our notation system as 'the greatest single asset of European classical music', he goes on to answer the question. Among other things, he cites the shackles 'our reliance on paper' has placed on many of our musical thoughts, and the resultant prejudices – and even fears – which unnotated music arouses.

He concludes with his oft-stated opinion that the most important influences on contemporary music, for perhaps as long as 50 years, have come from other cultures, with improvisation a case in point of how non-European traditions have helped gradually to release us from trying to write everything down. 'Only through them have we begun to realize that, by insisting on notation, we were insisting on throwing out a large portion of the emotional and theatrical and psychological and ethical and social and technical and sexual and religious and recreational and rhythmic and formal possibilities of music'.

As an improvising accompanist, you can lend weight to the growing movement towards more musical flexibility. And this could open new doors; the current breed of pan-cultural composers whose music is 'a deliberate rebuke to three decades of arid, overly intellectualized music produced by the post-war avant-garde'[23] is increasingly drawn towards dance and other theatrical milieux. I have known several good improvisers who were gradually enticed into choreographic projects with dancers or other forms of creative work in the theater, and are now happily functioning in the unexpected role of composer.

But, whatever your future, mastery of improvisation – with all that this implies – will inevitably stretch and enrich you as a musician and a person.

11   Improvisation 2 – Renaissance–rock excursion

> At this moment, it appears that we are on the edge of a synthesis in which composers
> will create, not pop, not rock, not folk, not art, but music that will embody the best
> qualities of each – the involvement of folk, the exuberance of dance and the
> dimensions of art music. The receptivity to that development, if it ever comes, must
> be credited to rock and its more inspired creators.
>
> Arnold Shaw, *The Rock Revolution*, 1971

Now that we have viewed improvisation within familiar styles conventionally used in the ballet studio, it may prove interesting to venture farther
afield. This will involve a dual excursion: to the worlds of late-
Renaissance–early-Baroque dance-music and rock. Although such a pairing may
seem startling to some, these two types of music share many characteristics,
sometimes to a surprising degree. And both contain clear, useful stimuli for
improvising.

The early dance-music and good rock (as opposed to commercial pop music) are
grounded in and permeated by improvisation. Neither could possibly be said to be
'composed' in the sense that a piece by Stravinsky, Tchaikovsky, Chopin,
Beethoven or Mozart is composed – that is, given to us on a written score which
contains all of the notes and as many details of interpretation as is customary for the
era. Anyone who has seen scores of the early dances or the 'songbooks' of the
Beatles, Dylan, Led Zeppelin, Yes, the Who, et al., and is familiar with the music *as
performed*, will know that the printed notes offer what are often barely sketches.

We are, of course, at a disadvantage with the sixteenth- to seventeenth-century
dance-music, having to approach it through theory rather than actual contemporary experience of its performance. But, at least three things are certain: (1) the
printed music was intended as a point of departure, not as a strict literal guide to be
repeated precisely at each performance; (2) not only the performer carrying the
melodic line and the continuo player were expected to elaborate on what was given,
but often most or all of the players, with only the restriction that they should not
interfere or 'run with' other instrumental parts (stated in a sixteenth-century
manual of orchestra technique by Agostino Agazzari); (3) the scores rarely
specified the instrumentation. This depended on the resources available on the
occasion, or preference. Such flexibility led to other things, such as the transcribing
of ensemble pieces for solo lute or virginals and vice versa. Both of these reinforced
the improvisatory tradition, for, while following the basic scheme, each instrumen-
talist would naturally add figurations native to the instrument he was playing.
Thus, a *galliard* performed by a quartet of crumhorns would turn out rather
differently when played by rebecs, violone, viols, lute and two harpsichords; the

275

extemporizing of passages suitable to each instrument would make this inevitable (for a modern attempt to reproduce this practice listen to *La Gamba* as played by two types of ensemble: tracks 10b. and c. on the Musica Reservata Italian collection, side II, see list in Section V. A).

All three of these characteristics – freedom from dependence on precise notation, improvisation throughout an ensemble, the generation of ideas and the over-all effect varying according to the instrumental composition of the group – also exist in rock performance. In addition, both show the virtue of simplicity, a particular type of inventiveness within this simplicity and the fallacy of total 'originality'. All of these are of value for the ballet improviser and the basis this chapter.

Choreographers, moreover, are turning, for their scores, to rock and the earlier periods, and not a few teachers recognize this and welcome such departures from the conventional music for class from time to time.

Finally, there is the problem of the performer's conditioning. As I remarked earlier, pianists are commonly trained to be unspontaneous. The widespread emphasis on correct procedures and 'fidelity' to the printed page gradually channels the musician's responses and conceptions into a narrow band. A certain passivity and dependency results. These not only detract from the performance of repertoire but they dam up the spontaneity which is so essential for improvising. Thus, although direct *imitation* of early Baroque and rock music can lead to usable improvisations, the purpose of this excursion is actually more one of *stimulation*. In my experience, free play with the materials and procedures of these two different yet similar styles is one of the most effective antidotes to constriction of performance and creation. But only if approached in the *spirit* of the originals; I have heard accompanists trying to improvise in a rock or an early style and the results were incongruous. The accompanists were using the language, the sounds, of each style, but their mentality was firmly entrenched in the formality of eighteenth- and nineteenth-century compositional control.

Above all, the spirit behind the best of the early dance-music and rock is an informal one, and it is also involved and unforced. These are just the mental qualities needed by the improvising accompanist, no matter in what style she may be creating.

I. Simplicity; inventiveness; 'originality'

I have called the mutual approach of our two styles informal, involved and unforced. These could be said to have their counterparts in the three musical qualities I mentioned: simplicity, inventiveness and 'originality'.

1. Simplicity

The majority of 'music-lovers' are put off by the simplicity (to them, simple-mindedness) of both the early dance-music and rock. This is understandable considering the conditioning of such listeners by the particular richness and creativity of the periods which come between. But it is also a misapplication of criteria and a rejection of 'elements that the fashion or habit of one's own particular epoch may arbitrarily have neglected: archaic elements, primal elements, irrational elements, neglected mutation and concealed survivals, often overlooked by the wise in their too narrow wisdom.'[1] If, however, one can alter a possibly too narrow wisdom into an appreciation of the seemingly limited creations of the sixteenth-century dance-music and rock, then you can see how their informality – of both composing and performing – make possible a kind of ingenuity or effectiveness of detail which is unattainable within the more imposing or controlled schemes and procedures of the eighteenth and nineteenth centuries. You will find a different sort of inventiveness.

2. Inventiveness

There are actually two kinds of inventiveness to be considered. Both depend on basic simplicity. First is the inventiveness of detail; in sixteenth-century dance and rock music, one melodic deviation, one altered harmony, one shifted accent, can amaze. In fact, in styles based on such limited, simple means, without the structural or emotive melodic and harmonic resources of the Classical–Romantic repertoire, special attention to detail is essential.

The second is the improvisational element. Through this the details of melody, harmony and rhythm of the basic scheme are varied and extended – both during one performance and in other, different, performances. The link with involvement should be clear; without it this sort of music-making is impossible – in fact, its very essence is destroyed. This can be seen vividly in academic, note-by-note renditions of early music and the formularized repetitiousness of mediocre pop groups. Simplicity becomes inanity.

3. 'Originality'

Both the early dances and rock are inherently resistant to the obsession with novelty of nineteenth- and twentieth-century serious music. Because of their base in simple, limited schemes, used unselfconsciously by all – what is called 'common practice' – they must lose their character if they depart too far from this, as in Mike Oldfield's *Tubular Bells*. Whatever this piece may be, or however attractive some sections, it is not rock but a grab-bag of undigested 'classical' and pop elements without an underlying simple vision and structure. Similarly, Deep Purple and Emerson, Lake and Palmer, among other rock groups, often mistook clutter, meandering and pretentiousness for richness of invention. And the rock groups and critics who succumbed to the contemporary disease of noveltyitis attack rock at its very roots by emphasis upon 'newness' and 'innovation'. It would be sad indeed to see the vital common practice of the good groups who continue to make music year after year, unselfconsciously yet freshly, be replaced by a free-for-all of competitive 'originality'. They continue to develop, but always retain the strong underlying simplicity of a limited and integrated base. This is primarily why their music is so exciting.

Fortunately, the majority of rock fans are not vulnerable to the disease, and seek good music-making rather than innovation – just as did the original audiences who heard countless pavanes, galliards, passamezzos and allemandes, written by men to whom the idea of expressing oneself in a radically different language and manner from his fellows would have seemed strange and perverse. 'The Beatles world is just another part of an International Academicism [read 'common practice'] wherein the question is to be better rather than different.'[2] This thought applies equally well to the worlds of rock and the early dances, as does the following assertion by John Lennon (who goes even beyond Rorem in rejecting the idea of 'better'): '. . . it's real, it's not perverted or thought about, it's not a concept, it is a chair, not a design for a chair, or a better chair, or a bigger chair, or a chair with leather or with design . . . it is the first chair. It is a chair for sitting on, not chairs for looking at or being appreciated. You sit on that music.'[3]

Although Lennon was talking about blues (as opposed to 'white middle class good jazz') he could as easily have meant unselfconscious rock or the early dance-music. All of these, of course, can be original in its best sense; it is the first chair because no matter how many times you hear the progression I–V–IV or VIII–VII–IV, it is itself at that time in that song if the song is good. A piece using one of these, or other common harmonic schemes, is not a concept or a design or bigger or even better than another good use of the scheme. 'Baba O'Reilly', 'When the Levee Breaks', 'Angelsea', 'Shelter from the Storm' and 'Jungleland' do not compete with one another. Although all are formed through the I–V–IV progression one is not compelled to choose only one as the biggest or best. They all, in fact, enrich and enlarge one another by the link. Each is good, each different, each similar. (This is a somewhat tricky point. It does not mean that I do not have certain decided favorites. Personal taste is unavoidable. And even objectively, not *all* uses of I–V–IV or the other schemes to be surveyed in Section V will be equally 'good'. They can range from magnificent to hackneyed. So, obviously, a certain level of merit must be attained for the scheme to be effective. But, while recognizing this, I maintain that the compulsion towards originality of basic *material* – as opposed to the *treatment* of it – is irrelevant and destructive to rock, which thrives on being 'better rather than different'. This esthetic does not, of course, suit those who believe that to be different is automatically to be better (see also below, pp. 281–2 and 299–300).)

The same philosophy applies, as I have said, to the hundreds of dances written over the four or five most popular ground basses from c. 1500 to 1630, or within the similarly limited harmonic schemes. The passamezzo or folia or romanesca bass is always similar, always different; ten dances built on the passamezzo are both ten ways of experiencing one thing and ten examples of diversity. This is quite a different concept from the one with which 'serious' music lovers today grew up. It is the span between our two types of music which saw the development of the search for the *idea* of a chair, a bigger chair, or, lately, a chair which has one, two and a half or five legs, hangs upside down, and is impossible to sit upon.

II. Listening

The vital sixteenth- and seventeenth-century men and women who heard, moved to and loved their dance music, and passionate rock fans today are united in that they *listen* differently from the audiences for eighteenth- to twentieth-century 'serious' music. For one thing, listening to and making music are not separated decisively for the sixteenth-century or rock listeners. An audience can also be an imminent group of performers. The same Elizabethans who spent many hours, regularly, dancing to the performing of paid musicians could turn round – in fact were expected to – and play or sing madrigals for the rest of the evening (in the same way that they danced their own dances also and did not rely exclusively on paid dancers to entertain them). Similarly, fans who attend a rock concert will huddle in the back of a van, happily making music on their way home. Lord Chesterfield, in contrast, in his advice to his son, grants that a gentleman may occasionally listen to music, but that it does not befit his dignity to take part in the performance of it, showing how the eighteenth century firmly crystallized a change in attitude towards the function of music.

Another, related, point is the *pervasiveness* of music in the Renaissance and rock worlds, or perhaps *integrality* is an even better term. Both worlds would find Dr. Burney's idea of music as an unnecessary innocent luxury incomprehensible. 'If man bound round the universe to make of it one harmonious whole, then man must let music creep into his ears till he, like the stillness of night or the very smallest activities of day, was touched by its immortal sounds.'[4] This was one of the deepest beliefs of the Elizabethans. Music belonged to almost every department of one's existence, going far beyond mere decoration or entertainment, as did dance. 'This was an age of music and dance – not the music of great composers or the professional ballet, but the native song, the familiar playing of instruments, the continual breaking out into country rounds or court measures.'[5] Furthermore, 'The great diversity of dance-forms in the renaissance springs from a tradition of real dance music whose vitality is the vitality of physical movement.'[6]

Music, and its vital sister, dance, illuminated everyday activities of the Renaissance to a degree which we can hardly imagine. But the degree or kind of involvement in rock music has not been understood by outsiders either. As in the Renaissance sphere, rock 'gives rise to dance; amateurs can play it . . . The audience is more directly involved than in the New Music and indeed has some control over the product',[7] and 'it is not an embellishment of living which one can take or leave; it *does something*, being "music of necessity"'[8] where, again, the very smallest activities of the day are touched by its immortal sounds, and people can and do make it themselves.

Here we come back to *playing* as a key element. Few people indeed now buy scores in order to play music at home – certainly not of serious music created in their own century. Yet, the huge increase in printed scores during the Renaissance was due just as much to domestic demand as to the needs of paid performers. 'The practice of instrumental "parlor" music was a veritable fad in all classes of society.'[9] Those who could not afford expensive instruments bought cheap lutes. The upper classes, all the way to Queen Elizabeth herself – who regularly played early in the morning, even at times of national crisis – took music for granted as a necessity. And so the scores poured forth to meet this need. (Remember, however, that part of the music-making was the ability to sing or play embellishments, variations and divisions on the *printed* notes.)

Similarly, today, the never-ending stream of rock songbooks continues, for much the same reason as in the Renaissance: as a point of departure for music-making within a social group or as an important part of everyday life. And, above all, in both cases the performers are compelled to listen and respond to what they are playing and to one another, in a way which no one who has a fully-composed, detailed score need equal (although fine players in this category will approach it).

III. Other similarities

Many observers have noted that record-buyers and audiences who favor early music also favor rock, and vice versa, passing over the Classical and Romantic periods to a large degree. Lovers of those, in turn, are unresponsive to Renaissance and rock music – unless unusually catholic in their tastes. This is not surprising: especially when one reflects that 'what turns one man off may turn another one on, not because of any absolute quality in the music itself but because of what the music has come to mean to him as a member of a particular culture or social group.'[10] Thus, rock fans often reject, as meaningless to them, 'serious' music, while Pablo Casals can say 'Rock and roll is poison set to sound.' And the average concert-goer is mystified and unentranced by Renaissance fare. Fortunately, more people now realize, with Ernst H. Meyer, that 'there is wonderful vitality and variety in this music, alike in its rich harmonic life, its colorful and often popular melodies, and especially its rhythms . . .'[11] He is speaking here of German dance-music c. 1600, but his comments apply just as well to the English, French, Italian and Spanish dances of 1500–1600. In an essay on rock, Mellers comments: 'the essential characteristics of beat music are that its phrases are very brief and are hypnotically repeated; that its rhythm is obvious and unremitting; and that its sonority is very loud.'[12] These qualities are also present, in different form, in much Renaissance dance-music: short patterns or grounds, repeated and varied rather than developed as in later music; clear, forthright rhythms rather than the subtle, pulseless interplay of polyphonic lines; and, in the loud consorts composed of mixed wind instruments and percussion, a high decibel level. (I should point out that in both rock and the Renaissance dance-music, soft, subtle sonorities are also frequent).

Another link is that both were generated by song. The instrumental dance-music actually began as transcriptions and variants of vocal models. Rock, similarly, took off from blues and other song-forms, and gradually developed great instrumental virtuosity; many tracks now are almost completely instrumental, or the voice is often treated as another instrument, the words being nearly incomprehensible. Yet, no matter how far each type of music seems to depart from the vocal base, its ghost remains. Early dance-music and rock, therefore, both contain a well-balanced synthesis of song, dance and instrumental techniques.

I have cited several similarities. The rest of this chapter will, in one way or another, be devoted to closer looks at these, including the repetition and variation of short ideas or phrases, vital, body-oriented rhythms, remarkably similar harmonic usage, which contrasts strongly with that of late seventeenth- to twentieth-century art-music, and what can be called primary tone-colors. I shall begin the following survey of details with a few comments on these sounds, for they are the medium through which all else passes.

1. Sonorities

Music-lovers who favor the smooth, rich sounds of modern orchestral instruments recoil from both the twang and the bite of electric guitars and drums, and 'peculiar' electronic sounds of rock, and the nasality or 'raucousness' of crumhorns, shawms, sackbuts, regals and other 'primitive' wind instruments, or the 'thinness' of viols, lutes and recorders. These sonorities only make all the more unbearable the other unfavored qualities of rock and early music. They are an affront to those who seek polished or lush sounds (neither of which, incidentally, would have been heard in orchestras of Mozart or Beethoven's time), and who believe that instruments have 'progressed' triumphantly – only to have regressed drastically into the cacophony of rock.

But the twangy, nasal, 'thin' and percussive sounds of Renaissance and rock music are integral to both. Impossible to blend in the manner of modern vibrato-hazed ensembles, they stick out and bounce back and forth in space. This is intensified by the use of terraced dynamics – alternation of loud and soft, without modulating crescendos and diminuendos – which is common to both musical styles. In Classical, Romantic and much contemporary music, the norm is modulated dynamics within an envelope of space; in the mixed-consort dance-music and rock it is more a contrasting or a splintering of areas of aural space.

The accompanist obviously cannot produce these sonorities, just as she is deprived of the orchestral colors when she plays excerpts from ballets and other orchestral pieces. Yet they can act as a powerful stimulus. A pianist who is familiar with the original sounds will be able to create and play improvisations in these styles differently from one who knows this music only through written examples. In addition, awareness of the spice and interest which unusual sonorities and sudden shifts in dynamic levels can bring will be likely to spill over into other styles and help to prevent the *mezzo-forte* monotony described in Chapter 9 or the middle-of-the-keyboard security blanket approach.

2. Common practice

The widespread use of certain procedures and 'formulas' – or common practice – prevailed, to a greater or lesser degree, in every era prior to the Romantic cult of originality (and does now in reggae, soul music, blues, jazz and folk music, in addition to rock). But, in my view, there are major differences between the common practice of the late-Baroque and Classical periods and that of Renaissance–early Baroque and rock music. For one thing, a distinction must be made between the 'serious' music written for cultured listening and the *pièces d'occasion* which were played unobtrusively behind social conversation and at the dinner table – the eighteenth-century Muzak. In earlier periods, all music was music *d'occasion*. If it also happened to be first-rate, so much the better. Rock, too, is basically music *d'occasion* (the pretentiousness of some groups notwithstanding), not divided into 'serious' and 'functional categories, for 'listening' *vs.* entertainment.

My point here is that in the eighteenth century it was the mediocre Muzak composers who relied exclusively on the common practice, using vapid melodic formulas, circumscribed harmonic schemes and cadential clichés, taking them at face value and, like their performers, doing little with them. This exaggerated the common practice similarities. In Renaissance dance-music (*and* other types) and rock, common practice is not an easy way out for utilitarian musicians; it is a positive, shared springboard for excellent (and often even middling) ones.

In the late Baroque and Classical periods it is a different story. Bach and Vivaldi use some extraordinary harmonies and melodic twists. Haydn is by no means always the genial conventional figure which the Romantics made of him. Mozart, in his mature works, deviates far more from standard practice than is usually supposed. A work like the Fortieth Symphony has little to do with the pleasant or insipid harmonic schemes of his or lesser men's dinner serenades. Constant Lambert was one of the first to make the point when he wrote, in 1933, 'Although the greatest achievements of the eighteenth century have probably never been surpassed [*sic*], the general level of everyday music has probably never been lower. There is a certain distinction about the minor composers of earlier periods, but the minor eighteenth century composers are merely garrulous and perfunctory. The same is true of the minor works of even such great masters as Mozart and Haydn.'[13]

Here we come back to the factor of improvisation. That the 'formula'-progressions in the early dances and rock are only points of departure gives them a different meaning; in later music they are schemes used for convenience in composition and unobtrusiveness in performance – in a situation where inventiveness by the performers would have been a liability because it demands attention. These *pièces d'occasion* were mere decorations and symbols of privilege, like the paintings on the walls and the elaborate costumes. Improvisation was out of place, and was, in fact, withering away (although preserved for a while in the solo concerto cadenza).

3. Harmony

We have seen two major differences between late-Baroque and Classical common practice and that of the Renaissance–early Baroque and rock music. One involves the function and 'place' of music, the other has to do with the encouragement of imagination and improvisation. Another important difference is that of the harmonic schemes. Tonality, or the supremacy of the major and minor scales, (which were originally merely two of the early church modes: see p. 250), was firmly established by the time of the Classical composers (Bach's *Well-tempered Clavier* being a decisive factor in this). In the late Renaissance and early Baroque, however, things were in flux; the medieval modal language co-existed happily with the gravitation towards tonality. This produced some unusual (wonderful to some modern ears, jarring to others) harmonic schemes. Tonal harmonies are used to achieve a sense of progression, resolution and structure; that is, not so much for their intrinsic sound as for what they can *do*. In this sense they are agents.

Modal harmonies, in contrast, are not agents, but rather results of melodic movement and combinations of inner voices; these originated in vocal music, but were taken over as attractive sounds in their own right by the new sixteenth-century instrumental music. They are non-schematic and non-functional. Thus, they are not agents but entities. The same holds true for rock harmonies. They are not chosen for where they can 'progress' to but for how they sound in juxtaposition.

The point of departure for countless rock songs is simply a sequence of chords, over which simple melodic ideas, motives and rhythmic patterns are added (unlike modern jazz, in which sophisticated chords underlie intricate polyphonic textures, into which the chords often nearly vanish). Similarly, in the early dance-music, with its frequent construction on ground-basses like the *passamezzo* and its implied harmonies, or on a characteristic 'free' progression, chords generate many of the pieces and persist throughout. With the Classical composers who relied mainly on simple common-practice harmonic schemes, the effect is that they are passively conforming to a language imposed by the theory and esthetic of their time: are, in fact, grasping a crutch; in contrast, the effect of the harmonies of the early dance-music and rock is that they are employed actively, with flexibility and responsiveness. The result, in both, is an ever-surprising and fresh juxtaposition of essentially simple elements.

Having been conditioned by tonal music, we cannot hear such harmonies as the original listeners did; they have an extra 'archaic' quality to modern ears. But it is interesting that the rock groups – from the Beatles, all the way up through the New Wave bands and after – gravitate so consistently to these earlier non-tonal harmonic schemes. Even when they use, as they frequently do, the I, IV and V chords of Classical common practice, there is a radical difference. These do not form the predictable progressions of eighteenth-century music, but are interspersed with II, III, VI and *lowered* (or flattened) VII chords as in modal music. And when the normally tyrannical dominant 7th appears, it as often as not ignores its normal resolution and floats off to another (equally non-functional) dominant 7th, or moves self-containedly to a II or other anarchic point. The dominant 7th is not, in other words, a typical chord in rock, unlike blues and jazz, and when it *is* used, it tends to evade its functional value partially or wholly.

In rock the dominant 7th is often ambiguous, in the Classical period it is the norm, and in the Renaissance and early Baroque it is a growing force which is challenging the old modal VII, with the two co-existing in a somewhat unpredictable balance.

This early harmonic language has a quality which was lost when tonality won out or, later, was complicated by Lisztian and Wagnerian chromaticism. It has been described as 'noble poignance'; this is apt, for in addition to the simple power of these chords, they are sharp and cutting – definitely not qualities for a graceful, elegant age like the Classical which considered the sixteenth- and early seventeenth-century harmonic practice to have been coarse, vulgar and uncouth. Likewise in rock: Tin Pan Alley's sentimental tonal harmonies of the 1930s–1950s, rooted in the diatonic–chromatic language of 'serious' music, were not only inadequate to convey the power and thrust of the new rock impulse, but utterly irrelevant to the spirit of its world in general.

The music created during the supremacy of tonality had its own, varied, virtues, but in doing away with the ambiguous, bittersweet modal harmonies, the expression of certain human qualities in music ceased. A few early twentieth-century composers went back, for various reasons, to the pre-tonal language; Debussy and Ravel, Bartók and Kodály, Holst and Vaughan Williams renewed interest in modal writing and made it respectable again. Later the popular folk-movement reinforced this trend (and also served as one of the sources of folk-rock). But no composers since the Elizabethan and Continental dance-composers of the sixteenth and seventeenth centuries have used these harmonies more authentically, forthrightly, dynamically and colorfully than do the rock-musicians.

4. Forms; Variations and Ostinatos

I have discussed the harmonic element on its own merits, but it is also part of a larger common practice – the ubiquitous variation-form, with its other materials of melodies and ostinatos. The majority of the dance-pieces were based on pre-existing popular tunes (which were often transformations of chansons and Protestant chorale-melodies), a handful of ground-bass patterns, harmonic sequences which were related to these – or all three at once. And these were used for not just a single dance, but often for two or three in the linked dances which were so popular: pavane–galliard, and passamezzo–saltarello–piva. These would use the basic scheme, altering the rhythm (duple to triple) and tempo (slow to fast). Many of the later four-, five- or six-movement dance suites used the same tunes, basses or harmonic schemes throughout.

Yet, these circumscribed bases were used with the greatest flexibility. Just as the popular tune often was not stated literally, the piece beginning with a variation of it which was then itself varied, so the ground-bass patterns could be altered, as could the harmonic schemes. And, of course, the pieces were seldom repeated exactly, the players improvising different versions on each occasion.

The passamezzo antico (a later form in dance of the pavane) was the most popular ground-bass. Its basic pattern followed that of the dance: an extended series of 8-measure choreographic patterns. As long as the dance continued – and this could be very long indeed – the players improvised on this scheme:

Ex. 1

Above this could be either a pre-existing tune or an original melody. Certain characteristics of this ground are of interest here. It features the modal lowered VII chord which is so important in rock. In addition, cross-relations are built into the scheme; the F naturals of the lowered VII and III chords challenge the F sharp of the V. This, as I have said, is also a familiar element in rock. In rock the cross-relations are linked closely to the blues-note, an essentially vocal phenomenon, where the singer aims in between the minor and major notes of a scale (in D major, for instance, what is sung is neither F♮ nor F♯, but 'inside' these. Instrumentalists took up the practice throughout the scale; in rock it is called 'bending' the notes, and the general sound affected their harmonic approach).

In addition, the passamezzo ground-bass being repeated over and over, in 8-measure periods, it forms an ostinato, or repeated pattern. While this would be varied by added notes and passing tones in all the voices, it remains implicit, no matter how disguised. Listen to David Munrow's *Two Renaissance Dance Bands* LP for a particularly sensitive and rich treatment of the passamezzo bass, on band 10, Side I. Extended enough to give one a proper feeling of the period, it is superb. (David Munrow died, shockingly prematurely, in 1976, but left a wonderful, if depressingly truncated, heritage on his LPs.)

There were several other popular grounds: the passamezzo moderno (which anticipates the coming tonality) romanesca, folia, ruggiero and passacaglia or chaconne. The latter two are the most familiar to the average listener. They appeared around 1600 and quickly became popular. In their original form they consisted of four descending notes – with their implied harmonies – paced in four equal beats. (An adequate distinction between the two has never been achieved, not even when they were first used.) Later versions extended this as in Purcell, Bach and, much later, Brahms. (I should mention here again the currently popular *Canon* by Pachelbel; this uses a completely tonal eight-note ostinato which never varies: one which was widely used by mid-to-late Baroque composers, with dropping fourths in the bass-line. With it, Pachelbel created one of the loveliest pieces of all time.)

Ex. 2   Passamezzo moderno   Ex. 3   Romanesca

Ex. 4   Folia

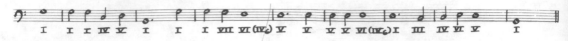

I   I   I IV V   I   I   I VII VI (IV) V   V   V V VI (IV) I   III   IV VI V   I

Ex. 5   Ruggiero

Ex. 6   Passacaglia (major)   Ex. 7   Passacaglia (minor)   Ex. 8   Passacaglia (chromatic)

As for parallels with rock: many of the pieces listed in Section V. A consist of invention over inexorably repeated ostinatos or shorter ostinato-sections plus contrasting material, or treatment in the freer style of the passamezzo. Three examples are particularly relevant here. In 'Hey Jude', the long C section consists of a four-chord ground which features the modal VII of the passamezzo and the inexorability of the passacaglia–chaconne. Led Zeppelin's 'Ballad of Evermore' is built almost completely on an undulating four-note ostinato, which contains the passamezzo lowered VII. Mott the Hoople's version of David Bowie's 'All the Young Dudes' combines an extended *passacaglia* ground with a wealth of cross-relations (see further discussion in Section V). In these, and in many songs, the one constant element is the harmonic ostinato. Bukofzer stresses this shared peculiarity of the early music based on grounds: 'In view of the fact that the harmonic scheme was the only stable element, the procedure may be called a variation on ostinato harmonies.'[14]

As for the over-all form, it could either be a continuous string of variations as in the passamezzo, or consist of two or three sections (A-B or A-B-C) each of which would be varied (A, A_1, A_2 – B, B_1, B_2) as the dance progressed. These sections could be based on grounds or freely composed, but were always linked to the form of the dances.

The ballet improviser can make use of these venerable schemes for her own flights of fancy. Many of the pieces which I improvised for class used such patterns, and I never tired of seeking new things to be done with them. The great value of working in this way is that, having a firm base, you are particularly free to invent and elaborate without losing your way.

5. Physicality

'The Beatles' music, made up by people who couldn't read notation, had to be in part improvised, in part aurally memorized; and this is why instrumental techniques had to be directly derived from the movements of hand and body.'[15] I have already mentioned the physicality which rock and Renaissance dance music share. In both cases, this acted as a powerful catalyst, challenging prevailing traditions. The clear, strong beat of the dances challenged the spiritual, pulseless polyphonic quality of the religious music of Palestrina, Lassus and Vittoria, paving the way for the forceful, more direct monody of Monteverdi and the New Music. Rock re-introduced the body into music, challenging the over-arranged mush of Tin Pan Alley and the physically enervating, 'head-music' convolutions of cool jazz. At the same time, rock challenged the concert-hall/Sinatra-Crosby-et al. concept of the performer as deified 'artist' – which even cool jazz accepted, and 'It has remained for the new rock musicians to demolish this model altogether, by the simple expedient of restoring dance to its rightful place alongside music. Of course, jazz was also once a music for dancing. But the jazz writers of that generation and the following ones, hypnotized (as are all good middlebrows) by the European idea of what constitutes "culture", were indecently eager to repudiate dancing so as to demonstrate that jazz was as "refined" (i.e. white and European) as "serious" or "classical" music'.[16] Wilfred Mellers claims: 'Pop music and dance have no truck with the separation of the dance as spectacle from the dance as activity, in which the audience participates by singing, and sometimes clapping, stamping and jigging and screaming.' And '. . . only in a very partial sense can we dismiss the teenager's orgiastic dancing as a tipsy escape from the hard realities of life. On the contrary, as compared with the romantic unreality of the previous generation's ballroom dancing (which is in turn related to the fairytale myth of classical ballet) one might rather describe teenage dance as practical and functional in Collingwood's sense; an inchoate attempt to rediscover the springs of being.'[17]

In all this, rock-listeners and dancers (not all 'teenagers' by any means) are clearly very close indeed to their late-Renaissance counterparts, who were uninhibitedly physical and have been often described as 'dance-mad'.

One of the major sources of the physicality in both types of music is the harmonic language. After pointing out the similarity of the Beatles' harmonic approach to that of pre-eighteenth-century music – including the flat VII, modal flavor, cross (or 'false') relations and lack of conventional dominant–tonic modulations – Mellers comments, 'Of course this doesn't necessarily mean that the Beatles have ever heard, or even heard of, medieval or Renaissance music, any more than the peasant folk-singer knew he was singing in the Dorian mode. It's rather that their melody and harmony welling up in their subconscious, discovers authentic affinities with music of an earlier, less "harmonic" stage of evolution, and thereby reinforces the primitivism of their rhythm.'[18] (The rhythm of Renaissance dance-music was, of course, "primitive" compared to sixteenth-century polyphonic rhythm.)

The improviser, I repeat, should not attempt to work within a harmonic language which she cannot feel clearly and physically. In Renaissance music and in rock, the easily heard and felt harmonic progressions and the absence of precise, detailed notation particularly encourages the performer to rely on the body rather than the mind for the remembering and invention of music. When the player cannot respond in this physical way to what she is playing, the inner ear will also be dull, and she will be in a defensive position, the notes continually threatening to overwhelm her. Let the principles behind early dance-music and rock help to show the way towards a physical simplicity.

IV. Spontaneity *vs.* rehearsal

I have touched on the subject of spontaneity several times already, but a few more points need to be made. For one thing, listeners whose only acquaintance with the early dance-pieces is through recordings, which means most of us, are misled. The short tracks which form these collections, sometimes as many as twenty to one side, lasting a half-minute to two minutes each, are no more than points of departure – which are not followed by the actual journeys. The picture we get is a miniature, trifling one, especially when the performance is the old-fashioned listless, piping-recorder travesty which prevailed until recent times. Actually, however, the music could have gone on and on – as did the enthusiastic dancers – and there is evidence that the performers intensified their variation as the piece continued. This prolongation can be inferred from a description of the galliard: 'The dancer traversed the hall once or twice with his partner, released her, and danced in front of her; she retreated dancing to the opposite end of the hall; the dancer here surpassed his previous performance, and so it went on with increasing intensity, until the musicians laid down their instruments.'[19]

Although it gradually lost this pantomimic quality, it remained 'bold and wanton', with its leaping and thrusting movements. These, obviously, could hardly develop in the brief samplings so often offered on record. Nor could the other stately or lively dances of the time. And all were dependent on and stimulated by the inventiveness of the musicians.

Two other examples may illustrate this even more vividly. In some forms of the tordion the music 'contains but twelve bars and consequently these would have had to be repeated between forty and fifty times, serving the purpose of a rhythmic stimulus to the intricate footwork of the expert dancers of the period.'[20] The pavane, also, could go on, used either as a set dance or as a processional; in the latter the short sections of the music were repeated, with varied embellishments and rhythmic figurations, for as many times as required by the number of dancers in the procession, which was often lengthy.

In his notes for the record, 'The Kynge's Musicke' (Decca 79434) John White describes the situation regarding performance and score:

[these] are reconstructed as examples of informal music-making. No scores survive to show exactly how the King's Music played for dancing and lively entertainments, and probably none ever existed. Dances and tunes in keyboard scores we have considered as sketches or 'versions' to be pre-empted by the performers of New York Pro Musica and realized in the same way Renaissance musicians would have realized them, playing partly by note and partly by ear and probably never the same way twice. Ornaments and embellishments are introduced freely, particularly at cadences and on the repetition of musical material, and whole passages of improvisation are captured here that existed only at the moment of recording and have never been written down.

(The first track of this record offers three enchanting popular dances, brilliantly played. The Pavane and Galliard on Side 1, especially the latter, are wonderful examples of the power and interest generated by performers with flexibility and a feeling for this music.) Although the Pro Musica is bound by the conventions of time-spans on recordings, it still manages to give an authentic picture of the early music.

The ornamentation of lines, with flurries of runs, skips and subdivisions (called 'divisions' or 'diminutions' in the Baroque era) is also integral to rock performance. Rock performers often vary these so much on different occasions as almost to make every live performance by a good group a potential re-creation. The intelligent rock musician knows that the more he tries to freeze a 'good' version, the more lifeless the music will become.

Jan Steele made this point also, in a prize-winning essay in *Melody Maker*.

All rock musicians know that however much the individual composer may attempt to control the materials of composition, however much he may write down, the eventual product will always be changed beyond recognition – the bass player will always make the bass line his own by changing it here and there, and, in fact, if he doesn't, the end result is insipid; the guitarist's solo is crystallized in the recording and becomes part of the piece, and so on . . . This is the exact opposite of what happens in classical music. Here the composer's idea is paramount and sacred. Even with certain so-called avant garde music where performers (and possibly audiences) are given a 'choice' as to what they may do in a composition, the final result must still accord with the composer's conception. The best illustration is to compare two different recordings of a symphony, which will be almost identical, given a slight interpretive difference, with two versions of the same pop song, which often vary so much as to be different songs.[21]

While this might seem to be overstating the case a bit, making classical performance a more rigid activity than it actually is, Steele's observations are certainly valid. It is a matter of perspective or degree. About the classics, David Barnett's perspective is that 'a performance is not the score but simply one idea of it. Since no two performances are alike, there are as many ideas of the score as there are performances . . . [But] a consensus about a given score acts to limit the extent to which performances of it differ.'[22] This may also be somewhat misleading, for convention, expectation and reverence for the composer's 'message' are far more weighty determining agents than are deviation and flexibility in interpretation. The basic rule of fidelity to printed notes and directions makes this inevitable. In rock and, to a lesser degree, in Renaissance dance-music, the score is the least important part of all. This is well-known regarding rock; exposure to the great differences in performance of the comparative versions of the early dances will show it to be true in this music also. The paramount rule of latter-day classical performance is that, no matter how many alterations, and even wild distortions of rhythm, tempo and phrasing may occur, the *notes* are sacrosanct. No leaving-out, adding-to or changing of the written notes is permitted, no transposition up or down an octave, no subtraction or addition of contrapuntal lines, no actual *changes* of rhythmic patterns: these are some major differences between classical music-performance and Renaissance-dance or rock performance.

This is a reflection of a general cultural condition, for 'the whole framework of Western political thought since the Enlightenment has rested on a repressive theory, one that did not allow for the expression of that which was or could be potentially disruptive.'[23] Now, in music nothing is a more potentially 'disruptive' force than personal or collective improvisation. It is unpredictable, without the secure controls of an invariant score. Rock music and the counter-culture returned ('regressed') to the dangers – and potentialities – of disruption.

True, and mainly unfortunately, many rock groups have tended more and more towards controlled rehearsal and super-produced albums, although the best groups regain much of their original spontaneity in live performance and try to maintain some flexibility even on recordings. But rock is a cruelly commercial form of expression, and because of economic pressures it often must subject the on-the-spot creativity of live performance (plus its beneficial hazards) to a more controllable record-product. This results in the dilemma described by Michael Wale: 'In the ultimate analysis everything in pop depends on what a group can bring out on record. Fantastic lengths are gone to in order to guarantee that the final performance shall be flawless, sometimes so flawless that it is impossible to reproduce on stage.'[24]

Rehearsal of 'improvisations' for class tends to negate their main value; practice at *improvising* is fine but pre-packaged creations will lack the response to a moment, a situation, which is the main value of improvising for dance. By all means attempt to remember the best ones, to add to your repertoire, but also try to keep them simmering, to allow new things to happen within them on other occasions. The improviser needs spontaneity, and spontaneity cannot be rehearsed or put in reserve.

V. The music on record

This section is totally dependent on listening; the more pieces heard from the following selection (and others the reader may discover) the stronger the message will be. Unheard, the lists will remain abstract and meaningless. The rock numbers should be, in the main, easily available from personal collections, those of friends, record sales, etc., but more effort may be needed to track down the collections of early dance-music. Try also local circulating record libraries, music-school libraries and classical radio stations.

For those who are unacquainted with the Renaissance and early Baroque sound it is essential to listen until it no longer seems 'archaic'. Only then can its special beauty be fully appreciated. There remains, of course, the problem of sketchy versions; the listener must eke out what *is* there with research, and some imagination of the vivid scenes and circumstances in which this music would originally have been performed, danced to and relished. This will help a great deal to counteract its often truncated presentation on LPs.

A. Renaissance–early-Baroque dance-music

1. Comparisons

Many of the dances appear on more than one record (see list of recordings on p. 295). This offers an opportunity to hear different approaches; the instrumentation may vary radically (as it did originally), and also such things as tempos, passing tones and melodic figurations, spacings, registers and inversions – all of which can alter the over-all effect considerably. Compare, for example, the versions of 'La Bataille' and 'La Mourisque' by the N.Y. Pro Musica and Musica Reservata (recordings D and B). There is a great feeling of *spine* in these dances, and others like them – a sense of proud erect carriage and tingling in the very fingertips of the dancers. Yet, in 'La Mourisque' one feels a curious difference between the Pro Musica version – which seems almost arrogant – and the faster Musica Reservata one, in which the quicker tempo produces a foot-tapping elation. But perhaps the most exciting version of the lot (I include six; it is a popular selection) is the one by David Munrow on the *Two Renaissance Dance Bands* LP (Q). This combines, strikingly, qualities of the two just cited, with an additional zest of its own. Munrow, again, provides an electrifying experience for those who know a dance through an ordinary or poor realization in his splendid and rich version of the *Bergerette sans roch*. This is a re-creative music-making that inspires a rare joy in the listener (it is also a particularly vivid example of the affinity between renaissance dance-music and rock).

On a somewhat less exalted level, compare also the pavane, *Si par souffrir*, by the Musica Reservata and the Musica Aurea (B and E) – a particularly clear illustration of the impact of an embellished rendition with a straight, skeletal one. Another such comparison is offered by the versions of the 'Pavane de Spaigne'; the brief, sketchy one of the Nonesuch Praetorius LP (G) is trivial compared with the longer, highly varied performance by the Pro Musica (C). Then there is the spectacular contrast between the monophonic version of 'Jouyssance vous Donneray' on the Nonesuch French Dances LP (H) and the ensemble one in Munrow's *Henry VIII* film-score (P). Each rendition is equally valid, but the Munrow is one of the most satisfying of any of the tracks listed below regarding vitality of performance, contrasting use of registers and sonorities, and *length*.

With these six dances I leave the reader to make other, equally surprising discoveries as to how radically this uncomplicated music can be affected by performance, and historical imagination and empathy.

2. *Vocal models*

The Musica Reservata Italian and French collections (A and B) point up beautifully the link between the vocal chanson and the instrumental dance (many chansons survived intact to become part of the popular dances – another similarity to rock). They give us a lovely contrast between the vocal model of *Gentil madonna* and its instrumental galliard metamorphosis. *Belle qui tient ma vie*, that most exquisite of pavanes, can also be heard in both vocal and instrumental form in the Musica Reservata collection (B), and, sung beautifully, on the Nonesuch French Dances LP (H).

A startling transformation of the vivacious chanson, 'Il estoit une fillette', into the ironically named pavane, *La Gaiette*, sombre and touching, also comes from the Musica Reservata (B). The Susato *Ronde* (on the same LP), however, stays close in spirit to the original song.

3. Pavane–galliard link

The clearest form of variation in these dances is the frequent use of the musical material of the duple pavane for the following triple galliard. An exciting example of this is contained in the pavane–galliard, *Au joli bois* (B), in which the stately, symmetrical phrasing of the pavane becomes excitingly displaced in the galliard. Another wonderful transformation occurs in the similarly conceived *Allemande-tripla* from Schein's Suite No. 1 (G), also a common pairing.

Such rhythmic alterations are, of course, valuable for the improviser who wishes to introduce variety when necessary, or refreshing yet not complex syncopation.

4. Harmonic physique

The harmonic language of these dances forms their spine; it is a major source of their beauty and strength. The dance-music is, interestingly, considering its worldly, physical nature, actually closely linked with the forthright, clear-cut, nonmystical hymns of the Protestant Reformation. Both were based on vital, vigorous tunes, often of folk-origin, clear metric rhythm, and stark and powerful harmonies, although the dance-music decked these out with colorful percussion and more extreme, 'unseemly' tempos. (Listen, for instance, to the Praetorius chorales (on G), and his three *Bransles Doubles* on the Munrow LP (O).) In these dances, the rhythms and harmonies work closely together indeed, for the straightforward, pungent block-chords, often modal or bi-tonal, underscore the kinetic thrust and vigorous rhythms of the fast pieces and add sinew and focus to those in slower tempos.

(i) Much wonderful dance-music was created with only I, IV and V chords, sometimes spiced with one or two others. The powerful pavane/galliard 'Au joli bois' (B) uses these chords with the inexorability of a novice punk-rocker. Only an occasional modal II chord leavens their reiteration (an interesting detail is the appearance of a melodic blues-note in the more improvisatory B sections of each, with its resultant cross-relation effect. Here a pianistic comparison of modal and tonal can prove instructive; for anyone with a feeling for the harmonic style of the dances, the alteration of minor Vs to major V_7s or the G minor II to a G major [major], sound weak and sickly.

Another almost exclusively I–IV–V scheme, again with an occasional II, is found in Haussmann's 'Tantz' (I). The marvelous 'Branle de Champagne' (I) likewise consists of I–IV–V, except for one VII in each A section. But this dance differs from the first two in that it vacillates, in the B section, between the major and minor forms of V – that popular device of the period. Remember, a minor V going to a major or minor I (or, as in 'Au joli bois', a minor II to V) has a lowered VII, i.e. in C, a $B^{\flat}$ rather than the tonal B♮. In both cases the flavor is singularly expressive. Many of the loveliest dances contain the minor V or minor–major vacillations. In addition to the decidedly rock-ish 'Branle de Champagne' (I, J) are Mainerio's 'Balli Anglese' and 'Francese' (O), the Allemande de Liège (I), 'La Scarpa' (the version on A, Band 7b.) and the 'Passamezzo pour les cornetz'.

Major–minor shifts of I are also common. A concentrated example of an ambivalent I occurs in Schein's powerful *Allemande – Tripla* from the Suite No. 4 (G) (and, in fact, throughout his dance-suites, which are permeated by major–minor shifts).

(ii) II and VII chords dominate or strongly color a great proportion of these early dances. The incomparable *La Gamba* (A) owes much of its dark beauty to the lowered VII which is prominent throughout; it also contributes, with the II chord, to the poignance of the *Allemande 8 et Tripla* (B, E, L) and, again with II, gives a piquancy to the *Bergerette sans roch* (E, K, M, Q). In the *Allemande de Liège* mentioned above, we hear an enchanting riot of major–minor shifts which create sparkling cross-relations, which include the F♮ of VII. The pavane, 'Belle qui tient ma vie', cited earlier as being particularly beautiful, has an outstandingly rich harmonic pallette; the lowered VII, both the major and minor forms of IV and V, and also III and VI. The wide expressive range which results makes it perhaps one of the best introductions to this music for those conditioned primarily by Romantic music.

'Bouffons', an Elizabethan popular dance-song (on M) sounds like a germinal idea for a song by Genesis, Yes, or Dire Straits. The lowered VII is very prominent, in addition to I, IV and V chords, with a cross-relation between VII and V. The three delectable dances from Mainerio's *Primo Libro di Balli*, played so wonderfully in Munrow's Medieval Renaissance album (O), similarly venture strikingly close to rock territory. The three rock-groups mentioned above, like many others, not only use the lowered VII with I, IV and V chords quite similarly to Mainerio, but also achieve, not deliberately, of course, a corresponding energy and spirit. (A performance of Mainerio's dances, among many others, could prove most interesting in this light if rock drum-patterns, the bite and twang of electric guitars and electric keyboard instruments were their medium, and some characteristic rock improvising filled out the written notes – although the 'classical' performers on the Munrow LP certainly rock in their own way).

5. *Cross-relations*

Here we have perhaps the most pervasive and moving element of these dance pieces. It has cropped up already in 4 above; technically, a cross-relation is the juxtaposition of two chords which share a common note, but in one chord this note is altered and 'crosses over' from one voice to another. (See also Ex. 12 in Section V. B. 7.)

Ex. 9

This can occur in quick succession – its most acute effect – or with intervening chords. In Ex. 9.3 it exists between the melodic line and the chord (an integral part of rock and blues). In each case it produces a feeling of bi-tonality, a restlessness not found in the predictable tonal consistency of purely diatonic music (see also examples below, in Section B, item 7).

Listen particularly to *La Gamba* and *La Scarpa* (A). The former, richly sombre, shows the graver aspect of cross-relations, and the latter, proud and muscular, their noble side. In a faster tempo they can convey other feelings; both the Gervaise *Branle de Champagne* and the Phalèse *Reprise/Galliard* (I) are spiky and pungent. The latter is a veritable orgy of cross-relations; during its short span there are three: between C#/C♮, F#/F♮ and B♮/B♭.

In all tempos, they produce the bittersweet, ambiguous quality so characteristic of this period. By Purcell's time they were being ousted by the new diatonicism, and he was considered old-fashioned for continuing to use them. They disappeared for all too long, but have now been rescued and given new life by rock musicians, few of whom will be aware of their historical role; theirs was a discovery of the ear, not the studious eye. Oddly, in earlier times the cross-relation similarly was generated by intuitive procedures.

6. Cross-rhythms

Cross-relations involve conflicting tonalities; cross-rhythms result from displaced accents. In both cases a norm is challenged or disrupted. Unusual stresses and syncopations are a feature of these dance-pieces, whether from melodic shifts or unexpected harmonic changes. These are, naturally, related to the dance patterns. The 6-beat tordion and galliard were based on the *cinque pas*, which had a marked accent on the fifth beat:

    step   step   step   step   jump   land in 5th pos.

    1   –   2   –   3   –   4   –   5   –   6

This must have been exciting to dance, particularly as the galliard music was often already syncopated as a result of its triple treatment of the duple pavane themes. I tried the *cinque pas* to the strong cross-accented gagliarda, Zorzi (A) and became breathless and exhilarated. Then I did it to the final galliard on the Renaissance Band LP (C); this was even better. The performance tempo of the former did not leave much time for such antics, being more for listening than for dancing, and, also, the particular cross-accents and unusual phrasing of the latter galliard combined electrically with the syncopated dance-phrase. There is, of course, an overall cross-accented relationship between dance and music (Ex. 10). (These conflicting groupings of three twos and two threes, with the resultant cross-accents, are an early form of the ambiguity found in the hemiola (see remarks in earlier chapters).)

Ex. 10

There were many variations upon the basic *cinque pas* (Arbeau devotes fifty pages of his *Orchesographie* to them) and the musicians, keeping pace with the zestful 'bold, wanton and thrusting' dancers, would no doubt have contrived ever more intricate and exciting syncopated cross-rhythms.

The above has been a necessarily brief discussion; I could cite only a handful of the pieces which I consider particularly pertinent, interesting and beautiful, but here are some related lists for the reader to investigate. They are based on these LPs. (All are good, but those marked † are, in my opinion, superlative – for music, performance or both.)

†   A.   16th century Italian Dance Music
         Musica Reservata   Phillips 6500 102

†   B.   16th century French Dance Music
         Musica Reservata   Phillips 6500 293

      C.   The Renaissance Band
         N.Y. Pro Musica   Decca 9424

      D.   Renaissance Festival Music
         N.Y. Pro Musica   Decca 9419

†   E.   Dances of the Renaissance (Susato-Phalèse)
         Ensemble Musica Aurea   Oiseau Lyre   SOL–R330

      F.   High Renaissance Dance Music
         Collegium Terpsichore   D G Archive 73153

      G.   Praetorius–Schein: Dances
         Ferdinand Conrad Ensemble   Nonesuch 71128

      H.   French Dances of the Renaissance
         Ancient Instrument Ensemble of Paris   Nonesuch 71036

†   I.   Golden Dance Hits of 1600
         Ulsamer Collegium Terpsichore   D G Archive 2533 184

      J.   Tanzmusik
         Ulsamer Collegium   D G Archive 2533 111

      K.   Medieval Instrumental Music
         Ricercare Ensemble   Oryx 1509 (also on Odyssey)

      L.   To Entertain a King
         Musica Reservata   Argo ZRG 566

      M.   The Medieval Sound
         David Munrow and Ensemble   Oryx EXP 46

      N.   Courtly Pastimes of 16th Century England
         St. George's Canzona   Oiseau Lyre SOL 329

*†   O.   Instruments of the Middle Ages and Renaissance
         David Munrow and the Early Music Consort   EMI SLS988

**   P.   Music for the film *Henry VIII and His Six Wives*
         (Arranged and composed by David Munrow)
         Early Music Consort of London   EMI CSDA 9001

†   Q.   Two Renaissance Dance Bands
         David Munrow, the Early Music Consort of London and the Morley Consort   EMI HQS–1249

      R.   Renaissance Suite
         David Munrow, the Early Music Consort of London   EMI HQS–1415

*   This superb album also contains two sides of medieval music, which lies outside our survey but is strongly recommended both for lovers of the early repertoire and the musically curious.

**   An illuminating example of the benefits obtained by assigning a knowledgable and imaginative musician to the production of a period film-score.

Selected pieces

The following pieces are identified according to the records on which they appear, as listed above.

1. Comparative versions

Allemaigne–Recoupe   D, E (All. 1), Q

Allemande 8   B (Band 3.b., Side I), E, L (Allemande Prince)

Ballet de feu   G, M

La Bataille: Pavane   B, D, Q

Belle qui tient ma vie: Pavane   B, H

Bergerette sans roch: Basse danse   E, K (Suite 1, Side I), M, Q

La Bourrée   C, F/I, M

Branle de Bourgogne   I (Band 12, Side I) and (Band 1, Side II)/J (Nos. 10 and 16, Side II), K

Le cuer est bon: Basse danse   B, K (Suite 3, Side II), N

Entrée du fol   E, K (Suite 3, Side II), N

Galliarde 1   E, K (Suite, Side I: 3rd dance)

Galliarde (Praetorius)   C (Band 6, Side I), R (Band 5, Side I)

Galliarde de la guerre   C, I

Galliarde de Monsieur Westron   C, I

La Gamba: Pavane – Gagliarda   A, B (Side II, *J'ameroye*)

Hoboeckendans   B, E

Il me suffit: Basse danse   B, L

Jouyssance vous donneray: (B) Basse danse   H, P

Mille regrets: Pavane   D, E, Q

Mon amy: Ronde – Branle   D (Band 2, Side I), E, M, Q

Mon desir: Basse danse   E, K (Suite 3, Side II)

La Mourisque: Basse danse   B, D, L, N, P, Q

Passamezzo d'Italie   A, E, J, K, L, Q (A, L and Q variants on original passamezzo ground-bass; E, J and K based on original passamezzo tune)

Pastime with Good Company   L, P

Pavane de Spaigne   C, G

Pour quoy: Ronde   B, N

Rocha el fuso (Larocque): Galliard   E, K (Suite 3, Side II)

Ronde   D (1st Ronde, Side I), I/J, Q (No. 3, Side I)

La Scarpa: Gagliarda   A (Bands 6 and 7, Side I), P (Band 2.b, Side II)

Schiarazula Marazzula   E, I, J

Si par souffrir: Pavane   B, E

La Traditora: Gagliarda   A, L (Version 1); E (Bands 3.b, 10, Side II), P (Version 2)

Ungarescha – Saltarello   I, J, M

La Volta   M, O

La Volunte: Basse danse   H, N

Zorgi (Giorgio): Gagliarda   A (Bands 5.b, 5.c, Side II)

2. Vocal models

Examples of song-versions of instrumental dances are included on these records:

16th century Italian Dances (A)

16th century French Dances (B)

French Dances of the Renaissance (H)

3. Thematic relationships between paired slow and fast dances

Allemaigne–Recoupe   D, Q
Allemande–Tripla (Schein), Suite
No. 1, in G   G
Allemande–Tripla (Schein), Suite
No. 2, in d   G*
Caro ortolano   O
Passamezzo–Gagliarda d'Italie   A, L/E,
J/Q

Pavane–Galliard d'angleterre   H
Pavane–Galliard (Au joli bois)   B
Pavane–Galliard (Mille ducats)   E
Pavana–Gagliarda (La Traditora)   A
Ronde (Salterelle)   Q, D, I/J
Ungarescha–Saltarello   I, J, M

* Other examples can be heard on F; Schein, in fact, habitually related the movements of his dance-suites thematically.

4. Harmonic language

a. Based primarily on I, IV and V (in one section or all)

La Bataille   B, D, Q
La Bourrée   C, F/I, M
Branle de Bourgogne (Gervaise)   I/J,
K
Branle de Champagne   I/J
Courante   I (Band 2, Side I)
The Fairie Round   O

Gagliarda   C (Band 6, Side I)
Gavotte   F/I
King Henry VIII Pavan   L, P
Passamezzo   C (Band 1, Side 1)
Pavane–galliard (Au joli bois)   A
Tanz   I
Volta CCI   F

b. II and/or lowered VII important

Allemaigne–Recoupe   D, E, Q (VII)
Allemande de Liège   E (VII)
Allemande 6   E (VII)
Allemande 8 et tripla   B, L, E (II and
VII)
Ballo Anglese   O (VII)
Belle qui tient ma vie   B, H (VII)
Bergerette sans roch   E, K, M, Q (II
and VII)
Bouffons   M (VII)
3 Bransles doubles   O (II)
La Brosse: Basse danse – Tripla –
Tourdion   J (VII)
Il buratto   L (II and VII)
Caro ortolano   O (VII)
Catkanei   I (II)
El Colognese: Pavana (vocal
version)   A (VII)
Danse du Roy   Q (II)
Desiderata: Pavana   M (VII)
Dont vient cela: Basse danse;
galliard   A, D (No. 4, Side I), R (II
and VII)

La Gaiette: Pavane   B (II)
Galliard   P (first on Side II)
La Gamba   A (VII)
La Gatta: Basse danse   J (II and VII)
Mille ducats: Pavane et Galliarde   E
(II and VII)
La Mourisque   B, D, L, N, P, Q (II)
Passamezzo d'Italie   A, L, Q (VII)
Pastime with Good Company   L, P
(VII)
Pavane de Spaigne   C, G (II and
Rocha el fuso   E, K (VII)
Ronde (-Salterelle)   D (1st ronde), I/J,
Q (No. 3, Side I) (II)
Ronde   Q (No. 9, Side I) (II and VII)
Ronde 3   E (II and VII)
La Rosette   G (VII)
La Scarpa   A, P (Band 2.b, Side II)
Schiarazula Marazzula   E, I, J (VII)
Ungarescha – Saltarello   I, J, M (VII)
Vegnando da Bologna: Pavana   L
(VII)

5. Cross-relations or major–minor

Allegmaigne–Recoupe   D, E, Q
Allemande de Liège   E
Allemande-tripla   I
Allemande 6   E
Ballo Francese   O
La Bataille   B, D, Q
Belle qui tient ma vie   B, H
Bergerette sans roch   E, K, M, Q
La Bourrée   C, F/I, M
Branle de Bourgogne (anon./le
   Roy)   I/J
Branle de Champagne   I/J
Branle double de Poictou   R
Il buratto   L
Caro ortolano   O
Cest a grand tort (Reprise)   B
El Colognese   A
Courante and Allemande-tripla
   (Schein: Suite No. 1, G)   F*
Courrant de la Royne   C
Dances and Galliards (Widmann)   F
Desiderata   M
Dont vient cela   A, D, R
La Gaiette   B
Galliard   P (1st on Side II)

Galliard (Dowland)   O (Band II, Side
   IV)
Galliarde de Monsieur Westron   C, I
La Gamba   A, B (*J'ameroye*)
Gentil madonna   A
Intrada (Hassler)   R
Jouyssance vous donneray   H, P
Mille ducats   E
Mille regrets   D, E, Q
Passameze pour les cornetz   C
Pavane 1   E
Pavane de Spaigne   C, G
Reprise–Galliard   I
Ronde   Q (No. 9, Side I)
Ronde   Q (No. 11, Side I)
La Rosette   G
La Scarpa   A
Spagnoletta   I
Tantz   I (melodic cross-relation)
La Traditora   A, P
Tripla (Allemande 8)   E
Turkeyloney/Staines Morris (arr.
   Munrow)   P
Variations on the Romanesca   O
Zorzi   A

* In addition to this example, cross-relations and major–minor shifts occur throughout Schein's dances on F and G.

6. Cross-rhythms

Basse galliarde   R (Band 5, Side II)
Bransle double de Poictou   R
Courante   I (Band 2, Side I)
Gagliarda   C (Band 6, Side I)
Galliarde (Au joli bois)   B (Band 1.c,
   Side II)
Galliarde de la guerre   C, I
Galliard (Haussmann)   I
Galliarde de Monsieur Westron   C, I
Galliarde (Praetorious)   C (band 6,
   Side I), R (Band 5, Side II)

Jouyssance vous donneray   H, P
Mille ducats (C section)   E
La Pastorella   P
Pavane et galliarde d'angleterre   H
Ronde 3   E
Tripla (La Brosse)   J
Volte   I (Band 3, Side I)
Volte   I (Band 5, Side I)
Wedding Music for Anne of Cleves
   (Irish Jigg)   P

I have not surveyed III and VI chords. Not only did pressures of space preclude it, one of my objectives here was to show the difference between the Renaissance-dance harmony and that of the eighteenth and nineteenth century. Thus, the focus had to be on harmonies atypical of the latter, or, in the case of the ubiquitous I, IV and V chords, on the difference in their use in the earlier music. The III and VI chords are strong agents in tonality, and their ambivalent use in sixteenth- and early seventeenth-century music both foreshadows it and resists it, as when they are used modally or to produce cross-relations. (The nineteenth-century repertoire contains many cross-relations, but their expressive effect is markedly different from that in the early music.)

The listener who is able to compare two or three recorded versions will have a taste of the variation possible in the original live performances in the sixteenth and seventeenth centuries. Improvisers, certainly, will be stimulated by it in proportion to the inventiveness of the performers. I suggest, therefore, that you seek out as many other recordings of this music as possible, paying particular attention to comparative versions.

B. Rock

After rock has been condemned because of its continually high decibel-level (which, of course, is not true of the good groups, who have many quiet sections or even entire songs), the next criticism is that it is 'repetitious' and limited. I hope to show in this section that the harmonic common practice of rock groups leads to anything but sameness and the purpose of the charts which begin on page 305 is to prove how *diversified* the music is from group to group, and even within the repertoire of one group.

Many Beatles songs, for instance, are based on the I–IV–V harmonic sequence, or permutations of it. Yet few listeners are conscious of this as a *primary* characteristic. If they do come to realize it later, as a background connection, it is still the foreground elements peculiar to each song which are decisive in one's reaction to it. And neither are Beatles I–IV–V songs 'like' Dylan's 'Idiot Wind' or the Rolling Stones' 'Get Off My Cloud'; the I–IV–V progression becomes transformed in each.

Yet underneath, as with the dance music of the Renaissance and early Baroque, is the great satisfaction (conscious or not) derived from the harmonic scheme which unites them. To me, 'Lucy In The Sky With Diamonds' is enhanced and enlarged by its organic I–IV–V link to 'You've Got To Hide Your Love Away', 'Rain', or 'Born to Run' – not diminished. They are related but different, rather than separate examples of sameness. It could be argued that this is true of any good music in a style which consists of simple, commonly used chords – such as the late-Baroque or Classical styles in serious music (although see above, III. 2). One difference with these, however, is that there is a great deal to divert the listener's attention from the simple harmonic language. Carefully shaped melodies, extended and often fascinating formal development and thematic interplay, intricate, exciting counter-point – these and other sophisticated elements found in serious music are not part of rock music-making. In this light, it (and the early dance-music) is spare indeed. The miracle is that music which is so elementary in certain ways, and so circumscribed harmonically, can offer such beauty, richness and seemingly inexhaustible invention. But more of this presently.

I have been talking about variety from song to song, but it is the frequent variety *within* a song which is perhaps most exciting. A very large number of rock songs consist mainly of repeated short patterns – similar to the passacaglia, chaconne and passamezzo frameworks of the early dance-music. Over these, the lead, rhythm and bass guitars can generate great interest and intensity through comparatively simple variations and flights away from and back to the basic pattern. Sometimes only one note or chord may be varied, sometimes a sequence, but even the tiniest alteration can send a shock of joy through the attentive listener. And, always, the richest cumulative effects come from the simplest means. True, even the best groups are sometimes led up the garden path in one way or another, but the ones who endure are those who find their way back to the basic core of rock, leaving the unassimilable tinsel – whether 'classical', technological or histrionic – behind. Influences which can be absorbed are utilized; those which threaten rock's simple substructure are sooner or later rejected.

Before we look at some of the common practice structures, a few necessary comments:

1. I consider the amount of attention given by many writers to rock lyrics so disproportionate, and often inane, that I am retaliating by concentrating on the music, for a change. In any case, we are concerned here with rock from a musical standpoint and for its value to the improviser.

2. Despite the strong rhythm-and-blues orientation of seminal groups like the Rolling Stones, Yardbirds, Beatles, Kinks and the Who, they and their successors gradually incorporated other influences: folk, 'pre-Bach', country and western, bluegrass, 'psychedelic', Eastern, classical, avant-garde electronic, minimalist and others. Thus, the following survey is primarily one of an *amalgamated* music, not of any one of the contributing influences in its 'pure' form. This means that blues, jazz, soul and reggae, *per se* lie outside the scope of this survey, which is a necessarily limited attempt to bring certain facets of rock to the improviser's attention rather than a comprehensive history of how rock developed, beginning with the rock 'n' roll of the 1950s. The early sixties 'rock-explosion' would have been impossible without the profound feeling and gritty energy of the various black influences, but the entire black musical ethos is radically different from that of the white.[25] Also, the treatment of often-shared techniques can differ greatly; even the simple classic blues' I–IV–I–V–IV–I – which is used repeatedly in rock songs – seldom sounds the same in multi-influenced rock as it does in its primal black outcry.

3. I had no difficulty at all finding enough good examples of songs in each category; the great problem was which of the masses of good or interesting songs to omit because of limited space. Of course any of the ubiquitous schemes of I–IV, I–IV–V, I–V–IV, VIII–VII–IV, and so on, can be used by one group to produce

captivating and beautiful music and by another to achieve paralyzing boredom or yet another evanescent pop novelty.

The problem of which songs to cite resolved itself into the practical considerations of time available for listening, and repeated access. I therefore restricted myself to recordings from my own collection which I consider *at least* above average in interest (and, in some cases, songs I do not particularly like but which were monster hits). Being human and not a tabulating machine, I naturally have quite a few favorites, which are marked. Since each song is taken from a recording, it represents only one version. Unused studio tapes, or out-takes, live performances and covers by other groups can vary considerably.

4. In many cases, the entire song is based on only one or two harmonic progressions. In others, the progression cited is one of several which occur during the song, but it is only included here if it is an important feature – whether in the verse, chorus or fade – as opposed to making only a casual, infrequent appearance. When a song uses two or more of the common schemes listed here, I have assigned it to the one which I feel represents the most effective part of the song.

5. Since rock harmonies are so often used in a non-functional unclear context, it is difficult at times to label them according to what is really a 'classically' academic tonal usage or system. Often the home 'key' is ambiguous, and I have argued many times – inconclusively – with fellow-musicians over a song's tonal center. This, of course, affects the numerical labeling of the chords.

A practice which often exaggerates the tonal ambiguity is the adding of foreign or non-triadic notes to a basic chord, say, D–F♯–A, plus the sixth degree of the scale, B: a clear enough entity to perceive, to be sure, but when it is used within the prevailingly non-functional harmony of rock, a theorist can be somewhat at sea as to whether this is a D-chord with an added sixth or a B minor 7th first inversion.

A further complication (and richness) exists in the practice of harmonizing a passage in more than one way during the course of a song. Again, this often involves added-notes and inversions. An ultimate in tonal ambiguity might be said to be the floating dominant 7th. The dominant 7th is already a minority-element in rock, but its semi-alien character is intensified by its frequent non-functional use, as in the Stones' 'The Last Time'. There are numerous examples of non-operative dominant 7ths – rather refreshing to many musicians like myself who were trained in a world which took for granted the tyranny of this agent of tonality.

6. Before the reader follows up the structure and techniques contained in the following lists, I would like to take a few characteristic examples and describe more fully some of their details. This should give an indication of how to approach the necessarily abstract, codified information of the lists, and show how much inventiveness may be masked by stark numbers or categories.

a. The inner c-pedal point which so enriches the I–I$_6$–IV–II–V scheme of the Raspberries' 'Overnight Sensation', especially in the glorious post-'radio' sequence. This was a master-stroke.

b. The enhancement of a basic I–IV–V progression, in Yes's 'Cord of Life', by added 6ths (to the IV and V chords), plus a low tonic D pedal point and the imaginative doubling of certain chord-tones in the bass (Yes uses the I–IV–V in 'Eclipse', to completely different effect – equally powerful – with all in inversion-form, exposed, without a pedal-point.)

c. Yes goes even further in the use of added 6ths in 'Heart of the Sunrise', where they often appear in the bass-line to sidestep or adorn the basic chord-pattern of I–IV (minor)–IV (major)–II–VII (lowered). The refrain 'Sharp Distance' appears six times (four in B minor and two in E minor). Each is different, although harmonically (and melodically) related. Varied by inversions, bass-lines, added notes (the 6ths, plus 2nds and 7ths), spacings, the vocal line and a pedal point at the end of the sixth refrain – each repetition is a different way of viewing (or hearing) the simple substructure.

d. The use of three common schemes: $I–V_7–I–IV–I–V_7–I$, a descending bass-line, and VIII–VII–IV in 'Hey Jude', one of rock's watersheds. The result is amazing, particularly in the long C section which transfigures the relentless, even pace of the four-chord ground-bass with layer upon layer of sound and invention. Throughout, instrumental and vocal embroideries emerge, to be joined and supplanted by others, leaving the listener with the impression, as with all good fades, that the variation is continuing, endlessly, somewhere out of earshot. Seldom, in my opinion, has this sequence been used more effectively or excitingly.

e. The jangly added-note chords which are such a strong feature of the Byrds' music. In 'Get Down Your Line', the basic VIII–VII–IV is made radiant by the added 2nds, 6ths, 7ths and 9ths, which also act at times to form inner pedal points from chord to chord. This technique of retained notes stems from the drone-note of the banjo, and can also be heard in the Byrds' equally beautiful 'Buglar', America's 'Don't Cross the River', Led Zeppelin's 'Gallows Pole', Aztec Two-Step's 'So Easy' and 'Dancers All', and, less overtly, in the Beatles' 'Ticket to Ride' and 'You've Got To Hide', America's 'Children' and Jefferson Airplane's 'We Can Be Together'. A most memorable use occurs in Tom Petty's 'American Girl', with its spectacular quadruple-note drone soon joined by *another* pedal point: an ostinato figure in the treble whose inner pedal persists, shining through a final, intensified clash with a cross-relations sequence. These added-note chords are very effective on the piano, with a fresh, ringing sonority in the treble and mid-range and a richness in the octave below middle C.

f. The *slight*, but often quite subtle, variations of extremely simple figures. Ian Hunter's 'It Ain't Easy When You Fall/Shades Off' is a compelling example. Here, there are two such delights – one melodic, one harmonic. For the refrain of 'It Ain't Easy', the backing chorus repeats an ambivalent melodic figure in thirds which seems unable to decide whether to ascend or descend – giving a somewhat non-committal effect; during the continuation, 'Shades Off', this figure suddenly metamorphoses into a more direct 'falling' pattern which is both surprising and compassionate in effect.

The second, harmonic, delight comes part way through this variation with the magical transformation of the thirds into strong, radiant three-part chords, that include a beautiful suspension and tied-over inner voice.

The entire song is, in fact, made up of simple variations and mutations of the opening four-note descending pattern. On a less grand scale, Blondie's '(I'm Always

Touched By Your) Presence, Dear' uses a simple three-note ascending figure. Not only does this form the beginning of the melody, it is soon picked up and echoed instrumentally, creating a fluid dialogue between Debbie Harry's tangy vocalizing and the player's bold figurations. The frequent use, also, of intervals of a third in voice and instruments are a logical extension of the third outlined by the three-note figure.

g. The passacaglia-approach of Ozark Mountain Daredevils' 'Giving It All To the Wind'. The four chords of this ground-bass produce a cross-relation and a major–minor shift, and the brief introduction generates a descending three-note figure which not only appears in poignant parallel fifths on the viola but also as part of the melodic line and as a recurrent motif throughout. In addition, an inner double-note pedal throughout the 4-chord sequence turns the basically triadic harmonies into added-note chords. Meanwhile, the viola's melodic variations, which expand upon the brief introduction, contribute their own added notes to the underlying chords.

h. The use of added notes with simple triads. In the chorus of 'They Say the Sunshines', the Shirts begin with a clear sequence comprised of V, I, II and IV chords, but by the time they reach the fade the original clarity has become dense and distorted by the addition of dissonances to the triads, or what is, in fact, a super-imposition of these notes in what could be called a harmonic partial eclipse. Whether this was done consciously or not, it effectively underscores and intensifies the lyric.

i. The motivic compression and integration of Wire's 'Outdoor Miner'. Based on two somewhat meager ideas – repeated notes and a brief descending figure – it has the compact drama of a madrigal and the ominous quality of a nightmare.

It would take ten times longer to read a detailed description of Wire's inventiveness than to listen to it. Therefore I urge all would-be improvisers to seek out this song so that they can discover how Wire gives life to dry repeated notes and a lean motive, with its inversion, by means of transformations, inter-relationships, an inner pedal point and harmonization, with major–minor vacillations intensifying the song's disquieting effect.

j. Using the same sort of concentrated, interwoven techniques as 'Outdoor Miner', Manfred Mann's thrilling version of Bruce Springsteen's 'Blinded By the Light' amplifies these within the spacious setting of a passacaglia (which is interrupted once by an interlude consisting of variations on the central idea). Bursting with brilliant treatment of the basic material, in effect large-scale variations on Springsteen's original version, it has two admirably clear and expressive (and closely related) tunes, recurrent forceful motives, inversions, descending bass-lines, repeated notes and, much of the time, a bass pedal point which roots and intensifies the passacaglia's chord-sequence – all of these gathered into the over-all unity by a *shape*, rather than one specific musical motive. Excepting the pedal point, all of the musical elements have a downward pull – yet, oddly, the impression throughout is not one of closing in but rather one of great expansion. And the flow is so strong that even 'Chopsticks' is swept into it as an organic idea.

Many of the details just described can be adapted by the improvising accompanist for use in class. Others may be picked up when listening to the songs in the lists which follow this section. More of this, however, at the end of the chapter.

7. Where I felt it to be desirable, I have made notations in the lists below, but I hope that the listener will soon be able to recognize all events without guidance (that is, in which section of the song the scheme appears and whether it uses inversions, added notes, etc.).

8. The disparity between the number of rock songs surveyed and the early dances listed in section A is not intentional. It simply reflects the comparative numbers available.

9. For practical reasons, I had to select a cut-off point for these lists, which is around the early 1980s. This requires me to make a brief historical summary here. The long period of this book's writing, which began during the late-sixties' flower-power euphoria, saw a gradual decline into musical confusion and technological decadence in certain quarters. This in turn was (abruptly) challenged by the pistol-shots of the New Wave/Punk nihilism. Its pioneers were often scornfully termed 'three-chord wonders', but they and their successors scoured off much of the corrosion of the more self-indulgent trends of the seventies. Tough and defiant, they were both a creation and an expression of the growing economic crisis, especially in Britain, and the best of this music is characterized by a driving, exciting iconoclasm. 'Mainstream' rock, good and bad, of course continued to pour forth, and does so now. Similarly, the New Wave persists in the 'New Music' – this despite the inundation of nostalgia which has dampened but not drowned the Punk-eruption. Punk was realistic and aggressive; nostalgia-pop, while also a product of a generally grim and rudderless society, is a commercialized, often-grotesque flight from reality. But – from the early sixties rock-explosion to the alarming torrent of today's Top Ten exploitations of rock-video (inherently a medium of great potential) – the harmonic world I discuss in this chapter provides an integrating thread, and I–V–IV, VIII–VII–IV, I–II–IV, cross relations, etc. go on being used to create fresh, beautiful and timely, or derivative and evanescent songs, amid a current co-existence of many types of rock.

Seemingly inexhaustible in potential, this common practice apparently is the heart, muscle and spirit of rock. No matter how much the style, presentation, costume, lyrics and philosophy may change, these seem secondary to the intrinsic musical language that developed in its essentials by the mid-sixties, to function within a framework of raw energy, comparative naivety, repetitive patterns, aural rather than printed-note orientation, and ritual function and audience participation. All of this continues to differentiate rock from both the sentimental, witty or pretty operetta-based songs of the 1930s–1950s, and the rarefied, convoluted, polyphonic cool jazz. Whatever happens to rock now – as the Grand Old Men of Rock become 'over-forties' and perhaps one by one fade away, with their enduring influence as yet uncertain – nothing can eradicate rock's existence as one of the richest musical phenomena of all time or its imperviousness thus far to the pronouncements, beginning in 1965, that 'rock is dead'.

10. The listener should always be aware of the value of a facility in each of the

elements which the following lists encompass. No improviser will be dull, limited and repetitious who can – even when using the simplest of chords and harmonic patterns – work with inversions, added-notes, cross-relations, ground-basses and descending bass-lines, modal harmonies, melodic variation, and rhythmic alteration and syncopation. I have presented these as they exist in the Renaissance – early Baroque dance pieces; now here they are as re-experienced by rock musicians. (* denotes songs I consider especially moving or exciting and/or to be good, clear illustrations.)

Rock structures

1. Chords: I–IV

This might seem the most limited of all; certainly prolonged alternation of, say, C and F chords docs not promise much. Yet remarkable music has been made within its restrictions (occasionally rounded off with one or two other chords). Certainly, while experiencing the immensity of songs like 'Biko' or 'Hymn', you can feel that no other chords but these two could ever be needed. Here are some examples which demonstrate how much can be done with a basic two-chord scheme.

*   Allman Brothers – Blue Sky   (+ I–V–IV, B section)
    Amazing Blondel – Easy Come, Easy Go   IV–I$_6$
*   Jon Anderson – Ocean Song   I (added 2nds, 6ths) IV–I (over pedal D)
*   Badfinger – Apple of My Eye   (B section)
*   Barclay James Harvest – Hymn
*   Beatles – Get Back   I$_7$–IV$_7$ (refrain and break)
              I've Got a Feeling   I–IV–I$_7$, over pedal point
              Love Me Do   (+ V–IV–I break)
              Paperback Writer
*   Blondie   Union City Blue
*   Eagles – Desperado/reprise (fade)
        Outlaw Man (A section & fade)
        Try and Love Again
*   Dan Fogelberg – There's a Place In the World For a Gambler
    Foghat – Gotta Get To Know You (opening and fade)   I$_7$–IV–I (over pedal point)
           It's Too Late
           Trouble In My Way (+ II)
*   Peter Gabriel – Biko   I–IV$_{6\atop4}$, (+ VII and II)
    Ian Hunter – You Nearly Did Me In
    Elton John – Tiny Dancer
    Led Zeppelin – Going to California   IV–I–IV–I–IV–I–I min.–IV–I maj.
              Night Flight (over pedal A)
              Your Time is Gonna Come (refrain)
*   Lovin' Spoonful – Do You Believe In Magic?
*   Mamas and Papas – No Salt On Her Tail (+ V)
    Dave Mason – Just a Song
    Men at Work – Down By the Sea
*   Van Morrison – Astral Weeks
              Moonshine Whiskey
    Mott the Hoople – Ready For Love
              Sweet Jane (refrain)
    Nazareth – This Flight Tonight

Rolling Stones – Not Fade Away
      Street Fighting Man
      Stupid Girl
      Winter
*   You Can't Always Get What You Want
Bruce Springsteen – Backstreets (refrain)
      I'm a Rocker I–V_6^4
*   Stolen Car
* Cat Stevens – Where Do the Children Play?
Stranglers – Five Minutes
Strawbs – We Must Cross the River
* Tir na Nog – The Same Thing Happening
* Turtles – Your Maw Said You Cried
The Who – Tommy Can You Hear Me?
* Wire – Sand In My Joints (A section) I–IV_6^4
Yardbirds – Putty (I minor)
Yes – I see All Good People (a. Your Move)
Neil Young – Crippled Creek Ferry (I–IV added 6th)

2. Chords: I–V–IV sequence

Here, with the addition of the V chord between I and IV, we have the basis of many of the most splendid songs in rock and numerous good ones. Whether it is used in pure triadic form, as in 'Bring On the Lucie' and 'Angelsea', or with ringing, clashing added-notes, as in 'Baba O'Reilly', 'We Can Be Together' and 'Sway' – this sequence, unlike the I–IV, seems to have a life of its own, an intrinsic expressivity. (Play it in 4-note chords, with the tonic doubled on top, i.e. G-B-D-G, D-F♯-A-D, C-E-G-C, and – minus rhythmic detail – you are following Cat Stevens' route in part of 'Angelsea', and Dylan's in 'Shelter From the Storm'.)

 Most of the following use all the chords in the major, but a few go from the major I to a minor V; this is less powerful or brilliant but more poignant (see comments on minor V, Section V.A.4. (i)).

Alice Cooper – Be My Lover
     Hello Hooray V–IV–I (refrain and fade)
* America – Never Found the Time (fade) I–V–IV–V
Argent – Dance In the Smoke; over pedal point
* Aztec Two Step – Prisoner (fade)
Badfinger – We're For the Dark
The Band – All la Glory
* Beach Boys – Feel Flows (in 1st phrase and refrain; alternating with III minor 7th)
* Beatles – Across the Universe (refrain) V_7–IV–I
    Baby's In Black I–V–IV–V–I–IV–I
Bee Gees – Trafalgar
* Blondie – Fan Mail I–V–V–IV
Boston – Long Time I–V–(IV with suspension)–IV; over pedal point
    More Than a Feeling V–IV–I_6–I
* Jackson Browne – Late For the Sky I–V–IV–I_6 (followed by II–VI–V–IV)
Byrds – He Was a Friend of Mine
Crosby, Stills, Nash and Young – Country Girl (C section) I–V_6 minor–IV_6–IV
       Helpless
Dire Straits – Romeo & Juliet I–V–IV (sometimes VI), with frequent inversions
* Dylan – Shelter From the Storm

Eagles – Take It Easy
* Dan Fogelberg – There's a Place In the World For a Gambler (refrain and fade)
* Peter Frampton – I Believe (When I Fall In Love With You It Will Be Forever)
Genesis – Where the Sour Turns to Sweet (A section)
* Murray Head – Say It Ain't So Joe   I–Vmin. (II–VII) IV (A section)
Hollies – Dear Eloise
J. Geils Band – Must Have Got Lost   (V minor)
* Jefferson Airplane – We Can Be Together   I–V_6 added 6th–IV added 2nd
Kinks – Village Preservation Society
*   Waterloo Sunset   I–V_6–IV_6–IV
* Led Zeppelin – Tangerine (B section)
*   When the Levee Breaks   I–V–IV–V–(VII)–I
* John Lennon – Bring On the Lucie (Freda People)
Lindisfarne – Nothing But the Marvelous   (V minor)
* Lone Star – Lonely Soldier   I–Vmaj. (1st half)/I–Vmin. (2nd half)
* Van Morrison – Tupelo Honey I–V_6 added 6th–IV
          St. Dominic's Preview   V–IV–I
Mott the Hoople – Roll Away the Stone (refrain)   I–V_6–IV–V
* Move – Do Ya
Mungo Jerry – Johnny B. Badde
Nazareth – Vigilante Man
Ozark Mountain Daredevils – Colorado Song   V–IV–I
* Pretenders – Bird of Paradise
Rolling Stones – Dead Flowers
          It's All Over Now (refrain) V_7–IV–I
          The Last Time V_7–IV–I
          Sway
* Roxy Music – Triptych (Vocal section B)
Bruce Springsteen – Badlands   I–V–IV (VI)–V, + I–IV–V
          Jungleland
Stealer's Wheel – You Put Something Better   I (VI) V IV
* Cat Stevens – Angelsea (alternating with I–IV–V)
Strawbs – Lady Fuschia (Intro., over pedal point)
          The Flower and the Young Man
Tom Robinson Band – 2–4–6–8 Motorway
          Up Against the Wall   I–V–IV (V)
* Who – Baba O'Reilly (+ VII in last section)
          Pure and Easy   over pedal point (A section)
*   Relax (C section)   I–V–IV–V–I
          Squeezebox

3. Chords: I–IV–V sequence and permutations

This category contains both the I–IV–V sequence *per se* and various juxtapositions. A statistical survey would probably show that these three chords appear more frequently in *all* music than any others (which is usually attributed to acoustical laws related to the overtone series). What is significant here is not their ubiquity but the striking sound achieved when rock musicians use them. Not only do they produce quite a different effect in rock from traditional blues (the I_7–IV_7–I–V_7–IV_7–I progression), but they often seem to be – as do the previous ones in the I–IV and I–V–IV categories – not the same chords at all when compared with their usage in Classical and Romantic music. This is due, among other things, to what I have called their non-functional, pre-tonal use, without the conventional modulatory element of the dominant 7th (which is, of course, a major part of blues and jazz – one of the things which differentiates them from rock). The only 'serious' music which is consistently similar to rock in its usage of these chords is that of the Renaissance and early Baroque dances and songs and the Protestant church chorales which were contemporary with these. All of these are united by the prevailing infrequency of the dominant 7th; it appears from time to time, of course, as a harbinger of the coming tonality, but seldom with the emphasis of the later diatonic-tonal music. (The habitual use of the dominant 7th in nineteenth-century hymns is one of the main reasons why they seem so sentimental and pretty when compared with the strong, stark sixteenth- and early seventeenth-century hymns).

Bear all this in mind when listening to the songs in this category. The 'pure' triads which are overwhelmingly in the majority offer a simple source of fresh sounds when improvising. They have a clarity and incisiveness which is softened when dominant 7ths are added. Or, when a non-functional dominant 7th is used skilfully, it can produce a pleasurable surprise and an interesting phrase.

(Occasionally the I–IV–V chords are varied by a passing II, VI or VII, which intensifies their unorthodox effect, but the fact that the three basic chords receive the greater emphasis warranted these songs' inclusion in this category.)

    Abba – Waterloo

    Jon Anderson – Flight of the Moorglade (entirely on I–IV–V and perm.)

    Beach Boys – Help Me Rhonda (refrain)   V–I–V–I–IV–(VI)–I–(II)–V–I

                 Salt Lake City   I–IV–I–IV–V–(II)–I

    Beatles – Here Comes the Sun   I–IV–V$_7$ (+ descending bass)

          Hey Jude   I–V$_7$–V$_7$–I–IV–I–V$_7$–I (A section)

*   Lucy In the Sky (refrain)

*   Rain (A section)

          Thank you Girl   I–IV–I–IV–I–V–I

*   You've Got To Hide Your Love Away (refrain)

* Bee Gees – I Laugh In Your Face   I–IV–I–V–(VII) (refrain)

    Byrds – All I Really Want To Do   IV–I–V–I

    Cheap Trick – Surrender   I–V–IV–I (2 ×) IV–V–I (2 ×) (A section)

    Elvis Costello – Oliver's Army

    Druid – Towards The Sun   I–IV–I–IV–I–IV–I–V–(VII)

    Dylan – A Hard Rain's Gonna Fall   I–IV–I–I–V/IV–V–I (A section)

                         I–V$_{6\atop4}$–I–IV$_{6\atop4}$/I–V$_{6\atop4}$–I (refrain)

*   Idiot Wind   I–IV–I–IV–V (refrain)

          The Mighty Quinn   I$_7$–IV$_7$, etc. – I–V–IV–V (A section)

                     I–V–I–I–V–IV–I (refrain)

*   Like a Rolling Stone (refrain)

*   Mr. Tambourine Man   IV–V–I–IV–I–IV–V

    Fairport Convention – Rosie   IV–I–V–I (refrain)

* Peter Frampton – Don't Fade Away

    Genesis – Window   IV–I–V–I–IV (refrain)

    Roy Harper – These Last Days, + lowered VII

    Kinks – Days   I–V$_7$–IV–I–IV–I–V$_7$–I

    Led Zeppelin – Houses of the Holy   IV–(VII–IV)–I–V

    Left Banke – Pretty Ballerina   I–IV–I (3 ×) –V–IV (VII–III–V)

    Lindisfarne – All Fall Down   V–IV–I–IV–I–IV (refrain)

    Moby Grape – I Am Not Willing   V–IV–I, + I–IV

* Mott the Hoople – I Wish I was Your Mother   I–IV–I–IV–I–(II)–V
                                       I–IV–I–IV–I–(II)–IV–V } (Vocal)

                                       I–IV–V$_7$ inversion–I$_6$–I (I$_7$)–IV–V–I

                                       (Inst.)

Mungo Jerry – In the Summertime   I–I–IV–I–V₇–IV–I

* Nazareth – Homesick Again   IV–V–I (alternated with III cross-relation) over pedal
point (fade)

In My Time   I–IV–I–IV–I–V

Love, Now You're Gone   I–V–I–IV–(III)–I

* Poco – A Good Feeling to Know   IV–I–V

* Alan Price – Between Today and Yesterday   I–I₆–IV–IV added 6th–V₇

Procol Harum – Pilgrim's Progress   V–V₇–I₆–IV (fade)

* Raspberries – Overnight Sensation   I–I₆–IV–(II)–V

Rolling Stones – Get Off My Cloud

Satisfaction

* Shirts – They Say the Sunshines   V–I–V–I–V–I (II)–I–V–I (II) I–V–IV (Chorus)

* Simon and Garfunkel – Only Living Boy in N.Y.   I–IV–I–IV–I–IV (passing tones)
–V–IV–I–IV

* Bruce Springsteen – Born To Run (A section and fade)

*   She's The One   I–IV–I–V–IV (VII)

Starry Eyed and Laughing – One Foot In the Boat   I–IV–V–I I (VI)–IV–V

Cat Stevens – Bitterblue   I–IV–I–I–IV (I–V–I)–V

Ruby Love   I–IV–V–IV–I (V–I)

* Rod Stewart – Mandolin Wind   IV–I, etc. – V–IV–I (A section)

V–IV–IV added 6th inversion [or II minor 7th]–V
(Intro. & fade)

Supertramp – Give a Little Bit   I–V₇–I–IV–V₇–IV–V₇ (IV with added 6ths, usually)

Turtles – Wanderin' Kind   IV–V–I–IV–I–IV–V

* Who – A Legal Matter

*   Slip Kid   I–IV–Vmin. (VII)

* Yes – Cord of Life   I–IV added 6th – V added 6th (over pedal D)*

Eclipse   I₆/₄–IV₆/₄–IV (vocal)

Neil Young – I Believe In You   IV–V–I

4. Chords: VIII (I)–VII–IV and permutations

Like the I V IV progression, this seems to have special expressivity. If, for instance, played
slowly, in ringing parallel chords (as with the I–V–IV) – all in major form – what I can only
describe as defiant jubilance is evoked (such matters being subjective, other listeners may react
differently, but I think all will hear *some* strong quality).

Of course, as with all of the harmonic schemes listed here, the effect will be altered by rhythm
and melodic detail. But the lowered VII chord always makes this harmonic sequence antithetical
to the raised VII/'dominant' 7th of classical procedures and sounds:

Ex. 11

Many of the following use the VIII–VII–IV *per se*; others use these chords in different order or
elongate certain chords of the sequence.

Amazing Blondel – Weaver's Market

* Angel – Flying With Broken Wings (over pedal point)

* Aztec Two-Step – Dancers All
   Bad Company – Wildfire Woman (refrain)
* Badfinger – Got To Get Out of Here   VIII–IV$^6_4$–VIII–IV$^6_4$–VII–VIII (+ II)
            When I Say
   Barclay James Harvest – Sweet Jesus (over pedal point (A section))
   Beatles – Another Girl   VIII–VII–VIII–IV
*   Hey Jude (C section)
           Lovely Rita   VIII–VII–IV–VIII–(V)
           The Night Before   VIII–VII–IV–(V)–IV–VII–IV–VIII
*   You Never Give Me Your Money   VII–IV–VIII (C section)
* Bee Gees – Every Christian Lion Hearted Man   VIII–IV$^6_4$–VIII–VIII–VII–IV
* Boston – Long Time (B section)
   David Bowie – Janine (refrain)
*   Memory of a Free Festival (fade)
* Bread – She Was My Lady
            This Isn't What the Governmeant (B section)
* Byrds – Get Down Your Line (with added-notes)
            Tiffany Queen   VIII–VII–IV$_6$
*   Well Come Back Home   (+ I–V–I–IV–I)
   Cheap Trick – Stiff Competition (refrain), + cross relations
   Clash – Guns on the Roof   VIII–VII–IV$_6$–VIII$^6_4$
* Dire Straits – Skate Away   VIII–IV–VII
* Dylan – Tangled Up In Blue   VIII–VII (3X) – IV
   Fairport Convention – Matthew, Mark, Luke and John
* Genesis – Dance On a Volcano
   Tim Hardin – If I Were a Carpenter
   Headboys – Shape of Things To Come   VII–IV–VIII (refrain), + I–V$_6$–IV$_6$
   Hollies – Charlie and Fred
           Hold On
*   King Midas In Reverse (refrain)
* Horslips – Stowaway (chorus and fade)
* Ian Hunter – It Ain't Easy When You Fall/Shades Off   VIII–VII–IV (V cross-rel.)
                                              (refrain)
* Jefferson Airplane – Good Shepherd
   Kinks – Animal Farm
*   Celluloid Heroes   VII–IV–VIII
           Demolition (refrain and end)
*   Lola   VIII–IV–VII–VIII, + cross-rel.
* Led Zeppelin – Gallows Pole (refrain)
*   Thank You   VIII–VII–IV$_6$
*   Your Time Is Gonna Come
* Lindisfarne – City Song   VIII–IV–VII
*   Road to Kingdom Come (refrain)   (II in 1st phrase)
   Men at Work – Helpless Automaton   VIII–VII (III)–IV, + cr.-ref.
   Steve Miller Band – Babes In the Wood
   Mott the Hoople – One of the Boys
* Nazareth – Child In the Sun
* Tom Petty & the Heartbreakers – The Wild One, Forever
   Pink Floyd – Remember a Day (A section)
   Poco – Angel (refrain)
   Quiver – I Know You So Well

Raspberries – I Can Hardly Believe You're Mine (refrain and fade)
R.A.F. – Change Your Ways   VIII (III) VII–IV
* Rolling Stones – Lady Jane
               Midnight Rambler
               Sympathy For the Devil   VIII–VII–IV$_6$–VIII
* Roxy Music – Prairie Rose (A section and fade)   VIII–VII–IV (V)
* Marian Segal – Raven   VIII–IV–IV–VIII (2 ×)–IV–VII–IV–VIII (2 ×)
               Amongst Anemonies
*   Mayfly
Bob Seger & the Silver Bullet Band – Hollywood Nights   VIII–IV–VII–VIII, over pedal
                                       point
* Sonny and Cher – I Got You Babe   VIII–IV$_6$–VIII–IV–VII (V)
* Status Quo – Mystery Song   VIII–VIII$_7$ inv. (2 ×)–VII–IV$_6$(2 ×) opening: instr.
                               VIII –IV–VII–IV–VIII (over pedal A) opening: vocal
* Cat Stevens – Sun/C79   VII–VIII–IV (refrain)
Stranglers – No More Heroes   VIII–IV–VII
Strawbs – All I Need Is You   VIII–VII–IV (V)
* Supertramp – Forever   VII–IV–VIII, over pedal point at first (B section and fade)
Who – Bellboy (*Quadrophenia*)   VIII–IV–VII (over pedal point)
*   Helpless Dancer (*Quad.*)   VIII–IV minor–VII (over pedal point)
*   Naked Eye (B section)   (V–IV–I, A section)
*   Nothing Is Everything (A section & end)
       Love Ain't For Keeping   VII–IV–VIII
       Magic Bus
       Won't Get Fooled Again
* Yes – Yours Is No Disgrace   VIII–IV–VIII–IV–VII–IV–IV–VII–IV–IV–VIII

5. Chords: I–II–IV sequence

The II chord is also important in rock, and, like the lowered VII chord, challenges traditional tonality. In rock, particularly in the popular I–II–IV progression, it appears usually in root-position. This creates parallel motion of the chords from I to II, a *bête noire* of late-Baroque, Classical and much Romantic music. When the II chord is used in these periods, it is handled carefully within tonal precepts, by means of inversions and gracefully-moving bass-lines. Rock musicians happily and unconcernedly ignore such niceties and thus create a peculiarly strong and forthright effect, often involving cross-relations.

It appears not only in the I–II–IV sequence, but as part of other characteristic rock progressions, which often include the lowered VII. These songs make up our next two lists (plus songs not in the VIII–VII–IV category which strongly feature the lowered VII).

* Alice Cooper – Only Women Bleed (over pedal point) + cross-relation
* Beatles – Eight Days a Week
* Bee Gees – To Love Somebody (+ lowered VII and V–IV$_7$–I)
Blondie – Presence, Dear   I–IV–I–IV–II (V)–II (V)–II–IV–I, + cross rel.
* Byrds – Buglar
Dylan – It's All Over Now Baby Blue   II–IV–I
       You Ain't Goin' Nowhere
Eddie and the Hot Rods – Do Anything You Wanna Do   I–IV–II, with added notes
                                         (refrain)
* George Harrison – Isn't It a Pity
* J. Geils Band – Must Have Got Lost   I–II–IV (V) (B section)

*   Ian Hunter – Standing In My Light   I–IV–II–IV$_4^6$ added 6th–I

      Lindisfarne – Road to Kingdom Come (A section)

      Moby Grape – It's a Beautiful Day Today, + I–V–IV (refrain)

      Van Morrison – Sweet Thing

*   Tom Petty and the Heartbreakers – American Girl

      Pure Prairie League – Give Us a Rise

*   Bruce Springsteen – N.Y.C. Serenade   I (VI) II–IV

      Troggs – Love Is All Around   I–II–IV (V)

*   Who – They Are All In Love   I–II–IV (V)

6. Chords: II and/or lowered VII prominent

*   America – To Each His Own   II and VII (B section and fade) + cross-relation

      Jon Anderson – Sound Out the Galleon   II

      Animals – It's My Life   VII

*   Association – Cherish   VII

*   Badfinger – Baby Blue   II and VII

               I Don't Mind   II and VII

*   Name of the Game   II and VII

*   Perfection II and VII

*   We're For the Dark   VII (+ I–V–IV)

*   When I Say   II (B section)

*   Barclay James Harvest – Crazy City   VII

*   Beach Boys – California Girls   II and VII (refrain)

*   Beatles – Every Little Thing   II and VII

*   Hard Day's Night   VII

*   Help   II and VII

               If I Needed Someone   VII

*   Norwegian Wood   II and melodic VII

*   Ticket to Ride   II

*   We Can Work It Out   VII

*   Yes It Is   II and VII

*   You've Got To Hide Your Love Away   VII

*   Bee Gees – Sinking Ships   VII (2nd part)

               Suddenly   VII

*   Bread – Everything I Own   II (B section)

      Byrds – Borrowing Time   II

*   Eight Miles High   VII

               I Come and Stand At Every Door   II and VII

*   I Knew I'd Want You   II and VII

               I'll Feel A Whole Lot Better   II and VII

               You Movin'   II and VII (B section)

      Cheap Trick – Taking Me Back   VII

      Dire Straits – Solid Rock   II and VII

*   Druid – Red Carpet For an Autumn   II and VII

               Shangri-la   VII (+ I–IV–V) (A section and middle)

      Dylan (+ Band) – Yea! Heavy and a Bottle of Bread   VII

*   Eagles – My Man   II, + I–V–IV

*   Emerson, Lake and Palmer – Lucky Man   II

*   Genesis   – Afterglow   II & VII, over pedal point

                     Undertow   II (refrain)

* Genesis – As Sure As Eggs Is Eggs   II and VII
  Roy Harper – The Lord's Prayer   VII, over pedal point
* Hollies – When Your Light's Turned On   II (+ I–V–IV–V–I)
* J. J. Jackson – But It's Alright   II
  Jefferson Airplane – Lather   VII
*   Somebody to Love   VII
* Led Zeppelin – Battle of Evermore   VII (1st inversion)
*   Tangerine   II
* Left Banke – Barterers and Their Wives   VII (+ cross-relation)
  Lindisfarne – Poor Old Ireland   VII
  Men at Work – Down Under   VII
* Nazareth – 1692 (Glen Coe Massacre)   VII
  Ozark Mountain Daredevils – Kansas You Fooler   VII (+ cross-relation)
* Pentangle – No Love Is Sorrow   VII
  Tom Petty and the Heartbreakers – Listen To Her Heart   VII
  Plainsong – Raider   II and VII
  Poco – I Can See Everything   II and VII (refrain)
* Alan Price – O Lucky Man   VII
  Queen – Some Day One Day   VII, over pedal point (A section), + cross-rel. (B)
  Rolling Stones – Dandelion   II
              I Am Waiting   II and VII
*   Wild Horses   II and VII (+ VIII–VII–IV, refrain)
  Crispian St. Peters – The Pied Piper   II (B section)
* Shirts – Reduced to Whisper   II and VII, + cross relations
* Simon and Garfunkel – Scarborough Fair/Canticle   VII
*   Sounds of Silence   VII
  Bruce Springsteen – Out on the Street   II II and VII VII (refrain)
  Cat Stevens – Lady D'Arbanville   VII
  Alan Stivell – Susy MacGuire   II and VII
* Strawbs – Round and Round   II and VII
  String Driven Thing – Going Down   VII
* Supremes – You Keep Me Hanging On   VII (+ cross-relation)
  Turtles – A Walk In the Sun   VII
  Who – The Seeker   VII (+ cross-relation)
  Wire – Too Late   VII
* Yes – Heart of the Sunrise   VII

7. Cross-relations or shifting major–minor

Cross-relations are inevitable in songs with both lowered VII and major II chords, or any other case which has major or minor triads a 3rd apart, except in two instances (1. and 7.)

Ex. 12

Along with shifting major–minor forms of any chord, they are one of the most beautiful characteristics of Renaissance and early-Baroque music; the following songs show how they work their magic in rock.

  Alice Cooper – Elected
* Jon Anderson – Moon Ra
  Argent – Like Honey
* Badfinger – Perfection
*   Shine On
*   Song For a Lost Friend
           We're For the Dark
*   Name of the Game
  Barclay James Harvest – For No One (refrain)   + VII, A and fade
  Beatles – Back In the U.S.S.R.
*   Eight Days a Week
*   Help
*   Lady Madonna
           Please Please Me
           Polythene Pam
*   Sergeant Pepper's Lonely Hearts Club Band
*   Ticket to Ride
           The Word
*   Yes It Is
*   You've Got to Hide Your Love Away
* Bee Gees – Every Christian Lion Hearted Man
           I Can't See Nobody
*   I Laugh In Your Face (refrain)
*   Sinking Ships (A section; melodic cross-rel. in B)
           Suddenly
  Blondie – Cautious Lip
  Bread – What a Change
  Kate Bush – Wuthering Heights
  Byrds – Here Without You
           I'll Feel a Whole Lot Better
* Dire Straits – Telegraph Road
  Bob Dylan – Lay Lady Lay
* Emerson, Lake and Palmer – Trilogy (middle section)
  Fleetwood Mac – Bare Trees (throughout song, and fade)
                 Dust
* Four Tops – Reach Out, I'll Be There
  Genesis – As Sure As Eggs Is Eggs
           Lilywhite Lilith
* George Harrison – Isn't It a Pity
  Jefferson Airplane – Lather
                 White Rabbit
  Kinks – All Day and All of the Night
*   Sleepwalker, + lowered VII
* Led Zeppelin – Battle of Evermore
*   Friends
*   Gallows Pole
           In My Time of Dying
*   When the Levee Breaks
*   Your Time Is Gonna Come
  Lindisfarne – Poor Old Ireland (refrain)
           Road To Kingdom Come

Manfred Mann's Earth Band – One Way Glass
Moby Grape – What's To Choose
* Mott the Hoople – All the Young Dudes
Graham Nash – Immigration Man
Nazareth – Love, Now You're Gone
*   Vigilante Man
* Ozark Mountain Daredevils – Giving It All to the Wind
Pink Floyd – Arnold Layne
REO Speedwagon – Runnin' Blind
Rolling Stones – Brown Sugar
            Gimme Shelter
*   Jumping Jack Flash
*   Wild Horses
Roxy Music – Out of the Blue
Shirts – 10th Floor Clown
Starry Eyed & Laughing – Lady Came From the South
Alan Stivell – Susy MacGuire
Strawbs – Pavan (from Tears and Pavan)
*   Round and Round
* Turtles – Love In the City (refrain and fade)
Unicorn – Easy (Break and fade)
Who – Anyway, Anyhow, Anywhere
            Bell Boy and The Rock (*Quadrophenia*)
*   I Can See For Miles
            The Seeker
* Wire – Outdoor Miner (refrain)
*   Used To   + lowered VII
Yardbirds – A Certain Girl
            Heart Full of Soul
            I'm a Man
* Yes – Heart of the Sunrise (refrain)
*   Würm

8. Recurring bass-patterns and descending bass-lines

Here is a direct link between rock and Renaissance to early-Baroque music. Of course, many composers of the intervening centuries have used these devices (often in a conscious return to the past). But the combination of their use with other shared characteristics makes the bass-patterns of the early dance-pieces and rock akin in a special way.

Recurring basses are perhaps best known in the form of *passacaglia* or *chaconne* (see Section III. 4), and these are, in fact, what many rock songs turn out to be, sometimes for the duration of the song, other times intermittently. Often the patterns closely resemble the original models (see examples in Section III. 4), but also may be simple variants and extensions of the older types. A *passacaglia* or *chaconne*-like pattern is by nature an ostinato, repeated over and over with melodic and rhythmic variations above it (or, in some cases, below).

Of all the songs listed 'All the Young Dudes' contains, in my opinion, one of the finest examples of the *passacaglia-chaconne* technique in rock. With its extended, spacious bass-line, rich cross-relations, asymmetry of phrase and splendid over-all quality, it does not seem to me far-fetched to say that it is very much in a Purcellian tradition.

'Stairway To Heaven' is an equally dazzling example, wherein the initial seven-note descending bass pattern – which is almost identical to the third type of passacaglia pattern shown in Section

III. 4 – is distilled and metamorphosed into a pounding three-note descending pattern later in the song (plus an interim transposed three-note pattern). (See also later song-analysis, No. 4.)

Some descending-bass patterns are simply part of the total effect; they recur without any significant variation above them [D]. Others are used clearly in a passacaglia–chaconne manner, ostinato-like, with variations and intensifications in other voices. These and other ostinato patterns I label [P–C] (Sometimes, however, it is hard to make a precise distinction between the two.) Both make frequent use of inversions and these should be carefully listened for.

*   Amazing Blondel – Young Man's Fancy [D] – (P–C in fade)
*   Angel – Tower [P–C], + lowered VII
*   Association – Changes [D, over pedal point]
     Bad Company – Call On Me [P–C] (middle and fade)
*   Badfinger – Apple of My Eye [D] (B section)
             Song For a Lost Friend [P–C] (fade)
*   Without You [P–C] (fade)
*   Barclay James Harvest – For No One [P–C] (C section and fade)
*   The Great 1974 Mining Disaster [P–C] (fade)
*   Titles [P–C] (chor.)
*   Beatles – All You Need Is Love [D]
*   A Day In the Life [D]
*   Dear Prudence [P–C, over pedal point] (+ VII–IV–VIII)
           For No One [P–C]
           Hello Goodbye [D]
*   Hey Jude (B section, descending /C section, P–C)
*   Let It Be [P–C] (refrain)
*   Something [D]
*   While My Guitar Gently Weeps [P–C]
*   Bee Gees – I Laugh In Your Face [P–C]
             Marley Purt Drive [P–C]
             Turn of the Century [D]
*   David Bowie – Drive-In Saturday [P–C] (fade)
        Bread – Everything I Own [D]
*   Make It By Yourself [P–C]
*   What a Change [D] (refrain), + VII
*   Byrds – Chestnut Mare [D/P–C]
     Elvis Costello – All I Want To Do [D]
*   Derek and the Dominoes – Bell Bottom Blues [D/P–C]
*   Dire Straits – Tunnel of Love [P–C]
*   Telegraph Road [P–C]
*   Eagles – Try and Love Again [P–C] (last section and fade)
     Emerson, Lake & Palmer – Tank [P–C] (1st half)
*   Genesis – The Carpet Crawlers [P–C] (A section)
           The Conqueror [P–C]
*   Roy Harper – One of These Days In England [P–C]
*   Ian Hunter – It Ain't Easy When You Fall [D] (A sect.) – Shades Off [P–C]
     Jefferson Airplane – She Has Funny Cars [D]
*   Kinks – Sleepwalker [P–C] (ending)
*   Robert Knight – Everlasting Love [P–C]
*   Led Zeppelin – Babe I'm Gonna Leave You [P–C]
*   In the Light [P–C] (middle and end)
*   Stairway to Heaven [P–C]
           What Is and What Should Never Be [D] (B section)

  Left Banke – Walk Away Renee [D]
* John Lennon – Steel and Glass [D]
* Lone Star – Lonely Soldier [P–C] (last half)
* Lovin' Spoonful – Summer In the City [D]
* Manfred Mann – Blinded By the Light [P–C]
  Dave Mason – Look At You Look At Me (opening chord-seq. used as P–C bass at end)
* Van Morrison – Tupelo Honey [P–C]
* Mott the Hoople – All the Young Dudes [P–C]
                Here We Are [P–C] (fade)
* Graham Nash – Sleep Song [P–C]
                There's Only One [P–C]
* Ozark Mountain Daredevils – Giving It All to the Wind [P–C]
                Lowlands [D]
  Pink Floyd – Eclipse [P–C]
  Poco – Go and Say Goodbye [D]
* Roxy Music – A Really Good Time [D]
                Bittersweet [D] (section A)
  Bob Seger and the Silver Bullet Band – Down On Mainstreet [P–C] (A section)
  Shirts – Poe [P–C], + cross-relations (last section)
  Simon and Garfunkel – A Hazy Shade of Winter [P–C]
*   America [D]
                The 59th St. Bridge Song [P–C]
  Chris Squire – Safe (Canon Song) [P–C]
                You By My Side [P–C]
* Steeleye Span – Saucy Sailor [P–C] (refrain and fade)
  String Driven Thing – The Machine That Cried [P–C]
* Turtles – House On the Hill [D] (refrain)
* Who – Our Love Was, Is [D]
                Sheraton Gibson [D] (Townshend solo album)
*   They Are All In Love [P–C] (A section)
* Yes – Awaken [P–C] ('Masters of images . . .')
*   The Preacher The Teacher [P–C]

The foregoing is not an exhaustive survey of rock structures and devices. I have not, for instance, included specific examples of the usage of III and VI chords, which also occur frequently. But space and time force me to stop somewhere, and these chords seem to me to be less relevant to the present inquiry, their usage lying as it does between the two extremes of the pronounced deviation from traditional tonal procedures of the II and VII chords, and the altered perspective which rock-musicians create in their primary-color use of the common I, IV and V chords.

Before leaving this survey, however, I would like to offer a parallel to the Renaissance–Baroque section about comparative recorded versions since this is such an important feature of rock also.

9. Comparative versions

One of the joys (and risks) of rock is what can happen to a song when another group does it – or when the original group records or plays it again. One interesting thing about this is that, as a rule, the results are not 'arrangements' in the sense of various presentations of 'Moon River', 'The Man I Love' or 'I Dream of Jeannie', but rather they are realizations in the Baroque or Renaissance manner. 'Arrangement' is a matter of adornment, or at times change in style, of a fully composed song; that is, a *closed*-form, derived from nineteenth-century Romanticism and operetta, of the Kern–Porter–Gershwin genre. Such adornment could be very beautiful, as in the complex, sophisticated arrangements of Gershwin's songs by Nelson Riddle in the 1950s, but realization, rather than being an exercise in beautification, is a basic rethinking of and playing around with an often sparse structure akin to a Renaissance passamezzo bass or melody, or a Baroque basso continuo. Here, decoration of an object can be replaced by elemental reassessment and frequent re-creation of raw material within an *open*-form. But even when a new version of a song is on a more modest scale, comparison offers a fine opportunity to increase your ability to hear and reproduce detail because of the basic simplicity of rock's language and approach.

For variety and freshness, accompanists should gamble as much as possible, and careful listening to the comparative realizations of generally simple songs will go far, both in demonstrating how important attention to fine detail within the overall effect can be, and – most important – offering another means for the developing of one's inner ear that I have stressed is so essential and which can give the gambler increasing security.

All I Really Want to Do: Byrds – Dylan
All the Young Dudes: David Bowie – Mott the Hoople (Studio and live LP versions) – the Skids
America: Simon and Garfunkel – Yes
And Then I Kissed Her: Beach Boys – Sonny and Cher
Anyway, Anyhow, Anywhere: David Bowie – Who
Better Change: Dan Fogelberg – Roger McGuinn
Beware of Darkness: George Harrison, All Things Must Pass LP – Bangla Desh LP
Cloudy: Cyrkle – Simon and Garfunkel
Dead Flowers: Rolling Stones – New Riders of the Purple Sage
Drive My Car: Beatles – Humble Pie
Eight Miles High: Byrds: studio – live versions
Every Little Thing: Beatles – Yes
Girl Talk: Elvis Costello – Dave Edmunds
I Am a Rock: Hollies – Simon and Garfunkel
Idiot Wind: Dylan: studio – Rolling Thunder versions
I Go to Sleep: Kinks – Pretenders
I See You: Byrds – Yes
I Shall be Released: Bob Dylan – Hollies
It Ain't Me Babe: Bob Dylan – Turtles
It's All Over Now, Baby Blue: Bob Dylan – Manfred Mann's Earth Band
Jumping Jack Flash: Peter Frampton – Rolling Stones
Laughing: David Crosby – Byrds
Let's Spend the Night Together: David Bowie – Rolling Stones
Like a Rolling Stone: Dylan – Spirit – Turtles
Lucky Man: Emerson, Lake and Palmer: Studio – live LP versions
Mr. Tambourine Man: Dylan – Byrds (*Preflyte* LP) – Byrds (2nd LP version)
Pure and Easy: Townshend solo LP – Who
Rain: Beatles – Humble Pie
Rosie: Fairport Convention: studio – live LP versions
Say It ain't So Joe: Roger Daltrey – Murray Head
She Said She Said: Beatles – Lone Star
Something: Beatles – Bangla Desh LP
Stay With Me: Peter Skellern – Rod Stewart
Stop Your Sobbing: Kinks – Pretenders
To Love Somebody: Bee Gees – Flying Burrito Brothers
We Can Work It Out: Beatles – Humble Pie – Stevie Wonder
When I Paint My Masterpiece: Band – Dylan

While My Guitar Gently Weeps: Beatles – Bangla Desh LP
Wild Horses: Flying Burrito Brothers – Rolling Stones
Without You: Badfinger – Harry Nilsson
You Ain't Goin' Nowhere: Byrds – Dylan – *Basement Tapes*
You Really Got Me: Kinks – Mott the Hoople
You've Got To Hide Your Love Away: Beatles – Silkie

10. Analysis of miscellaneous harmonic schemes

Some songs do not fit tidily into any of the above harmonic categories. I consider the following exceptional and that an analysis of their chordal structures will be revealing and inspiring to the ambitious improviser. There are, of course, many others which use equally economical means with as varied, rich and imaginative results. I have had to resort to academic shorthand to condense as much as possible into limited space, and hope this does not mask or nullify the wealth of invention in each song.

1. Quiver: Don't Let Go

(A Major)
(Brief introduction: A–A ninth alternated)
1. (INSTRUMENTAL) VIII–VII–IV$_6$–IV$_6$–VII–VIII–VII–IV$_6$–VIII (I)–V–IV$_6$
2. (VOCAL) I–I$_7$ inversion–IV$_6$–IV$_6$–VII–I–I$_7$–IV$_6$–I–V–IV–IV$_6^4$ (2 ×)
3. (INSTR.) Descending bass
[Shift to D]
4. (VOCAL) I–IV–VII–IV$_6$–V min.$_7$ (2 ×)–V$_7$
5. (INSTR.) (Inner pedal A throughout) I–V–V$_6$ min.–IV$_6$IV$_6$ min.–I$_6^4$–V$_9$–VI min.$_7$–II–I$_6$–V$_7$
6. (INSTR.) I (VIII)–VII–IV–IV$_6$–VII–VIII
[Shift back to A]
7. (VOCAL) I–V$_6$ min (with added 4th–6th–7th)–IV–IV$_6$–VII added 6th–I–V$_6$ added notes – IV–I–V–IV
8. (INSTR.) I–V$_6$ added 6th–IV–IV–V$_6$–I–V$_6$–IV–IV$_6$–V$_6$ etc. I–V$_6$ min.–IV–IV$_6$–VII, towards end of fade.
(Used as P–C type bass, with variations over)

This is a miracle of thematic concentration. Within 3.59″ of eight brief sections plus an extended fade, it combines the microcosmic with the macrocosmic. Based almost exclusively on the I (VIII) IV, V and VII chords, it includes: the chord-schemes of VIII–VII–IV and I–V–IV, effective use of inversions, added-note harmonies, an inner pedal point, variation of basic patterns by inversions, added-notes and chord substitutions, and a broad *passacaglia–chaconne* treatment of the VIII–VII–IV scheme in the fade, extracting these three chords from the original longer sequence (1), and fulfilling its brief taste in section 6.

2. The Who: Relax

[E major]
(Brief introduction I$_7$–IV$_6^4$–I–I$_7$–IV$_6^4$–I
A. (VOCAL) I$_7$–IV$_6^4$–I (4 ×) –VII–I–VII (repeat of phrase)–I
B. (VOCAL) V$_9$–I–IV–V min.$_7$–V$_9$–I–IV–VII
[Shift to D: now I]
C. (VOCAL) I–V–IV–V–I (3 ×) –I–V–IV–VII–I (pedal D)
D. (INSTR.) Free variation on pedal D

[Shift Back to E]

A. I_7–IV_6^4–I (4×) –VII–I–VII–I

Another striking example of variety within unity, '*Relax*' uses mainly I_7, IV, V and VII chords, in the schemes of I_7–IV–I and I–V–IV, with a bit of color, and ambiguity between the V_9 and V min_7, in section B. Its lowered VII is very important structurally, creating a quaint parallel, doubtless unintentionally, to a device in Mozart's Fortieth Symphony: the relating of a key-change or shift to basic properties of the motivic material. Mozart's half-tone shift of key at the beginning of the first movement's development section is startling, yet organically linked to the opening theme's falling half-tone. The Who's link is based on a descending whole-tone, heard first in the opening three-note motif, then, reinforcing this melodically *and* harmonically, in the quick I–II–I–*lowered* VII–I melodic twist that enlivens the end of the three-note motif – with the VII subtly setting up the unprepared tonal shift from E major, down a whole-step to D major, in section C.

The entire song in fact is based, however well disguised, on these two simple ideas: one melodic, one harmonic, with continual inter-relationships. It is frustratingly brief, but perhaps that is part of its charm.

3. Rod Stewart: Maggie May

Introduction 1. (INSTR.)

    (A minor) I–VII_6^4–I–VII–I I–III–VII–I (IV–III–I) (2×)

(E minor) I–VII–I–V–I–III–IV maj.–V maj.–I (2×: 2nd time final I is maj.)

Introduction 2. (INSTR.)

  (D major) I–II–IV–I (2×)

a. (VOCAL) V–IV–I V–IV–I

b. (VOCAL) IV–I–IV–V II–V added 6th (or III min. 7th)–II (I added 9th)

c. (VOCAL) II–V–II–V–II–V–I

  (3×)

Bridge (INSTR.) II–V–I–IV II–IV–V–I

(VOCAL) a., b., c.

Bridge (INSTR.) II–V–I–IV II–IV–I II–V–I–IV–II–V–(I)

Fade I–II–IV–I; pedal D at first

This song is notable for its treatment of 'ordinary' chords; through sensitive juxtaposition of these, and added notes – both melodic and instrumental – aided by the delightful sonorities, a quirky, poignant mood is evoked. There are many telling details, and I can mention only a few. The beginning is deliberately 'archaic', and the vocal section c. also has a pre-tonal flavor stemming from the juxtaposition of the minor II and the major V. The pedal D under the beginning of the fade is a lovely touch, as is the reticence of the whole ending, which only sketches in the I–II–IV–I of introduction 2 (this has, incidentally, a curious, somewhat ambiguous feeling because of the luminous added notes, which color yet are swept into the strong skeletal I–II–IV–I bass line). The delicate tremor of the mandolin-cum-lute adds a haunting flavor to the overall effect, and lends itself to imitation in the piano's treble range. I now leave it to the accompanist to discover the other imaginative elements in this fresh and touching little jewel.

4. Led Zeppelin: Stairway to Heaven

[A minor]

A. (INSTR.) Descending bass: 7-note pattern

    A–G sharp–G–F sharp–F–B–A (+ cross-relations; lowered VII)

B. (INSTR.) III–IV–VI min.$_7$–I–VII$_6$–III–VII–IV III–IV–VI min.$_7$–I

A. (VOCAL) Descending bass: 7-note pattern (2 ×)
B. (VOCAL) (2 ×)
A. (INSTR. 1 ×; vocal 1 ×) Descending bass: 7-note pattern
C. (VOCAL) I min.$_7$–IV$_7$
D. (VOCAL) Compressed descending bass: 3-note pattern (C–B–A–(B) C–B–(F)–A)
C. (VOCAL) I min.$_7$–IV$_7$
D. (VOCAL) Compressed 3-note bass
C. (INSTR.) I min.$_7$–IV$_7$
D. (VOCAL) Compressed 3-note bass
C. (VOCAL) I min.$_7$–IV$_7$
D. (VOCAL) Compressed 3-note bass
[shift to D]
E. (INSTR.) VIII (I)–VII–VIII–VII
[back to A min.]
F. (INSTR.) Compressed bass now in different tonal center: (A–G–F); metamorphosis of
bass in treble
F. (VOCAL) A–G–F bass, with new vocal variants of bass; rhythmic variation
F. (INSTR,) A–G–F bass, with new instrumental variants above; rhythmic lengthening in
treble.
(VOCAL) Solo voice: brief synthesis of major elements of song (two 3-note bass patterns;
previous vocal variations; lowered VII, etc.)

This is a paragon of variety within unity – a *tour de force* of enrichment and expansion of seemingly circumscribed materials. The principal elements are a passacaglia–chaconne approach, continual variation of variations, effective use of inversions, cross-relations, the lowered VII and a frequent modal flavor. Although it uses the identical chords of the preceding track of the LP, the 'Ballad of Evermore' – A minor (I), G major 1st inversion (VII$_6$) and C major (III) – in its D section, they are treated so freshly and differently that this only occurred to me after long acquaintance with both.

5. Nazareth: Please Don't Judas Me

[E minor]
(INTRO.) E pedal point; hints of motives; parallel 5ths
A. (INSTR.) I–V min.$_7$–I–IV–(VI–VII–I); parallel 5ths (2 ×)
A. (VOCAL) I–V min.$_7$–I–IV–(VI–VII–I) (2 ×)
B. (INSTR.) V min.$_7$–I–(III–VII–I) (2 ×)
C. (VOCAL) V (mutant, with A and G)–V min.$_7$–I (2 ×)
A. (INSTR.) I–V min.$_7$–V$_6$ min.$_7$–V min.$_7$–V$_6$ min.$_7$–I– (passing-tone) –I–IV–(VI–VII–I)
A. (VOCAL) I–V min.$_7$–V$_6$ min.$_7$–V min.$_7$–V$_6$ min.$_7$–I– (passing-tone) –I–IV–(VI–VII–I)
        (2 ×)
B. (INSTR.) V–I filled in with descending bass: B–A–G–F sharp –E–(III–VII–I) (2 ×)
C. (VOCAL) V mutant –VII (originally V min.$_7$)–I (6 ×)
B. (INSTR.) Descending bass – (III–VII–I) (2 ×)
C. (VOCAL) V mutant – VII–I (4 ×)
B. (INSTR.) Descending bass – (III–VII–I) (2 ×)
C. (VOCAL) V mutant – VII–I (4 ×)
B.–C.–B. (INSTR.) Fade – continual variations over repeated basses.

The longest track of these under scrutiny, 'Judas' builds, like 'Stairway', inexorably and compellingly by the most economical means. It resembles the Led Zeppelin achievement, in fact, in several ways. The alternation of closely related sections, a general *passacaglia*-like treatment throughout of a simple chord-pattern and a related descending bass, the permeation by a lowered VII (which in 'Judas' is of strong schematic importance: note the concluding patterns, in brackets, of A and B), and subtle variation from section to section.

It is like a gigantic *pavane*, not so much in specific parallels as in overall spirit and quality, which makes it peculiarly fitting as a close to these analyses. It combines the bittersweet grandeur of the solemn processional-type *pavanes* such as 'La Bataille', 'Desiderata', 'Au joli bois' and 'Belle qui tient ma vie' with the smaller-scale poignance of the more intimate ones like 'Mille regrets', 'La Cornetta', 'La Gaiette' and 'Si par souffrir', with similar drum-patterns to those of sixteenth-century dances.

VI. Hopes and reiterations

For those readers who love rock, I hope that this chapter will have added to their delight in this so-vital branch of twentieth-century music. To those who have always disliked it and dismissed it as mere noise, I say that my great desire has been to raise questions and stimulate at least a faint uncertainty about the wholesale dismissal of this twentieth-century renaissance of venerable practices.

I hope, similarly, that I have contributed something of value to those who already respond to the vitality and (deceptively) simple joys of the sixteenth-century dance-music, and aroused interest in those to whom it was unfamiliar or seemingly dull and limited. But, above all, I trust that I have clearly shown the great practical advantages for the improviser who can command the techniques and devices (and spirit) of the music reviewed in this chapter.

Here, to conclude, are a few distillations of what I feel are the most important points:

1. Both the early dance-music and rock are based primarily on the technique of continual variation, and often expansion, of small-scale, repetitious, additive patterns and sections. The ability to incorporate this into improvisations in class automatically implies a generally greater facility in a free flow of ideas than when the improviser is limited to mere repetition and contrast. But it is particularly valuable for those long stretches when playing for across-the-floor combinations or much-repeated centerwork in a crowded class. Neither the dancers nor you will enjoy a remorseless literal repetition of A–B–A (or even C) when it continues for as long as do some of these dance-marathons. If you can vary your basic ideas (or even pieces from repertoire) convincingly, you, and the class, are fortunate indeed.

2. Through the years, I have heard many accompanists attempt to improvise. And time after time they became bogged down because of harmonic weaknesses. Either they could not seem to find any effective chord-progressions to work with, or, if they did come up with some of the common (or uncommon) ones such as we have been examining here, they could not bring them to life. Whether because of boredom with these seemingly simple chords, lack of imagination or craft, or just inertia, they produced listless, static music without any kinetic vitality.

When, on the other hand, I was struck by unusually inventive improvising, it always turned out to have a strong, confident harmonic approach as a foundation. Although rhythm is the primary force in music, it is harmony in my opinion which is the improviser's Achilles' heel. For without a keen sense of harmonic movement and a sense of spacing of the component notes, good rhythm and phrasing are actually unattainable – not to mention melody (I am, of course, speaking of music in the Western harmonic tradition).

I have tried to show the wonderful variety and freshness which can be achieved – both *in spite* of limited harmonic schemes and *because* of them – by virtue of freeing the improviser to play around with rich melodic and rhythmic detail rather than floundering in an attempt to construct complicated chords and progressions. (Needless to say, the improviser who begins with simple harmonic schemes will gradually be able to work spontaneously with richer harmonies in more sumptuous styles.) A broad harmonic mastery, whether of simple or complex chords, depends very much – I must repeat for the last time – on skilful use of inversions and the resultant bass-line movement. Frequent, acute listening to music from the lists in Section V should demonstrate this conclusively. The improviser who has a feeling for inversions within a harmonic sequence, moreover, will use parallel chords in root-position far more effectively than one who simply uses them by default. Inversions are not always necessary, as can be seen with many of the pieces on the lists above, but a working knowledge of them is an essential ingredient of improvising.

One more point about harmony: variation is a technique which can be applied within any style or period, but harmonic language – the choice and usage of chords – is a more circumscribed element. Rock music *per se* is not suitable for continual, prolonged use in classes (at least not in traditional ones), but because rock harmonies do not have the gaudy sentimental quality of those in cocktail-music or showtunes, or the immediately recognizable implications of blues or many jazz chords, they can be used in improvisations which are not specifically traceable to rock. This would depend on how the other elements of melody, rhythm and phrase-structure were combined with the harmonic progressions.

3. Even if the accompanist does not wish to use the sixteenth-century dances or rock songs for literal models, the simplicity of this music provides an excellent starting-point for the novice in improvising, and a source of valuable ear-training for both the novice and the more advanced improviser.

A final thought: when performing pieces from repertoire, the accompanist is an ensemble player rather than a soloist, but this is especially true of the improviser. 'Like members of a great athletic team, like such partners in dance as Nureyev and Fonteyn, or like some jazz combos, the Beatles in performance seem to draw their aspirations and their energy not from the audience but from one another.'[26] This is true of both rock and the sixteenth-century dance-music performer, and in both cases the instrumental ensemble combines with a group of dancers to form a larger ensemble, all of whom are interacting. The ballet accompanist plays alone, but she, too, ideally, interacts with a dance group and teacher in this way and draws her aspirations and energy not from an audience but from her fellow-workers.

12   Rehearsal and real life

In the long run, a passive musical culture must inevitably be frivolous.

Wilfrid Mellers, *Music and Society*, 1946

Ye who dance not, know not what we are knowing.

Hymn of Jesus (Apocryphal)

Art has been perpetuated into a form of civilisation that is possible *without* art. We have therefore given art a new name: culture. Yet culture should refer to an environment in which a species is able to grow.

Peter Fletcher, *Roll Over Rock*, 1981

JUST AS technique is only a means to an end – communication through artistry – so the daily ballet class is the path to performance on stage. Many dancers, for one reason or another, become what one writer has called 'eternal students'. Their lives and aims are bounded by the studio, where they trudge diligently once or twice a day to work out and then, after class, to gossip about the world of ballet. Others, whose aims include that of actually performing in ballets rather than just talking about them, will eventually add rehearsals to their schedule. Rehearsals require rehearsal pianists and while many accompanists play only for technique classes, those who rehearse ballets are carrying their work in the class to its logical conclusion.

All of the attributes and skills which I have discussed so far, excepting the selection of music, are needed by the rehearsal pianist, although in somewhat different ways. Improvisation, for instance, is used less in rehearsals, yet the need for it can arise. The choreographer may be working with an incomplete score, or without any score at all as yet. The pianist must be able to follow his directions as to the style, quality, mood, texture, number of measures, etc., and supply a substitute while he is awaiting delivery of his score. Choreographers I have played for, moreover, sometimes gave exercises or studies in order to bring out certain qualities or illustrate points. Almost without exception, they preferred improvisations for these rather than set pieces because of the flexibility of an extemporaneous accompaniment.

Some skills, however, are either peculiar to the rehearsal situation or are more important there than in class.

I. Special rehearsal skills

The following four skills are essential if one is to become a first-rate rehearsal pianist:

1. Fluent sight-reading
2. Playing from orchestral scores
3. Reliable choreographic memory
4. Ability to become an orchestra

1. Fluent sight-reading

You may be able to avoid playing unfamiliar music at sight in the daily class, but you cannot possibly manage this during rehearsals. Although you can sometimes take the music home for perusal before it is used in rehearsal, there will be many other times when a score is shoved in front of you and, without preparation, you will have to produce some approximation of it. Choreographers vary in their appreciation of the difficulties involved. Some habitually confront you with the day's sections without any warning, others helpfully tell you what they plan to do on the morrow. Often, however, they cannot predict for they do not know themselves. Choreographers can be forced, for many reasons, to jump about in time like balletic Prousts. If you have only prepared the opening sections for the first rehearsal, and the choreographer is inspired to begin with the Finale – you sight-read.

As with improvisation, pianists range from expert, even amazing, to hopeless in ability to translate unfamiliar marks on a page into a performance. I have seen pianists whiz through a score as if they had known it for years, and I have also seen those who could barely read two measures in a row without stumbling.

From my experience, I would say that the single most effective, and the most enjoyable, approach to sight-reading is not one practiced in solitude, but in company. That is, the regular reading of four-hand music with a good friend. This will not only provide a companionable evening, it will pinpoint your weaknesses and help you to improve. The friend should be musical and sensitive to the style and quality of the music (far more important than technical perfection), and should be implacable regarding starting and stopping. If you practice sight-reading on your own, you will tend to be lenient and mentally lazy, like someone learning to type by the hunt-and-pick method. You will never learn to sight-read fluently this way. If you indulge yourself thus while playing four-hands, your friend will soon get disgusted and seek a more rewarding partner. You must keep going, no matter what tonal catastrophes occur.

How do you do this? A familiar word will answer the question – *rhythm*. But how do you bring rhythm into play when you cannot even manage to strike the right notes consistently? (I forgot to mention that you will be observing, as closely as possible, the 'right' tempo.)

Three factors

There are three ways in which you can develop and utilize a sense of rhythm – a continuity – while sight-reading. They will prevent your having to resort to a spasmodic grabbing at the notes:

  i. The strongest possible feeling of the pulse in your body
 ii. The process of *scanning* rather than reading note by note (a hopeless effort)
iii. The power of projection and imagination

i. Without a self-perpetuating pulse in your body the music will quickly fall apart. A mental preoccupation with notes and details will rush in to fill the physical vacuum of non-rhythm. Since, in any piece of greater difficulty than, say, 'Twinkle

Twinkle Little Star', various difficulties will lurk, waiting to trip you up, you must acquire the lofty knack of sailing right over them – or, rather, drawing them into your wake. The mind is capable of encompassing just so much detail in a given span of time; you must be able to discern which of the frequently overwhelming number of details are necessary to keep the flow. Rhythm is the only reliable source of this ability, and it begins with the referrent of the pulse. But pulse experienced kinetically and unwaveringly in your body, not pulse counted out in a lifeless, fluctuating manner.

Counting, in music or in dance, separates and distracts, and in complex passages it is often impossible in any case. Abby Whiteside illustrates this point with an anecdote:

Feats in sight-reading are accomplished only by people who work under the spell of a rhythm. I have been told of an orchestra that was rehearsing a contemporary score of great difficulty. There were multiple changes in meter and no one was getting the feel of the music except the flutist. When the men asked him how he did it he replied, 'Well, I couldn't count the stuff, so I just got a rhythm in my body and kept it going'. If only we could absorb that very fundamental and revealing truth we would constantly use the only productive technical means for learning to read music and play our instrument. Put a rhythm in your body and keep it going.[1]

ii. The ability to scan – to range quickly over long passages of print and pick out relevant information – is essential for anyone doing prolonged serious research. It is equally necessary for the sight-reader. Again, it is a matter of coping with detail. No researcher can afford to dwell on each 'and', 'but' and 'the, or laboriously follow every amplifying or subsidiary statement. He must distill from a paragraph its key words, its essence – not get bogged down in minutiae.

Similarly, the sight-reader must be able to perceive instantly which musical events keep the momentum going and which operate on a secondary or subsidiary level. In, for instance, an eighteenth-century keyboard *allegro*, with a racing Alberti bass, it would be madness to try to identify each note of the eighth- or sixteenth-note patterns. In sight-reading you would aim for the over-all effect of the bass-motion. Since these patterns are based largely on broken chords, you would scan the basic harmonic progressions; it would not matter if you played a different broken-form of a C major triad, or even interpolated some scale-wise notes – as long as you maintained the pulse and the rhythmic flow. In other words, sacrifice as many of the niceties of a passage as is necessary in order not to break the thread, rather than sacrificing everything to grab for the niceties. You are a sight-reader, not a proof-reader. Yet, there is a process which, gradually developed, will enable you to encompass more and more detail without getting sidetracked and lost. This is the use of the inner ear.

iii. A reliance on the eye alone will not get you far as a sight-reader. The driver who wishes to navigate his car safely cannot limit himself to hazards which he can see; he must also listen – for screeching brakes behind him, an unseen child's voice, the bark of a dog, the far-off siren of a fire engine. So must the musical navigator use his ear – to cope with technical hazards, and to enable him to take the necessary action.

Not so much the outer ear, however, for with this the pianist can only hear what has already happened. The inner ear is the one which can predict what is to come.

The operation in its entirety is amazingly complex: the eye functions in a continuing present, registering one notated musical event after another; the outer ear hears each event in turn – and the inner ear correlates, and forecasts on the basis of the information received by the eye and the outer ear. And this in an unimaginable instant. The inner ear, in other words, employs memory and premonition. As Vaughan Williams writes, of the listening process,

The physical ear plays only a small part in our understanding of music. The physical ear can do no more than receive one moment of sound at a time, and our grasp of even the simplest tune depends on our power of remembering what has come before and of co-ordinating it with what comes after. So that it seems that the mind and the memory play an even more important part than the ear in appreciating music.[2]

What Vaughan Williams refers to as the mind and the memory are what constitute the inner ear. And its faculties are even more crucial to the performer of music at sight than to the listener.

Beginning on the most basic level, an inner hearing of the key in which the music is written is needed. During innumerable hours spent in teaching piano, I was shocked at how many pupils could or would not remember the key in which they were supposed to be playing. After glancing dutifully at the sharps or flats of the key signature, all too soon one or more of these would revert to a natural.

This was because the remembering of key in sight-reading involves not so much *mental* memory as *quality*-memory. For whatever reasons, A major has a different quality than A minor. This quality must be continually experienced through the inner ear, while playing, after being absorbed at the outset – rather than viewed as just another irksome bit of notation. I found when I encouraged pupils with perfect pitch, who could automatically hear keys in their minds, to sit for a moment before beginning their sight-reading, and concentrate on the quality of the key, that they ignored it far less frequently than when they had just glanced at the key signature. With those who did not have perfect pitch, I suggested playing a few triads and melodic fragments in the major and minor forms of A in order to feel the different qualities. They became able, gradually, to spend less and less time on these preliminaries, and often the mere striking of the tonic triad in each was enough. They read through the piece with never a lapse (at least not of key).

This is not to say, of course, that the composer will not deviate from time to time. In general, however, the key prevails throughout a section or piece (although chromatic Romantic music will pose problems and be more demanding).

If the music is contemporary, in a freely shifting tonality or in none at all, the problem is quite different, and considerably more taxing on the eye, and the outer and inner ears. Tonal music is much easier to sight-read, partly because it is simply a more familiar and thus a predictable sound-world. But also because it possesses what Leonard B. Meyer calls redundancy; this means that more similarity and thus less new 'information' is being conveyed in a phrase of tonal music than in one from certain twentieth-century trends. In a phrase by Boulez, Stockhausen, Berio, Elliott Carter or Milton Babbit, the actual, as opposed to apparent, sound-information carried in one or two measures may exceed that contained in an entire eighteenth-century sonatina or a movement from Vivaldi's *Seasons*. Avant-garde music, in other words, almost completely does away with the 'ands', 'buts' and 'thes' of modal and tonal music (see Meyer: 'Music, the Arts and Ideas' for engrossing discussion).

Retaining a sense of key involves aural memory. More sophisticated uses of the inner ear bring into play projection and imagination, which utilize the inner ear in re-creative and creative activity. Since projection presupposes a starting point of known factors, one must be familiar enough with the style and period of the music one is reading to have a basis upon which to function. This basis offers a musical shortcut, for within every style there are progressions and events which are highly probable and others which are almost inconceivable. So, projection relies upon reduction. The inner ear, automatically discounting the *impossibilities*, will thus be more alert, free to deal with, and project, the *possibilities* within a given style which continually lie ahead.

A simple example: when sight-reading a piece by Mozart, no undue mental effort is necessary for the final cadence, since in this style the piece is bound to end on the tonic. Even the approach to it is surprisingly circumscribed much of the time. Look, for example, at the many uses made by Mozart of 5–4–3–2–1 melodically at full cadences (which can include, say, 3–5–4–2–1, or 5–3–4–2–1). Familiarity with such characteristics of composers or periods will offer frequent opportunities to project possibilities and soar over details, freeing the mind for higher-level work. But a piece in the Viennese style of the early twentieth-century, by Schoenberg or Webern might keep you always on tenterhooks, for part of this style is the deliberate avoidance of tonal formulas and clichés. Mozart accepted and transcended them; the Viennese school rejected them, striving instead to supplant them with ever-fresh events. (Some critics, however, consider that composers in this style gravitated to just as habitual, if less apparent, use of clichés as did those of earlier times.)

A more subtle area is that of melodic content and direction. In pre-twentieth century, Western, music, melodies seldom progress by wide, dissonant intervals. If there is a large leap in the melodic line, it is usually followed, and filled, by diatonic (or modal) stepwise and triadic progression, in the opposite direction.

Another consideration is that, as Meyer observes, the predictability of the ways in which the music will progress becomes more uncertain in developmental sections. The original ideas and phrases, which may have been very simple and easy to forecast, can deviate considerably while they are being developed and expanded. The composer may chop them up, invert them, or suddenly hurl them into tonal side-streets, *cul-de-sacs*, among infinite possibilities.

A recapitulation will, of course, return to the more predictable course of the opening, although Beethoven and others often introduce dramatic surprises and even shocks into their recapitulations.

I have been discussing the sight-reading of pieces new to the pianist. If one is reading a piece not actually learned from score but which one does know from several hearings, the inner ear will be stronger and more secure, bringing specific memory into action. You will indeed pre-hear, not just through projection but through acquaintance. (One simple manifestation of this process is the inner pre-hearing of the opening notes of the next track on any LP comprised of many short pieces or several rock tracks. The ending of one track leads, without conscious effort, to the aural forecasting of the beginning of the next. Even the students of mine who had the most difficulty with theoretical matters in class affirmed that this happened consistently to them.)

But the inner ear does not operate only through projection and memory; it also can involve imagination, or creation. The more times you have heard the piece you are now reading at sight, the more you will employ aural memory. The less familiar you are with it, the more creativity is necessary. This, in fact, is not too different from the imagination, or creativity, which goes into an improvisation. In both cases you are attempting to get inside the mind of a composer or inside a style, and to follow through with musical consistency.

Whether sight-reading music you already know to some degree or totally unfamiliar pieces, you will find, as I have said, that the process is much easier in late-Baroque, Classical and early-Romantic music. The patterns, rhythmic, harmonic and melodic, are either in widespread use during their era – 'common practice' – or they are somewhat circumscribed. As the Romantics searched further afield for the original or idiosyncratic, the predictability of a piece diminished proportionately until, by the twentieth century, many composers seemed to be intent upon a complete thwarting of expectations; in place of the soporific, almost totally eventless formulas of third-rate Baroque and Classical *pieces d'occasion*, composers now inflicted pieces of mind-boggling, numbing unpredictability, crammed with *too* many events.

Music in this esthetic is probably the most tightly controlled and calculated music of any ever written. Yet since this is not done from an aural standpoint, but rather a constructional one, the hearer – and performer – is unable to comprehend more than a portion of it through the ear. According to Meyer, 'experimental music is often a set of relationships to be studied, not music to be heard. It is not, like language, a means of communication, but like mathematics, an object of investigation.'[3] Needless to say, a piece of this sort is unreadable at sight.

Contemporary scores which are not so remorselessly cerebral, such as the Elliott Carter Eight Etudes for woodwind quartet (to which Antony Tudor choreographed a dance for dance students of the Juilliard School) offer many difficulties, but are at least manageable – as long as you do not attempt to proceed from note to note. The more correct notes you can get the better, but the main thing is the perception of patterns and phrases (admittedly more complex than those of pre-twentieth-century music, but still attainable, and aurally meaningful). At the same time, you must maintain the rhythmic pulse and flow while bringing the imagination into play as to where these patterns might go. Tenacity here will produce results – but do not expect them to come easily!

Psychological attitude

A fourth factor, or rather the foundation of the three just discussed, is one's psychological approach to sight-reading. As with any difficult undertaking it is (barring human frailty and fate) one's attitude toward it, while employing all possible skill, which determines the outcome. No matter what skills or techniques you may have acquired, they cannot help you during the project at hand – whether climbing Mount Everest, playing badminton, dancing *Giselle* or sight-reading – if your conscious or unconscious attitude impedes them. If, like Herrigel's archer, 'you do not wait for fulfilment, but brace yourself for failure',[4] the necessary skills will either fail to develop beyond a certain point, or fail to come into action when you need them.

It is not a matter of ego or arrogance; rather it is the release of energies into an activity of importance in itself. As with improvisation, the minute you watch yourself to see how well you are doing, or you approach the sight-reading through fear that you cannot do it, it will not happen. In other words, you do not search, beat by beat, for notes; you let them come to you. It is, in effect, the performer becoming the essence and flow of the music.

2. Playing from orchestral scores

The sight-reading of piano pieces or piano transcriptions can make even the best of pianists nervous; the sight-reading of orchestral scores can inspire terror – or at least partial paralysis. Of course this is a very special skill, one which most musicians are not normally required to master – with the exception of composers and conductors, who often excel at it.

The first and last thing to remember is that you can rarely manage to play, even with practice, *all* the notes in music written for a large ensemble. If it uses the various instruments well, and exploits their potential, it cannot possibly be encompassed in its entirety by two hands.

Since you can rarely play all the parts, the main challenge is to find quickly which are the important ones. When doing this at sight, you obviously need quicksilver reactions – based on a knowledge of the characteristics of orchestral writing.

Thus, concentrated study of scores, ranging from simple (early Classical string quartets and symphonies, for instance) to complex is helpful. One practical aid is the use of scores which have the main themes or ideas marked with arrows or other visual aids, as in the Norton Scores Anthology edited by Roger Kamien. Bring the scores to life by following them while listening to recorded versions of the pieces. This is, however, only a prelude to action and ultimately the time will come when you must sit at the keyboard and play. It is best to begin with music which is already very familiar, like popular ballet scores.

If you have never done this before, the first attempts may be chaotic – but perhaps you have managed a flute solo here, a slow string passage there, and some rhythmic patterns in between. As with reading from familiar piano music, you have the great asset of your inner ear to help predict what comes next, if you allow it to. Try a section again, this time playing only what is written for the string section, keeping the rhythm going. If you know the piece well, you should be able to hear inwardly the moments when something important happens in the winds, brass or percussion. Sing these moments, while you are maintaining the progress of the string parts. Then start again, this time trying to incorporate the lines you have just been hearing or singing into what your keyboard-strings are doing.

If you keep at it, no matter how discouraging the results seem at first, you should find it easier and easier – although never, of course, as easy as reading only two piano staves. Refer frequently to the recorded performance, with score in hand. The aural associations to all those patterns, leaps from one instrumental family to another, or the blending of two or more, reinforce and make added sense of all that the eye is struggling to take in.

Unfortunately, you cannot use records to help you when you are in the rehearsal studio, faced with a commissioned score. Your sessions with record and score, followed up by approximations at the piano will, however, have brought you a long way towards coping with a new score at sight. (Some composers make piano reductions for rehearsal, but often this is not possible because of over-crowded schedules.) You will be becoming familiar with the world of the large score.

Transposition

During your initial efforts you will have been trying to extend your basic equipment – that is, your ability to read piano music. But, in addition to the problem of visually-fragmented themes or patterns which leap from strings to winds to brass, and back again, you will have inevitably been brought up short at some point by another problem. This is *transposition* – probably the single greatest obstacle in the sight-reading of scores. It involves complex mental activity and can often seem impossible. There are various approaches to teaching transposition, one of which is the use of the *solfège* system. Reference to books on this subject will tell you whether or not you wish to learn it.

In any case, the problems of musical ideas which jump from one choir to another and transposition are, in a sense, related. For this reason, I shall now discuss them in conjunction with one another. Tracing the progress of the music as it traverses the orchestra, and the staves on the page, is both an aural and a visual process. I have touched on the aural aspect while describing how it functions in reading piano music. The same forces, prediction, memory and imagination, operate in the reading of orchestral scores – both in instrumental interchange and transposition. From a visual point of view, also, the two problems share the same solution.

The two main processes involved in transposition of orchestral instruments are those of playing notes in a different key from the one which you are reading, and what might be called simultaneity: doing this in two (or more) different frames of reference while, at the same time playing some instruments at the pitch at which you are reading them. A typical passage could, for example, feature a melody in the B$^\flat$ clarinet, a counter-melody in the English horn doubled by the violas, with an accompaniment in the violins and cellos. Here you must transpose the clarinet down a major 2nd, the English horn down a perfect 5th, read the alto clef in which the viola is largely notated and read and play the violins and cellos without any transposition. Four different mental efforts, all of which must be done quickly.

On one level this is a matter of memory-drill, for which *solfège* offers one solution. Another, the one which I used, involves writing and hearing. During my first years as a student-composer, I had great difficulty (mainly due to laziness) in mastering the skill of transposition. One of my greatest blocks was the reading of the alto clef used for the viola. I then wrote a 40-minute string quartet – in 'concert' score, the viola being notated in the treble or bass clefs rather than in the alto (which, of course, had to be used for the final score and viola part). By the time I completed the final manuscripts, I *knew* the alto clef – and never forgot it. And I believe that the thoroughness with which I then, finally, managed to master this troublesome clef was due to the fact that I always sang the notes of the viola line in my mind while I was notating it on the alto clef. Thus I associated certain sounds with the corresponding lines and spaces of the clef, reinforcing the visual memory-effort.

The same approach was, of course, effective in the written transposition of clarinet, horn, etc. Somehow the effort of singing a major 2nd or a perfect 5th lower than I was notating the part embedded it in my subconscious. And this is where it needs to be, so that the conscious mind does not have to make a separate effort to identify the notes. There is too much else to cope with for that to be practicable. What you are striving for is elimination of the step between the seeing and the playing-action, so that perception is immediate. This resembles the mental processes involved in learning another language. When reading French, for instance, the beginner must consciously translate each word; the advanced student, upon seeing the word 'chat' simply registers 'cat'. (It is, of course but another form of your early learning of the piano's treble and bass clefs.)

The memory-factor is only one part of transposition, however. Projection and imagination also play a large part. Just as you should use these to predict the course of a melodic line which passes from one instrument to another, so should you do so to make transposition easier. For instance, a melodic line, say a sinuous lyrical one, may pass from violins to $B^\flat$ clarinet to bass clarinet (also in $B^\flat$, but transposing down a 9th rather than a 2nd). Visually, you can project (always barring the element of surprise) that wherever the line goes, the instrument which picks it up will follow through and be consistent. Thus a main idea in the violins will maintain its visual shape further up on the page where you identify the continuing sinuous shape in the clarinet. You can, in other words, reasonably assume the probability that a Jekyll–Hyde transformation will not take place, the main melodic thread suddenly becoming jagged and percussive when it goes to the clarinet (we are, of course, not talking about very dramatic or avant-garde music).

Aurally, for the purpose of transposition, you can similarly project that if the violin was playing in, say, the key of E major, the clarinet which takes over will be unlikely to enter in the key of $B^\flat$ minor. Here you can reasonably assume a continuance either in E major, or in a key which is closely related. Thus you prevent the mental process from deteriorating into a wild guessing-game involving the twenty-four major and minor keys.

Or, if there *were* a sudden dramatic tonal-shift, it is highly probable that the *visual* aspect of the music would alter when the clarinet entered. A striking change in orchestration or texture might accompany such a shift. The ability to project these, and other, possibilities, using the aural and the visual in conjunction, reduces the amount of actual detail-work and guesswork.

Simple steps

For those who start off with good intentions and find, after many unproductive attempts, that score-reading is just too difficult, I recommend some back-tracking. Evade, for the moment, the complexity of a full orchestra and turn instead to the simplicity of songs by Schubert, Schumann or Hugo Wolf. Organ music, violin, flute or cello sonatas are good practice also. If one is used to reading only two staves, the addition of a third is a complication, but a modest one. Opera arias, in piano-vocal score, tend to be more florid than art-songs, thus a step forward in difficulty. Beyond these are sonatas for two solo instruments with piano, and piano scores of eighteenth century concertos for two or more solo instruments, by Vivaldi and others.

Preliminary work for transposition in orchestral scores can include the sight-reading of pieces for transposing instruments and piano (or, if you wish to reduce the initial strain still further, you may read only the solo line for the time being).

When you feel ready, you may choose pieces for larger ensembles: string quartets and quintets, clarinet and horn quintets, sextets and the like. Works for small orchestra as Mozart's divertimenti or *Eine kleine Nachtmusik* are not too difficult.

Whether you prefer to attack the problem head-on by beginning with orchestra scores, or approach it gently with songs, sonatas, quartets, etc., steady and consistent effort, not intermittent and disconnected odd moments, is the key.

3. Reliable choreographic memory

Here we leave, momentarily, the strictly musical skills and come to one which has also to do with dance. It is the ability to see and *remember* movement. In the technique class you are not actually compelled to develop this skill, although it is certainly to your advantage to do so. In rehearsal, however, you will tread a thorny path if you cannot retain at least key moments in the choreography.

A reasonable choreographer will not expect you to produce every single note of the orchestral score. He will, however, definitely expect you to know his ballet well enough to be able to pick up the music wherever he may wish to begin work. This is by no means impossible – although it may seem so to accompanists who never bother to look at the dancers. It does take a certain amount of doing, though, and requires the development of movement-memory, reinforced by continual, clear indications entered into your score.

These will include important entrances and exits, beginnings of sections (ensemble after soloist, soloist after quartet, etc.), spatial designs (diagonal, circle, etc.), movements which stand out (abrupt change of direction, *pas de deux* lift, flinging off of cloak, hand gesture, etc.) – in short, anything which is visually striking and easy to recall. Then, of course, there are the steps themselves, and the *enchainements* which combine them. These require a bit more mental activity on your part, but the more you can identify, quickly jot down, and eventually memorize, the better.

Your notations, needless to say, must be positioned at their exact musical moments in the score, particularly when they occur in the middle of a section or phrase. You will often be asked to pick up the music at odd moments here and there. The choreographer may stride into the studio, toss a brief 'good morning' to all, turn to you and say, 'Right, we'll take it from Jennifer's *pas de chat* . . . and – ONE . . .' If you fail to manifest a cat's quickness of reaction, Jennifer will find herself in mid-air, in silence. You, sitting there looking blank and woebegone (or blank and unconcerned), will have been responsible for a somewhat dampening beginning of the rehearsal.

At the other extreme, a prepared and knowledgable pianist can be of great value to the choreographer. It is not unusual for a choreographer to forget his own choreography. Both he and the dancers may be uncertain, particularly if it is a section which has repeatedly been altered. If *you* can remember the most recent version, or have cannily jotted it down, you will be treasured. You can be sure that your involvement with the proceedings will be appreciated and remembered.

4. Ability to become an orchestra

In rehearsal, even more than in class, you must transcend the piano. If you have given the dancers a *reductio ad absurdum* during the piano rehearsals, their shock during the first orchestral rehearsal may have serious results. You must, therefore, approximate as closely as possible what they will finally hear. The uniformity of tone-color of the piano presents great problems here. It can mask the subtle interplay of the tone-colors of the various instruments, thus distorting the composer's intentions. At the same time, ironically, it can lend a deceptive simplicity and clarity, leading the dancers to listen less carefully than they will have to when dancing to an orchestra, however 'orchestral' your playing may have been.

I was amused, some years ago, by the contrasting reactions of dance-students after the first orchestral rehearsal of *Sleeping Beauty*. We had rehearsed for months, yet some of the dancers apparently had not bothered to augment the daily piano sounds with reference to orchestral recordings of the score. Discussing the rehearsal afterwards, they split into two camps. The first exclaimed over the beauty and the kinetic stimulation of the orchestral sounds. The second complained about the problems of dancing with orchestra, saying how much easier it had been to 'follow' the piano compared with all those confusing instrumental entrances, exits and overlappings. Almost without exception, the most musical and alive dancers were in the first camp and the least aware were in the second.

Despite the drawbacks of the monochromatic piano as a substitute for an orchestra, it is surprising how much of the essence of the original a good rehearsal pianist *can* convey. I have heard pianists play even the most complex orchestral scores with spirit and assurance, miraculously creating the illusion of the massed forces and the dialogues between instruments which are so characteristic of good orchestral writing. They even managed to achieve a sense of the qualities peculiar to each instrument. I have, of course, also heard pianists transform orchestral works into a cross between a Czerny exercise and an Add-A-Part record.

It is, in addition to the necessary technical skills, primarily a matter of aural imagination. The challenge is even greater when playing from a piano reduction where you have only sketchy indications of the instrumentation (or none at all). Yet many rehearsal pianists plow through these often pedestrian and misleading transcriptions without ever troubling to become familiar with the orchestral version (Tchaikovsky has suffered less in piano transcriptions than most).

A piano *reduction* – which is what it actually is, not a literal transcription – can give you only a partial idea of the orchestral texture and almost none of the instrumental balance. Both are important for the dancers. Familiarity with the record or score is the only answer. In many of Tchaikovsky's most effective passages, the texture consists of high, spacious, brilliant flute accompanied by crisp *pizzicato* or *détaché* strings. You can destroy the clarity of texture if you play the flute part in a nondescript, running-notes-on-the-piano manner accompanied by flaccid, half-heartedly separated notes. If you have once heard the textural effect of the original – as in the Songbird variation from *Sleeping Beauty* – you will be unlikely to forget it.

Balance

Balance is crucial. One of the many delights in Tchaikovsky's ballet scores is the frequent dramatic antiphonal throwing back and forth of musical ideas from strings to brass or winds to strings. And not only is the tone-color of each group different, the *weight* of sound can vary considerably. A passage played by the brass, *fortissimo*, is quite a different matter when repeated in a string *fortissimo*. Strings at their loudest can never equal in actual decibels the power of the brass (this being borne in mind, of course, by the experienced composer, who uses it as a means of expression).

On the other hand, a *fortissimo* in the brass echoed by the strings, *pianissimo*, is calculatedly dramatic, and is likely to be exploited by the choreographer. Yet the notation of this on a piano reduction is only a pale ghost of the actual dynamic effect. Again, an inner memory of the original balance will help the pianist to convey an orchestral *ff–pp*, as opposed to a piano *ff–pp*. It seems, in the orchestra, a much more physical phenomenon than on the piano where it is more a matter of gradation of volume. The orchestral brass *ff*, with its overwhelming force, pitted against the silken whisper of the strings' *pp* conveys a primarily kinetic sensation, not an aural one.

Now we come to one of the benefits to the pianist which I promised in Chapter 4. A common fault is carelessness regarding dynamics. All piano teachers are familiar with the monotonous *mezzo-forte* which their pupils gravitate towards like water seeking its own level. It takes more concentration to play very loud or very softly than to play in the medium range. But, once you have begun to compare the effectiveness of varied dynamics as heard in the orchestral version with the lack-luster monotony which the piano reduction tempts accompanists to fall into, you may well consider the effort worth making (see also 'Dynamics' in Chapter 9, Section VIII). Thus, you will benefit in any performance situation. Awareness of the dancers' needs, also, can help to jolt you out of a dynamics-lethargy. If you are slipshod regarding dynamics and balance during rehearsals, you will mislead them, sometimes with dramatic (and unwelcome) results. One dancer was so devastated by a sudden brass *ff* in the first orchestral rehearsal – habitually played in a keyboard *mf* by the pianist – that she actually fell, twisting her ankle. That pianist was as responsible as if she had pushed the dancer. You must forewarn the dancers of any extremes; an unexpected *pianissimo* can be just as startling. Another dancer was so accustomed to hearing a *pp pizzicato* string passage played *mf* (*legato*) by the pianist that she missed her cue in the same rehearsal. Result: wasted time while they repeated the passage. (Dancers are especially vulnerable during actual perform- ance: Martha Graham said, during an English television interview (BBC, July 18, 1976) that on one occasion, a performance of *Herodiade*, she almost fell because the violist missed an important entrance and she was thus deprived of her 'support'. She did not, needless to say, mean this in a passive way.)

More difficult is the approximation of balance *within* an instrumental passage played on the piano. At night all cats are grey, and on the piano reduction all *f* or *p* notes appear equal in volume, as in the brass *vs.* strings problem discussed above. When the reduction is one of strings and brass – or other mixed ensembles – playing together, one can easily be misled. One or two voices, sometimes inner ones, can be more important than others. They often, in fact, will be carrying the main melodic thread while the notes printed above them will be merely accompaniment or parts of the harmony.

If the choreographer has heard and responded to these melodic threads in the orchestral version he will not be happy to hear them swallowed up on the piano, and the dancers will be unfamiliar with key musical moments when they dance to the orchestra. Reference to the recorded version when possible, again, will help you, showing what to emphasize and what to hold back. If you feel uncertain about moments in a newly commissioned score, you can consult with the composer, who should be happy to clear up any misunderstandings. The rehearsal pianist is a go- between, bridging the gap between the composer and the conductor. As such, you are very important.

Everything I have said about the rehearsal pianist can, of course, be made irrelevant by a simple action. That is the supplanting of the pianist by a tape, used for all rehearsals up to the orchestral ones in the theater. This practice is a sore point with musicians' unions and depressing for a dedicated rehearsal pianist, but convenient and economic for the choreographer and dancers. The convenience is, however, marred by certain drawbacks.

An attempt to compare tapes with a live rehearsal pianist could pit the reliability of an ever-repeatable performance, with predictable tempos, against the human capacity for response. The ballet conductor may well fluctuate during perform- ance; the dancers will be unprepared for this by the clockwork tempos of the tape. Their responses in this area will have been dulled during the rehearsals with tape.

The convenience is also impaired by psychological considerations. 'If the company', writes John Lanchberry,

has been well rehearsed to a piano, their first run with orchestra should give them a 'lift', an exciting feeling of suddenly being near to actual performance. This lift, alas, is absent if they have rehearsed to tape, for a live orchestra in a theatre pit cannot help but sound thin by comparison. Even more important is the stifling effect on a conductor's musicianship of not being able to mould a performance after his own heart but having instead to try to duplicate a taped performance, which is usually that of another conductor.[5]

On the other hand, we must weigh the undoubted value to the dancers of hearing the actual instrumental sounds – tone colors, dynamics, balance and attack.

A perplexing debate indeed – or at least it is if you feel that, despite all the aforementioned flaws and problems which accompany the use of piano for rehearsals, a live, participating, responsive pianist is somehow more desirable than the inescapably cold and detached quality of a tape.

A further consideration, and an alarming one to many, is the growing use of electronic music-tapes for performance. In doing away with live musicians, a new point has been reached in music. To some it is the dawn of a benign new world, in which no obstreperous performer need ever again be tolerated. To others it is the ominous foreshadowing of the death of music as it has always been experienced. Those in the middle see no threat in the occasional use of electronic music.

From a dance point of view there is the question of whether or not a jarring note is introduced – a discrepancy – when live dancers dance to canned music. (The use of recorded music in the performance of ballets from the repertoire is certainly never very satisfactory.) The use of the esoteric sounds of electronic tapes, moreover, is all very well when the choreography is expressing torment, fear, peculiarity, tension, sterility, alienation – all those frailties which cry out for expression. And without doubt the younger generation of composers is doing much to humanize electronics (both in 'serious' music and rock), and to add a sense of joy and freedom. Such music has been used with happy results by many choreographers. Perhaps coexistence is possible.

The debate has really only begun; at the moment, all that can be said decisively is that the economic and practical advantages of rehearsal and performance tapes are not unalloyed. Since, however, the rehearsal pianist has by no means been ousted by them, I mention them here merely to acknowledge that they are part of the current scene.

II. Other considerations

The skills discussed in Section I emanate from the pianist. Other aspects of rehearsal come from external circumstance. These are facets of rehearsal which the pianist must understand and cope with:

1. Tempos
2. The need for patience and objectivity

3. Moving from studio to stage

1. Tempos

Rehearsal speeds can be very problematical, and since this is a crucial aspect for the dancer on stage, we must give it close attention.

One cause of conflict between dancer and musician in rehearsal is 'the right tempo'. You will frequently be asked to play passages at tempos which seem to you, as a musician, unsuitable or even outrageous. Perhaps – but the question of speed in choreography is not a simple one. Many musicians however like to think that it should be. Rehearsal pianists I have known, mainly very ordinary ones, view tempo as sacrosanct, and not to be willfully distorted by cheeky dancers. This makes their job more difficult and themselves less than popular. Since, as I have observed elsewhere, even composers themselves fluctuate markedly when performing their works, and all *realistic* performers admit that circumstance can affect their tempos, this restrictive, puritanical attitude toward tempo in dance seems a bit arbitrary.

What the musical purist fails to understand, moreover, is that the tempos to which they object are usually the result of the difference between a concert performance of a work and a theatrical one. Things change when the music is used to accompany bodily action. You may find, for example, that an *allegro* musical climax must be somewhat broadened to give the movement space in which to breathe (or, on heightened occasions, quickened). On the other hand, music which can be spun out in a slow, meditative manner in concert usually needs to be tightened up a bit for dancing. This is done to give the movement pace and a heightened kinetic feeling.

In general, concert performers tend to take a piece faster in the bravura or scherzo-like sections than do ballet conductors, and, in the case of lyrical, romantic sections, the concert performer is often tempted to milk every possible drop of emotion to such a degree that it would be impossible for a dancer to sustain the movement at such a tempo. (This poses a problem concerning the use of records. When I taught classes in rhythm for dancers, I preferred to use them so that we could work to the original instrumental sounds. Frequently, however, I had to play the music on the piano because the tempos were so far outside the possible range for sensible dance movement. Yet, if they *had* been usable, the performance would have been less compelling and sensible as music to sit and listen to in its own right.)

Another source of tempo-trouble for the rehearsal pianist is the difficulty or awkwardness of certain orchestral passages on the piano. The scrupulous pianist – as opposed to the flexible rehearsal accompanist – will make the notes more important than the over-all effect and rhythmic continuity. 'I have often noticed', writes Lanchberry,

that pianists tend to have trouble with orchestral music which translates badly for piano. For instance, the end of Aurora's Variation in the last act of the *Sleeping Beauty* with its quick leaps from low octave A's to high tonic chords is not easy on the piano. An average pianist is tempted to slow down slightly so as not to play wrong notes, whereas a good *rehearsal* pianist will take a chance and maintain the tempo. Failure to do this will lead the dancer to expect a *rallentando* there, and time will be wasted later at the rehearsal with the orchestra while she asks for one from the conductor . . .[6]

Of course, not all tempo-problems are caused by the pianist. Dancers can also create difficulties, sometimes with justification, other times not. A dancer has the right to request a different tempo (within reason) from one used by another dancer who is sharing the part. (This is more acceptable in a separate variation than in a section of a continuous narrative ballet, for obvious reasons.) Just as Rubinstein may take a certain piece at a different tempo than Horowitz, so may various dancers differ to some degree. It is a matter of personality, temperament and approach to the role.

In another world entirely, however, is the dancer who demolishes the music, now insisting that the pianist or orchestra rush (to help her over a difficult technical moment), now slow down (to squeeze out the soul of an *arabesque* or a *pirouette*). Nothing matters to her but the pathos or glitter of her performance. Such music-manipulators are a trial to pianist and choreographer, although the latter has more authority over them. Verna Arvey writes critically of this tendency:

Dancers often change the entire character of a piece of music by merely changing the tempo. They ritard in impossible spots so that they can execute a difficult movement with ease. They sometimes command that their music be played slowly in rehearsal while they learn their dances. Unconsciously then, they add too much movement, which cannot be included when the music is later danced in tempo. Their simple remedy for such a situation is to play the music too slowly in performance.[7]

In addition there are the daily fluctuations. Tempos can vary from rehearsal to rehearsal, sometimes to a surprising degree. This may be due to the dancer's state of health or mind, or simply that the studio is 10° colder than it was the day before.

The choreographer himself may fluctuate regarding the tempo he wants for a certain section. This is not always deliberate. He is not infallible, and the passage in question may not yet have settled into its final, best tempo. He also may simply not be able to remember it from one day to the next. Just as musicians vary in ability to retain tempos – some almost incapable of doing so without the aid of a metronome – so do choreographers.

But why should absolute precision be expected? This seems to me unreasonable. Dance and music, and their combination, are not simple matters, and they are created by humans, not robots. With the exceptions of the solipsistic dancer and the habitually amnesiac choreographer, tempo problems really should not lead to pursed lips – or curses – from the rehearsal pianist. José Limón tried to explain the problem of tempo in dance to an audience which included both dancers and musicians:

... there is still that baffling and subtle human unpredictability which sets us apart from machines. I have known conferences between dancers and conductors where the arbiter was a metronome and/or a stop watch. Agreements have been made. Notations on scores carefully written: such and such a number equals such and such a note. Come the performance and all this is as if nothing had been arbitrated, agreed, notated and rehearsed to the point of mutual exhaustion.[8]

2. The need for patience and objectivity

Some pianists may feel that all those tempo issues are just too trying. Well, there are matters which can demand far more patience and tolerance – reinforced by a cool head. In fact, it often seems that a rehearsal pianist needs the patience of a Stoic and the tolerance of a saint. There have been times, for instance, when, tired and frazzled, I thought that the choreographer and dancers (and I) could not *possibly* repeat a phrase or section one more time without going berserk. Yet one, two, three more times I heard, 'We'll just try that bit again . . .' And patience is tested in another way. Not only do you face the problem of fluctuations in tempo, you also have the other extreme of having to imitate a phonograph record with some choreographers. You *are* expected to play the same phrase over and over like a machine even though this is against the normal impulses of the musician. Lanchberry comments upon this double-edged sword: 'The pianist has to play the same few bars of music, often an incomplete phrase, over and over again with the same inflections – or deliberately different ones to suit the requirements of a different dancer sharing a role; he must try at the same time to keep faith with the composer and his original intentions . . .'⁹

The need for tolerance arises when faced with the desecrations – real or fancied – committed by choreographers. They are not all equally respectful of their scores, and some have done very odd things indeed (at least from the musician's point of view). Balanchine, for instance, cut every other two bars of a section in the Finale of Tchaikovsky's *Serenade for Strings*, and Tudor combined Prokofiev's *Classical Symphony* and part of his Third Piano Concerto in *Gala Performance*.

Whether this sort of thing is wicked or not these choreographers are skilled and experienced. Others, especially novices, cut and paste for pure expediency, to avoid inconvenient tests of their talent. One choreographer, for whom I played, sacrificed the middle of the slow movement of Debussy's String Quartet to the corresponding section of the Ravel Quartet. He did this because he just could not be bothered to solve the movement problems posed by Debussy's music at that point, but 'loved' the rest of the work.

Be this as it may, the rehearsal pianist is there to play (what remains of) the music, not to play avenging angel. And, are these practices all that far from the quaint habits of nineteenth-century performers? A Beethoven symphony might have a Weber aria interpolated between movements and the order of movements was even shifted on occasion. Operas were performed with ballets as *divertissements* between acts, and ballerinas substituted favorite variations from one ballet to another without a qualm. We are very holier-than-thou about such goings-on now, but they happened, and other less-than-perfect practices will continue to occur.

If they are too grotesque, the work or the practice will die, deservedly. But I would hazard that the issue is not one of 'purity' or consistency but rather whether the alteration is made for expressive purposes or not. There seems to me to be a difference in intent between chopping up a phrase which happens to have 'too many' measures or repeats and welding two or more pieces together to some purpose. But it depends mainly on how convincingly it is done and why. I see no all-encompassing answer.

Still, patience and tolerance, not to mention objectivity, are unarguably demanded even at the best of times. The nature of the choreographic art makes this inevitable. Limón referred to a not untypical clash between dancer and pianist. In this anecdote the pianist was his wife, just out of high school, who was thrilled to be playing for a famous dancer but also faced with the problem that the dance and the music did not seem able to end simultaneously. Eventually,

in utter exasperation the dancer stalked to the piano, pointed a trembling finger at the music, and demanded to know why the final chord was not being played. My wife explained that there was no such chord, that she was playing the music as it was on the paper. The dancer, by now very irritated, pointed to a mark on the music and demanded, 'what's that?' 'That's a rest', said my wife. 'Well, play it anyway!' My wife did. She played the rest.[10]

I, for one, believe this story. Tudor did the same thing, although in a witty, not crass manner. He was likewise determined to be supplied with a suspect rest and we rehearsed the ending until he felt he had 'heard' it.

I found, as I played for rehearsals, significant things happening to my attitude. For one, as I began to understand the physical demands on the dancers in their repetitions *ad nauseam*, and the mental ones on the choreographer, preoccupation with my own discomforts diminished and was replaced by awe at their stamina.

Secondly, I became fascinated by the variations in execution by the dancers – deliberate or not – and the subtleties of the alterations and re-thinking of the choreographer. Some of my most valuable knowledge and understanding of choreography and dancing was gained during what could have been merely tests of my endurance.

Thirdly, repetitions of a phrase by the dancers offered me the best possible opportunity to memorize the choreography and to make more detailed notations in the score (I should add that you can also be of service to anyone who is recording the ballet in Labanotation. This is being done more and more, to prevent the elusive art of choreography from disappearing as it has done in so many ballets of the past. Many times I was approached by notators to help clear up certain points – particularly ones regarding just where the movement occurred in conjunction with the music.)

3. Moving from studio to stage

For practical reasons, the bulk of rehearsals will be in a studio, unless the company is in residence at a university, and there are no conflicts with opera or drama departments. As everyone who has worked on a ballet knows, stage rehearsals are quite different from studio ones. Movements and patterns which were effective and dynamic in the studio can nearly vanish on stage, seemingly swallowed up by its visual and physical space. Sections can seem too fussy or they can seem uneventful and simple-minded. The stage is a great exposer. As Morton Gould observes,

Often glaring defects of one sort or another don't show up until the ballet is well into rehearsal in the theater itself. This stage is perilously close to the first performance and is the most likely place for drastic disagreements and changes to occur. Tempos that were satisfactory in the rehearsal room and that are an integral part of the music from the composer's point of view have to be changed to fit either the theatrical requirements or the dancers' needs. There might be drastic cuts or deletions.[11]

Since for economic reasons there are few rehearsals with orchestra, the rehearsal pianist as well as the dancers must absorb any last minute changes. Ideally, there should be close contact between composer and pianist at this time, although it is not always possible.

The time available for all stage rehearsals (often alarmingly short) encompasses many activities. First there is the initial stage rehearsal, with piano, on a set-less though diagrammed stage. As many writers have observed, this rehearsal tends to be depressing and dampening; the coziness and security of the rehearsal studio is exchanged for the echoing stage which, as yet, lacks the magic of sets and costumes (although I find a functional beauty in the stark undecorated expanse and the motley rehearsal togs). A varying number of such rehearsals will follow.

Then, the technical and lighting rehearsal, sometimes with pianist standing by in case she is needed. Next the great (or shattering) day of the first orchestral rehearsal, and it is advisable for the rehearsal pianist to be present since her job is not yet done. Here will usually occur more tempo, and other musical, changes, requiring work in the studio. Then comes the piano dress rehearsal with sets and costumes. Staging, lighting and costume problems, among others, can still arise, and this rehearsal can be trying indeed.

At the final dress rehearsal(s) the pianist bows out and the conductor takes over (although if you are at all interested in the ballet you have worked on all this time, you may wish to be present). This rehearsal is closest to the actual performance for 'if the earlier rehearsals have been properly conducted no adjustments should be needed at this rehearsal. Everything should fit perfectly.'[12]

III. Envoi

These, then, are the aspects of rehearsal which concern the pianist. In some ways, rehearsing is more difficult than playing for class; in others it is easier. Most accompanists seem to have a strong preference for one or the other. I know three (excellent) rehearsal pianists who absolutely refuse to play for class, and many class pianists I have known disliked the idea of rehearsal work intensely, even if they had never tried it. Perhaps the necessary temperament for each is different. One could say that the rehearsal pianist needs to be more patient and willing to be directed, and the class pianist more inventive and enterprising.

I have been asked many times which I preferred. This is, to me, an unanswerable question, somewhat resembling those as to which is more important – music or movement, choreographer or dancer, form or content. Daily class and rehearsal are two parts of a process and are, for me, mutually enhancing. Ballet in the theater, whether in rehearsal or performance, would not have meant as much to me if I had not seen and worked in the unglamorous atmosphere of the daily ballet class. On the other hand, I could never have fully appreciated the function and beauty of the daily exercises if I had not been a part of their flowering within choreography with the opportunity to observe closely its mechanics and artistry.

Above all, however, there is the incomparable experience of a sustained group effort, continuing from class to rehearsal. The experiences within the technique class have their unique value, and so do the trials during the course of rehearsals – and the challenge, anticipation, comradeship, elation and apprehension. And these are experienced by everyone who is involved in the production.

The contrast to me between these shared moments and my experiences as a solo performer is so extreme as to be almost laughable. I realize that many musicians would consider my view equally laughable. But I do maintain that it will profit any performer to broaden her perspective by working with others (by which I do *not* mean the performing of a piano concerto with orchestra). Even if ballet rehearsals and class work are only an adjunct to a solo career they can still be of value, possibly affecting your work as a soloist.

The shared experience of class and rehearsal has its rewards, practical and otherwise, for the pianist. But, as Peggy van Praagh says, no ballet is ever complete until it meets its audience, and there I find yet more rewards. When I am a member of an audience, I react to a ballet in company with others and, at the same time, I evaluate and appreciate what I am seeing in a different way than if I had not worked with dancers. Not that I 'know' things which the bulk of the audience may not, but that I experience the performance in a different, less separate way than the average non-professional viewer because of my *own* participation in this activity that I am watching.

Most spectators or audiences are not so lucky. Our society has contrived increasingly since the seventeenth century to create two contrasted groups: the doers and the watchers. Both of these suffer. The performer must, for one thing, guard against the isolation which can result from a sense of herself as different from and superior to her audience. And the audience is encouraged to become passive, tending towards hero-worship and an illusory sense of activity obtained vicariously through the super-beings they applaud. The view of that remarkable virtuoso, Glenn Gould, was rather atypical of his breed: 'I'm not at all happy with words like "public" and "artist"; I'm not happy with the hierarchical implications of that kind of terminology.'[13] Zuckerkandl devotes an entire chapter to this problem. In it he is greatly concerned over the concept of music as a possession of an elite – a symbol of privilege – and a cause of passivity:

Composing and interpreting are the business of a few experts; all other people are confined to participating in music as mere listeners, as an audience. Music is largely something produced by a small minority for a larger public. This division of functions determines the attitude in which we experience music today: we sit in front of something – a stage, a podium, a record player, a radio set – and wait for the music to come to us. Music always comes to us from the other side, from beyond a boundary; it is given to us and we receive it.[14]

Hindemith, equally disturbed, uses stark statistics:

in former times the broad phalanx of those participating in music consisted predominantly of a vast middle field of amateurs: people who made music their hobby in the form of singing and playing but did not practice it professionally. At their right wing there was a relatively small group of professionals, and at the left, an equally small number of mere listeners . . .

If we assume that the former distribution of listeners, amateurs and professionals was, expressed in percent, about 5, 90, and 5, respectively, we can for our modern times take 95, 1, and 4 as a fair estimate. We cannot think of a musician who would not see in this remarkable change of powers a turn towards shallowness.[15]

(In the thirty years since this was written, things remain much the same. Only through the 'regressive' kinetic and communal ethos of rock, and its profound influence upon some 'serious' musicians, does there seem to lie a partial access to what we have lost.)

The same is true of dance, although less decisively. At least the untrained can easily find outlets in folk-dancing and the pop scene. And while the dazzling, skilled performance of ballet is restricted to an 'elite' few, because bodies and movement are integral to our daily, mundane round we are linked to what Stevens refers to as 'the way of life of dancers, and their work, the nature of their art, their world within our world and integral to our world and lives', in ways denied us with professional, virtuoso musicians, for 'we are all dancers . . . The impulse to dance comes naturally, spontaneously, instinctively, from the state of being alive'.[16]

There are always, of course, those miraculous music and dance performances during which the schism is bridged between the performer or ensemble and the audience, which unites not only the two opposing sides but the members of each side in a shared wonder. This bridging by no means depends on the usual trappings; I have felt it happen in an unglamorous hall, a loft or in a park, where not a celebrity is to be seen. What produces this is difficult to say, but when it occurs there is no mistaking it for the circusy uproar which greets a 'star' performance. And when the barrier between performer and audience is thus dissolved, both have returned briefly to the roots, when dance and music were, together, an integrated part of everyday life and there were no ticket-buying spectators and highly paid stars, but only participants.

Is there any chance at all of our somehow regaining that lost essentiality? The structure of our society makes it seem impossible that music and dance can once again become part of daily life and taken for granted as such. We have replaced general, integrated activity with 'products' which involve the chain of creator–performer–purchaser. As I said earlier, much may have been gained by this, but much, possibly of more crucial significance, has been lost. John Blacking, who believes that *everyone* is musical, writes

. . . technological development brings about a degree of social exclusion: being a passive audience is the price that some must pay for membership in a superior society whose superiority is sustained by the exceptional ability of a chosen few. The technical level of what is defined as musicality is therefore raised, and some people must be branded as unmusical. It is on such assumptions that musical ability is fostered or anesthetized in many modern industrial societies.[17]

(And I am sure he would apply this equally to dance.)

This handicaps audiences in at least partially breaking down the barrier between themselves and the performers. I believe that those members of an audience who dance or make music, however 'amateurishly', are far better able to penetrate the surface skill of a professional performance and experience it as participants. It is the difference between alienated awe and appreciation based on shared activity, no matter how modest theirs may be in comparison.

Those who only listen or watch are cheated, deprived through intimidation and the obsession with superior talent and perfect technique of the rewards and insight gained by performing themselves. To listen to even the finest performance can never equal the meaning and satisfaction of making music oneself, with others; to watch even the most spectacular dancing cannot produce the excitement and potency of moving one's body as part of a group of untrained but enthusiastic dancers.

To perform brings us a step closer to the experiencing of dance or music as what Mellers called a 'necessity'. And despite the domination of the professional in today's culture, a surprisingly large number of amateurs are challenging the separatist, elite esthetic. They cannot, by themselves, reverse something which has been centuries in the making, but they *can* counteract it to some degree, and perhaps even alter our concepts of 'performance'. Some take the step by playing four-hand music, others in joining madrigal or recorder groups. Dentists form string quartets and doctors create their own orchestras. The local military band has to turn away applicants, and other enthusiasts join small experimental music–dance–drama groups.

Perhaps the most striking reaction of all is to be seen in the thousands of young or not-so-young, often untrained, musicians who, during the past two decades, have formed small groups in the wake of the pop explosion, playing at home, or in cafés and pubs throughout America, Britain and elsewhere for beer or a bit of cash. Many, of course, are bewitched by a vision of success (or just employment, nowadays). But others, such as Jim Lias's M6 Breakdown Band, in Lancashire, play for the sheer joy of it – like Jim, Dave, Pauline and Colin, rehearsing enthusiastically, and sustaining through the years their excitement at creating such a world with friends. This music is 'amateur', i.e. created through love. This music dances and sparkles and draws others into its orbit.

We have been considering those who are cheated by the pressures toward passive listening, the non-professionals, and their potential for taking action. What of the trained musicians, aimed towards 'careers', who are also cheated on *their* side of the wall? Here, in some ways, the scene is rather bleak.

One great problem is that of competition, and here the amateur, being relieved of this pressure, has an enormous advantage. He may not achieve notoriety and glory, but, not having to worry about 'failure', he avoids the fate of the countless pianists who fall short of their unrealistic goals and begin to view their entire training (and lives) as pointless and fruitless. I have commented upon this already, but it deserves further attention in this present context. Questioning the preoccupation with skill and competition which prevails today, David Barnett makes some telling observations. After pointing out that the listener tires of mere performing skill, coming to consider it in the same light as the momentary, replaceable novelty of a juggler who is forgotten when the next act appears, with Performer A likewise ousted by Performer B, he continues:

The emphasis on skill created other disadvantages as well. It placed one performer in more direct competition with another – that is, since skill is naturally more widespread than individuality, it created many more competitors than each might otherwise have had. Where competition of this sort is the rule, there will always be a fearful waste of human resources. The young performer practices for many years, makes his presentation, may even enjoy momentary recognition. Then, by the process of elimination, he is relegated to a teaching position for which he is not properly trained and from which, presumably, he will prepare younger students to go through the same cycle. Furthermore, competition on the basis of skill alienates the less skilful from participation in music. Even when concert performance is not the object, they find little attraction in the prospect of overcoming others who are already further along on the same road.[18]

This passage is valuable because of its relevance to the re-directed professional, the 'failed' professional, and the amateur. After tracing the development of the problems facing today's performers, he concludes with a crucial issue:

The question, What is performance? must be asked, as the question What is Art? was asked many times in the past. It is a time for re-examination of basic principles, for redetermination of the relation of the composer, the historian, and the psychologist to performance. This is a time, too, for redefinition of musical talent so that many students who have been alienated from performance can return to it with confidence. Musical ability is surprisingly widespread and, provided that performance is not construed solely as concert performance, it would be utilized to great advantage.[19]

John Blacking pursues a similar line of thought, from the point of view of an ethnomusicologist. He goes a step beyond Barnett to relate the question of performance to an audience and the social situation within which the audience exists:

. . . the functional effectiveness of music seems to be more important to listeners than its surface complexity or simplicity. What is the use of being the greatest pianist in the world, or of writing the cleverest music, if nobody wants to listen to it? . . . Why sing or dance or play at all? Why bother to improve musical technique if the aim of performance is to share a social experience?

The functions of music in society may be the decisive factors promoting or inhibiting latent musical ability, as well as affecting the choice of cultural concepts and materials with which to compose music. We shall not be able to explain the principles of composition and the effects of music until we understand better the relationship between musical and human experience.[20]

While on the same tracks as Blacking, Fletcher is more blunt:

The common association of the word culture with the arts is not only etymologically incorrect; it has also perpetuated the notion that involvement in the arts creates a superior mode of existence. The prejudices that exist over the different facets of our musical scene arise from the cultural interchanges of a multi-racial and socially unequal society, whose various kinds of music have come to serve very different functions, conditioned by very different sensory and cerebral responses.[21]

These writers, and others – who are increasing in number all the time – question fundamentally the elitism which blights our society, the concept of art as an embellishment or a contest of 'globe-trotting virtuosos, who have acquired unprecedented technical skill'.[22] Professional pianists, those for whom music is a living rather than a non-competitive amateur activity, will benefit in many ways from efforts to change the prevailing values. Dim as their situation may seem in comparison to the carefree amateur, there are ways in which the waste of resources mentioned by Barnett can be prevented. These ways all involve, in one form or another, a change in consciousness and purpose – an integration of the amateur-element in its sense, 'love-of', and a growth from insularity to the concept of ensemble. Frustrated musicians can become newly inspired, and can discover a point to all their training by turning their energies to some form of relatedness and interaction. The question is, in what direction? For me, obviously, the first choice is dance, and I know that other musicians who dedicate themselves to it need never feel isolated or pointless again.

Dancers are fortunate in that they work primarily as parts of an ensemble; even soloists function in a relation to the company which is different from that of a solo pianist to her orchestra in a concerto. The dancer's relatedness, it is true, can be harmed by attacks of self-importance which upset the delicate balance of the elements of ballet. But she has a powerful antidote available; she can banish isolationist tendencies through music, both in its relation to her movement and as a bridge between the movement and the audience.

For both dancers and musicians these shifts in orientation will tend to improve skills and to increase artistry – but more, it will place performers in an entirely different relation to their art. The import of this book is not bounded by the title, for it goes beyond the relationship of music and movement to the relationship of both of these to artistic communication and, ultimately, to everyday life.

The world of ballet is certainly no Utopia; the same frailties, frustrations and conflicts exist as do in the world at large. And the integration of musicians and dancers will not in itself solve the problems which tend to separate music and dance from real life, and to degrade 'real life' into various forms of shoddy, sterile or ruinous forms of escapism. It can only be one step towards art as need rather than ornament. But *any* step in this direction is welcome, and greatly to be desired for its potential effect in other areas of our lives. I realized very early that music was an essential in my everyday life, not a commodity or a means towards ends, and also, gradually, that I found it richest when it was related, in diverse ways, to experience beyond 'pure sound' or 'form' – a perception that was accelerated by that deepening involvement with dance which so radically altered my original concept of art and, subsequently, my ideas about every area of life. True, we cannot all make music or dance a career, but we *can* all practice and experience them as arts of necessity, 'all' meaning the amateur too. Reflect upon Gustav Holst's wise jest: 'If a thing is worth doing at all, it is worth doing badly.'

In conclusion I say to the dancer that one person in the audience who is moved, and led to think new thoughts by her performance is worth a thousand who have nothing to do but avidly count off her thirty-two *fouettés*. To the pianist I say that one class or rehearsal played lovingly, which expands the dancers' world surpasses a season of concerts rattled off with detached precision. To both I say enter the other's world: musicians, dance; dancers, make music!

The true goal of all performers might, finally, be said to be the development of just as much skill as is necessary to create good music or dance *with others*, whether the others are musicians, dancers or a stirred and participating audience.

APPENDIX A

The dancer's impediment:
An exercise in imagination for the musician

To become a good performer is a difficult and challenging task, but it is peculiarly, even cruelly, difficult for dancers. While they have much in common with musicians, one inescapable difference makes the dancers' lot formidable to a degree which almost no musician I have known appreciates. No matter how many moments of frustration and seeming ineptitude musicians may suffer, they function within what can only be called luxury when compared with what dancers have to face and surmount. Thus, I ask the musical performer to embark upon the following exercise, bearing in mind her own experience and expectations, while also trying to enter the mind of the dancer.

Picture yourself as a novice, required to learn to produce various patterns that have some semblance of meaning – but with no actual instrument to play upon. Gradually, you laboriously *construct* an instrument *at the same time* as you are struggling to develop a basic technique on this object from which essential mechanisms are still missing. By the time you reach young adulthood, your instrument is nearing completion, and your technique and artistry become increasingly expert as parts are added. You will meanwhile have endured painful moments – even accidents – because of 'mechanical' gaps. For, rather than being securely *seated at* an instrument, you will have been *propelling* one (your own body) to and fro, up and down, in often risky conjunction with other instruments (and this adds the element of chronic potential embarrassment: your training consists not of a private lesson and practice in a secluded haven, but within daily communal classes, your scantily clad body and its awkwardness and mistakes subject to continual scrutiny by teacher and fellow-students).

Now, if you have luckily escaped serious physical injury during the years of struggle and various hazards, you are (hopefully) ready to enter the arena. (There remain, of course, ineradicable faults in the instrument itself, since no human body is perfectible to the degree of a piano. And bear in mind that, no matter how great your professional achievement, you will continue to take that daily, revealing class – like the merest neophyte).

Then, as you become more mature, gaining increasing insight and nuance, you find to your dismay that this arduously constructed instrument is already beginning to deteriorate and become ever less responsive to your esthetic demands. Of course, you always knew that yours would be a very short-lived career, and the years of that ideal equipoise between prime physical excellence and sensitive artistry are few indeed. By the age of, say, thirty-five, with your artistic potential far from realized, you have usually passed your physical crest, with your aging instrument increasingly sabotaging your interpretive vision. You become acutely aware of fresh young talents, with their strong instruments in prime condition. Some artists for a time surmount this through illusions created by experience and inspiration – but the end eventually comes to all. A piano is replaceable; a body is not.

Thus, at a time when you should reasonably be able to consider yourself at the mere mid-point of your career, and you see musical performers continuing into even late old age, you must retire, reflecting perhaps on Makarova's poignant words on the dancer's instrument: 'We wear it out to our last ounce of strength. And our masochistic labor is wiped away like marks in the sand, and years of grinding effort – all of that single combat with the body at rehearsal and in performance – pass away into nothing, as if they had never been.'* Not, of course, for the audiences that will always remember the beauty created by the 'grinding effort', but certainly for the dancers, whose chance to develop and mature is so prematurely curtailed. Their relentless daily round, with its immense physical and mental demands, had to be endured, however, no matter how exhausted the body or depressed the spirit. Thus, as A.V. Coton observed in a different context, 'dancers "live" dancing as no . . . singer (or other musician, for that matter) ever lived his performing material'.†

The dancers' so-brief achievement, their years of rigorous training and time-haunted heyday, surely must evoke in us a unique response – and respect.

I recommend that any musician who remains sceptical about my argument attend a beginner's ballet class regularly for at least three months. He may find both an unexpected sympathy and some of the intermittent exhilaration that results from the occasional transcendence of the body's frailties and enables the dancer to persist with her 'single combat' in the most comprehensively demanding of all forms of artistic endeavor.

---

* Natalia Makarova, *A Dance Autobiography*, introduced and edited by Gennady Smakov, Adam and Charles Black, London, 1980, p. 165.
† A.V. Coton, *Writings on Dance, 1938–68*, Dance Books, London, 1975, p. 25.

APPENDIX B

Books particularly recommended

Almost all of the books listed in the references are well worth reading, but I wish to focus attention on certain of these, plus others not quoted from. These are books which I feel provide valuable additional information, illuminate or challenge my basic arguments, or encourage us to relate music and dance more significantly to society and 'culture' – in addition to being simply outstanding. For reasons which should be clear from my text, I did not make segregated lists for musicians, dancers and general audiences. Also, the three categories of books are somewhat arbitrary, being used mainly to avoid an undifferentiated, perhaps confusing grab-bag of titles, and also to provide gentle nudges in certain directions for those who may have in the past been unimpelled to investigate unfamiliar 'fields', or even unusual aspects of their own. Of this select list, a few still demand special emphasis, and these are identified by (†).

1. General background; historical

Amberg, George, *Ballet in America*. Duell, Sloane & Pearce, New York, 1948

Brinson, Peter and Crisp, Clement, *Ballet and Dance: A Guide to the Repertory*. David & Charles, Newton Abbot, 1980

Clarke, Mary and Crisp, Clement, *The History of Dance*. Orbis, London, 1981
 Making a Ballet. Studio Vista, London, 1974

† Hall, Fernau, *An Anatomy of Ballet*. Andrew Melrose, London, 1953

Harman, Alec and Mellers, Wilfrid, *Man and His Music*. O.U.P., New York, 1962

Lawrence, Robert, *The Victor Book of Ballets and Ballet Music*. Simon and Schuster, New York, 1950

Machlis, Joseph, *The Enjoyment of Music*. W.W. Norton, New York, 1970

† Sachs, Curt, *The Commonwealth of Art*. W.W. Norton, New York, 1946
 World History of the Dance W.W. Norton, New York, 1957

Searle, *Ballet Music*. Dover, New York, 1973

Siegel, Marcia B., *The Shapes of Change: Images of American Dance*. Avon Discus Books, New York, 1981

2. Esthetic; technical

† Austin, Richard, *Images of the Dance*. Vision Press, London, 1975

Barnett, David *The Performance of Music*. Barrie & Jenkins, London, 1972

† Cooke, Deryck, *The Language of Music*. O.U.P., London, 1959

Cooper, Peter, *Style in Piano Playing*. John Calder, London, 1976

Copland, Aaron, *Music and Imagination*. New American Library, New York, 1952

† *What to Listen for in Music*. Mentor, New York, 1964

de Mille, Agnes, *To a Young Dancer*. Atlantic–Little, Brown, Boston, Toronto, 1962

350

† Denby, Edwin, *Looking at the Dance*. Pellegrini & Cudahy, New York, 1949

Herrigel, Eugen, *Zen in the Art of Archery* (in *Zen*). McGraw-Hill, New York, 1964

† Hindemith, *A Composer's World*. Anchor Books, Garden City, New York, 1961

Lawson, Joan, *Classical Ballet*. Macmillan, New York, 1960

Makarova, Natalia, *A Dance Autobiography*. (introduced and edited by Gennady Smakov). Adam & Charles Black, London, 1980

Mellers, Wilfrid, *Twilight of the Gods: The Beatles in Retrospect*. Faber & Faber, London, 1976

Monahan, James, *The Nature of Ballet*. Pitman, London, 1976

† Persichetti, Vincent, *Twentieth-Century Harmony*. W.W. Norton, New York, 1961

Seymour, Lynn, with Gardner, Paul, *Lynn: the Autobiography of Lynn Seymour*. Granada, London, 1984

† Stokes, Adrian, *Tonight the Ballet*. Faber & Faber, London, 1947

van Praagh, Peggy and Brinson, Peter, *The Choreographic Art*. Alfred A. Knopf, New York, 1963

Whiteside, Abby, *Indispensables of Piano Playing*. Coleman-Ross, New York, 1961

Zuckerkandl, Victor, *Man the Musician*. Princeton University Press, Princeton, 1973
Sound and Symbol. Pantheon, New York, 1956

3. Social; cultural

† Blacking, John, *How Musical Is Man?* University of Washington Press, Seattle and London, 1973

Cole, Hugo, *The Changing Face of Music*. Victor Gollancz, London, 1978

Dewey, John, *Art as Experience*. Capricorn Books, New York, 1958

Finkelstein, Sidney, *How Music Expresses Ideas*. Lawrence & Wishart, London, 1952

Fischer, Ernst, *The Necessity of Art: A Marxist Approach*. Penguin Books, Harmondsworth, Middlesex, 1963

† Fletcher, Peter, *Roll Over Rock*. Stainer & Bell, London, 1981

May, Rollo, *The Courage to Create*. Bantam Books, New York, 1976

Mellers, Wilfrid, *Caliban Reborn: Renewal in Twentieth-Century Music*. Victor Gollancz, London, 1968

Meyer, Leonard B, *Music, the Arts and Ideas: Patterns and Predictions in 20th-century Culture*. University of Chicago Press, Chicago and London, 1967

† Pichaske, David, *A Generation in Motion: Popular Music and Culture in the Sixties*, Schirmer Books, New York, 1979

† Watts, Alan, *The Wisdom of Insecurity*. Vintage Books, New York, 1951

Whone, Herbert, *The Hidden Face of Music*, Victor Gollancz, London, 1974

References

Preface

1. Hugo Cole, *The Changing Face of Music*, Victor Gollancz, London, 1978, p. 22.
2. *ibid.*, p. 110.
3. *ibid.*, p. 118.
4. *ibid.*, p. 10.
5. *ibid.*, p. 40.
6. In 'Baryshnikov – The Dancer and the Dance', shown on British ITV, December 23, 1983.
7. Christopher Booker, *The Neophiliacs*, Gambit, Boston, 1970, p. 359.
8. George Steiner, 'The Necessity of Music' in *The Listener*, September 19, 1974.
9. See his fascinating discussion of how this 'gives rebirth not only of feeling but of perception', in *Tonight the Ballet*, Faber and Faber, London, 1947, p. 13.

1. Introduction

1. Ruth Page, in *The Dance Has Many Faces*, ed. Walter Sorell, World Publishing Co., Cleveland and New York, 1951, p. 224.
2. George Balanchine, interview in Arnold Haskell, *Balletomania*, Simon and Schuster, New York, 1934.
3. Igor Stravinsky, quoted in John Gillespie, *The Musical Experience*, Wadsworth Publishing Co., Belmont, California, 1968, p. 356.
4. Selma Jeanne Cohen, in *Dance Perspectives*, No. 18, Brooklyn, New York, 1963, p. 86. See also, for relevant comments, James Monahan's article in *The Listener*, November 18, 1965, and his *The Nature of Ballet*, Pitman Publishing, London, 1976, p. 41 and Richard Austin, *Images of the Dance*, Vision Press, London, 1975, pp. 36, 66, 68, 70, 112, 124, and his *The Ballerina*, Vision Press, London, 1974 pp. 79–81.

2. The relationship of movement and music

1. Prince Peter Lieven, *The Birth of Ballets-Russes*, transl. L. Zarine, Allen and Unwin, London, 1956, p. 22.
2. *ibid.*, p. 131.
3. George Borodin, *The Charm of Ballet*, Herbert Jenkins, London, 1955, pp. 82–3.
4. Peggy van Praagh and Peter Brinson, *The Choreographic Art*, Knopf, New York, 1963, p. 149.
5. Curt Sachs, *World History of the Dance*, W.W. Norton, New York, 1937, p. 443.
6. *ibid.*, p. 175.
7. *ibid.*, p. 183.
8. John Dewey, *Art as Experience*, Capricorn Books, New York, 1958, p. 236.
9. *ibid.*, p. 237.

References 353

10. Craig Stark, in *Stereo Review*, September 1969.
11. Victor Zuckerkandl, *Sound and Symbol*, Pantheon (Bollingen Series), New York, 1956, p. 3.
12. *ibid.*, p. 4.
13. Victor Zuckerkandl, *Man the Musician*, Princeton University Press (Bollingen Series), New Jersey, 1973, p. 156.
14. Zuckerkandl, *ibid.*, p. 157.
15. Audrey Williamson, *Contemporary Ballet*, Rockcliff, London, 1947, p. 3.
16. Sachs, *Dance*, p. 443.
17. Williamson, *Contemporary Ballet*, p. 7.
18. *ibid.*
19. August Bournonville, in Foreword to *Études Chorégraphiques*, trans. Erik Bruhn and Lillian Moore, A. and C. Black, London, 1961.
20. Edwin Denby, *Looking at the Dance*, Pellegrini and Cudahy, New York, 1949, p. 249.
21. Arthur Jacobs, *A New Dictionary of Music*, Penguin, Harmondsworth, Middlesex, 1961.
22. Suzanne Langer, *Philosophy in a New Key*, Mentor, New York, 1964, p. 185.
23. Quoted disparagingly in Suzanne Langer, *Feeling and Form*, Charles Scribner's Sons, New York, 1953, pp. 198 and 169.
24. Lieven, *Ballet-Russes*, p. 71.
25. Adrian Stokes, *Tonight the Ballet*, Faber and Faber, London, 1947, p. 15.
26. Langer, *Feeling and Form*, p. 169.
27. *ibid.*, pp. 174, 175.
28. *ibid.*, p. 174.
29. *ibid.*, p. 180.
30. *ibid.*, pp. 180–1.
31. See discussion, *ibid.*, p. 177.
32. *ibid.*, p. 195.
33. *ibid.*, p. 203.
34. *ibid.*, p. 201.
35. *ibid.*, pp. 199–200.
36. Fernau Hall, *Modern English Ballet*, Andrew Melrose, London, 1951, pp. 89 and 199.
37. Stokes, *Tonight the Ballet*, p. 17.
38. Katherine Sorley Walker, *Dance and its Creators*, John Day, New York, 1972, p. 133.
39. Joseph Gregor, in *The Dance Has Many Faces*, ed Walter Sorell, World Publishing Co., Cleveland and New York, 1951, p. 138.
40. Siegmund Levarie and Ernst Levy, *Tone: A Study In Musical Acoustics*, Kent State University Press, 1968, p. 163.
41. *ibid.*, see discussion pp. 72–3.
42. Hall, *Modern English Ballet*, p. 211.
43. Denby, *Looking at the Dance*, pp. 45–6.
44. *ibid.*, p. 21.
45. Walter Sorell, in *The Dance Has Many Faces*, p. 122.
46. Stokes, *Tonight the Ballet*, p. 50.
47. Lucia Chase, quoted in *Dance Perspectives*, No. 18, Brooklyn, NY, p. 73.
48. Margaret Black, quoted in *Dance Perspectives*, No. 18, p. 76.
49. Sara Leland, quoted in *Dance Perspectives*, No. 55, p. 38.
50. Selma Jeanne Cohen, in *Dance Perspectives*, No. 18, p. 86.
51. Concise Oxford Dictionary (Fourth Edition), London.
52. *ibid.*
53. Richard Wagner, quoted in Langer, *Philosophy in a New Key*, p. 188.
54. Hans Mersmann, quoted in *ibid.*, p. 206.
55. *ibid.*, p. 206.

56. Hermann Keller, *Phrasing and Articulation*, transl. Leigh Gerdine, W.W. Norton, New York, 1965, p. 9.
57. Arnold Haskell, *Prelude to Ballet*, Thomas Nelson and Sons, London, 1947, p. 93.
58. *ibid.*
59. *ibid.*, p. 94.
60. Stokes, *Tonight the Ballet*, pp. 71–2.
61. *ibid.*, p. 68.
62. Arnold Haskell, *Ballet*, Pelican Books, Harmondsworth, Middlesex, 1938, pp. 41–2.
63. Joan Lawson, *Classical Ballet*, Macmillan, New York, 1960, p. 158.
64. *ibid.*, p. 158.
65. van Praagh and Brinson, *Choreographic Art*, p. 56.
66. Agnes de Mille, *To a Young Dancer*, Little, Brown and Co., Boston–Toronto, 1962, p. 31.
67. William Chappell, *Fonteyn: Impressions of a Ballerina*, Macmillan, New York, 1951, p. 52.
68. E.W. Wodson, in *Evening Telegram*, January 24, 1933.
69. Richard Austin, *Images of the Dance*, Vision Press, London, 1975, p. 77.
70. *ibid.*, p. 159.
71. James Monahan, *The Nature of Ballet*, Pitman Publishing, London, 1976, p. 82.
72. Richard Austin, *Lynn Seymour*, Angus and Robertson, London, 1980, p. 81.
73. Serge Eisenstein, *Film Form*, World, Cleveland and New York, 1965, pp. 21–2.
74. *ibid.*, p. 20.
75. Monk Gibbon, *An Intruder At the Ballet*, Phoenix House, London, 1962, p. 36.
76. *ibid.*, p. 108.
77. Austin, *Images of the Dance*, p. 81.
78. Antony Tudor, in letter to author; 8 April 1975.

3. Ballet music

1. Peggy van Praagh and Peter Brinson, *The Choreographic Art*, Knopf, New York, 1963, p. 40.
2. Ernst Fischer, *The Necessity of Art*, Penguin Books, Harmondsworth, Middlesex, 1970, p. 49.
3. van Praagh and Brinson, *Choreographic Art*, p. 38.
4. Fernau Hall, *An Anatomy of Ballet*, Andrew Melrose, London, 1953, p. 37.
5. Joan Lawson, *Classical Ballet*, Macmillan, New York, 1960, p. 100.
6. Antony Hopkins, in *Ballet Decade*, ed. Arnold Haskell, Adam and Charles Black, London, 1956, pp. 101–2.
7. Norman Lloyd, in *Dance Perspectives*, No. 16, Brooklyn, NY, p. 50.
8. Constant Lambert, in *Footnotes to the Ballet*, ed. Caryl Brahms, Peter Davies, London, 1947, p. 168.
9. *ibid.*, p. 167.
10. Quoted in Humphrey Searle, *Ballet Music*, Dover, New York, 1973, p. 79.
11. Paul Henry Lang, *Music in Western Civilization*, Norton, New York, 1941, see discussion, pp. 605–6.
12. Lucia Dlugoszewski, in *Dance Perspectives*, No. 16, pp. 23–4. (The German tradition is less strong in American music today than when this was written.)
13. Norman Lloyd criticizes this conclusion in his contribution to *Dance Perspectives*, No. 16, but it is dismaying to see the number of people who feel that a symphony or string quartet is automatically 'superior' to a song, a suite or a tone-poem – even when they greatly prefer listening to anything *but* a symphony or string quartet.
14. Fernau Hall, *Modern English Ballet*, Andrew Melrose, London, 1951, p. 199.
15. Edwin Denby, *Dancers, Buildings and People in the Streets*, Horizon Press, New York, 1965, p. 53.

References   355

16. Deryck Cooke, *The Language of Music*, Oxford University Press, London, 1959, pp. 7–8.
17. Lambert, in *Footnotes to the Ballet*, pp. 168–9.
18. Cooke, *Language of Music*, p. 202.
19. See Peter Fletcher's enlightening comments on Mussorgsky and traditional precepts, *Roll Over Rock*, Stainer and Bell, London, 1981, pp. 41–3.
20. Cooke, *Language of Music*, pp. 8–9.
21. Lambert, in *Footnotes to the Ballet*, p. 166.
22. van Praagh and Brinson, *Choreographic Art*, pp. 132–6.
23. *ibid.*, p. 133.
24. *ibid.*, p. 134.
25. John Martin, *Introduction to the Dance* (1939), Dance Horizons, Brooklyn, NY (reprinted 1965) pp. 67–8.
26. van Praagh and Brinson, *Choreographic Art*, p. 154.

4. The accompanist

1. Agnes de Mille, *To a Young Dancer*, Little, Brown and Co., Boston–Toronto, 1962, p. 22.
2. Paul Hindemith, *A Composer's World*, Doubleday and Co., Anchor Books, New York, 1952, p. 204.
3. Peter Cooper, *Style in Piano Playing*, John Calder, London, 1976, p. 152.

5. Teachers and Schools

1. Jane Robbins, *Ballet Studio – An Inside View*, Urc Smith, Australia, 1978, p. 109.
2. Oleg Kerensky, *The Guinness Guide to Ballet*, London, 1981, p. 217.
3. Described in Prince Peter Lieven, *The Birth of Ballets-Russes*, George Allen and Unwin, London, 1956, p. 91.
4. Muriel Bentley, quoted in *Dance Perspectives*, No. 18, Brooklyn, NY, p. 60.

6. Selection of music (1)

1. Deryck Cooke, *The Language of Music*, Oxford University Press, London, 1959, pp. 179–80.
2. George A. Wedge, *Rhythm In Music*, G. Schirmer, New York 1927, p. 4.
3. George Balanchine, in *New York Post* interview, August 21, 1971.
4. *The Oxford Companion to Music*, 7th edn, London, p. 795.
5. Grosvenor Cooper and Leonard B. Meyer, *The Rhythmic Structure of Music*, University of Chicago Press, 1960, p. 6.
6. Suzanne Langer, *Philosophy In a New Key*, Mentor, New York, 1964, p. 196n.
7. Cooper and Meyer, *Rhythmic Structure*, p. 1.
8. Ludwig Klages, quoted in Victor Zuckerkandl, *Sound and Symbol*, Pantheon (Bollingen Series), New York, 1956, pp. 169–70.
9. Cooper and Meyer, *Rhythmic Structure*, p. 7.
10. Victor Zuckerkandl, *Sound and Symbol*, Pantheon (Bollingen Series), New York, 1956, p. 159.
11. *ibid.*, p. 170.
12. *ibid.*, p. 160.
13. Leonard B. Meyer, *Emotion and Meaning in Music*, Phoenix Books, University of Chicago Press, 1956, p. 115.
14. Joan Lawson, *Classical Ballet*, Macmillan, New York, 1960, p. 94.
15. William E. Brandt, *The Way of Music*, Allyn and Bacon, Boston, 1968, p. 12.
16. *ibid.*, p. 11.

17. Lawson, *Classical Ballet*, p. 91.
18. Peggy van Praagh and Peter Brinson, *The Choreographic Art*, Knopf, New York, 1963, pp. 154–5.
19. Lawson, *Classical Ballet*, p. 26.
20. *ibid.*, p. 92.
21. Meyer, *Emotion and Meaning*, p. 6.
22. Edwin Denby, *Looking at the Dance*, Pellegrini and Cudahy, New York, 1949, pp. 248–9.
23. Cooper and Meyer, *Rhythmic Structure*, p. 3.
24. Lawson, *Classical Ballet*, p. 95.
25. Denby, *Looking*, pp. 20–1.
26. *ibid.*, pp. 20–1.

7. Selection of music (2)

1. Arnold Bennett, *Literary Taste*, Penguin Books, Harmondsworth, Middlesex, p. 64.
2. Kay Ambrose, *The Ballet Lover's Companion*, Knopf, New York, 1955, p. 69.

8. Selection of music (3)

1. John Dewey, *Art As Experience*, Capricorn Books, New York, 1958, p. 179.
2. *ibid.*, p. 155.
3. Leonard B. Meyer, *Music, the Arts and Ideas*, University of Chicago Press, Chicago and London, 1967, p. 45.
4. Antony Tudor, quoted in John Gruen, *The Private World of Ballet*, Penguin Books, Harmondsworth, Middlesex, 1976, p. 266.
5. Natalia Makarova, *A Dance Autobiography*, Adam and Charles Black, London, 1980, p. 128.
6. Adrian Stokes, *Tonight the Ballet*, Faber and Faber, London, 1947, p. 100.
7. *ibid.*

9. Performance

1. Peter Cooper, *Style In Piano Playing*, John Calder, London, 1976, pp. 18–19.
2. Harold Taylor, *The Pianist's Talent*, Kahn and Averill, London 1975, p. 75.
3. Jane Robbins, *Classical Dance*, David and Charles, Newton Abbot, 1981, p. 70.
4. Abby Whiteside, *Indispensables of Piano Playing*, Coleman-Ross, New York, 1961, p. 18.
5. Siegmund Levarie and Ernst Levy, *Tone: A Study in Musical Acoustics*, Kent State University Press, 1968, p. 116.
6. *ibid.*, p. 117.
7. Joan Lawson, *Classical Ballet*, MacMillan, New York, 1960, p. 79.
8. Cooper, *Style*, p. 55.
9. Whiteside, *Indispensables*, p. 4.
10. *ibid.*, p. 47.
11. *ibid.*, pp. 47–8.
12. *ibid.*, pp. 4–5.
13. *ibid.*, p. 37.
14. *ibid.*, p. 25.
15. Roger Sessions, *The Musical Experience*, Atheneum, New York, 1950, p. 12.
16. Edwin Denby, *Looking At the Dance*, Pellegrini and Cudahy, New York, 1949, pp. 241–2.
17. William Butler Yeats, 'The Second Coming' from *Collected Poems*, Macmillan, New York, 1951.

18. Kurt Adler, *The Art of Accompanying and Coaching*, University of Minnesota Press, Minneapolis, 1965, pp. 126–7.
19. Whiteside, *Indispensables*, p. 145.
20. Sidney Harrison, *The Young Person's Guide to Playing the Piano*, Faber and Faber, London 1966, p. 54.
21. Whiteside, *Indispensables*, p. 61.
22. Peggy van Praagh and Peter Brinson, *The Choreographic Art*, Knopf, New York, 1963, p. 268.
23. August Bournonville, in *Bournonville's Views On Choreography*, trans. Inge B. Kelly, *Dancing Times*, London, March 1976, p. 305.
24. Edward T. Cone, *Musical Form and Musical Performance*, W.W. Norton, New York, 1968, p. 32.

10. Improvisation (1)

1. Vincent Persichetti, in letter to author.
2. Thurston Dart, *The Interpretation of Music*, Hutchinson University Library, London, 1964, p. 59.
3. Dart, *Interpretation*, p. 59.
4. Herbert Whone, *The Hidden Face of Music*, Victor Gollancz, London, 1974, pp. 119, 120, 29.
5. Dart, *op. cit.*, pp. 62–3.
6. Vincent Persichetti, in letter to author.
7. Abby Whiteside, *Indispensables of Piano Playing*, Coleman-Ross, New York, 1961, pp. 135–6.
8. *ibid.*, p. 135.
9. John Blacking, *How Musical Is Man?* University of Washington Press, Seattle and London, 1973, p. 9.
10. Vincent Persichetti, *Twentieth Century Harmony*, W.W. Norton, New York, 1961, p. 35, p. 189.
11. *ibid.*, pp. 189–90.
12. *ibid.*, p. 190.
13. Blacking, *How Musical Is Man?*, p. 25.
14. *ibid.*, p. 111.
15. Colin Wilson, *Brandy of the Damned*, John Baker, London 1964, p. 82.
16. Eugen Herrigel, *Zen in the Art of Archery*, Pantheon, McGraw Hill, New York, 1960, p. 48.
17. Vincent Persichetti, in letter to author.
18. Herrigel, *Zen*, p. 61.
19. *ibid.*, p. 99.
20. Sallie Wilson, quoted in John Gruen, *The Private World of Ballet*, Penguin Books, Harmondsworth, Middlesex, 197, p. 247.
21. Herrigel, *Zen*, p. 68.
22. Tom Johnson, in the *Village Voice*, January 29, 1979.
23. Michael Walsh, Nancy Newman, in *Time*, September 20, 1982.

11. Improvisation (2)

1. Lewis Mumford, *The Condition of Man*, Secker and Warburg, London, 1944, p. 12.
2. Ned Rorem, 'Why the Beatles are Good', in *The Beatles Book*, ed. Edward E. Davis, Cowles, New York, 1968, p. 5.
3. Jann Wenner, *Lennon Remembers: The Rolling Stone Interviews*, Straight Arrow Books, San Francisco, 1971, p. 103.

4. Lu Emily Pearson, *Elizabethans at Home*, Stanford University Press, 1958, p. 517.
5. Allardyce Nicoll, *The Elizabethans*, Cambridge University Press, 1957, p. 120.
6. David Munrow, Sleeve notes for LP, *Two Renaissance Dance Bands*, EMI.
7. Christopher Ballantine, in *New Society*, November 13, 1969.
8. Wilfred Mellers, *Twilight of the Gods*, Faber and Faber, London, 1973, p. 23.
9. Paul Henry Lang, *Music In Western Civilization*, W.W. Norton, New York, 1941, p. 301.
10. John Blacking, *How Musical Is Man?*, University of Washington Press, Seattle and London, 1973, pp. 32–3.
11. Ernst H. Meyer, in *The New Oxford History of Music*, ed. Gerald Abraham, Oxford and London, 1968, p. 595.
12. Wilfred Mellers, 'New Music In A New World', in *The Age of Rock*, ed. Jonathan Eisen, Random House, New York, 1969, p. 181.
13. Constant Lambert, *Music Ho!*, Penguin, Harmondsworth, Middlesex, 1948, pp. 86–7.
14. Manfred Bukofzer, *Music in the Baroque Era*, W.W. Norton, New York, 1947, p. 41.
15. Mellers, *Twilight*, p. 190.
16. Frank Kofsky, 'The Scene', in *The Age of Rock*, pp. 58–9.
17. Mellers, *Twilight*, p. 184.
18. Mellers, 'New Music in a New World', in *The Age of Rock*, p. 183.
19. Curt Sachs, *World History of the Dance*, W.W. Norton, New York, 1937, p. 359.
20. Mabel Dolmetsch, *Dances of England and France, 1450–1600*, De Capo Press, New York, 1976, p. 36.
21. Jan Steele, in *Melody Maker*, London, 28 August 1976, pp. 24–5.
22. David Barnett, *The Performance of Music*, Barrie and Jenkins, London, 1972, p. 10.
23. Jonathan Eisen, Introduction to *The Age of Rock*, p. xiv.
24. Michael Wale, *Vox Pop*, Harrap, London, 1972, p. 59.
25. See Peter Fletcher, *Roll Over Rock*, Stainer and Bell, London 1981, Chs 5 and 6 and Sidney Finkelstein, *How Music Expresses Ideas*, Lawrence and Wishart, London, 1952, for instructive and disturbing accounts of black music in the United States.
26. Richard Poirer, *The Performing Self*, Oxford University Press, New York, 1971, pp. 122–3.

12. Rehearsal and real life

1. Abby Whiteside, *Indispensables of Piano Playing*, Coleman-Ross, New York, 1961, p. 14.
2. Ralph Vaughan Williams, *National Music and Other Essays*, Oxford University Press, London, 1963, p. 127.
3. Leonard B. Meyer, *Music, the Arts and Ideas*, University of Chicago Press, Chicago and London, 1967, p. 278.
4. Eugen Herrigel, *Zen in the Art of Archery*, Pantheon McGraw Hill, New York, 1960, p. 50.
5. John Lanchberry, 'The Conductor's Work' in *Ballet and Modern Dance*, Octopus Books, London, 1974, p. 140.
6. *ibid.*, pp. 136–7.
7. Verna Arvey, *Choreographic Music*, E.P. Dutton, New York, 1941, p. 416.
8. José Limón, Convocation Address, The Juilliard School, 5 October 1966, 'Dancers Are Musicians Are Dancers', reprinted in Juilliard News Bulletin.
9. Lanchberry, 'Conductor's Work', p. 136.
10. Limón, Convocation Address.
11. Morton Gould, 'Music and the Dance', in *The Dance Has Many Faces* (Walter Sorell, ed.), World Publishing Co., Cleveland and New York, 1951, p. 47.
12. Peggy van Praagh and Peter Brinson, *The Choreographic Art*, Knopf, New York, 1963, p. 260.
13. Glenn Gould, in *Glenn Gould: Variations*, Doubleday, Canada 1983, p. 29.

References
359

14. Victor Zuckerkandl, *Man the Musician*, Princeton University Press, Princeton, NJ, 1973, pp. 10–11.
15. Paul Hindemith, *A Composer's World*, Doubleday Anchor Books, New York, 1961, p. 250.
16. Franklin Stevens, *Dance as Life*, Avon Discus Book, New York, 1977, p. 102.
17. John Blacking, *How Musical Is Man?*, University of Washington Press, Seattle and London, 1973, p. 34.
18. David Barnett, *The Performance of Music*, Barrie and Jenkins, London, 1972, p. 6.
19. *ibid.*, pp. 9–10.
20. John Blacking, *How Musical Is Man?*, p. 35.
21. Peter Fletcher, *Roll Over Rock*, Stainer and Bell, London, 1981, p. 14.
22. *ibid.*, p. 166.

Index

Italic page numbers refer to illustrations.

LISTENING TO THEATRE

LISTENING TO THEATRE

THE AURAL DIMENSION OF BEIJING OPERA

ELIZABETH WICHMANN

UNIVERSITY OF HAWAII PRESS

HONOLULU

© 1991 University of Hawaii Press

All Rights Reserved

Printed in the United States of America

91 93 94 95 96 97   5 4 3 2 1

Library of Congress Cataloging-in-Publication Data

Wichmann, Elizabeth.

Listening to theatre : the aural dimension of Beijing Opera /

Elizabeth Wichmann.

p. cm.

Bibliography: p.

Includes index.

ISBN 0-8248-1221-2

1. Operas, Chinese—Analysis, appreciation. I. Title.

MT95.W49 1989

782.81'0951—dc19   88-38574

CIP

MN

Photographs of instruments by Douglas Peebles

University of Hawaii Press books are printed

on acid-free paper and meet the guidelines

for permanence and durability of the Council

on Library Resources

CONTENTS

ILLUSTRATIONS

MUSICAL EXAMPLES

PHOTOGRAPHS

This book is an introduction to the aural performance of Beijing opera. Its purpose is to describe the major components of aural performance as they are understood by Beijing opera practitioners and connoisseurs. Through this description, I hope to communicate an understanding of how those components are used to create a performance, and of how that performance is appreciated by its audience.

In China, theatre in its broadest conception embraces all types of dramatic stage performance, encompassing story-telling; puppet theatre; mask-drama; dance-drama; song-drama, including the various types of Western opera; song-and-dance drama, including Western musical theatre; spoken-drama, including Western representational and presentational theatre; and traditional Chinese theatre. The term for theatre broadly conceived is *xiju* (lit. "theatre [of] drama"). Traditional Chinese theatre, often called "Chinese opera" or simply "Chinese theatre" in English, is termed *xiqu* (lit. "theatre [of] song").

Xiqu dates from at least as early as the Yuan dynasty (1271–1368). There are more than 360 different forms of *xiqu* currently being staged, and there have been a number of thriving forms since at least the middle of the Ming dynasty (1368–1644). Each of these forms developed in a particular region of China; many therefore have names reflecting their region of origin. Perhaps the most widely known is Beijing (Peking) opera (*jingju,* lit. "capital drama"; also called *jingxi,* lit. "capital theatre," and *guoju,* lit. "national drama"), which developed in the Chinese capital during the Qing dynasty (1644–1911). Beijing opera has been the nationally dominant form of *xiqu* for more than one hundred years.

Although the many forms of *xiqu* differ to varying degrees in their movement, costumes, makeup, and staging, they are fundamentally quite similar in these respects. It is ultimately the aural performance of each form that characterizes it and distinguishes it from all other forms of *xiqu*.

For the purposes of this study, "aural" is defined as "all that is heard," which includes not only the actual sounds produced but also the scripts and music that are presented in performance. Following this definition, there are four major components of aural performance: language, musical system, voice, and orchestra. The intimate relationships in *xiqu* between vocal performance and language, and between the musical system of each form and its vocal and orchestral performance, necessitate this fairly comprehensive definition.

In the first chapter of this book, I introduce fundamental aspects of the total performance of Beijing opera and provide a brief outline of the context in which aural performance occurs. Chapters 2 through 6 constitute the main body of the study. Chapter 2 describes language levels and the language of both song and speech. Chapters 3 and 4 are concerned with the musical system, describing the major musical elements and the composition process respectively. Chapter 5 introduces the basic techniques of vocal production, song, and speech, and chapter 6 presents the instruments of the orchestra and their individual and collective functions. In chapter 7, I analyze the interrelation of these four major components of the aural performance of Beijing opera.

Although many comparisons can be drawn between the aural performance of Beijing opera and that of other forms of *xiqu,* this book focuses upon the aural performance of traditional plays in Beijing opera during the period 1977–1986. Traditional plays were developed by master performers before 1949; they are discussed in chapter 1. In China, the period covered by this study is sometimes known as "post Gang of Four" *(si ren bang zhihou)* and is characterized culturally by the resurgence of traditional arts after the ten-year hiatus of the Cultural Revolution. Most contemporary practitioners of Beijing opera, however, view their art as a continuous tradition extending from at least 1850 to the present, with a break in the performance of traditional and traditional-style plays from 1966 to 1976 caused by the Cultural Revolution. Their descriptions of aural performance and of their own practices are drawn freely from this entire period, and I have adopted that perspective in this study. No attempt is made to compare the aural performance of Beijing opera in the first half of the century with that of the second. Furthermore, such topics as the historical development of Beijing opera, its social milieu, the visual aspects of performance, and the process of training stage performers and musicians are dealt with only sparingly, when they have an important bearing upon actual aural performance. Although the study deals fairly extensively with material of potential interest to literary scholars, ethnomusicologists, vocal scientists, and linguists, it is written from a theatrical, performance-oriented perspective.

In this book I have translated Chinese terms into English whenever possible. Terms that require more than one English word in their translation are hyphenated to identify them as specific, translated terms—for example, the Chinese word *zi* is translated as "written-character." This system of hyphenation also avoids possible confusion; in this example, between characters in a play and the written-characters in the script of that play.

The romanization system used throughout the study is *pinyin,* the official romanization system of the People's Republic of China. In the case of quotations from English-language works that use other romanization systems, I have provided the *pinyin* romanization in brackets within the quotation, following the quoted term.

All musical transcription in this study is in cipheric notation. That system is briefly described in Appendix 1 at the end of this volume.

Because traditional Beijing opera performance practice does not distinguish between male and female performers but only between male and female characters, the terms "performer" and "actor" are used to refer to both male and female stage performers. Performers of musical instruments are referred to as "musicians."

Research for the dissertation on which this book is based was conducted in the People's Republic of China between August 1979 and August 1981. This period of field study was supported by a fellowship from the Committee on Scholarly Communication with the People's Republic of China, an organization under the auspices of the American Council of Learned Societies, the Social Science Research Council, and the National Academy of Sciences, with funding provided by the U.S. Information Agency and the U.S. Department of Education. The dissertation was completed in the Department of Drama and Theatre (now the Department of Theatre and Dance) at the University of Hawaii, and the degree was awarded in 1983. Additional research was undertaken in the summers of 1984, 1985, and 1986. Research was conducted for the most part at two institutions in Nanjing, the capital of Jiangsu Province. The full name for what I call the "Beijing Opera Company" in this study is the Jiangsu Province Beijing Opera Company (Jiangsu Sheng Jingju Yuan). Similarly, the "Theatre School" is the Jiangsu Province School of Xiqu (Jiangsu Sheng Xiqu Xuexiao). In the course of my research at these institutions, I adopted two major roles to gather data: that of the researcher, and that of the student performer.

As a researcher, I attended performances, attended rehearsals and workout sessions *(liangong),* and conducted interviews. During the seven-year period I also viewed a number of films of Beijing opera performances given by master performers in the 1950s and early 1960s.

As a student performer, I participated in workout sessions at both the

Beijing Opera Company and the Theatre School. At the school I also attended lecture classes, took individual lessons in performance from Shen Xiaomei, the youngest student of Mei Lanfang, and participated in several public performances of the play *The Favorite Concubine Becomes Intoxicated (Guifei zui jiu)*.

Without the assistance of a number of institutions and literally hundreds of individuals in both China and the United States, this study would not have been possible. I would like to take this opportunity to thank at least a few of them.

Bob Geyer and Ann Waigand of the Washington office of the Committee on Scholarly Communication with the People's Republic of China were very helpful in solving problems that arose during the initial research period, as was Professor John Jamieson, the academic advisor for fellowship recipients who was stationed at the American Embassy in Beijing throughout my initial tenure in China. I am extremely grateful to all three, and to the Committee itself.

Two organizations in Hawaii, the State Foundation on Culture and the Arts and the University of Hawaii Center for Asian and Pacific Studies (now the School of Hawaiian, Asian, and Pacific Studies), gave me generous grants in support of audiovisual recording. A number of University of Hawaii faculty members provided much-appreciated assistance. Those who served on my dissertation committee, Professors Edward A. Langhans, Roger Long, Lo Chin-t'ang, Stephen Uhalley, and most especially the chair of the committee, James R. Brandon, provided substantial support and guidance in structuring the analysis of data. Professors Barbara Smith, Annette Johansson, and Iovanna Condax were of great help in readying considerable portions of data for presentation, lending the perspectives of the ethnomusicologist, vocal scientist, and linguist, respectively. And Professor Daniel W. Y. Kwok was leonine in his support of this study from its initial conception through its final stages. Through correspondence and during the later summer research periods, Professor Hu Dongsheng of the Beijing Institute of Xiqu Research provided invaluable assistance in revising and editing the manuscript for publication.

The Chinese Ministry of Education and the Jiangsu Departments of Higher Education and Culture arranged my affiliation with the Beijing Opera Company and the Theatre School, making long-term, daily access to these two crucial institutions possible. I am also especially grateful to Nanjing University for assisting in making those arrangements. In particular, University President Kuang Yaming and Professor Xu Manhua devoted much time and effort to my project. I am also very thankful to Professor Xu for patiently helping me cope with the plethora of theatrical terminology, not defined in dictionaries, that confronted me at the outset of my field study.

My greatest debt of gratitude goes to the administrators, theatre practitioners, and students at the Jiangsu Province Beijing Opera Company and the Jiangsu Province School of Xiqu. They made me welcome and helped me to understand the aesthetics and techniques of their art.

Fang Jinsen, Tan Muping, Wang Xiurong, and Zhao Yuan, chief administrators at the Beijing Opera Company, went out of their way to assist my research activities. Ma Jian and Ying Yicheng of the Theatre School opened all facets of their education and training programs to me and were always available for assistance and guidance.

Because it is not possible to thank individually all the performers, musicians, directors, and playwrights of the Beijing Opera Company who shared with me their knowledge and expertise, I can only express to them as a group my sincere gratitude. I would, however, like especially to thank the following people, each of whom devoted literally hundreds of hours to demonstrating and discussing their art with me: Gong Suping, Huang Kailiang, Liu Debao, Liu Zhixiang, Lu Genzhang, Sha Yu, Wu Xingyue, Xu Meiyun, Ye Hexiang, and Zhu Ya.

Several instructors at the Theatre School were also particularly helpful, supplementing course materials and standard training procedures for the benefit of one who lacked the cultural background of the pre-professional students. I extend my heartfelt thanks to Bian Shuangxi, Hu Zhongwu, Liu Jingjie, Xu Xiaotao, Xu Yifang, Yang Shengming, and Yang Yimei.

Shen Xiaowei and Zhou Liping, senior students at the Theatre School, generously consented to perform with me in the presentations of *The Favorite Concubine Becomes Intoxicated;* without their expertise, those performances would not have been possible for this novice. I would also like to thank Zhou Lixia, who shared with me her "private" classes in the performance of specific plays and spent many hours describing for me her own experiences as a pre-professional student of Beijing opera performance.

Finally, I would like to express my gratitude to my two principal teachers, Wu Junda of the Theatre School and Shen Xiaomei of the Beijing Opera Company. Wu Junda met with me weekly throughout my second year in China and almost daily during my subsequent research trips, sharing with me his essays on the music of Beijing opera and often preparing lengthy, detailed lectures on specific questions that I had raised. Shen Xiaomei made

me a part of her family and professional life, introduced me to major performers and musicians all over China, taught me basic techniques of vocal
production, song, and speech, and trained me to perform her teacher Mei
Lanfang's play *The Favorite Concubine Becomes Intoxicated*. She enter-
tained and sought answers to all the questions that I posed and devoted
much time to devising training techniques that would help make Beijing
opera art accessible to a cultural outsider.

I owe Wu Junda and Shen Xiaomei a debt of gratitude for information,
insights, and personal concern that far exceeds the scope of the materials
presented in this study of the aural performance of Beijing opera. As I thank
them, I wish to apologize to them for the errors of fact and interpretation
that are surely present in this study. Such shortcomings are my own, and
have occurred in spite of their tireless efforts to prevent them.

CHAPTER I

BEIJING OPERA PLAYS
AND PERFORMANCE

THE aural dimension of Beijing opera is so fundamentally important to the identity of this theatrical form that attending a Beijing opera performance is traditionally referred to as "listening to theatre" *(tingxi),* and acting in a play is termed "singing theatre" *(changxi).* But when Beijing opera singers apply stylized makeup, dress in elaborate costumes, and go onstage to "sing theatre," they actually do much more than sing and speak. Beijing opera singers are in fact consummate performers who act, sing, speak, dance, and often perform acrobatics as well. A general understanding of the aesthetics that apply to the total performance of Beijing opera, and of the plays that provide the characters, plots, and overall performance structure, is therefore a prerequisite to the discussion of aural performance.

THE TOTAL PERFORMANCE OF BEIJING OPERA

The total performance of Beijing opera presents a kaleidoscopic array of theatrical elements—story, music, voice, movement, makeup, costume, and stage properties. The presence of these numerous elements justifies calling Beijing opera "total theatre," according to E. T. Kirby's general definition of the term: "Theatre as the place of intersection of all the arts is . . . the meaning of 'total theatre.' We most often find this totality indicated by a list of components such as music, movement, voice, scenery, lighting, etc." Kirby, however, goes on to establish a more specific criterion for "total theatre":

> More important . . . is the understanding that there must be an effective interplay among the various elements, or a significant synthesis of them. Totality may, in this sense, be more or less extensive, including a greater or lesser number of aspects, but it must always be intensive, effecting an integration of the components. While totality as an ideal is extensive and all-inclusive, it is this relationship between elements, rather than an accumulation of means, which actually distinguishes the form.[1]

I

By this more specific standard, Beijing opera not only qualifies as "total theatre" but in fact exemplifies the concept. Its performance elements are bound together—are almost organically related to one another—by the fundamental aesthetics of traditional Beijing opera performance: the aesthetic aim, the basic aesthetic principles, and the role types of its dramatic characters. Beijing opera performers refer to the importance of these fundamental aesthetics by saying that they make Beijing opera a complete, integrated art *(wanzheng yishu)*, possessed of "a complete set of things" *(yitao dongxi)*— that is, a complete set of performance elements and techniques.

AESTHETIC AIM

In the performance of traditional Beijing opera, the stage is perceived as a platform upon which to display the performers' four skills *(gong):* song *(chang);* speech *(nian);* dance-acting *(zuo),* which includes pure dance, pantomime, and all the visible, physical results of "acting" in the Western sense; and combat *(da),* which encompasses not only actual fighting with fists, knives, swords, and spears, but also acrobatics as well. These skills are displayed within the context of a drama, in which each performer portrays a dramatic character.

The display of skills, however, is not an end in itself. Even the most virtuoso technique will be criticized as "empty" *(kong)* if in performance it does not contribute to the pursuit of a larger aesthetic aim. The fundamental aesthetic aim of traditional Chinese painting, to "write [i.e., draw/paint] the meaning" *(xieyi)* rather than to "write realistically" *(xieshi),* is frequently referred to by Beijing opera practitioners as being analogous to their own. Traditional painting is not realistic in the Western sense; for example, landscape paintings are rarely identifiable as portraying a precise portion of a specific place. Rather, a painting of a particular mountain will resemble that mountain in broad terms, and will convey the essence of that mountain and the spirit of the total concept "mountain." Beijing opera likewise aims first to strike the audience with a resemblance to life—and then to convey the very essence of life. It is through the display of skills, externalizing the thoughts and feelings of major characters and elaborating upon their actions and interactions, that Beijing opera performance transcends a resemblance to life and builds an overall effect that conveys its essence.

In the pursuit of this aesthetic aim, performers adhere strictly to a basic aesthetic value: everything within the world of the play must above all be beautiful *(mei)*. In its simplest applications the demand for beauty requires, for instance, that a beggar be dressed in a black silk robe covered with mul-ticolored silk patches rather than in actually dirty or tattered clothes, which would not be considered beautiful.

The demand for beauty also affects the portrayal of certain emotions; a performer playing a young woman who has just received heart-breaking news should never cry real tears, for the accompanying red eyes and runny nose are considered anything but beautiful. Instead, the act of crying is sug-gested, both vocally and physically; when done skillfully, the resulting por-trayal is very moving as well as almost painfully beautiful.

The demand for beauty actually affects the display of every performance skill. Song, speech, dance-acting, and combat should at all times appear effortless *(bu shi li)* in order to be beautiful. Any hint of strain at hitting a high note, performing a complex series of somersaults and flips, or speaking an extended declamatory passage is perceived as indicating that the per-former's command of technique is insufficient. When skills are not dis-played adequately—when strain or effort is noticeable—the build to an overall effect capable of conveying the essence of life rather than its mere resemblance is destroyed by the evident, un-beautiful actuality of a strug-gling performer.

In training schools and rehearsal halls, the criticism heard with much the greatest frequency, directed at song, speech, dance-acting, and combat alike, is that the particular sound or action being performed is incorrect because it is not beautiful. And the highest praise that can be given a perfor-mance is to say that it is beautiful. Ultimately, beauty as an aesthetic value connotes conformance to the aesthetic aim and principles of Beijing opera—anything that is not within the aesthetic parameters of Beijing opera is not beautiful within that world.

Aesthetic Principles

Every aspect of traditional Beijing opera performance is governed by three aesthetic principles: synthesis, stylization, and convention. Together, these principles provide the basic fabric of Beijing opera performance—the over-all patterns *(guilü)* that characterize each aspect of Beijing opera perfor-mance, as well as the relationships among them.

Synthesis

Story, music, song, speech, and dance-acting are present in almost every Beijing opera performance; many include stage combat and acrobatics as well. These elements are not simply presented in sequence, however. It is their synthesis *(zonghexing)* that is characteristic of Beijing opera performances.

Song and speech in performance occur simultaneously with the dance-like movement of the performer; dance-acting and combat are interwoven on the stage with melodic and/or percussive accompaniment. The primary skill displayed in some passages is an aural one—song or speech. In others it is visual—dance-acting or combat. However, if the focus at a given moment is aural, as when a singer relates a sad separation from a loved one, that song is performed within the complementary visual fabric presented by the unceasing gentle synchronized movements of eyes, hands, torso, feet, and often the body through space. And if the focus is visual, as upon a brave warrior ascending a steep mountain, that pantomime is enacted within a texture of percussive sound provided by the orchestra. Percussive sound also provides aural punctuation to speech, which is performed within a visual fabric of movement punctuation as well. Extended speech and song without dance-like movement and accompanying melodic or percussive sound rarely occur in traditional Beijing opera, nor does dance-acting or combat without melodic or percussive accompaniment. Both the eyes and the ears of the audience are engaged at all times.

Stylization

Stylization refers to the divergence between the behaviors of daily life and their presentation on the stage—that is, the representation of those behaviors in performance, within a particular style. In Beijing opera, stylization is considered to be the act of raising and refining *(tilian)* the behaviors of daily life, with the aim of making them beautiful—making them a part of the world of Beijing opera performance.

The most basic physical, visually perceived characteristic of stylization in the performance of Beijing opera is roundness *(yuanxing)*. Roundness applies to posture and movement, both of various parts of the body in isolation and of the entire body in or through space. Straight lines and angles are to be avoided; positive aesthetic value is perceived in the presentation of a three-dimensional network of circles, arcs, and curved lines.

In stasis, this means, for instance, that an outstretched arm will be held in an extended curve unbroken at either the shoulder or elbow by angles. In movement, this aesthetic applies to action as small as the gaze of an eye, and as large as the blocking of major characters. For many types of characters, the performer's eyes are used to focus the attention of the audience; to lead it with the movement of a gaze. In such an instance, if the performer intends to indicate an object on the ground, the gaze of his or her eyes will begin away from the object with a sweep up, and then curve down to rest on the object. Conversely, if the gaze is to end in an indication of something above eye level, it will travel down as it moves toward that object and then sweep up to light upon it. This same use of the arc is made in pointing gestures, which first curve away from the direction in which the hand will ultimately point; to point directly in front of his or her body, a performer will begin by sweeping the pointing hand in towards the body before sending it out to point. To point to the left, the performer will begin with a sweep of the pointing hand to the right, and vice versa.

In movement through space, the performer similarly avoids straight lines and angles. For instance, a move from facing downstage at downstage center to facing downstage in front of a chair at upstage center is begun by circling to either the left or the right while gradually turning the entire body to face upstage. The performer then crosses upstage on a slight diagonal to the side of the chair and circles again in the opposite direction to face downstage once more, this time directly in front of the chair. The resulting S-shaped curve has been compared to the movement of a marionette puppet, necessary to keep the puppet's strings from entangling, and hypotheses have been drawn on this basis concerning the origins of traditional theatre movement in puppet theatre.[2] Whatever the origin, the ceaseless pattern of curved lines, arcs, and circles running throughout all Beijing opera performances helps to create a characteristic visual world for Beijing opera.

The foundation for Beijing opera's aurally perceived stylization is its musical system (shengqiang xitong); the elements of the musical system as presented orchestrally and vocally in the performance of Beijing opera plays serve to create a characteristic aural world for Beijing opera. This aural dimension, like the visual one, is perceived by the practitioners and connoisseurs of Beijing opera as being characterized by roundness. But while roundness in visual stylization is fairly direct and therefore readily appreciated by Western audiences, roundness in aural stylization is a more complex concept. Its appreciation requires that the auditor be cognizant of the aesthetics, elements, and techniques of the musical system, and of composition and performance within that system. These topics are discussed in detail in chapters 3–7 of this study.

Conventions

In the broadest sense, conventions (chengshi) are an aspect of stylization; conventions are also departures from daily reality. But conventions are more specialized: they include specific practices to which fairly precise meanings have been ascribed by tradition. The use of a particular conventional sign serves to signal its ascribed meaning to the audience. A great many such conventions are utilized in Beijing opera performance; the meanings of some are immediately recognizable to an uninitiated audience member while others require preknowledge for comprehension.

Dance-acting conventions most frequently fall in the former category, especially pantomimic actions such as opening and closing doors and windows, mounting and descending stairs, tending fowl, sewing, and movement over rough terrain and in conditions of darkness, heat, cold, rain, and wind—these actions are directly communicative and require no informed expertise of the spectator. Other dance-acting conventions are more formal, such as the act of walking in a large circle, which connotes traveling a considerable distance, and the straightening of costume and headdress parts upon entrance to signal the presence of an important character who is about to speak; these conventions do require familiarity from audience members, as do the visual conventions associated with the staging of Beijing opera.

The traditional Beijing opera stage is bare, with a decorative rather than realistic backdrop, and a carpet covering the floor for the protection of acrobatic performers. The only scenery used is one or more tables and one or more chairs. Although recent years have seen the advent of more elaborate scenery and certain technological innovations—including lighting and sound effects—in the performance of some plays, the staging of Beijing opera remains fundamentally quite simple.

This simple staging achieves a high degree of plasticity through the use of conventions. The table(s) and chair(s), through their placement and use, conventionally serve as a city wall, a mountain, a bed, a throne, or simply as a table and one or two chairs. Conventional use of stage properties frequently signals the presence and use of large objects not visually present on the stage; a whip signals the presence of a horse, an oar that of a boat, and large blue banners swung in wide arcs close to the stage floor that of rushing water.

Aural conventions require that audience members learn beforehand their ascribed meanings—very few aural conventions are immediately understandable without preknowledge of their significance. The most important aural conventions are individual elements of the musical system, which through their appropriate combination conventionally express specific emotions. Chapters 3 and 4 of this study are devoted to describing these elements and the way in which they may be combined in musical composition.

ROLE TYPES

The four principal role types in Beijing opera are *sheng* (standard male characters), *dan* (female characters), *jing* (painted-face male characters), and
chou (lit. "ugly" characters, who are usually male). During Bejing opera's
early development and nineteenth-century maturation, all were played by
men. Although the majority of performers in contemporary China play role
types of their own gender, most major subcategories in most role types do
have both male and female performers. Each of the role types, and even
more specifically each of their major subcategories, is itself indicative of a
particular age, gender, and level of dignity; makeup, headdress, and costume conventions indicate visually the role type and subcategory of every
character in each play.

Most Beijing opera performers specialize in the performance of only one
role type—for instance, the term *sheng* refers both to *sheng* characters and
to performers who play *sheng* characters—and most perform only one particular subcategory. This does not imply that actors perform stereotypes,
however; the characters included in each of the several role types and subcategories may be good or bad, strong or weak, intelligent or stupid. Role-
type specialization produces patterns *(guilü)* of performance technique
rather than dramatic characters with stereotyped personalities. Performers
of each role type specialize in the display of certain selected performance
skills. And the performance of each role type is characterized by certain
physical and vocal conventions and patterns of stylization specific to it.
Although some of the major physical conventions and patterns of stylization
are touched upon in the following descriptions of each role type, the fundamental role-specific vocal characteristics are not discussed here—they are
dealt with in chapter 5.

Sheng

Sheng characters are intrinsically dignified male characters. Generally, they
are of high social status or deserving of such. There are three major subcategories of *sheng* roles: older *sheng (laosheng)*, martial *sheng (wusheng)*, and
young *sheng (xiaosheng)*.

Older *sheng* roles are those of scholars, statesmen, and faithful retainers;
although the vagaries of fortune as dictated by the plot may place them in
positions of low social status, the intrinsic dignity of older *sheng* implies
that they are deserving of respect. Their makeup is fairly simple, consisting
of black-rimmed eyes and sharply rising black eyebrows on a flesh-colored

face tinged slightly peach around the eyes and in the center of the forehead. All older *sheng* wear beards *(rankou)*, which are usually waist-length and may be black, gray, or white depending upon the age of the specific character being portrayed. Every beard is divided into three separate parts—two sideburns and a central chin portion. Black cloth boots with thick white wooden soles (*guan xue,* also called *houdi xue,* lit. "thick bottom boots") enhance the dignity of the older *sheng*'s gait, lending weight and solidity to each step. Costumes for older *sheng* frequently include water sleeves *(shuixiu);* these are extensions of the sleeves proper, made of white silk from twelve to eighteen inches long. They may be held folded at the wrist, or dropped and moved by the arm in a variety of gestural patterns. Older *sheng* roles feature primarily song, speech, and dance-acting skills. There is an important further subdivision of the role, martial older *sheng (wulao-sheng),* in which combat skills are featured as well. These characters wear stage armor *(kao),* which may include four flags attached to the back at the shoulders.

Martial *sheng* roles are those of warriors and bandits. Their makeup is identical with that of older *sheng,* but they usually do not wear beards. In some cases, however, martial *sheng* characters who are over thirty years old and/or married are bearded.

There are two major subcategories of martial *sheng: changkao* (lit. "long armor") and *duanda* (lit. "short combat"). The former are high-ranking warriors and are dressed in stage armor, like the martial older *sheng.* *Duanda* martial *sheng* are lower-ranking warriors, bandits, criminals, or supernatural characters. They wear close-fitting costumes that facilitate movement, flat soft-soled boots (*bodi xue,* lit. "thin bottom boots"), and rarely use water sleeves. The major skills of all martial *sheng* are combat and dance-acting, though some song and speech are used, most extensively by the *changkao* martial *sheng,* who tend to be more dignified.

Young *sheng* characters are under thirty and/or unmarried. Their make-up follows the overall design of the older *sheng*'s; however, the basic color is much paler, and the tinge around the eyes pinker. Young *sheng* are always unbearded but usually wear the thick-soled boots. Their major skills are song, speech, and dance-acting. Lovers and young scholars are played by civil young *sheng (wenxiaosheng)* actors; they frequently use water sleeves and folding fans. Princes and young warriors are played by martial young *sheng (wuxiaosheng)* actors; they often wear two long pheasant feathers *(zhiwei,* also called *lingzi)* attached to their headdresses that figure prominently in their gestures, and utilize combat skills as well.

Dan

The second principal role type in Beijing opera is *dan,* female characters. There are four major subdivisions: older *dan (laodan),* "blue cloth" *dan (qingyi),* "flower" *dan (huadan),* and martial *dan (wudan).*

Older *dan* are almost always dignified characters, respected because of their great age. They wear essentially no makeup and have unadorned hair in a simple bun on the top of the head. Older *dan* usually walk with a long staff *(guaizhang)* in a quite realistic portrayal of extreme old age, with a bent back and a slow and painful gait. Most older *dan* roles use costumes with water sleeves. Their major skills are song and speech, supported by dance-acting.

The remaining subcategories of *dan* are all young women. Although hair styles and headdresses differ among the subcategories and for specific roles within them, the makeup is the same throughout. It is similar to that of the young *sheng,* but the tinge around the eyes and on the cheeks is a deep rose that does not appear on the center of the forehead, and the mouth is red or deep rose and quite small.

Blue cloth *dan* are demure young and middle-aged women, usually of high social status and/or high intrinsic dignity. The name for the role type may come from the fact that a blue cloth is used to wrap the head of blue cloth *dan* who are poverty-stricken or traveling.[3] Blue cloth *dan* usually wear costumes with long skirts and water sleeves. Their main skill is song, supported by speech and dance-acting. Very young blue cloth *dan* are sometimes called "boudoir" *dan (guimendan).* They are usually of high social status, but have a somewhat livelier movement style than other blue cloth *dan* because of their extreme youth.

Flower *dan* are vivacious young women, usually of fairly low social status. They may be dressed in either long skirts or trousers but rarely use water sleeves since the role type features much hand gesture. Whereas the eyes of blue cloth *dan* are usually downcast, those of flower *dan* are used extensively and flirtatiously. And while blue cloth *dan* roles are usually serious, flower *dan* roles generally are quite humorous. The main skill of flower *dan* performers is dance-acting, supported by speech and sometimes song.

Martial *dan* characters may be of high or low social status; they are generally more dignified than flower *dan* but less so than blue cloth *dan.* They may be dressed in the female version of stage armor, often with pheasant feathers in their headdresses, or in a feminine version of the close-fitting garments of the *duanda* martial *sheng;* the latter are sometimes called "sword and horse" *dan* *(daomadan)*. The main skill of martial *dan* is combat, supported by dance-acting, speech, and in some instances song.

A fifth major subcategory of *dan,* the "flower shirt" *(huashan),* was developed by *dan* performers of the first half of the twentieth century, including Mei Lanfang (1894–1961), one of the foremost Beijing opera actors of all time. The flower shirt role is a combination of the three young *dan* role types. Such characters may or may not use water sleeves, depending upon the particular play being performed. Flower shirt roles combine the natures and skills of martial, blue cloth, and flower dan, allowing the performer to display all four skills: song, speech, dance-acting, and combat.

Jing

The third principal role type in Beijing opera, *jing,* is also known as "painted face" *(hualian,* lit. "flower face"). Painted-face characters are men of great strength—men with suprahuman physical or mental powers, or supernatural beings. One of the most striking features of the role type is its makeup. The entire face is completely painted in bright colors and striking designs from high on the forehead, which is shaved, to the jawline. The designs of painted-face makeups *(lianpu)* range from faces that are a single, solid, brilliant primary color, broken only by white eye areas between black eyebrows and black-rimmed eyes, to complex, multicolored abstract designs and carefully rendered, realistic paintings of real and mythical animals that are totally unrelated to the natural features of the face. The colors and designs used have specific connotations, telegraphing every character's nature to the audience and identifying many characters specifically. Most painted-face characters wear beards that are as long or longer than those of *sheng* characters and are broad and solid rather than in three separate parts. All painted-face characters wear padded shoulder jackets under their costumes and very high thick-soled boots to increase their physical size.

There are three main categories of painted-face roles: great-painted-face *(dahualian),* supporting *jing (fujing),* and martial *jing (wujing).* Great-painted-face roles, also called "great face" *(damian),* "black head" *(heitou),* and "copper hammer" *(tongchui),* are usually major roles, and feature singing skill. Supporting *jing* roles, also called "posture-painted-face" *(jiazi hualian)* and "second-painted-face" *(erhualian),* are usually secondary roles, and feature speech and dance-acting skill. Characters in both of these civil role categories frequently use water sleeves. Martial *jing* roles feature dance-acting and combat skills, and in some cases acrobatics; such characters often wear stage armor *(kao).*

Chou

The fourth principal role type in Beijing opera, *chou,* is often referred to in English translation as "clown" or "jester." Although they frequently portray humorous characters, the actors of this role type may also play villains, young lovers, and other characters who are not necessarily humorous. The major distinguishing features of the role are that actors in performance may improvise, ad lib, and talk directly to the audience as actors, activities in which performers of other role types generally do not engage. *Chou* characters therefore serve as a direct link to the audience, clarifying and commenting upon the actions of other characters. Perhaps for this reason, *chou* characters are rarely leading characters but are important supporting characters.

There are three major subcategories of *chou*: civil *chou (wenchou),* martial *chou (wuchou),* and *choudan.* Civil and martial *chou* are male characters of less intrinsic dignity than *sheng,* though they may be of any social status, high or low. They are often called "small-painted-face" *(xiaohualian)* because of their makeup—a patch of white in the center of the face, enclosing the eyes and nose. Black eyebrows, soft red blush on the cheeks, and black-outlined reddish-brown mouths are frequently featured in their makeup as well. *Chou* may wear beards when appropriate for the age of the character being portrayed—most *chou* beards, however, are short and patchy in comparison with those of *sheng* and *jing.* Civil *chou* often use water sleeves and feature speech and dance-acting skills in their performance. Martial *chou* dress in the manner of *duanda* martial *sheng* and feature combat skills supported by dance-acting and speech.

Choudan (also called *chou* "old ladies," *choupozi*) are usually somewhat older, ugly female characters—matchmakers, nagging wives, and other older women who usually have certain undesirable qualities and are of rather low social status. Though younger *choudan* characters (sometimes called "colored" *dan, caidan*) were once the province of *dan* performers, all *choudan* characters are now usually considered to be *chou* roles.[4] The makeup, hair, and costume for *choudan* are designed for each specific character, often in parody of the young *dan* aesthetics—tiny eyes, large red mouths and red circles on the cheeks, faint downward curving eyebrows, and large black moles are common makeup features, accompanied by skirts that are too long or too short, water sleeves that are too narrow or improperly manipulated, or other comically reinterpreted young *dan* costume features. *Choudan* roles, like civil *chou* roles, feature speech and dance-acting skills in performance.

Every Beijing opera troupe aims for a playable balance of role types. This balance is often described through analogy to a table whose top is supported by four beams that in turn are supported by four legs. The top represents the full repertoire of Beijing opera plays; to perform them, four "beams," i.e., four principal performers, are required to portray leading roles. These principal performers are an older *sheng,* a martial *sheng,* a young *dan,* and either a young *sheng* or a *jing.* These four "beams" are then supported by four "legs," the absolutely essential performers of supporting roles: a secondary older *sheng,* an older *dan,* a *chou,* and a young *sheng* or a *jing* (whichever has not already been employed as a "beam").[5] Every troupe also requires a number of tertiary performers to serve as additional supporting characters, foot soldiers, attendants, and servants of both sexes.

THE PLAYS

Most Beijing opera plays are anonymous, having been devised by actors as vehicles through which to display their own performance skills. Many have never been published and exist only as part of the oral acting tradition or in handwritten copies in the possession of individual actors. Many of those that have been published contain no stage directions or descriptions of action; they include only the language that is spoken and sung in performance. In addition to this important component of aural performance, however, Beijing opera plays provide the plots and thereby the characters in whose portrayal performers display their skills, as well as the overall structure of each performance.

PLOT

The plots of most Beijing opera plays are well-known stories concerning familiar characters. Most early plays were adaptations of the *chuanqi* plays of *kunqu,* the predominant national theatre form before the ascent of Beijing opera, or of the plays of *kunqu's* major predecessors, *nanxi* and *zaju.* At least half of the 272 Beijing opera plays listed in 1824 had the same titles as plays performed in those earlier theatre forms.[6] The most comprehensive listing of Beijing opera plays to date, Tao Junqi's *Jingju jumu chu tan (An Initial Exploration of the Beijing Opera Repertoire),* first published in 1957 and updated in 1964 and 1980, includes 1,389 play synopses. According to the scholar Hwang Mei-shu, the plots of more than one-third of these plays can be found in just thirteen novels. Most of the remaining plays in the Beijing opera repertoire are based upon "history, true stories, sketches, note-books, legends, [other] novels, and earlier plays."[7]

The "earlier plays" to which Hwang refers include not only *kunqu's* *chuanqi* plays, *nanxi* plays, and *zaju* plays, but also plays from other regional forms of *xiqu*, forms that developed earlier than or concurrently with Beijing opera. Many of these plays are also based upon the sources listed by Hwang. In quite a few cases, a single plot has been dramatized in a number of regional forms, and several of these versions have been sepa-rately adopted by Beijing opera. Often, these different versions of what is essentially the same play have different titles as well. For instance, *The Fish-erman's Revenge (Dayu sha jia)*, *The Lucky Pearl (Qing ding zhu)*, and *Demanding Fish Tax (Tao yu shui)* share the same plot and characters; the story of *The Butterfly Dream (Hudie meng)* also occurs as *Zhuangzi Fan-ning the Grave (Zhuangzi shan fen)* and *Breaking Open the Coffin (Da pi guan)*.[8]

Because they are based upon well-known stories, the plots of Beijing opera plays may "unfold in a leisurely and natural way, without the tension and violence that characterize Western plays. . . ."[9] Dramatic interest does not arise from the plot, for there is very little question as to eventual out-come. As Sophia Delza points out, "This theatre is not one of suspense, as is our Western theatre."[10] Dramatic interest instead arises from the interpreta-tion given these familiar characters, and especially from the expression of their reactions to the circumstances in which they find themselves. In the expression of those feelings and emotions, performers make the greatest, most concentrated display of their performance skills.

Not surprisingly, this large body of plays with overlapping plots and characters has been classified according to a number of systems during the course of its development.[11] In contemporary China, Beijing opera plays are classified according to three main systems. Although each system is con-cerned primarily with plot and subject matter, all are related to performance as well. In the first classification system, inaugurated after Liberation in 1949, plays are each placed in one of three categories according to thematic content. This system is based upon the various historical periods during which Beijing opera plays were developed and reflects certain basic, overall performance considerations. The second two systems are traditional and can be represented as continuums along which each given play is placed. The characterizing extremes of the continuum in the first system are civil *(wen)* and martial *(wu)*, and those in the second system are serious *(daxi*, lit. "great play") and light or comic *(xiaoxi*, lit. "small play"). These two classification systems reflect the different purposes served by each of the four performance skills—song, speech, dance-acting, and combat—and the relationship of these skills to one another in performance.

Thematic Content

Since the establishment of the Drama Reform Committee in July of 1950, less than a year after Liberation, all Beijing opera plays have been divided into three categories that are based upon the thematic content of the plays and the historical period in which they were created.[12] The first category, that of traditional plays *(chuantongju/chuantongxi)*, includes all plays that were in performance before 1949 and were devised or written without the intention of conveying post-Liberation values and concerns. Some of them have been altered somewhat to remove or replace objectionable attitudes and situations, particularly those with overt erotic content. But the aesthetic principles and performance techniques of all aspects of traditional Beijing opera performance are exemplified in the performance of these plays.

The second category is most often referred to as newly written historical plays *(xinbian de lishiju/lishixi)*, though it is sometimes given broader names, such as newly written ancient plays *(xinbian de gudaiju/gudaixi)*, or newly written ancient-costume plays *(xinbian de guzhuangju/guzhuangxi)*. When the term "historical" is used, it is used loosely—although some of these plays do concern historical figures, many have well-known mythological heroes such as the Monkey King Sun Wukong and the legendary Judge Bao. Whether strictly historical or not, these plays have newly created plots, many of which are constructed to consciously embody contemporary values and concerns and all of which are set in the past. Although no newly written historical plays were produced from 1966 to 1976, from the beginning of the Cultural Revolution until the overthrow of the Gang of Four, they are currently a major focus for many Beijing opera playwrights. Because newly written historical plays are set in the past—usually the traditional Chinese past—the entire body of traditional performance techniques may be utilized in their performance. Except for their thematic content, such plays are therefore often quite similar to traditional plays in both script and performance, and the descriptions of traditional aural performance in chapters 2–7 of this study apply in many respects to the performance of most newly written historical plays as well.

The final category of plays is termed contemporary plays *(xiandaiju/xiandaixi)*. Like many newly written historical plays, contemporary plays consciously embody contemporary values and concerns. However, their plots and characters are all of the twentieth century. The aesthetic principles and performance techniques of traditional Beijing opera, developed for the presentation of plays concerning familiar characters in traditional Chinese society, are not necessarily directly applicable to the performance of contemporary plays. Contemporary plays in performance are experimental theatre pieces. Though they share the basic aesthetic aim of all Beijing opera plays, contemporary plays require the creative adaptation of aesthetic principles and the development of new performance techniques. The aural components of Beijing opera performance described in the chapters that follow are an important foundation to the aural performance of contemporary plays; however, the experimental aspects of that performance exceed the scope of this study.

Civil and Martial

The civil and martial classification system is the oldest and most generally used. In this system, civil plays *(wenxi)* have plots involving personal, social, domestic, and romantic situations; the plots of martial plays *(wuxi)* center upon wars, military encounters, the activities of bandits, and other such situations that feature heroic, martial activity.

The performance skills of Beijing opera serve different purposes, purposes that are related to these two types of plots. Civil plays are concerned with the relationships between characters, and especially with those characters' feelings and emotions. In the performance of civil plays, the expression of feelings and emotions is achieved primarily through the display of song skill. Although martial plays also include sometimes highly emotional character portrayal, they are generally more concerned with situation and action —with the representation of martial activity, portrayed through the display of combat skill. Dance-acting occurs in both types of plays. It is always performed in synthesis with song, combat, and/or speech, its display supporting the display of those skills. Dance-acting may also be featured as a major display of skill; in such cases, it usually serves to establish environment, and in some instances to advance the plot. The display of speech skill occurs in all civil plays, and in most martial plays as well, serving in both types of plays primarily as the means of interaction—i.e., communication—between characters, and therefore as a major means of furthering the plot. The content of dialogue in Beijing opera (though not necessarily the style) is quite accurate in its reflection of conversation in daily life. In traditional Chinese society, the direct expression of emotion, both physically and vocally, is strongly discouraged. In the civil plays of Beijing opera, where the expression of emotion is a major aim, emotions are most often expressed through the stylized display of song skill—a departure from the standard modes of social interaction.

In keeping with this distribution of performance skills, civil and martial plays feature those role types whose performers specialize in the appropriate skills. The leading performers in martial plays are martial *sheng,* martial young *sheng,* martial *dan,* and martial *jing* actors, supported by martial *chou* actors. Civil plays feature performers of the older *sheng,* civil young *sheng,* older *dan,* blue cloth *dan,* flower *dan,* and civil *jing* role types, supported by actors of civil *chou* and *choudan* roles.

Very few full-length plays, however, are limited entirely to either civil or martial elements. Most predominantly civil plays feature some martial elements, usually performed by supporting martial-role characters. Sometimes, however, combat skills are displayed by the leading characters as well. The play *The White Snake (Bai she zhuan)* provides a good example. In this primarily civil play, a white and a blue snake spirit descend to earth in human form—that of a blue cloth *dan* and a flower *dan,* respectively. The love affair between the White Snake and a young man (a young *sheng*), their marriage, and their domestic life together are portrayed through song, speech, and dance-acting skills. However, after the young man is turned against his wife by a powerful Buddhist monk and locked away from her in that monk's impregnable temple, the two snakes lead an army of water spirits in an attack upon the temple—and the two leading performers playing the snakes are called upon to display combat skills themselves during the battle. In such cases, performers such as flower shirt *dan* actors, capable of displaying all four skills—song, speech, dance-acting, and combat—are required if the major characters are to be played by the same performers throughout. The majority of predominantly martial plays likewise include some civil elements. However, the song and speech skills in martial plays are almost always displayed by the performers playing the leading roles.

Whatever the balance of martial and civil elements in a given play, the inclusion of both is in keeping with the basic aesthetic principle of synthesis. It also requires that performers of all role types be trained in the aural performance skills—song and speech—because at least one of those skills is displayed in the vast majority of plays. Even in those few strictly martial plays, such as *Yandang Mountain (Yandang shan),* in which no song or speech is performed, there remains a strong aural dimension to performance, for the percussive orchestra accompanies and punctuates all displays of combat and dance-acting skill.

Serious and Light

Every Beijing opera play is also classified as being a predominantly serious play (*daxi*, lit. "great play") or a primarily light or comic play (*xiaoxi*, lit. "small play"). The play *Silang Visits His Mother (Silang tan mu)* is one of the most serious. It concerns divided national and familial loyalties and a conflict between the considerations due past and future generations in terms of filial piety. Among the lightest are plays involving the Monkey King Sun Wukong and plays of lighthearted romance, such as *Picking Up the Jade Bracelet (Shi yu zhuo)*, in which the only real hindrance to the joining of two lovers is their own shyness.

The performance skills of Beijing opera serve different purposes in relation to serious and light plays, purposes that parallel their functions as represented by the civil and martial classification system. In civil plays, the display of song skill is the primary means whereby the feelings and emotions of major characters are expressed to the audience; it is therefore the major source of serious elements. In martial plays, combat skill is used to portray the serious, martial activity with which these plays are concerned. Light elements in both civil and martial plays are presented primarily through the display of speech and dance-acting skills.

This does not imply that speech and dance-acting skills are always a source of humor. In both civil and martial plays, as discussed above, they are important means of advancing the plot and establishing environment as well. And dance-acting may even serve as the primary, serious dramatic focus, as in the danced portrayal of tragic suicide in *Investigating the Jade Bracelets (Kan yu chuan)*, and of the death of a fallen horse and his heroic rider in *Overturning the War Machine (Tiao huache)*. However, in the vast majority of serious civil plays, serious emotions are expressed through song. "The more complicated the internal feelings and emotions of the major characters, the more song is needed." And in martial plays, "the more immediate the martial situation [i.e., the more serious], the more combat is needed."[13] The aural performance of serious civil plays features the display of both song and speech skill, as well as the music of the orchestra. The aural performance of light civil plays features primarily speech skill, and orchestral music. In the performance of martial plays, whether serious or light, speech is often the major aural performance skill, and the percussive accompaniment of the orchestra is an important component of the aural performance.

Even the most serious plays are by no means required to end tragically.

The vast majority of traditional Beijing opera plays, no matter how serious, are given *tuanyuan* endings. *Tuanyuan,* which literally means "round round" and in common usage connotes "reunion," is perhaps best defined theatrically as a "modified happy" ending. Even if the major positive character(s) dies as a result of the machinations of negative characters or the general pressures of an unjust society, he or she will be vindicated in the end, his or her name cleared or revered, and his or her descendants rewarded for the virtue of their ancestor. And much more often than not, the still-living major positive character(s) is cleared and rewarded for his or her virtue by the end of the play.

Furthermore, even the most serious plays include some light elements, provided in the aural dimension of performance through the display of speech skills. The serious, primarily civil *Silang Visits His Mother* provides a good example.

While the barbarian Princess is trying to come to terms with the fact that for fifteen years she has not known the true identity of her husband, and Silang is tearfully mustering the courage to tell her his real name, their baby son, Ah Ge, cries, and she holds him off to the side so that he can urinate through the slit in his trousers. Silang says, "Ah, Princess, I am talking to you. Why are you disturbing Ah Ge in this way?" And the Princess replies, "Say what you have to say but don't prevent my son from making water."[14] Performers usually must pause after this exchange to allow the audience's laughter to die down before proceeding to the more serious matter of Silang's real identity. Because the Princess is a flower shirt *dan* role, which includes the skills of flower *dan,* and comedy is primarily the province of flower *dan* and *chou* roles, it is not surprising that humorous elements are to be found in scenes involving this character.

The basic aesthetic principle of synthesis supports the practice of mixing serious and light elements, as well as civil and martial elements, in one play. Humor as conveyed through speech also increases the variety of skill displayed in the performance of speech, thereby enriching the aural dimension of performance.

STRUCTURE

In Beijing opera, play structure is generated by the demands of performance. The structure of every play is designed to display the skills of major performers through the portrayal of the feelings and reactions of major characters arising from the dramatic situation provided by the plot. Generally the focus is on one skill at any given time, with a second and often a third skill simultaneously displayed in support of the first. As discussed above, when song or speech is the featured skill, dance-acting supports it; when combat is the featured skill, it is also supported by dance-acting, and occasionally by brief displays of speech or song skill as well.

Many Beijing opera performances in pre-Liberation China consisted of *zhezixi,* short plays or selected scenes from longer plays; several *zhezixi* were performed together as a single bill.[15] Although such performances are no longer as common as they once were, they do still occur; this performance practice is directly related to the structure of Beijing opera plays. The short plays have simple plots featuring one basic situation. In civil plays, the major character expresses his or her emotional reaction to the situation; in martial plays, he or she carries out a plan of action arising from the situation. The performer portrays these emotions or actions through several virtuoso displays of skill. The longer plays may have much more complex plots but are also structured to feature one basic situation and a concentrated display of skill in each major scene; these scenes, when excerpted, can stand alone as complete performance pieces. Generally, a bill of *zhezixi* is composed to feature as wide a range of the four performance skills as possible.

A short play usually consists of one act. In Chinese such a play is termed a *xiaoxi* (lit. "small play"), the same designation used for a light, or comic, play. A longer play, which may consist of from six to fifteen or more scenes, is called a *daxi* (lit. "great play"), the same designation used for a serious play. Since the introduction of Western drama into China in the late nineteenth and early twentieth centuries, a short Beijing opera play may also be referred to as a one-act play *(dumuxi,* lit. "single curtain play"), and a long play is often referred to as a full-length play *(quanbenxi)* or multi-scene play *(duochangxi).* For purposes of clarity, they will be referred to in this study as one-act plays and multi-scene plays, respectively.

All plays—light and serious, civil and martial—may be composed in either one-act or multi-scene structure. In the following description of play structure, the examples cited are from serious civil plays because these plays feature the aural performance skills—song and speech—most predominantly. In light civil plays, the same types of structure are used to feature dance-acting, speech, and sometimes song; in martial plays, to feature combat and dance-acting, and in many instances speech and song as well.

The primary structural features that will be discussed are the use of emotional-progression structure (*cengcixing buju,* lit. "progressional composition") and the conceptions of time *(shijian de gainian).* These features are fundamental to the structure of both one-act and multi-scene plays.[16]

Emotional-Progression Structure

The structure of most one-act plays and of most major scenes in multi-scene plays consists of a series of emotional states, each the reaction of the major character(s) to developments in the basic situation. After presenting as little expositional material as possible through speech and dance-acting, the major part of each one-act play and major scene is devoted to the concentrated display of performance skill in the presentation of these successive emotional states. When song is the featured skill, the successive emotional states of the major character(s) being portrayed are the foundation of musical composition, as discussed in chapters 3 and 4.

In the one-act play *The Favorite Concubine Becomes Intoxicated (Guifei zui jiu,* sometimes translated as *The Drunken Beauty),* the first emotional state is the proud joy the Favorite Concubine feels in strolling through the moonlit gardens to an appointed rendezvous with the Emperor. This is expressed through song, speech, and dance-acting skills. She is then informed by her attendants that the Emperor has gone to visit another concubine instead, and enters a second emotional state. Her anger and jealousy are controlled by her desire to appear undisturbed before her attendants; after an initial outburst in a short monologue conventionally not overheard by the other characters onstage *(beigong),* she proceeds to drink the wines of the feast alone in an attempt to demonstrate the desired lack of concern. The performer conveys this emotional conflict through dance-acting skills. The character enters the third emotional state through increasing intoxication. Playfulness alternates with progressively more obvious displays of anger and jealousy, conveyed by song and dance-acting skills. In the fourth, very brief emotional state she accepts defeat and the uncertainties of her fate; sadness and loneliness are expressed through song, speech, and dance-acting skills as the character submits to the urging of her attendants and departs for her chambers without seeing the Emperor.

Not all scenes in multi-scene plays are composed in emotional-progression structure. The simplest multi-scene plays use an overall structural pattern termed focal-scene structure *(zhongdian tuchuxing buju,* lit. "highlighting the focus composition"). Such plays feature only one or two major focal scene(s). The major focal scene(s) is preceded by several shorter, expositional scenes and often followed by one or more concluding scenes as well. Only the major focal scene(s) is composed in emotional-progression structure, and may be excerpted for performance as *zhezixi.*

More complex multi-scene plays are composed in contrast structure *(duibixing buju,* lit. "contrast nature composition") and feature several major scenes, most of which are composed in emotional-progression structure and may be performed as *zhezixi*. Contrast in such plays is achieved by alternating between scenes concerned with positive characters *(zhengmian renwu)* and scenes concerned with negative characters *(fanmian renwu)*, between civil *(wen)* and martial *(wu)* scenes, or between scenes set in two different "worlds" *(shijie)*.

In the first two instances, one type of scene usually features the major character(s), and the other, the supporting characters; the scenes featuring the major character(s) are of course the major scenes. For instance, in the six-scene play *The Fisherman's Revenge (Dayu sha jia)*, the scenes alternate between those concerned with the fisherman and his daughter, the positive characters, and those concerned with the negative characters and their attempts to tax and drive out the fisherman and his daughter. However, the scenes that feature the older *sheng* actor playing the fisherman and the young *dan* performer playing his daughter include more extensive, concentrated displays of song, speech, and dance-acting skills than those featuring the negative characters; generally, only the former are excerpted for performance as *zhezixi*.

Plays concerning the exploits of the legendary Judge Bao perhaps best exemplify the contrast between "worlds." They often alternate between scenes involving officials and aristocrats, and those concerned with peasants and outcast members of society. The Judge himself then moves between these two "worlds" of society in the course of making his investigation, and arrives at a true and just solution. In most such plays, there are several major scenes in which the great-painted-face actor playing Judge Bao has ample opportunity to display song, speech, and dance-acting skills. These major scenes are usually composed in emotional-progression structure and can be excerpted for performance as *zhezixi*.

The most complex multi-scene plays are said to follow emotional-progression structure throughout. In such plays the majority of scenes are composed in emotional-progression structure, with each scene beginning its emotional build at the point where the preceding scene concluded. The performance of these plays requires enormous stamina of their leading performer(s), who must almost constantly perform concentrated displays of skill. The thirteen-scene play *Silang Visits His Mother (Silang tan mu)*, a virtuoso performance piece for the older *sheng* actor in the title role, provides a good example.

Within the overall emotional-progression structure of this complex play, contrast structure is also utilized. There are seven major scenes: the first two are set in the "barbarian world" of which Silang has become a member through marriage, as is the final scene in the play. Scenes seven through ten occur in the "Chinese world" where Silang's Chinese family is encamped. Scenes three through six, eleven, and twelve are short and transitional. All major "Chinese world" and "barbarian world" scenes are civil, with martial scenes performed "on horseback" occurring in the transitions from one world to the other.

In the first two scenes, Silang reveals his true identity and persuades his barbarian wife to help him in his effort to visit his Chinese family, and she tricks her mother the Empress into giving her a pass, good until dawn, with which Silang may cross the border. During the first transition, the first transitional scene is set in the "barbarian world" (scene three) and is civil; the last is set in the "Chinese world" (scene six) and is martial. The two intervening scenes occur on the border rather than in either world and are both martial. This progression takes Silang from the peaceful life he has known for fifteen years and thrusts him into the tense, unsettled milieu of the deposed Chinese ruling class in exile.

In the four major scenes set in the "Chinese world," Silang is briefly joined with his Chinese family in tearful reunion. Then, despite their protests, he painfully tears himself away and returns to the "barbarian world" to prevent his barbarian wife and son from suffering for their part in his unlawful visit to enemy territory. Upon his return, he once again passes through the martial border transition (scenes eleven and twelve), and once again suffers for having done so; he is imprisoned and sentenced to death. However, in the final scene of the play, the barbarian Princess pleads with her mother and succeeds in saving her husband's life. This tight structure of multiple contrasts—Chinese and barbarian worlds and the transitions between, and civil and martial activities—creates a total theatrical piece of strong cohesion. None of the major "world" scenes is of less importance than any other, and each features major displays of song and speech skills. Furthermore, all thirteen scenes are integral, successively building parts of the full play.

Nonetheless, four separate *zhezixi*, each an integral theatrical piece in itself, can be excerpted from the play. The first, second, and final scenes, each of the major scenes of the "barbarian world," are composed in emotional-progression structure. Each may be performed alone as a complete theatrical piece. The major "Chinese world" scenes are usually not separated from one another because together they constitute a single, unbroken emotional progression for the major character, Silang. However, as a set they are frequently performed as a single, complete, and quite complex *zhezixi*.

Multi-scene plays composed in focal-scene structure with only one focal scene are rarely performed in their entirety. Such plays simply do not present enough concentrated display of skill. This concentration is best created by *zhezixi,* each of which is a focal scene or one-act play composed in emotional-progression structure, or by a multi-scene play composed in contrast structure or in emotional-progression structure throughout, in the manner of *Silang Visits His Mother.*

The Conception of Time

Time on the Beijing opera stage is conceptualized in three separate ways: as stage time *(wutai shijian),* also referred to as the span of time covered by the action of the play *(juqing shijian de kuandu,* lit. "breadth of dramatic plot time"); as performance time *(yanchu shijian);* and as script length *(juben changdu).* [17]

In terms of stage time, a number of Beijing opera plays cover very short periods of time; the action of *Silang Visits His Mother* occurs within a twenty-four-hour period, from early morning of one day, when the barbarian Princess learns of Silang's plight and helps him to visit his Chinese family, to early morning of the next day, when he returns from that visit and the Princess must plead for his life. However, many plays may be considered "epic" in the sense that the action of the play may span years or even decades; *The White Snake,* with its final scene in which the Blue Snake returns to free her friend and mistress from imprisonment, spans more than thirty years.

In the exposition of plot, stage and performance time in a Beijing opera play are often compressed. For instance, a journey of several hours' or months' duration may be portrayed by a few lines of speech and several circles of the stage. The passage of many years may not even be enacted at all, with a character simply stating at the beginning of a scene that a certain number of years have passed since the last action portrayed.

In the expression of emotional states, however, the opposite phenomenon often occurs; stage and performance time are expanded, with, for instance, several minutes of song or speech occurring in the several "seconds" it takes a watchman to strike the hour. Reactions to surprising events are often extended in this manner, so that every step and realization of the reaction may be fully portrayed through song, speech, and/or dance-acting. This manipulation of time serves an important purpose: it allows a greater proportion of performance time to be devoted to the display of skill.

One-act plays usually have a performance time of approximately one hour, and multi-scene plays generally take from two to three hours to perform. Because most post-Liberation performances are approximately three hours in length, one or two complete traditional plays may be performed on one bill. A single bill may therefore consist of a single, long multi-scene play, or of a one-act play and a short multi-scene play. In either case, the multi-scene play selected for this type of performance generally utilizes contrast structure or emotional-progression structure throughout, rather than focal-scene structure, in order to provide the concentrated display of skill necessary to create a build of effect; this is especially true when only one long multi-scene play is performed. And, as previously noted, a single performance may also consist of *zhezixi;* a combination of from three to five one-act plays or excerpted scenes may be performed on one bill, the number depending upon the exact performance time of each piece.

Performance time is not necessarily reflected in script length, however. Because many published scripts contain no stage directions or descriptions of action, dance-acting and combat skills do not appear; but the display of these skills may occupy a considerable portion of actual performance time. Scripts for predominantly civil plays are therefore in most cases considerably longer than those for predominantly martial plays, because civil plays contain more song and speech. Even with civil plays, however, the scripts for two plays with the same performance time vary markedly in length if one features more song than speech; the performance time required to sing a given number of written-characters *(zi)* is often much longer than that needed to speak the same number.

When compared with the scripts of plays for Western-style Chinese theatre (*huaju,* lit. "spoken drama") and translated realistic Western plays of the same performance time, even the scripts for predominantly civil Beijing opera plays are quite short. The Western and Western-style plays average ten thousand written-characters each, while the longest multi-scene civil plays of Beijing opera contain approximately five thousand written-characters, and most multi-scene Beijing opera plays average only two thousand five hundred written-characters.[18] This difference in script length of course reflects the importance of dance-acting and combat skills. However, it is also due in large measure to the display of aural performance skills in Beijing opera; whereas speech in Western and Western-style realistic theatre is delivered rather naturalistically, and therefore fairly rapidly, a large portion of the performance time of civil Beijing opera plays is occupied by the music to which song lyrics are sung, and by the stylization of the spoken passages. The unique language of Beijing opera facilitates this prolonged delivery.

CHAPTER II

LANGUAGE

THE language of Beijing opera, sung and spoken by Beijing opera performers in their display of song and speech skills, is a major component of aural performance. Because song and speech serve different purposes in performance—song is used primarily to express emotion, and speech to advance the plot through the social interaction of dramatic characters, or to provide humor—song lyrics *(changci)* and stage speech *(nianbai)* have certain very different characteristics. These elements are therefore discussed separately below. All Beijing opera stage language, however, is composed within a system of language levels; an understanding of the specific language of song and speech requires knowledge of these language levels.

LANGUAGE LEVELS

There are two basic levels of language used in Beijing opera plays. The first and more heightened level is classical Chinese *(wenyan wen),* the language of classical Chinese literature. This is actually an old written language, differing markedly from all of the numerous contemporary Chinese dialects. Its grammar is different from that of contemporary Chinese, and its syntax is made up almost exclusively of single written-character words *(zi),* each of which represents a complete unit of meaning and is spoken in a single-syllable pronunciation. There are very few compound words such as those in contemporary language, compounds that consist of two or more syllables joined together to express a single unit of meaning, and that are recorded by a corresponding number of written-characters. The meaning for each written-character in classical Chinese therefore can be broader than it is for the same written-character in contemporary language, since it is not narrowed by the presence of other directly associated written-characters, and fewer written-characters are required in classical Chinese than in contemporary language to express the same general meaning. For the modern listener, this gives spoken classical Chinese a distinctly poetic flavor. Moreover, the meanings of an appreciable number of written-characters are somewhat different in classical Chinese than they are in contemporary language; spoken classical Chinese creates an imposing, "ancient" impression as a result.

The second level of language is vernacular *(baihua)*. This level consists primarily of standard spoken "Mandarin" Chinese *(putonghua,* lit. "common speech"), which was historically the regional dialect of Beijing and its environs. Mandarin has been the official language of all twentieth-century Chinese governments; because it is a tool for mass communication, it is understood throughout China, including Taiwan, but is somewhat "antiseptic" because of its standardization. In certain instances, contemporary Beijing slang is therefore inserted in vernacular stage language. As with classical Chinese, the meanings of some of the written-characters used to record this slang differ from those used to record Mandarin. In this case, however, the divergence is experienced as colorful and immediate rather than as erudite and removed. The occasional use of other regional dialects and their slang achieves this same effect.

The level of language sung and spoken by each character reflects the role type and therefore the level of dignity, social status, age, and sex of that character. Pure classical Chinese usually occurs only in passages quoted directly from classical writings.[1] A practical function is served by this practice; famous passages from classical writings are known and therefore understandable to the majority of audience members, whereas original composition in classical Chinese would, when spoken or sung, be understandable only to the most highly educated members of the audience. Characters in all role types may quote from the classics, though *chou* roles frequently quote them incorrectly.

In most cases, the level of language used by each role type is in fact a blend of classical Chinese and vernacular. Characters of a higher social status and/or level of dignity—older *sheng, changkao* martial *sheng,* older *dan,* blue cloth *dan* and the young *sheng* paired with them, and *jing* roles—use a blend of language levels that is closer to classical Chinese than it is to vernacular. *Duanda* martial *sheng* and flower *dan* and the young *sheng* paired with them, being characters of lower status and/or intrinsic dignity, use language that contains more vernacular than classical Chinese. Only characters of the lowest social status and/or least intrinsic dignity—*chou,* minor characters like servants and attendants, and the very young (i.e., children)—generally speak in straight vernacular. And only *chou* make regular use of slang, regional dialects, and topical ad libs. In a given play, the language level of a specific character usually varies somewhat, becoming more classical in formal situations and more vernacular in informal situations.

Language level also varies according to whichever skill it helps display; the language of song often contains more classical elements than does the language of speech. This is due primarily to the different purposes served by the display of song and speech skill. Plot exposition and humor are more readily understandable if presented in language that is closer to vernacular. The expression of emotion, however, is frequently heightened by the poetic flavor of classical Chinese in the language of song lyrics.

SONG LYRICS

A fairly complex system of common practices and techniques exists for the composition of song lyrics *(changci)* in Beijing opera. Four fundamental practices are the composition of lyrics according to lyric types, the use of a basic lyric structure, the use of rhyme, and the composition of speech-tone patterns within every passage of lyrics.

LYRIC TYPES

Six basic types of song lyrics facilitate the expression of emotion through the display of song skill: emotive, condemnatory, narrative, descriptive, disputive, and "shared space separate sensations" lyrics. These types all share the same basic lyric structure discussed separately below, but differ in kind and degree of emotional content and expression. Each type facilitates the expression of a different facet of the personality of the character singing it by revealing a different sort of reaction to the circumstances in which that character is involved.[2]

Emotive *(shuqing)* lyrics are introspective, direct statements of a character's feelings. In many cases, they occur when there is only one character onstage; that character can therefore commune only with himself or herself, or directly with the audience. For example, in the opening section of the first scene of *Silang Visits His Mother,* Silang (Yang Yanhui) is alone onstage and sings of his own emotional state in this passage of emotive lyrics:

> Yang Yanhui sits in the palace
> And thinking to himself sighs
> While reflecting on events of years ago.
> How sad and dispirited.
> I am like a bird in a cage,
> I have wings but cannot stretch them;
> I am like a tiger forgotten in the mountain
> Alone and suffering.

> I am like a wild goose come from the South
> Lost from the flight.
> I am like a dragon out of water
> Besieged on a sandbank.[3]

In other instances, emotive lyrics are used when more than one character is onstage; however, under such circumstances the emotive lyrics are by convention generally not heard by the other character or characters.

Condemnatory *(zhize)* lyrics are pointed, direct statements of a character's feelings, expressed purposively in criticism of another character. After learning that her husband has taken another wife, Silang's Chinese wife sings in condemnatory lyrics:

> When I hear your words I am unhappy.
> You married the Iron Mirror Princess.
> Because of you I did not wear flowers in my hair.
> Because of you I did not wear embroidered shoes.
> I did not eat, I could not drink tea.
> For fifteen years I have not sat down at my dressing table to do my coiffure.[4]

Narrative *(xushu)* lyrics are indirect statements of a character's reactions to circumstances expressed through a description and/or explanation of those circumstances. In the course of the narrative, the character's feelings are made clear, as are Silang's in this passage of narrative lyrics, which immediately follows the emotive lyrics quoted above:

> I think of that year and the meeting at Shatan,
> A bloody battle they fought,
> Rivers of blood and the dead piled up in mountains.
> A bloody battle,
> The Yang family fled and scattered East and West.
> A bloody battle,
> All the young men fell from their horses.
> I was captured and assuming another name escaped disaster.
> Dividing my name character Yang, I turned it into Mu Yi and married.
> Now Xiao Tianzuo prepares for battle.
> Both sides are ready to fight, my mother guides
> Troops to the Northern barbarian country.
> I wish I could return to the Song camp to see my mother,
> But what am I to do in a barbarian place as distant as the skies?[5]

Descriptive *(xingrong)* lyrics are metaphorical, indirect statements of a character's feelings, expressed through the description of physical surroundings. In the first section of *The Favorite Concubine Becomes Intoxicated,* as she walks proudly with her attendants through the palace gardens on her way to the appointed rendezvous with the Emperor, the Favorite Concubine sings in descriptive lyrics:

> How I am like Chang E [the goddess of the moon] descending from heaven;
> clear, clear and empty is the palace of the moon. Ah, the palace of the moon.
> A jade bridge over a stream; I take the rail and lean.
> Now two ducks come to play.
> Golden carp swim in the stream and watch me. Ah, swim and watch me.
> Boundless space, geese in flight. Wild geese, fly; I rejoice to see you!
> Wild geese in pairs ascend,
> hearing my singing settle in the flowers' shade.
> This landscape intoxicates me;
> without noticing, I've reached Fragrance Hall.[6]

The first two lyric types, emotive and condemnatory, are for the direct expression of emotion; the second two, narrative and descriptive, are for more indirect emotional expression. A complete song in each of these four lyric types is usually sung entirely by one character. Songs in both the remaining two lyric types, however, are sung by two or more characters in alternation.

Disputive *(zhengbian)* lyrics are for the direct expression of opposing views. They resemble condemnatory lyrics in that they are pointed, and expressed with a purpose. They may occur as formal debate between opposing parties in trial scenes or between ministers of a court, or as argument between family members or friends. Scene ten in *Silang Visits His Mother* utilizes disputive lyrics in a family argument; the statement of opposing views is made in speech, with song serving to express the intense emotions involved in the conflict:

> WIFE: *(speaking)* Aiya, mother-in-law, he has only just returned home and he wants to go back to the foreign state.
> MOTHER: *(speaking)* Aiya, my son! You have only just come back. Why do you want to return? Do you not know that to put filial loyalty first is the greatest thing in heaven and on earth?
> SILANG: *(speaking)* Aiya, my mother. Does your son not know that the greatest thing in heaven and on earth is to put filial loyalty first? If I do not return by the fifth watch at dawn your foreign daughter-in-law and her child will be beheaded. It is truly bitter.
> MOTHER: *(singing)* I weep, weep for my son Yanhui.
> SILANG: *(singing)* My old mother.

BROTHER: *(singing)* My fourth elder brother.

SILANG: *(singing)* My worthy sixth brother.

SISTERS: *(singing)* Our fourth elder brother.

SILANG: *(singing)* Ah, my two kind sisters.

WIFE: *(singing)* Hard-hearted husband.

SILANG: *(singing)* My unfortunate wife.

ALL: *(singing)* Ai . . .

SILANG: *(singing)* Mother, your son . . .

MOTHER: *(singing)* My son . . .

BROTHERS AND SISTERS: *(singing)* Fourth elder brother . . .

WIFE: *(singing)* My husband . . .

SILANG: *(singing)* Aiya.

    The fifth watch has struck in the drum tower.

    I bid goodbye to my family.

    I must leave the tent.

    I, Yang Silang, feel my heart pierced as by a knife.

MOTHER: *(speaking)* Ai, my son.

SILANG: *(singing)* I am unable to stay,

    Old mother advanced in years.

BROTHER: *(speaking)* Fourth elder brother.

SILANG: *(singing)* I am unable to stay,

    Worthy sixth elder brother with your great talents.

SISTERS: *(speaking)* Fourth elder brother.

SILANG: *(speaking)* I am loath to leave my worthy sisters not yet married.

WIFE: *(speaking)* Cruel-hearted husband.

SILANG: *(speaking)* I am loath to leave my first wife. We must part. I, Yang Silang, am resolved in my mind to return to the foreign outpost. I must not delay but leave the whole family and go from this tent.[7]

In these disputive lyrics, the emotional intensity of the opposing view is expressed through the use of relational terms; in traditional Chinese society, an individual's sense of self is primarily defined by his or her relationships with others. The repeated calling of Silang by his relational names is the strongest argument that could be advanced against his leaving.

Lyrics of shared space and separate sensations (*tong chuang yi meng,* lit. "same bed different dreams") express the thoughts and emotions of two characters who are onstage at the same time, but who are either unaware of each other's presence or unable to hear one another. Many plays that involve love affairs use lyrics of shared space and separate sensations in the former situation; each of the two lovers sings of his or her own thoughts and feelings alternately, with the passages becoming progressively shorter until finally the two meet. In the play *Black Dragon Residence (Wu long yuan)*, two lovers who have just quarreled bitterly are locked together in one bedroom for the night by the girl's mother, who hopes that this arrangement will encourage reconciliation. Song Jiang and Yan Xijiao awake alternately, sing of their feelings and intentions towards the other, and then resume sleeping:

SONG: The watchtower has announced the first part of the night;
In silent melancholy I retreat to serious thinking.
Suddenly I have a desire to make up with her . . .
But she treats me as if I were a stranger, a real stranger.

YAN: The watchtower slowly drumming
Recalls to me his kindliness;
I'd better go embrace him . . .
But I've sworn to cut him away, ah, to cut him away.

SONG: The watchtower has sounded a third time.
My anger shoots up high from my heart.
Going forward, I'll settle my score with her . . .
A man should think thrice before he acts, yes, to think thrice.

YAN: The watchtower strikes the fourth watch.
A desire for murder comes over me;
With this scissors I could stab his heart . . .
But I'm afraid it'll ruin my plan, my long held plan.[8]

Lyrics of shared space and separate sensations may be introspective, direct expressions that resemble emotive lyrics, as in the above example, or may be indirect expressions resembling narrative or descriptive lyrics.

In addition to these basic lyric types, there are lyrics not designated by a specific name; some serve conventionalized purposes, and some serve as dramatic dialogue. "Conventionalized" lyrics are usually quite short, and are not intended to express the emotions of the character singing; they are rather intended to convey the status of that character in society and/or to stress certain elements important to the plot. Conventionalized lyrics are usually sung immediately after a character enters or just before he or she exits, thereby marking transition points in the play. In the first scene of *Silang Visits His Mother*, the Princess sings the following conventionalized lyrics just after entering:

The peonies are in flower, masses of red blossom;
How glorious the spring with the birds all singing!
I must go to my husband and banish his everyday cares with play;
What is to be done? He sits all day, his brows knit in sorrow.[9]

The first three lines suggest the Princess's status; she is definitely a woman of the aristocracy, with time to view the pleasures of spring, and no duties other than the entertainment of her husband. The last line introduces the Princess's function in the plot of this scene—she will try to solve her husband's problem. Within scenes, such conventionalized lyrics may also mark a transition from one subject to another.

Lyrics that serve as dialogue function in part as speech; they are statements made to other characters that directly further the plot and only indirectly express emotion. Such lyrics may be considered "elevated speech."[10] Elevated speech lyrics occur in the final scene of *Silang Visits His Mother:*

> PRINCESS: Why are you bound as though for execution?
> SILANG: A little while ago they bound me up.
> I am confused, I cannot make it out. . . .
> Keep your tears and if you remember what a faithful wife
>   should do,
> Go quickly to the Silver Hall and intercede for me, Yang
>   Silang, the man you married.
> PRINCESS: Husband, bear your bonds a little while.
> I will go to the Palace and intercede for you.
> Taking my pretty child in my arms, I enter the Silver
>   Hall.[11]

All but the last line in this exchange are urgent, sung dialogue; the final line is a conventionalized lyric, marking the transition from this portion of the scene to the portion in which the Princess pleads with the Empress for Silang's life.

The several types of lyrics are in many instances combined with one another, or with conventionalized or elevated speech lyrics, to achieve the precise emotional content and expression appropriate to each individual character and specific situation. Furthermore, there are some lyrics that are atypical and simply do not fit into one of these categories. However, the majority of lyrics in traditional Beijing opera plays either conform to or seem based upon these categories.

It should be clear from this description of the basic types of lyrics that most lyrics are sung either by one character or by two characters in alternation; in most cases there is only a single, solo performer displaying his or her song skill at any one time. Occasionally, however, two or more performers sing in unison. The disputive lyrics in scene ten of *Silang Visits His Mother* are sung in sequence by Silang, his mother, his brother, and his wife as solo lines, by his two sisters in unison, and once by the entire family in unison.

Because the two sisters are minor, primarily functional characters whose other actions in the play are also performed basically in ensemble, their singing in unison serves to underscore the fact that emotionally and functionally they are as one; their singing serves an atmospheric purpose and is not a featured display of skill. The lyric for the single line sung in unison by the entire family is an onomatopoeic syllable expressive of crying; though Silang's determination to leave and his family's desire that he stay with them constitute an irresolvable conflict, the misery of that situation is shared by all. As a general practice, unison singing, whether by two or more characters, tends to occur in situations in which the characters participating are functioning as one. And generally, such singing features minor, supportive characters, as in the unison lines of the two sisters, and is a brief section of a full passage that primarily features the individual display of song skill.

LYRIC STRUCTURE

The basic structural unit for all types of lyrics is a couplet *(lian)* consisting of two lines *(ju,* lit. "sentences"). A given passage of lyrics includes as many couplets as necessary to convey the desired dramatic content—passages of from one to more than twenty couplets occur. The first line in each couplet is termed the opening line *(shang ju),* and the second is called the closing line *(xia ju).* The full couplet may consist of two complete sentences, or may be a single grammatical sentence in which the opening and closing lines are independent clauses. In either case, each line is a complete unit, independent of the other line in the couplet grammatically and syntactically but related to it in meaning.

Couplets may be written in two lines of ten written-characters each, or in two lines of seven written-characters each. Internally, each line is further divided into three semantic and rhythmic units, each of which is called a *dou* (lit. "pause"). The usual division of a ten-written-character line is into

Figure 1
Basic Structure of a Couplet

	10 written-characters/line			7 written-characters/line		
	1st *dou*	2nd *dou*	3rd *dou*	1st *dou*	2nd *dou*	3rd *dou*
Opening line	X X X	X X X	X X/X X	X X	X X	X X X
Closing line	X X X	X X X	X X/X X	X X	X X	X X X

Each 'X' represents a single written-character.

three *dou* of three, three, and four written-characters, respectively; a seven-written-character line is usually divided into three *dou* of two, two, and three written-characters. The third *dou* of a ten-written-character line may then be subdivided into two equal portions; if this is done, each half of the third *dou* must also be a discrete semantic and rhythmic unit. (See Figure 1.)

This basic lyric structure facilitates the creation of extremely effective, "dense" antithetical couplets *(duizhang)*. The corresponding *dou* of the opening and closing sentences can be composed so as to match written-character to written-character—monosyllable to monosyllable—in syntax, creating couplets of a strong rhythmic nature.

Lyric structure is fairly flexible, however, allowing for a number of variations to facilitate emotional expression. The simplest variations are created by subdividing a given line differently, producing, for instance, in a ten-written-character line, *dou* of four, three, and three written-characters, respectively. Three techniques for producing more substantial variations are frequently employed, each changing the basic couplet structure to a progressively greater extent: the insertion of "padding written-characters" *(chenzi,* also termed *cunzi,* lit. "accumulated written-characters," and *duozi,* lit. "piled written-characters"); the insertion of "padding lines" *(chenju,* also termed *chenzi,* lit. "padding written-characters"); and the use of the "sweephead" *(saotou)* technique.[12]

The insertion of padding written-characters increases the number of written-characters in a seven-written-character line to eight or nine written-characters, and the number in a ten-written-character line to as many as sixteen written-characters. A brief look at the script of almost any Beijing opera play will reveal a number of such lengthened lines. In most cases, padding written-characters do not "pad" in the sense of adding only sound, and not meaning, to a line. Rather, they extend the line beyond its standard length to clarify its meaning. Padding written-characters are usually added within *dou* and are an integral part of the *dou* as a semantic and rhythmic unit. Practically speaking, therefore, padding written-characters cannot be isolated as individual written-characters; it is only possible to point to a particular *dou* and say that, because it has more than the basic number of characters, it includes padding written-characters. There is no common practice governing the insertion of padding written-characters; one padding written-character may be inserted into any one *dou,* two may be inserted into any one or two *dou,* three into any one, two, or three *dou,* and so on. In Figure 2, the possible line structures produced by inserting one and two padding written-characters within *dou* are illustrated.

Figure 2

Line Structure Varied by Insertion of Padding Written-characters Within *Dou*

Basic Line Structure	10 written-characters/line			7 written-characters/line		
	1st *dou*	2nd *dou*	3rd *dou*	1st *dou*	2nd *dou*	3rd *dou*
	xxx	xxx	xx /xx	xx	xx	xxx
Possible Line Structure with One Padding Written-character	x̲x̲x̲x̲	xxx	xx /xx	x̲x̲x̲	xx	xxx
	xxx	x̲x̲x̲x̲	xx /xx	xx	x̲x̲x̲	xxx
	xxx	xxx	x̲x̲x̲ /xx	xx	xx	x̲x̲x̲x̲
	xxx	xxx	xx /x̲x̲x̲			
Possible Line Structure with Two Padding Written-characters	x̲x̲x̲x̲x̲	xxx	xx /xx	x̲x̲x̲x̲	xx	xxx
	x̲x̲x̲x̲	x̲x̲x̲x̲	xx /xx	x̲x̲x̲	x̲x̲x̲	xxx
	x̲x̲x̲x̲	xxx	x̲x̲x̲ /xx	x̲x̲x̲	xx	x̲x̲x̲x̲
	x̲x̲x̲x̲	xxx	xx /x̲x̲x̲			
	x̲x̲x̲x̲	x̲x̲x̲x̲	xx /xx	x̲x̲x̲	x̲x̲x̲	xxx
	xxx	x̲x̲x̲x̲x̲	xx /xx	xx	x̲x̲x̲x̲	xxx
	xxx	x̲x̲x̲x̲	x̲x̲x̲ /xx	xx	x̲x̲x̲	x̲x̲x̲x̲
	xxx	x̲x̲x̲x̲	xx /x̲x̲x̲			
	x̲x̲x̲x̲	xxx	x̲x̲x̲ /xx	x̲x̲x̲	xx	x̲x̲x̲x̲
	xxx	x̲x̲x̲x̲ -	x̲x̲x̲ /xx	xx	x̲x̲x̲	x̲x̲x̲x̲
	xxx	xxx	x̲x̲x̲x̲/xx	xx	xx	x̲x̲x̲x̲x̲
	xxx	xxx	x̲x̲x̲ /x̲x̲x̲			
	x̲x̲x̲x̲	xxx	xx /x̲x̲x̲			
	xxx	x̲x̲x̲x̲	xx /x̲x̲x̲			
	xxx	xxx	x̲x̲x̲ /x̲x̲x̲			
	xxx	xxx	xx /x̲x̲x̲x̲			

Each 'X' represents a single written-character.
Underlining denotes *dou* that contain padding written-characters.

Two or more padding written-characters may also be placed before, between, or after the *dou* of a line, effectively constituting an additional *dou*. In this case, they are an integral part of the line as a unit of meaning; it is usually not possible to state which of the four *dou* is additional. One is only able to observe that a given line has an additional *dou*. For instance, a line whose basis was ten-written-character structure could be varied to read: [xxx xxx xxx xx/xx]; and a line whose basis was seven written-characters could be varied to read: [xx xx xx xxx]. In both instances there is no way to tell which *dou* is the added unit, for the additional dou in no way differs from the regular units.

Padding written-characters simply produce lines of irregular length; they do not change the basic semantic or rhythmic nature of the couplet-line-*dou* structural system. Occasionally a written-character, or rarely, more than one, is omitted from a line. Here, also, the basic nature of the system is not altered, because the line and each of its three *dou* remain the semantic and rhythmic units.

When the second technique for variation is employed, however, the balance of the couplet structural system is altered. Padding lines *(chenju)* are inserted before, between, or after either of the basic two lines. Padding lines may consist of from one written-character to a full grammatical sentence; unlike the padding written-characters, padding lines function as discrete semantic units unto themselves. The insertion of a padding line between the opening and closing lines of a couplet, for instance, can create the following altered couplet structure:

$$xxx \quad xxx \ xx/xx$$
$$xxxxx$$
$$xxx \quad xxx \ xx/xx.$$

According to Dolby, padding lines generally consist of

> words of slighter meaning than the rest of the song, very often more colloquial words or conventional phrases which are easily recognized as such. Many of them have meanings such as, 'You might think he would . . .', 'Do they not say that . . .', 'there is a saying that . . .', and '[By] good fortune it happened that . . .'; they are somewhat similar to the storyteller's stock phrases and impart a similar narrative intimacy and directness.[13]

Single word or sound interjections may also function as padding lines. The overall effect produced by the presence of padding lines is the unbalancing of the two lines per couplet structure, interrupting the rhythm and creating a sense of suspense, urgency, or casualness depending upon the context.

A similar effect is produced by the "sweephead" *(saotou)* technique. In it, a three-line lyric is sung, with the implied fourth line played by the percussive orchestra, as discussed below in chapter 6. The three-line lyric consists of one complete couplet and the opening line of a second couplet; the orchestra may be seen therefore as taking the closing line of the second couplet. The sense of interruption produced by this divergence from basic couplet structure is quite strong and can be used for dramatic effect in situations where a character is startled or surprised.

In fact, the couplet structure, by creating the expectation that an opening line will be followed by a closing line, lends itself generally to a technical enhancement of dramatic tension. As Rulan Chao Pian points out, there is "a feeling of suspense in line one [i.e., in the opening line] and a sense of repose in line two [the closing line]."[14] In disputive lyrics, the assignment of the opening line to one character involved in the contention, and the closing line to the other, technically creates a situation in which the former character is questioning or attacking and the latter is successfully responding. This basic structure can then be elaborated upon: a summation can be made by the former character in a complete couplet, after which the latter character may take up the attack with the opening line of the next couplet, with the former character responding in the closing line; the latter character may fail to respond, indicating temporary or final defeat, with the closing line taken up by either character after a pause, thereby changing the direction of the contention. If the closing line is omitted altogether, the sense of interruption and non-resolution is strongest, in the manner of the "sweephead" technique.

Speech may be inserted between the opening and closing lines, similarly creating a sense of interruption and expectation. Speech interruption frequently heightens leavetaking and the giving of orders—for instance, by speaking after an opening line of farewell or dismissal to call the parting character or recipient of the orders back, and then making a final statement in the sung closing line. Interruption by speech may be used to further increase the dramatic tension in disputive lyrics. It may also be used to create an entertaining pattern, as in the first scene of *Silang Visits His Mother,* where the Princess is trying to guess the reason for Silang's unhappiness. Each guess is sung by the Princess in one line and is followed by spoken discussion as to why that guess was incorrect. The first guess is sung on an opening line, suggesting that it is the first in a series: "Is it that my mother the Empress has not treated you well?" The second guess, sung on a closing line, therefore has the flavor of "then it *must* be . . .": "Is it that you are tired of me?" The third guess, on the opening line of the second couplet, has the sense of "Well, then, is it this?": "Are you not longing to go and enjoy yourself in the Pavilion of Qin and the Chu Hall [courtesan quarters]?" And the fourth guess suggests, "Aha, it's got to be this!": "Do you not wish to take a concubine?" When this guess is also proven in discussion to be wrong, the Princess engages in serious thought in the opening line of the third couplet: "It is not this, it is not that, then what is it?" And her final guess is given an air of certainty by being sung on the closing line: "You are thinking of your family, and would like to flee to them."[15] Rulan Chao Pian believes that this sort of guessing sequence, "which stretches out a simple question-and-answer episode over a long time, usually does not really build up tension. . . . What the audience looks for is a playful patterning for its own sake. . . . The audience enjoys in a relaxed manner the virtuosity of the performers."[16] Variations in lyric structure, through enhancement of dramatic tension and the creation of entertaining patterns, directly serve the display of song skill in the expression of emotion.

Rhyme in Lyrics

Rhyme in Beijing opera lyrics is of course a function of the Chinese language. Both classical and vernacular Chinese are based upon the monosyllable. In classical Chinese, each written-character and the monosyllable with which it is pronounced constitute a complete unit of meaning—a "word." A given monosyllable and the written-character with which it is recorded are not necessarily a complete unit of meaning in vernacular Chinese, in which monosyllables are in many instances used only as one of the two or more components joined to form a compound word. However, in both classical and vernacular Chinese, monosyllables are the smallest morphemes, or units of sound that can carry a meaning. And it is upon these individual monosyllabic morphemes—referred to henceforth as "words" for convenience—that rhyme is based.

All words are composed of an initial consonant *(shengmu)* and a final vowel *(yunmu)*. The latter may be either simple or compound, and may end in a terminal /n/ or /ng/.[17] Classical Chinese and all vernacular dialects are fairly "sound poor." In Mandarin Chinese there are twenty-one sounds that function as initial consonants: /b, c, ch, d, f, g, h, j, k, l, m, n, p, q, r, s, sh, t, x, z/, and /zh/. Additionally, the vowels /i/ and /u/ may serve as initial consonants; when they do so, they are viewed as "semi-vowels,"[18] and are written 'y' and 'w', respectively. Thirty-six sounds function as final vowels—they are listed in Figure 4. Twelve of these final vowels may serve as words without initial consonants. Theoretically, then, there are fewer than eight hundred and ninety possible discrete monosyllabic pronunciations in Mandarin Chinese. The actual number is substantially smaller (405), because certain combinations of initial consonants and final vowels do not occur.

Rhyme is a function of the composition of final vowels. At their most complex, compound final vowels consist of a medial vowel *(yuntou,* lit. "vowel head"), a central vowel *(yunfu,* lit. "vowel belly"), and a terminal vowel or consonant *(yunwei,* lit. "vowel tail"). For instance, in the word *guai* (strange), 'g' is the initial consonant, 'u' is the medial vowel, 'a' is the central vowel, and 'i' is the terminal vowel; in the word *guan* (official), 'n' is the terminal consonant. Simpler words have no medial vowel, such as *gan* (to dare) and *gai* (to alter). The simplest words have no initial consonants, such as *an* (peace), and *ai* (short), or consist of only an initial consonant and a single, central vowel, as in *lu* (deer) and *bi* (brush). Rhyme exists in words that have no terminal vowel or consonant if the central vowel is the same in any given two words. In all other cases, it exists if the central vowel and terminal vowel or consonant are the same. The range of final vowel composition in relation to rhyme determinants is shown in Figure 3.

Beijing opera uses thirteen rhyme categories *(yunbu)* that are based upon this definition of rhyme; they are commonly referred to as the thirteen *zhe*. These thirteen rhyme categories are each designated by two words that represent the rhyme sounds they include. Figure 4 lists the thirteen rhyme categories, and the final vowels that are included in each category.[19] The final vowels are shown in the four standard divisions of Chinese vowels; the name of each division suggests the correct oral placement for pronouncing the initial sound of all vowels included in that division, and the pronunciation of the first written-character in each name places the mouth and throat

Figure 3
The Range of Final Vowel Composition in Relation to Rhyme Determinants

Word	Initial Consonant	Final Vowel		
		Medial Vowel	Central Vowel	Terminal Vowel or Consonant
ai¹			a	i
an¹			a	n
ye	y²		e	
li	l		i	
lie	l	i	e	
luo	l	u	o	
lei	l		e	i
lan	l		a	n
liao	l	i	a	o
liang	l	ī	a	ng
		Rhyme Determinant		

1 These two words are examples of final vowels serving as words without initial consonants.

2 This is an instance of a "semi-vowel" serving as an initial consonant; were there a standard initial consonant, this sound would be a medial vowel and would be written 'i,' as in *lie* above.

Figure 4
Final Vowels and Their Placement in Rhyme Categories[1]

Vowel Classification	Rhyme Category	Vowel Type (Kai) Opened-mouth	(Qi) Level-teeth	(Huo) Closed-mouth	(Cuo) Scooped-lips	Vowel Classification
SIMPLE VOWELS: have a single, central vowel (6)	yi qi		i[7]		ü[9]	**SIMPLE VOWELS:** have a single, central vowel
	gu su			u[8]		
	fa hua	a[2]	ia	ua		Medialized diphthongs (*hou xiang*, lit. "rear sounded"): have medialized central vowels, and the central, final vowel is prolonged (5) — **COMPOUND VOWELS**
	suo bo	e, o[3]		uo		
	mie xie	ê[4]	ie		üe	
Simple diphthongs (*qian xiang*, lit. "front sounded"): have central and terminal vowels, and the central, first vowel is prolonged (4) — **COMPOUND VOWELS**	huai lai	ai		uai		Triphthongs (*zhong xiang*, lit. "middle sounded"): have medial, central, and terminal vowels, and the central, second vowel is prolonged (4) — **VOWELS**
	hui dui	ei		uei (usually written "ui")		
	yao tiao	ao	iao			
	you qiu	ou	iou (usually written "iu")			
Front nasal vowels (8) — **VOWELS WITH TERMINAL CONSONANTS**	yan qian	an	ian	uan	üan	Front nasal vowels — **VOWELS WITH TERMINAL CONSONANTS**
	ren chen	en[5]	in	uen (usually written "un")	ün	
Rear nasal vowels (8) — **VOWELS WITH TERMINAL CONSONANTS**	jiang yang	ang	iang	uang		Rear nasal vowels
	zhong dong	eng[6] ong	ing iong	ueng		

1. The pronunciations for all final vowels in Mandarin Chinese given in Appendix 2 at the back of this volume are arranged according to rhyme category for easy reference with this figure. Pronunciation guides (including the International Phonetic Alphabet spellings, in brackets) for those final vowels discussed in these notes are given here, as well.

2. All the opened-mouth vowels except /ong/ may serve as words without initial consonants. A twelfth final vowel, /er/, which does not appear in the figure, may do so as well; it is the only sound in standard Mandarin to use /r/ as a terminal consonant, and is included in the *yi qi* rhyme category.

3. The *suo bo* rhyme category includes sounds that would not be considered rhymes in English:

/e/, [ɤ] pronounced like "uh," but with the tongue pulled back in the mouth; and

/o/, [ɔ] pronounced like the 'o' in "boy."

A practical reason for this might be simply that both sounds occur infrequently without terminal vowels or consonants.

4. The /ê/, [ɛ] sound in the *mie xie* and *hui dui* rhyme categories is pronounced like the 'e' in "bet"; except as an exclamatory sound, it occurs only after /i/ and /ü/, and before /i/.

5. The *ren chen* rhyme category also includes sounds that would not be considered rhymes in English:

/en/, [ən] pronounced like the 'en' in "chicken"; and

/in/, [in] pronounced like the 'ean' in "leen."

In fact, in everyday speech these two sound are frequently indistinguishable.

6. The *zhong dong* rhyme category then incorporates the "exceptional" rhyme sounds of both the *suo bo* and *ren chen* categories, making the following sounds rhyme:

/eng/, [əŋ] pronounced like the 'ung' in "lung";

/ing/, [iŋ] pronounced like the 'ing' in "sing"; and

/ong/, [ɔŋ] pronounced like the 'o' in "boy," plus the 'ng' in "sing."

7. When not preceded by a standard initial consonant, this sound is written 'yi'; the /i/ sound serves in such instances as both a "semi-vowel" initial consonant and as a final vowel. Sounds in its vowel type without standard initial consonants are written 'ya, ye, yao, you, yan, yin, yang, ying', and 'yong', respectively.

8. When not preceded by a standard initial consonant, this sound is written 'wu'; the /u/ sound serves in such instances as both a "semi-vowel" initial consonant and as a final vowel. Sounds in its vowel type without standard initial consonants are written 'wa, wo, wai, wei, wan, wen, wang', and 'weng', respectively.

9. The *yi qi* rhyme category also includes sounds that would not be considered rhymes in English:

/i/, [i] pronounced like the 'ee' in "see"; and

/ü/, [y] pronounced like the 'u' in French *tu* and the 'ü' in German *müde*.

As with the *suo bo* rhymes, the scarcity of the /ü/ sound as a terminal vowel may account for this.

In addition to the /er/ final vowel mentioned in note 2 above, there are two other sets of sounds included in the *yi qi* rhyme category that are not present in the figure. This first set consists of:

/zhi/, [tʂ ɭ] pronounced like a voiced vocalic prolongation of the retroflex 'j' in "jaw";

/chi/, [tʂʰɭ] pronounced like a voiced vocalic prolongation of the retroflex 'ch' in "chaw";

/shi/, [ʂ ɭ] pronounced like a voiced vocalic prolongation of the retroflex 'sh' in "shawl"; and

/ri/, [ʐɭ] pronounced like a voiced vocalic prolongation of the retroflex 'r' in "run."

The sounds in the second set are:

/zi/, [ts ɿ] pronounced like a voiced vocalic prolongation of the alveolar 'dz' in "adze";

/ci/, [tsʰɿ] pronounced like a voiced vocalic prolongation of the alveolar 'ts' in "cats"; and

/xi/, [s ɿ] pronounced like a voiced vocalic prolongation of the alveolar 's' in "sew."

These sounds include no vowels in their common speech pronunciation, and therefore have no place in the vowel type classification. Their inclusion in the *yi qi* rhyme category gives that category the largest number of possible rhyme sounds, and hence the largest number of words to be used in the composition of lyrics.

in approximately that position: "opened-mouth" *(kaikou)*, "level-teeth" *(qichi)*, "closed-mouth" *(hekou,* often pronounced *huokou)*, and "scooped-lips" *(cuochun)*. Each final vowel is placed in its division according to its medial or, if it does not have a medial, its central vowel sound, because it is upon that sound that the entire portion of the syllable relevant to rhyme begins.

It should be noted that in practice there is some flexibility within these rhyme categories; certain sounds are accepted as imperfect rhymes. The most usual such rhyme sounds are /yi ei/, which combines the *yi qi* rhyme category with the *hui dui* rhyme category; /ai ei/, which combines *huai lai* with *hui dui;* /an en/, combining *yan qian* and *ren chen;* /an ang/, combining *yan qian* and *jiang yang;* /en eng/, combining *ren chen* and *zhong dong;* and /ang eng/, combining *jiang yang* and *zhong dong.*[20]

Although the rhyme categories themselves are somewhat complex, standard rhyming practice is quite simple. Generally, one rhyme category is used throughout a given passage of lyrics, and most lines end on a word within that rhyme category. For example, in the *yan qian* rhyme category, the rhymes for a two-couplet lyric might be:

> xxx xxx xx/x *yan*
> xxx xxx xx/x *qian.*
> xxx xxx xx/x *bian*
> xxx xxx xx/x *lian.*

Within this practice, dramatic tension can be created by using a non-rhyming word at the end of one of the first three lines, most frequently the opening line of the first couplet, so that the rhyme scheme is not resolved until the second couplet is completed, i.e.:

> xxx xxx xx/x *gong*
> xxx xxx xx/x *yan.*
> xxx xxx xx/x *bian*
> xxx xxx xx/x *lian.*

In some cases the same rhyme category is used in all the lyrics of a given scene. However, in most instances the rhyme category changes when another character enters, or there is a major change in topic.

The final vowels, initial consonants, and rhyme categories are all associated with specific aesthetic and emotional qualities. These qualities are important considerations in the choice of words throughout a passage of lyrics, as well as in the actual end rhymes.

Each type of vowel is perceived as having its own aesthetic and emotional qualities. Opened-mouth vowels are seen as having a "frank, straight-forward, open and clear, firm, unyielding, ringing flavor." Level-teeth vowels on the other hand are experienced as "relatively soft and gentle, graceful, elegant, and eloquent." Closed-mouth and scooped-lips vowels are felt to be "short and impetuous, with a clear and fresh flavor."[21]

Similar aesthetic and emotional qualities are attached to the initial consonants. The nasal initial consonants (/m, n/ and /l/) and the semi-vowels used as initial consonants (/i/, written 'y', and /u/, written 'w') are known as "thick sounds" (zhuoyin, termed "voiced sounds" in linguistics) and are perceived as "most expressive of sluggish, weak, slow, and dilatory situations." All other initial consonants (/b, d, g, p, t, k, f, j, q, x, zh, ch, sh, r, z, c/, and /s/) are known as "clear sounds" (qingyin, termed "voiceless sounds" in linguistics) and are experienced as "lucid, lively, and sprightly."[22]

A third set of aesthetic and emotional qualities is seen in the rhyme categories themselves; each rhyme category is perceived as representing one of two fundamental principles, yin and yang. Yin is the feminine or negative principle in nature according to Chinese philosophy and its application in medicine and the arts; yang is the masculine or positive principle. The two exist not in opposition but ideally in a state of balance. A disruption of that balance produces illness in physiology and dissonance in aesthetics. It is therefore important that every play have a balanced—that is, equal—representation of yin and yang sounds. The four rhyme categories with terminal consonants—yan qian, ren chen, jiang yang, and zhong dong—and the fa hua category are experienced as "clear and sonorous," and are termed the yang rhyme categories (yangzhe). The remaining eight categories are known as the yin rhyme categories (yinzhe) and are further divided into two levels. Suo bo, huai lai, yao tiao, and you qiu are a lower level of yin, felt to be "soft, gentle, and mild." Yi qi, gu su, mie xie, and hui dui are a higher level of yin—experienced as even more yin—and are felt to be "slight, fine, and subtle."[23]

In linguistic terms, yang sounds include all those that end with nasals, all simple low back vowels, and all diphthongs that end with low back vowels. Low-level yin sounds include all simple mid back vowels, all diphthongs and triphthongs that include mid back vowels, and all diphthongs and triphthongs that begin with or include—but do not end on—low back vowels. High-level yin sounds include all simple high front and high back vowels, and all diphthongs and triphthongs that include mid front or lower mid front vowels. Yang as an aural concept is therefore either nasal or low and back, while yin is high or frontal.

In the composition of lyrics, the most firm, straightforward, clear, and sonorous sounds possible are those from the *yang* rhyme categories that utilize opened-mouth vowels and "clear sound" initial consonants—sounds such as /da, gan, ren, bang, leng/, and /zhong/. And the most graceful, subtle, slow, and elegant sounds possible are those from the higher level *yin* rhyme categories that have level-teeth vowels and "thick sound" initial consonants—sounds such as /ni, ya/, and /mie/. The range of aesthetic and emotional possibilities between these two extremes is quite broad. Words are selected for a given passage of lyrics so that the nature of the character singing and the emotion being expressed are enhanced and supported by the appropriate, specific balance of these qualities.

Speech-tone Patterns in Lyrics

Classical Chinese and all vernacular Chinese dialects are tonal languages. Mandarin Chinese uses four speech-tones, or inflections; a single sound, such as *ma*, may have at least four completely different meanings, indicated in writing by four different written-characters and in speech by the use of the four speech-tones. As a third component of monosyllabic pronunciations, speech-tones serve to increase the number of discrete sound units in Mandarin Chinese almost fourfold (certain syllables do not occur with all four speech-tones). The four speech-tones in Mandarin Chinese are listed in Figure 5, together with their internal pitch progressions. Although the overall pitch of each speech-tone may be raised or lowered in song and speech to convey emotion, as discussed in chapters 3, 4, and 5, these internal pitch progressions and relative pitch relationships between tones are standard.[24]

The first and second tones are for historical reasons collectively known as level- *(ping)* tones; the third and fourth tones are collectively known as oblique- *(ze)* tones. In the writing of lyrics in couplets, as previously described, patterns of level-tone and oblique-tone words considered pleasing to the ear are followed. The most basic common practice is that the closing line of every couplet in each aria must end with a level-tone word; exceptions are made only when the expression of meaning absolutely requires an oblique-tone word. General patterns of level-tone and oblique-tone words are also followed within each line. Most two-couplet lyrics with seven written-characters per line adhere fairly closely to one of the following two patterns (— represents a level-tone; | an oblique one):[25]

Pattern One   **Pattern Two**

```
— —   | |   — — |        | |   — —   — | |
| |   — —   | | —        — —   | |   | — —
| |   — —   — | |        — —   | |   — — |
— —   | |   | — —        | |   — —   | | —
```

The most common, standard variation of these two patterns is the use of a level-tone word for the last written-characters in the opening line of the first couplet. The first, third, and fifth written-characters in a line also frequently vary in tone from those prescribed by these two patterns; tones for words in these places are considered relatively unimportant. Patterns such as the following therefore also occur quite frequently in seven-written-character lines:

```
| |     — —     | | —
— —     | |     | — —
— —     | |     — — |
| |     | —     | | —
```

No basic set of speech-tone patterns exists for couplets with ten-written-character lines; patterns are developed for each specific passage of lyrics. However, there is a strong tendency for opening lines to end with one type of tone and closing lines with the other. Most frequently, opening lines end with oblique-tone words and closing lines with level-tone words.

Because speech-tones require a relative pitch progression in the pronunciation of each word to make its meaning clear, patterns of speech-tones within the lyric structure create lyrics with a strong musical flavor. This musical quality of the language in song lyrics is heightened by the use of rhyme, and by the rhythmic effect of *dou* in the lyric structure itself.

A broad and subtle range of emotional expression is possible through the use of appropriate lyric type, variations in lyric structure and common rhyming practices, and the specific balance of aesthetic and emotional qualities perceived in initial consonants, final vowels, and rhyming categories. This range and subtlety are further increased by the poetic nuances possible in the primarily classical Chinese language of song lyrics. In conjunction with the highly rhythmic and musical quality produced by the basic lyric structure and the use of rhyme and speech-tone patterns, song lyrics eminently well suited to the display of skill in the expression of emotion can be created.

Figure 5
Tones in Mandarin Chinese

Order	Tone category	Tone name	Tone pitch	Pitch diagram	Tone mark	Example
First tone	*yin ping sheng* (*yin* level tone)	(high) level-tone	high and level		—	i —　*mā* (mother)
Second tone	*yang ping sheng* (*yang* level tone)	(middle) rising-tone	begins in middle, and rises high		\	6 i.　*má* (hemp)
Third tone	*shang sheng* (ascending tone)	turning-tone	from 1/2 low, falls, then rises to 1/2 high		>	5 3. 6　*mǎ* (horse)
Fourth tone	*qu sheng* (going tone)	falling-tone	from high, falls to low		/	i 3.　*mà* (to curse)

Each horizontal line in the pitch diagram represents a half-step in pitch; do (1) is at the bottom, and do an octave higher (i̇) at the top. The horizontal lines are elongated at the pitch intervals that form the standard seven-tone scale: do (1), re (2), mi (3), fa (4), so (5), la (6), and ti (7).

STAGE SPEECH

There are three major types of stage speech *(nianbai)* in Beijing opera, all of which may be spoken by characters of any role type: prose speeches, the recitation of quotations from classical poetry, and conventionalized stage speeches. Each type of speech serves a different structural and dramatic purpose.[26]

PROSE SPEECHES

The majority of stage speech consists of prose speeches (*taici,* lit. "stage lines"), the monologue and dialogue of Beijing opera. In the early years of Beijing opera, prose speeches were frequently improvised; in the twentieth century, this practice is continued by *chou* roles. Improvisation is possible because even the most heightened prose speeches contain much more vernacular than do song lyrics. There are no prescribed forms for prose dialogue or monologue. However, most prose speeches are short, achieving their most common purposes—plot advancement through conversation, or the injection of humor—as directly as possible.

Yet prose speeches are by no means colorless. All have strong rhythmic elements, achieved in performance through the stylized articulation of monosyllabic sound units, and all have a musical flavor, attained in performance through the stylized pronunciation of speech-tones. The more heightened prose speeches make use of literary allusion; alliteration is used for both serious and comic effect. Their very brevity causes prose speeches to stand out in contrast to song lyrics—they are sparkling compressions of a character's nature as evidenced in social interaction, set amidst the extended emotional expressions of song.

CLASSICAL POETRY

Quotations from classical poetry *(gushi)* are used sparingly; few plays include more than one or two such quotations, and many plays have none at all. In most instances, the quotation of classical poetry provides a heightening effect; these poems are the only occurrences of pure classical Chinese in the vast majority of Beijing opera plays. However, incorrect quotation is occasionally made, especially by *chou* and flower *dan,* for comic effect.

In quotations of classical poetry, the poetic form is of course that in use at the time the poetry was written; Han (206 B.C.–A.D. 220) *fu,* Tang (618–907) *shi,* Song (960–1279) *ci,* and Yuan (1271–1368) *qu* forms are all quoted, as are their even earlier predecessors.[27] Classical poetry is indisputably beautiful, as well as complex in form, and its proper reading and interpretation—or skillful misreading and misinterpretation—constitute a major display of speech skill.

CONVENTIONALIZED STAGE SPEECHES

Conventionalized stage speeches *(chengshi nianbai)* are spoken in almost every play, at important transition points. There are three major types of conventionalized stage speeches, which provide a standard procedure for entrance, exit, and for plot recapitulation.

Entrance *(shangchang)* speeches, collectively called self-introduction speeches *(zi bao jiamen),* are the most complex. Unlike the prose speeches described above, each type of conventionalized entrance speech has a prescribed style and structure, inherited from Yuan, Ming, regional, and folk forms of *xiqu.*[28] The initial entrance of a major character frequently includes the delivery of three distinct kinds of entrance speeches in a prescribed order: a prelude poem, a set-the-scene poem, and a prose set-the-scene speech.

The prelude poem *(yinzi)* is delivered immediately upon entrance, often at downstage center before sitting. Prelude poems may be entirely spoken or may be partly spoken and partly sung *a cappella.* They serve to establish the general atmosphere of the scene that is to follow. Most do not exceed four lines in length; those that do are termed "large" prelude poems *(da yinzi).* Two standard patterns of equal-length lines are frequently followed: two lines of seven written-characters each, and four lines of five written-characters each, the latter of which is termed "tiger head" prelude poem *(hutou yinzi).* However, prelude poems often do not occur in pairs of related lines; they are not bound by the couplet *(lian)* structure of the lyrics. An odd number of lines and unequal line length are in fact considered to be of greater aesthetic value in prelude poems. *The Ruse of the Empty City (Kong cheng ji)* includes a "large" prelude poem in seven lines of four, three, four, four, three, three, and four written-characters, respectively. *Silang Visits His Mother* includes a prelude poem in three lines of five, four, and four written-characters, respectively. Nor is rhyme a necessary attribute of prelude poems. Those that do rhyme do so within one of the thirteen rhyme categories utilized by the lyrics. Rhymes may occur at the end of lines, internally within lines, or in a combination of these two placements, as in *Silang Visits His Mother* (rhyming words are underlined):

jin	*jin*	*suo wu*	*tong,*		(The *wutong* tree locked in a golden courtyard,)	
chang tan	*sheng*	*sui*			(A long sigh)	
yi	*zhen*	*na*	*feng.*		(carried away on the breeze.)[29]	

A prelude poem may be replaced in the sequence of three entrance speeches by an opening song that fulfills the same atmospheric function, as in *The Favorite Concubine Becomes Intoxicated.*

The second conventional entrance speech, a set-the-scene poem (variously termed *chuchang shi, dingchang shi,* and *zuochang shi* in Chinese), is spoken after the prelude poem and usually after the character doing the speaking is seated.[30] Set-the-scene poems describe the basic situation in which the character speaking is involved, and convey his or her general state of mind. Unlike prelude poems, set-the-scene poems are bound by the couplet *(lian)* structure of the lyrics; the equal-length lines of each poem occur in related pairs, with each line divisible into three *dou.* Most set-the-scene poems are composed of two couplets, with seven written-characters in each of the four lines. However, poems of four couplets do occur, as do poems with ten written-characters per line. A special type of set-the-scene poem, called "single couplet" set-the-scene poem *(shangchang dui),* is composed of only one couplet, often with five written-characters per line instead of seven; it is conventionally used to indicate that the character speaking is poor, but has a soaring, beautiful spirit. Each set-the-scene poem is rhymed, usually at the end of every line, in one of the thirteen rhyme categories. The set-the-scene poem in *The Favorite Concubine Becomes Intoxicated* is in the standard two couplets (rhyming words are underlined):

Li	*zhi*	*tian*	*sheng*	*nan zi*		*juan;*
Cheng huan	*shi*	*yan*	*jiu*	*wei*		*nian.*
Liu	*gong*	*fen*	*dai*	*san qian*		*zhong;*
San	*qian*	*chong ai*	*yi*	*shen*		*zhuan.*

In translation, this poem reads (rhyming words are underlined):

True beauty is heaven sent, not one's <u>own</u>;
So bestowed, gratefully, I serve the <u>throne</u>.
Concubines numbering three thousand souls;
Of them all, he adores myself <u>alone</u>.[31]

The last major conventional entrance speech is for self-introduction. It begins with a statement of the character's name *(tongming),* which is followed by a prose set-the-scene speech *(dingchang bai)* in which the character speaking more explicitly identifies himself or herself by describing family and social relations, and explains in some detail the situation and his or her feelings about it. Self-introductions vary greatly in length, depending primarily upon the complexity of the situation involved. Their language is of the level appropriate to the role type and specific character speaking, as is all the monologue and dialogue following the conventional entrance speeches in each scene. In *The Favorite Concubine Becomes Intoxicated,* the Favorite Concubine speaks the following self-introduction: "I am Yang Yuhuan; by my lord adored, and named his Favorite. Last night he ordered me to arrange a feast at Fragrance Hall today. Gao, Pei, my lords; is the feast well prepared? Then lead on, to Fragrance Hall."[32]

Simplified conventions are applied when major characters make subsequent entrances, and for all minor character entrances that utilize conventionalized entrance speeches. In the simplest instances, a cough, a cry, or a prose line is delivered off-stage; the character then enters and proceeds immediately to the action of the scene. In other cases, an entrance poem (*shangchang shi* or *shangchang bai,* lit. "entrance speech") may be delivered. An entrance poem is a simplified, combined version of a set-the-scene poem and a set-the-scene speech; most consist of a single couplet with five written-characters per line. When two or more characters enter together, they frequently speak the lines of an entrance poem in alternation.

In some plays the first entrance of a *chou* character is marked by the recitation of "counted beats" *(shuban).* Usually these speeches have the same content and function as set-the-scene poems or speeches; in the latter instance, however, they are rarely preceded by a statement of the character's name *(tongming).* "Counted beats" speeches are usually fairly long and have no prescribed number of lines. They often have seven or ten written-characters per line, though they are not bound by the lyric couplet *(lian)* structure and hence may be of unequal line length. Lines are generally divisible into two semantic and syntactic units that may be separated by pauses in delivery. Units of four and three written-characters are common in seven-written-character lines; three- and seven-written-character units often occur in ten-written-character lines. "Counted beats" speeches are rhymed, usually at the end of each line and in one of the thirteen rhyme categories throughout. They are recited to a strong rhythm that is punctuated by the clapper and are usually quite humorous, in keeping with the *chou* role type. However, they can also be used quite tragically and movingly, as they are by the character Zhang Yunxiu in *Qing Feng Pavilion (Qing feng ting).* Such serious "counted beats" speeches are referred to as "tearful yearning" *(ku xiangsi).*

Entry may also be marked by the singing of conventionalized lyrics, followed directly by the action of the scene, as in the barbarian Princess's entry in the first scene of *Silang Visits His Mother*. If the entering character is coming from a distance, this singing may occur offstage, with action commencing immediately upon the performer's physical appearance on the stage. In all cases except the cough or cry and the single prose line, entrance-speech conventions utilize verse.

Whereas the focus in conventionalized entrance speeches is upon opening a scene, that in conventionalized exit *(xiachang)* speeches is upon closing a scene, and frequently upon setting up the succeeding entrance as well. In many ways, however, conventionalized exit speeches are similar to simplified entrance conventions. An exit poem *(xiachang shi* or *xiachang bai,* lit. "exit speech") may be delivered, sometimes followed by a single spoken line. Like set-the-scene poems, exit poems describe the basic situation in which the character speaking is involved and convey his or her general state of mind. They are also bound by the lyric couplet structure, occurring therefore in related pairs of equal-length lines, each divisible into three *dou*. When a set-the-scene poem of two couplets is used at the beginning of a scene, an exit poem with the same number of couplets and matching line length (usually seven written-characters per line) is often recited. When a scene opens with a "single couplet" set-the-scene poem, it almost invariably closes with a "single couplet" exit poem *(xiachang dui)*. However, while the "single couplet" set-the-scene poem is usually in seven-written-character lines, the "single couplet" exit poem may occur in either seven- or five-written-character lines. Like those of entrance poems, the lines of exit poems may be divided among two or more characters. Exits may also be marked by "counted beats" speeches, or by singing. In the latter case, the singing is sometimes followed by spoken lines, laughing, or crying. All exit speech conventions begin in verse, though they frequently end in prose.

Recapitulation (*diaochang,* lit. "hanging/ or suspending the scene"), the third major type of conventionalized stage speech, may occur during the course of any scene other than the first and is spoken by supporting more often than major characters.[33] It consists of a prose recapitulation of the major plot developments up to that point in the play. Recapitulation occurs primarily because of the *zhezixi* performance tradition; a recapitulation reminds the audience of the entire plot when a scene is excerpted from a full play and performed separately. Recapitulation serves a second purpose as well, however; in recapitulation, plot development and the character's feelings are stated clearly in predominantly vernacular prose. Because the lyrics and many heightened speeches may not be readily understandable to many audience members, recapitulation also serves a useful clarifying function in the production of an entire play.

In fact, all conventionalized stage speeches, in the course of marking transition points within a given play, serve to clarify plot and character relationships and thereby to facilitate the *zhezixi* performance tradition. Perhaps even more important, however, they provide a conventionalized aural framework that runs throughout all Beijing opera performances. The marking of transition points with conventionalized speeches highlighting the importance of major characters is an important element in creating a separate, aural world for Beijing opera. And performances of prelude poems, set-the-scene poems, and exit poems constitute major displays of speech skill within that world.

The display of speech skill serves primarily to support—to lead into and out of—the principal, extended emotional expression that occurs in the display of song skill. Prose speech does so by advancing the action of the plot, creating the situations that produce emotional reactions. The conventionalized stage speeches of major characters do so by conveying the basic emotional states of those characters at transition points—by clearly stating the emotions that are to be expressed. Featured within this focusing, supportive fabric of speech are the concentrated, extended expressions of emotion made through the display of song skill. In performance, the lyrics sung in the display of song skill can be wedded to those melodic and rhythmic practices of the Beijing opera musical system that best convey the precise emotions being expressed.

CHAPTER III

THE MUSICAL SYSTEM:
MUSICAL ELEMENTS

In Beijing opera, the musical system (*shengqiang xitong,* lit. "vocal melodic-passage system") is conceptualized as the source of vocal music. The musical system used in Beijing opera is known as *pihuang;* it is so important to this "sung theatre" that Beijing opera is sometimes referred to as *pihuang* theatre *(pihuangxi).* But no music for any passage of lyrics in any Beijing opera play is entirely fixed. Specific musical passages are to varying extents actually created by the singing performers themselves, both in rehearsal and in performance.[1]

The *pihuang* musical system is characterized by three major elements: melodic-phrases *(qiang),* metrical types *(banshi),* and modes *(diaoshi)* and modal systems *(shengqiang xitong).*[2] These elements are hierarchically related and influence one another to considerable extents. Collectively, melodic-phrases, metrical types, and modes and modal systems provide performers with patterns *(guilü)* of melody, meter, tempo, and rhythm. The smallest meaningful elements are melodic-phrases, which have certain melodic tendencies—tendencies toward certain patterns of pitches. Metrical types are a more comprehensive element; the meter, tempo, and melodic tendencies of melodic-phrases are modified by metrical types. Modes and modal systems are the most comprehensive element. Specific metrical types are each associated with a specific mode, and each mode is associated with a modal system. Every mode significantly modifies the rhythm and melodic tendencies of both its associated metrical types and its individual melodic-phrases, and each modal system has regular procedures for modulation between its associated modes. In composing the music for a specific play, performers select and interpretively arrange modal systems and modes to suit the overall atmosphere of that play and the fundamental psychology of its major characters. They then select and interpretively arrange metrical types, and finally compose specific melodic-phrases, to express the specific emotional content of each passage of lyrics.

Two modal systems are included in the *pihuang* musical system, *xipi* and *erhuang*. The term *pihuang* is simply an abbreviated statement of their names *([xi] pi [er] huang)*. Because the melodic-phrases of the two modal systems share several important characteristics, as do the metrical types, the following analysis of the major elements of the *pihuang* system begins with discussions of these two smaller elements and then proceeds to an analysis of the modes and modal systems themselves.[3]

MELODIC-PHRASES

A melodic-phrase *(qiang)* can be defined as "the joining of written-character and song."[4] Although the term is often loosely applied to any passage of singing in Beijing opera, it also has a much more specific meaning. The couplet structure of song lyrics provides the structural framework for *pihuang* music; within this framework, a melodic-phrase is the melodic progression (i.e., passage of specific pitches) for singing a single written-character. The two or more melodic-phrases needed to sing a *dou* are termed a melodic-section *(qiangjie,* lit. "section of melodic-phrases"), and the three or more melodic-sections required to sing an entire opening or closing line are termed a melodic-line *(qiangju,* lit. "line of melodic-phrases").

Collectively, these progressively larger units of melodic-phrases are called melodic-passages *(changqiang,* lit. "sung melodic-phrases"). Each song consists of a complete melodic-passage *(wanzheng changqiang)* in which the written-characters of a complete passage of lyrics are joined with music in melodic-phrases, -sections, and -lines that correspond to the individual written-characters, *dou,* and lines of lyrics.

The following example of a melodic-passage is a single melodic-line. Vertical dashed lines separate the individual melodic-phrases; those dashed lines with horizontal lines at top and bottom indicate *dou,* and therefore melodic-section, divisions. The pitches in parentheses are instrumental interludes and are not sung.[5]

Example 1 A Melodic-passage

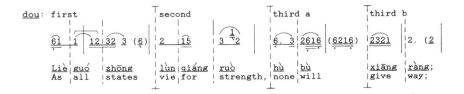

In this melodic-line, the direct correspondence between written-characters and melodic-phrases is evident, as is that between melodic-sections and *dou*.

Each mode and metrical type influences the melodic progressions of melodic-phrases, -sections, and -lines. However, melodic-phrases themselves have certain innate melodic tendencies. These tendencies arise from two types of influence: the influence of language, and the influence of age and gender.

THE INFLUENCE OF LANGUAGE ON MELODY

The meaning of every written-character, when pronounced in Mandarin Chinese, is conveyed not only through articulation but through the use of speech-tone as well, as discussed in chapter 2. In the melodic-phrase used to sing a given written-character, the appropriate speech-tone should be made clear or the meaning of that written-character might be lost. Hence, melodic-phrases are based upon four very fundamental pitch progressions, one for each speech-tone: 1 1 for the level-tone, 6 1 for the rising-tone, 5 3 6 for the turning-tone, and 1 3 for the falling-tone. But these pitches are relative rather than absolute, so that, for instance, a level-tone may be sung 2 2, and a rising tone 1 2 relative to it.

The general rule in singing is "first set the written-character, then move the melodic-phrase."[6] In other words, the first several pitches of a given melodic-phrase usually make the speech-tone of that written-character clear; further pitches sung during a continuation of that syllable need not convey speech-tone and can therefore be sung without denotative restrictions in melodic contour, except that the final pitch of a given melodic-phrase must be one that allows the speech-tone of the following written-character to be set clearly relative to it. For instance, the melodic-phrase used to sing a turning-tone word should probably not end on 5 if a level-tone, rising-tone, or falling-tone word is to follow, because 6 is above many performers' vocal ranges.

Certain standard variations in the pitch progressions used to indicate speech-tone are made for word emphasis. As in English, a given word may be stressed by raising or lowering the pitch at which that word is spoken or sung—i.e., a turning-tone word, 5 3 6, may be stressed by the initial pitch progressions 6 5 1 and 3 2 5. In Mandarin Chinese, word emphasis may also be attained by stressing the speech-tone of the written-character; a turning-tone word may therefore also be stressed by enlarging the pitch

Figure 6

A Comparison of Speech-tones in Mandarin Chinese and in Selected Regional Dialects

Tone name in Mandarin	Mandarin word example	Fundamental pitch progressions			
		Mandarin	Nanjing	Henan	Huguang
Level	*mā* (mother)	1 –	5 3.	5 1.	1 –
Rising	*má* (hemp)	6 1.	6 1.	1 3.	53 6
Turning	*mǎ* (horse)	53. 6	1 –	1 –	6 3.
Falling	*mà* (to curse)	1 3.	1 –	13 5	5 1.

range of the pitch progression indicative of its speech-tone, as in 5 2 6. Because of the influences of metrical types and modes upon melody, which will be discussed below, in some instances it is not possible to sing clearly the speech-tone of every written-character. However, even in such cases an attempt is made to indicate speech-tone, if only conventionally.[7]

Although no fixed, absolute pattern of pitch progression is followed for each speech-tone, the indication of speech-tone in each melodic-phrase—through fundamental pitch progressions, standard variations for word emphasis, or more conventional means—ultimately gives melodic-phrases certain characteristic melodic tendencies. Cumulative patterns of melodic tendencies in melodic-sections, melodic-lines, and arias are the result of the patterns of level and oblique speech-tones followed in the couplet structure of the lyrics. If, for instance, the speech-tone pattern followed in a given line is — — | | — — | (level, level, oblique, oblique, level, level, oblique), a finite though large number of speech-tone placement possibilities are prescribed: level level, rising rising, level rising, or rising level for the first *dou;* turning turning, falling falling, turning falling, or falling turning for the second *dou;* and level level turning, level level falling, rising rising turning, rising rising falling, level rising turning, level rising falling, rising level turning, or rising level falling for the third *dou.* Because the speech-tone of each written-character is in its melodic-phrase indicated by one of several melodic tendencies, the finite though large number of speech-tone placement possibilities in melodic-lines give to melodic-lines a large but also finite number of possible patterns of cumulative melodic tendencies. The melodic tendencies of melodic-phrases and melodic-lines are integral to Beijing opera's *pihuang* musical system; the change to another dialect of Chinese would necessitate a corresponding change to another set of melodic tendencies to indicate the tones peculiar to that dialect, and on that basis alone the musical system would no longer be Beijing opera's. Figure 6 illustrates the differences such a change would make in the fundamental pitch progressions indicative of speech-tone.[8]

The Influence of Gender and Age on Melody

Whether a character is male or female makes an important difference in the melodic tendencies of the melodic-phrases, -sections, and -lines that a performer sings to express that character's thoughts and feelings. Melodic-passages that by association are indicative of masculinity are called male melodic-passages *(nanqiang)*; those that convey the sense of femininity are termed female melodic-passages *(nüqiang)*. Although certain specific melodic tendencies and contours of male and female melodic-passages arise from the influence of metrical types and modes, three basic differences between male and female melodic-passages are evident in all melodic-passages: female melodic-passages are pitched higher than male, are more melismatic (i.e., have more individual pitches within each melodic-phrase) than male, and tend to be slower in tempo.

The following example compares a male with a female melodic-line, both of which are in the same metrical type, mode, and modal system.[9]

Example 2 A Male and a Female Melodic-line Compared

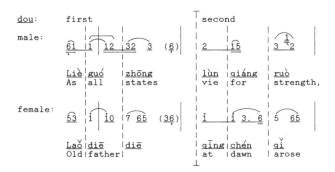

(continued)

Example 2 (continued)

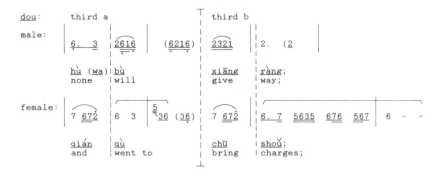

The female melodic-line is much higher in overall pitch than the male, is in $\frac{4}{4}$ rather than $\frac{2}{4}$ meter (and is therefore slower in tempo, because of the relationship between meter and tempo in *pihuang* music, to be discussed below), and contains appreciably more melisma—the male melodic-line has twenty-four notes and one grace note, and the female melodic-line has thirty-eight notes and one grace note.

Female melodic-passages, characterized by these three important features, are used when musically interpreting the lyrics of most *dan* characters; male melodic-passages are sung in the interpretation of most *sheng* and all *jing* and *chou* lyrics. However, age rather than gender is the basis for interpreting the lyrics of older *dan* characters and young *sheng* characters. Young *sheng* characters have not yet entered the state of adult manhood; their lyrics are sung with female melodic-passages containing slightly less melisma than other female melodic-passages and frequent uncharacteristically low pitches, to convey the strength of potential manhood. Older *dan* characters have the same intrinsic dignity associated with older *sheng* characters; their lyrics are sung with male melodic-passages pitched slightly higher and containing slightly more melisma than male melodic-passages for other role types, to convey the dignified, time-honed femininity of older *dan*.

These melodic tendencies are modified somewhat by each individual role type. Role types that feature the expressive display of song skill are in most instances interpreted musically with somewhat higher overall pitch and somewhat more melisma than are those in which song is not the major expressive skill. Of those roles that are interpreted with male melodic-passages, older *sheng*, older *dan*, and great-painted-face roles are therefore in most instances sung with a higher overall pitch and more melisma than are martial *sheng,* martial *jing,* and *chou* roles. And of those roles that are interpreted with female melodic-passages, blue cloth *dan* and the young *sheng* paired with them are usually interpreted with higher overall pitch and more melisma than are flower *dan,* the young *sheng* paired with them, and martial *dan.* The fundamental difference, however, is between male and female; all role types and the melodic-passages used in their musical interpretation are classified as either male or female.

METRICAL TYPES

The second basic element of the *pihuang* musical system is metrical type (*banshi,* lit. "accented beat style"; also called *qudiao,* lit. "song air"); *pihuang* music includes ten major metrical types. Each metrical type has a characteristic tempo, is associated with certain characteristic melodic tendencies, and is perceived as appropriate for certain dramatic situations. Metrical types are classified in two categories: metered metrical types (*shangban de banshi,* lit. "accented beat styles that use accented beats") and free metrical types (*ziyou banshi,* lit. "accented beat styles free of accented beats"). To facilitate comparison between metrical types, all examples in the following descriptions of specific metrical types are opening-line male melodic-passages in the same mode unless otherwise noted.[10]

METERED METRICAL TYPES

The *pihuang* musical system includes six principal metered metrical types: primary-meter *(yuanban),* slow-meter *(manban),* fast-meter *(kuaiban),* fast-three-eyes-meter *(kuaisanyan),* two-six-meter *(erliuban),* and flowing-water-meter *(liushuiban).* Every metered metrical type provides a pattern of accented beats *(ban)* and unaccented beats (*yan,* lit. "eyes") by which melodic-lines and melodic-passages are organized. In performance, each accented beat is usually marked by the percussive sounding of the wooden clapper (*ban,* lit. "accented beat [marker]"), described in detail in chapter 6 below.

Primary-meter (*yuanban,* lit. "primary/original accented beat [type]") is perceived as the most fundamental metrical type; all other metrical types are defined relative to it. Primary-meter is "designed to be about seventy-two beats per minute, like a healthy resting heart."[11] In other words, its tempo is moderate. Primary-meter is characterized by performers as having "one

accented beat [for every] one eye" *(yi ban yi yan);* that is, one accented beat
and one unaccented beat in each measure. In Western musical analysis, it is
duple meter, in most instances $\frac{2}{4}$. Lyrics with either ten or seven written-
characters per line may be sung in primary-meter, although the latter occurs
somewhat more frequently. In the following example, accented beats *(ban)*
are marked with an X, and unaccented beats *(yan)* with an O.[12]

Example 3 Male Primary-meter in Ten- and Seven-written-character Lines

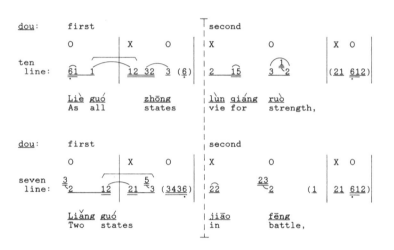

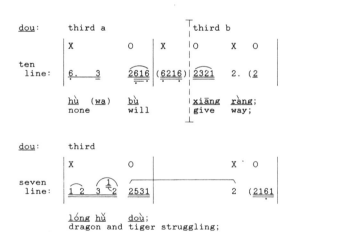

Primary-meter is used most often in fairly straightforward, relatively unemotional situations for the narration of events or the setting forth of facts and
explanation.

Slow-meter (*manban,* lit. "slow accented beat [type]") is the slowest metrical type. "Its special characteristic is that you have to wait five minutes for
the next word."[13] Performers characterize slow-meter as having "one
accented beat [for every] three eyes" *(yi ban san yan);* that is, one accented
and three unaccented beats in each measure. Slow-meter is sometimes also
called "slow-three-eyes" *(mansanyan).* In Western musical analysis, it is
quadruple meter, in most instances $\frac{4}{4}$. Every accented and unaccented beat
of slow-meter has a longer duration than do those of primary-meter. Slow-
meter is generally used to sing lyrics with ten written-characters per line,
although occasionally lyrics with seven written-characters per line are sung
in slow-meter. In the following example, the third *dou* is divided into two
syntactic and melodic-sections; this in some instances occurs in primary-
meter with lines of ten written-characters, but almost always occurs in slow-
meter.[14]

Example 4 Male Slow-meter

As is evident from this example, slow-meter is considerably more melismatic than is primary-meter—several melodic-phrases in every line of slow-
meter have extended, highly ornamented melodic progressions. Slow-meter
is usually sung in relatively peaceful, introspective situations.

Fast-meter (*kuaiban,* lit. "fast accented beat [type]") is the fastest metrical type. "Fast-meter is used when you've got a lot to say, fast!"[15] Performers characterize fast-meter as having "four accented beats [and] no eyes" *(si ban wu yan),* or as "having accented beats [but] no eyes" *(you ban wu yan);* each measure of fast-meter contains only one, accented beat. Every beat has a shorter duration than do those of primary-meter. In Western musical analysis, fast-meter is single-beat meter, in most instances $\frac{1}{4}$. Fast-meter is almost always used to sing lyrics with seven written-characters per line. As is evident in the following example, fast-meter melodic-lines are quite short.[16]

Example 5 Male Fast-meter

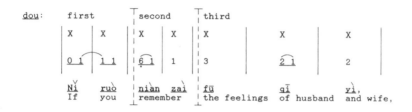

Whereas slow-meter is extremely melismatic, fast-meter is basically syllabic —many melodic-phrases contain only one pitch, and only a very few contain more than two. Fast-meter is highly animated,[17] and usually occurs in situations of excitement or anticipation.

Slow-meter, primary-meter, and fast-meter encompass the entire range of possible tempos and degrees of melisma in the metered metrical types of *pihuang* music. Slow-meter, which is slow in tempo and has strong melismatic melodic tendencies, and fast-meter, which is fast in tempo and strongly syllabic in its melodic tendencies, define the two extremes of this range. Primary-meter is firmly in the center, moderate in both tempo and degree of melisma. The three other metered metrical types, fast-three-eyes-meter, two-six-meter, and flowing-water-meter, fall within the range thus demarcated.

Fast-three-eyes *(kuaisanyan)*-meter is "approximately twice as fast as slow-meter, and twice as slow as primary-meter."[18] It takes its name from its metrical organization, which is the same as that of slow-meter *(yi ban san yan,* lit. "one accented beat [for every] three eyes [i.e., unaccented beats]"). Each beat in fast-three-eyes-meter is of longer duration than a beat in primary-meter, but of shorter duration than a beat in slow-meter. Like slow-meter, fast-three-eyes-meter is in quadruple meter according to Western musical analysis, in most instances $\frac{4}{4}$. It is generally used to sing lyrics with ten written-characters per line, as in the following example.[19]

Example 6 Male Fast-three-eyes-meter

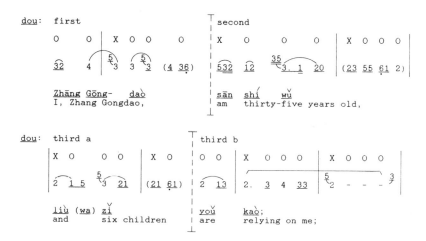

Fast-three-eyes-meter is less melismatic than slow-meter, but more melismatic than primary-meter, as can be seen through a comparison of the above examples: there are thirty-two notes and seven grace notes in the fast-three-eyes-meter in Example 6; forty-one notes and seven grace notes in the slow-meter in Example 4; and twenty-four notes and one grace note in the ten-written-character primary-meter in Example 3. Fast-three-eyes-meter is sung in introspective situations, like slow-meter, and in relatively unemotional, straightforward situations, like primary-meter.

When fast-three-eyes-meter is sung in interpretation of a young *sheng* character, it is given a special name: children's-tunes-meter *(wawadiao)*. As mentioned above, certain important melodic tendencies differentiate male and female melodic-passages; young *sheng* roles are sung with female melodic-passages. However, male melodic-passages with occasional especially high pitches are used by young *sheng* performers when singing fast-three-eyes-meter. In spite of its name, children's-tune-meter, through its use of male melodic tendencies, gives the impression of great strength—perhaps the strength peculiar to youth.

Between primary-meter and fast-meter there are two metered metrical types of faster tempo and less melisma than primary-meter: two-six-meter *(erliuban)* and flowing-water-meter *(liushuiban)*. Two-six-meter is faster and more syllabic than primary-meter; flowing-water-meter is faster and more syllabic than two-six-meter, but still less so than fast-meter.

Two-six-meter in most instances uses the metrical organization of primary-meter—"one accented beat [for every] one unaccented beat," or $\frac{2}{4}$ meter.[20] In some instances, however, male melodic-passages of two-six-meter use the metrical organization of fast-meter—"four accented beats [and] no unaccented beats,"or $\frac{1}{4}$ meter. In such cases the metrical type is referred to as fast two-six *(kuai erliu)*; the more standard two-six-meter metrical organization, which can be used for both male and female melodic-passages, may be called slow two-six *(man erliu)* in contradistinction. The pulse of slow two-six is slower than that of fast two-six, with each accented and unaccented beat of $\frac{2}{4}$ meter two-six-meter being held longer than those of $\frac{1}{4}$ meter. However, a single beat in either meter of two-six-meter is shorter in duration than one in primary-meter and longer than one in flowing-water-meter.

Flowing-water-meter uses the metrical organization of fast-meter—"four accented beats [and] no unaccented beats," or $\frac{1}{4}$ meter. Flowing-water-meter also occurs in both fast *(kuai)* and slow *(man)* versions. Both versions have the same metrical organization, but beats in the latter are of longer duration than those in the former. Each beat in either version of flowing-water-meter is longer in duration than each beat of fast-meter and shorter than each beat of fast two-six. Flowing-water-meter is sometimes referred to as piled-up-meter *(duoban)*.[21]

Lyrics of both ten and seven written-characters per line may be sung in both two-six-meter and flowing-water-meter. Example 7 compares ten- and seven-written-character lines in $\frac{2}{4}$ meter two-six-meter, and in flowing-water-meter.[22] Two-six-meter is more syllabic and less ornamented than primary-meter, as can be seen through a comparison of Examples 3 and 7: the ten-written-character primary-meter melodic-line in Example 3 contains twenty-four notes and one grace note, while the ten-written-character two-six-meter melodic-line in Example 7 contains only nineteen notes and no grace notes; the seven-written-character primary-meter melodic-line in Example 3 contains eighteen notes and five grace notes, while the seven-written-character two-six-meter melodic-line in Example 7 contains sixteen notes and two grace notes. However, two-six-meter is less syllabic and more ornamented than flowing-water-meter; the ten- and seven-written-character flowing-water-meter melodic-lines both contain only twelve notes and no grace notes. And flowing-water-meter in turn is less syllabic than fast-meter,

**Example 7 Male Two-six-meter and Flowing-water-meter
in Ten- and Seven-written-character Lines**

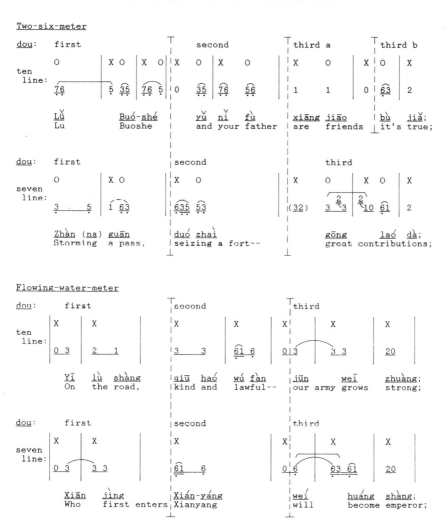

whose illustrative melodic-line in Example 5 contains only ten notes and no grace notes. Two-six-meter is sung in situations that are fairly straightforward but nonetheless have a sense of excitement or anticipation about them. Excitement or anticipation approaching (but not quite reaching) that conveyed in fast-meter calls for flowing-water-meter.

Figure 7

Metered Metrical Types

Tempo	Metrical Type	Metrical Organization — Chinese analysis	Metrical Organization — Western analysis	Number of notes per line in examples — 7 w-c* lines	Number of notes per line in examples — 10 w-c* lines	Number of grace notes per line in examples — 7 w-c* lines	Number of grace notes per line in examples — 10 w-c* lines
slow ↓	slow-meter	XOOO	$\frac{4}{4}$		41		7
	fast-three-eyes-meter	XOOO	$\frac{4}{4}$		32		7
	primary-meter	XOXO	$\frac{2}{4}$	18	24	5	1
	two-six-meter	XOXO	$\frac{2}{4}$	16	19	2	0
	flowing-water-meter	XXXX	$\frac{1}{4}$	(14	15	1	0)**
↓ fast	fast-meter	XXXX	$\frac{1}{4}$	12	12	0	0
		XXXX	$\frac{1}{4}$	10		0	0

melismatic ←——————————→ syllabic

*The letters "w-c" refer to "written-characters."

**These figures for male, single beat two-six-meter are based on several unidentified examples provided by Wu Junda, not given in the above discussion.

Figure 7 lists the names and metrical organization patterns of the six principal metered metrical types, and illustrates the overall relationship of their tempos and melodic tendencies.

FREE METRICAL TYPES

The *pihuang* musical system includes three principal free metrical types, dispersed-meter *(sanban),* lead-in-meter *(daoban),* and shaking-meter *(yaoban).* A fourth metrical type, undulating-dragon *(huilong)*-meter, is associated with the free metrical types although it is actually metered. The free metrical types have no rhythmic regulation. In each melodic passage in every free metrical type, the duration of every pitch is regulated relative to all other pitches in the melodic passage. However, all free metrical types are free of patterns of accented and unaccented beats, and therefore of regulating percussive accompaniment. For this reason, free metrical types are perceived as being "like the stopping of the heartbeat."[23] The freedom from a regulating pulse allows each free metrical type to be sung at a fairly broad range of tempos.

Dispersed-meter *(sanban,* lit. "dispersed/loosened/scattered accented beat [type]") is the basic free metrical type. It is generally sung at moderate tempos—within the tempos of fast-three-eyes-meter, primary-meter, and two-six-meter. Lyrics with either ten or seven written-characters per line may be sung in dispersed-meter; lines of both lengths are compared in Example 8.[24] Dispersed-meter is perceived as "less tense, more gentle" than the other free metrical types discussed below.[25]

Example 8 Male Dispersed-meter in Ten- and Seven-written-character Lines

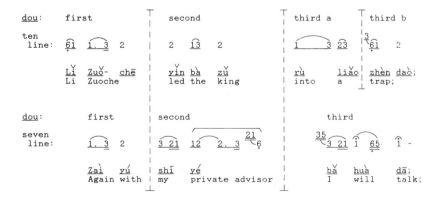

Lead-in-meter (*daoban,* also written as "collapsed" meter) is slower than dispersed-meter; its tempos range from those slower than slow-meter to those of slow-meter and fast-three-eyes-meter. Like dispersed-meter, it may be sung with lyrics of either seven or ten written-characters per line. Unlike dispersed-meter, lead-in-meter is in many instances only one melodic-line long; when it is used, it is usually sung with the first line of a multi-couplet passage of lyrics. One of its unique features is that although it is sung with an opening line of lyrics, it uses the song structure pattern for closing lines described below in the analysis of modes.

Undulating-dragon (*huilong,* lit. "turning/circling dragon")-meter, although a metered metrical type, is associated with the free metrical types because it is sung only after a melodic-line in lead-in-meter. Although lead-in meter can be used without undulating-dragon-meter, the latter must follow a melodic-line in lead-in-meter. A melodic-line in undulating-dragon-meter begins with the closing line of a couplet, using the song structure pattern for closing lines. Undulating-dragon-meter is almost always followed by slow-meter, fast-three-eyes-meter, or primary-meter, and takes the meter and tempo of the metered metrical type that succeeds it. A melodic passage in undulating-dragon-meter may be only one melodic-line in length or may include several melodic-lines. In most instances, the first line (i.e., a closing line) of a multi-line passage in undulating-dragon-meter has the same number of written-characters as the line that precedes it (i.e., an opening line); successive lines may continue with that number or may switch to the line length of the lyrics sung in a metered metrical type that follow. Undulating-dragon-meter is often used for a line containing padding written-characters, and frequently concludes with a very melismatic, extended melodic-phrase. The following example illustrates a ten-written-character line sung in lead-in-meter and followed by a ten-written-character line sung in undulating-dragon-meter.[26]

Lead-in meter tends to be quite high in pitch. Undulating-dragon-meter, as its name suggests, has melodic progressions that tend to undulate—rising and falling progressions of pitches within a fairly narrow range. Both are considerably more melismatic and ornamented than dispersed-meter. The ten-written-character dispersed-meter in Example 8 has sixteen notes and one grace note, whereas in Example 9 the lead-in-meter has fifty-two notes and nine grace notes, and the undulating-dragon-meter has forty-six notes and four grace notes. There is considerable leeway for individual passages of free metrical types in melisma and ornamentation, but these figures represent average ratios. Lead-in-meter, often followed by undulating-dragon-

Example 9 Male Lead-in-meter and Undulating-dragon-meter

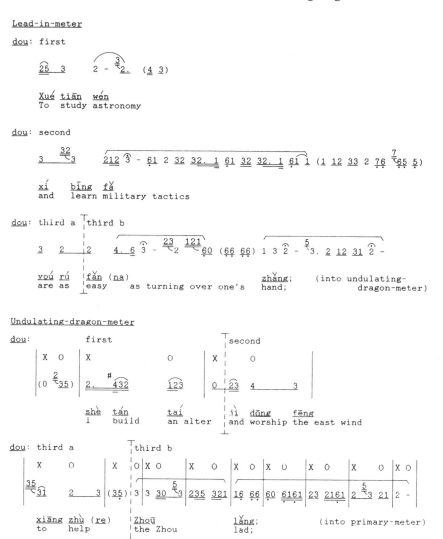

meter, is perceived as expressive of sudden grief, extreme unhappy surprise, and other intense, unexpected emotions. It may be sung onstage during a scene in which the singing character has just been startled, or offstage, preceding the character's highly emotional entrance.

The third free metrical type, shaking-meter *(yaoban),* is somewhat faster than dispersed-meter; its tempos are those of primary-meter and two-six-meter. Shaking-meter is distinct from the other two free metrical types in that it uses the single-beat-meter percussive accompaniment of flowing-water-meter. However, the singing itself is free from this rhythmic accompaniment; shaking-meter is frequently referred to as "beat urgently sing slowly/freely" *(jin da man/san chang)* for this reason. Like the other free metrical types, shaking-meter may be sung with lyrics of either seven- or ten-written-character lines, though the former is more common. In the following example, the first and third *dou* of a seven-written-character line both include padding written-characters.[27]

Example 10 Male Shaking-meter

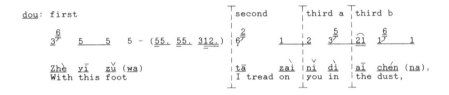

Shaking-meter is somewhat less melismatic than dispersed-meter, although it can be equally as ornamented. There are thirteen notes and four grace notes in this example of shaking-meter, and nineteen notes and four grace notes in the seven-written-character dispersed-meter in Example 8; these examples are representative of average ratios. Shaking-meter is expressive of exterior calm and interior tension—the emotions of lead-in-meter under control—with the singing character frequently in pursuit of a particular aim.

Figure 8 is a graphic representation of the general relationship between the free and the metered metrical types.

The melodic-phrases used to sing a melodic-line in each metrical type must cumulatively produce the proper degree of melisma for that metrical type. Simultaneously, they must indicate the speech-tone of each written-character being sung, and must be representative of either the male or female category of melodic-passages. In even the most melismatic metrical type, male melodic-passages are less melismatic than female; they have a lower overall pitch and a somewhat faster tempo as well. Each metrical type provides the overall tempo for its melodic-passages and, in the case of metered metrical types, a rhythmic organization for melodic-phrases, -sec-

Figure 8
A Comparison of Tempo and Melodic Tendencies
in Free and Metered Metrical Types

Tempo	Free Metrical Types	Metered Metrical Types	Melodic Tendencies
slow			melismatic
	lead-in-meter	slow-meter	
	undulating-dragon-meter	fast-three-eyes-meter	
	dispersed-meter	primary-meter	
shaking-meter		two-six-meter $\frac{2}{4}$	
		two-six-meter $\frac{4}{4}$	
		flowing-water-meter	
fast		fast-meter	syllabic

tions, and -lines. Most metrical types have at least two major versions, how-ever—a version in the *xipi* mode, and a version in the *erhuang* mode. All *xipi* metrical types share certain rhythmic and melodic characteristics, and differ substantially from their *erhuang* versions as a result.

MODES AND MODAL SYSTEMS

Modes *(diaoshi,* also called *qiangdiao)* and modal systems *(shengqiang xitong)* are the most comprehensive elements of the *pihuang* musical system. Each of the two modal systems encompasses a principal mode, whose rhythmic and melodic characteristics are shared by all of its associated metrical types, and several secondary modes. The *xipi* modal system takes its name from its principal mode, *xipi; erhuang* is the principal mode of the *erhuang* system. In each modal system, the secondary modes include an inverse *(fan),* tragic version of the principal mode as well as one or more additional secondary modes that share antecedents with the principal mode, and for which the accompanying musical instruments are tuned the same as for either the principal or the inverse mode.

PRINCIPAL MODES

Each principal mode *(zheng diaoshi)* has an identifiably different modal identity *(diaoshixing,* lit. "mode nature") established by four types of structural patterns *(guilü,* which may also be translated as "rules"). Each is identified by its unique, characteristic patterns of modal rhythm, song structure, melodic contour and construction, and keys and cadences. As a result of the modal identity established by the combination of specific structural patterns, each principal mode is experienced as having its own characteristic atmosphere *(qifen).*[28] The following sections describe each of these types of structural patterns and compare the specific patterns followed in *xipi* and *erhuang* modes. The initial comparison is made in male primary-meter for clarity; alterations in these patterns for female melodic-passages and different metrical types are discussed thereafter.

Modal Rhythm

Modal rhythm *(diaoshi jiezou)* concerns the placement of the written-characters of the lyrics within metrical organization. Each mode follows a different, specific pattern of association between written-characters and accented and unaccented beats. In *xipi,* the melodic-phrase for singing the first written-character of each line begins on an unaccented beat; the melodic-phrase for singing the last written-character begins on an accented beat. In *erhuang,* the melodic-phrases for both the first and last written-characters in each line begin on accented beats. Within each melodic-line, a more flexible pattern of written-character placement is followed in each mode. The melodic-phrases for the internal written-characters in each line begin in many instances between beats; however, each internal written-character centers *(wei zhongxin)* on an accented or unaccented beat, depending upon its order within the melodic-line. For instance, in Example 3 above, the first *dou* of the opening line of ten-written-character male *xipi* primary-meter is

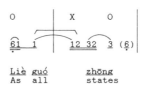

Lie begins on an unaccented beat; *guo* begins between beats but centers upon an accented beat; and *zhong* begins between beats but centers upon an unaccented beat. Figure 9 illustrates the patterns of modal rhythm in ten-

Figure 9
Patterns of Modal Rhythm in Opening Lines

Mode	Number of Written-characters per Line	First *dou*	Second *dou*	Third *dou*
Xipi	ten	O̲ X O	X O O	X O O X̲
	seven	O̲ X	X O	X O X̲
Erhuang	ten	X̲ O X	X O X	X O O X̲
	seven	X̲ O	X O	X O X̲

X = written-character on an accented beat

O = written-character on an unaccented beat

and seven-written-character opening lines in *xipi* and *erhuang* modes. The underlining identifies those written-characters that must begin on the beat indicated; melodic-phrases for all other written-characters need only center upon the indicated beat.

These patterns of modal rhythm are modified somewhat when line length is not standard, as when padding written-characters are used. Specific words are in some instances given interpretive stress by deviating from these patterns; for instance, a word that should center on an unaccented beat may be stressed by centering it on an accented beat, and a word that should center on an accented beat may be underplayed by centering it on an unaccented beat. However, the tendency to follow these patterns is quite strong.

In *xipi* mode, the patterns for placing written-characters within metrical organization in ten- and seven-written-character lines are the same in both opening and closing lines. In *erhuang*, however, the second *dou* in both ten- and seven-written-character closing lines have different placement patterns than in the opening lines: O O O and O O, respectively, in the closing lines, rather than the X O X and X O of the second *dou* in the opening lines.

Hypothetically, then, assuming one beat per melodic-phrase, these patterns of modal rhythm give *xipi* a single, standard melodic-line according to metrical organization, and give *erhuang* two standard lines—a standard opening line and a standard closing line. All three of these lines are seven measures long and are adaptable to lines of both ten and seven written-characters. In the following example of this hypothetical standard metrical organization, beats in parentheses do not serve as centers for written-characters in either the ten- or the seven-written-character pattern.

**Example 11 Hypothetical Standard Metrical Organization of Melodic-lines
in *Xipi* and *Erhuang***

```
                              Xipi

Hypothetical
Opening and Closing Melodic-lines

dou:              first        ⊤ second      ⊤ third

beats:    |(X) O | X  O  | ⌐ X  O  | X  O  | ⌐ X  O  |(X) O  | X (O)|
lyrics:       t     t  t    ⎸ t  t       t    ⎸ t  t       t    t
              s     s       ⎸ s  s            ⎸ s          s    s
                            ⌞_                ⌞_


                              Erhuang

Hypothetical
Opening Melodic-line

dou:              first        ⊤ second      ⊤ third

beats:    | X  O | X (O) | ⌐ X  O  | X (O) | ⌐ X  O  |(X) O  | X (O)|
lyrics:     t  t    t      ⎸ t  t      t     ⎸ t  t       t    t
            s  s          ⎸ s  s            ⎸ s          s    s
                         ⌞_               ⌞_

Hypothetical
Closing Melodic-line

dou:              first     ⊤ second            ⊤ third

beats:    | X  O | X ⎸O  | (X) O  |(X) O  | ⌐ X  O  |(X) O  | X (O)|
lyrics:     t  t    t ⎸t      t       t     ⎸ t  t       t    t
            s  s    ⎸ s       s            ⎸ s          s    s
                   ⌞_                      ⌞_
```

"t" indicates the placement of a written-character in a line of ten;
"s" indicates the placement of a written-character in a line of seven.

Song Structure

Song structure (*qushi*, lit. "song-style") concerns the relationship of the melodic-sections in the opening line of each couplet to the corresponding melodic-sections in the closing line—that is, the relationship of the first *dou* in the opening line to the first *dou* in the closing line, etc. Because the lyrics of both *xipi* and *erhuang* are in couplet structure, both use couplet song structure *(duiju qushi de jiegou)*. However, each uses a different type. The couplet song structure of *xipi* is termed changed-tail-structure (*huanweishi*, lit. "change the tail style"); it is a parallel couplet structure, with melodic-lines of equal length. *Erhuang*'s couplet song structure is called extended-pattern-structure (*yanshenxing*, lit. "extend the pattern"); it is a contrast couplet structure, with melodic-lines of unequal length.

In the changed-tail-structure of *xipi,* the first *dou* of the opening and closing lines are sung with the same melodic-section; likewise, the melodic-section for the second *dou* is the same in both lines. The third *dou,* however, has a different melodic-section in each line.

In the extended-pattern-structure of *erhuang,* the opening line is almost twice as long (i.e., contains almost twice as many measures) as the closing line; the standard is ten measures for the opening line and five for the closing line. And because note values are not simply lengthened, the opening line therefore has approximately twice as many notes per melodic-phrase as does the closing line. In practice, the melodic-phrases for the final written-characters in the first and second *dou* of the opening line are usually extended the most, and the melodic-sections for the first and second *dou* of the closing line are the most compact (i.e., have the fewest notes per melodic-phrase), allowing the melodic-section for the third *dou* of the closing line to be a bit more elaborate than those for the first two *dou*. Example 12 illustrates standard lines in changed-tail-structure and extended-pattern-structure. In this and following examples, beats that have no associated melodic-phrase are shown in parentheses. Parentheses within the melodic-line enclose the notes for connective instrumental accompaniment; when it can be extended for one or more additional measures, accompaniment is simply indicated and specific notes are not given.[29]

As can be seen in Example 12, the standard lines in the changed-tail-structure song structure of *xipi* are nearly identical to the hypothetical standard line constructed in Example 11 on the basis of *xipi's* modal rhythm patterns. The actual standard lines are both seven measures long, with melodic-sections of two, two, and three measures, respectively. The effects of the extended-pattern-structure of *erhuang* are in keeping with its name. The actual standard opening line is extended to ten measures, with melodic-sections of three, four, and three measures, respectively; the actual standard closing line is compacted to five measures, the first two of which complete the first two melodic-sections.

Within a multi-couplet passage of lyrics in *erhuang,* the first couplet almost always follows this extended-pattern-structure. However, in later couplets the opening line is sometimes tightened to parallel the closing line in both individual melodic-section and overall line length. This is done by assuming a different center for written-character placement in the first two *dou*. In the standard seven-written-character closing *erhuang* line, the second written-character in the first *dou* centers on the unaccented beat in the first measure, and the first written-character in the second *dou* centers on the unaccented beat in the second measure. In the tightened opening line, the latter written-character is perceived as centering on the accented beat in the second measure. In the standard ten-written-character closing *erhuang* line, the third written-character in the first *dou* is perceived as centering on

Example 12 Actual Standard Metrical Organization of Melodic-lines in *Xipi* and *Erhuang*

```
                                    Xipi
                        Changed-tail Song Structure

Actual
Opening and Closing Melodic-lines

dou:              first        ⊤second        ⊤third
                               |               |
beats:   |X)    O |X  (O) | |X  O|(X  O)   ||X O|(X)  O |X (O
                           |               |
opening
  line: i.c.) 12ⁱ23 (36) | 22 2 |(21 612) | 2 1 |(61) 3 |2 (i.c.
                           |               |
closing
  line: i.c.) 12ⁱ23 (36) | 22 2 |(21 612) | 2 3 |(61) 2 |1 (i.c.
                           |               |
lyrics:          tt  t   |tt  t        |t  t      t  t
                 ss      |s   s        |s        s  s
                         ⊥             ⊥


                                  Erhuang
                        Extended-pattern Song Structure

Actual
Opening Melodic-line

dou:              first              |second           ⊤third
                                     |                 |
beats:  |X O)|X  O |X   O |(X  O)  | |X   O|X O| X  (O |X O)||X O|(X)  O |X (O
                                     |                 ||
        i.c.)|2  3|2   -  |(21 612) | 1  3|2 6| 1 (i.c.| )||2 3|(36) 2 |1 (i.c.
                                     |                 ||
lyrics:      t    t   t           |t   t  t        |t  t     t  t
             s    s               |s   s           |s       s  s
                                  ⊥                 ⊥

Actual
Closing Melodic-line

dou:            first    ⊤2nd ⊤third
                         |    |
beats:      |X  O| X  | O ||X   O  |(X)  O |X (O
                         ||           |
            22 7 |(6)| 66 5||5  6   |(6)  2 |2 (i.c.
                         ||           |
lyrics:     tt  t   |tt  t|t   t      t  t
            s   s   |s   s|s          s  s
                    ⊥     ⊥
```

"i.c." indicates an extendable instrumental connective;
"t" indicates a written-character in a line of ten;
"s" indicates a written-character in a line of seven.

the accented beat in the second measure, and all three written-characters in the second *dou* center on the unaccented beat in the second measure. In the tightened ten-written-character opening *erhuang* line, the first written-character in the second *dou* is perceived as centering on the accented beat in the second measure (along with the last written-character in the first *dou*), the second on the unaccented beat in the second measure, and the third on the accented beat in the third measure (along with the first written-character in the third *dou*). When the opening and closing *erhuang* lines are made parallel in this fashion, it does not constitute a change to *xipi* because the other fundamental patterns of *erhuang* remain unchanged.

In addition to sung sections, songs in *pihuang* music also include instrumental connectives (*guomen*, lit. "through the door"). They are integral to song structure in both *xipi* and *erhuang*. Most metrical types in each mode have their own identifiable instrumental connectives, which come in three basic lengths. Small instrumental connectives *(xiao guomen)* are quite short, in most cases only one or part of one measure in length. Large instrumental connectives *(da guomen)* average eight measures in length, though they may be even longer. The third basic instrumental connective length is from one and one-half to three and one-half measures; such instrumental connectives are termed half-line instrumental connectives *(banju guomen)*.

Most passages of song are introduced by instrumental connectives that serve as preludes and are played before the singing of the lyrics begins; in the case of *xipi,* the final pitches of the prelude instrumental connective occupy the first, accented beat of the first measure in the opening melodic-line of an initial couplet, as can be seen in Example 12. Prelude instrumental connectives are in many cases large instrumental connectives, though small ones are used as an indication of surprise or sudden determination, especially in the faster metrical types.

All three lengths of instrumental connectives may serve as interludes within and between melodic-lines. Interlude instrumental connectives punctuate song structure, clarifying textual meaning by making the units of meaning (*dou* and lines) clear. By connecting closing lines to successive opening lines, they also tie together successive couplets in multi-couplet passages of lyrics.

Patterns for the placement of instrumental connectives are provided by the changed-tail song structure in *xipi* and by the extended-pattern song structure in *erhuang*. In both lines of a *xipi* couplet, small instrumental connectives occur at the end of the first *dou* and at the end of the second *dou.* Instrumental connectives, which may be either large or small, occur within the third *dou* and at the end of the third *dou;* the latter instrumental connective then continues through the first beat of the first *dou* of the succeeding line. In *erhuang* opening lines, instrumental connectives occur at the end of the first *dou* and at the end of the second *dou;* the first is small and the second is half-line. A small instrumental connective may also be placed within the third *dou,* and a large or small instrumental connective may be placed at the end of the third *dou,* if their occurrence in these positions enhances emotional expression in a particular passage of lyrics. *Erhuang* closing lines have only one prescribed instrumental connective, which may be either large or small, at the end of the third *dou;* it ties the closing line to the succeeding opening line. If helpful for emotional expression, a second, small instrumental connective may be used, in most instances placed either at the end of the first *dou* (usually in seven-written-character lines only) or within the third *dou* (in either line length).

The following example illustrates the placement and function of instru-

Example 13 Placement and Function of Instrumental Connectives in *Xipi* and *Erhuang*

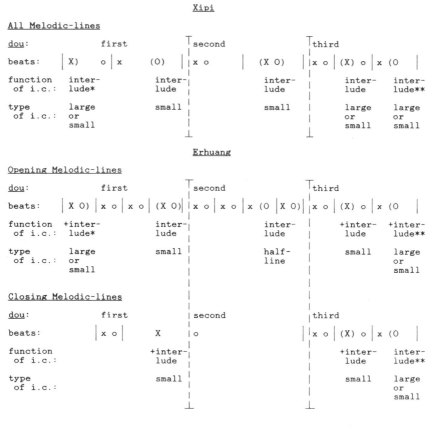

*   or prelude in the opening line of an initial couplet;
**   this connects to the successive line, except in the closing line of a concluding couplet, where it serves as a coda;
\+   these instrumental connectives are optional in <u>erhuang</u>, except for the opening line of an initial couplet, which requires a prelude.

mental connectives in song structure. Parentheses indicate the beat or beats devoted to each instrumental connective (i.c.).

The song structure of both principal modes is quite detailed. Yet it is a pattern, rather than an unbending rule. Within either mode, song structure may be modified—an instrumental connective may be omitted or added, melodic-phrases and melodic-sections may be lengthened or shortened—in the process of interpreting a specific passage of lyrics. However, such modification has impact and effectiveness as an interpretive technique precisely because of the strength of the basic patterns of song structure in *xipi* and *erhuang*. Changed-tail-structure and extended-pattern-structure are the standard conventional musical structures for emotional expression in the display of song skill.

Melodic Contour and Construction

Xipi and *erhuang* modes each have a basic melodic contour (*jichu changqiang*, lit. "basic melodic-passage") in two lines—an opening line and a closing line. The basic melodic contour for each mode is constructed upon characteristic pitch progressions. In *xipi* the characteristic pitch progressions are 1 2 3 and 3 2 1; in *erhuang,* they are 2 3 2 and 1 2 1. Example 14 illustrates these basic melodic contours.

Specific melodic-passages are composed for specific passages of lyrics following these basic melodic contours, frequently using their characteristic pitch progressions as figures (i.e., clearly recognizable melodic themes) as well. Each mode uses a different type of melodic construction (*changqiang jianzhu*, lit. "melodic-passage construction"). *Xipi*'s melodic construction is more disjunct. "Its melodics rise and fall over a rather wide pitch range, often in a series of step-wise [i.e., sequential] pitch progressions, but frequently soaring or dropping" as much as a sixth or a seventh.[30] Most second *dou,* however, are given melodic-sections with relatively level pitch progressions. The usual pitch range is 2 to 6. *Erhuang*'s melodic construction is more conjunct, using step-wise pitch progressions within a narrower pitch range, 5 to 6. "While sometimes small skips up or down in pitch are used, the melodies tend to be stable, smooth and steady, and relatively complex."[31] In both modes, the specific melodic progression for each melodic-phrase is of course influenced by the speech-tone of the word being sung.

In Example 15, the basic melodic contour for each melodic-passage is notated above the specific melodic-passage. Although in most instances each specific melodic-passage contains more individual pitch occurrences than does its basic melodic contour, the overall correspondence is evident.[32]

Example 14 Basic Melodic Contours in Male *Xipi* and *Erhuang*

Xipi Opening Line

dou:		first		second		third	
beats:	X)	0	X	(0)	X	0	(X | 0)	X	0	(X)	0	X	(0
bmc:	i.c.)	12	23	(36)	22	2	(21 | 612)	2	1	(61)	3	2	(i.c.

Xipi Closing Line

dou:		first		second		third	
beats:	X)	0	X	(0)	X	0	(X | 0)	X	0	(X)	0	X	(0
bmc:	i.c.)	12	23	(36)	22	2	(21 | 612)	2	3	(61)	2	1	(i.c.

Erhuang Opening Line

dou:		first			second			third	
beats:	X 0)	X	0	X	0	(X | 0)	X	0	X	0	X	(0 | X | 0)	X	0	(X)	0	X	(0
bmc:	i.c.)	2	3	2	-	(21 | 612)	1	3	2	6	1	(i.c. |)	2	3	(36)	2	1	(i.c.

Erhuang Closing Line

dou:		first	2nd	third	
beats:		X	0	X	0	X	0	(X)	0	X	(0
bmc:		22	7	(6)	66	5	5	6	(6)	2	2	(i.c.
	or	55	7					6	2	

(bmc = basic melodic contour)

The basic melodic contour and melodic construction patterns of *xipi* and *erhuang* apply to their instrumental connectives as well. Interlude small instrumental connectives in most cases follow their basic melodic contours quite closely. The melodies of interlude large and half-line instrumental connectives are composed according to their mode's pattern of melodic construction, as are prelude instrumental connectives. "*Xipi*'s contain pitch progressions with a relatively large range of rising and descending flow; *erhuang*'s are a progression of small jumps or leaps in pitch within a narrower range."[33] Example 16 illustrates the standard prelude large instrumental connectives in male *xipi* and *erhuang* primary-meter.[34]

When describing the experiential differences between the prelude instrumental connectives for *xipi*'s metrical types and those for *erhuang*'s, performers regularly mention three characteristics: a *xipi* prelude "drops one," like a rubber ball, and the opening pitch of the singer's melody rebounds from the falling, closing pitches of the prelude; an *erhuang* prelude "lifts the

**Example 15 Basic Melodic Contours and Specific Examples
in Male *Xipi* and *Erhuang* Primary-meter**

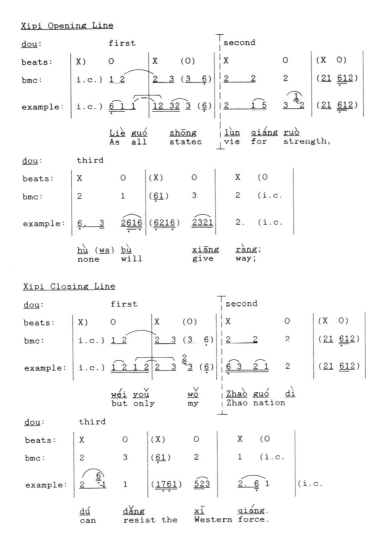

(continued)

Example 15 *(continued)*

Erhuang Opening Line

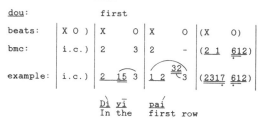

dou: first

beats:	X O)	X O	X O	(X 0)
bmc:	i.c.)	2 3	2 -	(2 1 612)
example:	i.c.)	2 15 3	1 2 ⌢32⌣3	(2317 612)

Dì yī   pai
In the   first row

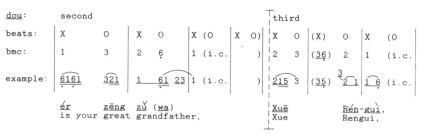

dou: second   ⊤third

beats:	X 0	X 0	X (0	X 0)	X 0	(X) 0	X (0
bmc:	1 3	2 6	1 (i.c.	)	2 3	(36) 2	1 (i.c.
example:	6161	321	1 61 23	1 (i.c. |)	215 3	(35) 3⌢21	1 6 (i.c.

ér   zēng   zǔ (wa) |Xuē   Rén-guì,
is your great grandfather, |Xue   Rengui,

Erhuang Closing Line

dou: first   second

beats:	X 0	X 0
bmc:	5 5 7	(6) 6 6 5
example:	5635 6⌢27	0 2 2

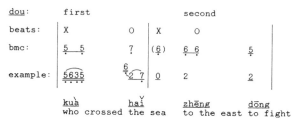

kuà   hai   zhēng   dōng
who crossed the sea to the east to fight

dou: third

beats:	X 0	(X) 0	X (0
bmc:	5 6	(6) 2	2 (i.c.
example:	6. 765 5 6	(65) 2 2	2 (i.c.

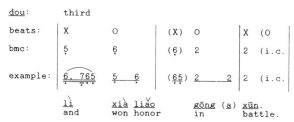

lì   xià liǎo   gōng (a) xūn.
and   won honor   in   battle.

singer," whose opening pitch continues the rise of the rising, closing pitches of the prelude; and most *erhuang* preludes prominently include the characteristic rhythm of the second measure in the closing sung melodic-line (i.e., in primary-meter, 56 5 61 in the prelude, and 6 66 5 in the melodic-line).[35]

Within the patterns provided by the basic melodic contour and the type

**Example 16 Standard Prelude Large Instrumental Connectives
in Male *Xipi* and *Erhuang* Primary-meter**

Xipi

Erhuang

of melodic construction of each mode, there is a great deal of flexibility. These patterns are by no means "set melodies"; they are rather modal melodic tendencies. The experience of one learning *pihuang* music is that familiar melodic progressions occur periodically; just as one begins to hum along, however, the melodic progression becomes unfamiliar once again. These familiar melodic progressions occur most often at the beginning of individual melodic-phrases, due primarily to speech-tone indications, and at the end of melodic-sections, particularly of those for singing third *dou*. The frequency of familiar melodic progressions at the end of melodic-sections is due to the cadence patterns of *xipi* and *erhuang*.

Keys and Cadences

Pihuang music is based upon the ancient Chinese pentatonic scale. The five tones of this scale are called *gong, shang, jiao* (also pronounced *jue*), *zhi,* and *yu*.[36] They are written in cipheric notation as 1, 2, 3, 5, and 6, respectively; contemporary Beijing opera performers refer to them as do, re, mi, so, and la. The tones 4, fa, and 7, ti, are not a part of this basic scale. They are used, however, in both *xipi* and *erhuang,* as coloration tones *(secaiyin)* and for modulating between the keys of the two modes. With two exceptions, the relative pitches are the same as those in the standard Western octave. However, the Beijing opera fa is between a sharp and a natural Western fa, and the Beijing opera ti is slightly lower than a Western ti.

In *pihuang* music, key *(diao)* is defined as the centering *(wei zhongxin)* of melodic-passages around a particular relative pitch. The shifting between melodic-passages centering around 1 (i.e., the tonic; do) to those centering around 2 (i.e., the supertonic; re) is considered modulation *(zhuandiao,* lit. "shifting keys"). *Xipi* is perceived as 1-centered, or in the key of do, and *erhuang* is perceived as 2-centered, or in the key of re; more melodic-phrases in *xipi* center around 1 than around any other tone, and more in *erhuang* around 2 than around any other tone. The word for mode, *diaoshi,* literally means "key style." The tuning of the two strings of the spike fiddle *(jinghu),* which provides the primary melodic accompaniment to *pihuang* singing, facilitates this modal difference. In *xipi* they are tuned to 6 and 3, and in *erhuang* to 5 and 2; in both cases, there is an interval of a fifth between the two strings.

However, melodic-phrases centering around any of the basic tones—1, 2, 3, 5, and 6—are in practice used in both modes. The most important factor in determining the keys of *xipi* and *erhuang* is their pattern of cadences *(zhongzhiyin,* lit. "finishing note[s]"). Because *xipi* is 1-centered, what can best be termed resolution (i.e., completion) in the analysis of most nineteenth-century European concert music is achieved in *xipi* by the use of 1 as the cadential tone; in *erhuang,* this sense of completion occurs when 2 is the final tone.

Xipi and *erhuang* each have a pattern of cadential tones; both patterns complement the lyric structure and the type of song structure specific to each mode. In *xipi,* the first *dou* of both lines often end on 1, and the second *dou* on 2, creating a sense of parallelism and balance. In almost all cases, the third *dou* of the opening line, and therefore the opening line itself, ends on 2; because *xipi* is 1-centered, this line ending gives the opening line a feeling of incompleteness and a need to continue. The closing line then ends on 1, creating a sense of completeness and resolution. In *erhuang,* the first *dou* of the opening line frequently ends on 2, and the second *dou* on 1. The line itself then ends on 1, an unfinished cadence in this 2-centered mode. The first *dou* of the closing *erhuang* line often ends on 6, 7, or 3; the second *dou* has no prescribed cadential tone, perhaps because it is extremely short, and the line itself ends on 2, achieving resolution.

In both modes, performers interpretively vary the cadential tones for the first and second *dou* fairly frequently. However, deviation from the pattern of cadential tones at the ends of lines occurs only in the expression of the most intense emotions; these cadences are essential to modal identity.

Figure 10 compares *dou* and line cadence patterns in *xipi* and *erhuang;*

Figure 10
Cadence Patterns in Male *Xipi* and *Erhuang*

	Xipi			*Erhuang*		
Opening Line	3	2	2	2	1	1
Closing Line	3	2	1	6/7/3	—	2

(Passages more than one measure long devoted entirely to instrumental connectives are not included in the underlining that indicates relative *dou* length in measures.)

single underlining indicates *dou* endings, and double underlining, line endings. The length of the underlining indicates relative *dou* length.

The specific combination of modal rhythm, song structure, basic melodic contour and construction, and key and cadence patterns in *xipi* and *erhuang* gives each mode its modal identity. *Xipi*'s modal rhythm is regular, with an equal number of written-characters centering on accented and unaccented beats in each line. Its changed-tail song structure creates parallel melodic-lines of equal length, in which its more disjunctly constructed melodies rise and fall over a wide pitch range. *Xipi* is in the key of 1, with resolution achieved through the return to 1 at the end of the melodic-passage for each couplet.

Erhuang's modal rhythm is irregular, with more written-characters centering on accented beats in opening lines, and more centering on unaccented beats in closing lines. Especially in opening couplets, its extended-pattern song structure creates contrasting melodic-lines of unequal length—opening lines are twice as long as closing lines—in which its more conjunctly constructed melodies are complexly woven within a relatively narrow range of pitch. And *erhuang* is in the key of 2, with resolution achieved through a return to 2 at the end of the melodic-passage for each couplet.

Performers and audience members experience two very different atmospheres *(qifen)* as a result of these two modal identities, somewhat comparable to a Westerner's experience of the difference between major and minor modes. *Xipi* is experienced as "sprightly, bright and clear, energetic, forceful, and purposeful." And *erhuang* is experienced as "relatively dark, deep and profound, heavy and meticulous."[37] *Xipi* is therefore considered best suited to expressing joy, delight, and vehemence, while *erhuang* is considered most expressive of grief, remembrance, and lyricism. Although these patterns are in certain respects applied differently in female melodic-passages and in other metrical types, these basic modal identities as described in male primary-meter remain constant, as does the atmosphere created by each mode.

Patterns of Modal Identity for Female Melodic-passages

In most respects, both male and female *xipi* and *erhuang* follow the same patterns of modal identity. However, the female versions differ from the male in melodic contour, certain aspects of melodic construction, and in their cadence patterns. The melodic tendencies characteristic of female melodic-passages are the primary source of these differences.

The most striking contrast between the male and female versions of both modes is the difference in pitch. The male and female pitch ranges in each mode span the same number of pitches; however, the female pitch ranges are much higher than the male. Each mode employs a different standard relationship between its male and female pitch ranges. In female *xipi* the pitch range is 6 to 3, a fifth higher than that of the male (2 to 6). In female *erhuang,* the ideal pitch range is 5 to 6, a full octave higher than that of male *erhuang* (5 to 6). These different pitch-range relationships make ideal female *erhuang* considerably higher in average pitch than female *xipi*. For this reason it is said that "women are afraid of *erhuang*."[38] As a result, the actual pitch range used in female *erhuang* is in practice usually 2 to 3. Female *xipi* and female *erhuang* have different basic melodic contours, serving to maintain the separate modal identities in the female versions. They are not, however, direct transpositions of the male basic melodic contours. The following example compares the basic melodic contours of male and female *xipi* and *erhuang*.

The male and female basic melodic contours are more nearly similar in *erhuang* than they are in *xipi*, especially at the end of *dou* and in the closing *erhuang* line, as can be seen in Example 17. This is due at least in part to the interval relationships produced by the different pitch-range relationships. In *erhuang,* the octave difference between the male pitch range and the ideal female pitch range produces the same interval relationships in ideal female *erhuang* as exist in male *erhuang*. However, the fifth difference in pitch range between male *xipi* and female *xipi* gives the two versions different interval relationships. Figure 11 compares these interval relationships. Although the upper range of the ideal female *erhuang* pitch range is not used in the female basic melodic contour, the interval relationships in male and female *erhuang* are in fact the same.

The patterns of melodic construction used in female *xipi* and *erhuang* are

Example 17 Basic Melodic Contours in Male and Female *Xipi* and *Erhuang*

Male Xipi Basic Melodic Contour

```
dou:            first        ⌐second          ⌐third
                             |                |
beats:  |X)    0   |X    (0) ||X  0 |(X  0)  ||X   0 |(X)    0 |X (0
                             |                |
opening                      |                |
  line: |i.c.) 12‾|23   (36) ||22  2 |(21 612)||2   1 |(61)   3 |2 (i.c.
                             |                |
closing                      |                |
  line: |i.c.) 12‾|23   (36) ||22  2 |(21 612)||2   3 |(61)   2 |1 (i.c.|
                             ⊥                ⊥
```

Female Xipi Basic Melodic Contour

```
dou:            first           ⌐second              ⌐third
                                |                    |
beats:  |X 0)  0 0 |X 0 0 (0) ||X 0 0 0 |(X  0  0  0)||X 0 0 0 |X (0)  0 0 |X (000
                                |         [ optional ]|
opening                         |                    |
  line: |i.c.) 5 1‾|1 7 6 (36) ||5 3 5 6 |(34 36 12 3)||5 7 6 3‾|3 (36) 5 7|6 (i.c.
                                |                    |
closing                         |                    |
  line: |i.c.) 5 61‾|1 7 6 (36)||5 3 5 6 |(34 36 12 3)||5 3 5 6 |3 (6)  4 3|5 (i.c.|
                                ⊥                    ⊥
```

Male Erhuang Basic Melodic Contour

```
dou:            first              ⌐second               ⌐third
                                   |                     |
beats:  |X 0) |X 0|X 0|(X     0)  ||X 0|X 0|X (0  |X 0)||X 0|(X)  0|X (0
                                   |                     |
opening                            |                     |
  line: |i.c.) |2 3|2 -|(21   612)||1 3|2 6|1 (i.c.  )||2 3|(36) 2|1 (i.c.
                                   ⊥                     ⊥
```

```
dou:             first  ⌐2nd ⌐third
                        |    |
beats:          |X  0| X | 0 ||X 0|(X)   0 |X (0
                | 55 7|   |   ||   | 6    2 |
closing    or   | ⊷  ⁙|   |   ||   | ⁙      |
  line:         |22 7|(6)|66 5||5 6|(6)   2 |2 (i.c.|
                        ⊥    ⊥
```

Female Erhuang Basic Melodic Contour

```
dou:            first           ⌐second              ⌐third
                                |                    |
beats: |X 0) |X 0|X 0|(X    0)  ||X 0|X 0|X (0  |X 0)||X 0|(X)   0|X (0
                    [optional] |                    |
opening                        |                    |
  line: |i.c.) |5 6|5 -|(5643 235)||7 6|5 6|1 (i.c.  )||5 6|(65)  6|1 (i.c.
                                ⊥                    ⊥
```

```
dou:            first  ⌐2nd |third
                       |    |
beats:         |X   0| X | 0 ||X 0|(X)  0 |X (0
                       |    |
closing                |    |
  line:         |5   7|(6)|5  6||5 6|(67) 26|5 (i.c.|
                       ⊥    ⊥
```

87

Figure 11

Interval Relationships in the Pitch-ranges of Male and Female *Xipi* and *Erhuang*

	Xipi	*Erhuang*
	Keynote	Keynote
Male intervals	2 3 5 6 1̣ 2 3 5 6 M2 m3 M2 m3 M2 M2 m3 M2	5 6 1 2̇ 3 5 6 M2 m3 M2 M2 m3 M2
Female intervals	6̣ 1 2 3 5 6 1̇ 2̇ 3̇ m3 M2 M2 m3 M2 m3 M2 M2	5 6 1̇ 2̇ 3̇ 5̇ 6̇ M2 m3 M2 M2 m3 M2

M2 = a major second; i.e., two "half-steps"
m3 = a minor third; i.e., three "half-steps"

fundamentally the same as the male versions. Female *xipi*'s melodic construction is more disjunct; melodies often leap, soaring or dropping as much as a sixth or a seventh, and have a wide pitch range (6̣ to 3̇). Female *erhuang,* like male *erhuang,* is more conjunct; melodies generally utilize level or step-wise pitch progressions or small jumps up or down in pitch, and have a narrower pitch range (ideally 5 to 6̇, but actually usually 2 to 3̇). And in the female versions of both modes, the specific melodic progression for each melodic-phrase is of course influenced by the speech-tone of the word being sung.

However, the female versions of both modes are more melismatic than the male, in keeping with this basic melodic tendency of female melodic-passages. This is especially true in female *xipi;* whereas the basic melodic contour for male *xipi* primary-meter is in $\frac{2}{4}$ meter, the female *xipi* primary-meter is in $\frac{4}{4}$ meter, as can be seen in Example 17. This means that there are more beats per melodic-phrase in female *xipi,* and therefore, because pitches are not merely extended, more pitch occurrences per melodic-phrase. Additionally, in specific female melodic-passages, the third *dou* in both *xipi* lines and in the closing *erhuang* line are lengthened, especially in slow-meter, much more frequently and to greater extents than they are in specific male melodic-passages.

The altered patterns of melodic contour and construction in the female versions are apparent in their instrumental connectives as well. In the female versions of both *xipi* and *erhuang,* interlude small instrumental connectives are frequently omitted at the end of the second *dou* in the closing *xipi* line and at the end of the first *dou* in the opening *erhuang* line, as can be seen in Example 17. Although such omission does not create more melisma per se, the absence of these instrumental connectives does make song more concentrated in the female versions.

The prelude large instrumental connectives in female *erhuang* are essentially the same as those in male *erhuang,* but an octave higher, in keeping with the octave difference in pitch range and the relatively high degree of resemblance between male and female *erhuang* basic melodic contours. However, the female prelude large instrumental connectives in *xipi* primary-meter, like the sung melodic-passages of female *xipi* primary-meter, are in $\frac{4}{4}$ meter instead of the $\frac{2}{4}$ meter utilized by the male versions. They use more high pitches as well. The following example compares standard prelude large instrumental connectives in male and female *xipi* primary-meter.[39]

Example 18 Standard Prelude Large Instrumental Connectives in Male and Female *Xipi* Primary-meter

Male

X	O	X	O	X	O	X	O	X	O	X	O
	(62	1 65	32 1	6	1 1	2	3 5	6535	25.5	5532	1235 6535

X	O	X	O	X
2165	3212	6125	3612	1 6)

Female

X	O	O	O	X	O	O	O	X	O	O	O
(1	6 5	3 2 1		0 5 1̇ 3	5 1̇ 6 5			3 6 3 5	1̇ 3 5 5		

X	O	O	O	X	O	O	O	X	O	O	O
3 6 3 5	1̇ 3 5 5			2 3 5 1̇	6 5 3 2			1 2 3 5	6̇1̇36 5 1		

X	O	O	O	X	O	O	O	X	O
2 3 5 5	21 6 1 2			7 72 6 4	3 2 12 6			1 1 6)	

The cadence patterns in female *xipi* and *erhuang* are fundamentally in keeping with the pitch-range difference and resulting interval relationships in the male and female versions of each mode. The correspondence is closest in *xipi*: the cadential tone for the female opening line is 6, and that for the female closing line is 5. Both of these tones are a fifth higher than their male counterparts (2 and 1, respectively), and the interval between the two is the same as the male version, a major second. The pattern of cadential tones for the first and second *dou* in each line of female *xipi* is simpler than that for the male version; both first and second *dou* often end on 6 in female *xipi,* as opposed to 3 and 2, respectively, in male *xipi.* The second *dou* cadential tones in the female version are therefore frequently a fifth higher than in the male, while the first *dou* cadential tones are often only a fourth higher.

In *erhuang,* the ideal octave difference in pitch range between the male and female versions is preserved in the cadential tone for the opening line: the male final tone is 1, and the female final tone is 1̇. The final tone for the second *dou* in the opening line often preserves this same relationship (1 in the male version, and 1̇ in the female version), as does the first *dou* in the closing line (6, 7, or 3 in the male version, and 6, 7, or 3̇ in the female version). However, the cadential tone for the closing line in female *erhuang* is only a fourth higher than the male counterpart: the male final tone is 2, and the female final tone is 5. The cadential tone for the first *dou* in the opening line frequently follows this relationship as well (2 in the male version, and 5 in the female). The final tone for the female *erhuang* closing line is therefore a fourth lower than that for the opening line. This is a different interval than the one between the cadential tones for the two male *erhuang* lines (the male closing line is a second higher than the opening line), but it is also different than the interval between the cadential tones for the two female *xipi* lines (the female *xipi* closing line is a second lower than the opening line). The integrity of modal identity in the female versions is maintained by this difference in female *xipi* and *erhuang* cadential patterns. Figure 12 compares the cadence patterns in male and female *xipi* and *erhuang.*

Figure 12
Cadence Patterns in Male and Female *Xipi* and *Erhuang*

	Xipi			*Erhuang*		
Male						
Opening Line	3	2	2	2	1	1
Closing Line	3	2	1	6/7/3	—	2
Female						
Opening Line	6	6	6	5	1̇	1̇
Closing Line	6	6	5	6/7/3̇	—	5

(Passages more than one measure long devoted entirely to instrumental connectives are not included in the underlining that indicates relative *dou* length in measures.)

Patterns of Modal Identity for Other Metrical Types

Like primary-meter, most metrical types have a *xipi* and an *erhuang* version. All metrical types associated with each mode follow that mode's basic patterns *(guilü)* of modal rhythm, song structure, melodic contour and construction, and key and cadences. Each has a male and a female version as well.

The major additional difference between the metrical types of the two modes is one of tempo. The same metrical type in *xipi* is faster (i.e., the duration of each of its beats is shorter) than it is in *erhuang*. Additionally, two-six-meter and fast-meter do not have *erhuang* versions. *Erhuang* does have a version of flowing-water-meter, termed piled-up-meter *(duoban)*. However, in *erhuang* this is a subsidiary metrical type, comprising only a single melodic line (see note 21). The absence of the faster metrical types in *erhuang,* and the reduced tempo of all other metrical types in their *erhuang* versions, contributes to the "relatively dark, deep and profound, heavy" atmosphere associated with *erhuang* modal identity. Figure 13 lists the metrical types associated with each primary mode.

Within each mode, certain adaptations in modal rhythm and basic

Figure 13
Primary Modes and Their Associated Metrical Types

Metrical Type		*Xipi*	*Erhuang*
Metered	slow-meter	X	X
	fast-three-eyes-meter	X	X
	primary-meter	X	X
	two-six-meter	X	—
	flowing-water-meter	X	(piled-up-meter)
	fast-meter	X	—
Free	lead-in-meter	X	X
	undulating-dragon-meter*	X	X
	dispersed-meter	X	X
	shaking-meter	X	X

Xipi undulating-dragon-meter occurs only rarely, and when it does occur, usually consists of only a closing line. Undulating-dragon-meter is used much more often in *erhuang*, and can function much more independently, often continuing for several lines. Although metered, undulating-dragon-meter is categorized with the free metrical types because it always follows lead-in-meter, and has no meter and tempo of its own, taking those of the metered metrical type that follows it in each instance.

x = presence
— = absence

melodic contour and construction are made to accommodate the meters and melodic tendencies of each associated metrical type. Because slower metrical types are more melismatic and ornamented than primary-meter, their melodic-passages in both *xipi* and *erhuang* are more melismatic and complex than those of primary-meter. This is generally the case throughout melodic-passages in slower metrical types; it is often intensified in certain melodic-phrases. For instance, in both *xipi* and *erhuang* slow-meter, the last written-character in the third *dou* of both lines is frequently lengthened by one or more measures. The instrumental connectives of the slower metrical types are also longer and/or more melismatic.

Similarly, melodic-passages in the faster metrical types in *xipi* are tighter, less melismatic, and simpler than those of primary-meter. And modal rhythm is occasionally sacrificed to speed, especially in flowing-water-meter and fast-meter, which have no unaccented beats. In these metrical types, the characteristic modal rhythm is suggested in the first *dou* of each line by preceding the first pitch with a rest of equal duration (i.e., 0 1). Generally no attempt is made in the remaining *dou* in each line to suggest the pattern of written-character placement within accented and unaccented beats followed in the other metrical types associated with *xipi*. The instrumental connectives in the faster meters are shorter and/or less melismatic; in fast-meter, interlude small instrumental connectives are occasionally omitted altogether. Fundamentally, however, the basic patterns that establish modal identity are followed by every metrical type in each mode.

The following four examples illustrate the close correspondence between the principal metrical types in each mode and the basic patterns of modal identity. Examples 19 and 20 compare specific instances of fast-meter, primary-meter, and slow-meter in male and female *xipi,* respectively; Examples 21 and 22 compare specific examples of primary-meter and slow-meter in male and female *erhuang,* respectively. *Dou* divisions, beats, and the basic melodic contour applicable to each example are notated as well.[40]

Example 19 Fast-meter, Primary-meter, and Slow-meter in Male *Xipi*

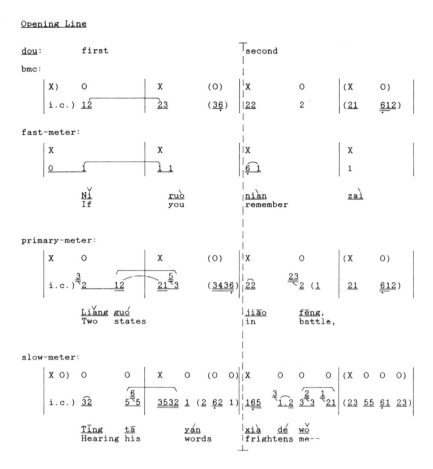

(continued)

Example 19 *(continued)*

<u>dou</u>: third

bmc:

X		O		(X)		O		X		(O
2		1		(6̣1)		3		2		(i.c.

fast-meter:

X		X		X	
3		2⌢1		2	

fū   qī   yì,
the feelings   of husband   and wife,

primary-meter:

X		O		X		(O	
1⌢2	3⌢2	2531		2		(i.c.	

lóng hǔ   dòu;
dragon &   tiger   struggling;

slow-meter:

X	O	O	O	(X	O)	O	O	X	O	O	O	X	O	O	O	(X	O	O	O
1	1	5̣3̣	7̣6̣	5̣	(5̣	5̣6̣)	2 ³5̣.6̣	1	1.6̣	3̣ ²3̣	55	2 ³2	3.1̣	2 -		(i.c.			

xīn (na)   jīng   dǎn   pà;
my heart   is shocked   and my   courage gone;

94

Example 19 *(continued)*

Closing Line

dou: first   │ second

bmc:
```
 │X)     O      │ X     (O)   │ │ X       O    │(X       O)   │
 │i.c.) 12      23    (36)   │ │ 22      2    │(21     612)  │
```

fast-meter:
```
 │X            │ X           │ │ X            │ X            │
 │0     1      1 1           │ │ 2 1          │ 6 1          │
        qù            daò    │ Jīn-          líng
        then go       to     │ Nan-          jing
```

primary-meter:
```
 │X)     O     │ X     (O)   │ │ X       O    │(X       O)   │
 │i.c.) 12   12  21   5 (3536)│ │ 61     3 2  │(21     612)  │
                3            │
        gè    wèi            │ qí      zhǔ
        each one  for        │ its own sovereignty
```

slow-meter:
```
 │X O ) O   O  │(X) O O (O) │ │ X   O    O  O │(X  O  O)  O │
 │i.c.) 31   135 (5) 76 5 (6 5)│ │ 63  261  1 1 2 (6 23 55 61  2) 1│
                                           6
        bèi  zhuǎn  shēn     │ zì  mán  yuàn              wǔ
        I    turn  my back   │ and blame myself           for
```

(continued)

Example 19 *(continued)*

<u>dou</u>: third

bmc:

X	O	(X)	O	X	(O
2	3	(6̣1)	2	1	(i.c.

fast-meter:

X		X		X	
1		6͡ 2		1	

<u>bān</u>   <u>jiu</u>   <u>bīng</u>;
and   get   troops;

primary-meter:

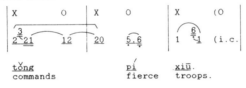

<u>tǒng</u>   <u>pí</u>   <u>xiū</u>.
commands   fierce troops.

slow-meter:

X	O	O O	X	O	O	O	X	O	O O	(X O O O
1̂6̲̲1	6.1	5 32	76	50	6.1	6.1	3̂2̲3	2.6	1 -	(i.c.

<u>zì</u>   <u>jǐ</u>   <u>zuò</u>   <u>chā</u>.
having   done   badly.

Example 20 Fast-meter, Primary-meter, and Slow-meter in Female *Xipi*

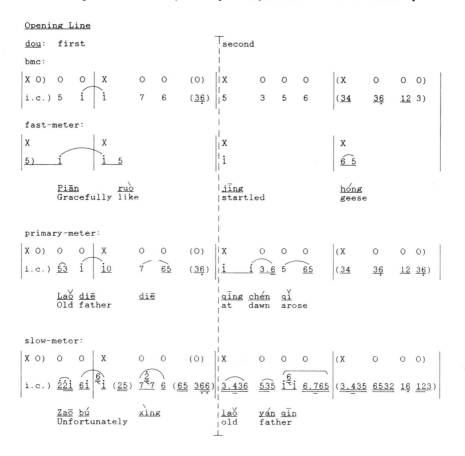

(continued)

Example 20 *(continued)*

<u>dou</u>: third

bmc: | X   O   O   O | X (O)   O   O | X   (O   O   O |

5   7   6   3| 3 (3̲6̲) 5   7 | 6   (i.c.

fast-meter:

| X | X | X |

3   3̲ | 0̲ 5̲ | 6̲ |

lái zhaò   yĭng,
seeing their   reflections,

primary-meter:

| X   O   O   O | X (O)   O   O | X   O   O   O | X O O (O |

7   6̲7̲2̇ 6   3 | 3̲6 (3̲6̲) 7   6̲7̲2̇ | 6. 7   5̲6̲3̲5̲   6̲7̲6̲ 5̲6̲7̲ | 6 – – (i.c.

qiǎn   qù   chū   shoŭ;
and   went to   bring   charges;

slow-meter:

| X   O   O   O | X (O)   O   O | X   O   O   O |

7.̲ 7̲ 6̲7̲2̇ 6̲ 7̲ 3̲ 3 | (6̲6̲) 5̲.6̲ 7̲6̲2̇ | 7̲6̲ 6̲ 3̲ (3̲6̲) 5̲.6̲ 1̇.̲2̲5̲ |

yún   biān   sàng   míng;
far   away   met his death;

| X   O   O   O | X O (O O |

6̲ (6̲1̇) 3̲. (2̲3̲) 5̲ 6̲.2̲̇7̲6̲ 6̲5̲6̲7̲6̲7̲ 7̲ | 7̲6̲6̲ 6 (i.c.

Example 20 *(continued)*

Closing Line

<u>dou</u>: first   second

bmc:

```
|X 0)  0   0  |X      0   0    (0)  ||X   0      0   0    |(X    0   0   0)|
|i.c.) 5  6̱1̱ |1      7   6    (36̣)  |5   3      5   6    |(34   36̣  12  3)|
```

fast-meter:

```
|X            |X           ||X        |X        |
|    2        |2  3        |43       |46       |
```

    wǎn   shì   shén   lóng
    like   a   magic   dragon

primary meter:

```
|X 0)  0   0  |X      0   0    (0)  ||X   0      0   0    |
|i.c.) 5  6̱1̱1̱0̱  7̱  6̱5̱  (36̣)  |5̱3̱  1     5̱  6̱5̱   |
```

    dǎo jiào   wǒ   Guì-yīng ér
    this makes   me,   Guiying   his child,

slow-meter:

```
|X 0)  0   0  |X      0   0     0   ||X   0      0   0    |
|i.c.) 2̱2̱1̱ 6̱1̱ 1 (25)  7̱7̱ 6.7̱ (65̱ 366̣)|1̱6̱ 1̱.2̱3̱.6̱ 5̱3̱1̱ 6̱65̱5̱ |
```

    piē bú   xià   mǔ zi mén
    left   behind,   mother and child

```
|X 0   0   0  |X   0   0   0   |X   0 (0  0
|5̱4̱ 3̱3̱ 51.2̱ 3243 |235̱ 6̣.1̱ 2.532 1.2123 |3̱2̱ 2̱1̱ 2 (i.c.
```

(continued)

Example 20 *(continued)*

<u>dou</u>: third

bmc:

```
| X   O    O    O  | X   (O)   O    O  | X  (O   O    O
| 5   3    5    6  | 3   (6)   4    3  | 5  (i.c.
```

fast-meter:

```
| X            | X         | X
| 4643         | 2.3       | 5 (36
```

xì   hǎi   bīng.
playing   on the   seashore.

primary-meter:

```
| X   O    O    O  | X    O    O    O  | X  O  O  O | X  O (O  O
| 5   3    5   3.5 6| 30   6   06  43 | 3 2 3 2.3 5 | 5  -  (i.c.
```

guà   zài   xīn   tóu.
uneasy   in   heart and   mind.

slow-meter:

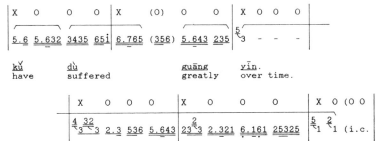

```
| X   O    O    O  | X    (O)   O    O  | X  O  O  O
| 5.6 5.632 3435 651| 6.765 (356) 5.643 235| 5/3 - - -
```

kǔ   dù   guāng   yīn.
have   suffered   greatly   over time.

```
      | X   O  O  O  | X    O    O    O  | X  O (O  O
      | 4 32 2.3 536 5.643| 23 2 3 2.321 6.161 25325| 5 2 1 (i.c.
      |  3 3             |                |
```

Example 21 Primary-meter and Slow-meter in Male *Erhuang*

Opening Line

dou: first

bmc: | X O) | X   O | X   O | (X   O) |
        | i.c.)| 2   3 | 2   - | (2 1   612) |

primary-meter:

        | X O) | X   O | X   O | (X   O) |
        | i.c.)| 2 15   3 | 1 2   32⌣3 | (2317 612) |

                Dì yī   pái
                In the   first row

slow-meter:

        | X O) | X O   O   O | X O   (O   O) |
        | i.c.)| 35⌢3 (6) 323 453 |1⌢2 2 (3 65 612) |

                Yī   lún
                A   round

dou: second

bmc: | X   O | X   O | X   (O | X   O) |
        | 1   3 | 2   6 | 1   (i.c. |) |

primary-meter:

        | X   O | X   O | X   (O | X   O) |
        | 6161   321 | 1   61   23 | 1   (i.c. |) |

                ér   zēng   zǔ (wa)
                is your great   grandfather,

slow-meter:

        | X O   O   O | X O   O   O | X O (O O | X O O O) |
        | 21⌢30 6.1 234 | 4̄33 4̄3.2 1.2 326 | 1⌢1 1 (i.c. |) |

                míng   yuè
                bright   moon

(continued)

Example 21 (continued)

<u>dou</u>:   third

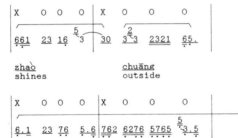

bmc: | X   O | (X)   O | X (O

          | 2   3 | (<u>36</u>) 2 | 1 (i.c. |

primary-meter:

    | X   O | X   O | X (O

    | <u>215</u> 3 | (<u>35</u>) $\overset{3}{\frown}$ 2 1 | 1 6 (i.c. |

    <u>Xuē</u>   <u>Rén</u>-   <u>guì</u>,
    Xue   Rengui,

slow-meter:

    | X O O O | X O O O |

    <u>661</u> <u>23</u> <u>16</u> $\overset{5}{\frown}$3 <u>30</u> $\overset{2}{\frown}$ 3 3 <u>2321</u> <u>65.</u>

    <u>zhaò</u>   <u>chuāng</u>
    shines   outside

    | X O O O | X O O O |

    <u>6.1</u> <u>23</u> <u>76</u> <u>5.6</u> | <u>762</u> <u>6276</u> <u>5765</u> $\overset{5}{\frown}$3.5

    <u>xià</u>;
    the window;

    | X O O O | X O O O | X O (O O

    <u>6535</u> <u>61</u> <u>212</u> <u>32</u> $\overset{6}{\cdot}$71 <u>7276</u> <u>56</u> <u>65</u> $\overset{5}{\cdot}$6 - (i.c.

Example 21 *(continued)*

Closing Line

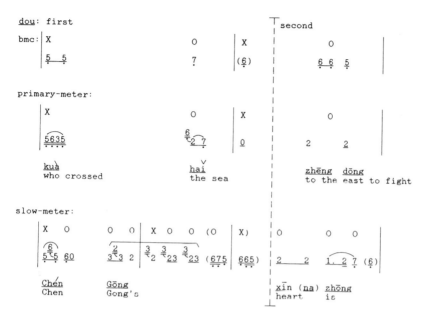

(continued)

Example 21 *(continued)*

dou: third

bmc: | X   O | (X)   O | X (O |
       | 5̰   6̣ | (6̣)   2 | 2 (i.c. |

primary-meter:

       | X   O | (X)   O | X (O |
       | 6͡.765   5   6 | (65͟)   2   2 | 2 (i.c. |

         lì   xià liǎo   gōng (a)   xūn.
         and   won honor   in   battle.

slow-meter:

       | X   O   O   O | X   O   O O |
       | 6͡5͜5 37 676 523 | 2͡3 3 (235) 5͡3 5.35 |

         luàn   rú mǎ.
         confused   as hemp.

       | X   O   O   O | X   O   O O | X O O (O |
       | 5͡6   5͡6 5͡6   67 | 46   23   5 6͡7͜6 | 5 - - (i.c. |

Example 22 Primary-meter and Slow-meter in Female *Erhuang*

Opening Line:

dou: first

bmc:

X O)	X O	X O	(X O)
i.c.)	5 6	5 -	(5643 235)

primary-meter:

X O)	X O	X O
i.c.)	5 1 656i	5. (643 235)

Chǔ bīng
The troops of Chu,

slow-meter:

X 0 0 0)	X 0 0 0	X 0 0 0
i.c.)	51 65 i2 i6i	5 3 (66 36 43 2356)

Xiǎng dāng nián
Thinking of that year

dou: second

bmc:

X O	X O	X (O	X O)
7 6	5 6	i (i.c.	)

primary-meter:

X O	X O	X (O
7 7 66	656 7265	i (i.c.

fēn fēn
rank on rank,

slow-meter:

X O 0 0	X 0 0 0	X 0 (0 0	X 0 0 0)
57 6765 7 65 535	66 6 72 506	ii i (i.c.	)

jié   jiāng shì
when I was intercepted at the river,

(continued)

105

Example 22 (continued)

dou: third

bmc:
X	O	(X)	O	X	(O
5	6	(65)	6	i	(i.c.

primary meter:

X	O	X	O	X	(O)
53	767	65 35	6i56	i27	(6 561)

zhā   liǎo   duì;
are   forming   lines;

slow-meter:

X	O	O	O	(X)	O	O	O
2̇2̇2̇	765	7˙5	6˙6	(5327) 6.657)	6i̇	2̇3̇	5.656

xīn   zhōng   huí
my   heart is filled   with regret

X	O	O	O	X	O	O	O
2̇3̇2̇	2̇66	7.2̇76 5306		762̇	2.376 656	5.672̇

hèn;
and hate;

X	O	O	O	X	O	O	O	X O	(O O
676535 6 (561) 2̇.3i̇2̇ 3̇2̇				76.7	2̇276	5.656 72̇55		6.	(i.c.

Example 22 (continued)

Closing Line:

dou: first ⊤ second

bmc:
| X | O | | X | | O | |
| 5 | 7 | | (6) | | 5 6 | |

primary meter:

| X | | O | |
| 2̇ 76 | | 5 6 7̇2̇ | |

jūn chén   taó mìng
the emperor and officials   flee for their lives,

slow-meter:

| X O | O | O | X | O | O | O | (X) | O | O | O | |
| 5 65 | 3 | 2.36i | 2.2 | 1.23 | 2̇ i | 6 | (657 | 6.276) | 2̇7 | 2̇376 | 63 | |

bei fū jūn   piě jiāo ér
I forsook my husband,   cast aside my son--

(continued)

Example 22 (continued)

<u>dou</u>:   third

bmc: | X   O | (X)   O | X   (O |
      | 5   6 | (<u>67</u>)   2̇6 | 5   (i.c. |

primary-meter:

      | X   O | (X)   O | X   (O) |
      | <u>6765</u>   <u>356</u> | (<u>67</u>)   2 <u>6276</u> | <u>643</u>   (<u>235</u>) |

      | haǒ   bù | shāng | beī. |
      | and   all | is | tragedy. |

slow-meter:

      | X   O   O   O | (X   O)   O   O |
      | <u>5.3</u>   <u>63</u>   <u>5535</u> <u>66</u> | (<u>6.276</u> <u>5356</u>) 72̇   <u>630</u> |

      | liǎng   dì | lí |
      | in two   distant places | we now |

      | X   O   O   O | X   O   O   O |
      | 2̇2̇2̇   <u>7̇2̇5</u> 6   - | 66   <u>530</u> <u>767</u> 2̇7 |

      | fēn. |
      | dwell apart. |

      | X   O   O   O | X   O   O   O | X   O (O O |
      | <u>6.72̇2̇</u> <u>76</u>   <u>4323</u> <u>43623</u> | <u>5.</u> ³↗5 <u>16̇2̇</u> <u>76.1</u> <u>3561</u> | 5 ⁶↘5 (i.c. |

The four examples just given also illustrate the complex interrelation of the major elements of the *pihuang* musical system. Each principal mode sets patterns of modal rhythm, song structure, melodic construction, and key—patterns that are followed by both its male and female versions in all metrical types associated with that mode. Each male and female version of each mode sets patterns of basic melodic contour and cadences, and influences melodic construction through its inherent melodic tendencies (i.e., female versions are more melismatic). And each metrical type in each mode sets patterns of meter and tempo, and influences melodic construction through its inherent melodic tendencies (i.e., the slower metrical types are more melismatic, the faster metrical types more syllabic); the faster metrical types adapt modal rhythm as well. In every specific melodic-passage, the precise melodic progression for each melodic-phrase is composed according to these patterns; simultaneously, each indicates the speech-tone of the word being sung by means of one of the fundamental relative pitch progressions, standard variations, or conventional techniques. Figure 14 diagrams this interrelation of basic elements and patterns.

Figure 14
The Interrelation of Basic Elements and Patterns in the
Principal Modes of the *Pihuang* Musical System

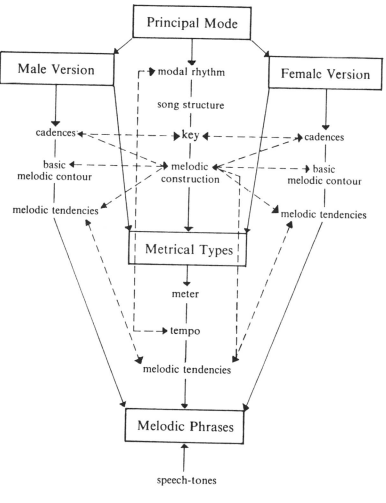

SECONDARY MODES

In addition to their principal modes *(zheng diaoshi)*, the *xipi* and *erhuang* modal systems include several important secondary modes.[41] Both modal systems have an inverse *(fan; zheng* may also be translated as "obverse") version of their principal modes. The *xipi* modal system includes one other important secondary mode, *nanbangzi,* and the *erhuang* modal system includes two additional important secondary modes, *sipingdiao* and *gaobozi.* The additional secondary modes in each modal system share antecedents with, and developed in relation to, the principal and inverse modes, and the spike fiddle used to accompany each is tuned the same as for either the principal or the inverse mode. All the secondary modes in each modal system have their own basic patterns of modal identity, which are related to those established by the principal mode; there are standard procedures based upon those patterns for modulating between the modes of each system. Like the principal modes, each secondary mode is experienced as producing its own characteristic atmosphere and is therefore considered most appropriate for certain dramatic situations.[42]

Inverse Modes

The inverse modes are a fourth higher in overall pitch than the principal modes. The spike fiddle for inverse *xipi* is therefore tuned to 2–6 (*xipi*'s is tuned to 6–3), and that for inverse *erhuang* to 1–5 (*erhuang*'s is tuned to 5–2). The inverse tunings, like those of the principal modes, preserve an interval of a fifth between the two strings. Within this pitch range difference, the basic melodic contours remain essentially similar: in a given male melodic-passage in an inverse mode, some pitches are the same as those in the melodic contour for the principal mode, some are a fourth higher, and some are an octave higher. The same is true in female melodic-passages. In spite of the higher pitch ranges, the inverse modes use the patterns of cadential tones characteristic of the principal modes, especially at the end of melodic-lines. However, both the male and female patterns of cadential tones in each principal mode may be freely used by either the male or the female version of the inverse mode; when male cadential tones are used in female melodic-passages in the inverse modes, the tones are generally an octave higher in pitch.

Both inverse modes follow the same patterns of modal rhythm, song structure, melodic construction, and key as do their respective principal modes. The metrical types associated with each inverse mode have the same characteristic meter and melodic tendencies as do their principal mode counterparts, and their tempos remain the same relative to one another. However, the overall tempo of each metrical type associated with each inverse mode is slower than that of its principal mode counterpart. This slower tempo contributes to the atmosphere created by the inverse modes; each is experienced as "more carefully detailed and profound, more tragic, and more lyric"[43] than its principal mode. The atmosphere produced by inverse *xipi* is therefore substantially different than that of principal *xipi*, whereas inverse *erhuang*'s atmosphere is simply a heightening of the atmosphere characteristic of principal *erhuang*. Perhaps for this reason, inverse *erhuang* is used much more often than is inverse *xipi*, and is a much more complete mode, including many more associated metrical types: inverse *xipi* includes only primary-meter, two-six-meter, dispersed-meter, and shaking-meter, the last of which is used very infrequently; inverse *erhuang*, however, includes slow-meter, primary-meter, lead-in-meter, undulating-dragon-meter, dispersed-meter, and shaking-meter.

In Example 23, female *erhuang* primary-meter is compared to female inverse *erhuang* primary-meter.[44] The general correspondence between the patterns of melodic contour and cadences in these two melodic-passages is fairly clear. The melodic-phrase for the last written-character in the third *dou* of the opening line in both passages uses what is called a 6 (la) tone large melodic-phrase (la *yin da qiang*); the term refers to the use of 6 as the cadence tone in a long, highly melismatic melodic-phrase. When the last melodic-phrase in a line of these two modes is greatly extended in this fashion, 6 is the usual cadence tone for the female opening line and 5 for the closing; 1 is most often used for the male opening line and 5 for the closing. The cadential tone in the third *dou* of the closing line in the *erhuang* example is 5, characteristic of the pattern of female *erhuang* cadences; that in the inverse *erhuang* is 2̇, an octave higher than the corresponding male *erhuang* cadence. Other patterns of modal identity are closely followed in both melodic-passages.

Modulation to and from each inverse mode is accomplished through three standard procedures. Modulation between inverse and principal modes may occur within the same metrical type (i.e., from inverse *xipi* primary-meter to principal *xipi* primary-meter, and vice versa). Modulation may also occur between two metrical types that have similar meter and tempo (i.e., from principal *xipi* primary-meter to inverse *xipi* two-six-meter, and vice versa). And it may occur between two commonly associated metrical types: from inverse *erhuang* lead-in-meter to principal *erhuang*

Example 23 Female *Erhuang* and Inverse *Erhuang* Primary-meter

<u>Opening Line</u>

dou: first

bmc: | X O) | X   O | X   O | (X   O)
      | | | | [optional]
i.c.) | 5 | 6   5 | – | (5643 235)

<u>erhuang</u>:

| X O O O) | X   O   O O | X (O   O   O) |
| i.c.) | 5i 665 (6) i2 i.26i|5⁶5 (566   3646   2356) |

Wǒ   xīn zhōng
In   my heart

inverse <u>erhuang</u>:

| X O O O) | X   O   O O | X   O   O   O |
| i.c.) | 255 32i   i6i 2.53i|2   2 (3) 3 2.32i 6 (13) |

Wǒ   zhè lǐ
Here   I   am

dou: second

bmc: | X   O | X   O | X   (O | X   O) |
      | 7   6 | 5   6 | i   (i.c.|) |

<u>erhuang</u>:

| X   O   O O | X (O)   O   O | X O   (0 0 | X 0 0 0) |
| 57 665 (6) 765 535 | 6 (7656) 72   5.6 | i i (23 i.c.|) |

zhǐ   bǎ nà
there   is only

inverse <u>erhuang</u>:

| X   O   O O | X O   O   O | X O   (0 0 | X 0 0 0) |
| 2355 3 (3212) i6i 2.3434|3   3022   7622 7.656|i i (12 i.c.|) |

jiǎ   yì ér
pretending,

112

Example 23 *(continued)*

<u>dou</u>: third

bmc:

X	O	(X)	O	X	(O	
5	6	(<u>65</u>)	6	i̇	(i.c.	

<u>erhuang</u>:

X	O	O	O	X	(O)	O	O	X	O	O	O
7.2̇	<u>663</u>	(6̇) <u>535</u>	6	6	(<u>63</u> <u>5616</u>)	<u>5.5</u>	35	<u>666</u> <u>50</u>		<u>767</u>	<u>266</u>

Tāng   zéi   lái   hěn;
hate   for that   evil   Tang;

<u>inverse erhuang</u>:

X	O	O	O	(X)	O	O	O	X	O	O	O
<u>235</u><u>5</u> <u>3i</u>		<u>5.2̇ 3</u> (<u>12</u>		<u>3256</u>)	<u>3.233</u>	<u>2.321</u> 6 (<u>13</u>)		2̇	<u>225.6</u>	<u>7.276</u>	<u>76567672</u>

lǎn   zēng   xìng   yǎn;
lazily   opening   almond   eyes;

<u>erhuang</u>, cont'd:

X	O	O	O	X	(O)	O	O
2̇7	2̇76 6 <u>507</u>		<u>6755</u>	3	(<u>643</u> <u>235276</u>)	<u>55</u>	6̇5 (<u>66</u>)

X	O	O	O	X	O	O	O	X O	(O O
<u>5i</u>	<u>305</u> <u>6.756</u> <u>762̇</u>			<u>672̇</u>	<u>305</u>	<u>672̇2̇</u>	<u>725</u>	7̇6 6	(<u>67</u> i.c.

<u>inverse erhuang</u>, cont'd:

X	O	O	O	X	O	O	O	X O	(O O
<u>67653235</u> <u>6.i</u>	<u>2.3i2</u> <u>322̇</u>			<u>276767</u> <u>2.327</u>		<u>676i7i2̇</u> <u>72766i5</u>		6 6	(<u>67</u> i.c.

(continued)

Example 23 (continued)

Closing Line

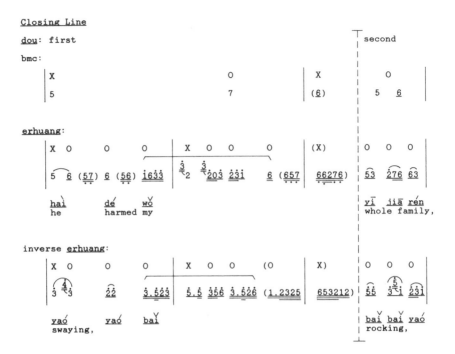

Example 23 *(continued)*

dou: third

bmc:
X	O	(X)	O	X	(O
5	6	(67)	2̇6	5	(i.c.

erhuang:

X	O	O	O	X	(O)	O	O
5.3	663	535	6	6	(276 | 5356)	72̇	5	(356)

liǎng xià lǐ   lí
in two places   separating

inverse erhuang:

X	O	O	O	(X)	O	O	O
2̇1̇4	3̇1̇	2.3̇1̇2	3̇	(3256)	1.2̇	3̇2̇5	5̇6̇3̇2̇

niǔ niè   xiàng
bashfully   coming

erhuang, cont'd:

X	O	O	O	X	(O)	O	O
2.³≠2 725 6	6	6 (78 5356)	767 2³≠27

fēn.
us.

X	O	O	O	X	O	O	O	X	O	(O O
62̇.3 766 466 2.3	506	1̇7	6.1̇	3.5651	6 5̇·5 5	(66 i.c.

inverse erhuang, cont'd:

X	O	O	O	X	O	O	O
2̇≠1̇	-	-	-	2̇≠1̇	1̇ (1̇) 2̇	3̇6̇	5.6̇4̇3̇

qián.
forward.

X	O	O	O	X	O	(O O
2̇ (2̇) 7 6.761̇	2̇1̇2̇3̇2̇ 1̇0̇2̇1̇2̇3̇	2̇ 2̇	(35 i.c.

115

undulating-dragon-meter; from inverse *erhuang* undulating-dragon-meter to principal *erhuang* slow-meter, fast-three-eyes-meter, or primary-meter; or from the principal versions of these metrical types to their inverse versions.

Nanbangzi Mode

Nanbangzi is used only for female melodic-passages (i.e., those of young *dan* and young *sheng*) and therefore has no male version. There are only three metrical types associated with *nanbangzi:* primary-meter, lead-in-meter, and dispersed-meter. Primary-meter *nanbangzi* has two patterns of metrical organization, $\frac{2}{4}$ and $\frac{4}{4}$; the latter is slower than the former (i.e., the duration of each beat is longer in $\frac{4}{4}$ *nanbangzi* than in $\frac{2}{4}$ *nanbangzi*), and both are somewhat slower than *xipi* primary-meter. *Nanbangzi* (which literally means "southern clapper") represents *pihuang*'s adaptation of the numerous regional clapper operas of northern China; it is most directly descended from Gansu clapper opera *(Gansu bangzi)*.

Nanbangzi's modal rhythm is parallel, like that of *xipi*. However, both the first and second *dou* in most *nanbangzi* melodic-lines follow the modal rhythm of the first *dou* of *xipi*: O X O in ten-written-character lines and O X in seven-written-character lines. Third *dou* in *nanbangzi* follow the modal rhythm of *xipi*'s third *dou*: X O O X and X O X. Similarly, *nanbangzi*'s song structure is parallel, like *xipi*'s. The melodic-phrases for the last written-character in the first and third *dou* of both lines are generally extended, however, particularly in the former case.

The overall pitch range in *nanbangzi* is about the same as that in *xipi*. But *nanbangzi* has its own basic melodic contour and does not use that of *xipi*. Its melodic construction is very similar to *xipi*'s but somewhat simpler. *Nanbangzi*, like *xipi*, is in the key of 1, and the spike fiddle is tuned the same in *nanbangzi* as it is in *xipi*: 6–3. Cadence patterns in *nanbangzi* are generally the same as those of female *xipi*, especially at melodic-line ends: 6 and 5. *Nanbangzi* is experienced as more graceful than *xipi*. It is considered appropriate for expressing "smooth and exquisite or happy sentiments, as well as meditation and silent thought."[45]

The following example compares $\frac{2}{4}$ and $\frac{4}{4}$ *nanbangzi* primary-meter melodic passages with the *nanbangzi* basic melodic contour.[46]

Modulation to and from both meters of *nanbangzi* primary-meter, as well as *nanbangzi* lead-in-meter and dispersed-meter, is usually made from *xipi* primary-meter or two-six-meter. *Nanbangzi* is perceived as most resembling these two *xipi* metrical types.

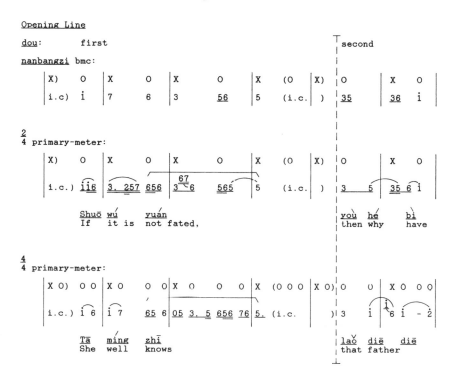

Opening Line

dou: first   second

nanbangzi bmc:

| X) | O | X | O | X | O | X | (O | X) | O | | X | O |
| i.c) | i | 7 | 6 | 3 | 56 | 5 | (i.c. |) | 35 | | 36 | i |

$\frac{2}{4}$ primary-meter:

| X) | O | X | O | X | O | X | (O | X) | O | | X | O |
| i.c.) | 116 | 3. 257 656 | 3⌢6 | 565 | 5 | (i.c. |) | 3 | 5 | 35 6 i |

Shuō wú yuán   yoù hé bì
If   it is not fated,   then why have

$\frac{4}{4}$ primary-meter:

| X O) | O O | X O | O O | X O | O | O | X | (O O O | X O) | O | U | X O O O |
| i.c.) | i 6 | i 7 | 65 6 | 05 3. 5 656 76 | 5. | (i.c. |) | 3 | i | 6 i - 2 |

Tā ming zhī   laǒ diē diē
She well knows   that father

(continued)

Example 24 *(continued)*

<u>dou</u>: third

<u>nanbangzi</u> bmc:

	X	O	X	O	X	O	
	5	<u>75</u>	6	<u>57</u>	6.	(<u>5</u>	

$\frac{2}{4}$ primary-meter:

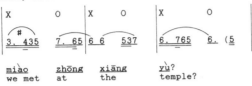

	X	O	X	O	X	O	
	3. 435	7. 65	6 6	537	6. 765	6. (5	

<u>miào</u>   <u>zhōng</u>   <u>xiāng</u>   <u>yù</u>?
we met   at   the   temple?

$\frac{4}{4}$ primary-meter:

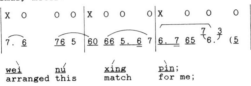

	X O	O O	X O O	O	X	O	O	O	
	7. 6	76 5	60 66 5. 6	7	6. 7 65	6.		(5	

<u>wèi</u>   <u>nú</u>   <u>xíng</u>   <u>pìn</u>;
arranged this   match   for me;

118

Example 24 *(continued)*

Closing Line

dou: first

nanbangzi bmc:

X)	O	X	O	X	O		X
i.c.) 6		2̇	1̇	1̇	6		5

2
4 primary-meter:

X)	O	X	O	X	O		X
i.c.) 6. 1̇6̇1̇		2̇. 5̇3̇2̇	1̇6̇1̇	1̇	6. 2̇7̇6̇		5635

ruò   yǒu   yuán
if   it is fated,

4
4 primary-meter:

X O)	O	O	X	O	O	O	(X	O)	O	O	X	O
i.c.) 6. 1̇ 6̇1̇			2̇. 5̇ 3̇2̇	1̇6̇ 1̇			(13 21)	6. 5̇ 6̇1̇	3 (4 3) 5			

fǎn   jiāng   tā
but   she   has sent

(continued)

Example 24 (continued)

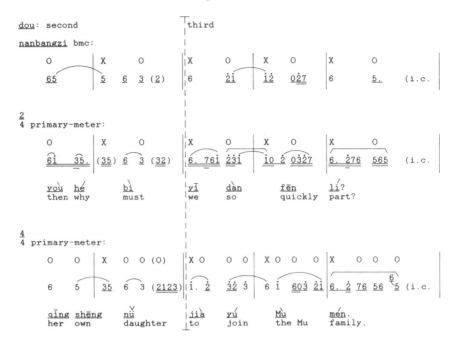

Sipingdiao Mode

Sipingdiao may be used by all role types but *jing*. It is the most highly developed mode after *xipi* and *erhuang* and has its own inverse mode, pitched a fourth higher. *Sipingdiao* developed out of *kunyiqiang* and historically is *erhuang*'s ancestor; however, *sipingdiao* retained its own characteristics after the subsequent development of *erhuang*.[47]

Sipingdiao's modal rhythm resembles *erhuang* only in the most basic respect—it is not parallel. Opening lines in *sipingdiao* usually begin on an accented beat, like *erhuang,* and closing lines on an unaccented beat, like *xipi*. Within lines, the placement of written-characters within the pattern of accented and unaccented beats is quite flexible, accommodating lines of extremely irregular length.

Sipingdiao's song structure also resembles *erhuang* only in that it is not parallel. Like its modal rhythm, *sipingdiao*'s song structure is highly flexible, easily accommodating not only lines of irregular length (including lines with padding written-characters), but also lines not a part of couplet structure (padding lines).[48]

Male and female melodic-passages in *sipingdiao* share the same basic melodic contour, which is different from that of *erhuang*. Female melodic-passages in *sipingdiao* are an octave higher than male and therefore more nearly adhere to the ideal *erhuang* female pitch range than do *erhuang*'s female melodic-passages.

The pattern of melodic construction in *sipingdiao* is similar to that in *erhuang*, with an even stronger tendency to step-wise pitch progressions. *Sipingdiao* uses the same large instrumental connectives as does *erhuang*, and many of the same half-line and small instrumental connectives as well. The latter two types, however, are frequently placed differently than they are in the *erhuang* extended-pattern song structure and basic melodic contour.

Sipingdiao is considered to be in the same key as *erhuang*. The spike fiddle tuning is the same: 5–2. However, the cadence patterns are quite flexible, generally resembling those of *xipi* more than those of *erhuang*. Opening lines often end on 2 (or 2̇ in female melodic-passages) and closing lines on 1 (or 1̇), as in male *xipi*; opening lines also frequently end on 6 (or 6̇) and closing lines on 5 (or 5̇), as in female *xipi*. Lines that precede padding lines, and padding lines themselves, often end on 2 or 6 (or 2̇ or 6̇).

Sipingdiao utilizes slow-meter, primary-meter, lead-in-meter, undulating-dragon-meter, and dispersed-meter. Each metrical type in *sipingdiao* is somewhat faster (i.e., each beat has a shorter duration) than its *erhuang* counterpart.

Sipingdiao is also quite flexible in atmosphere. It is considered expressive of a wide variety of emotional states: "relaxed lightness, remembrance, impelling indignation, and sorrowful desolation,"[49] depending upon its compositional relationship to other modes and upon the compositional relationship of its metrical types.

Example 25 compares male and female *sipingdiao* primary-meter melodic-passages with the male *sipingdiao* basic melodic contour. Each melodic-passage, as well as the basic melodic contour, is preceded by a prelude large instrumental connective not noted here (as in other musical examples, internal instrumental connectives more than one measure long are indicated simply by the letters "i.c." in parentheses). The opening melodic-line of the female melodic-passage is sung twice—first with a seven-written-character line of lyrics and then with a nine-written-character line—before proceeding to the closing melodic-line. Two lines of lyrics are sung within the closing melodic-line. The first of these is a six-written-character line; the second, a five-written-character line, begins within the second *dou*.[50]

Example 25 Male and Female *Sipingdiao* Primary-meter and the
Sipingdiao Basic Melodic Contour

<u>Opening Line</u>

<u>dou</u>:   first

<u>sipingdiao</u> bmc:

| X   O | X   (O |
| 6̣   3 | 2   (i.c. |

male:

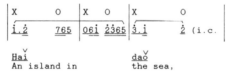

        Sòng Gōng-   míng
        I, Song Gongming,

female (initial opening line):

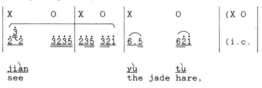

        Hǎi   daǒ
        An island in   the sea,

female (repeated opening line):

| X   O | X   O | X   O | (X O |
| 2̇3̆2̇   3̇2̣3̇5̇ | 2̇3̇5̇ 3̇2̇1̇ | 6̣.5̣   6̣2̇1̇ | (i.c. |

        jiàn   yù   tù
        see   the jade hare,

Example 25 *(continued)*

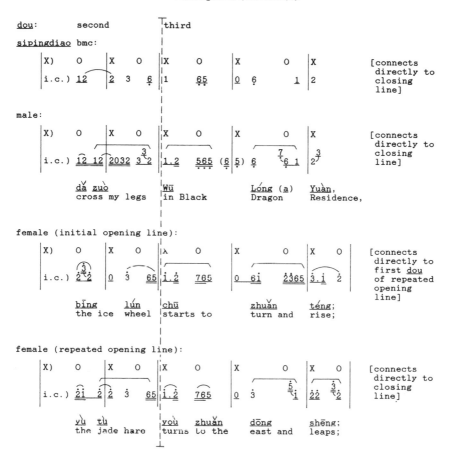

(continued)

Example 25 *(continued)*

Closing Line

dou: first   second

sipingdiao bmc:

	O	X		O		X	O	X	O		X	(O)	
	1	0	5	6		7	6	0	5	6	5	(6)	

male:

	O	X		O		X	O	X	O		X	(O)	
	1	0	3	3 6	35 3.5	615	(6 5)	35	6276		635	(656)	

cai   yi   cai | da   jiě
and   try to   guess | big   sister's

female:

	O	X		O		X	O	X	(O	X O)	X	O	
	76	2	2	76 5		7276	567	6 6	(i.c.	)	3	5.6	

na   bīng lún   lí haǐ | daǒ   qián kūn
that ice wheel leaves | the sea,   all   heaven

Example 25 (continued)

<u>dou</u>: third

<u>sipingdiao</u> bmc:

```
 | X    O | X    O  | X
 | 1    65| 06   2  | 1
```

male:

```
 | X     O   | X    O    | X  O
 | 1216  565 | 0 61 2321 | 6  1
   fù          nei        qing.
   most        inner      thoughts.
```

female:

```
 | X    O  | X    O    | X  O
 | 1.2  765| 0 61 2321 | 6  1
   fēn       wai        ming.
   glows     so         bright.
```

Modulation to and from *sipingdiao*'s metrical types is usually made in *erhuang* primary-meter or dispersed-meter. Because the large instrumental connectives are the same in both modes, it can be achieved quite smoothly.

Gaobozi Mode

Gaobozi may be sung by all role types, although male *gaobozi* occurs much more often than does female. The instruments that provide its major musical accompaniment are different from those used in *pihuang*'s other modes. The primary melodic accompaniment in *gaobozi* is provided by a spike fiddle that is slightly larger than that which accompanies other modes; it is called the *bohu* (lit. "stirring/turning stringed instrument"). A small version of the double-reed instrument used only for special situations in other modes (the *suona*, described in chapter 6) often supports the *bohu* and occasionally serves without it as the primary melodic instrument.[51] *Gaobozi*'s primary percussive accompaniment is usually provided by the *bangzi* clapper rather than the *ban* clapper described in chapter 6, which accompanies all other modes. The *bangzi* clapper consists of two unconnected pieces of hardwood, one cylindrical and the other a rectangular solid, that are struck together by the player. *Gaobozi* developed out of the mutual influences of *qinqiang,* Anhui folk music, and *kunyiqiang.* It is a principal mode in *huiju* and only in recent years has come to be used in Beijing opera.[52]

The modal rhythm of both lines in *gaobozi* resembles that of the closing line in *erhuang* (the beats in parentheses indicate the additional beats required by ten-written-character lines):

both *gaobozi* lines: X O (O), O O (O), X O (O) X;
closing *erhuang* line: X O (X), O O (O), X O (O) X.

The only difference is in the ten-written-character line, where written-characters centering on unaccented beats are even more predominant than in *erhuang.* The song structure in both lines of *gaobozi* is also very similar to that of the closing line in *erhuang;* the first two *dou* in each line are very short, and the third *dou* is longer. As a result, *gaobozi*'s song structure and modal rhythm are parallel, resembling *xipi* in this respect rather than *erhuang.*

Gaobozi's spike fiddle is tuned to 1–5, like that for inverse *erhuang,* and *gaobozi*'s pitch range is higher than that of *erhuang,* as this would suggest. However, *gaobozi* is irregularly higher rather than a fourth higher throughout as in inverse *erhuang;* unlike *erhuang* or inverse *erhuang, gaobozi*'s male and female pitch ranges are approximately the same.

The basic melodic contour is different from that of *erhuang.* It is quite simple, built around a strong pattern of cadences, and is the same for both male and female melodic-passages. Although *gaobozi* is considered to be in the key of 2, like *erhuang,* its cadences are very dissimilar. Resolution (i.e., a return to 2 at the end of closing lines) is generally avoided; the opening line usually ends on 5 and the closing line on 1̇. The final tone in the closing line is higher than that in the opening line, as in male *erhuang,* but the interval between the two is a fourth instead of a major second (*erhuang*'s male lines end on 1 and 2, respectively). Sometimes, especially for female melodic-passages, the opening line ends on 3 and the closing line on 5; they may also end on 6 and 1̇, respectively. In such cases, the cadential tone for the closing line is a third higher than that for the opening line, rather than a fourth lower as in female *erhuang* (*erhuang*'s female lines end on 1̇ and 5, respectively). All of these cadence patterns are closer to those of *erhuang* than to those of *xipi,* however; in *xipi,* the final note of the closing line in both the male and female versions is a major second lower than the final note in the opening line.

Within this pattern of cadences, *gaobozi* follows a pitch range that is even narrower than that of *erhuang* and a melodic construction that, though containing more leaps and jumps than *erhuang*'s, is quite simple; all metrical types associated with *gaobozi* are more syllabic than their *erhuang* counterparts. The tempos of all metrical types in *gaobozi* are faster (i.e., each beat is of shorter duration) than those of their *erhuang* counterparts as well. *Gaobozi* uses essentially the same instrumental connectives as does *erhuang*, though they are placed differently; in *gaobozi*, instrumental connectives are commonly at the end of the second and third *dou* in both lines. They may be either small or half-line and may be replaced by rhythmic rhyming sounds spoken in these positions.

   Gaobozi has even more metrical types than *sipingdiao*: primary-meter, piled-up-meter, lead-in-meter, undulating-dragon-meter, dispersed-meter, and shaking-meter. Free metrical types not only are more numerous, but are also used more extensively than primary-meter in the melodic passages of *gaobozi*. All are more independent than in *erhuang*; entire long melodic-passages may be sung in any one of *gaobozi*'s free metrical types. *Gaobozi* is

**Example 26 Male and Female *Gaobozi* Primary-meter and the
Gaobozi Basic Melodic Contour**

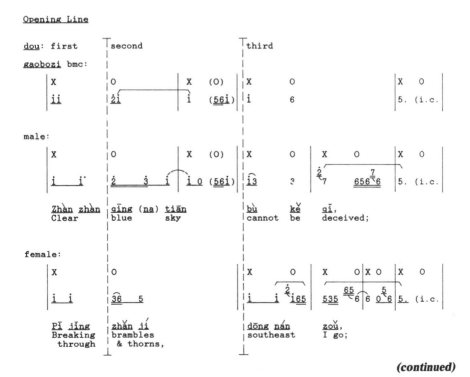

(continued)

Example 26 *(continued)*

Closing Line

considered most expressive of indignant grief. Its name, which literally means "high stirring," reflects this atmosphere, the high pitch range (for male melodic-passages), and the faster tempos of *gaobozi*.

Example 26 compares male and female *gaobozi* primary-meter with the *gaobozi* basic melodic contour.[53]

Modulation between *gaobozi* and *erhuang* may occur in the same metrical type, between metrical types with similar meter and tempo, or between commonly associated metrical types, such as lead-in-meter and undulating-dragon-meter. However, *gaobozi* is most frequently employed as the only mode used in an entire scene or play.[54]

The secondary modes increase the dramatic and musical potential of the two modal systems. Every secondary mode has a characteristic atmosphere different from that of the principal mode in each modal system, thereby expanding the expressive capabilities of each system. By modifying the patterns of modal identity to produce these different atmospheres, the second-

Figure 15
The Modal Systems, Modes, and Metrical Types of the *Pihuang* Musical System

Modal System		Xipi			Erhuang				
	Mode:	Xipi	Inverse Xipi	Nanbangzi	Erhuang	Inverse Erhuang	Sipingdiao	Inverse Sipingdiao	Gaobozi
Metrical Type									
M	slow-meter	X	–	–	X	X	X	X	–
E	fast-three-eyes-meter	X	–	–	X	–	–	–	–
T	primary-meter	X	X	X	X	X	X	X	X
E	two-six-meter	X	X	–	–	–	–	–	–
R	flowing-water-meter	X	–	–	(piled-up-meter)	–	–	–	(piled-up-meter)
E D	fast-meter	X	–	–	–	–	–	–	–
F	lead-in-meter	X	–	X	X	X	X	X	X
R	undulating-dragon-meter	X	–	–	X	X	X	–	X
E	dispersed-meter	X	X	X	X	X	X	–	X
E	shaking-meter	X	X	–	X	X	–	–	X

X = presence ; – = absence

ary modes also increase the rhythmic and melodic variety of each modal system. The combination of these two modal systems makes the *pihuang* musical system one of the most varied, complex, and expressive musical systems in *xiqu*.[55]

Figure 15 illustrates the more comprehensive elements of the *pihuang* musical system, indicating the metrical types associated with each mode in both modal systems. Performers thoroughly trained in the various patterns provided by the elements of this system interpretively apply these patterns when composing and singing the lyrics of specific Beijing opera plays.

CHAPTER IV

THE MUSICAL SYSTEM:

MUSICAL COMPOSITION

Musical composition for Beijing opera plays is often called *buju*, which literally means "arrangement of the parts." The composition process is perceived as occurring in three sequential stages. In the first stage, modal systems and modes are selected and arranged for an entire play; in the second, metrical types are selected and arranged for passages of lyrics. Certain standard compositional patterns *(guilü)* are usually followed in these first two steps. In the third stage, individual melodic-passages are interpretively composed.

The selection and arrangement of modal systems and modes for a given play provide the basic musical interpretation of that play's overall atmosphere and of the fundamental psychology of its major characters. In the selection and arrangement of metrical types for specific passages of lyrics, the emotional content of each passage is more explicitly interpreted. Finally, through the interpretive composition of specific melodies for individual melodic-passages, the precise emotional content of each written-character, *dou*, line, and couplet is given specific musical expression.

For newly written historical plays, contemporary performers often have a great deal of compositional freedom. During rehearsals, they first select and arrange modal systems and modes, and then metrical types, frequently in consultation with one or more musicians. When the fairly general interpretation entailed in these first two stages is agreed upon, performers alone or in conjunction with one or more musicians then compose the specific melodies that they will sing—this composition is based on the patterns provided by the specific modal system, mode(s), and metrical type(s) selected, the speech-tones of the words being sung, and the performers' interpretations of the characters whom they portray.

When composing for traditional plays, contemporary performers usually do not select and arrange modal systems, modes, and metrical types; traditional plays have been sung a number of times before, in many cases by master performers, and the selection and arrangement of these more comprehensive musical elements are already essentially fixed. However, contemporary performers do, to varying extents, interpretively compose their own specific melodies for traditional plays.

In the following discussion of the three compositional stages, the examples used are from traditional plays. Because the more comprehensive musical elements have already been selected and arranged in traditional plays, the basis for that selection and arrangement can be analyzed.[1]

STANDARD PATTERNS OF MODAL COMPOSITION

Depending upon its atmosphere and the psychology of its major characters, a traditional Beijing opera play is composed in one of three standard patterns of modal composition: entirely in one mode of one modal system, in more than one mode of one modal system, or in one or more modes of both modal systems. The overall atmosphere of a specific play and the fundamental psychology of its major characters provide the basis not only for selecting the pattern of modal composition, but also for selecting and arranging the specific modal system(s) and modes. Music for both one-act and multi-scene plays may be composed according to any of the three patterns, although the first two are used most frequently for one-act plays.

SINGLE MODE COMPOSITION IN ONE MODAL SYSTEM

When one atmosphere and one psychological trait dominate an entire play, that play is generally composed in one mode of one modal system. The one-act play *Xu Ce Runs on the City Wall,* excerpted above as an example of *gaobozi,* is characterized by a highly charged, tense atmosphere throughout and is composed entirely in the *erhuang* modal system's *gaobozi* mode. The entire play is primarily an expression of Xu Ce's indignation and grief at his plight and is therefore well suited to *gaobozi.*

The multi-scene play *Silang Visits His Mother* is one of the most complexly structured Beijing opera plays (see chapter 1). Yet its music is composed entirely in the *xipi* modal system's principal mode. This single mode composition is extremely important to the interpretation of Silang's character; he is a strong, purposive individual, not given to self-pity. Though homesick and reflective in the first scene, Silang is determined to find a way to visit his Chinese family. Were *erhuang* sung in the first scene, remembrance would be clearly indicated, but it would be imbued with grief; Silang loves his barbarian wife, has no desire to leave her permanently, and is therefore not grief-stricken. Even more important, the use of *erhuang* would suggest that Silang was overcome by the sadness of separation from his Chinese family and had no purposeful desire to go and see them once more. Through the use of *xipi*'s slower metered metrical types and free metrical types, Silang's sadness can be expressed; simultaneously, *xipi* clearly conveys his strength and determination. *Xipi* is similarly appropriate to Silang's character in the "Chinese world" scenes (scenes seven through ten); though he is distressed to part with his Chinese family once again and sympathizes with their desire to have him remain, he is determined to return to the barbarian Princess and his son.

Xipi is quite suitable as an interpretive vehicle for the other characters as well. The barbarian Princess is a practical, loving woman who demonstrates in scene one that she trusts her husband despite his unusual past; she is determined to help him see his Chinese family and to save his life after he has done so and returned. The confident, regal power of the barbarian Empress and the strong desires of Silang's Chinese family are also well expressed in *xipi*.

MULTIPLE MODE COMPOSITION IN ONE MODAL SYSTEM

When the basic atmosphere remains the same throughout a play but the major characters experience an important psychological change or conflict, that play is generally composed in two or more modes of the same modal system. In the one-act play *The Favorite Concubine Becomes Intoxicated,* the basic atmosphere is that of the regal beauty associated with an imperial concubine; limited power and unlimited prestige with an uncertain future. The *erhuang* modal system, with its fairly deep and profound atmosphere and its ability to convey lyricism, is more suitable than the energetic, purposeful *xipi* system. In the first portion of the play, during the Favorite Concubine's walk through the imperial gardens to her appointed rendezvous with the Emperor, *erhuang*'s *sipingdiao* is sung. She is proud of her beauty, feels sure of her high position, and sees both reflected in the scenery around her—the relaxed lightness of *sipingdiao* helps to convey this mood. However, after the Favorite Concubine learns that the Emperor has gone to visit another concubine instead, the certainty that she originally felt in her position evaporates, and she becomes angry, jealous, and hurt. During the central portion of the play, in which she drinks alone to hide her feelings from her attendants, there is no song. As she becomes intoxicated, that desire to "save face" lessens, and she abandons herself to her pain. Her first song after drinking alone is therefore in principal *erhuang*, a lyrical, contemplative mode expressive of grief and remembrance. The final portion of the play, in which she abandons herself to the uncertainty of her fate, is then sung in *sipingdiao,* which with this principal *erhuang* introduction is expressive of sorrowful desolation.

The majority of songs in the multi-scene play *Yu Tangchun* are concentrated in its two focal scenes, "A Woman Traveling Under Guard" ("Nü qi jie") and "The Tripartite Joint Trial" ("San tang hui shen"). The dominating atmosphere of both scenes is one of tension, characterized by Yu Tangchun's desire to vindicate herself. Except for two melodic-passages at the beginning of the first, both scenes are sung entirely in the *xipi* modal system; its energetic, forceful atmosphere is best for the expression of such vehement determination. The play is in fact considered a model for the use of the *xipi* modal system in female roles. Yet the two *erhuang* melodic-passages are extremely important in setting up the blend of *xipi* modes that then dominates the focal scenes.

As "A Woman Traveling Under Guard" opens, Yu Tangchun is in prison; her fate is extremely uncertain, she doubts the likelihood of any happy outcome, and she is without any plans. When she is called out of her cell to begin her journey to trial, she sings first of her fear in principal *erhuang* and then of her doubts in inverse *erhuang.* The first mode is experienced as heavy and profound and the second as even more profound and tragic; a clearer expression of her helplessness could not be made within the *pihuang* musical system. Yu Tangchun then rallies her strength and determination; throughout her journey to trial in the rest of this first focal scene, she sings in principal *xipi,* expressive of vehemence and purpose.[2]

Once she arrives at the provincial court, however, she is intimidated by its grandeur and power, and some of her original fear and helplessness return. Throughout the second focal scene, "The Tripartite Joint Trial," she is therefore in psychological conflict; she knows she must defend herself well if she is to live, yet she doubts her chances of succeeding. This is expressed musically through a blend of principal *xipi,* which conveys her determination to vindicate herself, and *nanbangzi.* The latter is more graceful, smooth, and contemplative than principal *xipi,* suggesting her fear and potential weakness. Principal *xipi* and *nanbangzi* are at various points in the scene both blended in the same melodic-lines and sung in alternation, subtly expressing her ongoing psychological conflict.[3]

MULTIPLE MODE COMPOSITION IN TWO MODAL SYSTEMS

When the basic atmosphere itself undergoes a major change in a given play, that play is usually composed in one or more modes of both modal systems.

In *Catching and Releasing Cao Cao,* principal *xipi* is used for the first half of the play and principal *erhuang* for the second. The first half is action-oriented, concerned with the capture of Cao Cao and the subsequent murder of the entire Lü family. The major character, Chen Gong, undergoes violent changes of mood. *Xipi,* experienced as energetic and forceful and expressive of vehemence, is considered best for the music of arias sung in such a situation. The second half of the play is concerned with Chen Gong's recollection and assessment of all that Cao Cao has said and done that day. Because the arias must therefore express a complex state of mind, *erhuang* is considered most appropriate; it is experienced as deep, profound, and meticulous, and best for expressing remembrance and thought.

In *Shepherd's Story (Muyang juan),* the mode changes from principal *erhuang* to principal *xipi.* The play uses the focal scene structure discussed in chapter 1, with the first eight scenes setting up the lengthy focal scene that follows. In the first half of scene nine, the hero weeps at the tomb that he believes contains his mother and wife, and the mother and her daughter-in-law beg for food. The second half begins with the daughter-in-law relating her feelings and ends with the hero recognizing his mother and wife. *Erhuang* best expresses the remembrance and grief in the first half, while *xipi* best conveys the vehemence and joy in the second.

Occasionally some plays alternate back and forth between modal systems —for example, *The Luo River Spirit (Luo shen),* which begins and ends in *xipi,* with a central section in *erhuang.* Each of the three sections ends after the completion of a song. This is a standard practice—switching modes normally takes place between songs and not within them. Only very rarely is there modulation between modal systems within a single passage of lyrics in traditional Beijing opera.

In this first stage of the composition process, then, the selection and arrangement of modal system(s) and mode(s) for a given play provide the basic musical interpretation of that play's atmosphere and the fundamental psychology of its major character(s). In the second stage, the emotional content of each passage of lyrics is interpreted through the selection and arrangement of metrical types within those modes.

STANDARD PATTERNS OF METRICAL-TYPE COMPOSITION

Although appropriateness of emotional expression is the most important consideration in selecting and arranging metrical types for passages of lyrics, it is not the first factor considered in this second stage of the composition process. The first consideration is a practical one, concerning the timing of the entire play. Stage and performance time are extended in the expression of emotion through the display of song skill—yet even the longest multi-scene plays generally should not run more than two to three hours in playing time, as discussed in chapter 1. Because some metrical types are more melismatic and slower than others, expanding stage and performance time to a greater extent as a result, a balance of slower and faster metrical types needs to be maintained so as not to expand performance time excessively.

In common practice, the most frequently used metrical types are dispersed-meter and shaking-meter, with fast-meter, flowing-water-meter, and two-six-meter occurring quite often as well in plays that include principal *xipi* in their composition. Primary-meter is sung less often, "three or four times in one play." Fast-three-eyes-meter is used even less, and slow-meter the least, "one or two times in one play."[4] Because slow-meter is the most introspective metrical type, directly expressive of emotion, the effect of its scarcity is to make a passage of lyrics sung in slow-meter an important, featured moment in any play. Lead-in-meter and undulating-dragon-meter are also slow and melismatic and are also sung only once or twice in each play, similarly creating important focal moments.

From the perspective of composing in metrical types, there are three major types of song in Beijing opera. The first two types are both considered arias *(changduan)*: large arias *(daduan)* and small arias *(xiaoduan)*. Any of the six types of lyrics discussed in chapter 2 may be composed as a small aria or as all, or more often part, of a large aria, and all except emotive lyrics may be interspersed with speech. The third type of song is referred to only as song *(chang)*, rather than as aria *(changduan),* and is hereafter referred to as "small song" for clarity. Small songs are primarily for conventionalized lyrics and elevated speech.

Large Arias

Large arias are composed in two or more metrical types, at least one of which is metered. Analysis reveals that there are two basic subtypes of large arias: large arias of alternation and large arias of acceleration. A third type of large aria may be composed by combining these first two; such large arias are referred to here as complex large arias. All are designed to express and interpret two or more emotional states presented by the emotional-progression structure of one-act plays and the focal-scenes of multi-scene plays discussed in chapter 1.

Large Arias of Alternation

Large arias of alternation alternate melodic-passages composed in a free metrical type (i.e., dispersed-meter, lead-in-meter, or shaking-meter) with melodic-passages composed in a metered metrical type (i.e., slow-meter, fast-three-eyes-meter, primary-meter, two-six-meter, flowing-water-meter, or fast-meter). They may begin in either type of metrical type, alternate only once or several times, and may end in either type of metrical type. Although they may include lyrics of more than one lyric type, such large arias are more frequently composed for one complete passage of lyrics in one lyric type.

The one-act play *The Favorite Concubine Becomes Intoxicated* contains an excellent example. After her entrance and the opening sequence, the Favorite Concubine sings a long passage of descriptive lyrics composed as a large aria of alternation. It opens in primary-meter, conveying her relaxed state as she indirectly describes her own beauty and happiness through a description of her resemblance to the legendary goddess Chang E, who lived in the moon, and of the beauty of the garden's curved bridges, colorful carp, and mandarin ducks. She then sees geese in flight, a rare and excellent omen, and her "heart stops"; she initially sings of this sighting in dispersed-meter. She then continues her description of the geese in a more relaxed fashion in primary-meter, relating them to herself, until she arrives at her destination, enters the pavilion, and begins to speak.

In some instances, large arias of alternation are composed entirely in metered metrical types. This occurs most frequently in disputive lyrics in which the opening lines in a series of couplets are taken by one character and the closing lines by a second character, as discussed in chapter 1. The lines for the first character may be composed in one metrical type and those for the second character in another; in this way, for instance, primary-meter may alternate with two-six-meter for a number of successive melodic-lines. As the direction of the argument changes, the assigned metrical types may also change (i.e., the two characters may switch metrical types, or both may change to new metrical types).

Large Arias of Acceleration

Large arias of acceleration are composed in two or more metered metrical types; they begin in a slower metrical type and then switch to a faster one. More, progressively faster metrical types are frequently used as well. Although they may be composed for lyrics of only one lyric type, large arias of acceleration in many instances include two or more lyric types.

In the play *Yu Tangchun,* the major, *xipi* portion of the first focal-scene, "A Woman Traveling Under Guard," includes a large aria of acceleration composed for a sequential passage of emotive and condemnatory lyrics; it is interspersed with the speech of the official who is taking Yu Tangchun on her journey to trial.

The large aria of acceleration begins with a passage of emotive lyrics in which Yu Tangchun expresses her grief at the difference between her present state as an accused murderer and her former state as an elegant courtesan; the passage is composed in slow-meter, implying an introspective, passive state. She then sings a passage of condemnatory lyrics in which she condemns all who are responsible for this downfall. The first several couplets are composed in primary-meter; the increase in tempo suggests that she is coming to terms with her situation and feels wronged but no longer hopeless. In these couplets she condemns her parents for selling her, the merchant for buying her, his wife for poisoning him, the wife's servant for helping carry out the crime, and the corrupt officials for arresting her, accepting bribes, and torturing her to force a confession. The final couplets of condemnatory lyrics, in which she condemns all residents of the district in which her downfall occurred but excepts the kindly official accompanying her, are composed in flowing-water-meter. Its still faster tempo expresses Yu Tangchun's rising anger at her situation and her growing determination to vindicate herself.

Complex Large Arias

Alternation and acceleration are combined in the composition of complex large arias. An initial melodic-passage, often in a free metrical type, is followed by successive passages in increasingly faster metered metrical types that "reach such a high [emotional] pitch that the only way to bring it [i.e., the full passage] to a close is to break down the rhythm in the last line." Such a progression from increasingly faster metered metrical types to a free metrical type—for example, from slow-meter to primary-meter, to fast-meter, and then to the free meter dispersed-meter—is known as "singing it loose" *(chang sanle).* Although "singing it loose" does occur in large arias of alternation that conclude in free metrical types, the emotional "contrast . . . is not always as striking"[5] as it is in complex large arias, where appreciable acceleration occurs before the free metrical type is sung.

The second focal scene in *Yu Tangchun,* "The Tripartite Joint Trial," features such a complex large aria. The entire trial scene, from the time Yu Tangchun formally presents herself before the three judges until the adjournment and exit of the two overseeing judges, consists primarily of a long passage of narrative lyrics sung by Yu Tangchun, interspersed with the questions and comments of the judges. During the course of this long passage of lyrics, Yu Tangchun experiences four different basic emotional states: fear of the trial situation, a reexperiencing of her love for Wang Jinlong, anger at the merchant's wife and the corrupt local authorities, and a desire to see Wang Jinlong again. In her first emotional state, Yu Tangchun gives her name in lead-in-meter and appeals in undulating-dragon-meter for a chance to explain her situation, conveying her tension and anxiety. She then tells of her initial sale to the brothel and her first meeting with Wang in slow-meter, expressive here of her tentativeness and fear. Having begun to speak of her lover, she reexperiences her love for him and sings of their life together, his fall into poverty, and the financial assistance she gave him in primary-meter, suggesting the importance of this man and their love to her life. She switches to the faster two-six-meter at the end of this passage, emphasizing the determination of her vow to wait for him. In her third emotional state, Yu Tangchun tells the story of her forced association with the merchant and his family, the resulting false accusation of murder, and the corrupt local trial; her anger and desire for vindication are conveyed through the use of fast-meter. Finally, her "heart stops" as she sings in dispersed-meter of her desire to see her lover one more time.

Complex large arias may be considerably shorter than this, but are always characterized by successive metered metrical types of mounting tempos that are "sung loose," that is, concluded by a passage in a free metrical type. One such shorter complex large aria is sung after the opening sequence of the first scene of *Silang Visits His Mother*. Silang first sings a passage of emotive lyrics in the introspective slow-meter, expressing his sadness at having been away from his Chinese family for so long. He then sings narrative lyrics that relate the circumstances of battle, capture, and marriage that have prevented him from seeing his family; all but the last line of this passage is sung in two-six-meter, suggesting his determination to overcome these obstacles. Finally, he cries out his desire to see his mother once more in a last line composed in dispersed-meter; by "singing it loose" after the previous acceleration, the composition sets off and emphasizes the depth of that desire.

In the longest complex arias, the composition may revert to a slower meter before continuing the tempo acceleration and may include interspersed free metrical types. Such composition is capable of expressing subtle details of thought and emotion; a character's reassessment of his or her position, the effect of the speech of other characters upon the character singing, sudden remembrance of relevant past experience, and so on. However, the overall progression is from slow to fast, and the final metrical type is a free one, usually dispersed-meter.

SMALL ARIAS

Small arias consist of only one type of lyric composed in only one metrical type, usually slow-meter, fast-three-eyes-meter, primary-meter, or dispersed-meter. Every small aria is designed to express and interpret only one emotional state.

A good example of a small aria can be found in *The Ruse of the Empty City (Kong cheng ji)*. Zhuge Liang sings a passage of emotive lyrics in which he expresses his belief in his own prowess and in his ability to reunite the Han dynasty. The passage is sung in the introspective slow-meter; better than could the faster meters, this metrical type helps express his calm assurance in his power to transcend all difficulties.

Both *Yu Tangchun* and *The Favorite Concubine Becomes Intoxicated* contain important small arias. In the former play, Yu Tangchun sings two couplets of emotive lyrics as soon as she enters the courtroom in the second focal scene, expressing in dispersed-meter the incapacitating fear that strikes her as soon as she sees the provincial high court. In the latter play, the Favorite Concubine's first entrance is marked by a passage of descriptive lyrics instead of a prelude poem. The five lines (the first couplet has two successive opening lines) are sung in primary-meter, clearly expressing her confidence in and reliance upon the Emperor's preference for her beauty.

Some plays that feature several major characters are composed almost entirely of small arias; in such plays, specific metrical types may be assigned to each major character. Assignment is made on the basis of social status and overall emotional state. In *Ascending the Heavenly Altar (Shang tian tai)*, Emperor Guangwu of the Eastern Han dynasty (A.D. 25–220) sings primarily in slow-meter, indicating that he is an Emperor with unchanging policy. Lady Guo, whose father was killed by Yao Gang, has come before the Emperor to plead that the murderer be punished; she sings primarily in shaking-meter, simultaneously expressing her high state of tension and purposive control. Yao Qi, the murderer's father, takes his son before the Emperor and pleads for his life in lead-in-meter and dispersed-meter, indicating his nervous and frightened state. Yao Gang, the murderer, sings in dispersed-meter for the same reason. When the murderer is pardoned, his father sings his gratitude to the Emperor in primary-meter, expressing his return to a relaxed state.

SMALL SONGS

Small songs are composed for conventionalized lyrics and elevated speech lyrics. Although such lyrics usually are not directly expressive of emotion in their textual content, they are considered more emotionally expressive than straight speech because they are sung and therefore expressed with the atmospheric, psychological, and emotional connotations of mode and metrical type.

Small Songs for Conventionalized Lyrics

Small songs for conventionalized lyrics are composed in only one metrical type, usually in one of the faster metrical types that occupy less performance time. The specific metrical type for each set of conventionalized lyrics is chosen to reflect the mood of the scene at the time of the transition point. Shaking-meter is the most frequently used. It is the fastest free metrical type, and its connotations of exterior calm and interior tension are often appropriate for transitional situations; in small songs composed for conventionalized lyrics, shaking-meter suggests that something is about to happen, or that what has just happened has larger implications that will become known in the next scene. At the end of scene two of *Silang Visits His Mother,* the Empress sings conventionalized lyrics in which she adjourns the royal court until dawn, when the arrow of command is to be returned. They are composed in shaking-meter, suggesting that difficulties will arise at that time. At the beginning of scene ten, Silang's mother sings conventionalized lyrics in shaking-meter, announcing that she hears Silang and his Chinese wife crying; the implication is that the difficulty soon will affect her.

Conventionalized lyrics are also frequently composed in dispersed-meter for less tense situations; in fast-meter, flowing-water-meter, or two-six-meter for more animated, excited situations; and occasionally, for very calm situations, in primary-meter. Those composed in the metered metrical types may conclude by being "sung loose"; however, this non-metered conclusion is relatively rare, with the vast majority of small songs for conventionalized lyrics composed in only one metrical type.

Small Songs for Elevated Speech Lyrics

Small songs for elevated speech lyrics are also composed only in the faster metrical types. Among these, shaking-meter, with its connotations of inner tensions under control, is again the most commonly used metrical type. In scene seven of *Silang Visits His Mother,* Silang and his brother discuss their mother's whereabouts and current activities, and Silang asks his brother to take him to see her; these elevated speech lyrics are composed in shaking-meter, suggesting the intense emotions of reunion controlled by the demands of proper social intercourse. Elevated speech lyrics may also be composed in dispersed-meter, lead-in-meter, fast-meter, flowing-water-meter, and two-six-meter.

Unlike the small songs for conventionalized lyrics, those for elevated speech lyrics may be interspersed with speech, and may be composed in more than one metrical type, resembling large arias in their use of alternation, acceleration, or the combination of both patterns. However, small songs that employ these more complex compositional patterns (referred to henceforth as complex small songs) always use only the faster metrical types. The elevated speech lyrics of the Princess and Silang in scene thirteen of *Silang Visits His Mother* are composed as a complex small song, using alternation composition; the Princess expresses her surprise and concern in dispersed-meter, Silang tells her of his difficulties and pleads for her assistance in lead-in-meter, and the Princess assures him that she will intercede on his behalf in flowing-water-meter.

Narrative, condemnatory, and disputive lyrics may also be composed, like elevated speech lyrics, in small songs or complex small songs composed in one or more of the faster metrical types, respectively. Such composition heightens their urgency and implies great excitement. In scene seven of *Silang Visits His Mother,* before Silang's brother learns the identity of his prisoner, the two brothers sing a passage of disputive lyrics composed as a complex small song. Silang first declares in flowing-water-meter that he will only answer when questioned. His brother then asks his name, nationality, and intentions in the same metrical type. Silang responds in fast-meter, which conveys the excitement he feels at revealing his identity and their relationship. His brother then greets him brokenly in dispersed-meter, which expresses the heart-stopping surprise he feels at Silang's return.

The Relationships Between Metrical Types, Lyric Types, and Song Types

It is apparent from this discussion of the standard patterns of metrical-type composition that this second stage of the composition process is quite flexible; there are a number of possible permutations to the patterns of metrical-type composition. A single metrical type may be used to compose a given passage of lyrics, expressing one specific emotional state; more than one metrical type may be used instead, connoting an emotional progression within that passage of lyrics. A given passage of lyrics may be composed independently as a complete song, or may be joined with passages in one or more different lyric types to form a complete song expressing a more varied range of emotions.

The aim of metrical-type composition, however, is the musical interpretation of the overall emotional content of each passage of lyrics; because each lyric type facilitates a different kind and degree of emotional expression, the specific lyric type of a given passage of lyrics appreciably influences the metrical-type composition of that melodic passage.

Certain tempos are considered most appropriate for specific lyric types. Emotive and descriptive lyrics are rarely composed in the faster metrical types; condemnatory and disputive lyrics are rarely composed in the slower. Narrative lyrics may be composed in any metrical type and are frequently composed in more than one. Lyrics of shared space and separate sensations, depending upon their specific content, may be composed like emotive, descriptive, or narrative lyrics.

Because metrical types are not applied directly to lyric types but are composed according to the compositional patterns provided by the specific song types, these compositional patterns also influence metrical-type composition. The compositional pattern of each song type specifies the number of lyric and metrical types that may be used in one song composed according to that pattern. Most specify the tempos that may be used as well.

A single large aria may include one or more lyric types and uses two or more metrical types in its composition; any of the several metrical types may be selected. Small arias include only one lyric type and use only one metrical type in their composition, in most instances one of the slower ones. Small songs for conventionalized lyrics also include only one lyric type and use only one metrical type, but usually one of the faster metrical types. Small songs for elevated speech lyrics include only one lyric type but may be composed in one or more metrical types. Like those for conventionalized lyrics, small songs for elevated speech lyrics use only the faster metrical types.

The compositional patterns of certain song types are therefore considered most appropriate for certain lyric types. Small aria composition is considered appropriate for emotive, narrative, descriptive, and shared-space-separate-sensations lyrics; it is rarely used for disputive or condemnatory lyrics. Large aria composition is considered appropriate for all six lyric types. However, disputive and emotive lyrics are only infrequently composed as large arias. In large arias, emotive lyrics often occur as a first passage, followed by narrative, descriptive, or condemnatory lyrics; disputive lyrics are more frequently composed as small songs. Small-song composition is used for conventionalized and elevated speech lyrics and for disputive lyrics that function as elevated speech. Narrative and condemnatory lyrics are also composed as small songs when they function as elevated speech.

These relationships between lyric types, song types, and metrical types are in fact complex musical conventions that serve to heighten the communicative value of metrical-type composition. Their flexibility allows for the sensitive and precise musical expression of emotion in the display of song skill.

Figure 16 illustrates the complete metrical-type composition of three plays excerpted frequently as examples in this discussion: *The Favorite Concubine Becomes Intoxicated, Yu Tangchun,* and *Silang Visits His Mother.* In the latter two, multi-scene plays, it is possible to see the predominance of faster metrical types, as required by the demands of performance time. In *Silang Visits His Mother,* the resulting predominance of small songs is evident as well. In the listing of metrical-type composition throughout Figure 16, free metrical types are underlined, and lyric types are given in parentheses before the metrical types used in their composition. Asterisks mark those specific songs excerpted as examples of lyric and song types in the descriptions above and in chapter 2.

When the overall emotional content of each passage of lyrics has been interpreted through metrical-type composition in this second stage of the composition process, each performer then develops his or her own specific melodies for each melodic-passage.

INDIVIDUAL MELODIC-PASSAGE COMPOSITION

Performers compose specific melodies for each melodic-passage to establish clearly the speech-tone and therefore the meaning of each written-character, and to express musically their interpretation of nuances of dramatic character and of the specific emotional content of the lyrics. In this third stage of the composition process (called *xingqiang,* lit. "doing the melodic-phrase"; also called *shiqiang,* lit. "making the melodic-phrase"), certain standard interpretive techniques are applied. However, unlike the standard patterns of modal and metrical-type composition, these standard techniques of melodic-passage composition are discretionary rather than prescribed. While these standard techniques are used in composition as appropriate, the process of composing a specific melodic-passage is fundamentally one of

Figure 16
Mode, Song, and Metrical-type Composition in
The Favorite Concubine Becomes Intoxicated, Yu Tangchun, and *Silang Visits His Mother*

Character	Mode	Song Type	Metrical-type Composition
		A. The Favorite Concubine Becomes Intoxicated	
Favorite Concubine	*Sipingdiao*	Small aria*	(descriptive) primary-meter
Favorite Concubine	*Sipingdiao*	Large aria of alternation*	(descriptive) primary-meter → dispersed-meter → primary-meter
Favorite Concubine	*Sipingdiao*	Small aria	(narrative) primary-meter
Favorite Concubine	*Erhuang*	Large aria of alternation	(descriptive) lead-in-meter → undulating-dragon-meter → dispersed-meter
Favorite Concubine	*Sipingdiao*	Large aria of alternation	(narrative) primary-meter → dispersed-meter → primary-meter dispersed-meter
"A Woman Traveling Under Guard"		*B. Yu Tangchun*	
Yu	*Erhuang*	Small aria	(narrative) shaking-meter
Yu	Inverse *Erhuang*	Small aria	(narrative) slow-meter
Yu	*Xipi*	Small aria	(narrative) flowing-water-meter
Yu	*Xipi*	Small aria	(narrative) fast-meter
Yu	*Xipi*	Small song	(elevated speech) lead-in-meter
Yu	*Xipi*	Large aria of acceleration*	(emotive) slow-meter → (condemnatory) primary-meter → flowing-water-meter
Yu	*Xipi*	Small song	(conventional) shaking-meter
"The Tripartite Joint Trial"			
Yu	*Xipi*	Small aria*	(emotive) dispersed-meter
Wang	*Xipi* *Nanbangzi*	Large aria of alternation	(narrative) dispersed-meter → primary-meter
Yu	*Xipi*	Complex large aria*	(narrative) lead-in-meter → undulating-dragon-meter → slow-meter → primary-meter → two-six-meter → fast-meter → dispersed-meter

(continued)

Figure 16 (*continued*)

Character	Mode	Song Type	Metrical-type Composition
Wang	*Xipi*	Small song	(narrative as elevated speech) shaking-meter
Yu	*Xipi*	Complex small song	(elevated speech) two-six-meter → dispersed-meter → fast-meter → dispersed-meter → flowing-water-meter → shaking-meter →fast-meter → shaking meter

C. Silang Visits His Mother

Scene 1

Silang	*Xipi*	Complex large aria*	(emotive) primary-meter → (narrative) two-six-meter → dispersed-meter
Princess	*Xipi*	Small song*	(conventional) flowing-water-meter
Princess	*Xipi*	Large aria of alternation	(narrative) lead-in-meter → slow-meter
Silang	*Xipi*	Complex small song	(elevated speech) flowing-water-meter → shaking-meter → flowing-water-meter
Princess	*Xipi*	Small song	(elevated speech) dispersed-meter
Silang	*Xipi*	Large aria of alternation	(narrative) lead-in-meter → primary-meter → shaking-meter
Princess	*Xipi*	Small song	(narrative as elevated speech) flowing-water-meter
Princess / 5x Silang Princess / Silang / Princess	*Xipi*	Small song	(elevated speech) flowing-water-meter→ fast-meter → fast-meter → flowing-water-meter → shaking-meter → flowing-water-meter
Silang	*Xipi*	Small song	(conventional) fast-meter → dispersed-meter

Scene 2

Empress	*Xipi*	Large aria of alternation	(narrative) lead-in-meter → slow-meter → dispersed-meter
Princess	*Xipi*	Small song	(conventional) shaking-meter
2x Empress Princess	*Xipi*	Small song	(elevated speech) shaking-meter → shaking-meter →

Figure 16 (*continued*)

Character	Mode	Song Type	Metrical-type Composition
2 x Princess Empress			flowing-water-meter → flowing-water-meter
Princess	*Xipi*	Small song	(conventional) <u>shaking-meter</u>
Empress	*Xipi*	Small song*	(conventional) <u>shaking-meter</u>
Scene 3			
Silang	*Xipi*	Small song	(narrative as elevated speech) flowing-water-meter
Princess	*Xipi*	Small song	(conventional) <u>shaking-meter</u>
Silang	*Xipi*	Small song	(elevated speech) fast-meter
Silang	*Xipi*	Small song	(conventional) <u>dispersed-meter</u>
Princess	*Xipi*	Small song	(emotive as elevated speech) <u>shaking-meter</u>
Scene 4			
Officials	*Xipi*	Small song	(conventional) <u>dispersed-meter</u>
Silang	*Xipi*	Small song	(narrative as elevated speech) flowing-water-meter
Silang Officials Silang Officials	*Xipi*	Small song	(elevated speech) flowing-water-meter → <u>shaking-meter</u> → <u>shaking-meter</u> → <u>shaking-meter</u>
Officials	*Xipi*	Small song	(conventional) <u>shaking-meter</u>
Scene 5			
Nephew	*Xipi*	Large aria of alternation	(narrative) <u>lead-in-meter</u> → slow-meter
Silang	*Xipi*	Small aria	(narrative) slow-meter
Scene 6			
Brother	*Xipi*	Large aria of alternation	(narrative) <u>lead-in-meter</u> → primary-meter → <u>dispersed-meter</u> → <u>shaking-meter</u>
Nephew	*Xipi*	Small song	(conventional) <u>shaking-meter</u>
Scene 7			
Silang	*Xipi*	Small song	(conventional) flowing-water-meter
Silang	*Xipi*	Small song	(elevated speech) <u>dispersed-meter</u>

(*continued*)

Figure 16 (*continued*)

Character	Mode	Song Type	Metrical-type Composition
Silang	*Xipi*	Complex small song*	(disputive as elevated speech) flowing-water-meter →
Brother			flowing-water-meter →
Silang			fast-meter →
Brother			<u>dispersed-meter</u>
Silang	*Xipi*	Small aria	(narrative) primary-meter
Brother	*Xipi*	Small aria	(narrative) primary-meter
Brother	*Xipi*	Small song	(elevated speech) primary-meter
Nephew	*Xipi*	Small song	(conventional) <u>shaking-meter</u>
Silang	*Xipi*	Small song*	(elevated speech) <u>shaking-meter</u> →
Brother			<u>shaking-meter</u> →
Silang			<u>shaking-meter</u>

Scene 8

Character	Mode	Song Type	Metrical-type Composition
Mother	*Xipi*	Small song	(conventional) <u>dispersed-meter</u>
Brother	*Xipi*	Small song	(elevated speech) <u>dispersed-meter</u> →
Silang			<u>dispersed-meter</u>
2 x Mother	*Xipi*	Small aria	(emotive) <u>lead-in-meter</u> →
Silang			<u>lead-in-meter</u> →
Both			<u>lead-in-meter</u> →
Mother			<u>lead-in-meter</u> →
Silang			<u>lead-in-meter</u>
Mother	*Xipi*	Small aria	(narrative) flowing-water-meter
Mother	*Xipi*	Small song	(elevated speech) <u>shaking-meter</u>
Silang	*Xipi*	Small aria	(narrative) two-six-meter
Silang	*Xipi*	Small song	(elevated speech) two-six-meter →
Silang			<u>dispersed-meter</u> →
Brother			<u>shaking-meter</u> →
Silang			<u>dispersed-meter</u> →
Sisters			<u>dispersed-meter</u> →
Mother			<u>dispersed-meter</u> →
Silang			<u>dispersed-meter</u> →
Sisters			<u>dispersed-meter</u> →
Silang			<u>dispersed-meter</u> →
Silang			<u>dispersed-meter</u>
Mother	*Xipi*	Small song	(conventional) <u>dispersed-meter</u>

Scene 9

Character	Mode	Song Type	Metrical-type Composition
Wife	*Xipi*	Small song	(conventional) <u>dispersed-meter</u>

Figure 16 (*continued*)

Character	Mode	Song Type	Metrical-type Composition
Sisters	*Xipi*	Small song	(elevated speech) <u>dispersed-meter</u>
Wife	*Xipi*	Small song	(narrative as elevated speech) <u>lead-in-meter</u>
Wife	*Xipi*	Small song	(elevated speech) flowing-water-meter
Silang	*Xipi*	Small song	(narrative as elevated speech) flowing-water-meter
Wife	*Xipi*	Small song*	(condemnatory as elevated speech) flowing-water-meter
Silang	*Xipi*	Small song	(disputive as elevated speech) flowing-water-meter →
2 x Silang			dispersed-meter →
Wife			dispersed-meter →
Silang			<u>dispersed-meter</u>

Scene 10

Character	Mode	Song Type	Metrical-type Composition
Mother	*Xipi*	Small song*	(conventional) <u>shaking-meter</u>
Silang	*Xipi*	Small song	(conventional) <u>shaking-meter</u>
Wife	*Xipi*	Small song	(conventional) <u>dispersed-meter</u>
Mother	*Xipi*	Small song*	(disputive as elevated speech) <u>dispersed-meter</u> →
Silang			<u>dispersed-meter</u> →
Brother			<u>dispersed-meter</u> →
Silang			<u>dispersed-meter</u> →
Sisters			<u>dispersed-meter</u> →
Silang			<u>dispersed-meter</u> →
Wife			<u>dispersed-meter</u> →
Silang			<u>dispersed-meter</u> →
All			<u>dispersed-meter</u> →
Silang			<u>dispersed-meter</u> →
Mother			<u>dispersed-meter</u> →
Sisters & Brother			<u>dispersed-meter</u> →
Wife			<u>dispersed-meter</u> →
Silang			<u>shaking-meter</u>
Mother	*Xipi*	Small song	(conventional) <u>shaking-meter</u>

Scene 13

Character	Mode	Song Type	Metrical-type Composition
Silang	*Xipi*	Small song	(conventional) fast-meter → <u>dispersed-meter</u>

(*continued*)

Figure 16 (*continued*)

Character	Mode	Song Type	Metrical-type Composition
2 x Empress Silang	*Xipi*	Small song	(disputive as elevated speech) <u>dispersed-meter</u> → <u>dispersed-meter</u>
Empress	*Xipi*	Small song	(elevated speech) fast-meter
Silang	*Xipi*	Small song	(narrative as elevated speech) <u>shaking-meter</u> → <u>dispersed-meter</u>
Princess	*Xipi*	Small song	(conventional) flowing-water-meter
Princess Silang Princess	*Xipi*	Small song*	(elevated speech) <u>dispersed-meter</u> → <u>lead-in-meter</u> → flowing-water-meter
Princess	*Xipi*	Small song*	(conventional) flowing-water-meter
Princess	*Xipi*	Small song	(narrative as elevated speech) flowing-water-meter
Princess Empress 2 x Princess Empress	*Xipi*	Small song	(disputive as elevated speech) flowing-water-meter → <u>dispersed-meter</u> → <u>dispersed-meter</u> → dispersed-meter
Princess	*Xipi*	Small song	(narrative as elevated speech) flowing-water-meter
4 x Princess Silang Princess Both Silang	*Xipi*	Small song	(elevated speech) <u>dispersed-meter</u> → dispersed-meter → dispersed-meter → dispersed-meter → dispersed-meter
3 x Princess Empress	*Xipi*	Small song	(disputive as elevated speech) flowing-water-meter → flowing-water-meter
Princess	*Xipi*	Small song	(elevated speech) <u>dispersed-meter</u>
Silang Silang Princess Silang	*Xipi*	Small song	(elevated speech) flowing-water-meter → <u>dispersed-meter</u> → <u>dispersed-meter</u> → dispersed-meter

interpretively applying the patterns provided by the modal system, mode, and metrical type(s) selected for that passage of lyrics to make the meaning of the lyrics clear and, even more important, to give specific musical expression to emotions and character interpretation.

STANDARD INTERPRETIVE TECHNIQUES

Three standard interpretive techniques are frequently used in the composition of melodic-passages: empty-words *(xuzi)*, extended tones *(yanyin)*, and a gradual decrease in tempo *(che,* or *jianman)*. The latter two are used for emphasis; empty-words increase the ease with which language is sung.

Empty-words, a concept perhaps most accurately represented in English by the ethnomusicological terms "vocable" or "non-lexical syllable," are sounds, such as "ah" and "oh," that have no denotative meaning but are considered easy to sustain when singing. The pronunciations of certain written-characters are considered difficult to sustain; if one of those written-characters is located in a position that calls for an extended melodic-phrase —i.e., at the end of a third *dou*—it is often sung quickly, with just one or two notes. An empty-word is then used to sing the remainder of the melodic-phrase. The selection of appropriate empty-words is discussed in detail in chapter 5.

Extended tones function much like the *fermata* in Western music; in fact, they are indicated in cipheric notation by that mark, as can be seen in many of the examples cited in chapter 3. When a performer decides to make a certain note an extended tone, it is freed from its rhythmic relationship to other notes and may be held for as long as the performer deems dramatically appropriate. Tones may be extended in both metered and free metrical types. When they are extended in the former, the effect is that of one note sung in free meter; however, because the original meter is immediately resumed, the use of extended tones is not considered a switch to free meter. The final tones in melodic-sections and melodic-lines are those that are most often extended.

A gradual decrease in tempo is most frequently employed at the end of a melodic-passage and is used only in metered metrical types. It also does not constitute a change to free meter but rather functions much like the use of *ritard* in Western music; all notes in the melodic-phrase or melodic-section selected for a decrease in tempo retain their original rhythmic relationships, but the duration of each beat becomes progressively longer.

Every performer is adept at the use of these techniques and applies them discretionarily in the composition of specific melodies. Extended tones and gradual decreases in tempo serve to emphasize—and empty-words to facilitate—the expression of emotion in the singing of specific words. The melodies to which those words are sung are composed through the creative, interpretive application of the compositional patterns provided by mode, metrical type, and role type.

Once the modal system, modes, and metrical types have been selected for a given play, the patterns governing the composition of individual melodic-passages are clear. Each mode provides patterns of modal rhythm, melodic construction, and keys for every melodic-passage composed in that mode; its appropriate male or female version provides patterns of melodic contour, cadences, and melodic tendencies. Each metrical type provides meter, tempo, and additional melodic tendencies for every melodic-passage composed in that metrical type. The script itself provides the speech-tone to be indicated by one of several patterns in each melodic-phrase. These patterns, and their atmospheric, psychological, and emotional connotations, are second nature to Beijing opera performers. "All these factors are molded into what one may call the 'artistic instinct of the singer,' who is able to compose orally musical lines from written text, on the spur of the moment, without any apparent conscious effort."[6]

Through the application of this trained, musical instinct, each performer develops a specific melody for each line of text he or she is to sing. The melody developed for a given line of text is a detailed musical expression of the performer's interpretation of that line's emotional meaning within the patterns of the *pihuang* musical system.

COMPARISONS OF INTERPRETIVE COMPOSITION

The interpretive precision and variety possible in the third stage of the composition process can most clearly be seen through three sorts of comparison: a comparison of different lines as sung by the same performer in the portrayal of the same character in the same play, composed in the same mode and metrical type; a comparison of the same lines as sung by different performers in the portrayal of the same character in the same play, also composed in the same mode and metrical type; and a comparison of the same lines as sung by the same performer on two different occasions in the portrayal of the same character in the same play, again composed in the same mode and metrical type.

Different Lines by the Same Performer

Cheng Yanqiu is famous for his interpretation of the title role in the play *Yu Tangchun;* the analysis of mode, song, and metrical-type composition for that play in Figure 16 is based upon the published notation of a transcription of his performance.[7] This traditional play was performed in the nineteenth century in several different regional versions; the original Beijing opera version was probably that of the master actor and teacher Wang Yaoqing. By the time Cheng Yanqiu composed his interpretation in the early twentieth century, Wang's mode and metrical-type arrangement for the play as performed in Beijing opera had become standard. For instance, it was standard to sing the complex large aria and the complex small song in the second focal scene, "The Tripartite Joint Trial," in *xipi,* with certain passages in two-six-meter. Cheng followed this arrangement; in fact, he developed at least parts of his interpretation under Wang's tutelage.[8] He pointed out, however, that "although both the earlier and later songs each have a two-six-meter passage, the inner feelings expressed are not the same." In the complex large aria that constitutes Yu Tangchun's testimony before the

**Example 27 Two Different Female *Xipi* Two-six-meter Melodic-passages
Composed by Cheng Yanqiu**

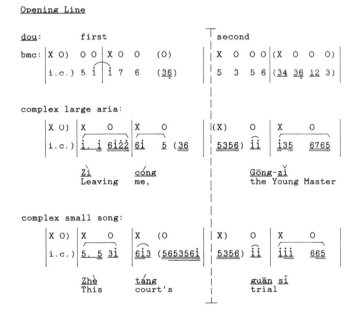

(continued)

Example 27 *(continued)*

<u>dou</u>: third

bmc: | X O O   O | X (O) O O | X (O O O |
| 5 7 6   3 | 3 (3̲6̲) 5 7 | 6 (i.c. |

complex large aria:

| X   (O | X)   O | X (O |
| 3̲5̲3̲ (5̲5̲3̲6̲ | 5̲1̲̇3̲5̲) | 1̇1̇ | 6̲5̲ (i.c. |

Nán-   jīng   qù,
to Nanjing   went;

complex small song:

| X   O | X   O | X   O |
| 3̲2̲2̲ 1̲7̲ (6̲2̲ | 1̲3̲2̲1̲) | 6 (6̲1̲) | 2̲̇2̲̇2̲̇ 1̇ (i.c. |

wèi   dòng xíng,
has been without   torture;

<u>Closing Line</u>

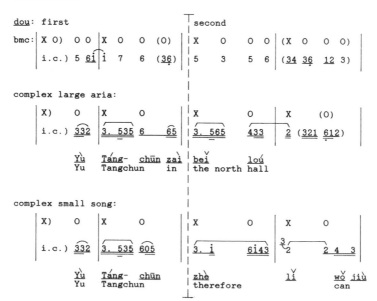

<u>dou</u>: first   second

bmc: | X O) O O | X O O (O) ‖ X O O O | (X O O O) |
| i.c.) 5 6̲1̲ 1̇ 7 6 (3̲6̲) ‖ 5 3 5 6 | (3̲4̲ 3̲6̲ 1̲2̲ 3) |

complex large aria:

| X) O | X   O | ‖ X   O | X   (O) |
| i.c.) 3̲3̲2̲ | 3. 5̲3̲5̲ 6 6̲5̲ ‖ 3. 5̲6̲5̲ | 4̲3̲3̲ | 2 (3̲2̲1̲ 6̲1̲2̲) |

Yú Táng- chūn zài ‖ bèi   lóu
Yu Tangchun in ‖ the north hall

complex small song:

| X) O | X   O | ‖ X   O | X   O |
| i.c.) 3̲3̲2̲ | 3. 5̲3̲5̲ 6̲0̲5̲ ‖ 3. 1̇ | 6̲1̇4̲3̲ | 2 | 2 4 3 |

Yú Táng- chūn ‖ zhè   lǐ   wǒ jiù
Yu Tangchun   ‖ therefore   can

154

Example 27 *(continued)*

<u>dou</u>: third

```
bmc:  X        O      O      O    | X  O  O  O  | X (O  O  O
      5        3      5      6    | 3 (6) 4   3  | 5 (i.c.
```

complex large aria:

```
      X        O    | X      O    | X      O    | (X   O
      22       722  | 672    7643 | 233    23235 | (i.c.

      zhuāng   bing        xing;
      pretended illness;
```

complex small song:

```
      X        O    | X      O    | X      O    | X (O
      3
      2       22 33 | 0 643 233   | 43466 4. 323 | 5 (i.c.

      fàng    liǎo  kuān          xīn;
      relax,  greatly             relieved;
```

court, the two-six-meter passage "is a kind of recollection, a reminiscence." In the complex small song sung after the trial is adjourned, the two-six-meter passage "has a kind of light, relaxed feeling, as if [Yu Tangchun is] relieved of a heavy load."[9] The difference between the specific melodies composed by Cheng Yanqiu for these two passages is quite great, as can be seen in Example 27.[10]

These two melodic-passages in two-six-meter differ in three major respects: pitch, length of melodic-phrases, and the use of coloration tones. These compositional differences are interpretive, designed to express the specific emotional content of each passage.[11]

Both melodic-passages have the characteristic disjunct melodic construction of *xipi,* with frequent large rises or falls in pitch. But the placement of those rises and falls is different in the two passages, expressing the different emotional states. For example, in the third *dou* of the opening line in the complex large aria, the first syllable of the word Nanjing is low and relatively level in pitch; the pitch then leaps, and the second syllable is sung a sixth higher. The pitch drops a third to begin the final melodic-phrase, for the word *qu* (went), and falls stepwise a major second to conclude the line. This progression, in the context of the emotional content of the lyrics, produces a lonely, plaintive effect. In the same *dou* of the same line in the complex small song, the melodic-phrase for the initial word *wei* (has been without) is a falling, step-wise pitch progression that leaps a seventh at the end; the pitch then falls slightly for *dong* (the first syllable of "torture"), and leaps again, a fourth, for *xing* (the second syllable of "torture"). This combination of melody and lyrics produces a celebratory, happy effect.

The relative length of melodic-phrases is also different in the two passages, contributing to the expression of their different emotional content. For example, in the third *dou* of the closing line in the complex large aria, the word *zhuang* (pretended) has a short melodic-phrase; *bing* and *xing* (the two syllables of "illness") both have considerably longer melodic-phrases. The effect is that the concept and remembrance of illness are stressed; this phrasing also implies, as is explained in the following line of lyrics, that while Yu Tangchun pretended physical illness to avoid being forced to entertain other patrons of the brothel, her internal pain was real. In the same *dou* of the same line in the complex small song, the first two melodic-phrases are both very short—*fang* and *liao* (both syllables of the word "relaxed"). The third melodic-phrase, for the word *kuan* ("greatly"; lit. "broadly"), is a very long, melismatic one, stressing the enormity of the relief that is named in the single-tone melodic-phrase at the end of the line. The combination of phrasing and lyrics creates a feeling of freedom and lightness.

The use of coloration tones constitutes a third important expressive, compositional difference in these two passages. In both closing-line, third *dou* sections, coloration tones are used extensively; there are three 7's and one 4 in the second melodic-phrase of the complex large aria, enhancing the word *bing* (ill), and four 4's in the third melodic-phrase of the complex small song, enhancing the word *kuan* (greatly). In combination with the meaning of the respective words, these coloration tones in the first instance have a haunting flavor, and in the second are suggestive of an actual sigh of relief.

The Same Lines by Different Performers

Mei Lanfang and Xun Huisheng also studied *Yu Tangchun* with Wang Yaoqing and composed their own, equally famous interpretations of the title role. All three performers agreed that there are certain basic demands made of the composition of melodic-passages in the second focal scene of this play, "The Tripartite Joint Trial":

> The primary expressive medium is song; because very few supplementary mediums are used, the musical expression of Su San's [Yu Tangchun's] emotions and

psychology is extremely important. . . . But she is a prisoner, and her expressions cannot be too complex. . . . If melodic-passages are too complex, they will seem "oiled"; if they are excessively simple, however, they will seem insipid and pedestrian. . . . Obviously, they must be just right, not damp, and not fiery.[12]

The melodic-passages composed by each of these three performers for the opening small aria in *xipi* dispersed-meter, given in Example 28, illustrate the balance between these two extremes that each has achieved. In the differences between the three passages, one can see each performer's unique interpretation of the role.[13]

Of the three, Xun Huisheng's melodic-passage appears the simplest; how-

Example 28 The Same Female *Xipi* Dispersed-meter Melodic-passage as Composed by Mei Lanfang, Cheng Yanqiu, and Xun Huisheng

First Couplet

Opening Line

```
dou:          first              | second
bmc: | X 0)  0 0 | X 0 0 (0)     | X 0   0 0  | ( X    0    0    0) |
     | i.c.) 5 1 | 1 7 6 (3 6)   | 5 3   5 6  | ( 34   36   12   3) |

Mei Lanfang:
                           2
     i.c.)   1   1    3 5    |(5 5   5 5)
             Lai  zai
             Arriving at

Cheng Yanqiu:
                                          5
     i.c.) 5          6  3 6 | 5 3  0    (5 5      3)
           Lai        zhi    | zai
           Arriving   here   | at

Xun Huisheng:
     i.c.)   1   1    - 3 5 - |(5 5   5 5)
             Lai  zai
             Arriving at
```

(continued)

Example 28 *(continued)*

<u>dou</u>: third

bmc: | X   0   0 0 | X (0)   0   0 | X   (0 0 0
     | 5   7   6 3 | 3 (3 6) 5   7 | 6   (i.c.

Mei Lanfang:

2̇   3̇²₂ i   ³̇₂ - ³̇₂³̇₂ ³̇₁ ²̇₁ - (i.c.

<u>Dū</u>   <u>Chá</u>   <u>Yuàn</u>,
The Capital Law   Court,

Cheng Yanqiu:

2̇   i. 2̇₁ 6   (i 6) 2̇ - - ᵢ₂ ³̇₁ ²̇₁ - (i.c.

<u>Dū</u>   <u>Chá</u>   <u>Yuàn</u>,
The Capital Law   Court,

Xun Huisheng:

2̇   i - 6 i   (i 6) 2̇ - 2̇ i i - (i.c.

<u>Dū</u>   <u>Chá</u>   <u>Yuàn</u>,
The Capital Law   Court,

Example 28 *(continued)*

Closing Line

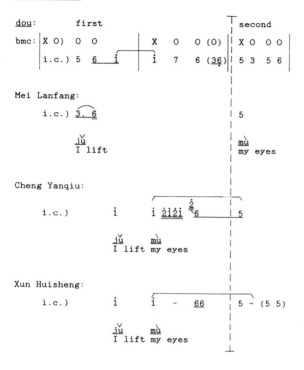

(continued)

Example 28 (continued)

Example 28 *(continued)*

Opening Line

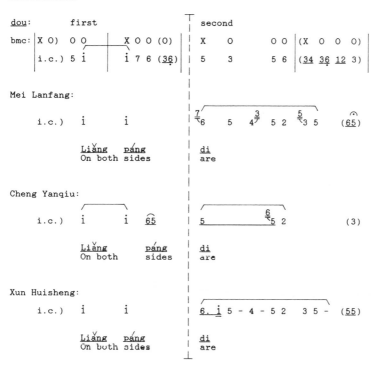

(continued)

Example 28 *(continued)*

dou: third

bmc:| X   O   O   O | X (O) O O | X   (O O O |
| 5   7   6   3 | 3 (3̲6̣) 5 7 | 6   (i.c. |

Mei Lanfang:

5̲.̲ 6̲   7̲.̲ 2̣   6   3   5   ₃⁵5   6 - (i.c.

g̲u̲i̲   z̲i̲   s̲h̲o̲ǔ̲,
executioners [lit., "chop-off-hands"];

Cheng Yanqiu:

i ⁽²i⁾ 0̲ 5̲   6 6̲6̲ 4̲2̲ 3̲2̲3̲ 2̲. 3̲   5 4̲3̲2̲ ⁵32 ¹2 2̲2̲ ³1 ²1 - (i.c.

d̲a̲ō̲   f̲ǔ̲   s̲h̲o̲ǔ̲,
executioners [lit., "knife-axe-hands"];

Xun Huisheng:

5̲ 6̲   7̲ 2̣ 0 6   3   5 -   5   6 - (i.c.

d̲ā̲o̲   f̲ǔ̲   s̲h̲o̲ǔ̲,
executioners;

Example 28 *(continued)*

Closing Line

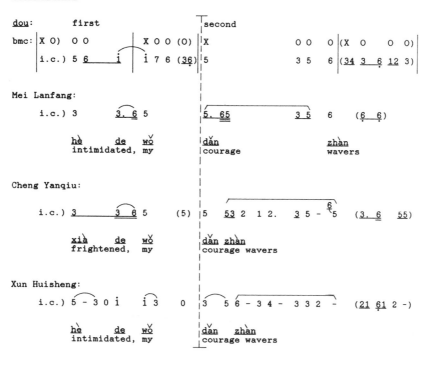

(continued)

Example 28 *(continued)*

dou: third

bmc: | X O   O   O |

     | 5 3   5   6 |

Mei Lanfang:

xīn
and my spirit

Cheng Yanqiu:

xīn
and my spirit

Xun Huisheng:

xīn
and my spirit

Example 28 (continued)

dou: third (cont'd)

```
bmc: |X     (0)   0        0                              | X    (0 0 0
     |
     |3     (6)   4        3                              | 5    (i.c.
```

Mei Lanfang:

```
7. 2  6 5  5 2    5 3 2 1 2  3.   2   1 2.  2 1          1     - (i.c.

you       hán!
is        cold!
```

Cheng Yanqiu:

```
7 - -  6 6  5 5 -  35 3  5  66  (6 6)  7 -  7  7  7  7.  6  5 6 6  5  5  - (i.c.

you       hán      (na)!
is        cold     (oh)!
```

Xun Huisheng:

```
6 5  5 2    5 3 2 1 2 5 - 3 2   2  2                    1     - (i.c.

you hán!
is  cold!
```

ever, its notation is "relatively sketchy; ornamentation is not included. In performance, Xun's ornamentation was approximately as extensive as Mei Lanfang's."[14] Cheng Yanqiu's melodic-passage is the most complex, with the longest final melodic-phrases in the third *dou*, and the most ornamentation. The differences in character interpretation can be seen most clearly in the three areas discussed above—pitch, length of melodic-phrases, and the use of coloration tones—and in the use of standard interpretive techniques.[15]

By far the greatest difference between the three melodic-passages is their interpretive use of pitch. The opening line of the first couplet in Mei Lanfang's melodic-passage is high, indicating initial courage as Yu Tangchun enters the court. The first two *dou* of the closing line are low, suggesting tentativeness as Yu Tangchun sings that she will lift her eyes; these low melodic-sections also imply that her initial show of bravery was perhaps an attempt to bolster her own spirits. In the last melodic-phrase of the third *dou*, Mei's passage returns to the high pitch, again suggesting bravery, as Yu

Tangchun begins to sing the word *guan* (gaze). However, the pitch falls a fifth in the course of the melodic-phrase, with the connotation that her sudden burst of courage is ebbing.

The opening line of the second couplet in Mei's passage begins high once again, here indicating that she is startled by what she sees. The pitch falls quite low in the second *dou*, suggesting tentativeness and fear. The third *dou* rises steadily in pitch in the first two melodic-phrases and then falls, wavers, and rises somewhat in the last. The impression conveyed is one of extreme, frightened tension—as though Yu Tangchun had had the breath knocked out of her by the sight before her eyes. The closing line is basically low—and hence fearful—with occasional sudden high notes indicative of actual trembling. The final melodic-phrase falls extremely low, suggesting an almost stark terror.

Cheng Yanqiu's first couplet opening line, unlike Mei's, begins low, "expressing Su San's [Yu Tangchun's] experience of torture and suffering in a situation of injustice hard to redress." However, in the third *dou* of the line, Cheng's melodic-passage is high in pitch, expressing "an attempt at courage as she prepares to look at the court."[16] In the closing line, Cheng's pitch remains high and brave for the first *dou*, as Yu Tangchun announces her intention to lift her eyes. The third *dou* is quite similar to Mei's in pitch; low and tentative for the first two melodic-phrases, high and courageous as she begins the final melodic-phrase for the word *guan* (gaze), and progressively falling during the course of that phrase, connoting the ebb of Yu Tangchun's courage.

Cheng's pitch for the first two *dou* in the opening line of the second couplet is also similar to Mei's, beginning with startled high notes and falling quite low in the suggestion of fear. However, Cheng begins the third *dou* fairly high and then follows a weaving but steadily dropping pitch progression to conclude a full octave lower, creating the strong impression that Yu Tangchun's courage has entirely left her at the sight of the executioners. In the closing line, the first two *dou* are basically low, like Mei's, indicating fear; the middle of the second drops even lower in pitch than Mei's, on the word *zhan* (wavers). The first melodic-phrase of the third *dou* also includes occasional sudden high notes indicative of trembling. In the final melodic-phrase, however, Cheng's pitch progression gradually falls, rises quite high, and falls again, suggesting that Yu Tangchun feels an enormous frustration mixed with her fear.

Xun Huisheng sings the opening line of the first couplet high, like Mei, indicating initial courage. The bravery is continued in the first *dou* of the closing line, which is also sung high, like Cheng's. However, in the third *dou,* Xun's pitch steadily falls—the final note in the last melodic-phrase for the word *guan* (gaze) is a full octave lower than the note that began the line, indicating that the actual contact with the court has drained Yu Tangchun's courage and left her quite frightened.

The opening line of the second couplet in Xun's melodic passage is very similar to Mei's; it begins with startled high notes, falls quite low in the second *dou,* indicating fear, and rises, falls, wavers, and rises somewhat in the third, suggesting extreme tension and fright. The closing line also resembles Mei's but is even lower in overall pitch, with fewer but more abrupt occasional high notes indicative of trembling; the final melodic-phrase, like Mei's, falls extremely low in pitch, suggesting helpless terror.

As a result of the interpretive use of pitch, even line cadence tones are different in the three melodic-passages; some are different from the pattern of cadences prescribed for the *xipi* mode as well. In the first couplet, Mei and Cheng end the opening and closing lines on 1̇ and 5, respectively; female *xipi* cadences are commonly 6 and 5. The use of the female *erhuang* opening line cadential tone (1̇) for the opening line gives the couplet a tragic air. Xun also concludes the opening line with this tone; his closing line ends with 1, the male *xipi* cadential tone, to facilitate that line's progressive fall in pitch.

In the second couplet, Mei and Xun use the cadential tones 6 and 1; the former is the common final tone for female *xipi* opening lines, and the latter is the final tone for male *xipi* closing lines, the use of which makes possible the gradual, extreme fall in pitch used by both these performers in the closing line. Cheng's opening line concludes on 1, the male *erhuang* cadential tone, which simultaneously facilitates his octave fall in pitch during the third *dou* and lends a feeling of tragedy to the couplet. Cheng's closing line ends on 5, the common female *xipi* closing line cadential tone.

Melodic-phrase length also differs in some instances among the three melodic-passages. For instance, in the second *dou* of the closing line of the second couplet, Mei uses a fairly long melodic-phrase for the word *dan* (courage) and a single-note melodic-phrase for the word *zhan* (wavers). This composition creates a sense of the courage "breaking," as well as indicates that further description is to follow. Cheng and Xun, however, use very short melodic-phrases for "courage"—one and two notes, respectively —and much longer melodic-phrases for "wavers," in which the pitch progressions themselves suggest wavering.

Coloration tones are not used extensively by any of the three performers for these two couplets; however, those that are used are employed differently. In the third *dou* of the closing line of the first couplet, Mei and Cheng enhance the sense of tentativeness and fear by using five and four 7's, respectively, in the melodic-phrase for the word *guan* (gaze). Xun, however, follows a step-wise downward pitch progression for this phrase that includes only the tones 3, 2, and 1. In the third *dou* of the opening line of the second couplet, Cheng sings the coloration tone 4 twice in the melodic-phrase for the final syllable of the word *shou* (execution). The effect heightens the impression that Yu Tangchun has lost her courage. In their considerably shorter and somewhat higher-pitched corresponding melodic-phrases, Mei and Xun use only the tones 6, 5, and 3. And in the second *dou* of the closing line of the second couplet, Xun uses the coloration tone 4 to heighten the sense of wavering in the melodic-phrase for the word *zhan* (wavers); Mei sings only the single note 6 whereas Cheng uses the tones 6, 5, 3, 2, and 1. All three performers employ the coloration tone 7 in the third *dou* of the closing line in the second couplet. Mei and Xun use it sparingly, however, in the first half of the melodic-section; in Cheng's fall, rise, and fall in pitch in the last melodic-phrase, 7 is repeated five times as the highest basic pitch (i.e., pitch that is not a grace note) in the melodic-phrase, greatly enhancing the musical expression of Yu Tangchun's sense of frustration in Cheng's interpretive composition of that melodic-phrase.

Two standard interpretive techniques are applied in these three melodic-passages: empty-words and extended tones. Only Cheng Yanqiu uses an empty-word, in the last melodic-phrase of the third *dou* in the closing line of the second couplet. In the word *han* (cold), the final vowel ends with a terminal consonant. As will be discussed in chapter 5, such final vowels require a special type of vocal projection that is very difficult to achieve. Cheng sings the word *han* with a fairly short melodic-progression and then switches to the empty-word *na* for the major portion of the melodic-phrase. Because *na* contains no terminal consonant and its vowel is regarded as one of the easiest to sustain, the use of this technique facilitates Cheng's exceptionally long melodic-phrase. Mei Lanfang and Xun Huisheng also sing fairly long melodic-phrases for the word *han;* however, theirs are not as long as Cheng's, and they do not utilize the empty-word.

Extended tones are used twice in the melodic-passages composed by Mei Lanfang and Cheng Yanqiu. Both Mei and Cheng use an extended tone in the third *dou* of the closing line of the first couplet, for the final melodic-phrase sung for the word *guan* (gaze). However, they extend different tones in the phrase. Mei extends the final tone in the melodic-phrase, 5. Because the pitch falls a fifth in this melodic-phrase and 5 is the lowest tone as well as the final tone, its extension heightens the implication that Yu Tangchun's courage is ebbing. Cheng extends the opening tone, $\overset{.}{2}$, instead. Therefore, although Cheng's pitch progression is essentially the same as Mei's, his interpretation of the melodic-phrase puts more emphasis upon Yu Tangchun's initial attempt at courage.

Both performers use extended tones in the third *dou* of the closing line of the second couplet as well, for the word *han* (cold); again, the two place the extended tones differently. Mei extends the final tone, 1. The melodic progression for his melodic-phrase begins fairly high and falls extremely low; by extending this final, lowest tone, Mei heightens the expression of Yu Tangchun's terror. Cheng extends the first of the five successive 7 coloration tones that characterize his melodic-phrase; the expression of Yu Tangchun's frustration at her unjust fate is thereby further enhanced.

Through their melodic-passage compositions, these three performers have expressed three quite different interpretations of Yu Tangchun. Cheng Yanqiu's Yu Tangchun is a strong woman, aware of and frustrated by the injustice of her fate. She experiences extremes of emotions in this melodic-passage. Initially she is preoccupied by her fate and therefore fearful of the court. She then makes a strong attempt at courage, which is overcome by extreme fear after she sees the executioners—both of these emotions are given a tragic flavor. The melodic-passage concludes with Yu Tangchun experiencing great frustration at her fate.

Mei Lanfang's Yu Tangchun is a more reserved woman, not demonstrably aware of the injustice of her fate, who tries to be brave but is reduced to terror by the visible powers of the court. She is never as brave as Cheng's and is a much more tender individual. Her attempts at courage are interspersed with tragic tentativeness and fear, which give way to frightened tension, trembling, and finally to terror after she sees the executioners.

Xun Huisheng's Yu Tangchun is a simpler woman. Like Mei's, she is not perceptibly aware of the injustice of her fate in this melodic-passage. Initially, she is a stronger woman than is Mei's Yu Tangchun—she expresses more genuine courage in the first half of this melodic-passage. She is then more psychologically affected by the court and is reduced to terror every bit as great as Mei's by the sight of the executioners.

The Same Lines by the Same Performer on Different Occasions

Mei Lanfang, Cheng Yanqiu, and Xun Huisheng are now recognized as three of the "four great *dan* performers" *(si da ming dan);* they are regarded as masters.[17] Each trained a number of other performers in his style of interpretive composition and performance (*liupai,* henceforward translated as "school"). A great many more performers follow each of their schools, learning from their students, their recordings, and the published notation of plays for which they have composed the melodic-passages; *Yu Tangchun* has a recognized, standard Mei Lanfang version (Mei*pai xi*), Cheng Yanqiu version (Cheng*pai xi*), and Xun Huisheng version (Xun*pai xi*). However, even these standard versions are not entirely fixed and are open to further musical interpretation in performance.

While watching a respected older *sheng* performer trained in the Tan Xinpei school rehearse a young professional for the leading role in the Tan version of *Silang Visits His Mother,* I recorded the following advice: "You must go off, work on your own, and find alternate ways of singing the major melodic-passages. Find a high, strong method as well as a lower, softer one for performances in which your voice is not as good or you feel tired. This is the only way in which to have art. Otherwise you are a faulty tape recorder. The stage must be alive and malleable, not rigid."[18]

Even the master performers themselves varied their melodic-passage composition at different performances, following this principle. Example 29 compares the published notation for the Cheng Yanqiu version of the melodic-passage analyzed above with the same passage as performed by Cheng at the 1957 Forum on *Xiqu* Music (Xiqu Yinyue Zuotanhui) in Beijing:[19]

Except in the closing line of the second couplet, the transcription of the 1957 performance is generally less melismatic than the published notation, with shorter melodic-phrases. In the closing line, the second *dou* and the second melodic-phrase of the third *dou* are longer and more melismatic in the 1957 performance, as though Cheng Yanqiu were "saving himself" for this final line.

Although no interview is available to corroborate this hypothesis, it is further substantiated by the pitch of the 1957 performance, which has fewer high notes and assigns shorter durations to those high notes that are sung. Additionally, the 1957 version does not use extended tones, which require exceptional breath control.

In a few instances, these pitch changes produce interpretive differences. For instance, the octave fall in pitch during the third *dou* of the opening line of the second couplet is lessened to the fall of a seventh in the 1957 performance. This alters the cadential tone from 1, the male *erhuang* opening line final tone that gives the published notation a tragic flavor, to 2, the standard male *xipi* cadential tone for opening lines. However, no new overall character interpretation is evident in the 1957 performance.

Example 29 The Same Female *Xipi* Dispersed-meter Melodic-passage as Performed by Cheng Yanqiu on Two Different Occasions

First Couplet

Opening Line

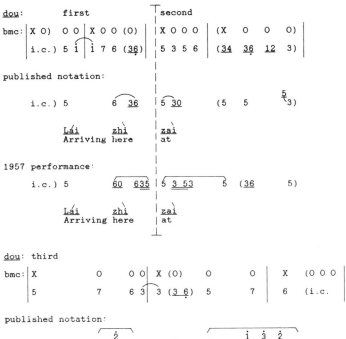

dou: first   second

bmc: X 0) 0 0 | X 0 0 (0) | | X 0 0 0 | (X 0 0 0) |

    i.c.) 5 1̂ | 1̂ 7 6 (3̣6̣) | 5 3 5 6 | (3̱4̱ 3̱6̣ 1̱2̱ 3) |

published notation:

    i.c.) 5   6 3̱6̱ | 5 3̱0̱   (5 5 ⁵⌣3)

    L̀ái   zhì | zaì
    Arriving here | at

1957 performance:

    i.c.) 5   6̱0̱ 6̱3̱5̱ | 5 3̱ 5̱3̱ 5 (3̱6̱   5)

    L̀ái   zhì | zaì
    Arriving here | at

dou: third

bmc: | X   0   0 0| X (0)   0   0 | X (0 0 0

    | 5   7   6 3| 3 (3̱ 6̣) 5   7 | 6 (i.c.

published notation:

    2̇   1̇. ⌣2̇̇1̇ 6 (1̇ 6) 2̇ - - ⌣1̇2̇ ⌣3̇1̇ ⌣2̇1̇ - (i.c.

    Dū   Chá   Yuàn,
    The Capital Law   Court,

1957 performance:

    2̱̂2̱   1̇. 1̇ 6 1̇1̇ 0 ⌣1̇2̇ - 2̱̇2̱̇ ⌣3̇1̇ ⌣2̇1̇ 1̇ (i.c.

    Dū   Chá   Yuàn,
    The Capital Law   Court,

(continued)

Example 29 *(continued)*

<u>Closing Line</u>

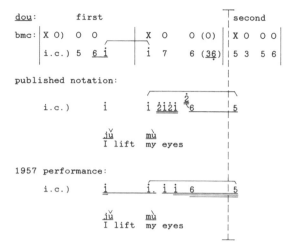

<u>dou</u>: first | second

bmc: X 0) 0 0 | X 0 0 (0) | X 0 0 0
i.c.) 5 6 i | i 7 6 (36) | 5 3 5 6

published notation:

i.c.) i   i 2i2i 2̇₆   5

jǔ   mù
I lift my eyes

1957 performance:

i.c.) i   i. i i 6   5

jǔ   mù
I lift my eyes

<u>dou</u>: third

bmc: X   0 0 0 | X   (0) 0   0 | X (0 0 0
5   3 5 6 | 3   (6) 4   3 | 5 (i.c.

published notation:

wǎng   shàng   guān.
in an upwards gaze.

1957 performance:

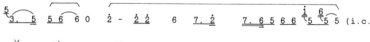

wǎng   shàng   guān.
in an upwards gaze.

Example 29 *(continued)*

<u>Second Couplet</u>

<u>Opening Line</u>

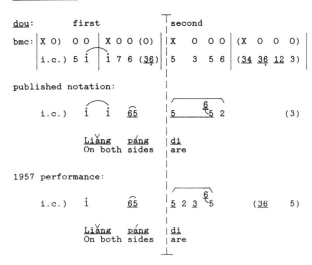

<u>dou</u>: first | second

bmc: X 0) 0 0 | X 0 0 (0) || X 0 0 0 | (X 0 0 0)

i.c.) 5 1 | 1 7 6 (36) || 5 3 5 6 | (34 36 12 3)

published notation:

i.c.) 1 1 65 | 5 6 5 2 (3)

Liǎng páng | di
On both sides | are

1957 performance:

i.c.) 1 65 | 5 2 3 6 5 (36 5)

Liǎng páng | di
On both sides | are

<u>dou</u>: third

bmc: X 0 0 0 | X (0) 0 0 | X (0 0 0

5 7 6 3 | 3 (36) 5 7 | 6 (i.c.

published notation:

(2) 1 1 0 5 6 66 42 3 23 2. 3 5 432 5 32 1 2 22 3 2 1 1 - (i.c.

daō fú shǒu,
executioners;

1957 performance:

(2) 1 1 0 5 6 66 4 3 3 5 2 3 2 2 (i.c.

daō fú shǒu,
executioners;

(continued)

Example 29 *(continued)*

Closing Line

dou: first   ⌐ second

bmc: | X 0)   0 0 | X 0 0 (0) || X   0   0   0 |(X 0   0 0) |
     | i.c.) 5 6   i | i 7 6 (36)|| 5   3   5   6 |(34 3 6 12 3) |

published notation:

     i.c.) 3   36 5   (5) | 5   5 3 2 1 2. 3 5 - 6·5   (3. 6   55)

           xià   de wǒ | dàn zhàn
           frightened, my | courage wavers

1957 performance:

     i.c.) 3   35 5   0 | 5   5·3 2 1 2. 3 5 3. 5 35 5 0

           xià   de wǒ | dàn   zhàn
           frightened, my | courage wavers

dou: third

bmc: | X 0   0   0 | X   (0)   0   0 |
     | 5 3   5   6 | 3   (6)   4   3 |

published notation:

     2̇ - 2̇2̇ 7. 6 565 06   7 ³·2 - - (22) 7   - - 6 6 5   5 - 353

     xīn   yōu   hán,
     and my spirit   is   cold,

1957 performance:

     2̇ 2̇2̇   2̇ 2̇ 2̇ 656 7 2̇ ²·7272 6   5 0 5   353

     xīn   yōu   hán,
     and my spirit   is   cold,

Example 29 *(continued)*

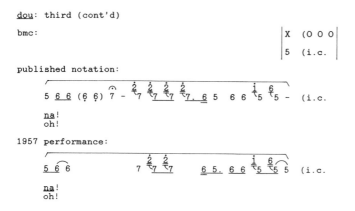

It is therefore quite probable that the composition for the 1957 performance was adapted primarily for ease in singing. Perhaps Cheng was more tired, felt his voice was less strong, or was singing in a hall with poorer acoustics at this performance than at the one that was transcribed for the published notation. In such circumstances, the somewhat simplified melodic-progressions of the 1957 melodic-passage would help avoid strain, thereby facilitating the display of apparently effortless song skill under adverse conditions.

Through the application of the performer's trained, musical instinct in this third stage of the composition process, a startlingly wide range of character interpretations may be given extremely precise musical expression in the same mode and metrical type. The flexibility of melodic-passage composition also permits carefully composed melodic-passages to be adapted to different performance conditions, allowing the performer to make the best possible display of his or her song skill under less than ideal circumstances.

In fact, musical composition is prominently featured in the emotionally expressive display of song skill. In the performance of a given play, each performer's compositional skill is displayed in the musical expression he or she gives to overall atmosphere and to the psychology and emotions of the character being portrayed. Different Beijing opera performers are like different speakers of the same language. Using the same basic vocabulary and syntactic structure, one speaker can be dull and matter-of-fact, and another, a moving orator; similarly, one performer can be "an automatic converter of speech into passable [*pihuang*] melodies, [and another,] a truly artistic singer."[20]

CHAPTER V

THE VOICE

I̶N the aural performance of Beijing opera, two types of sounds are actually heard: song and speech vocalized by the stage performers, and instrumental music played by the musicians of the orchestra. The voice (*sangzi*, also termed *sangyin*, lit. "voice sound") of the Beijing opera performer, accompanied and punctuated by the orchestra, is the featured component of aural performance. The voice of every Beijing opera performer is developed through lengthy, rigorous training, during which a complex body of vocal techniques is learned; it is therefore an artificial voice, in the sense of displaying artifice, or art. It is also stylized, and makes use of characterizing vocal conventions. The same basic techniques of vocal production are used in both song and speech, which are sometimes jointly referred to as "singing and reading" *(changbai),* and as vocal music *(shengyue).* However, some techniques are employed primarily in song, and others primarily in speech—and the vocal performance of each role type has certain unique characteristics. In vocal performance, the performer displays his or her skill at employing these techniques of basic vocal production, song, and speech. Simultaneously, he or she clearly indicates the role type of the character being portrayed by displaying the vocal characteristics unique to that role.

VOCAL PRODUCTION

From the perspective of vocal production (*fasheng,* lit. "production of sound"), rather than that of dramatic purpose, all vocalized sound in Beijing opera is conceptualized as song. There are said to be four "levels of song: songs with music; verse recitation; prose dialogue; and [vocalizations like] crying, laughing, and coughing."[1] Because the same basic techniques of vocal production are used for all types of vocal performance, there is no feeling that a character suddenly stops talking and starts singing, or stops singing and begins talking; "a very smooth transition from speech to song and vice versa [is achieved], contributing to the unity of a whole play."[2] The basic techniques of vocal production shared by all four "levels of song"—by song, verse speech, prose speech, and wordless vocalizations—may be classified in three categories: the use of breath *(yongqi)*, pronunciation *(fayin)*, and special Beijing opera pronunciation *(shangkouzi,* lit. "go-to-the-mouth written-characters").[3]

THE USE OF BREATH

In Chinese theatrical terminology, breath *(qi,* which may be translated as both "breath" and "air," and often implies the act of breathing) is based in the pubic region *(dantian);* the abdominal muscles support the breath. The basic principle governing the use of breath is that "strong centralized breath moves the melodic-passages" *(zhong qi xing qiang).*[4] A central breathing cavity is seen as extending from the pubic region to the top of the head, and breath is conceptualized as being drawn up this cavity from the pubic region, becoming sound by vibrating over the larynx *(houtou).* Specific methods of breathing (generically known as *qikou,* lit. "breath mouths") are employed to control the way in which breath enters, leaves, and is held within this central breathing cavity; these methods allow the exiting breath to then control the pitch, timbre or tone color, and energy of the sound produced, and to be employed in certain special techniques of vocal projection.

Breath Control

Controlling or operating the breath *(caozong qi)* is of paramount importance to the entire process of taking breath into, holding it within, and expelling it from the central breathing cavity; the breath must be under firm, purposeful control at all times.

Exchanging breath *(huan qi)* and stealing breath *(tou qi)* are the two major methods of taking breath into the cavity. Exchanging breath is a relatively relaxed, unhurried process in which air remaining in the lungs is first exhaled, and "new" air is then inhaled. Although relaxed and therefore fairly "natural," exchanging breath should not be obvious—obvious breathing is not in keeping with the aesthetic demand for effortlessness. Breath is exchanged when there are no pressures of time, such as during an instrumental connective following a melodic-passage, or in the course of dialogue when another character is speaking. Stealing breath is a rapid inhalation that is not preceded by exhalation, and that should be undetectable to the audience. Breath is stolen when a sung or spoken line is too long to be delivered in one breath, and no vocal pauses are desired. In both exchanging breath and stealing breath, only slightly more than the precise volume of air needed for the following vocal passage should be inhaled. Excess as well as insufficient breath indicate that the performer has not "aimed at the breath" (qu qi) properly.

When exchanging breath, air is drawn in through the nose with the mouth closed; when stealing breath, the nose is also used, but the mouth can be used as well if it is open at the time for the pronunciation of a vowel. In both cases, the breath should be "low"—the inhaled air should be drawn to its base in the pubic region. Because the use of the nose for inhalation requires that the inhaled air travel the entire length of the central breathing cavity to reach that base, nasal inhalation helps assure that the entire cavity is in use and under control at all times. Because it precludes a "fish-like" gasping for air, it also contributes to the aesthetic demand for effortlessness. The emphasis on low breathing is considered critical to proper breath control and the aesthetic of effortlessness as well. Breathing in which the chest and/or shoulders rise to accommodate breath (termed "superficial breathing" [fu qi] and "horizontal breathing" [heng qi]) is to be strictly avoided. Performers are instead instructed to hold their chest and abdominal muscles as though moving a heavy object, and to breath directly to the pubic region. Only in certain highly emotional passages of speech is a sharp, audible inhalation (bie qi, lit. "suppressing the breath") considered an aesthetically positive technique.

In all song and much speech, precisely placed intervals are set for both exchanging and stealing breath; even the latter should never be done arbitrarily, because controlling the breath implies that no unforeseen need for more breath will arise. The precise intervals for inhalation (also called "breath mouths," qikou) are set according to the demands of sense and dramatic interpretation made by the text, as well as the practical need for breath. In singing, breath is frequently stolen within the melodic-phrase of a single written-character, allowing an important succeeding written-character to follow immediately, without a pause for inhalation. Published scripts that include musical notation often mark these inhalation intervals with carats (ˇ), as in the following example from the Mei Lanfang version of The Favorite Concubine Becomes Intoxicated:[5]

Saving the breath *(cun qi)* is the most important principle governing exhalation made for the production of vocalized sound in Beijing opera vocal practice. The breath should not be expended all at once; rather, it should be conserved throughout a line of song or speech, with somewhat more breath saved to support important words or phrases. The central breathing cavity should never be entirely depleted of air. When a vocalization is completed, it is stopped—i.e., cut off—by closing the lips, and there should be no hint of "pushing" the breath to make it stretch to that cutoff. In song, a breathy quality caused by releasing more breath than is necessary for sound production is also to be scrupulously avoided. Both "leaking the breath" slowly *(lou qi)* and "pounding the breath" suddenly to stress a particular word *(za qi)* are highly undesirable vocal qualities. It is quite acceptable to stress a particular note with controlled volume and/or energy *(za yin,* lit. "pound the note"), but the note should be kept within the precise resonating area *(gongming dian),* with no audible exhalation of air. Conversely, unstressed words and notes should be both clearly audible and precisely focused and concentrated—the breath should never be loose or scattered *(san qi).*

Generally, the same is also true for speech. However, "releasing the breath" audibly *(xie qi),* which constitutes a problem if it occurs in song, is a technique that may be used for emotional expressiveness in speech. For instance, in the phrase "kill his entire family" *(sha ta de chuan jia),* hissing air may be consciously expelled on the word "kill" *(sha)* for effect.

Within an exhalation made for the production of vocalized sound, a pause is often taken, termed "resting the breath" *(xie qi).* In this pause, no sound is produced, and no exhalation or inhalation occurs; the lips cut off the sound and remain closed until the sound is recommenced. This technique is most often used in song, either between words or within a single word. It is employed when a pause is called for, but breathing would break the feeling of the moment. In describing the effect attained through this technique, performers say that "the sound breaks, but the breath/melodic-passage does not" *(yin duan qi/qiang bu duan).*[6]

Breath held within the central breathing cavity is conceived of as being under constant pressure, whether it is being rested, or being exhaled in the production of sound. The experience is described as one of being physically aware of "holding" the breath within the central breathing cavity at all points along the cavity; the exertion of controlled pressure makes air tangibly felt at all points within the cavity—from the top of the head to the pubic region.

Functions of the Controlled Breath

The controlled breath of the Beijing opera performer is further relied upon
to control four fundamental aspects of vocalized sound. By "relying on the
breath" *(tuo qi),* each performer controls the pitch, timbre, energy, and
manner of projection of every vocalization.

Through adjusting the breath *(tiao qi),* breath is used to control the pitch
of a tone. Controlled breath, rather than the larynx *(houtou)* alone,
produces the pitch desired by placing the breath and the sound that it is producing at the proper pitch level. This is considered important for every individual pitch in all types of vocal performance. It is considered especially
important when vocalizing glides *(huayin;* i.e., continuous step-wise pitch
progressions, especially those that fall in pitch at the end) and sudden jumps
in pitch in all types of vocalizations, and when singing the ornamented
melodic-passages *(huaqiang)* of the more melismatic metrical types, which
contain numerous grace notes *(zhuangshiyin).* In these instances, reliance
on the larynx alone is perceived as resulting in sound that changes pitch too
slowly, and is "dead" or "overly fixed" *(si):* controlling pitch through adjusting the breath, however, allows rapid, flexible, vibrant pitch changes.

Adjusting the breath also refers to the use of breath to control tone color,
or timbre. In Beijing opera vocal practice, the human body is conceptualized
as having five principal resonating cavities *(wuqiang):* the chest *(xiong),* the
throat *(hou),* the mouth *(kou),* the nose *(bi),* and the head *(tou).* These cavities are seen as highly interrelated and are often combined in discussion into
three: the chest cavity; the central cavities, which include the throat, mouth,
nose, and the paranasal sinus *(bidou);* and the head cavities, which include
the frontal sinus *(edou)* as well as cavities discussed below that are perhaps
more metaphorical. By causing certain cavities to resonate more than others, the breath controls the timbre of the tone produced as well as its pitch.
In fact, the way in which the cavities are utilized is one of the main distinguishing characteristics of the several role types, as will be discussed in more
detail below. However, in all role types, utilization of any one cavity alone,
untempered by other cavities, is regarded aesthetically as a negative vocal
quality. Skill in adjusting the breath implies the simultaneous utilization of
all the cavities, with carefully placed relative emphasis. For instance, blue
cloth *dan* performers place greatest emphasis upon resonation in the head
cavities and least upon resonation in the chest cavity:

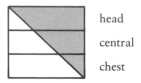

head

central

chest

Jing performers, on the other hand, generally concentrate their resonation in the chest cavity and use the least head resonation:

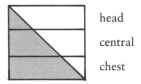

head

central

chest

When singing, all performers use less chest and more head resonation for higher pitches, and the reverse for lower.

Breath is also used to control the energy flow *(jin)* of vocal production. There are numerous terms for specific types of energy flow, many of which are associated with only certain schools *(liupai),* or are interpreted differently in different schools and hence serve as matters of dispute among them. However, the concept of controlled variation in energy for interpretive purposes is a basic one. Although variation in energy often produces a variation in volume, the latter change is not the primary one; energy variation primarily indicates different types of intensity. For instance, "growing the breath" *(xu qi)* is the gradual increase of energy in the course of a vocal passage; intensity and volume may mount together, or volume may remain unchanged.

Related to the control of energy flow is the technique of "accommodating the breath" *(jiu qi).* If a performer's voice is not in good form, or if he or she for some reason has less breath remaining than is ideal for singing or speaking a particular passage, the performer will drop the energy level somewhat and exert further control so as to make the best use possible of the remaining breath. Similarly, if after a sequence of strenuous movement a performer is out of breath, he or she will "push down the breath" *(an qi)* or "press down the breath" *(ya qi)* to avoid panting.

Basic vocal projection is achieved through breath control, but the concept of the use of breath *(yong qi)* also includes two special techniques of vocal projection. "Spray [or 'spurt']-mouth" *(penkou)* projection and "back-of-the-head-sound" *(naohouyin,* lit. "behind the brain sound") projection are primarily utilized for speaking or singing the last written-character in a given sentence, when sound has the greatest tendency to "die away" and hence has the greatest need for additional projection.

Spray-mouth projection is described as "heavily spitting out the sound of the written-character."[7] This technique is best utilized with written-characters enunciated mainly with the lips or the tip of the tongue against the teeth. It also requires that the sound be fairly short; a melismatic sung passage or an extended reading of the written-character does not lend itself to spray-mouth projection. In spray-mouth projection, the written-character, especially its initial consonant, is heavily enunciated with strong impulse from the abdominal muscles. The spray of saliva that frequently results from the use of this technique is the source of its name.

Back-of-the-head-sound projection is regarded as every bit as essential to vocal production as spray-mouth projection, but more difficult to achieve. It is most often utilized with written-characters whose final vowel sound is /i/ (pronounced like a long 'e' in English), or which contain a terminal consonant. And it is best utilized with relatively lengthy sound production; melismatic sung passages and extended readings of written-characters with the /i/ vowel sound or with terminal consonants are ideal for back-of-the-head-sound projection. In back-of-the-head-sound projection, the sound is first directed out with abdominal support and is fairly open. The /i/ or nasal consonant sound is then "received" or "closed" *(shou)*; the throat closes a bit, and throat resonation is joined with resonation in the nasal cavity. The sound then grows and resonates throughout the cavities of the head, including the perhaps metaphorical cavities at the back of the head; the resonation at the end of the delivery of the written-character seems to be projected from the entire head as a whole.

PRONUNCIATION

The controlled breath and projected sound achieved through the "use of breath" techniques are then articulated into precise units of meaning through attention to the techniques of pronunciation *(fayin)*. Basic pronunciation is viewed as having two major aspects; the throat and mouth must take on the shape necessary for producing the desired vowel sound, and the initial consonants must be clearly and precisely articulated. The basic shapes for the throat and mouth are categorized as the four vowel types *(sihu,* lit. "four exhalations"), and the basic means of articulating consonants are categorized as the five consonant types *(wuyin,* lit. "five sounds").

In Beijing opera vocal practice, a further aspect of pronunciation is extremely important—the pointed or rounded quality of certain sounds.

The Four Vowel Types

The four vowel types discussed briefly in chapter 2 are standard divisions of Mandarin Chinese vowels; the name of each division suggests the correct oral placement for pronouncing the initial sound of all vowels included in that division, and the pronunciation of the first written-character in each name places the mouth and throat in approximately that position. The four divisions are "opened-mouth" (*kaikou*), "level-teeth" (*qichi*), "closed-mouth" (*hekou*, often pronounced *huokou*), and "scooped-lips" (*cuochun*). Opened-mouth vowels are those vowel sounds that require a fully opened mouth: separated lips and teeth, and a definite distance between the tongue and palate. The pure opened-mouth vowels are the simple vowels /a/, /e/, /ê/, and /o/ (for pronunciation of these vowels and those that follow, see Appendix 2); in phonetic terms, these are a low back unrounded vowel, a mid back unrounded vowel, a lower-mid front unrounded vowel, and a lower-mid back rounded vowel, respectively. Compound vowels that begin with opened-mouth sounds are /ai, ei, ao, ou, an, en, ang, eng/, and /ong/. Level-teeth vowels require only slightly separated lips and an even alignment between the upper and lower front teeth that brings them almost to touch each other; the tongue is raised in the center to almost touch the palate and dropped in the front so that the tip almost touches the back of the lower front teeth. The simple level-teeth vowel is /i/, a high front unrounded vowel in phonetic terms; /ia, ie, iao/, /iou/ (usually written 'iu'), /ian, in, iang, ing/, and /iong/ are all compound vowels that begin with level-teeth sounds.

The pronunciation of closed-mouth vowels necessitates that both the lips and teeth are almost closed, with the lower front teeth placed behind the upper; the tongue lies lower in the mouth than it does for level-teeth vowels, but not as low as in opened-mouth vowels. The simple closed-mouth vowel is /u/, a high back rounded vowel; the compound vowels are /ua, uo, uai/, /uei/ (usually written 'ui'), /uan/, /uen/ (usually written 'un'), /uang/, and /ueng/.

Scooped-lips vowels require that the teeth and tongue be placed as for level-teeth vowels, but that the lips be brought together, projecting outward in an "o" shape. The simple scooped-lips vowel is /ü/, a high front rounded vowel; the compound vowels are /üe, üan/, and /ün/. The four vowel types are customarily listed in this order to present a progression from the most "opened" sounds to the most "closed." This listing also reflects the number of different vowel sounds in each division; there are a total of thirteen simple and compound vowels in the opened-mouth division, the level-teeth division contains ten, the closed-mouth division nine, and the scooped-lips division only four.

The Five Consonant Types

Each of the five consonant types is denoted by the portion of the mouth deemed most critical to the articulation of the consonant sounds within its category. The five types are throat, or larynx *(hou)*; tongue *(she)*; molars, more specifically the jaw and palate *(chi)*; front teeth *(ya)*; and lips *(chun)*.

The category of throat or larynx sounds includes the vowels /i/ and /u/ when used as "semi-vowel" initial consonants for the pronunciation of written-characters (written 'y' and 'w', respectively), and certain gutteral exclamatory sounds. The consonants /g, k/, and /h/, formed by the back of the tongue and the soft palate at the back of the mouth, are sometimes included in this category as well.

The tongue consonants, /d, t, n/, and /l/, are produced by the tip of the tongue against the alveolar ridge at the front of the roof of the mouth, just behind the upper front teeth. Although the production of the consonant sounds in other categories also utilizes the tongue, these sounds are viewed as being produced solely by the tongue. In phonetic terms, /d/ and /t/ are alveolar stops—the tip of the tongue is pressed firmly against the alveolar ridge; /n/ is an alveolar nasal (the soft palate is lowered so that air may go out through the nose), and /l/ is an alveolar lateral (the air stream flows over the sides of the tongue). The final consonant /er/ is also considered a tongue consonant, probably because it is produced solely by movement of the tongue in the mouth.

The molar, or jaw and palate, consonants are /g, k, h/, /zh/ (pronounced like the 'j' in "jaws"), /ch/ (pronounced like the 'ch' in "chaws"), /sh/ (pronounced like the 'sh' in "shawl"), and /r/. In the first three, the back of the tongue together with the soft palate produces the consonant sound, as mentioned above; in the latter four, the tip of the tongue is curled back to the back part of the alveolar ridge, termed retroflex articulation in phonetics. The consonants /sh/ and /r/ are retroflex fricative consonants, produced by narrowing the distance between the tongue and the alveolar ridge so that the air stream is partially obstructed; /zh/ and /ch/ are retroflex affricative consonants—stops produced by the tongue against the alveolar ridge, followed by the production of sound through a partially obstructed air stream at the same point.

The front teeth consonants are /j/ (like the 'j' in "jeans"), /q/ (like the 'ch' in "cheat"), /x/ (like the 'sh' in "she"), /z/ (like the 'dz' in "adze"), /c/ (like the 'ts' in "cats"), and /s/. The first three are formed by the front portion of the tongue, but not its tip, and the back portion of the alveolar ridge, where the ridge meets the hard palate. This is termed alveopalatal articulation: /x/ is an alveopalatal fricative, and /j/ and /q/ are alveopalatal affricatives. The latter three front teeth consonants use the tip of the tongue and the forward portion of the alveolar ridge, termed alveolar articulation: /s/ is an alveolar fricative, and /z/ and /c/ are alveolar affricatives.

Lip consonants are /b, p, m/, and /f/. For all four sounds the tongue is held low and fairly relaxed in the mouth, and the sound is produced by the lips: /b, p/, and /m/ are produced by both lips, termed bilabial articulation (/b/ and /p/ are bilabial stops, and /m/ is a bilabial nasal); /f/, which utilizes only the lower lip and the upper front teeth, is termed a labiodental fricative in phonetics.

The precise, clear formation of the proper vowel and articulation of the proper consonant are critical to listening comprehension; they also form an important aural aesthetic value of Beijing opera. The proper pronunciation of the appropriate vowel type and consonant type for each written-character in Beijing opera performance is termed "biting the written-character" *(yao zi)* or "spitting out the written-character" *(tu zi)*. Even in the vocalization of an extremely melismatic sung or drawn-out spoken written-character, this precise, proper pronunciation should never be changed or distorted. Although the categories and specific vowels and consonants described above are those of Mandarin Chinese, it is widely accepted that the clearest pronunciation and articulation of Mandarin is that of the Beijing opera performer.

Pointed and Rounded Sounds

Within the aural realm of Beijing opera, certain sounds are viewed as being either pointed *(jian)* or rounded *(tuan)*. Strictly speaking, these qualities are associated only with certain consonant and vowel combinations. In this strict sense, only fricative and affricative consonants produced by the front portion of the tongue and the alveolar ridge are perceived as pointed or rounded; in Mandarin Chinese, all such consonants are in the molar, or jaw and palate, and the front teeth categories of consonants. Those that are produced with the forward portion of the alveolar ridge are considered pointed sounds, while those produced with the back portion of the alveolar ridge are considered rounded. The pointed consonants are therefore /z, c/, and /s/, from the front teeth category of consonants; the rounded consonants are /j, q/, and /x/, from the front teeth category, and /zh, ch, sh/, and /r/, from the molar category.

In this same strict sense, only written-characters whose pronunciations are composed of a pointed consonant followed by the simple vowel /i/ or /u/, or a compound vowel beginning with one of those two vowels, are considered to have the pointed sound quality. In standard Mandarin Chinese, there are therefore only eighteen pointed pronunciations: /zi, zu, zuan, zui, zun, zuo, ci, cu, cuan, cui, cun, cuo, si, su, suan, sui, sun/, and /suo/. Of these, /zi, ci/, and /si/ actually have no standard vowel; the 'i' in these cases represents vocalization of the consonant. Only written-characters with pronunciations composed of a rounded consonant followed by the simple vowel /i/ or /ü/ (simplified to 'u' after /j, q/, and /x/, as these consonants can take the /ü/ sound but not the /u/ sound), or a compound vowel beginning with one of these two vowels, are considered to have the rounded sound quality. In standard Mandarin Chinese, the forty-six rounded pronunciations are therefore: /zhi, chi, shi, ri, ji, jia, jian, jiang, jiao, jie, jin, jing, jiong, jiu, ju, juan, jue, jun, qi, qia, qian, qiang, qiao, qie, qin, qing, qiong, qiu, qu, quan, que, qun, xi, xia, xian, xiang, xiao, xie, xin, xing, xiong, xiu, xu, xuan, xue/, and /xun/. Here too, /zhi, chi, shi/, and /ri/ have no standard vowel; the 'i' represents vocalization of the consonant. By this strict definition, then, the ratio of pointed to rounded sounds is approximately 1 to 2.6.

In a somewhat broader application of the concept of pointed and rounded sounds, all pronunciations that begin with pointed consonants are considered pointed sounds, and all that begin with rounded consonants are considered rounded. In this sense, there are thirty-one additional pointed sounds: /za, zai, zan, zang, zao, ze, zei, zen, zeng, zong, zou, ca, cai, can, cang, cao, ce, cen, ceng, cong, cou, sa, sai, san, sang, sao, se, sen, seng, song/, and /sou/. This brings the total number of pointed sounds in standard Mandarin to forty-nine. In this same sense, there are sixty-eight additional rounded sounds: /zha, zhai, zhan, zhang, zhao, zhe, zhei, zhen, zheng, zhong, zhou, zhu, zhua, zhuai, zhuan, zhuang, zhui, zhun, zhuo, cha, chai, chan, chang, chao, che, chen, cheng, chong, chou, chu, chua, chuai, chuan, chuang, chui, chun, chuo, sha, shai, shan, shang, shao, she, shei, shen, sheng, shou, shu, shua, shuai, shuan, shuang, shui, shun, shuo, ran, rang, rao, re, ren, reng, rong, rou, ru, ruan, rui, run/, and /ruo/. This brings the total number of rounded sounds in standard Mandarin to 114 and increases the ratio of pointed to rounded sounds slightly, to 1 to 2.3.

In the broadest sense given to these two qualities, all pronunciations that do not begin with pointed consonants are considered rounded sounds. This brings an additional 242 rounded sounds to standard Mandarin, making a total of 49 pointed and 356 rounded sounds, a ratio of approximately 1 to 7.3.

Although more words exist with some pronunciations than with others, these ratios are close to the actual ratios of words with pointed sounds to those with rounded. And by all three applications of the pointed and rounded qualities of sound, there are appreciably more of the latter than the former. But this does not imply a relative difference in importance. In Beijing opera vocal practice, pointed and rounded sounds are most frequently discussed in terms of the thirteen rhyme categories; even when these qualities are applied in their strictest sense, three rhyme categories contain both types of sound. Pronunciations in the *yi qi* rhyme category include both the pointed sounds /zi, ci/, and /si/, and the rounded sounds /zhi, chi, shi, ji, qi, xi, ju, qu/, and /xu/; the *yan qian* category includes the pointed sounds /zuan, cuan/, and /suan/, and the rounded sounds /jian, qian, xian, juan, quan/, and /xuan/; and the *ren chen* category includes the pointed sounds /zun, cun/, and /sun/, and the rounded sounds /jin, qin, xin, jun, qun/, and /xun/. In the broader applications of these qualities, all rhyme categories except the *mie xie* include both pointed and rounded sounds.

Especially in singing the rhymed lyrics of Beijing opera, the pointed or rounded quality of each written-character's pronunciation should be clearly distinguished and articulated. Even in speech in which written-characters' pronunciations are not being used as rhymes, these qualities are considered extremely important for both listening comprehension and aesthetic effect. The precision and exaggeration of the pointed and rounded qualities of sound is in fact one of the most outstanding features of all Beijing opera vocalization.

Special Beijing Opera Pronunciation

The Mandarin Chinese spoken and sung on the Beijing opera stage is the most clearly and precisely pronounced and articulated rendition of that spoken language. However, certain written-characters have special pronunciations in Beijing opera theatrical language that differ from their normal Mandarin pronunciations. There are two major reasons usually given for these differences.

Historically, Beijing opera came into being through the creative combination and development of a number of regional theatre forms and *kunqu*. In the process of this development, certain regional pronunciations of written-characters were adopted into the newly emerging form, primarily from Anhui, Hubei, Sichuan, and Suzhou dialects.[8] Many of these regional pronunciations are still retained in Beijing opera's stage language. For example, the word *ni,* which is the Mandarin pronunciation of the written-character meaning "you," may be pronounced /li/ in Beijing opera, following the Anhui dialect pronunciation. *He,* Mandarin for "what," may be pronounced /huo/ as in Hankou dialect, the regional speech of a city that is now a part of Wuhan in Hubei. *Liu,* Mandarin for "six," may be pronounced /lu/ according to its Sichuan pronunciation, and *wo,* for "I," often becomes /ngo/, following the pronunciation of Suzhou, the home of *kunqu.* Such special pronunciations are referred to as "accustomed (or 'traditional') sounds" *(xiguanyin)* when they occur in Beijing opera.

Second, during the development of Beijing opera, alterations have been made in the Mandarin pronunciation of certain written-characters for ease or variety in pronunciation and projection of sound. Certain sounds are frequently given altered endings, making them much easier to sustain and complete. For instance, /zhi, chi, shi/, and /ri/, which do not contain standard vowels, do not carry well and are difficult to sustain because they occur quite far back in the mouth; they are frequently delivered with the additional simple vowel /i/ (ē), enhancing the ease with which they can be pronounced and projected: /zhrii, chrii, shrii/, and /rii/. As discussed above, there are many more rounded sounds in standard Mandarin than there are pointed; the number of pointed sounds is increased by altering the initial consonants of certain words. For example, the word for "elder sister," *jie* in standard Mandarin, may be pronounced /zie/. *Jiu,* Mandarin for "rice wine," may be pronounced /ziu/. "One thousand," *qian* in Mandarin, may become /cian/, and "just," *qie* in Mandarin, may become /cie/. The pronunciation of the word for "west" may be altered from *xi* to /si/, and that of "night" from *xiao* to /siao/. Special pronunciations of this type are termed "go to the mouth" written-characters *(shangkouzi).*

Although the specific pronunciation changes just discussed are recognizable as having been made for ease and variety in sound production, the reasons for alteration of pronunciation in the majority of "go to the mouth" written-characters are not readily discernible. In fact, both types of special pronunciations are usually referred to in practice as "go to the mouth" written-characters, translated here as "special pronunciations." All are established by tradition; no overall set of rules or regulations exists by which special pronunciations can be logically established. For instance, most sounds represent a number of words with very distinct meanings; they are differentiated from one another by speech-tone, and of course by written-characters, as discussed in chapters 2 and 3. For each sound that may have a special pronunciation, there are only certain specific words that will take that pronunciation; all others will not. The performer must simply memorize the sounds and specific written-characters whose pronunciations may be given special pronunciations, as well as those special pronunciations themselves. This process of memorization is an ongoing one; it occurs each time a student or professional performer learns an established play from a particular school, in which the words that have special pronunciations and their specific altered pronunciations have been set by tradition. And this body of memorized special pronunciations is then applied by every performer who participates in developing a new play, and must decide which words will have what special pronunciations.

The following two figures list many, but by no means all, of the sounds and specific written-characters that may be given special pronunciations. Because of the traditional nature of these pronunciations, such a listing can only present those that have been brought to the attention of the compiler to date. The first figure, Figure 17, lists those written-characters whose special pronunciations maintain the same rhyme category as that of the original pronunciations; the second, Figure 18, lists those in which the rhyme category is altered by the special pronunciations. The special pronunciations in the second figure are regarded as more extreme than those in the first, because such alterations affect the textual rhyme scheme as well as the sound in performance, and their use therefore must be considered in the composition of the text.

The special pronunciations of these written-characters may occur in all sung passages and in certain types of speech, as will be discussed below. However, the special pronunciations of these written-characters are not always used. Generally speaking, the last written-character in a sentence will be given its special pronunciation; however, if that written-character is spoken or sung very quickly, it often will not. And the special pronunciations of written-characters occurring in the middle of a sentence are frequently not used, especially if that sentence is sung.

The use of these special pronunciations produces two major effects in performance. First, they serve to link northern and southern language. Northern dialects have more rounded sounds, and southern dialects more pointed; standard Mandarin Chinese is primarily a northern language. Spe-

Figure 17
Written-characters With Special Pronunciations
That Maintain the Same Rhyme Category

Mandarin Pronunciation	Special Pronunciation	Written-characters	Rhyme Category
zhi	zhrii	know; spider	*yi qi*
chi	chrii	eat; slow; gallop; shame; relax	
shi	shrii	lose	
ri	rii	day	
ni	li	you	
xi	si	west	
ge	guo	elder brother; song; dagger/axe; pavilion; pigeon	*suo buo*
ke	kuo	division; severe; thirst; class; a measure word	
he	huo	peace; standing grain; wheat; river; lotus; combine; box; entire; congratulate	
e	ngo	mistaken; soon; pretty young woman; evil; calyx; hold back	
wo	ngo	I	
bo	be	silk; meagre	
qie	cie	just	*nie xie*
jie	zie	elder sister	
ai	yai	short; receive; get close to; dust	*huai lai*
hai	xai	skeleton	
mao	miao	cat; flag; anchor	*yao tiao*
xiao	siao	night	
jiu	ziu	rice wine	*you qiu*
ban	buan	kind; remove; scar; half; accompany; stumble	*yan qian*
pan	puan	a surname; lose; betray; judge; scatter; side; plate; nirvana; boulder; coil	
man	muan	evade truth; steamed; full	
lian	luan	love; golden rain tree; contraction	
lian	jian	face	
han	xian	shout	
qian	cian	one thousand	
rong	yong	dissolve; contain; a kind of flower; glory; lofty; misty	*zhong dong*

Figure 18

Written-characters With Special Pronunciations That Change the Rhyme Category

Mandarin Pronunciation	Special Pronunciation	Written-characters	Original Rhyme Category	New Rhyme Category
lü	lu	green	*yi qi*	*gu su*
zhu	zhrü	vermilion; a surname; tree trunk; pearl; spider; pig; host; all; shuttle; explain; casting; halt	*gu su*	*yi qi*
chu	chrü	get rid of; store up; kitchen; livestock; dwell; toad; out		
shu	shrü	book; stretch; transport; different; skill; relate; tree; forgive; vertical; office; hub; rat; millet; express		
ru	rü	as if; eat; scholar; child; you; breast; haltingly		
yu	yo	desire	*gu su*	*suo buo*
ya	yai	cliff	*fa hua*	*huai lai*
zuo	zhu	sit	*suo buo*	*gu su*
lue	lio	brief; plunder	*nie xie*	*suo buo*
jue	juo	role/part; sense; nobility		
jue	qüo*	chew		
que	qüo*	retreat; authentic		
que	cüo*	sparrow; magpie		
nue	nio	cruel; tease		
xue	xüo*	study		
xue	suo	whittle		
yue	yo	high mountain; arrange; music; leap		
jie	jiai	all; steps; street; between; boundary; avoid; fall due; divide	*nie xie*	*huai lai*
xie	xiai	shoes; in accord; crab; slack		

Figure 18 *(continued)*

Mandarin Pronunciation	Special Pronunciation	Written-characters	Original Rhyme Category	New Rhyme Category
bai	be	white; 100; brother-in-law; cypress	*huai lai*	*suo buo*
mai	mo	wheat; vein		
chai	che	take apart		
wei	wui (no implied e before the i)	not; flavor; tireless; tiny; only; hold together; tail	*hui dui*	*yi qi*
bei	be	north	*hui dui*	*suo buo*
mao	mieou	spear	*yao tiao*	*you qiu*
jiao	jüo*	foot	*yao tiao*	*suo buo*
qiao	cüo*	sparrow		
yao	yo	medicine		
liu	lu	six	*you qiu*	*gu su*
rou	ru	meat		
geng	jin	change; plough	*zhong dong*	*ren chen*
heng	hun	horizontal		

*There is no /üo/ sound in the original *suo buo* rhyme category.

cial pronunciations enlarge the number of pointed sounds in Beijing opera language by both including certain specific southern pronunciations and creating new pronunciations with the pointed quality, suggesting the flavor of southern language. The language of Beijing opera is thereby made more appealing to speakers of the diverse range of dialects throughout China than is Mandarin alone. Second, the use of special pronunciations in essence creates for Beijing opera a language of its own; this special stage language heightens and stylizes the effects of speech and song in Beijing opera.

SONG

Beijing opera song *(chang)* in performance consists of lyrics, music for those lyrics composed in the elements of the *pihuang* musical system, and the performer's voice, employing fully all the basic techniques of vocal production. In song, however, the performer uses two additional vocal techniques as well, including segmented *(qieyin,* lit. "cut sound") and direct *(zhinian,* lit. "straight reading") pronunciation, and empty-words *(xuzi)*. These techniques serve both aesthetic and practical functions, functions that are related to the different dramatic purposes of speech and song, and to the different uses of stage and performance time that stem from those dramatic purposes. Although speech is most often used in conversation, it is also one of the primary means for the compression of stage time—the events of days, weeks, or years are frequently recounted in a few moments of performance time through speech. However, both stage and performance time are often expanded in song for the expression of emotion. And although words are occasionally prolonged for dramatic or stylistic effect in speech, the pronunciation of a single monosyllabic word often occupies many seconds of performance time in song. Several of Beijing opera's metrical types are quite slow and melismatic; even fast-meter allows ample time to present the speech-tone and pronunciation of the sound of each written-character very clearly. The vowel types, consonant types, and pointed or rounded quality of each word therefore become even more important as aesthetic and communicative factors in song, and are frequently exaggerated to an even greater extent than in speech. Together, segmented and direct pronunciation and the use of empty-words serve to further clarify the precise sound of each written-character being sung, and simultaneously to further stylize the emotional expression of song. In conjunction with lyric structure, song structure, and vocal production techniques, they produce the complex and varied phrasing characteristic of Beijing opera song.[9]

SEGMENTED AND DIRECT PRONUNCIATION

Segmented pronunciation (*qieyin,* lit. "cut sound") is based upon two-part pronunciation (*fanqie,* lit. "two-sided cut"), one of two major traditional Chinese methods for indicating the pronunciation of written-characters without the use of a phonetic alphabet. In two-part pronunciation, a single written-character's pronunciation is indicated by two other written-characters, the first having the same initial consonant as the given character, and the second having the same vowel (including nasal final if appropriate) and tone. For instance, the pronunciation of *tóng* ("similar") is written as *tu* ("on foot") *hóng* ("red"), indicating a combination of the consonant from *tu* and the central vowel, nasal final, and tone from *hóng.*

This concept of "cutting" the sound is applied aurally in segmented pronunciation, which is employed in singing words with complete, complex sound structures when they are prolonged either through duration or melisma. To be given segmented pronunciation, the sound of a written-character must be divisible into three distinct parts: the "head" *(tou),* the "belly" *(fu),* and the "tail" *(wei);* these three portions of the sound are directly related to the sound structure of Mandarin Chinese and the rhyme categories of Beijing opera, discussed in chapter 2. Each segment is individually pronounced, clearly and precisely, and then blended or modulated into the next.

The head consists of the initial consonant or "semi-vowel," and the medial vowel /i/, /u/, or /ü/ if the particular sound includes one. Articulation of the head is called "putting out the written-character" *(chu zi).* In vocalizing the head, the vowel type of the "semi-vowel" or the consonant type of the initial consonant and its pointed or rounded nature must be clear, as must the vowel type of the medial vowel if one is present. Only in words with a medial vowel can the head itself be appreciably prolonged.

The belly follows the head and consists of the central vowel. It is the belly that is prolonged throughout the major portion of the melodic-phrase for a written-character, especially in more melismatic passages. Singing this portion of the word is referred to as "moving the melodic-phrase" *(yun qiang)* or "returning to the rhyme" *(gui yun);* it is begun by "opening the mouth" *(zhang kou)* for the central vowel, whose vowel type must be clear and unaltered throughout.

The tail of the written-character is composed of its terminal vowel or consonant. Pronunciation of this portion of the sound is termed "closing the sound" *(shou sheng);* the central vowel must modulate into the clearly and precisely articulated terminal vowel or consonant. In "closing the sound," the entire pronunciation, and hence the specific meaning, of the written-character is made evident.

The pronunciation of the speech-tone may occur in the head and the first part of the belly in relatively melismatic melodic-phrases, as described in chapter 3. The latter portion of such a melodic-phrase is not associated with speech-tone in meaning, except in its ending pitch, which must accurately reflect the relationship of the particular written-character's speech tone to that of the next. But the demands made upon the clarity of the central vowel and terminal vowel or consonant remain the same throughout. The speech-tone may also, however, be extended throughout a melodic-phrase, particularly in those that are less melismatic. In these instances, the approximate speech-tone in relation to that of the preceding written-character is indicated in the head. Internal pitch relations of the speech-tone are established in the belly, and the ending pitch of the speech-tone in relation to that of the succeeding written-character is made clear in the tail. When the breath is rested in the middle of a melodic-phrase, all three portions of the written-character's sound are pronounced before the pause; when the singing resumes, the performer once again "opens the mouth" for the central vowel in the belly, and then again "closes the sound" with the tail. In such cases, except for the ending pitches, the second partial singing of the written-character is free of speech-tone restrictions as well.

All words that have terminal vowels or consonants, and can therefore be closed, may be given segmented pronunciation. Such words always have a central vowel as well, and their pronunciation therefore always involves vowel modulation from the central vowel to the terminal vowel or consonant. All words in the *huai lai, hui dui, yao tiao, you qiu, yan qian, ren chen, jiang yang,* and *zhong dong* rhyme categories are so structured; when prolonged in song, they are therefore given segmented pronunciations. Some of these words do not have heads; for instance, those that are in the opened-mouth vowel category and do not have initial consonants or vowels, such as *ai, an, ang, ao, ei, en, eng, er,* and *ou.* In these cases, "putting out the written-character" occurs at the beginning of the belly portion, and is followed by vowel modulation to the terminal vowel or consonant. When words in these eight rhyme categories are sung quickly with very little or no melisma in their melodic-phrases, they are still given a type of segmented pronunciation, but it is quite rapid—the sound modulates quickly but precisely from head to belly to tail. This type of segmented pronunciation is called the "fast cut method" *(ji qie fa).*

Direct pronunciation *(zhinian,* lit. "straight reading") takes its name from the second major traditional method of indicating the pronunciation of written-characters without the use of a phonetic alphabet. In this method, a single written-character's pronunciation is indicated directly by another, single written-character with the same pronunciation; the speech tone is not necessarily the same as that of the written-character indicating pronunciation, and is listed after it by name. For instance, the pronunciation of *dà* ("large," pronounced with the fourth, falling tone) is written as *dá* ("extend," pronounced with the second, rising tone) *qu sheng* (lit. "going tone," the fourth, falling tone).

This concept of directly presenting a single sound is aurally applied in Beijing opera's direct pronunciation, which is used for both the prolonged and the rapid singing of written-characters whose pronunciations do not have terminal vowels or consonants and therefore cannot be closed. Most such words consist of a belly alone—a single, central vowel, such as *a, e,* and *o*—or are composed of only an initial consonant head and a belly, such as *la, che,* and *po.* Whether prolonged or sung rapidly, the pronunciation of

words with this simple structure proceeds quickly and directly to the concluding, central vowel, and is not closed through vowel modulation. Some
words without terminal vowels or consonants do involve modulation from
an initial or a medial vowel in the head to the central vowel in the belly, and
therefore include two distinct segments of sound, such as *ya* (y-a), *guo* (gu-
o), and *jie* (ji-e). But the initial or medial vowel is not extended in direct pronunciation, and none of these words is completed by internal vowel modulation; the sound still proceeds directly from the head to the concluding,
central belly vowel, whether sung rapidly or in an extended fashion. All
words in the *yi qi, gu su, fa hua, suo buo,* and *mie xie* rhyme categories have
this simpler, "incomplete" sound structure and are therefore given direct
pronunciation in song.

Both segmented and direct pronunciation involve the clear, precise pronunciation of each part of a written-character's sound—direct pronunciation demands the same clarity in "putting out the written-character" and
"moving the melodic-phrase" as does segmented pronunciation. In addition
to heightening clarity of meaning, however, both segmented and direct pronunciation are perceived as producing a beautiful aural aesthetic effect. For
both these reasons, they are also employed in pronouncing those words that
are prolonged for dramatic or stylistic purposes in speech.

Figure 19 lists the segments of every possible sound in Mandarin Chinese,
arranged according to rhyme category. Each initial consonant or "semi-
vowel" and the central vowel and terminal vowel or consonant on each line
together compose at least one Mandarin word. Except as otherwise noted,
the medial vowels are always used with the initial consonants, but are not
used with the initial vowels. Asterisks denote those bellies, and bellies and
tails, which also stand alone as words, without initial vowels or consonants.

Empty-words

Empty-words *(xuzi)* were discussed briefly in chapter 4 as one of the standard interpretive techniques for the composition of individual melodic-
passages. They have no denotative meaning; when an empty-word is
employed, the sound of a written-character is sung completely but briefly,
and then the empty-word is used to sing the remainder of the melodic-
phrase. Empty-words are used primarily in long, extended melodic-passages, for both dramatic and aesthetic purposes.

Because empty-words have no denotative meaning and are therefore not
bound by speech-tones even in their ending pitches, they may be melodically

Figure 19

Possible Sounds in Mandarin Chinese and Their Segmentation in Pronunciation

Words given direct pronunciation (rhyme categories: yi qi, gu su, fa hua, suo bo, mie xie)

Rhyme Category	"semi-vowel"	Head: initial consonant	medial vowel	Belly: central vowel	Tail: terminal vowel or consonant
yi qi	y	b, d, j, l, m, n, p, q, t, x; c, ch, r, s, sh, z, zh[1]		i	
yi qi	y	j, l, n, q, x		ü	
yi qi				*e	r[2]
gu su	w	b, c, ch, d, f, g, h, k, l, m, n, p, r, s, sh, t, z, zh		u	
fa hua		b, c, ch, d, f, g, h, k, l, m, n, p, s, sh, t, z, zh		*a	
fa hua	w, y	j, l, q, x	i	a	
fa hua		ch, g, h, k, sh, zh	u	a	
suo bo	w, y	c, ch, d, g, h, k, l, m, n, r, s, sh, t, z, zh		*e	
suo bo		b, f, m, n, p		*o	
suo bo		c, ch, d, g, h, k, l, n, r, s, sh, t, z, zh	u	o	
mie xie	y[3]	b, d, j, l, m, n, p, q, t, x	i	e	
mie xie	y	j, l, n, q, x	ü	e	

Words given segmented pronunciation (rhyme categories: huai lai, hui dui, yao tiao, you qiu)

Rhyme Category	"semi-vowel"	Head: initial consonant	medial vowel	Belly: central vowel	Tail: terminal vowel or consonant
huai lai	w, y	b, c, ch, d, g, h, k, l, m, n, p, s, sh, t, z, zh		*a	i
huai lai		ch, g, h, k, sh, zh	u	a	i
hui dui	w	b, f, g, h, l, m, n, p, sh, z, zh		*e	i
hui dui		c, ch, d, g, h, k, r, s, sh, t, z, zh	u	(e)[4]	i
yao tiao	y	b, c, ch, d, g, h, k, l, m, n, p, r, s, sh, t, z, zh		*a	o
yao tiao		b, d, j, l, m, n, p, q, t, x	i	a	o
you qiu	y	c, ch, d, f, g, h, k, l, m, n, p, r, s, sh, t, z, zh		*o	u
you qiu		d, j, l, m, n, q, x	i	(o)	u

Rhyme Category	Head		Belly		Tail
	"semi-vowel"	initial consonant	medial vowel	central vowel	terminal vowel or consonant
		Words given segmented pronunciation, continued			
yan qian	y, w	b, c, ch, d, f, g, h, k, l, m, n, p, r, s, sh, t, z, zh		*a	n
		b, d, j, l, m, n, p, q, t, x	i	a	n
		c, ch, d, f, g, k, l, m, r, s, sh, s, z, zh	u	a	n
	y	j, q, x	ü	a,	n
ren chen	w	b, c, ch, f, g, h, k, m, n, p, r, s, sh, z, zh		*e	n
	y	b, j, l, m, n, p, q, x		i	n
	y	j, q, x		ü	n
		c, ch, d, g, h, k, l, r, s, sh, t, z, zh	u	(e)	n
jiang yang	w, y	b, c, ch, d, f, g, h, k, l, m, n, p, r, s, sh, t, z, zh		*a	ng
		j, l, n, q, x	i	a	ng
		ch, g, h, k, sh, zh	u	a	ng
zhong dong	w	b, c, ch, d, f, g, h, k, l, m, n, p, r, s, sh, t, z, zh		*e	ng
	y	c, ch, d, g, h, k, l, m, r, s, t, z, zh		o	ng
	y	b, d, j, l, m, n, p, q, t, x		i	ng
	y	j, q, x	i	o	ng

1 The /i/ after the sounds in the second group of initial consonants — /c, ch, r, s, sh, z/, and /zh/ — indicates vocalization of the consonant, and is not given the long "ē" pronunciation (see Appendix 2).

2 *Er* is the only word in the *yi qi* rhyme category which has both a belly and a tail and is therefore given segmented pronunciation.

3 When /y/ is the "semi-vowel" initial consonant, the medial /ī/ is not used, as in *ye*. However, the "semi-vowel" /y/ is used with the medial vowel /ü/, as in *yüe* and *yüan* (written 'yue' and 'yuan').

4 Letters in brackets are not actually included in the possible spellings, but are clearly pronounced.

* Asterisks denote those bellies, and bellies and tails, which also stand alone as words, without initial vowels or consonants.

interpreted quite freely to express affective meaning. In the extended
melodic-passages in which they are employed, they afford the opportunity
for both especially striking and subtle, nuanced melodic expressions of emotion.

Aesthetically, empty-words are often used to increase the variety of
sounds in a particular song or aria. The same rhyme sound is usually
employed throughout a multi-couplet passage of lyrics; inserting an empty-
word at the end of a third *dou,* where extended melodic-passages most often
occur, serves to vary the rhyme pattern without actually breaking it. More
important, however, empty-words are used aesthetically to create more
pleasing sounds. Sounds in the *gu su, suo bo, mie xie, hui dui,* and *you qiu*
rhyme categories are considered insufficiently resonant, and unpleasant
when sustained for very long. The *ren chen* rhyme category is regarded as
containing the most strictly nasal, and therefore the most unpleasant,
sounds. Words in these categories are therefore often augmented by empty-
words when they occur in positions that call for extended melodic-phrases.
All empty-words have central vowels of the "opened-mouth" type, vowels
that, as discussed in chapter 2, are seen as having the most open, clear, and
ringing sounds. These vowels are considered the most beautiful when prolonged in extended melodic-passages.

Figure 20
Rhyme Categories and Their Preferred Empty-words

rhyme category	empty-word	a	ai	e *	na	nei	wa	ya
yi	qi	x				x		
gu	su	x					x	
fa	hua							x
suo	buo	x						
mie	xie							x
huai	lai		x					
hui	dui					x		
yao	tiao						x	
you	qiu						x	
yan	qian				x			
ren	chen				x			
jiang	yang			x				
zhong	dong			x				

* (or /ngo/)

A fairly strict set of regulations governs the use of empty-words. Sounds in each rhyme category usually take only one or two specific empty-words. The only major exception to this is the *ren chen* rhyme category; because it is regarded as containing the most unpleasant sounds, there is quite a bit of flexibility in the empty-words that may be used with *ren chen* words. However, the *ren chen* category also has one preferred empty-word. Figure 20 matches the several rhyme categories with their appropriate empty-words.

Overall Aesthetics of Song

Many of the aesthetic values concerning song in Beijing opera are specific to role types and will be discussed below. However, certain fundamental aesthetics concerning vocal range and timbre are common to all roles.

The majority of songs in Beijing opera are within a pitch-range of an octave and a fifth (i.e., nineteen "half-steps"). At the same time, high pitch is a positive aesthetic value for all role types. Performers therefore generally pitch their songs as high as possible, so that the highest notes in the songs approach the upper limits of their vocal ranges. This is of course done with the aesthetic demand for effortlessness as a prime consideration; to pitch a song so high as to give the appearance of strain in the highest notes would be counterproductive aesthetically. As a result of this value placed on high pitch, key in its Western conception functions solely as a technical tool of the performer, rather than as an interpretive technique; if he or she can properly produce the high notes of a song sung in the key of F, that key will be used rather than the lower keys of C, D, or E.[10] Only when a song or aria alternates passages between two different performers, or when one song or aria is followed very closely by another, is it common practice to compromise in choice of key to accommodate more than one voice. In cases where one performer sings an entire song or aria that is preceded and followed by speech or action, the choice of key is usually up to that performer, and the key may be changed for the next song or aria by the next performer. This practice frequently necessitates retuning the accompanying stringed instruments or switching instruments or players.

The ideal basic timbre for singing in all role types may be described in Western terms as a controlled nasal tone; the nasal resonating cavities are almost always in use. However, nasality alone, untempered by the use of other cavities, is a negative aesthetic value. At least one other resonating cavity must always be employed as well, modifying and augmenting the nasal tone.

Vibrato is extremely important in Beijing opera singing; for many role types, a single pitch is rarely extended without it. Performers frequently discuss two different types of Beijing opera vibrato, "shaking (or 'trill') tone" (*chanyin,* the term most often used for "vibrato" in general), and "wave-tone" *(bolangyin)*. Both are characterized by performers as slow *(man)* and wide *(kuan);* the tremors in the tone are fairly long in duration and are separated by fairly wide pitch intervals. Tremors in shaking-tone vibrato are somewhat longer than those in wave-tone vibrato; their production is in fact consciously controlled and timed by the singer, and each pitch is precisely produced individually. Shaking-tone vibrato is actually very similar to the use of grace notes *(zhuangshiyin)*. Tremors in wave-tone vibrato are not quite as long and are more "naturally" produced; the effect is somewhat more flowing than that of shaking-tone vibrato. But Beijing opera performers contrast the vibrato of "Western opera" to both shaking-tone and wave-tone vibrato by saying that the Western opera vibrato is fast *(kuai)* and narrow *(zhai,* or *xia)*. In the context of Beijing opera singing, a fast, narrow vibrato is a negative aesthetic value, indicative of lack of control and therefore improper use of breath; such a vibrato is felt to enlarge the pitch being sung, to make it less specific. The aesthetic effect of both these Beijing opera vibratos is perceived as clearly presenting the tone and then producing variations on it; for the untrained listener, it is at times difficult to discern which is the basic pitch and which pitches are the result of the use of vibrato.

Sophia Delza was probably referring to this phenomenon when she wrote, "The voice, which violates every familiar conception of human intonation, covers the gamut of sound . . . with the confused nonchalance of an orchestra tuning up on a damp day . . . ."[11] In both types of Beijing opera vibrato, the singing of a particular pitch may begin and/or end above or below that pitch and will clearly move to and from it in the course of singing that note. The variations in pitch produced by the vibrato are usually not, however, considered a part of the melodic progression and are generally not included in the notation of those plays that are transcribed. For example, in the published notation of the Mei Lanfang version of the play *The Favorite Concubine Becomes Intoxicated,* the following melodic-passage occurs:[12]

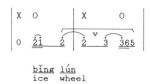

In actual performance, more notes are sung quite precisely through shaking-tone vibrato:[13]

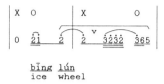

The apparent expansion of the melodic progression is stylistic rather than compositional; such melodic expansion through the use of vibrato requires that the performer be well versed in the vocal techniques of Beijing opera. A singer untrained in Beijing opera vocal production and singing aesthetics cannot, as a result, sing from notation and "sound like" Beijing opera; pitch movement is often around pitches rather than from one directly to another.

The overall effect of this controlled nasal tone and distinctive vibrato is perceived as an intense voice with a precise focus. Beijing opera performers characterize the singing of "Western opera" as presenting round but empty and hollow tones in straight, or direct, melodic-passages; they perceive their own song as presenting round but sharply focused tones in weaving, "round" melodic-passages. In fact, a basic overall demand in Beijing opera song is that the written-characters be delivered accurately and precisely and the melodic-passages be round *(zi zheng qiang yuan)*.

SPEECH

The single most striking feature of Beijing opera theatrical speech *(nianbai)* is its wide variety of speech style. Much of this variety is provided by the two distinctly different types of speech, heightened speech and colloquial speech. Heightened speech *(yunbai,* lit. "rhymed speech") is used for delivering prose as well as verse; it is employed for most speeches in poetry and for prose speeches written in classical Chinese, or in a blend of classical and vernacular language in which the classical language is dominant. Because language in which classical Chinese predominates is characteristic of the speech written for characters of high social status and/or intrinsic dignity, as discussed in chapter 2, heightened speech is therefore spoken primarily by performers playing such characters. There are two types of colloquial speech: colloquial Mandarin speech *(jingbai,* lit. "Beijing colloquial") and the colloquial speech of regional dialects *(fangyanbai,* lit. "regional colloquial speech"). Either type of colloquial speech may be employed for prose speeches with a blend of classical and vernacular language in which the vernacular language is dominant, and for prose speeches written entirely in vernacular language. Colloquial speech is therefore spoken for the most part in the portrayal of characters of lower social status and / or intrinsic dignity.[14]

HEIGHTENED SPEECH

Heightened speech has very strong musical qualities, and frequently has the flavor of declamation as well. It uses special pronunciations extensively, to an even greater extent than does song, and is slower than colloquial speech, with greater extremes in pitch. However, its overall pitch range is somewhat narrower than that of song. Heightened speech has been described as "exaggerated, cadenced half-singing and half-spoken intonation."[15] In heightened speech, the pitch of each written-character relative to those that precede and follow it is much more important for denotative meaning than any internal variations in pitch.

The pitches of written-characters in heightened speech follow the speech-tones of the Song (960–1279) and Yuan (1271–1368) dynasty dialect of Zhongzhou, a district in Henan province.[16] These Zhongzhou speech-tones are called Zhongzhou *yun* (lit. "Zhongzhou rhyme"), and it is from this terminology that heightened speech takes its name *(yunbai)*. They are appreciably different than the speech-tones of Mandarin Chinese, which stress internal pitch modulation as well as relative pitch. Zhongzhou dialect does not distinguish between the level-tone (*yinpingsheng,* lit. "feminine-principle level-tone": the first tone in Mandarin Chinese) and the rising tone (*yangpingsheng,* lit. "male-principle level-tone": the second tone in Mandarin). The same pitch is used for both types of "level" *(ping)* tones; it is not as high as the high level pitch used for the level-tone in Mandarin, because the highest pitch in Zhongzhou dialect is reserved for the turning-tone (*shangsheng,* the third tone in Mandarin Chinese), which in Zhongzhou dialect is perceived as vigorous and strong. Zhongzhou dialect's lowest pitch is that of the falling-tone (*qusheng,* the fourth tone in Mandarin), which in Zhongzhou dialect is regarded as plaintive. Finally, in contrast to Mandarin, in which written-characters with entering-tone *(rusheng)* pronunciations have been distributed among the other four tone categories, Zhongzhou dialect preserves the entering-tone, a speech-tone most recognizable by its short duration. Because they are not a feature of Mandarin, Beijing opera performers must simply memorize entering-tone words to give

Figure 21

Speech-tones in Mandarin Chinese and the Zhongzhou Dialect of Heightened Speech Compared

Order in Mandarin	Tone Category	Tone Name	Mandarin		Zhongzhou Dialect	
			Pitch Diagram	Example	Pitch Diagram	Example
first tone	*yinpingsheng* (yin level tone)	(high) level-tone				
second tone	*yangpingsheng* (yang level tone)	(middle) rising-tone				
third tone	*shangsheng* (ascending tone)	turning-tone				
fourth tone	*qusheng* (going tone)	falling-tone				
- - - - -	*rusheng* (entering tone)	entering-tone				

Figure 22

Relative Pitches of the Zhongzhou Dialect of Heightened Speech

Order (in common speech)	Tone Category	Tone Name	Pitch Diagram	Example
third tone	*shangsheng* (ascending tone)	turning-tone		
first and second tones	*yin* and *yang pingsheng* (*yin* and *yang* level tones)	level- (and rising-) tone (s)		
– – – – –	*rusheng* (entering tone)	entering-tone		
fourth tone	*qusheng* (going tone)	falling-tone		

them their proper pitch in heightened speech. Among the most important entering-tone words are the four that change their speech-tone in Mandarin according to that of the word that follows them: *yi* (one), *qi* (seven), *ba* (eight), and *bu* (not).[17] In the original Zhongzhou dialect, level-tones and entering-tones had the same pitch, in between those of turning-tones and falling-tones, and were distinguishable from each other only by the brevity of the entering-tones. So as not to confuse the two types of speech-tones, heightened speech allows level-tones a slightly higher pitch than entering-tones while maintaining the shorter duration of the entering-tones. Figure 21 compares the speech-tones of Mandarin with those of Zhongzhou dialect as adapted for heightened speech; Figure 22 illustrates the relative pitches of the latter.[18]

It is easiest to see the basic application of these relative pitches in simple phrases with no consecutive, like speech-tones. The sentence *Kè kǔ nài láo* ("Work hard [and] endure labor") is made up of a falling-, a turning-, a falling-, and a level (rising)-tone. In Mandarin speech, it is read:[19]

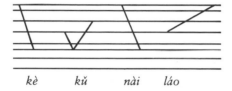

However, in heightened speech it becomes:

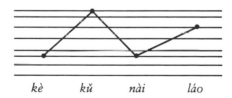

Not only are the tones different; the internal modulations in pitch are replaced by sliding connectives between the relative pitches. A second example is provided by the sentence *Nǎ gè gǎn lái dào cǎo?* ("Who [lit. 'which one'] dares [to] come [to] steal herbs?") In Mandarin, it is read:

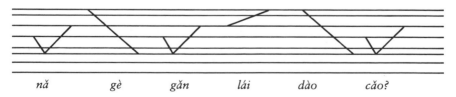

In heightened speech:

nǎ   gè   gǎn   lái   dào   cǎo?

Of course, in actual performance some leeway is necessary for interpretation and variety. In the second example, it is unlikely that the three turning-tones would all be read at exactly the same pitch; however, all would be higher than the pitch of *lái,* a level (rising)-tone written-character.

Pauses and variations in intonation within the parameters of the relative pitch relationships are used not only to separate *dou,* but also, on a lesser scale, to set off level-tones (i.e., both level-and rising-tones). For example, following the basic rules of Zhongzhou speech-tones, the sentence *Jiàoxué wéi zhǔ* ("Education receives priority") would be read:

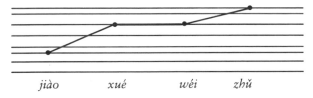

jiào   xué   wéi   zhǔ

However, this is an unbroken upward progression; it is difficult to say and judged to be unpleasing to the ear. It becomes:

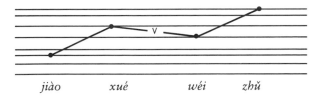

jiào   xué   wéi   zhǔ

The carat (ˇ) represents a slight pause, separating the two level (rising)-tones and setting them both off.

In fact, there are rules governing variations in intonation to deal with both two and three consecutive written-characters with the same tone. When there are two level-tones, as is evident above, the second one is pitched slightly lower than the first. With two turning-tones, the first is low and the second is high; the pitch dips even lower than it begins, in transit to the second written-character:

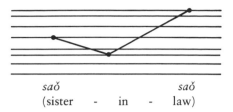

saǒ *saǒ*
(sister - in - law)

When there are two falling-tones in succession, both are low; however, the pitch rises quite high before falling low again in transit to the second written-character:

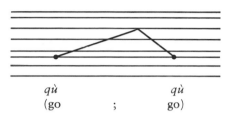

qù *qù*
(go ; go)

This sliding with a variation in pitch is an important instance of the use of controlled breath to control pitch—it is perhaps the major application of the glide *(huayin)* technique mentioned above. With two entering-tones, both are cut off; there is no sliding connective:

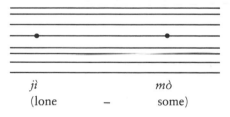

jì *mò*
(lone – some)

Three consecutive level-tones are described as sounding like flowing water; they may have a downward progression of pitches, or the pitch of the second may be slightly higher than the first and the pitch of the third slightly lower:

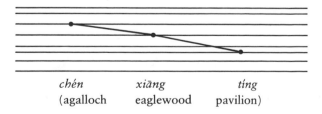

chén *xiāng* *tíng*
(agalloch eaglewood pavilion)

Or:

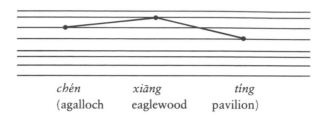

chén   xiāng   tíng
(agalloch   eaglewood   pavilion)

With three consecutive turning-tones, it is the third that rises high; the first two are low:

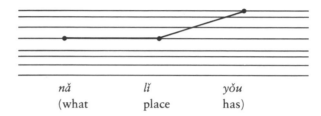

nǎ   lǐ   yǒu
(what   place   has)

The second may in fact drop even lower:

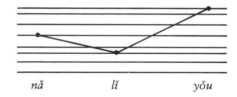

nǎ   lǐ   yǒu

In the case of three consecutive falling-tones, the glide technique is used twice; once between the first two written-characters, and on a rising slide at the end of the third:

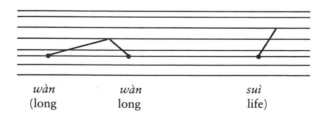

wàn   wàn   suì
(long   long   life)

Three consecutive entering-tones may have the third slightly lower than the first, as in the case of level-tones; however, the second drops lower than either the first or the third:

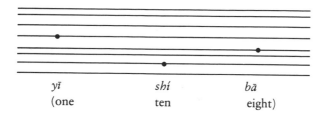

yī   shí   bā
(one   ten   eight)

They are cut off, with no sliding connective.

Although relationships between pitches remain constant, the overall range may vary considerably. In calm or formally polite situations, it is relatively narrow; in excited situations, the pitch range becomes more extreme.

Because heightened speech is used primarily for portraying characters of high social status and/or intrinsic dignity, it is spoken most often by older *sheng*, martial *sheng*, young *sheng*, blue cloth *dan*, martial *dan*, older *dan*, and *jing*. However, under certain circumstances it is also spoken by flower *dan* and *chou*. For instance, the flower *dan* character Li Fengjie in *Meilong Town (Meilong zhen)* speaks in heightened speech for symmetry with the Emperor, Zheng De, an older *sheng*. When *chou* play young scholars they frequently speak in heightened speech, as does Zhang Wenyuan in *Black Dragon Residence (Wu long yuan)*. Other *chou* may also use heightened speech occasionally, for comic purposes. Mu Xuan, in the newly written historical play *The Battle of Shouzhou (Zhan Shouzhou)*, opens in heightened speech, with highly formal accompanying physical movements. He is feeling quite self-important at this point, and the use of heightened speech helps to convey this attitude. However, he quickly switches into colloquial speech, which is more appropriate for his role type, for the duration of the play.

COLLOQUIAL SPEECH

Colloquial speech in Beijing opera has a smaller pitch range than does heightened speech. Most colloquial speech is colloquial Mandarin speech *(jingbai)*. It follows the pronunciation, intonation patterns, and tones of Mandarin Chinese. Different levels of speech can be achieved in colloquial Mandarin through the degree of use of special pronunciations; the more special pronunciations that are used, the more heightened the speech level. However, even in the most heightened colloquial Mandarin, special pronunciations are used to a much lesser extent than in heightened speech, and the level of speech is consequently considerably lower.

The colloquial speech of regional dialects *(fangyanbai)* follows the pronunciation, intonation patterns, and tones of the particular regional dialect in use. It does not use special pronunciations, probably because the pronunciations of regional dialects are already different from those of Mandarin. Regional colloquial is used much less frequently than is colloquial Mandarin; the former is generally considered a lower speech level than colloquial Mandarin and becomes even lower when it employs regional slang expressions.

Colloquial speech is used primarily for portraying characters of low social status and/or intrinsic dignity. Regional colloquial is spoken primarily by *chou;* for example, the merchant Shen Yanling in *Yu Tangchun* speaks in Shanxi dialect. Colloquial Mandarin is spoken most often by flower *dan* and *chou.* However, under certain conditions older *sheng, jing,* and young *sheng* may use colloquial Mandarin. In the play *Kaishan Prefecture (Kaishan fu),* Zou Yinglong, an older *sheng* role, and Yan Song, a *jing* role, speak primarily in heightened speech. However, in highly emotional situations, both occasionally break into colloquial Mandarin; the technique is highly moving, underlining the humanity of the characters. Additionally, older *sheng* and *jing* usually employ colloquial Mandarin pronunciation, intonation patterns, and tones when the characters being portrayed are eunuchs, even when the language spoken is predominantly classical Chinese; the older *sheng* role Chen Lin in *Nine Songs Bridge (Jiu qu qiao)* and the *jing* role Liu Jin in *Dharma Gate Temple (Fa men si)* are typical. Young *sheng* may use colloquial Mandarin in plays in which they are paired with a flower *dan;* the young *sheng* role Yang Zongbao speaks colloquial Mandarin with the young *dan* Mu Guiying in *The Capture of Hongzhou (Po Hongzhou),* as does Lu Kunjie with Di Yunluan in *Pleasurable Predestiny (Deyi yuan).* Finally, all children's roles use colloquial Mandarin no matter what their social status. In *Qing Feng Pavilion (Qing feng ting),* the young *sheng* role Zhang Jibao is a child in the first half of the play and therefore speaks colloquial Mandarin; in the second half of the play, after he has become an official, he switches to heightened speech.

OVERALL AESTHETICS OF SPEECH

Because the overall pitch range in song is greater than that in speech, the lowest notes in song are lower and the highest notes higher than those in speech. However, the median speaking pitch for each performer is usually the same as, or at most a single full tone higher than, his or her median sing-

ing pitch. As with singing, the ideal speaking tone is in Western terms a controlled nasal tone that is augmented by other resonating cavities as well.

In the performance of rhymed speech, certain patterns of overall intonation and rhythm are discernible. Such patterns do not change the relative
pitches or internal pitch movement required by the tones of written-characters in heightened and colloquial speech, respectively, nor do they alter the
placement of pauses required by level-tones, *dou,* and the ends of sentences
and poetic lines. These patterns instead vary the range of pitch placement or
movement, the length of pauses, and the length of syllable prolongation in
the interest of enhancing overall lyricism and euphony.

For instance, in the performance of prelude poems *(yinzi),* there is a basic
pattern for the reading of each poetic line. The first half of each line is to be
given a relatively sturdy, stable reading, within a minimal, fairly flat range
of pitch. The second half of each line rises and then falls in overall pitch,
with the reading tempo slowing down at the end. This basic line reading
pattern is then modified within the reading of the full prelude poem. In a
four-line prelude poem, the first two lines have less overall pitch-range than
does the third, which rises in pitch throughout to a "long drawn out utterance of the final syllable. . . . [The] fourth line [is then] taken very
smoothly, or alternatively given a brisker emphasis as an indication of following action."[20]

Generally, however, there are two major demands made of all stage
speech, both heightened and colloquial speech and both poetry and prose.
The first is for variety. Every spoken passage must have variety within the
range of high *(gao)* and low *(di)* pitches. It must vary between light, soft
(qing) speech and heavy, loud *(zhong)* speech. And each spoken passage
must include variation between slow, prolonged *(man* or *xu)* speech and
rapid, more staccato *(ji)* speech. Second, the impetus for this variety must be
the meaning of what is said and the interpretation of the character being
portrayed. Without this interpretive impetus for variety, stage speech
"sounds like that of children who have memorized passages; it cannot satisfy the listener."[21] These same demands are in fact also made of song, for
the same reason.

ROLE-SPECIFIC VOCAL CHARACTERISTICS

All role types in Beijing opera are divided into two categories according to
their basic vocal timbre: small-voice *(xiaosangzi),* also called "false-voice"
(jiasangzi), and large-voice *(dasangzi),* also called "true-voice" *(zhensangzi).*

The performers of all small-voice roles sing and speak in a falsetto voice—those of large-voice roles do not.[22] Within each of these two categories, every role type has a characteristic vocal timbre (i.e., sound quality), produced by the use of specific placement and resonating cavities. Each role type is characterized as well by certain distinctive song, speech, and wordless vocalization practices. These role-specific vocal characteristics are referred to generally as "the characteristic uses of the voice in each role type" *(mei yige hangdang/jiaose* [or *juese*] *yunyong sangzi de tedian).*[23]

SMALL-VOICE ROLES

All young *dan* and young *sheng* role types sing in female melodic-passages, as discussed in chapter 3; they also sing and speak with the small-voice, in falsetto. For two major reasons, performers of these roles feel that the ideal sounds for important, extended words, whether sung or spoken, are those in the *yi qi* rhyme category. First, it is believed that the falsetto voice can be best displayed in the production of these sounds. Second, these sounds are pronounced with a nearly closed mouth; because young *dan* roles require that the teeth rarely be shown and the mouth never open wide, these sounds enhance visual aesthetics as well. In addition to the *yi qi* rhyme category, performers who speak and sing with the small-voice are partial to the *hui dui, yan qian, ren chen,* and *jiang yang* rhyme categories; the mouth need not be opened very widely for the pronunciation of most sounds in these categories.

The *yi qi* and *hui dui* rhyme categories are considered representative of the feminine principle *(yin),* as discussed in chapter 2; the latter three rhyme categories are considered representative of the male principle *(yang).* Sounds in the *yi qi* category are sung with direct pronunciation while those in the other four categories are given segmented pronunciation in song. Together, these five most frequently used rhyme categories provide performers who use the small-voice with a sufficient number of both male *(yang)* and female *(yin)* sounds to achieve the necessary balance between the two required of the song and speech of every performer. They also provide for both direct and segmented pronunciations, contributing to the required variety and color in sung stage language discussed above. Beijing opera playwrights must of course write lyrics and speech with these preferences for certain rhyme categories in mind.

From the perspectives of playwriting, musical composition, and basic vocal timbre, then, young *dan* and young *sheng* are considered quite similar; performers of these role types prefer the same rhyme categories, compose in female melodic-passages, and sing and speak with the same basic vocal timbre. However, in performance both these major role types, as well as their several subcategories, are characterized by certain distinctive practices affecting specific vocal timbre, song, speech, and in some cases, wordless vocalizations. These distinguishing practices function as conventions, aurally establishing the identity of each role type.

The Young *Dan* Voice

The voice of the young *dan* is an especially clear falsetto. It has a high, light, buzzing quality, yet the sound is very penetrating; "although it must have strength, it is not robust."[24] The head is considered the principal resonating area.

The basic young *dan* vocal timbre, that of the blue cloth *dan,* is described as "mellow and full, bright and clear; in composing and singing melodic-passages, it should be gentle and flexible, graceful and elegant, but with strength in the gentleness."[25] However, there is more variation in vocal timbre among the various schools of young *dan* than among those of any other role type. The vocal technique of the Mei Langfang school places the voice in the mask of the face. It is not, however, purely nasal, which would be a negative aesthetic quality. The entire mask of the face is used in resonation; performers describe this process as placing each tone high in the head and forward in the face. It results in a vocal timbre that is "sweet, fragile, clear and crisp, round, embellished and liquid." This timbre is considered ideal for portraying "natural, graceful and poised, dignified, gentle and lovely traditional women."[26] The vocal timbre of the Cheng Yanqiu school is markedly different. In the Cheng school, the voice is placed more directly in the center of the face and somewhat farther back than in the Mei school; it also makes some use of back-of-the-head-sound and spray-mouth projection and is augmented by a bit more resonation in the chest cavity. Additionally, slight breaks or pauses in singing are used much more frequently within the melodic-phrases of individual written-characters. The resultant vocal timbre and singing style are "rather dark and close, with melodic-passages apparently severed but actually still very much connected."[27] The overall effect is seen as a "smokier" sound; that sound is considered ideal for portraying faithful and unyielding tragic heroines. Performers who follow the Cheng school generally use a somewhat lower median pitch in both speech and song than do those who follow the Mei school, which contributes to the "smoky" effect of the sound.

Flower *dan* and martial *dan* roles feature much less singing than do blue cloth *dan* roles. When they do sing, flower *dan* and martial *dan* do so in the manner of blue cloth *dan,* but in somewhat simpler versions. For instance, they rarely use metrical types slower than primary-meter, thereby avoiding extended melisma, and usually sing in *xipi* rather than *erhuang,* with the major exception of *erhuang*'s *sipingdiao,* because *xipi* female melodic-passages are pitched lower than are *erhuang* female melodic-passages.

Styles of speech vary somewhat more among the various subcategories of young *dan* than do styles of song. Blue cloth *dan* of course speak in heightened speech. They have a fairly wide range of pitch in their speech and use more modulation of pitch within each given word in heightened speech than do performers of any other role type. Blue cloth *dan* frequently break the pronunciation of single words, sounding the major vowel twice in succession; overall, they take more time in the pronunciation of each word than do martial and flower *dan.* Martial *dan* specialize in combat and dance-acting; perhaps to harmonize with the relatively high degree of stylization in their movement, they often speak in heightened speech as well. Flower *dan,* on the other hand, generally use colloquial speech.

Speech pitch and tempo for younger *dan* roles are, however, primarily based on the age, emotional state, and social status of the characters being portrayed. Older, troubled characters who are upper class, such as the flower shirt role Zhao Nü in *The Cosmic Blade (Yuzhou feng),* speak in a relatively steady manner at a lower median pitch. The younger, happier flower shirt character Cheng Xue'e in *The Phoenix Returns to Its Nest (Feng huan chao),* who is also of an aristocratic family, speaks in a more lively manner at a higher median pitch. Her maid, a flower *dan* character, is about the same age—but she is a lower-class character and therefore speaks more rapidly and at a higher median pitch. The young, carefree, lower-class flower *dan* character Sun Yujiao in *Picking Up the Jade Bracelet (Shi yu zhuo)* is also about the same age. But she has no connection whatsoever with an aristocratic household and therefore speaks even more rapidly and at an even higher pitch. In plays about her youth, the martial *dan* character Mu Guiying, the daughter of a Robin Hood–type local ruler, speaks at a tempo and pitch similar to that of Sun Yujiao, as in *The Mu Family Axhandle Stockade (Mu ke zhai).* Her voice, however, is somewhat crisper than Sun Yujiao's, as befits a martial *dan.* In plays about Mu Guiying's middle age, such as *Mu Guiying Assumes Command (Mu Guiying gua shuai),* her tempo is slower and her overall pitch is lower. Minor female roles, such as maids *(yatou),* ladies in waiting *(gongnü),* and female troops *(nübing),* are usually younger, untroubled characters and therefore speak at an overall pitch that is higher than that of major *dan* characters; however, they have the least range of pitch of all young *dan* roles.

The young *dan* roles all make considerable use of "steeply rising and descending cadences as the conclusion to emotionally charged passages of speech."[28] With blue cloth *dan* especially, the final one or two words of an emotional speech are very drawn out and almost sung. These words are not melismatic but are rendered on a long, rising and/or falling glide *(huayin),* as described above.

The Young *Sheng* Voice

The basic voice of the young *sheng* is actually a combination of the small-voice and large-voice, known as "tiger sound" *(huyin).* It is somewhat more nasal than that of the young *dan* and has less of the buzzing quality associated with the latter. Furthermore, the young *sheng* voice encompasses a much broader range of timbre; as with the young *dan,* the head is considered the principal resonating area—but more of the central and chest registers are used as well. In a manner that stylistically suggests a young man whose voice is changing, the young *sheng* voice "breaks" periodically from the small-voice (falsetto) into the large-voice. The breaks occur both in speech and song but are especially marked in the former. In some schools, the breaks from small- to large-voice are accompanied by a gravelly vocal quality; in others, a quality "purer" and sweeter than young *dan* vocalization is used.

When a vocalization is primarily falsetto, that falsetto is controlled so as to include elements of the large-voice; it is therefore unlike the falsetto of the young *dan.* Primarily large-voice vocalizations are similarly controlled and include elements of the falsetto, making them unlike those of the older *sheng.* Precise and fluent use of breath is considered especially important in attaining the necessary control. The basic young *sheng* voice is described as "broad, loud and clear, with a lovely timbre as rich as early morning air"; the civil young *sheng*'s voice is "strong yet gentle and flexible," while the martial young *sheng* is more "robust and vigorous."[29]

In most role types, characters in the martial subcategory sing less frequently and in shorter passages than do those in the civil subcategory. However, the most important song in the young *sheng* role type is that of the martial young *sheng;* plays that primarily feature the young *sheng* role and song skill usually have a martial young *sheng* as the leading character. Civil young *sheng* sing less frequently and in shorter passages than do martial young *sheng*. When they do sing, it is in a simplified version of the martial young *sheng*'s singing style; civil young *sheng* usually sing in primary-meter or in an even faster metrical type, and at an overall pitch somewhat lower than that of martial young *sheng*. But the speech of the martial young *sheng* has a more abrupt, militant quality than that of the civil young *sheng*. As mentioned above, young *sheng* generally match their speaking style to that of the young *dan* playing opposite them; with blue cloth *dan,* they speak in heightened speech, and with flower *dan* or martial *dan,* in colloquial speech.

Both civil and martial young *sheng* share a stylized type of laughter that is characteristic of the overall role category. A. C. Scott describes it as "prolonged and high but rich in quality."[30] It is open to wide variations in interpretation and can be expressive of states ranging from boyish exuberance to lustful exhaltation.

LARGE-VOICE ROLES

All older *dan,* older *sheng, jing,* and *chou* role types sing in male melodic-passages, as discussed in chapter 3; they also sing and speak with the large-voice (i.e., the non-falsetto voice). Performers of these role types find sounds in the *jiang yang* rhyme category ideal for displaying the large-voice when singing or speaking important, extended words. All such sounds end in a nasal terminal consonant, which is excellent for back-of-the-head-sound *(naohouyin)* projection, a technique used most frequently by performers who sing and speak with a large-voice. *Yan qian* and *ren chen* category words are also favored for the same reason. Sounds in all three of these rhyme categories are considered representative of the male principle *(yang)* and are given segmented pronunciation in song. Words in the *zhong dong* rhyme category, also classified as male and given segmented pronunciation, are used less frequently, and are almost solely the province of older *sheng*.

Performers of large-voice roles are also partial to *fa hua, huai lai,* and *yao tiao* category words. *Fa hua* category sounds are considered male but are given direct pronunciations. *Huai lai* and *yao tiao* sounds are considered representative of the feminine principle *(yin),* although less so than the *yi qi* and *hui dui* category words used by the small-voice role types; they are given segmented pronunciations. In the pronunciation of words in all three of these categories, the mouth must be fully open; that such sounds are considered very appropriate for the large-voice, male melodic-passage role types perhaps indicates that an open mouth is a sign of masculine strength.

Together, words in these six (or seven, including *zhong dong*) rhyme categories provide performers who use the large-voice with a variety of male and female sounds for use in both song and speech (four—or five—categories of male sounds, and two of female sounds), as well as with both direct (the *fa hua* rhyme category) and segmented pronunciations (the *huai lai, yao tiao, yan qian, ren chen, jiang yang,* and *zhong dong* rhyme categories) for song. As in the case of small-voice roles, playwrights must follow the preferences of large-voice performers for certain rhyme categories when writing their lyrics and speech.

All large-voice roles are quite similar in their use of male melodic-passages, rhyme categories, and in their basic vocal timbre. However, in performance every major large-voice role type, as well as each subcategory, is characterized by certain distinctive practices affecting specific vocal timbre, song, speech, and in some cases, wordless vocalizations.

The Older *Dan* Voice

Older *dan* speak and sing with the large-voice, as do older *sheng,* but with a higher overall pitch and a higher and more forward placement. The head is considered the principal resonating cavity, as it is for the young *dan.* Older *dan* use a vocal style known as *tangyin* (lit. "thorax [or 'chest'] sound"), which is generally broad, loud, and clear. *Tangyin* for older *dan* emphasizes supporting resonance in the mouth, the throat, and the chest cavities; the nose is used as well, as is some back-of-the-head-sound projection. When speaking and especially when composing and singing melodic-passages, older *dan* performers must convey the hardy strength of age while preserving the gentleness, flexibility, and delicacy of femininity. In the words of A. C. Scott, the performer's voice "combines qualities of both [young] *dan* and [older] *sheng,* and must possess a vibrant power typifying the dignity and pride as well as the sadness of old age."[31]

Older *dan* are among the most elderly characters in Beijing opera; only white-bearded older *sheng* and *chou* characters are as physically and vocally aged. The physical techniques used to convey this great age are supportive and usually do not occur as focal exhibitions of skill. As a result, song and speech are the primary skills of all older *dan* and are of critical importance to the portrayal of every older *dan* character.

In song, the entire range of metrical types may be used by older *dan;* long melismatic passages sung by older *dan* are especially striking, utilizing extreme ranges in pitch. In these passages, older *dan* frequently employ grace notes in a specific pattern known as "trembling (or 'enlivening') tone" *(souyin);* a number of grace notes are followed by a break and then by a number of grace notes again. Older *dan,* however, use less wave-tone vibrato than do older *sheng.*

Older *dan* speak in heightened speech and make much interpretive use of the interjection "ah." This interjection is used in a wide variety of situations, ranging from anger to consuming sadness; in the former instance, it is an extended exhalation that rises progressively in volume and pitch; in the latter, it is a somewhat shorter exhalation that begins both low and soft, rises a bit in pitch, and then falls in pitch as it diminishes even more in volume.

The Older *Sheng* Voice

Like older *dan,* older *sheng* speak and sing in the large-voice. The older *sheng* voice is fairly high in overall pitch but less so than that of the older *dan;* it is placed somewhat lower and farther back than that of the older *dan,* and the mouth is considered the principal resonating area. Especially in song, the older *sheng* voice must clearly convey the hardy strength and forcefulness of maturity.

There are two basic vocal styles for older *sheng—tangyin,* which is the basic style used by older *dan,* and *yunzheyue* (lit. "clouds screen the moon"). *Tangyin* for older *sheng* emphasizes supporting resonance in the head, the throat, and the chest cavities; some nasal resonation is used as well, and back-of-the-head-sound projection is quite important. *Yunzheyue* is described as producing an aural experience similar to the visual experience of "looking at scenery in the moonlight—some bright and some dark— producing a somewhat dim and hazy beauty."[32] *Yunzheyue* is a slightly throaty, husky timbre and can be very moving. Both basic styles principally involve central and head resonance; the precise timbre used for a given character is blended to best portray that character and best display the vocal technique of the performer.

Older *sheng* make considerable use of the wave-tone vibrato in their singing. As in the young *dan* role type, civil characters sing more often and in longer passages than do martial. The songs of martial older *sheng* are simpler and lower in overall pitch than those of civil older *sheng* and are rarely slower than primary-meter. Civil older *sheng* themselves, however, generally do not use metrical types as slow as those used by *dan;* fast-three-eyes-meter is usually featured in the songs of older *sheng,* rather than slow-meter.

Older *sheng* speak primarily in heightened speech. Pitch modulation is greatest between written-characters, rather than internally within each written-character as it is for young *dan*. The speech of martial older *sheng* is generally more abrupt and somewhat faster than that of civil older *sheng*, whose speech is usually fairly slow and even in tempo. When aroused, however, civil older *sheng* characters deliver speech quite rapidly, as in *Qing Feng Pavilion (Qing feng ting), Stealing the Ancestral Scroll (Dao zong juan),* and in *Examining the Head and Executing Tang (Shen tou ci Tang).*

The weeping style of older *sheng* is perhaps that role's single most characteristic vocalization. The cry begins with an extended, melismatic pattern of sound, which is followed by several short stylized sobs. The first scene of *Silang Visits His Mother* features several instances of virtuoso older *sheng* weeping.

The *Jing* Voice

The chest is considered the principal resonating area for the *jing* voice. But *jing* actors are trained to use all the resonating cavities and to support chest resonation with simultaneous resonation in as many other areas as possible. Their vocal placement is farther back than in any other role type, and back-of-the-head-sound projection is most important for *jing* performers. The *jing* voice produces a harder, fuller, more nasal sound than that of the older *sheng*. However, the sound, especially of *jing* singing, is still high to Western-trained ears; in fact, the attainment of high pitched tones while utilizing all possible resonating cavities is one of the most valued aesthetic achievements for *jing* performers. This achievement entails "loud and sonorous, deep and powerful" sound production at a remarkably great volume.[33] A. C. Scott describes it by saying that the voice of the *jing* performer "is full and . . . has great carrying power. . . . The vocal technique of the *jing* actor is quite extraordinary; his voice is robust and full, nasal, even raucous in quality, and characterized by protracted enunciations of tremendous volume. It is common for Chinese dramatic writers to say of their favorite *jing* actor that the walls of a theatre still echo three days after he has sung on stage."[34]

Jing speak primarily in heightened speech. Their speech is by far the most guttural stage speech in Beijing opera, as well as the deepest. Contrary to the general practice, *jing* speech is lower in pitch than *jing* singing. It is also generally harsher and gruffer in quality. *Jing* take considerably less time in the pronunciation of each written-character than do other role types, and have the least modulation in pitch within words. This characteristic rapid tempo is also found in *jing* singing; they rarely sing slower than primary-meter, and display a breath control in singing that is "forceful, vigorous,

and firm."[35] A special technique termed "exploding sound" *(zhayin)* is sometimes used in *jing* singing. It involves the rough, loud vocalization of a word
in a sung line, and is used in excited situations. Although it was originally
employed only by supporting *jing* and martial *jing,* who sing less often and
in shorter passages than do great-painted-face *jing,* the "exploding sound"
technique is now also used by some great-painted-face *jing* performers as
well.

The most striking *jing* vocalization is a protracted ululation within a narrow, fairly high pitch range, produced at a tremendous volume. It is known
as "making a sound like *wayaya*" *(da wayaya)* and is done with the tongue;
performers practice it by pushing up and down on the tongue rapidly with
chopsticks. It is expressive of astonishment and anger, or of threat to an
enemy. The *wayaya* vocalization was originally and is still primarily performed by supporting *jing* and martial *jing;* it is not for upper-class characters and therefore is not used for all characters in these subcategories.

The *Chou* Voice

Chou performers also speak and sing in the large-voice, and generally utilize
the same resonating cavities as do older *sheng* performers. However, their
vocal timbre is somewhat thinner than that of older *sheng* performers, as
well as much more nasal. The overall pitch of the *chou* voice, moreover, is
appreciably lower than that of the older *sheng* voice.

The *chou* voice is the least stylized Beijing opera voice; its vocal style is
much closer to that of popular comedians *(xiangsheng)* than to that of any
other role type in Beijing opera. Popular comedians usually speak in Beijing
dialect, a dialect that is known for its nasality and emphasis on the round
quality of sound.[36] *Chou* generally speak in Beijing opera's colloquial Mandarin speech, which is based on the Beijing dialect, and frequently use Beijing and/or regional slang as well. Like popular comedians, *chou* performers further exaggerate nasality, further emphasize all round-quality sounds,
and increase the tempo of everyday Mandarin speech while maintaining its
characteristic patterns of intonation, phrasing, and rhythm. Their speech is
considered quite beautiful, "clear, melodious, and pleasing to the ear, with a
brisk and neat enunciation."[37]

Most *chou* roles do not feature singing. When *chou* do sing, it is frequently in parody of other role types; for instance, Zhang Wenyuan in *Black
Dragon Residence* sings in parody of a young *sheng.* Like popular comedians, *chou* performers also occasionally sing folk and popular songs *(changger,* lit. "sing songs"), songs that are not a part of the *pihuang* musical sys-

Figure 23
A Comparison of the Overall Pitch-range and Vocal Timbre of
Major Role Types in Beijing Opera

Type of Melodic-passage and Voice	Role Type	Range of "Feminine" and "Masculine" Qualities	Overall Pitch Range and Vocal Timbre
female melodic-pasages, small-voice	Blue-cloth *dan* Flower *dan* Martial *dan* Civil young *sheng* Martial young *sheng*	Most "Feminine"	Thinnest sound, highest overall pitch
male melodic-passages, large-voice	Older *dan* Civil older *sheng* Martial older *sheng* *Jing* *Chou*	Most "Masculine"	Fullest sound, lowest overall pitch

tem of Beijing opera; when singing such songs, *chou* performers use a "natural" *(ziran)* voice rather than singing in the trained, stylized fashion of Beijing opera (*changxi,* lit. "sing theatre").[38]

Figure 23 compares the overall pitch-range and vocal timbre of the major role types in Beijing opera. Important subcategories that differ appreciably from one another in vocal stylization are included separately in the comparison. The *chou* role type is listed in the figure as a large-voice role; however, because it is not a part of the spectrum of overall pitch-range and vocal timbre presented by the highly stylized voices of the other role types, it is not included in the comparison.

The specific vocal characteristics of each role and subcategory serve as aural conventions, clearly identifying the role type and subcategory, and therefore the level of dignity, social status, gender, and age of every character portrayed. In combination with the more comprehensive techniques of vocal production, song, and speech, they also help to create a separate, stylized aural "world" for Beijing opera. Within this world, performers demonstrate their mastery of this body of vocal techniques in the display of song and speech skill. And their display is supported and accompanied by the musicians of the orchestra.

CHAPTER VI

THE ORCHESTRA

The musicians of the Beijing opera orchestra *(yuedui,* also termed *changmian)* play in intimate ensemble with the stage performers. Because the focus of Beijing opera performance is the stage performers' display of skills in the expression of character and emotion, the vast majority of orchestral music accompanies the song, speech, and dance-acting of the stage performers; only very rarely is orchestral music featured independently. But the aesthetic and interpretive importance of this accompanying role cannot be overemphasized. The Beijing opera orchestra provides a fabric of punctuating and integrating sound that runs throughout every Beijing opera performance, serving simultaneously to aurally characterize every performance as Beijing opera, and to express the musical interpretation of each play's atmosphere and emotional content. The *pihuang* music of Beijing opera is characterized not only by the elements and composition process of the *pihuang* musical system, but also by the specific instruments that make up its orchestra, the sound and use of each, and the functions that they perform together.[1]

INSTRUMENTS

The instruments that make up the Beijing opera orchestra for the performance of a given play are selected according to the musical requirements of that play. No performance, however, is without two or more two-string spike fiddles *(huqin),* a *yueqin,* a clapper *(ban),* a clapper-drum *(bangu),* a large gong *(daluo),* a small gong *(xiaoluo),* and cymbals *(naobo).* Other instruments that may be included are a *ruan,* a *sanxian,* a *pipa,* a *suona,* horizontal and vertical bamboo flutes *(dizi* and *xiao),* a *sheng,* a *guan,* a *tang* drum *(tanggu),* a large *tang* drum *(datanggu),* cymbals of different sizes and timbres including large cymbals *(dabo)* and "hoarse" cymbals *(yabo),* a large "screen" gong *(dashailuo),* "bump bells" *(pengling),* a nine-tone gong *(jiuyinluo),* and a *bangzi* clapper.

Descriptions of the Instruments

The instruments of the Beijing opera orchestra are divided into two sections, the melodic orchestra (*wenchang,* lit. "civil section"; also referred to as *guanxian yuedui,* lit. "wind and string orchestra") and the percussive orchestra (*wuchang,* lit. "martial section"; also termed *daji yuedui,* lit. "percussive orchestra," but usually referred to as *luogu,* lit. "gongs and drums"). Although the melodic orchestra may be somewhat more prominent in the performance of civil plays, and the percussive in martial plays, almost every performance includes both sections. In all plays, the two sections are combined to form a full orchestra *(quan yuedui)* for the accompaniment of singing, some dance-acting, and some speech. In other situations, the percussive orchestra performs alone.

Melodic Instruments

The traditional melodic orchestra is itself divided into three groups of instruments: bowed *(la)* instruments, plucked *(tan)* instruments, and blown *(chui)* instruments. All bowed instruments are two-string spike fiddles *(huqin,* lit. "introduced-from-abroad stringed-instruments"), which were originally indigenous to the areas north and west of China but were adopted by Chinese musicians in the Song dynasty (960–1279).[2]

Spike fiddles are played with a bamboo bow strung with horsehair. One of the two, closely placed strings of the instrument runs between the bamboo and the horsehair of the bow—the bow can therefore be removed from the instrument only by detaching that string. By controlling the direction of the pressure exerted by the bow, the musician selects the string to be sounded at any given time. The string enclosed by the bow is played with outward pressure and is referred to as the outer string *(waixian).* The string not enclosed by the bow is played with inward pressure and is called the inner string *(neixian).* The inner string is thicker than the outer and is tuned to the lower of the two pitches appropriate to whatever mode is being played. The body of the instrument is a hollow cylinder, covered in front with a taut skinhead and pierced at a right angle by the spike, a longer, thinner, solid cylinder. All spike fiddles are held vertically, with the body resting on the musician's left thigh, the skinhead facing forward in the same direction as the musician, and the spike supported and the two strings fingered by the left hand. The bow, held parallel to the ground, is drawn diagonally across the strings by the right hand. The strings are secured at the base of the instrument to the bottom end of the spike, where it pierces the underside

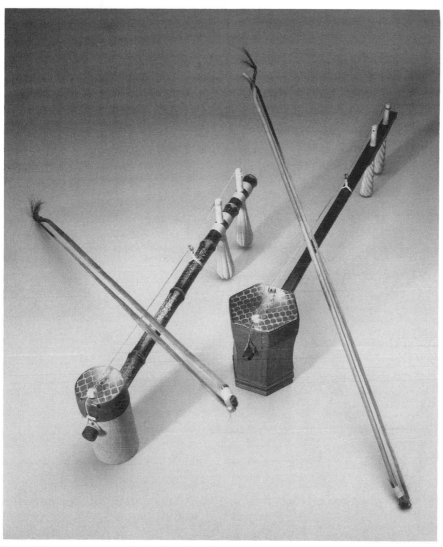

Bowed instruments: *jinghu* (left) and *erhu* (right). [Described on pages 226 and 231 in text.]

Plucked instruments: *yueqin* (center), *ruan* (left), and *sanxian* (right). [Described on pages 231–232 in text.]

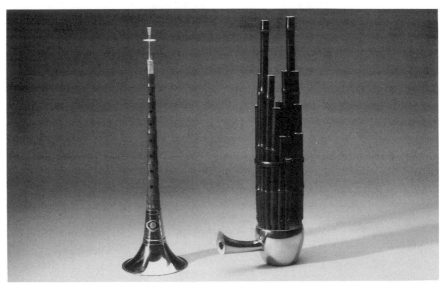

Blown instruments: *suona* (left) and *sheng* (right). [Described on pages 232–233 in text.]

Leading percussive instruments: clapper drum *(bangu)* (right, on a wooden stand) and clapper *(ban)* (left, resting on an upturned clapper drum). [Described on pages 233–234 in text.]

Principal brass percussive instruments: small gong *(xiaoluo)* (upper left), large gongs *(daluo)* (upper center and right), and cymbals *(naobo)* (lower left and center). The cloth handles of the cymbals are wrapped around the hands of the player, who therefore does not actually touch the cymbals themselves when playing. [Described on pages 234–235 in text.]

Supplementary percussive instruments: *tang* drum *(tanggu)* (center) and brass "bump bells" *(pengling)* (lower left). [Described on pages 235–236 in text.]

of the body. They are drawn up over a bamboo bridge near the center of the head, through a metal hook attached to the spike, and are wrapped around two wooden tuning pegs inserted through the spike near its upper end. In fingering the strings, the musician exerts pressure upon them with the left hand but does not press them against the spike.

The *jinghu* (lit. "Beijing opera introduced-from-abroad stringed-instrument," i.e., *jing* [*ju*] *hu* [*qin*]) is the principal spike fiddle in Beijing opera. It is the smallest spike fiddle used in Beijing opera, and its body and spike are constructed of bamboo. The size, construction, and playing technique result in a piercing, high-register sound.

The major supporting spike fiddle is the *erhu* (lit. "second introduced-from-abroad stringed-instrument," i.e., "second *hu* [*qin*]"). The *erhu* is somewhat larger than the *jinghu* and its strings are slightly thicker. The body and spike of the *erhu* are constructed of red-wood.[3] These differences in size and construction give the *erhu* a lower-pitched, gentler tone quality (i.e., timbre) than the *jinghu;* at least one of each accompanies every Beijing opera play.

Several other types of tertiary spike fiddles may also be used, generically termed *zhonghu* (middle *hu* [*qin*]), *dahu* (large *hu* [*qin*]), and *dihu* (bass *hu* [*qin*]). These vary in size, most being larger than either the *jinghu* or the *erhu,* and in the materials with which they are constructed. As a result, each has a unique pitch-range and timbre. However, none is so large as to require a different playing position—all are rested on the left thigh and supported vertically by the left hand.

The plucked instruments group is composed of the *yueqin, ruan, sanxian,* and *pipa.* All are much more mellow in timbre than is the *jinghu.*

Of these, the *yueqin* (lit. "moon [shaped] stringed-instrument") is the principal instrument; only it is included in the orchestra for every traditional Beijing opera play. The *yueqin* takes its name from its circular body. Outside of Beijing opera, most *yueqin* have four strings—however, the Beijing opera *yueqin* usually has only two. When the instrument is played, it rests on its side on the thighs of the musician, with the rather short neck slanting to the left. The *yueqin* has ten frets and is usually plucked with a single plectrum.

The *ruan* is visually quite similar to the *yueqin,* and like the *yueqin* is constructed for four strings. However, the Beijing opera *ruan* also usually employs only two. The *ruan* is played in the same position as the *yueqin,* is also fretted, and is also usually plucked with a single plectrum.

The *sanxian* (lit. "three strings") is, as its name suggests, a three-stringed instrument. It has no frets and may be plucked with either a single plectrum held in the hand or with multiple plectra attached to the fingers. The body is a flattened oval with a snakeskin head, and the neck is quite long. The instrument is held virtually horizontally in the lap, face out, when played. It has the most piercing sound of all the plucked instruments but is still quite gentle and soft in comparison with the *jinghu.*

The *pipa,* often called a "lute" in English translation, is a four-stringed, fretted instrument that is generally plucked with individual plectra attached to the fingers. The body of the *pipa* is long and pear-shaped, and its face is indented in a shallow curve. When played, the body rests on the thighs and is held upright.

None of the blown instruments is used in every Beijing opera play. The *suona* and horizontal bamboo flute *(dizi)* are used more frequently, however, than are the vertical bamboo flute *(xiao),* the *sheng,* and the *guan.*

The *suona* is used more often than is the horizontal bamboo flute. It is constructed of a conical red-wood body, a metal mouthpiece fitted with a small double reed, and a movable flared metal bell that is shaped like the end of a trumpet. Different pitches are produced by fingerings of the seven front and one rear finger holes on the red-wood body, and by moving the trumpet-shaped bell, which alters the tone quality as well. Because of the movable bell, the *suona* is capable of producing a wide variety of timbres.

The horizontal bamboo flute *(dizi)* produces a clear, sweet sound. There are ten holes in the top of the flute; the mouth hole is on the far left as the flute is held horizontally and played. The hole to its right is covered with a thin membrane that enhances tone quality, and the next six are finger holes; there are two additional holes, in some flutes on the top and in others on the bottom, on the far right.[4]

The secondary blown instruments are used less often, with approximately equal frequency. The vertical bamboo flute *(xiao)* is similar to the horizontal with regard to holes other than the mouth hole; one open end of the tube serves as the mouth hole, into which air is blown as the flute is held nearly vertically and played.

The *sheng* is a multiple reed-pipe instrument. It is constructed of bamboo pipes resembling the pipes of a pipe organ in miniature, each equipped with a single free reed. The pipes are set into a cup-shaped hollow wooden or metal holder, into which the player alternately blows out and sucks in air through a protruding mouthpiece.

The *guan* is a cylindrical wooden instrument with a broad double-reed inserted into the mouth end. It has seven holes in the front and one in the rear for fingering, as does the *suona,* but does not have a movable bell; it is therefore more consistent in tone quality than is the *suona.*

Percussive Instruments

The percussive orchestra is said to have four basic instruments: the drum-and-clapper *(guban)*, the large gong *(daluo)*, the small gong *(xiaoluo)*, and the cymbals *(naobo)*. None of these instruments is constructed so as to have a specific pitch in relation to the voices of the stage performers or to the melodic instruments of the orchestra. All four are included in the orchestra for every Beijing opera play.

The first and most important percussive instrument, the drum-and-clapper, is in fact two separate instruments: the clapper *(ban,* lit. "accented beat [marker]") and the clapper-drum *(bangu,* lit. "accented beat drum"; also called *danpigu,* lit. "single-skin drum").[5] Both these instruments are played, often simultaneously, by the conductor *(sigu,* lit. "manager of the drum"), who conducts not only the percussive orchestra but the full orchestra as well.

The clapper consists of three pieces of hard red-wood that are just over ten inches long and taper slightly in a convex curve from a little over two inches wide at their tops to about two-and-a-half inches wide at their bottoms. Two of these pieces are three-sixteenths of an inch thick, and one is twice that. The thick piece is firmly bound to one of the thinner pieces at top and bottom with fine cord, forming a single piece nine-sixteenths of an inch thick. This thick piece and the remaining thin piece are tied together loosely with a thick cord that runs through two holes bored in each piece one-third of the way down from the top on either side of longitudinal center. When the clapper is held preparatory to playing, the thin piece is held thirty degrees off vertical in the left hand with the cord draped over the thumb, suspending the thick piece on the other side of the thumb, which is thereby sandwiched between the two pieces; the lower portion of the thick piece rests on the lower portion of the thin piece. The forearm rotates counterclockwise rapidly at the elbow when the clapper is played, causing the thick piece to travel up to approximately forty-five degrees off vertical; it is then caught by the thin piece as it descends, producing a sharp, clear percussive sound.[6] The volume may be modulated by the speed of the forearm rotation; a faster rotation causes the pieces to be struck together more firmly and produces a louder sound.

The clapper-drum is made of a solid piece of hard wood a little over ten inches in diameter and about three inches thick. A relatively small hole, less than two inches in diameter, is bored through the instrument in the center of its convex top. The inside is then carved out in a funnel shape, producing inside walls that are less than an inch thick at the bottom but become considerably thicker as the carved-out area tapers to the dimensions of the small hole at the top. The hole, and in fact the entire top of the drum, is covered with tightly stretched skin nailed around the sides. The clapper-drum is mounted on a tripod and struck with unpadded, knobless bamboo beaters *(qian)* resembling chopsticks. Only one is used, held in the right hand, when the conductor is also playing the clapper; two are used, one held in each hand, when the clapper-drum is played without the clapper. Striking the skin directly over the hole produces a sharp, piercing sound that carries very well. The volume may be modulated by striking firmly or more gently. Striking the wooden portions of the drum head produces a much softer, quieter sound with very little resonance.

The remaining three basic percussive instruments are constructed of brass. The large gong *(daluo)* comes in two types; at least one type of large gong is used in every Beijing opera play. The *jingluo* (lit. "Beijing opera gong," i.e., *jing [ju] luo*) is about a foot in diameter, with a slightly convex face that is flattened in the center. The *suluo* (lit. "Suzhou gong," i.e., *Su [zhou] luo*) is larger in diameter and often has a flatter face.[7] The former is used more frequently. Both large gongs are held in the left hand by a rope attached through two holes in the rim, struck with a padded stick held by the right hand, and produce loud, sonorous, intense sounds. In the collection of instruments examined, the *jingluo* produces fairly strong and clear basic pitches. When it is hit lightly, the pitch falls slightly and then rises a half step in the duration of the ringing tone; when the gong is hit more firmly, the pitch falls slightly and then rises a minor third. The overall pitch of the *suluo* is considerably lower and less specific than that of the *jingluo*. When struck, the initial sound is complex, containing a wide range of pitches (inharmonic partials—overtones not within the harmonic series). When the *suluo* is struck firmly, many of these pitches are quite high. In the duration of the ringing tone, whether the gong is struck lightly or firmly, a central pitch is heard rising slightly and then falling, with numerous lesser pitches rising as the central one falls. The interval of the central descending pitch is a major third.[8]

The small gong *(xiaoluo)* is about half the diameter of the *jingluo* and has a convex face composed of a flat circle in the center, a little over an inch in diameter, and sloping shoulders. The small gong is held by balancing the rim, which extends to the back, on the fingers of the left hand. It is struck in the center of the face with the corner of a thin, flat piece of wood about six inches long and less than two inches wide. This beater is held in the right hand, upright, with the edge of the long side perpendicular to the face of the gong, and manipulated by the ring finger, thumb, and a clockwise rotation of the wrist—the hand itself does not move toward or away from the face of the gong. The small gong must be struck within the flat circle to produce the proper sound—a clear, melodious, bounding tone quality. When struck lightly, one pitch predominates; it is a fifth below the primary pitch of the *jingluo*. When struck firmly, a clear rising progression of three pitches is produced (i.e., 1 2 3, with 1 being the single pitch produced by the light striking).

The cymbals are about six inches in diameter and are each composed of a flat outer ring and an inner cup-shaped portion with a small central hole through which a cloth "handle" is attached. The pitch of the two cymbals is not the same, and the interval separating the two pitches is a small, dissonant one to Western ears. When struck and then muffled (stopped/closed) by holding the two cymbals together, only the two "dissonant" pitches are heard. When struck and immediately separated, the pitch of each cymbal rises slightly and then falls a minor third, with more overtones emerging in the duration of the ringing tone. When the two cymbals are rubbed together in a continuous circular motion, a wave of rising, falling, and rising pitches within a full octave pitch-range is produced. Although this third method creates a rather gentle overall sound, the first two produce penetrating, stimulating, jarring effects that are rather shrill.

The percussive orchestra frequently includes one or more of these supplementary percussive instruments as well: the *tang* drum (*tanggu,* lit. "hall drum"), the large *tang* drum *(datanggu),* the large cymbals *(dabo),* the "hoarse" cymbals *(yabo),* the large "screen" gong *(dashailuo),* the "bump bells" *(pengling),* the nine-tone gong *(jiuyinluo;* also called the "cloud gong," *yunluo),* and the *bangzi* clapper described in chapter 3.

The *tang* drum has a barrel-shaped smooth wooden body to which two skinheads about the same diameter as the head of the clapper-drum are nailed. It is a little over a foot tall and is suspended by ropes from a stand so that one head faces up and the other down; the ropes run through equally spaced rings around the center of the *tang* drum's body. It is struck with two knobless, unpadded sticks. The large *tang* drum comes in various sizes, all larger than the *tang* drum, and all in the shape of a truncated cone; the larger the diameter of the head that is struck, the more squat the body and the smaller the diameter of the lower head. In other respects, it resembles the *tang* drum.

The large cymbals, the "hoarse" cymbals, and the large "screen" gong are, as their names imply, versions of the basic brass percussive instruments in different sizes and timbres. The "bump bells" and nine-tone gong are also made of brass. The former consists of two small brass cups connected by a cord; the center of the cord is held in the hand, causing the two cups to be suspended as bells and allowing them to hit against one another. The latter consists of nine small, tuned gongs, all less than three inches in diameter, suspended from a small wooden frame. A tenth gong is in some instances attached to the top of the frame, belying the name of the instrument. The small gongs are struck with a small wooden hammer.

USE OF THE INSTRUMENTS

Every musical instrument has a characteristic pitch-range and/or timbre. Many are associated with certain aesthetic values as well. The use of each instrument within the two sections of the Beijing opera orchestra is based upon these characteristics and values.

The Melodic Instruments

As will be described below in detail, the major function of the melodic orchestra is the accompaniment of singing. The *jinghu* provides the principal accompaniment; it follows the melody composed and sung by the stage performer. The other melodic instruments then follow the melody played by the *jinghu,* supporting and accompanying it. The piercing, high-register sound of the *jinghu* characterizes the sound of the melodic orchestra. It cuts through the sounds of all other melodic instruments and is clearly audible at all times, facilitating its use as leader of the melodic orchestra. The similar *bohu* replaces the *jinghu* in the *gaobozi* mode, as discussed in chapter 3.

The *erhu* and the *yueqin* are the major supporting melodic instruments. Because the *erhu* is a spike fiddle, like the *jinghu,* their sounds blend well; however, the *erhu* is lower in pitch than the *jinghu* and has a gentler tone quality. It therefore serves to broaden the pitch-range and tone quality of the bowed instruments in every Beijing opera performance. The *yueqin,* which is the only plucked instrument used in every performance, provides a very different tone quality than either bowed instrument; the sound of plucked instruments is experienced in Beijing opera as lilting and lyrical.

Together, the *jinghu, erhu,* and *yueqin* are known as the "three major pieces" *(san da jian)* of the melodic orchestra.

When they are used, the tertiary spike fiddles serve to further broaden the pitch-range and tonal qualities of the bowed instruments. Similarly, the secondary plucked instruments increase the range of pitch and timbre in the plucked instruments group. In doing so, they of course expand the pitch-range and tonal qualities of the entire melodic orchestra.

The two most frequently used blown instruments, the *suona* and the horizontal bamboo flute, unlike the stringed instruments, do not follow the *jinghu* throughout a given play, but are used for specific occasions. The sound of the *suona* is often quite strident, and the instrument is frequently used in martial situations. Because of its broad range of tone quality, the *suona* is also used extensively for sound effects; for instance, in *Silang Visits His Mother,* the *suona* provides both the cry of his baby and the neigh of his horse. It is also featured in the music that opens plays, that accompanies formal processions, and that closes plays ending with weddings, processions, and other auspicious occasions. A small version of the *suona* often supports the accompaniment for singing when a scene or play is composed in the *erhuang* system's *gaobozi* mode, as discussed in chapter 3; occasionally the small *suona* serves as the primary melodic instrument in *gaobozi.* In such situations, the *suona* follows the singer, and the other melodic instruments follow the *suona;* the *suona* becomes both the principal accompanying instrument and the leader of the melodic orchestra.

The clear, sweet sound of the horizontal bamboo flute, like that of the plucked stringed instruments, is considered lilting and lyrical in Beijing opera. The horizontal bamboo flute provides the principal accompaniment for singing in *kunqu,* the predominant national theatre form before the ascent of Beijing opera. It is most frequently used in Beijing opera to accompany songs *(qupai,* lit. "song types," translated below as "fixed-melodies") taken from that older form, from other forms of *xiqu,* and from folk music. When such pieces are played, the horizontal bamboo flute in some instances replaces the *jinghu* as the principal accompanying instrument and as the leader of the melodic orchestra; in other instances, the horizontal bamboo flute follows the *jinghu,* which retains its position of leadership.

The secondary blown instruments, when used, follow the principal accompanying instrument. In most cases, this is the *jinghu;* in *gaobozi* compositions, however, they follow the *bohu* or the *suona,* and in compositions in which the principal accompanying instrument is the horizontal bamboo flute, they follow that instrument. The sounds of the vertical bamboo flute and the *sheng* are experienced as lilting and lyrical in Beijing opera whereas that of the *guan* is considered more martial. These instruments serve to broaden the pitch-range and tone quality of the blown instrument group, and thereby of the entire melodic orchestra, much as do the secondary plucked instruments and the tertiary spike fiddles.

The Percussive Instruments

The principal percussive instrument is the set of two instruments known collectively as the drum-and-clapper: the clapper and the clapper-drum, both of which are played by the conductor *(sigu)*. Usually only the latter instrument is used to conduct the percussive orchestra. However, both may be played when the conductor directs the combined, full orchestra.

When the full orchestra is combined, the conductor maintains the tempo and rhythm established by the singing performer, so important to each metered metrical type, with the drum-and-clapper. The clapper is usually struck together firmly on every accented beat (i.e., on the one accented beat for every three unaccented beats in slow-meter, on the one accented beat for every one unaccented beat in primary-meter, and throughout the unbroken series of accented beats in fast-meter). On unaccented beats, the conductor may strike the clapper-drum with one stick. In some instances, the clapper is struck together lightly on unaccented beats; this may occur alone or in conjunction with the striking of the clapper-drum. For free metrical types, there is of course no regular clapper beat. However, the clapper is often struck together firmly between musical lines. Only when conducting melodic-passages composed in the *gaobozi* mode does this system alter. For that mode, the *bangzi* clapper replaces both the clapper and the clapper-drum; it is struck firmly on accented beats and may be struck lightly on unaccented beats. The *bangzi* clapper is also used occasionally for sound effects such as the sound of horses' hooves.

The use of each of the three brass percussive instruments carries certain conventional connotations. A predominance of large gong connotes the presence of male characters who are of high status or are bold, fierce warriors. It is used extensively in accompaniment for older *sheng,* martial *sheng,* martial young *sheng,* and *jing;* older *dan,* who share the same dignity associated with older *sheng,* are also frequently accompanied by large gong. It is considered the most appropriate brass percussive instrument for expressing solemn, stately grandeur and heroism, as well as for battle or intense situations in which emotions suddenly burst forth. The small gong dominates percussive accompaniment for elegant, refined characters such as blue cloth *dan,* civil young *sheng,* and some older *dan;* for commoners or characters of low intrinsic dignity, including flower *dan,* some older *sheng,* and most *chou;* and for secondary negative characters, often played by *chou.* A predominance of cymbals indicates a tense and/or confused atmosphere; they are also frequently used to produce sound effects. Together, the three basic brass percussive instruments and the drum-and-clapper are known as the "four major pieces" *(si da jian)* of the percussive orchestra.

The supplementary percussive instruments are used only in certain, special circumstances. The *tang* drum and large *tang* drum are usually associated with formal, often martial activities. However, they may also be used in conjunction with lyric melodic accompaniment to dance-acting. Occasionally they are employed in the percussive accompaniment of melodic-passages composed in inverse *erhuang* mode as well.[9] The large cymbals, "hoarse" cymbals, large screen gong, bump bells, and nine-tone gong are used primarily for special effects, such as temple bells and the sounds of ritual instruments in ceremonial scenes.

Each of the four major pieces of the percussive orchestra may be struck in several ways. These methods of striking are all named and are each represented by a written-character for which a romanized symbol based on that written-character's pronunciation is sometimes substituted. Percussive scores may therefore be written down, in a manner similar to cipheric notation, using either written-characters or romanized symbols. Such percussive scores are termed "percussive classics" *(luogu jing).*[10] Figure 24 lists the basic methods of striking the instruments and the names of these strikes; although the methods and names do vary a bit from musician to musician and from company to company, those given here are fairly standard. Romanized symbols for each of the methods of striking are also assigned to facilitate the examples in the discussion below.[11]

These strikes are joined together to make more than one hundred named, identifiable percussive passages *(luogu dian,* lit. "gong and drum points"; "points" signifies "beats," as in "drumbeats").[12] The passages are of different lengths; some are as short as one measure while others are as long as or longer than an opening melodic-line composed in female *erhuang* slow-meter—up to twelve or more measures in length. Each named percussive passage may vary somewhat from musician to musician and company to company, as do the methods of striking themselves; again, however, those given below as examples are fairly standard.

There are more methods for striking the clapper-drum than for any other percussive instrument. This reflects the use of the clapper-drum as the prin-

Figure 24

Methods of Striking the Four Major Pieces of the Percussive Orchestra

Predominant Instrument	Method of Striking	Other Instruments Involved	Name	Romanized Symbols
large gong:	one firm beat	none, or with the small gong	*kang/kuang*	Z
	one light beat	none	*kong*	K
	one firm beat	small gong and cymbals	*cang*	C
	one light beat	small gong and cymbals	*qing*	q
small gong:	one firm beat	none	*dei/tei*	D
	one light beat	none	*ling*	L
	one muffled beat	none, or with the cymbals	*za*	$\dot{z}$
cymbals:	one firm clap	none	*qi/qie*	Q
	one muffled clap	none, or with the small gong	*pu*	P
clapper:	one firm clap	small gong	*cei/cai*	I
	one firm beat	none	*zha*	X
	one light beat*	none	*yi*	E
clapper-drum:	one firm beat of the right stick	none	*da*	d
	one light beat of the right stick	none	*duo*	$\dot{d}$
	two successive light beats of the right stick	none	*longdong*	ïd
	short roll (2 "bounces") of the right stick	none	*duoluo*	ḍï
	one firm simultaneous beat of both sticks	none	*ba/beng*	B
	one firm beat of each stick in succession (left then right)	none	*bada*	bd
	continuous rapid roll of both sticks	none	*duer*	$d_{///}$

Additionally, a rest in which no instrument is played is usually called *ge* or *yi*, represented below by the symbols G and O.

* *yi* as played by the clapper generally occurs on the unaccented beats in passages of singing; *zha* marks the accented beats.

cipal instrument employed by the conductor in directing the percussive orchestra.

The conductor utilizes the clapper-drum in three basic ways when conducting the percussive orchestra. The first is via an extensive set of gestural signals *(shoushi)*, made by placing and moving the two knobless drum sticks *(qian)* across the face of the clapper-drum. These signals are visual and hence produce no sound; they indicate the specific percussive passages to be played. The first sound heard is then that of percussive instruments other than the clapper or clapper-drum. Basic examples of such signals include pointing with one stick to the center of the drum, pointing with two sticks to the center of the drum, placing one stick on the rim of the drum, placing both sticks on the rim of the drum, placing both sticks on the center of the drum and then moving them together to one side, and placing both sticks on the center of the drum and then moving them to opposite sides of the drum face.

In the second method of conducting, the conductor plays a specific passage of strikes on the clapper-drum; such passages are called "basic drummings" *(digu)*. These aural directions alone may serve to indicate the specific percussive passage to be played, or they may be followed by a single gestural signal, further clarifying the direction, after which the percussive orchestra joins in. Frequently used "basic drummings" include d, b̲d̲, B̲d̲$_{///}$, b̲d̲b̲d̲, and d̲d̲ d̲d̲ d̈d̲ d̈.

Certain "basic drumming" passages are classified as a third means of conducting the percussive orchestra. These passages, called "raising the gong" *(tiluo),* end with a strike of the small gong: for instance, d̲D̲, d̲ḋD̲, b̲d̲D̲, B̲D̲, and b̲d̲B̲D̲. They are frequently used to introduce percussive passages that give predominance to the large gong. The conductor uses a gestural signal to let the small gong player know when to play and for how long. A second gestural signal may follow the strike of the small gong to further clarify the nature of the percussive passage to be played.

The conductor selects and times percussive passages on the basis of the song, speech, dance-acting, and combat of the stage performers; his or her eyes are therefore at all times focused on those performers. The remaining members of the percussive orchestra, however, concentrate their attention throughout every performance on the face of the clapper-drum.

THE MUSICIANS AND THEIR PLACEMENT ON STAGE

The basic orchestra consists of eight musicians: the conductor playing drum-and-clapper, a large gong player, a small gong player, and a cymbals player, providing the four major pieces of the percussive orchestra; a *jinghu* player, an *erhu* player, and a *yueqin* player, providing the three major pieces of the melodic orchestra; and one other musician, often a *sanxian* player. Performers of stringed instruments other than the *jinghu* generally play the horizontal bamboo flute and *suona* as needed for each play in such a basic arrangement. Frequently it is the *erhu* player who plays the horizontal bamboo flute when it is called for, because the flute is most often played in conjunction with the plucked instruments. And conversely, it is usually the *yueqin* or *sanxian* player who plays the *suona* when it is needed, the *suona* most often being played with the percussion instruments alone, or with the spike fiddles. The *jinghu* player often plays supplementary percussive instruments when they are played in conjunction with the blown instruments, or with other percussion instruments only.

When an orchestra has more than eight musicians, a *ruan* and a *pipa* are often the next additional instruments, followed by a second *erhu* or tertiary spike fiddle. A second *jinghu* may be added as well. When plays that require a considerable amount of horizontal bamboo flute, *suona,* or supplementary percussion accompaniment are being performed, separate musicians are also added for these instruments. An enlarged Beijing opera orchestra of seventeen musicians might include the conductor, large gong player, small gong player, cymbals player, one or two *jinghu* players, one or two *erhu* players, a *yueqin* player, a *sanxian* player, a *ruan* player, a *pipa* player, a horizontal bamboo flute player, a *suona* player, and three to five other musicians who might be players of tertiary spike fiddles, additional plucked string instruments, supplementary blown instruments (a vertical bamboo flute, *sheng,* and/or *guan*), or supplementary percussive instruments, as appropriate for the play being performed.

The overall sound of the orchestra is therefore open to some variation. The use of numerous plucked string instruments produces an effect quite different from that in which horizontal and vertical bamboo flutes are used extensively, though both create a lyric, lilting atmosphere; the latter is a more "classical" sound to a Chinese audience, being more like *kunqu*. A preponderance of spike fiddles, *suona, guan,* and supplementary percussion instruments on the other hand produces a much more martial atmosphere. However, except when playing *gaobozi* compositions and certain fixed-melodies, the full orchestra is conducted by the drum-and-clapper and led melodically by the *jinghu;* the percussive orchestra is led by the clapper-drum and dominated by the sounds of the three basic brass percussive instruments.

Figure 25
Standard Seating in a Basic Eight-member Full Orchestra

house	downstage left

(diagram)

jinghu   erhu   yueqin   sanxian   conductor   small gong   cymbals   large gong

The musicians are seated just offstage at the downstage left corner. Seating is arranged so that the conductor and the *jinghu* player have an unobstructed view of the stage performers, the *jinghu* player can clearly hear the conductor's drum-and-clapper, and the percussive instrument players have a close and unobstructed view of the face of the clapper-drum. The conductor is therefore seated in the center of the musicians, facing the playing area; often, his or her chair is placed on a raised platform. The *jinghu* player is seated in front and to the left of the conductor, in the front row of the orchestra, where the closest possible proximity to the stage performers is obtained, and yet the conductor is also very close. The other members of the percussive orchestra are seated in a semicircle around the conductor. Although the specific placement of musicians may vary from performance to performance and troupe to troupe, the diagram in Figure 25 represents the standard arrangement for a basic, eight-member full orchestra; the percussive orchestra is generally seated farther back from the stage than the melodic orchestra, because the sounds of their instruments have much greater carrying power.[13]

FUNCTIONS OF THE MELODIC ORCHESTRA

The melodic orchestra always performs in conjunction with the percussive orchestra, as a part of the combined, full orchestra—it never performs independently. The most important function of the melodic orchestra is accompaniment for singing. It also performs two important, related functions: it plays instrumental connectives *(guomen),* and it plays action-strings *(xingxian)* and fixed-melodies *(qupai).*

ACCOMPANIMENT FOR SONG

By far the greatest part of accompaniment for Beijing opera singing is led
melodically by the *jinghu*. Only in the *gaobozi* mode and in pieces taken
from other forms of *xiqu* and from folk music do other instruments sometimes lead instead; the *bohu* or the *suona* in the former case, and usually the
horizontal bamboo flute in the latter. The *jinghu* player plays in close
ensemble with the singing stage performer.

Accompaniment for Beijing opera singing is not chordal. Chordal texture
is in fact not a part of traditional Chinese music.[14] However, accompaniment for singing is also not strictly in unison—the *jinghu* player does not
play exactly the same notes the singer is singing. It is instead heterophonic—
although the basic melodic contour played by the *jinghu* is the same as that
sung by the singer, there is appreciable divergence. In most instances, the
jinghu plays more notes per measure than the singer sings. The effect is that
the two melodies seem regularly to "cross" one another, with the *jinghu*
elaborating upon and weaving around the vocal line. The following
melodic-line illustrates this relationship; it is a closing line in *sipingdiao* primary-meter, from the Mei Lanfang version of the one-act play *The Favorite
Concubine Becomes Intoxicated*.[15]

Example 30 A Comparison of *Jinghu* and Vocal Melodies

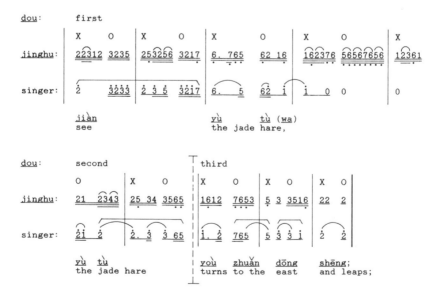

The two melodies are quite similar; they share the same meter and overall melodic contour. However, it is obvious that they differ in both rhythmic detail and in specific notes, and that the *jinghu* accompaniment contains many more pitch occurrences than does the singer's line. In this example, as is often the case, the *jinghu* is an octave lower than the singer and has a slightly larger pitch-range (5̇–6) than does the singer (5̇–5̇).

For the accompaniment of melodic-passages composed in a free metrical type, the *jinghu* does play essentially the same melody that the singer sings —frequently, however, an octave lower. When accompanying these metrical types, the *jinghu* player audibly and literally "follows" the singer; as a result, the melody in the accompaniment is often slightly behind the melody sung by the performer, repeatedly producing what to a Western ear sounds like dissonance quickly corrected.

In the performance of metered metrical types, specific notes shared by the *jinghu* and singer are played and sung simultaneously, as is evident in the above example. The *jinghu* player develops his or her own specific variation on the singer's melody during the course of rehearsals. In performance, the tempo and rhythm for the singing, and therefore for the accompaniment, are established by the singer and maintained by the conductor with the drum-and-clapper. However, the *jinghu* player does follow the melody of the singer in performance as well; when the performer adapts his or her composition to different performance conditions, the *jinghu* player follows these adaptations. Chapter 4 presents transcriptions of the same couplet as sung by Cheng Yanqiu at two different performances; the specific melodies sung on these two occasions are somewhat different, and the *jinghu* player on each occasion instinctively adapted the *jinghu* melodic variation as a result.[16]

This instinctive ability of the *jinghu* player is analogous to that of the singing performer; both have mastered the elements and patterns of the *pihuang* musical system and are able to use those elements and patterns as an interpretive vocabulary. However, accompaniment makes an additional demand of *jinghu* players; they must be extremely well attuned to the singing performers with whom they play. Because of this need, every major stage performer traditionally employed his or her own *jinghu* player; the two worked together exclusively onstage and offstage.[17] In contemporary China, each troupe has several *jinghu* players; most stage performers work with only one of them.

The most basic element of the *pihuang* musical system is the melodic-phrase, as discussed in chapter 3. In performance, the most important melodic-phrases are those sung by the singer; second in importance, however, are the *jinghu* variations on those melodic-phrases, played in accompaniment. The relationship of the other melodic instruments to the *jinghu* is analogous to the *jinghu*'s relationship to the singing; they follow it heterophonically. Their primary functions are to broaden the pitch-range and expand the types of tone quality—and to increase the number of variations upon the melody being sung by the singer.

INSTRUMENTAL CONNECTIVES

The melodic orchestra plays instrumental connectives *(guomen)* that serve as preludes to the sung melodic-passages, as interludes between them, and often as codas to them, as discussed in chapter 3; instrumental connectives are therefore closely related to the accompaniment of song, because they introduce, connect, and sometimes conclude that accompaniment. In spite of this close connection, however, instrumental connectives are usually classified as a function separate from the accompaniment of song by both musicians and stage performers. There are two major reasons for this classification.

The first reason may be termed the "source of the melodic initiative."[18] The specific melody of every sung melodic-passage originates with the singing performer; the melody played by the *jinghu* player in accompaniment is a variation on that specific melody, and the *jinghu* player follows the singer when playing that accompaniment. However, instrumental connectives are purely instrumental; when the *jinghu* player leads the melodic orchestra in playing them, he or she follows only the tempo and rhythm set and maintained by the conductor with the drum-and-clapper. Because there is no sung melody during instrumental connectives, the melodic initiative is, within the patterns of the mode and metrical type, the *jinghu* player's own.

Second, the purpose of instrumental connectives is somewhat different than that of accompaniment for song. In the accompaniment of singing, the *jinghu* provides the major variation on the melody sung by the singing performer, with the other instruments of the melodic orchestra providing additional variations. Prelude instrumental connectives, however, introduce and establish the atmosphere and emotional color of the sung melodic-passages that follow; interlude instrumental connectives maintain that atmosphere and emotional color when the singer is not actually singing but the song has not yet concluded, and concluding instrumental connectives "round off" that atmosphere and emotional color. Additionally, interlude instrumental connectives serve to punctuate the *dou,* clarifying meaning by making the units of meaning distinct. Instrumental connectives are therefore interpretively quite important. But the focus of every song is on the display of song skill by the singer(s) in the expression of emotion. Although the singer may adapt his or her melody to suit performance conditions, instrumental connectives are more melodically fixed, serving as constants between the more melodically flexible melodic-passages of the singer and his or her accompaniment.

Most metrical types in each mode of both modal systems therefore have standard instrumental connectives with relatively set melodies, which conventionally establish and maintain the atmosphere and emotional color associated with that metrical type, mode, and modal system. However, some standard instrumental connectives are shared by different metrical types in the same mode, or by the same metrical types in different modes. These shared instrumental connectives serve important interpretive functions. For instance, shaking-meter, the free metrical type that expresses exterior calm and interior tension through the use of the single-beat-meter drum-and-clapper accompaniment of flowing-water-meter, is performed with the same instrumental connectives that are employed in the performance of compositions in flowing-water-meter in the same mode. These flowing-water-meter instrumental connectives introduce and maintain the urgency of the drum-and-clapper accompaniment in shaking-meter. Similarly, compositions in each of the metrical types of *sipingdiao* mode are performed with the same instrumental connectives that are employed for those metrical types in principal *erhuang* mode compositions. *Sipingdiao* differs from principal *erhuang* in certain major respects, as discussed in chapter 3; the shared instrumental connectives serve to clarify *sipingdiao*'s resemblance to *erhuang* in atmosphere and emotional color.

There is also a prelude instrumental connective that serves to modify the atmosphere and emotional color of the metrical types that it introduces. It is called "colliding-meter" *(pengban)*. Despite its name, it is not a metrical type but rather an abrupt, three-note prelude instrumental connective that may be used to introduce slow-meter, fast-three-eyes-meter, and primary-meter melodic-passages. Frequently, the tempo of the metrical type that follows it is somewhat faster than usual (i.e., each beat is of somewhat shorter duration than usual). The "colliding-meter" instrumental connective serves to express anxiety or surprise in those slower meters, without switching metrical types. Its use is decided upon in the course of the compositional process.

As discussed in chapter 3, there are three major types of instrumental connectives—large instrumental connectives *(da guomen)*, small instrumental connectives *(xiao guomen)*, and half-line instrumental connectives *(banju guomen)*. The first type is longer than the latter two; the standard instrumental connective for each metrical type in each mode is usually its large instrumental connective. The shorter instrumental connectives may consist of an excerpt from the large instrumental connective, or may be a simplified version of the entire large instrumental connective. Both large and small instrumental connectives may serve as prelude, interlude, or concluding instrumental connectives; half-line instrumental connectives most frequently occur as interludes, and are usually found in the *erhuang* mode. Because the display of song skill in the expression of emotion is usually performed in synthesis with dance-acting, instrumental connectives serve a third function; in addition to establishing and maintaining atmosphere and emotional color, and to clarifying meaning by punctuating *dou,* instrumental connectives also accompany the dance-acting movements of the stage performers. When longer sections of dance-acting movement are appropriate, large instrumental connectives are played. And when shorter sections of dance-acting movement are called for, small instrumental connectives are performed. In some instances speech is interjected during instrumental connectives as well.

A common rehearsal practice attests to the interpretive and structural importance of instrumental connectives. In early rehearsals, the orchestra is not present. But the stage performers themselves sing the melodies of instrumental connectives to onomatopoetic sounds (e.g., *ling ker long ker*) before and in between their melodic-passages; the instrumental connectives are an integral part of the performer's emotional expression.

Action-strings and Fixed-melodies

All instrumental music played by the melodic orchestra other than instrumental connectives and accompaniment for song is collectively known as "scene music" *(changjing yinyue)*. Scene music is not a part of melodic construction—unlike instrumental connectives, scene music is not required by the *pihuang* musical system, and its placement is not prescribed. Scene music is played only when melodic accompaniment for physical performance is desired, or for specific atmospheric purposes. There are two major types of scene music, action-strings *(xingxian)* and fixed-melodies *(qupai)*.[19]

Action-strings are fairly short, relatively set musical lines that are quite flexible—they can be played only once or repeated almost any number of times, and can be altered and elaborated upon by raising or lowering pitch and by adding grace notes. They are played between full passages, lines, or *dou* of lyrics when singers want to perform interpretive dance-acting or pantomime without breaking the flow of orchestral accompaniment, and instrumental connectives are too short or are inappropriate. Speech may be interjected during action-strings as well.

Movements of set duration and short interjected speeches can often be performed during instrumental connectives, as described above. But performers frequently want more expressive flexibility. Because action-strings are so adaptable, they allow performers the freedom to expressively lengthen or shorten the duration of movement and interjected speech to fit the precise conditions of each particular performance. Because they are melodically different from instrumental connectives and accompaniment for song, they also serve to indicate musically a change in action or emotional state.

The *jinghu* player provides the melodic lead in passages of action-strings. He or she and the conductor pay careful attention to the stage performer and conclude the action-strings as the passage of speech or movement concludes. Action-strings connect easily and directly to instrumental connectives. Each mode has its own set of action-strings, of different lengths and with different cadence notes, to allow for this ease in connection as well as for maximum expressiveness and flexibility. For example, a short *xipi* 2 (re) cadence passage of action-strings is[20]

121 02 ||: 121 02 | 12 62 | 12 43 | 2321 6123 | 121 02 :||

Fixed-melodies (*qupai*, lit. "song types") are longer, more complete melodies, often in irregular-length lines, in which rhythm and basic melodic progression are essentially set. Each is individually named. In a number of forms of *xiqu*, lyrics are written to fixed-melodies in the composition of songs—*kunqu* is composed in this fashion.[21] Folk melodies are also occasionally used in some forms of *xiqu* as fixed-melodies. In Beijing opera, fixed-melodies from other forms of *xiqu* and from folk music are only rarely used in the composition of sung melodic-passages. However, they are employed quite frequently as scene music; technically, fixed-melodies used as scene music are referred to as "instrumental fixed-melodies" (*qiyue qupai*).

Instrumental fixed-melodies may be played in conjunction with song or completely separately from it. When played in conjunction with song, they are used before or after a complete song or aria, rather than within it like action-strings, to set the mood and atmosphere and/or to accompany movement. They are also used to accompany interpretive dance-acting, pantomime, and pure dance (such as that of a concubine before an Emperor) that are performed independently of song, and to set atmosphere and mood at transition points in a play that are not marked by song. Speech may also be interjected during fixed-melodies, as it may during instrumental connectives and passages of action-strings.

When instrumental fixed-melodies are used in conjunction with song, they are adapted to the *pihuang* musical system at least minimally, in terms of meter (i.e., they are arranged in $\frac{1}{4}$, $\frac{2}{4}$, or $\frac{4}{4}$ meter, rather than in $\frac{3}{4}$, $\frac{6}{8}$, etc.). Those used after song are usually preceded by the standard instrumental connective appropriate to the mode and metrical type being sung. The musicians then modulate to the fixed-melody via the use of 7 and 4 tones, and a change in rhythm and tempo if necessary. Those used before song usually begin independently and conclude with modulation into the instrumental connective appropriate to the mode and metrical type of the following sung melodic-passage.

For instance, in the play *The Favorite Concubine Becomes Intoxicated,* the fixed-melody "Near the Makeup Table/Boudoir" *(Pang zhuangtai)* is played while the Favorite Concubine drinks the wines of the feast alone.[22] For this fixed-melody, the *jinghu* should be tuned to 1–5, as in inverse *erhuang,* rather than to 5–2, as in the *sipingdiao* composition that follows. The fixed-melody is followed by a small instrumental connective representative of inverse *erhuang,* which then modulates to a principal *erhuang* primary-meter large instrumental connective, played with the standard *erhuang* 5–2 tuning. This instrumental connective then connects to the *sipingdiao* primary-meter sung melodic-passage that follows. In performance, the fixed-melody may be played by an additional *jinghu* player; the *jinghu* player who accompanies song then joins in the passage of modulation to the principal *erhuang* primary-meter large instrumental connective, and the additional *jinghu* player drops out when that modulation is complete. The fixed-melody may also be played by a single *jinghu* player, who modulates from inverse *erhuang* to primary *erhuang* through fingering alone.

Instrumental fixed-melodies played completely independently of song are also usually adapted to the *pihuang* musical system in terms of meter. However, because they are not connected to instrumental connectives, they are free of the need for modulation. Fixed-melodies performed to open or close a play, or to provide musical transitions between scenes, do not necessarily accompany specific stage action, but rather musically express the overall atmosphere of the entire play at these transition points. They are therefore usually free of any specific relation to the stage performer as well. For most plays, however, transitional music is primarily the responsibility of the percussive orchestra, as will be discussed in more detail below.

Instrumental fixed-melodies are selected on the basis of appropriateness for plot, atmosphere, and the particular situation in the scene being depicted. Many are reserved for very specific uses. For instance, "Ten-thousand Year Joy" (Wan nian huan) is for happy, celebratory occasions such as marriages and banquets. "Small Door Opening" (Xiao kai men) accompanies practical physical activities, such as walking, writing a letter, or changing clothes. And "Large Door Opening" (Da kai men) accompanies the formal entrances of high officials. Instrumental fixed-melodies are usually classified by the instruments they feature, in two main categories: "blown and struck fixed melodies" (chuida qupai), which feature a wind instrument and/or the full percussive orchestra, and "silk string fixed-melodies" (sixian qupai), which feature stringed instruments and just the clapper, clapper-drum, and/or tang drum from the percussive orchestra.

Some blown and struck fixed-melodies feature the suona as the main melodic instrument; they are known as "rough blown" (cuchui) fixed-melodies. Those that feature the horizontal bamboo flute are considered "delicate blown" (xichui) fixed-melodies. There is also a type of struck fixed-melody that is played by the percussive orchestra alone. Such fixed-melodies originally included song as well; however, only the percussive rhythm was retained, as in the pattern "Fish at the Bottom of the Water" (Shui di yu). These percussive fixed-melodies are called "dry" (gan) fixed-melodies when performed with movement, and "dry reading" (gan nian) fixed-melodies when performed with speech. They are usually considered percussive passages since they are played solely by the percussive orchestra.

All silk string fixed-melodies are considered delicate (xi). For most, the jinghu is the main melodic instrument. Some, however, feature plucked instruments—for example, the "Zither Song" (Qin ge), which is used in the play The Ruse of the Empty City (Kong cheng ji) when the character Zhuge Liang plays the zither (qin) as part of his defense strategy.

Instrumental fixed-melodies are quite adaptable. Length is often flexible, and many can be repeated a number of times in succession—for example,

"Willow Shakes Gold" *(Liu yao jin),* which is repeated several times in the play *The Favorite Concubine Becomes Intoxicated* to express intoxication. Instrumentation can also be changed, as in "Willow Green Maiden" *(Liu qing niang),* which features the *suona* when used to accompany the night battle in *Battle with Ma Chao (Zhan Ma Chao),* but becomes a silk string piece for the needlework scene in *Mistake at Huatian (Huatian cuo).*

Action-strings and fixed-melodies, then, serve both interpretive and aesthetic purposes. They establish mood and atmosphere. They make physical expression more flexible while adding an aural dimension to the movements of stage performers, and serve as part of a melodic fabric into which speech can be interjected as well. And by providing melodies that do not occur in song, they increase the melodic variety of aural performance.

FUNCTIONS OF THE PERCUSSIVE ORCHESTRA

The percussive orchestra plays in conjunction with the melodic orchestra whenever the latter performs, as a part of the full, combined orchestra. Numerous times during the course of every play, the percussive orchestra also performs independently of the melodic orchestra. The percussive orchestra creates a fabric of sound that runs throughout every Beijing opera performance, simultaneously characterizing those performances as Beijing opera and significantly contributing to the expression of atmosphere and emotions specific to each play.

In Conjunction with the Melodic Orchestra

In conjunction with the melodic orchestra, the percussive orchestra performs three basic functions. The first of course is actually provided by the conductor alone, who marks rhythm and tempo in passages of singing, instrumental connectives, action-strings, and fixed-melodies, primarily using the drum-and-clapper to do so. Under the direction of the conductor, the entire percussive orchestra plays percussive passages that serve two additional functions: they introduce and punctuate passages of singing, and of instrumental music.

Introductions

Introductory percussive passages are called "openers" *(kaitou).* They indicate the meter of the passage of singing or instrumental music that they precede, and conventionally establish the overall emotional state. For passages of singing, openers very rarely introduce the sung melodic-passages directly; in most instances, they serve to open the prelude instrumental connective, which in turn introduces the sung melodic-passage itself. The prelude instrumental connectives to passages of song almost invariably are introduced by an opener. Within a given sung melodic-passage, modulation between metrical types may include a short opener, which introduces the instrumental connective leading into the new metrical type; however, modulation may also be made by the melodic orchestra alone.

There are numerous openers, all of which are named, and each of which is expressive of a particular emotional state; for instance, several openers are used only to introduce melodic-passages composed in lead-in-meter, which are expressive of intense, unexpected emotions. A standard one is called "Lead-in-meter Opener" (*Daoban tou*, lit. "lead-in-meter head") and is played:

| d D | C d$_{///}$ | I D | C C | X

The final measure may also be played | ż d |.[23] The following examples illustrate openers frequently used to introduce the prelude instrumental connectives to sung melodic-passages in other metrical types. All are used in relatively calm situations; different openers are employed to indicate surprise, excitement, anger, fear, and other strong emotions.

"Slow Long Hammer" *(Man chang chui),* for slow-meter, fast-three-eyes meter, and primary-meter, in $\frac{4}{4}$ time:[24]

D ||: C Q D Q :|| C Q DQ D | C LQ ED C | dP DC O |

It may also be played in $\frac{2}{4}$ time:[25]

D | CQ DQ ||: ZQ DQ :|| ZQ DQD | C

"Fast Long Hammer" *(Kuai chang chui),* for two-six-meter, flowing-water-meter, fast-meter, and shaking-meter, in $\frac{2}{4}$ time (it may also be played in $\frac{1}{4}$ time):[26]

dd | E E ||: CQ DQ :|| Cd E | qQ | C LQ | ED C |

"Lightning Hammer" *(Shan chui),* also for two-six-meter, flowing-water-meter, fast-meter, and shaking-meter, in $\frac{1}{4}$ time (it may also be played in $\frac{2}{4}$ time):[27]

| 1́d́E | d́ED ||: C̲L̲ | I̲D̲ :|| C̲L̲ | I̲D̲ | C |

"Twisted Silk Threads" *(Niu si),* for dispersed-meter:[28]

| 1́d́ b̲d̲D̲ | $\widehat{C\,I}$ | $\widehat{C\,I}$ ||: C̲D̲ Q̲D̲D̲ :|| C̲D̲ I̲D̲D̲D̲ | C C |

It may also be played:[29]

| 1́d́ b̲d̲D̲ | Z̲D̲ I̲D̲ ||: Z̲D̲ I̲D̲. | Z̲D̲ I̲D̲. :|| Z̲D̲ I | Z̲O̲ C | CC |

Fixed-melodies also begin with openers, which serve the same functions as for sung melodic-passages; they indicate the meter and tempo of the instrumental music that will follow and conventionally establish the overall emotional atmosphere.

Punctuation

Playing in conjunction with the melodic orchestra, the percussive orchestra also punctuates passages of singing and instrumental music. In Chinese, this punctuating function is termed "emphasizing" *(jiazhong)* and "strengthening" *(jiaqiang)* the "tone of voice" *(yuqi)* and the dance-acting movement skill *(zuogong)* of the stage performer.

In passages of singing, the percussive orchestra may play passages after lines or couplets, creating structural markers that "simultaneously drive the music forward."[30] For instance, lines of dispersed-meter are often separated by the short percussive passage "One Hit of the Large Gong" *(Daluo yi ji),* which may be played in several different ways: B̲d C, d̲D C, d$_{///}$ C, or simply Z or C.[31] Percussive passages may also accompany performer's movements before or after songs, or between melodic-lines or couplets in place of action-strings. When they do so, there is a much greater feeling of urgency than with melodic instrumental music.

There are two important interpretive techniques for punctuating passages of singing: the "withdrawn gong" and the "sweep head" techniques. Percussive passages known collectively as the "Withdrawn Gong" *(Che luo)* may be used between melodic-lines or couplets in passages of continuous singing in which two different types of characters sing alternately. Such percussive passages are divided into two sections; the first section emphasizes one gong, and the second a different gong. For instance, a "Withdrawn Gong" passage that initially emphasizes the large gong and then emphasizes the small gong may be used to indicate a switch from an older *sheng* singer to a young *dan* singer:[32]

dD | C I Z I ||: C D I D :|| C D I D | C D I L ||: D L D L :|| D. d̲ D D |

The "sweep head" technique was discussed in chapter 3 as one of the three major techniques for varying couplet line length, one that creates a sense of interruption indicative of surprise, expectancy, or urgency. When it is employed, the percussive orchestra replaces the closing line of a couplet (other than the first couplet) with the percussive passage known as "Sweep Head" *(Sao tou)*.

In the second focal scene of the play *Yu Tangchun,* "The Tripartite Joint Trial," the dispersed-meter small aria that the title character sings just after entering the courtroom is punctuated between lines by "One Hit of the Large Gong" in one of its simplest versions: K. It is introduced by the opener "Twisted Silk Threads," as described above, and followed by the percussive passage "Sweep Head," which serves both as the final line of the last couplet and as a "dry" fixed-melody accompanying her frightened dance-acting movement:[33]

BEdd | Z̲O̲D̲ Z̲I̲ | Z̲I̲ Z̲I̲ | Z I ||: Z̲D̲ I̲D̲ :|| Z̲L̲ I̲E̲D̲ | Z d̲D | Z I | Z O |

Throughout the small aria, these percussive passages "join and extend her feelings, engulfing the audience in the mood."[34]

Within the instrumental connectives of a sung melodic-passage, or within passages of action-strings, percussive passages may be played that are related to the movement of the performer rather than to the emotional color or structure of the music. They may be subtle, not interrupting the musical piece, as for instance a strike of the small gong marking the opening of a fan or the toss of a sleeve. They may also mark a major interruption, as in the unexpected entrance of another major character or the sudden beginning of a battle. The interruption may be permanent—the passage of singing may not be returned to and concluded—or it may be temporary, with an eventual resumption of the singing. In either case, such percussive passages are usually played after the opening line of a couplet, so that the interruption of the couplet structure serves to heighten the effect.

Percussive passages may also be used in fixed-melodies. There also, they may serve to punctuate and integrate the instrumental music itself, or to punctuate the interpretive movements of the stage performer, highlighting eye, hand, head, sleeve, and foot movements as appropriate.

INDEPENDENT FUNCTIONS

The percussive orchestra performs four major functions completely independent of the melodic orchestra. It punctuates the speech of the stage performers, punctuates their movement, provides sound effects, and provides structural punctuation for each play as a whole. In all four of these functions it is still of course the conductor who controls the timing of percussive passages, so that the strikes correspond to what is transpiring on the stage, and leads the rest of the percussive orchestra in carrying out that timing.

Speech Punctuation

The percussive orchestra's speech punctuation is termed "emphasizing" (*jiazhong*) and "strengthening" (*jiaqiang*) the "tone of voice" (*yuqi*) of the stage performer—the same terminology applied to the punctuation of song in conjunction with the melodic orchestra, as discussed above. The function is indeed similar. When punctuating the speech of stage performers, the percussive orchestra plays percussive passages that serve as veritable aural punctuation marks—commas, periods, question marks, exclamation points, etc. Percussive speech punctuation may occur at regular intervals, often for syntactical purposes, or it may be used to provide dramatic stress.

Regularized punctuation is played most often for conventionalized speeches written as poetry (i.e., during the recitation of prelude and set-the-scene poems). Such punctuation is usually played for every punctuation mark that occurs in the text, serving to set off units of meaning, thereby making the meaning clearer, and to provide a rhythmic frame. For instance, in the three-line prelude poem in the first scene of *Silang Visits His Mother*, the percussive orchestra provides the following punctuation:[35]

> The *wutong* tree locked in a golden courtyard, | D D |
> A long sigh
> carried away on the breeze.   d̲ d̲ | D D |

The first percussive passage functions as a comma; the second, as a period. This formal, literal punctuation serves to heighten the effect of the recited poetry, and to set if off from the following prose speech, which lacks this regularized percussive punctuation.

The percussive orchestra also serves a regular, conventionalized purpose in its accompaniment of "count beats" (*shuban*), the rhythmically recited type of speech frequently spoken in place of other conventionalized entrance and exit speeches by *chou* performers. Here, however, there are no syntactical denotations; the clapper maintains a steady beat while the performer recites in a regular but syncopated rhythm that generally groups the written characters of each line into two units separated by a pause, as discussed in chapter 2. During the performance of a passage of "count beats," the tempo of both the strikes of the clapper and the syncopated recitation gradually increases, "each serving to drive the other on."[36]

Percussive speech punctuation that provides dramatic stress is not played at regular points. It is used rather to stress and highlight words, phrases, and pauses of special dramatic importance, much as intonation is used in English. The second focal scene of *Yu Tangchun,* "The Tripartite Joint Trial," provides a good example of such percussive speech punctuation:[37]

WANG JINLONG: Prisoner!

YU TANGCHUN: Yes.

WANG: Do you have a statement?

YU: Yes, I do.

WANG: Submit it.

YU: It . . . I can not. | d d | d dO | D — |

WANG: The court asks if you have a statement, and you say yes; when told to present it, you say you can not. Obviously you are a scheming woman.

GUARD: Judge Liu, apply torture.

JUDGE LIU: Slap her mouth!

      d̂/// | b d D Q | Z C | C C | C C | Cd D | Z I | Z I | Z — |

YU *(during percussive passage):* Your Honor!

YU *(cont'd):* I have not finished speaking—I can explain!

The first percussive passage is unnamed in the script. It serves as a period, indicating finality—it is not in Yu Tangchun's power to give Wang the written statement, because it is inside the lock of the cangue that chains her. This passage also creates an emphasized pause after her statement, stressing both characters' separate realization of what her inability means; during the pause filled by the percussive passage, the performer playing Yu Tangchun continues and builds her expression of fear, while the actor playing Wang builds his expression of anger. In this way, the impact of the following statement by Wang is increased.

The second percussive passage is known as the "Calling-out Head" *(Jiao tou).* It is expressive of fear, surprise, and urgency. The first portion of the passage serves as an aural "slap in the face" to Yu Tangchun. As the passage continues and she cries out "Your Honor!" with the gong strikes, Yu Tangchun's past history of torture and her resulting extreme fear of it are aurally recalled for the audience. The percussive passage makes it seem as though she is crying out in the midst of actually being tortured—or of vividly remembering that past experience. This central portion of the passage thereby serves to heighten Yu Tangchun's fear—to underline the words of her plea. The final portion of the passage stresses the pause in which she gathers up her courage, and pleads for the chance to explain her predicament. During the same pause, her extreme fear causes Wang to soften in his attitude toward her and prepare to hear her explanation.

Examples of percussive speech punctuation for dramatic stress in tense situations are perhaps the most striking. However, such punctuation is also used to enhance the aural expression of the full gamut of human emotions, from intense joy to utter despair, and from complacent satisfaction to raving insanity.

Movement Punctuation

Percussive passages that punctuate movement are played in conventional situations such as entrances, exits, and formal stage crosses, and throughout the dramatic action of each scene. Such punctuation is termed "emphasizing" *(jiazhong)* and "strengthening" *(jiaqiang)* the dance-acting skill *(zuogong)* of the stage performer—the same terminology applied to the punctuation of movement in conjunction with the melodic orchestra. The two applications of the independent percussive punctuation of movement are analogous to the use of percussive punctuation for both conventionalized speeches and dramatic stress.

In conventionalized situations, percussive punctuation does not punctuate specific movement per se—that is, it does not specifically mark a footfall or the swing of a hand. It rather creates a rhythmic framework for movement, which is primarily indicative of role type. For instance, the entrance walk of an older *sheng* scholar may be accompanied by the percussive passage "The Large Gong Hits the Entrance" *(Daluo da shang):*[38]

d̲D̲ ||: C̲Q̲ Q̲Q̲ | D̲Q̲ Q̲Q̲ :|| C̲Q̲ C̲Q̲ | C̲Q̲ D̲Q̲ | C̲D̲ Q ||: CQ :|| CQ̂ | C— ||

This is a stable, regular, relatively slow passage, providing a good framework for formal movements. The faster, more forceful entrance of a martial *sheng* warrior dressed for battle may be accompanied by the passage:

| Q P̲l̲d̲ | b̲d̲ D | D̂. C̲ ||

This is more suitable for several rapid movements culminating in a fierce pose. The vivacious entrance of a flower *dan* may use the pattern "Solitary Small Gong Entrance" *(Xiaoluo dan shangchang):*

D || : D D : || D d̲d̲ | D D̂O̲d̲ | D — ||

And the slower, more formal entrance of a blue cloth *dan* character may use the passage "*Dan* Small Gong Entrance" *(Xiaoluo dan shangchang):*

d̲L̲. ||: D̲.d̲ d̲d̲ | d̲d̲ d̲L̲. :|| D d̲i̲L̲ | D̲L̲ D | d̲ d̲i̲O̲ | D — ||

The punctuation of conventional movement is not, however, simply formulaic. There are numerous percussive passages for every role type, each of which connotes a different sort of entrance, exit, or cross. For the same role type, a major character's entrance is punctuated with a different percussive passage than that used for a minor character, a first entrance is punctuated differently than a later entrance, hurried entrances are punctuated differently than leisurely entrances, and so on. Moreover, many percussive passages can be used to punctuate the conventional movements of more than one role type; for example, the rapid entrance of a flirtatious flower *dan* bent on mischief may be punctuated by the same percussive passage as the rapid entrance of a mischievous *chou* with the same sort of intentions. The percussive punctuation of conventionalized movement is a highly flexible system for aurally indicating role type and general atmosphere at transition points within each play.

Percussive passages for punctuating dance-acting movements performed during the dramatic action of a play are even more numerous and have a broader range of complexity. Frequently the simplest movements of a major character are punctuated by single percussive strikes; that is, each completed movement in the process of writing a letter, having a drink, miming the opening of a window or door, or miming going up or down stairs may be punctuated by a percussive strike, lending aural substance to those commonplace actions. The more interpretively significant head and eye movements of a major character going through a process of thought and realization or decision are likewise accented by percussive strikes, as are gestures of anger, frustration, and determination. The walk of a major character pacing in frustration is punctuated throughout by a percussive passage; the same character's walk while pacing in fear is punctuated by a different percussive passage, selected for its suitability to the precise mood and conditions as well as the role type. The emotional reactions of two lovers meeting after a long separation are accented by percussive strikes and passages; two old friends meeting after years apart also have their emotional reactions accented, but with different strikes and passages, placed and played in a different manner, making clear the difference in the two types of relationships.

Percussive strikes and passages also punctuate the performance of combat skill. The percussive orchestra performs "fight openers" *(kaida)* that vary in composition and duration according to the type of combat that is to follow. Within the combat itself, all major movements and postures are punctuated by the percussive orchestra—such punctuation is vital in coordinating entrances, exits, and complex group combat sequences. Moreover, this punctuation provides an aural expression of the combat itself. The percussive punctuation of dance-acting and combat movement gives aural expression to the physical expression of emotion and action.

Sound Effects

The two functions of the independent percussive orchestra already described are concerned with the accompaniment of specific words or actions of the stage performers. The third major function deals with general atmosphere, and the conventionally evoked mise-en-scene—the percussive orchestra provides the sound effects of the natural and man-made environments.

Rain, snow, wind, darkness, cold, heat, and the presence of large bodies of water are among the features of the natural environment whose presence can be evoked by specialized percussive strikes and passages. Some are readily recognizable; the waves of rising and falling pitches of sound produced by rubbing the two cymbals together in circular motions directly resemble the gentle creaking of the metal fittings on a floating boat as well as the soft lapping of small waves. Supplementary percussion instruments provide immediately recognizable sounds such as the clop of horses' hooves and the cries of birds. The *suona* sometimes joins the percussive orchestra in providing immediately recognizable sound effects, as discussed above; its broad range of timbre allows it to sound like both the neigh of a horse and the cry of a baby. Other sound effects are more conventionalized and require prior knowledge on the part of the audience. For instance, the short passage "Cold Gong" *(Leng luo)* can be used to signal that it is in fact cold. It is most

often played b̲ d̲. O Z̲ O or b̲l̲d̲ Z̲.[39] These strikes, however, evoke cold solely by convention. The more lengthy pattern "Nine Hammers and a Half" *(Jiu chui ban),* which has several possible playing methods, most of which include nine *cang* (C) and one *kang* (Z), is often used to punctuate movement in the dark, especially the search for objects and other groping actions. It likewise conventionally rather than directly suggests the absence of light.

Sounds of the man-made environment are usually immediately recognizable rather than conventional. For instance, *kang* (Z) or *kong* (K) is played for the striking of a nightwatch, a *dei* (D) for the slipping home of a bolt on a door or window, a *da da da* (ddd) or *zha zha zha* (XXX) for a knock on the door. Supplementary percussion instruments likewise provide sounds such as the creak of hinges and the thud of falling objects.

Structural Punctuation

The fourth major function of the independent percussive orchestra is to provide structural punctuation within the context of each whole play. The percussive orchestra opens each play with one of several percussive passages known collectively as "scene openers" *(kaichang)*, provides transitions between scenes with passages known collectively as "scene shifters" *(zhuanchang)*, and closes each play with one of several passages known as "tail sounds" *(weisheng,* often translated as "coda"; these closing passages are also known as "conclusions," *jieshu).* The melodic orchestra may join the percussive to play fixed-melodies for these transitional situations. When it does, "rough blown" fixed-melodies featuring the *suona* are most often employed. But the melodic orchestra is not necessary—the percussive orchestra is responsible for punctuation and transition within the play as a whole, just as it is in movement and speech and even, to a considerable degree, in song. These passages of structural punctuation are the only instances of orchestral music featured independently of the song, speech, and movement of the stage performers.

Many different percussive passages can be used to open a play. One of the most frequently used is "Charging Head" *(Chong tou):*[40]

d d$_{///}$ ||: C I :|| $\underline{C\ I}$ $\underline{C\ O}$ ||

In pre-Liberation China, scene openers were played to announce that the action of the play was about to begin. Since 1949 and the advent of the act curtain and darkened auditorium throughout *xiqu* performance, scene openers generally begin as the lights start to dim and continue throughout the opening of the curtain. When these opening passages are completed, they are then frequently followed by a second percussive passage, accompanying the conventional movements of the first character's entrance. The pre-Liberation purpose of the percussive scene opener, then, is simply accentuated by this addition of lighting change and curtain—the percussive orchestra signals that the play is opening and serves to draw attention to the stage before the action of the play actually begins.

Scene shifters were traditionally played while stage assistants arranged or removed tables and/or chairs between scenes. In contemporary China, they occur in conjunction with the curtain; it is closed, the scene is changed behind it, and it opens again, all to the sound of percussive passages. Such passages are generally designed to begin with the atmosphere present at the end of the scene that has just closed, and then to "modulate" to the atmosphere present at the opening of the next scene. For instance, if a scene in which an older *sheng* has presided as judge or high official has just been completed, the transitional percussive passages will probably begin with passages that are fairly slow in tempo and feature the large gong. Then, if a battle scene is to occur next, the passages will increase in tempo and volume of sound, adding a greater number of cymbal strikes while maintaining the dominance of the large gong. If the scene change is from one featuring an older *sheng,* a martial *sheng,* or a *jing* to one featuring a young *sheng* or a *dan,* the "withdrawn gong" technique mentioned above may be used, switching dominance from the large gong to the small gong. The same is of course true in reverse.

In pre-Liberation times, tail sounds were played until all characters had exited the stage. In contemporary China, tail sounds begin as the last sounds or movements of the play are occurring and continue until the curtain is closed. Because most plays have modified happy *(tuanyuan)* endings, most end with the percussive orchestra playing "rough blown" fixed-melodies in ensemble with the *suona,* thereby indicating the auspiciousness of the occasion.

The percussive orchestra creates a fabric of sound and rhythm that runs throughout every Beijing opera performance. By adding this aural dimension to all movement, and highlighting and punctuating speech and song, the percussive orchestra appreciably enlarges the "life" presented on the stage. Its importance is perhaps most clearly illustrated by an all-pervasive rehearsal technique. The percussive orchestra does not participate in early rehearsals. Throughout these rehearsals, every performer speaks those percussive strikes and passages that accent his or her song, speech, and movement, just as each sings the instrumental connectives between his or her sung melodic-passages; these percussive strikes and passages are also inseparable from each performer's vocal and physical expression.

CHAPTER VII

THE INTERRELATION

OF COMPONENTS IN

AURAL PERFORMANCE

THE aural performance of Beijing opera consists of four components in interrelation—language, musical system, voice, and orchestra. Each of these components is internally a highly complex system; their interrelationships are complex as well. The most fundamental relationship among these components may be described as that of substance to sound—the relationship of the material that is performed to the actual sound in performance. An examination of the meaning of this relationship will help to clarify the more complex relationships among the four components, and to relate the components of aural performance to the overall aesthetic aim of the total performance of Beijing opera.

The substance of aural performance—the material that is performed—is supplied by the first two components, language and musical system. In a very important sense, both of these components may be considered languages—both aim to convey specific meanings through the arrangement of basic compositional units within specified structural patterns. In the Chinese language of the script, words—individual written-characters—are the smallest compositional units. They are arranged in sentences according to grammatical structure and the compositional patterns provided by speech types and lyric types. In the *pihuang* language of the music, individual pitches are the smallest compositional units. They are arranged in melodic-phrases, *dou,* lines, and couplets according to the structural patterns provided by metrical types, modes, and modal systems, and the compositional patterns provided by song types.

The Chinese language of the script occurs independently of the *pihuang* musical system in speech. And the language of the *pihuang* musical system is employed independently of the Chinese language in instrumental connectives. The two languages coexist in those instrumental connectives and pas-

THE CHINESE LANGUAGE OF THE SCRIPT

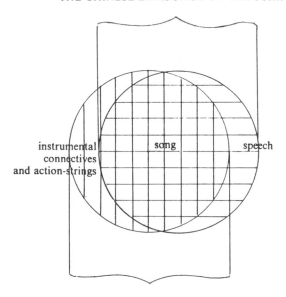

instrumental
connectives
and action-strings
song
speech

THE *PIHUANG* MUSICAL SYSTEM

sages of action-strings that include interjected speech. But in song, they are joined in a vital, symbiotic relationship.

Each of the written-characters in a script denotes a specific meaning by itself. Through combination with other written-characters, larger units of meaning are created. Individual pitches in the *pihuang* music for song are not indicative of specific meanings in themselves. Within melodic-phrases, they serve first of all to clarify the denotative meaning of each written-character by indicating its speech-tone. Within the larger context of *dou,* lines, and couplets, however, melodies interpretively composed according to the patterns of a specific metrical type, mode, modal system, and song type musically express the connotations of words as well as the emotional implications of words and sentences. In other words, the *pihuang* music composed for a given play expresses specific affective meanings—evokes specific emotions, feelings, and moods—that are based upon, but not directly expressed by, the Chinese language of the script.

There are several levels of denotative meaning in the Chinese language of the script, and several levels of affective meaning in the *pihuang* language of the music. The language of the script ranges from quite realistic language, in which denotation is the major aim and vernacular Chinese predominates, to

very stylized language, in which the aesthetic as well as the denotative qualities of sound are highly valued and classical Chinese predominates. The
most realistic language is that of prose speeches (principally dialogue),
which advance the plot and convey humor. Prose speeches are written primarily in vernacular language, though the amount of classical Chinese
included in prose speeches varies somewhat with role type. Conventionalized speeches and quotations from the classics are more stylized. Conventionalized speeches, which occur at transition points within the structure of
each play, contain classical Chinese language more regularly than do prose
speeches and provide a conventional aural structure running throughout all
Beijing opera plays. Passages quoted directly from classical writings are
written entirely in classical Chinese and are often employed to convey emotion through analogy. The most stylized language, however, is that written
for song lyrics. Song lyrics are stylized both in content, expressing emotion
within lyric types in predominantly classical language, and in form—that is,
in the use of lyric structure, rhyme, and speech-tone patterns.

The language of the music ranges from densely affective expression, in
which subtle nuances of emotion are conveyed in detail, to more conventional affective suggestion. The densest affective expression occurs in arias
composed in the melismatic, slower metrical types. Such arias have the most
pitch occurrences per melodic-phrase (that is, per written-character), and
therefore the most opportunity for the musical expression of emotion; arias
composed in more syllabic, faster metrical types are of necessity briefer in
their affective expression. Small songs composed for conventionalized lyrics
and elevated speech in essence telegraph affective statements—they are too
fast and syllabic to contain an appreciable amount of nuanced expression.
Instrumental connectives, which do not have the compositional flexibility of
sung passages, are limited to conventional affective suggestion made
through the introduction, continuance, and conclusion of specific metrical
types within specific modes. Action-strings similarly provide conventional
affective suggestion.

In song, the most highly stylized verbal language is joined with that range
of the musical language that includes the most densely nuanced affective
expression. To comprehend and appreciate the substance of song, audience
members must therefore be fluent in both these languages. They must
instantly understand the denotative meaning of every written-character in
the Chinese language of the lyrics and be fully aware of the aesthetic values
attached to the stylization of the lyrics in content and form. Equally importantly, they must immediately understand the affective meaning of each

melodic-passage in the *pihuang* language of the music, as conveyed by the combination of selected modal system, mode, metrical type, and song type, and by the composition of the specific melodic progression. Only when fluent in both the Chinese language and the language of the *pihuang* musical system can audience members both appreciate skillful composition in the two languages and be moved by the thoughts and emotions that they respectively convey.

Actual sound in aural performance is provided by the second two components—the voice of the stage performer and the instruments of the orchestra. The featured component of aural performance is the stage performer's display of the vocal skills—song and speech. The orchestra supports and accompanies that display. In displaying vocal skill, the stage performer gives sound to both the Chinese and the *pihuang* languages. Individual techniques of vocal production, song, and speech serve different purposes in relation to the two languages.

Some techniques, while aesthetically important, are designed primarily to clarify the denotative aspects of the Chinese language. These techniques include careful pronunciation of the four vowel types *(sihu)*, the five consonant types *(wuyin)*, and the pointed and rounded qualities of sound in both

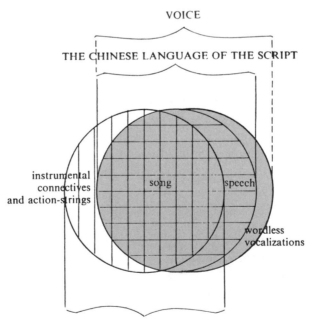

song and speech, and the use of segmented and direct pronunciation in song. Other techniques are primarily intended to enhance the aesthetic qualities of the Chinese language as sound: the delivery of rhymed speech with pleasing patterns of intonation and rhythm, and the delivery of all speech with both variety and emphasis. Finally, certain techniques both enhance the aesthetic sound qualities of the Chinese language and, through their selective use by certain role types, serve as conventional aural indicators of those role types. It might be useful therefore to refer to such techniques, which serve conventional, typifying purposes as well as aesthetic purposes, as typic techniques. They include special Beijing opera pronunciation in both speech and song, and heightened and colloquial speech and wordless vocalizations in speech. Because wordless vocalizations do not give sound to the Chinese language per se, but rather give direct expression to feelings, these techniques of the voice are in a sense actually outside the scope of the Chinese language.

The Chinese language is joined with the language of the *pihuang* musical system in song. Certain vocal techniques are therefore designed to enhance the aesthetic qualities of sound in both languages simultaneously. These techniques, all of which apply to both song and speech, include breath control; use of the controlled breath to control the pitch and timbre *(tiao qi)* and the energy flow *(jin)* of vocal production, and to produce spray-mouth *(penkou)* and back-of-the-head sound *(naohouyin)* projection; and apparently effortless high pitch. Other techniques also enhance the aesthetic sound qualities of both languages, but additionally serve as conventional aural indicators of role type (i.e., they are typic techniques). These typic techniques, all of which apply to both song and speech, include the large-voice and the small-voice, and emphasis upon particular resonating cavities to produce specific vocal timbres. Finally, certain vocal techniques—the majority of the specialized techniques for song—serve solely to enhance the aesthetic qualities of sound in the language of the *pihuang* musical system. These vocal techniques are therefore used only in song. They include empty-words, the Beijing opera vibrato *(chanyin* and *bolangyin),* and the production of round but sharply focused tones in weaving, "round" melodic passages.

The different purposes served by vocal techniques in relation to the two languages of Beijing opera divide the entire body of vocal techniques into three main types: those that serve denotative as well aesthetic purposes, those that serve typic as well as aesthetic purposes, and those that serve solely aesthetic purposes. Figure 26 illustrates the interelation of these three

Figure 26

The Interrelation of Languages, Vocal Skills, and Vocal Techniques

Language	Type of Technique			Skill
	Denotative and Aesthetic	Typic and Aesthetic	Solely Aesthetic	
Chinese	four vowel types five consonant types pointed and rounded sounds	heightened speech colloquial speech wordless vocalizations	patterns of intonation and rhythm in ryhmed speech variety and emphasis in all speech	Specialized Speech Techniques
Chinese and *Pihuang*	segmented and direct pronunciation	special Beijing opera pronunciation		Techniques for Both Song and Speech
		large-voice small-voice emphasis on particular resonating cavities to produce specific vocal timbres	breath control control pitch control timbre control energy flow spray-mouth projection back-of-the-head-sound projection effortless high pitch	
Pihuang			empty-words Beijing opera vibrato round but sharply focused tones in weaving, "round" melodic-passages	Specialized Song Techniques

types of vocal techniques, two languages of Beijing opera, and two skills of vocal performance.

Denotative techniques are associated primarily with the Chinese language; typic and aesthetic techniques with both languages. The majority of techniques in all three categories are employed in both speech and song. However, although the specialized techniques of speech derive from the Chinese language, those of song derive from both the Chinese and the *pihuang* languages. Because the language of the *pihuang* musical system and the Chinese language of the script are joined in song, it is in the display of song skill that the widest variety of vocal techniques is required.

Facility in the performance of vocal techniques is the primary emphasis in the display of speech skill in performance, and is an important part of the display of song skill. It requires not only technical ability on the part of the stage performer, but also the skillful cooperation of script writers. Script writers must pay careful attention to certain aspects of writing that affect the performance of typic and aesthetic techniques in both song and speech. Among these are role-type preferences for rhyme categories; role-type preferences for language levels; lyric structure; rhyme in lyrics; speech-tone patterns in lyrics; structure and rhyme in conventionalized speeches; and the aesthetic qualities of vowels, consonants, and rhyme categories. If a script were to be written without these aspects in mind, the full utilization of typic and aesthetic techniques in the display of both song and speech skill would not be possible.

The major aim of the display of skill, however, is the expression of emotion—and in the aural performance of Beijing opera, emotion is expressed most fully in song. The stage performers themselves are responsible for the composition of affective meaning—for the composition of the music of song. The performance of song not only gives sound to the Chinese and *pihuang* languages, but also displays the skill with which affective meaning has been composed in the *pihuang* language. The display of compositional skill is an integral part of the total display of song skill. It is also the source of affective meaning in aural performance—it is the actual expression given to emotion. The display of speech skill, which gives sound only to the Chinese language, provides the focusing vocal setting for the expression of emotion in song.

The sound of the orchestra supports and accompanies the stage performer throughout every Beijing opera performance. To see clearly the relationships of the orchestra to the other three components of aural performance, it is helpful to consider the two sections of the orchestra—the melodic and the percussive—separately.

The melodic orchestra is employed almost entirely within the spheres of the *pihuang* language and the voice—its primary function is the accompaniment of song. In fulfilling this function, the melodic orchestra serves both affective and aesthetic purposes—it supports and assists the stage performers in their expressions of emotion in the *pihuang* language. However, song accompaniment serves an important additional aesthetic function as well—it provides variations on the melody of the stage performer. In playing instrumental connectives *(guomen)*, which are closely related to song, the melodic orchestra introduces, connects, and concludes affective expression by giving sound to conventional affective suggestion. Instrumental connectives, while separate from the performance of vocal techniques, are still part of the *pihuang* language, as are action-strings *(xingxian)*. Only in playing fixed-melodies *(qupai)*, whose principal purposes are the primarily affective and aesthetic ones of setting atmosphere and/or providing melodic accompaniment for movement, does the melodic orchestra exceed the bounds of the *pihuang* language.

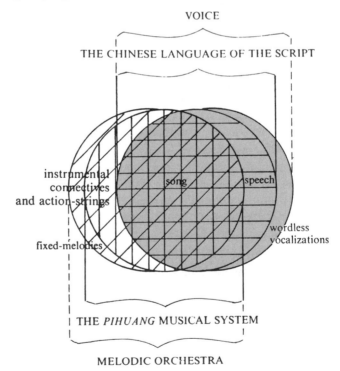

The percussive orchestra joins the melodic orchestra in supporting and accompanying the sung vocalization of the *pihuang* language, and in playing action-strings and fixed-melodies. Independently, it also provides speech and movement punctuation, sound effects, and structural punctuation for every performance.

Dramatic punctuation for speech may be considered affective as well as aesthetic, because it heightens the expression of emotion in the Chinese language. Regularized speech punctuation is both denotative and aesthetic in this sense, because it emphasizes and clarifies the expression of meaning in the Chinese language. But it also serves a typic purpose by aurally identifying conventional, transitional speeches. Sound effects, movement punctuation, and structural punctuation are independent functions of the percussive orchestra that occur completely outside the bounds of both the Chinese and the *pihuang* languages.

Sound effects may be considered denotative as well as aesthetic in that they denote the sounds of the natural and man-made environment within the aural performance of Beijing opera. Dramatic movement punctuation is affective and aesthetic, serving to emphasize and characterize emotionally the physical expression of the stage performers. Conventional movement punctuation is both typic and affective, aurally identifying role type and indicating state of mind. Structural punctuation can likewise be considered both typic and affective—each passage sets a particular atmosphere while collectively they give an aural structure to every Beijing opera performance that serves to typify those performances as Beijing opera.

Figure 27 illustrates this interrelation of aural components, orchestra sections, and orchestral function.

The percussive orchestra provides a pervasive fabric of sound running throughout the totality of every Beijing opera performance. It joins with the voices of the stage performers in giving sound to the Chinese language in speech, and with the melodic orchestra and the voices in giving sound to both the Chinese and the *pihuang* languages in song. Those of its functions that are independent of the other three components of aural performance then serve to unify the full performance aurally, typifying all performances as Beijing opera and lending an aural dimension to the visual, physical expression of the stage performers.

Only in the performance of song are all four components of aural performance—the Chinese language of the script, the *pihuang* language of the music, the voices of the stage performers, and the sounds of both the melodic and the percussive orchestras—simultaneously combined. Song is

Figure 27

The Interrelation of Orchestral Sections, Orchestral Functions, and the Other Components of Aural Performance

Orchestral Section	Type of Orchestral Function			Other Components
	Denotative and Aesthetic	Typic and Aesthetic	Affective and Aesthetic	
Melodic and Percussive			song accompaniment / instrumental connectives / action-strings / fixed-melodies	Chinese, *Pihuang*, and Voice
Percussive	regularized speech punctuation / sound effects	regularized speech punctuation	dramatic speech punctuation	Chinese and Voice
		conventional movement punctuation	conventional movement punctuation	
		structural punctuation	dramatic movement punctuation	
			structural punctuation	

Figure 28
The Interrelation of Components in Aural Performance

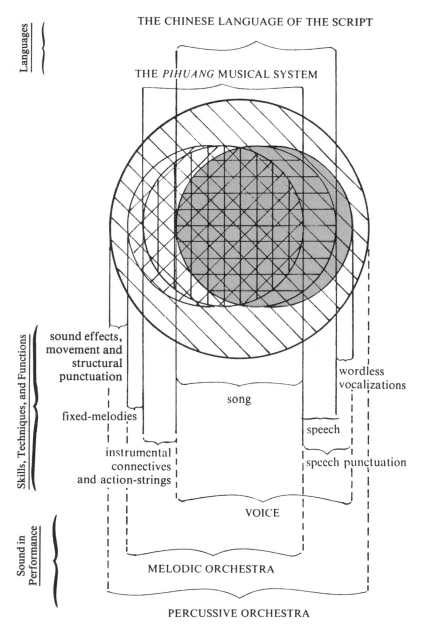

Languages {

THE CHINESE LANGUAGE OF THE SCRIPT

THE *PIHUANG* MUSICAL SYSTEM

Skills, Techniques, and Functions {

sound effects,
movement and
structural
punctuation

fixed-melodies

instrumental
connectives
and action-strings

song

wordless
vocalizations

speech

speech punctuation

Sound in Performance {

VOICE

MELODIC ORCHESTRA

PERCUSSIVE ORCHESTRA

dramatically, structurally, and aesthetically the heart of aural performance. Figure 28 illustrates this focal position of song within the interrelated components of aural performance.

The total performance of Beijing opera aims first to strike its audience with a resemblance to life, and then to transcend that resemblance and convey the very essence of life. This aim is facilitated by the interrelation of the components of aural performance. The most denotative aspect of aural performance—speech as conversational dialogue in the furtherance of plot— allows the performance of Beijing opera to strike its audience with a resemblance to the social interaction of everyday life in traditional China. The pervasive percussive orchestra and the entire body of vocal techniques in conjunction with the combined percussive and melodic orchestras create a separate, aural world for Beijing opera, one in which the transcendence of mere resemblance is possible. This separate aural world is further established through the performance of the typic techniques of the voice, and the typic functions of the orchestra. The typic techniques of the voice ceaselessly identify the role types of Beijing opera throughout vocal performance. Together, the voice and the orchestra give sound to conventionalized lyrics, marking transitions; independently, the percussive orchestra provides a typifying aural structure for all Beijing opera performances.

The aural performance of Beijing opera fully transcends everyday life in song. Through the display of song skill, fully utilizing the techniques of the voice, and supported and accompanied by both the melodic and the percussive orchestras, the stage performer vocalizes the Chinese language of the script and the *pihuang* language of the music. In this concentrated expression of affective and denotative meaning, presented in a synthesis of denotative, typic, aesthetic, and affective sound, the essence of human feeling in traditional Chinese society is captured and movingly displayed.

MUSICAL NOTATION

All musical transcription in this book is in cipheric notation *(jianpu)*. In this system, numbers are assigned to relative pitches: 1 = do, 2 = re, 3 = mi, 4 = fa, 5 = so, 6 = la, 7 = ti. With two exceptions, the relative pitches are the same as those in the standard Western octave. However, the Beijing opera fa is between a sharp and a natural Western fa, and the Beijing opera ti is slightly lower than a Western ti. Silence (a rest) is indicated by zero. Dots placed under numbers lower their register one octave (i.e., 1̣ is an octave lower than 1); dots above numbers raise their register one octave (i.e., 1̇ is an octave higher than 1). Metric divisions are shown by bar lines: | 1 2 | 3 4 | is duple meter; | 1 2 3 4 | 5 6 7 0 | is quadruple meter.

Duration is indicated in this system by underlining: a single underline halves the duration of a pitch, a double underline quarters duration, a triple underline reduces duration to one-eighth of the original value, etc. For example, in the measure | 1 2 3 4 5 6 7 0 7 |, each of the four groups of pitches has the same duration. The 1, 2, 4, and 5 are each half as long as the 3; the 6, 7s, and 0 (a rest) are each one-quarter as long as the 3. Uneven rhythmic divisions are shown by internal dots: a dot following a note increases its duration by one-half of its original duration. For example, in the measure | 1 2 3. 4 5 6 7 |, each group of pitches again has the same duration. The 1, 2, 5, and 6 are each half as long as the 7; the 3 is three-quarters of the 7, and the 4 is one-quarter of the 7. In most Beijing opera cipheric scores, a note represented by a number with no underlining is analogous to a quarter note in staff notation.

A note sounded before or after another note as an accessory to it *(zhuang-shiyin,* grace note) is written higher than the main row of numbers, is attached to the note with which it is associated, and "steals" its duration from the associated main note. For example, in $\overset{3}{\leq} 2$, the 3 accounts for one-quarter of the duration assigned to the 2; and in $5 \overset{6}{7}$, the 6 accounts for one-half the duration of the 5.

All Beijing opera performers and musicians are trained in cipheric notation, and most read and write it fluently. It is a very convenient notation system for Beijing opera. Key in the Western sense can change many times in the same Beijing opera performance, and performers often use different keys for different performances of the same play. The principal melodic accompaniment for Beijing opera is provided by stringed instruments that can be retuned quite easily to accommodate these key changes. Cipheric notation therefore obviates the need for laborious, written transpositions of scores. Because it is the system in general use in China and is simple to read and understand, it is employed in this study.

THE SOUNDS IN MANDARIN CHINESE †

A. Initial Consonants

Aesthetic Quality	Pinyin Spelling	I.P.A. Symbols	Linguistic Description	Pronunciation Guide
Clear sounds (*qingyin*)	b	p	voiceless unaspirated bilabial stop	'b' as in *box*
	d	t	voiceless unaspirated alveolar stop	'd' as in *day*
	z	ts	voiceless unaspirated alveolar affricate	'dz' as in *adze*
	j	tɕ	voiceless unaspirated alveolopalatal affricate	'j' as in *jeans**
	zh	tʂ	voiceless unaspirated retroflex affricate	'j' as in *jaws**
	g	k	voiceless unaspirated velar stop	'g' as in *go*
	p	pʰ	voiceless aspirated bilabial stop	'p' as in *put*
	t	tʰ	voiceless aspirated alveolar stop	't' as in *tame*
	c	tsʰ	voiceless aspirated alveolar affricate	'ts' as in *cats*
	q	tɕʰ	voiceless aspirated alveolopalatal affricate	'ch' as in *cheat**
	ch	tʂʰ	voiceless aspirated retroflex affricate	'ch' as in *chaw**
	k	kʰ	voiceless aspirated velar stop	'k' as in *keg*
	f	f	voiceless labiodental fricative	'f' as in *fair*
	s	s	voiceless alveolar fricative	's' as in *so*
	x	ɕ	voiceless alveclopalatal fricative	'sh' as in *she**
	sh	ʂ	voiceless retroflex fricative	'sh' as in *shawl**
	r	ʐ	voiced retroflex fricative	'r' as in *run*
	h	x	voiceless velar fricative (sometimes glottal)	'h' as in *hot*
Thick sounds (*zhuoyin*)	m	m	bilabial nasal	'm' as in *mut*
	n	n	alveolar nasal	'n' as in *nut*
	l	l	alveolar lateral	'l' as in *low*

(*continued*)

†Compiled with the assistance of Professor Iovanna Condax of the Department of Linguistics, University of Hawaii.

*In English, each of these three pairs of sounds is very similar. However, there is a small difference in each case caused by the quality of the following vowels. While these differences are not phonemic—i.e., critical to distinguishing meaning—in English, they are in Chinese.

The Sounds In Mandarin Chinese (*continued*)

B. Terminal Consonants [Nasal Finals]

Pinyin Spelling	I.P.A. Symbols	Linguistic Description	Pronunciation Guide
n	n	alveolar nasal	'n' as in *run*
ng	ŋ	velar nasal	'ng' as in *ring*

C. [Final] Vowels

Aesthetic Quality	Rhyme Category	*Pinyin* Spelling	I.P.A. Symbols	Linguistic Description	Pronunciation Guide
Yang	fa hua	a	ɑ	low back unrounded vowel	'a' as in *father*
		ia	jɑ	diphthong consisting of unrounded palatal on-glide followed by low back unrounded vowel	'ya' as in *yacht*
		ua	wɑ	diphthong consisting of rounded labiovelar on-glide followed by low back unrounded vowel	'wa' as in *wattle*
	yan qian	an	ɑ̃n	low back unrounded nasalized vowel followed by alveolar nasal	'an' as in *Khan*
		ian	jɛ̃n	unrounded palatal on-glide followed by lower-mid front unrounded nasalized vowel followed by alveolar nasal	*yen*
		uan	wɑ̃n	rounded labiovelar on-glide followed by low back unrounded nasalized vowel followed by alveolar nasal	'wan' as in *wander*
		üan	yɛ̃n	rounded palatal on-glide followed by nasalized lower-mid front unrounded vowel followed by alveolar nasal	'u' as in French *tu* and 'ü' in German *müde*, plus 'en' as in *yen*

ren chen	en	ə̃n	nasalized schwa followed by alveolar nasal	'en' as in *chicken*
	in	ĩn	nasalized high front unrounded vowel followed by alveolar nasal	'ean' as in *lean*
	uen (un)†	wə̃n	rounded labiovelar on-glide followed by nasalized schwa followed by alveolar nasal	*one*
	ün	ỹn (ɥə̃n)	nasalized high front rounded vowel followed by alveolar nasal (schwa optional)	'u' as in French *tu* and 'ü' in German *müde* plus 'n', or optionally 'un', as in *run*
jiang yang	ang	ɑ̃ŋ	nasalized low back unrounded vowel followed by velar nasal	'a' as in *father* plus 'ng' as in *ring*
	iang	jɑ̃ŋ	unrounded palatal on-glide followed by nasalized low back unrounded vowel followed by velar nasal	'ee' as in *see* plus 'a' as in *father* plus 'ng' as in *ring*
	uang	wɑ̃ŋ	rounded labiovelar on-glide followed by nasalized low back unrounded vowel followed by velar nasal	'o' as in *who* plus 'a' as in *father* plus 'ng' as in *ring*
zhong dong	eng	ə̃ŋ	nasalized schwa followed by velar nasal	'ung' as in *lung*
	ong	ɔ̃ŋ	nasalized lower-mid back rounded vowel followed by velar nasal	'o' as in *boy* plus 'ng' as in *ring*
	ing	ĩŋ	nasalized lower-high front unrounded vowel followed by velar nasal	'ing' as in *sing*
	iong	jɔ̃ŋ	unrounded palatal on-glide followed by nasalized lower-mid back rounded vowel followed by velar nasal	'ee' as in *see* plus 'o' as in *boy* plus 'ng' as in *ring*
	ueng	wə̃ŋ	rounded labiovelar on-glide followed by nasalized schwa followed by velar nasal	'wo' as in *won* plus 'ng' as in *ring*
Low-level Yin *suo bo*	e	ɤ	mid back unrounded vowel	*uh*, but with the tongue pulled back in the mouth
	o	ɔ	lower-mid back rounded vowel	'o' as in *boy*
	uo	ɔw	diphthong consisting of rounded labiovelar on-glide followed by lower-mid back rounded vowel	'wa' as in British *war* ('r' not pronounced)
huai lai	ai	ɑu	diphthong consisting of low back unrounded vowel followed by unrounded palatal off-glide	'ie' as in *lie*
	uai	wɑu	triphthong consisting of rounded labiovelar on-glide followed by low back unrounded vowel followed by unrounded palatal off-glide	'wi' as in *wide*

(continued)

The Sounds In Mandarin Chinese (*continued*)

C. [Final] Vowels (*continued*)

Aesthetic Quality	Rhyme Category	*Pinyin* Spelling	I.P.A. Symbols	Linguistic Description	Pronunciation Guide
Low-level *Yin* (cont'd)	*yao tiao*	ao	ɑʊ	diphthong consisting of low back unrounded vowel followed by rounded labiovelar off-glide	'ou' as in *loud*
		iao	jɑʊ	triphthong consisting of unrounded palatal on-glide followed by low back unrounded vowel followed by rounded labiovelar off-glide	*yeow!*
	you qiu	ou	oʊ	diphthong consisting of mid back rounded vowel followed by rounded labiovelar off-glide	'ow' as in *low*
		iou (iu)†	joʊ	triphthong consisting of unrounded palatal on-glide followed by mid back rounded vowel followed by rounded labiovelar off-glide	'yo' as in *yodel*
High-level *Yin*	*yi qi*	i*	i	high front unrounded vowel	'ee' as in *see*
		ü	y	high front rounded vowel	'u' as in French *tu* and 'ü' in German *müde*
		zhiᴬ	tʂɻ̩	initial consonant followed by retroflex vowel	a voiced vocalic prolongation of the retroflex 'j' in *jaw*
		chiᴬ	tʂʰɻ̩	initial consonant followed by retroflex vowel	a voiced vocalic prolongation of the retroflex 'ch' in *chaw*
		shiᴬ	ʂɻ̩	initial consonant followed by retroflex vowel	a voiced vocalic prolongation of the retroflex 'sh' in *shawl*
		riᴬ	ʐɻ̩	initial consonant followed by retroflex vowel	a voiced vocalic prolongation of the retroflex 'r' in *run*

*zi*ᐃ	tsɿ]	initial consonant followed by apical vowel	a voiced vocalic prolongation of the alveolar 'dz' in *adze*
*ci*ᐃ	tsʰɿ]	initial consonant followed by apical vowel	a voiced vocalic prolongation of the alveolar 'ts' in *cats*
*si*ᐃ	sɿ]	initial consonant followed by apical vowel	a voiced vocalic prolongation of the alveolar 's' in *sew*
gu su u*	u	high back rounded vowel	'o' as in *who*
mie xie ê	ɛ	lower-mid front unrounded vowel (except as an exclamatory sound, occurs only after /i/ and /ü/, and before /i/)	'e' as in *bet*
ie	jɛ	diphthong consisting of unrounded palatal on-glide followed by lower-mid front unrounded vowel	*yeh*
üe	yɛ	diphthong consisting of rounded palatal on-glide followed by lower-mid front unrounded vowel	'u' as in French *tu* and 'ü' in German *müde*, plus 'eh' as in *yeh*
hui dui ei	eɪ	diphthong consisting of mid front unrounded vowel followed by unrounded palatal off-glide	'ay' as in *hay*
uei (ui)†	weɪ	triphthong consisting of rounded labiovelar on-glide followed by mid front unrounded vowel followed by unrounded palatal off-glide	*way*

†In these three instances, the *pinyin* spelling used in practice is a shortened version of the actual sounds pronounced. The initial entry gives the full complement of sounds, and the spelling in common use follows in parentheses.

*/i/ and /u/ sometimes serve as initial consonants. They are termed "semi-vowels" when they do so, and are written 'y' and 'w' respectively. Hence in the *fa hua* rhyme category /ia/ may occur as *ya* and /ua/ as *wa*; in *yan qian*, /ian/ may occur as *yan* and /uan/ as *wan*; in *ren chen*, /in/ as *yin* /uen/ (/un/) as *wen*; in *jiang yang*, /iang/ as *yang* and /uang/ as *wang*; in *zhong dong*, /ing/ as *ying*, /iong/ as *yong*, and /ueng/ as *weng*; in *huai lai*, /uai/ as *wai*; in *yao tiao*, /iao/ as *yao*; and in *you qiu*, /iou/ (/iu/) as *you*.

ᐃThese sounds are not in fact final vowels, since they consist of both an initial consonant and a vowel. However, retroflex and apical vowels occur in Mandarin Chinese only when preceded by these consonants; they are therefore listed in this manner here.

(continued)

Certain combinations of final vowels and initial consonants are restricted. Any final vowel beginning with /u/ may not be preceded by /j/, /q/, /x/, or the semi-vowel /y/; and any final vowel beginning with /ü/ may be preceded only by /j/, /l/, /n/, /q/, /x/, and the semi-vowel /y/. A /ü/ following /j/, /q/, /x/, or the semi-vowel /y/ is therefore usually not written with the umlaut sign, because only that sound is possible. Any final vowel beginning with /i/ may be preceded only by /b/, /d/, /j/, /l/, /m/, /n/, /p/, /q/, /t/, /x/, and the semi-vowel /y/. Additionally, the initial consonant /q/ must be followed by a final vowel beginning with /i/ or /ü/.

NOTES

CHAPTER I: BEIJING OPERA PLAYS AND PERFORMANCE

1. E. T. Kirby, "Introduction" to *Total Theatre: A Critical Anthology*, xiii.

2. See Sun Kaidi, *Kuilei xi kao yuan*, for a well-supported thesis aiming to prove that puppetry was the origin of theatre in China, and that theatre therefore imitates the techniques of puppetry. See Sun Rongbai, *Jingju changshi jianghua*, 7, for a description of S-shaped movement patterns in Beijing opera.

3. The origin of the name for this role type, *qingyi*, is somewhat obscure. *Qing* may mean blue, green, or black. *Yi* means clothing, clothes, or garment. Poverty-stricken blue cloth *dan* in fact wear black robes, trimmed in turquoise-blue piping; when they are traveling, their heads are wrapped in a cloth of the same blue color. Because the majority of blue cloth *dan* performers with whom I worked equated the name to the blue head covering, I have followed that interpretation in my translation of the name.

4. See A. C. Scott, *The Classical Theatre of China*, 74.

5. Gui Weizhen and Wang Qinsheng of the Jiangsu Province Beijing Opera Company.

6. Zhou Yibai, *Zhongguo xiju shi*, 682. See William Dolby, *A History of Chinese Drama*, and Colin Mackerras, ed., *Chinese Theatre: From Its Origins to the Present Day*, for descriptions of these three important predecessors of Beijing opera.

7. Hwang Mei-shu, "Peking Opera: A Study of the Art of Translating the Scripts with Special Reference to Structure and Conventions," 29–31.

8. Ibid., 34–35. In Tao's listing, all plays with essentially the same plot are listed only once, with alternate titles following each play synopsis.

9. Liu Wu-ch'i, *An Introduction to Chinese Literature*, 174.

10. Sophia Delza, "The Classical Theatre of China," 228.

11. See Dolby, *History of Chinese Drama*, and Lo Chin-t'ang, *Zhongguo xiqu zongmu huibian*, for descriptions, analyses, and applications of these earlier systems; Lo's work includes synthesis of antecedent classification systems as well.

12. The policy of "simultaneously develop the three" *(san zhe bing ju)*, prevalent throughout the late 1970s and early 1980s, is associated with Zhou Enlai's policies of the 1950s and early 1960s regarding theatrical development. For a fairly comprehensive history of theatre in China from the perspective of cultural officials in the late 1970s, see "Zai Zhongguo Xijujia Xiehui disanci huiyuan daibiao dahui shang, Zhao Xun tongzhi zuo Ju Xie gongzuo baogao."

13. Wu Junda of the Jiangsu Province School of Xiqu; translations of quotations from personal interviews and conversations here and throughout are by the author.

14. Translation by A. C. Scott, *Traditional Chinese Plays*, 1:45.

15. Technically speaking, only short scenes from longer plays were traditionally considered *zhezixi,* although both complete short plays and selected scenes from longer plays were performed together on the same program. Perhaps because of this performance practice, both short plays and selected scenes have come to be referred to individually as *zhezixi;* a program of such pieces is also referred to as *zhezixi.*

16. The discussions of emotional-progression structure and the conceptions of time are based primarily on information provided by Wu Junda and Liu Jingjie of the Jiangsu Province School of Xiqu and Huang Yuqi of the Jiangsu Province Beijing Opera Company, and on analysis of live and recorded performances and available play scripts.

17. Although contemporary practitioners and connoisseurs frequently refer to these conceptualizations, they are not in fact traditional. As articulated concepts, they are products of the introduction of Western dramatic theory into China in the twentieth century. See Zhang Geng, *Xiqu yishu lun.*

18. Wu Junda.

CHAPTER II: LANGUAGE

1. Because the majority of traditional plays were developed by actors who in most cases had received only a minimal academic education, this is not surprising. See Colin Mackerras, *Rise of the Peking Opera,* and Scott, *Classical Theatre of China,* for descriptions of pre-Liberation actor training practices.

2. The description of lyric types is based on information provided by Huang Yuqi, and on analysis of live and recorded performances and available scripts.

3. Translation by A. C. Scott, *Traditional Chinese Plays,* 1:35–36. The Wade-Giles romanization in this and all subsequent translations by Scott has been changed to *pinyin* at his suggestion.

4. Translation by Scott, ibid., 75.

5. Translation by Scott, ibid., 36.

6. Translation by the author from the tape of a performance by Shen Xiaomei of the Jiangsu Province Beijing Opera Company in Nanjing, 1980.

7. Translation by Scott, *Traditional Chinese Plays,* 1:78–79.

8. Translation by Daniel Shih-p'eng Yang, "Black Dragon Residence."

9. Translation by Scott, *Traditional Chinese Plays,* 1:51.

10. Rulan Chao Pian, "Aria Structural Patterns in the Peking Opera," 76–77.

11. Translation by Scott, *Traditional Chinese Plays,* 1:82–83.

12. For the first technique, the term *chenzi* is used by Yu Dagang in *Guoju jianjie,* as Hwang Mei-shu points out in "Peking Opera," 187. William Dolby (*History of Chinese Drama,* 183) uses the term *duozi,* and the term used most frequently by contemporary practitioners and connoisseurs is *cunzi.* Yu Dagang refers to the second technique as *chenju,* whereas contemporary practitioners and connoisseurs most frequently use the term *chenzi.* I have chosen to use the terms employed by Yu

Dagang because in translation they most clearly contrast the nature of the two techniques.

13. Dolby, *History of Chinese Drama*, 57.

14. Pian, "Aria Structural Patterns," 66.

15. Translation by Scott, *Traditional Chinese Plays*, 1:40–42.

16. Pian, "Aria Structural Patterns," 71.

17. The symbols / / enclose *pinyin* transliterations of sounds; single quotes indicate letters used in spellings, and italics are used for actual Chinese words. For a guide to pronouncing the vowels and consonants discussed, see Appendix 2 in this volume.

18. Hwang Mei-shu, "Peking Opera," 185.

19. Figure 4 was provided by Wu Junda, as was much of the information in the discussion of rhyme categories and their aesthetic and emotional qualities that follows it.

20. Donald Chang and William Packard in the introduction to their translation of *The White Snake*, 54; and Wu Junda.

21. Wu Junda.

22. Wu Junda.

23. Wu Junda.

24. Figure 5 was provided by Wu Junda. The discussion of speech-tone patterns in lyrics is based on information provided by Wu Junda and Huang Yuqi; on Hwang Mei-shu, "Peking Opera," 164–165; and on analysis of live and recorded performances and available scripts.

25. In standard Mandarin Chinese speech, when two third-tone words occur in succession the first is changed to a second-tone word for ease in delivery: e.g., *hěn hǎo* (very good) becomes *hén hǎo*. This means that two successive oblique-tone words become a level-tone word followed by an oblique-tone word. However, in writing and singing lyrics, both words in such instances are given their unaltered, oblique-tone readings.

The four Mandarin Chinese words that change their tones according to the tone of the word that follows them—*yi* (one), *qi* (seven), *ba* (eight), and *bu* (not)—are read with the tone appropriate in each specific context. See chapter 5, note 17.

26. The description of stage speech is based on information provided by Wu Junda and Huang Yuqi, and by performers including Liu Debao of the Jiangsu Province Beijing Opera Company; and on Yang Mao, *Jingju changshi*, 15–16; Scott, *Traditional Chinese Plays*, 1:150; Qi Rushan, "Shang Xia Chang," in *Qi Rushan quan ji*, vol. 1; Qi Rushan, *Guoju yishu huikao*, 45–77; Hwang Mei-shu, "Peking Opera," 37, 138–139; Pian, "Aria Structural Patterns," 78; and analysis of live and recorded performances and available scripts.

27. For a description of these poetic forms, see Liu Wu-ch'i, *Introduction to Chinese Literature*.

28. See Dolby, *History of Chinese Drama*, and Mackerras, *Rise of the Peking*

Opera, for discussions of the development of Beijing opera and the influence of other forms of *xiqu* upon that development.

29. Translation by Scott, *Traditional Chinese Plays,* 1:34; the Chinese is transcribed from the tape of a performance by Liang Huichao of the Jiangsu Province Beijing Opera Company in Nanjing, December 1979.

30. According to Wu Junda, it is possible that these terms at one time specifically designated the number of couplets in a given set-the-scene poem.

31. Translation by the author; the Chinese is transcribed from the tape of a performance by Shen Xiaomei in Nanjing, 1980.

32. Translation by the author from the tape of a performance by Shen Xiaomei in Nanjing, 1980.

33. The name for this type of speech dates from the Yuan dynasty (1271–1368), according to Xu Fuming, *Yuandai zaju yishu,* 119–120.

CHAPTER III: THE MUSICAL SYSTEM: MUSICAL ELEMENTS

1. Rulan Chao Pian makes the same point in J. I. Crump and William P. Malm, *Chinese and Japanese Music Dramas,* 232: "I have watched my husband sing to entries in a telephone book. As long as the syllables are distributed correctly, he can do it. Of course, this would be the dullest opera possible. . . ." During rehearsals for newly written plays, performers develop their melodies as they develop their characters and receive notes from directors concerning both. Melodies for traditional plays are more fixed; however, even for these plays there is considerable creative leeway, as will be discussed in chapter 4.

2. The Chinese term *shengqiang xitong* (lit. "vocal melodic-passage system") is translated in the preceding paragraph as "musical system" and here as "modal system." The differing translations are intended to clarify the fact that *pihuang* is a complete system, while its modes are associated in groups or subsystems within it. The concept is the same, however; both individually and collectively, the groups of associated modes are systems of related elements that provide patterns for the creation of Beijing opera vocal music.

The complete *pihuang* musical system developed in the eighteenth and early nineteenth centuries out of the mutual influence of a number of forms of *xiqu,* including *hanju* and *huiju.* Today Beijing opera is the major form that features *pihuang* music; however, many other forms, such as *hanju,* also use music from this system.

3. The discussion of Beijing opera's musical elements is based primarily on information provided by Wu Junda; on Hu Qiaomu, *Zhongguo da baike quanshu: Xiqu quyi;* Rulan Chao Pian, "Aria Structural Patterns"; Shanghai Yishu Yanjiu Suo and Zhongguo Xijujia Xiehui Shanghai Fenhui, *Zhongguo xiqu quyi cidian;* and on analysis of live and recorded performances and available musical notation.

4. Wu Junda.

5. The example is from *The General and the Prime Minister Are Reconciled*

(Jiang xiang he), transcribed by Wu Junda. It is an opening line in male *xipi* primary-meter. For a description of the notation system used in this and all succeeding musical examples, see Appendix 1. The translation here and in all following examples is by the author unless otherwise noted.

6. *Xian ding zi, hou yun/xing qiang*. Lu Genzhang, an older *sheng (laosheng)* performer with the Jiangsu Province Beijing Opera Company.

7. Sun Rongbai, *Jingju changshi jianghu*, 50. Conventional indications of speech-tone are to a large extent the province of specific role types and subcategories, and of specific schools or styles *(liupai)* of performance. Generally, however, most involve shortened forms of the full pitch progressions and/or variations in vocal intensity.

8. Figure 6 was provided by Wu Junda.

9. In Example 2, the male melodic-line is from *The General and the Prime Minister Are Reconciled (Jiang xiang he)*; the female is from *The Fisherman's Revenge (Dayu sha jia)*. Both were transcribed by Wu Junda; they are opening lines in *xipi* primary-meter.

10. The mode is *xipi*.

11. Wu Junda.

12. In Example 3, the ten-written-character line is from *The General and the Prime Minister Are Reconciled (Jiang xiang he)*, and the seven-written-character line is from *The Ruse of the Empty City (Kong cheng ji)*. Both were transcribed by Wu Junda.

13. Lu Genzhang.

14. From *Catching and Releasing Cao Cao (Zhuo fang Cao)*, transcribed by Wu Junda.

15. Lu Genzhang and Huang Yuqi.

16. From *The Battle of Taiping (Zhan Taiping)*, in *Jingju chuantong changqiang xuanji*, 119; hereafter cited as *JCCX*.

17. This characterization is borrowed from Pian, "Aria Structural Patterns," 67.

18. Ye Hexiang, a conductor *(sigu)* with the Jiangsu Province Beijing Opera Company.

19. The example is from *First Place Imperial Examinees (Zhuangyuan pu)*, transcribed by Wu Junda.

20. The origin of the name two-six-meter is obscure—Wu Junda simply notes that it does not refer to $\frac{2}{6}$ meter. Since 1949, some Chinese scholars and theatre practitioners have begun to refer to this metrical type as two-flowing-meter *(erliuban)*, pointing out that it is approximately twice as slow as flowing-water-meter.

21. Piled-up-meter, a metrical type found only in the *erhuang* mode, is similar to flowing-water-meter in beat duration. It is also usually in $\frac{1}{4}$ meter, although $\frac{2}{4}$ meter piled-up-meter passages do occur, as in the following example. Piled-up-meter is very flexible, delivered in a style somewhat comparable to recitative—Wu Junda describes it as being similar to reading poetry tunefully. It consists of an unrestricted

number of short phrases, three to seven written-characters in length, all of which taken together equal a single melodic-line (usually a closing line). In a sense, these short phrases may be considered multiple padding *dou*. Piled-up-meter is generally not an independent metrical type and therefore usually occurs as part of a longer passage including primary-meter, shaking-meter, or undulating-dragon-meter. The following example of male piled-up-meter is from *Entering the Palace Twice (Er jin gong)* in Zhongguo Xiqu Yanjiu Yuan, *Jingju changqiang, di yi ji, xia bian: laosheng, xiaosheng,* 82–83.

Male Piled-up-meter

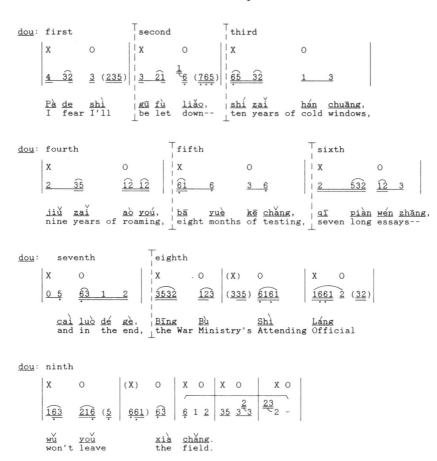

22. The ten-written-character two-six-meter melodic-line is from *Catching and Releasing Cao Cao (Zhuo fang Cao)*, in *JCCX*, 215; the seven-written-character two-six-meter melodic-line is from *Dingjun Mountain (Dingjun shan)*, in *JCCX*,

176. Both flowing-water-meter examples are from *The Pursuit of Han Xin (Zhui Han Xin)*, in *JCCX*, 158–159. Ten-written-character flowing-water-meter in male passages is rare; the example is actually a seven-written-character line with one padding written-character in the first *dou*, and two in the second.

23. Wu Junda.

24. The ten-written-character dispersed-meter example is from *The Hegemon King Parts with His Favorite (Bawang bie ji)*; it was transcribed by Wu Junda. The seven-written-character example is from *Dingjun Mountain (Dingjun shan)*, in *JCCX*, 178. It is a closing line; dispersed-meter in many instances is used in this position, as is discussed in chapter 4.

25. Wu Junda.

26. From *Borrowing the East Wind (Jie dong feng)*, in Zhongguo Xiqu Yanjiu Yuan, *Jingju changqiang*, 99, with corrections by Wu Junda. Both passages are in *erhuang* mode; although lead-in-meter is used frequently in *xipi* mode, it is rarely followed by undulating-dragon-meter, which traditionally occurs only in *erhuang* mode. *Erhuang*'s lead-in-meter is almost always followed by undulating-dragon-meter, as in this example.

27. From *The Battle of Taiping (Zhan Taiping)*, in *JCCX*, 118.

28. The concept of mode in *xiqu* is not the same as the major/minor dichotomy in common practice in nineteenth-century European concert music. It is more analogous to the Church Modes of medieval Europe, according to Professor Emeritus Barbara Smith of the Department of Music of the University of Hawaii.

29. The melodic-passages that accompany the standard lines in Example 12 are the basic melodic contours for male *xipi* and *erhuang*; they were provided by Wu Junda and are described in detail below, under melodic contour.

30. Wu Junda.

31. Wu Junda.

32. The *xipi* passage is from *The General and the Prime Minister Are Reconciled (Jiang xiang he)*, and the *erhuang* from *Raise the Cauldron and Look at the Painting (Ju ding guan hua)*; both were transcribed by Wu Junda.

33. Wu Junda.

34. Transcribed by Wu Junda.

35. Gong Suping, Huang Kailiang, Liu Debao, Liu Zhixiang, Lu Genzhang, Sha Yu, Wu Xingyue, Xu Meiyun, Ye Hexiang, and Zhu Ya of the Jiangsu Province Beijing Opera Company.

36. John Hazedel Levis, *Foundations of Chinese Musical Art*, 68.

37. Wu Junda.

38. Li Qingsen, "Weishenma nan pa xipi nü pa erhuang?" The full saying is "Women are afraid of *erhuang*, and men are afraid of *xipi*." The reason for the latter statement is that a wider pitch range is commonly used in *xipi* than in *erhuang* because of the different patterns of melodic construction—this is in fact true for female *xipi* as well as male, because the pattern of melodic construction is basic to modal identity.

39. Transcribed by Wu Junda.

40. The male *xipi* fast-meter is from *The Battle of Taiping (Zhan Taiping)*, in *JCCX*, 119. The primary-meter is from *The Ruse of the Empty City (Kong cheng ji)*, and the slow-meter is from *Catching and Releasing Cao Cao (Zhuo fang Cao)*; both were transcribed by Wu Junda.

The female *xipi* fast-meter is from *The Luo River Spirit (Luo shen)*, in Zhongguo Xiqu Yanjiu Yuan, *Mei Lanfang yanchu juben xuanji qupu*, 65, with corrections by Wu Junda. The primary-meter is from *The Fisherman's Revenge (Dayu sha jia)*, and the slow-meter from *Lian Jinfeng*; both were transcribed by Wu Junda.

In Example 21, the male *erhuang* primary-meter is from *Raise the Cauldron and Look at the Painting (Ju ding guan hua)*, and the slow-meter from *Catching and Releasing Cao Cao (Zhuo fang Cao)*. In Example 22, the female *erhuang* primary-meter is from *Wuzhao Pass (Wuzhao guan)*, and the slow-meter from *Memorial to the River (Ji jiang)*. All *erhuang* examples were transcribed by Wu Junda.

41. The term "secondary" is my own; I know of no generic Chinese term inclusive of all the modes other than the principal modes in both modal systems. They are simply referred to as related to *xipi* and *erhuang*.

42. There are also less important modes in the *pihuang* system. One of the most frequently used is *chuiqiang*, which is associated with the *erhuang* modal system, according to Wu Junda. *Chuiqiang* developed in the late Ming (1368–1644) and early Qing (1644–1911) dynasties, through the influence of *kunshanqiang* upon *yiyangqiang*. Both of these musical systems use joined-song-form *(lianquti)* musical structure, described in note 55; early in its development *chuiqiang* also followed joined-song-form musical structure, but later came to use seven- and ten-written-character lyric lines. However, *chuiqiang* still employs some fixed-melodies in irregular-length lines *(qupai)*, the primary element in joined-song-form musical structure, taken from the *yiyangqiang* and especially the *kunshanqiang* musical systems. *Chuiqiang*'s main accompanying melodic instrument is a horizontal bamboo flute *(dizi)* rather than a spike fiddle *(huqin)*; when fiddles are used as well, they are tuned as in *erhuang*.

Chuiqiang, like *gaobozi*, is one of the principal modes in *huiju* (described in note 47). Some *huiju* plays using the *chuiqiang* mode were taken into Beijing opera by *huiju* actors who joined developing Beijing opera troupes in the capital in the late eighteenth and early nineteenth centuries—those plays are now a part of the Beijing opera repertoire and still have *chuiqiang* characteristics. Major examples include *Opportune Double Meeting (Qi shuang hui)*, also known as *Story of the Horse Peddler (Fan ma ji)*, and *Death in the Hall of Sutras (Zhan jing tang)*.

Some music not actually within the *pihuang* musical system is also occasionally sung in Beijing opera, including music from other theatre forms and popular folk melodies. Most important is probably that of *kunqu* (lit. "songs of Kun"; also called *kunju*, lit. "Kun drama"). *Kunqu* was the predominant national theatre form before the ascent of Beijing opera, and therefore exerted considerable influence on the latter's development. *Kunqu* is the principal form in the *kunshanqiang* musical system, and uses joined-song-form *(lianquti)* musical structure with fixed-melodies in irregular-length lines *(qupai)*. Its main melodic accompaniment is provided by a horizontal bamboo flute *(dizi)*, as in *chuiqiang*.

Kunqu was created in the mid-sixteenth century in Kunshan, Jiangsu province, under the influence of the *yiyangqiang* musical system, several regional theatre forms, and the classical northern and southern rhymed verse for singing *(qu)*. A number of regional styles of *kunqu* developed during the late sixteenth and seventeenth centuries, giving rise to two major schools: the northern and the southern. Popular with the educated elite until the mid-nineteenth century, both schools were ultimately overshadowed by various regional theatre forms, especially Beijing opera. Although both are still performed by independent *kunqu* companies, they have also been partially incorporated in a number of newer forms. Sung passages from particular *kunqu* plays as well as entire scenes are sometimes performed in the northern style on the Beijing opera stage.

43. Wu Junda.

44. The *erhuang* is from [*Examining the Head and*] *Executing Tang (Ci Tang)*, in *JCCX*, 86-87; the inverse *erhuang* is from *The Cosmic Blade (Yuzhou feng)*, in *JCCX*, 26-29. Both passages include corrections by Wu Junda.

45. Wu Junda.

46. The $\frac{2}{4}$ *nanbangzi* primary-meter is from *Spring Lantern Riddles (Chun deng mi)*, and the $\frac{4}{4}$ primary-meter is from *The Phoenix Returns to Its Nest (Feng huan chao)*; both were transcribed by Wu Junda.

47. *Kunyiqiang* is a musical mode in *huiju*, a regional form of *xiqu* popular throughout southern China that originated in Anhui province. This mode developed in Anhui in the late Ming (1368-1644) and early Qing (1644-1911) dynasties through the mutual influences of *kunshanqiang* and *yiyangqiang*—two musical systems that use joined-song-form *(lianquti)* musical structure (see note 55)—as well as several local forms of *xiqu*.

48. According to Wu Junda, special techniques must be used to accommodate padding written-characters and padding lines in other modes. For padding written-characters, melodic-phrases may be added within melodic-sections (the technique is termed *kuoqiang*, lit. "expanding melodic-passages") and at the end of melodic-sections (termed *jiaqiang*, lit. "adding/additional melodic-passages"). For padding lines, melodic-phrases and melodic-sections may be added between lines (also termed *jiaqiang*), before opening lines (termed *jiamao*, lit. "adding a hat"), and after closing lines (termed *jiawei*, lit. "adding a tail").

49. Wu Junda.

50. The male *sipingdiao* is from *Black Dragon Residence (Wu long yuan)*, transcribed by Wu Junda. The female is from *The Favorite Concubine Becomes Intoxicated (Guifei zui jiu)*, in *JCCX*, 60-61.

51. During *gaobozi*'s development in regional theatre forms, plucked stringed

instruments and/or the small *suona* served as primary melodic accompaniment. The *bohu* came to dominate in Beijing opera.

52. *Qinqiang* is a regional form of *xiqu* that uses the same type of musical structure—melodic-phrases, metrical-types, and modes and modal systems—as does Beijing opera. This type of musical structure is called *banqiang*-form (*banqiangti;* see note 55). However, *qinqiang* is a member of the *bangziqiang* musical system, rather than the *pihuang,* and uses the *bangzi* clapper rather than the *ban* clapper for its primary percussion accompaniment. It arose in approximately the fifteenth century in Shaanxi and Gansu provinces and is popular today throughout northern and northwestern China. *Kunyiqiang* and *huiju* are described in note 47.

53. The male version is from *Xu Ce Runs on the City Wall (Xu Ce pao cheng),* in Hao Dequan, Li Buhai, and Lo Xuanbing, *Xu Ce pao cheng: Zhou Xinfang yanchu ben,* 27. The female version is from *Women Generals of the Yang Family (Yang men nü jiang),* in Liu Jidian, *Jingju yinyue gailun,* 489, with corrections by Wu Junda.

54. The play just quoted, *Xu Ce Runs on the City Wall (Xu Ce pao cheng),* is such an instance—it is sung entirely in *gaobozi.*

55. At present, there are four principal *xiqu* musical systems: *pihuang, bangziqiang, yiyangqiang* (also called *gaoqiang*), and *kunshanqiang.* Each of the first two systems has its own patterns of modal identity and its own metrical types, which are combined with the speech-tones of the language in the composition of vocal music. This type of musical structure is known as *banqiang*-form *(banqiangti); ban* refers to metrical types, and *qiang* to both melodic-passages *(changqiang)* and modal systems *(shengqiang xitong).* Each of the second two systems has a large number of basic fixed-melodies in irregular-length lines *(qupai,* lit. "song types"), which are usually arranged in a specific order in sets. Lyrics are written to these fixed-melodies for a given play; composers or performers, depending upon the specific form of theatre, then compose precise, full melodies for the lyrics. This type of musical structure is called joined-song-form *(lianquti); lian* (to join) refers to the specific order in sets, and *qu* (song) to the fixed-melodies.

CHAPTER IV: THE MUSICAL SYSTEM:
MUSICAL COMPOSITION

1. The discussion of the three compositional stages is based primarily on information provided by Wu Junda, Huang Yuqi, Yao Mingde, and Yao Tongsheng of the Jiangsu Province Beijing Opera Company; on Pian, "Aria Structural Patterns"; and on analysis of rehearsals, live and recorded performances, and interviews.

2. This scene is available in English as "A Girl Setting Out for Trial" in A. C. Scott, *Traditional Chinese Plays,* 3:63–92.

3. The description of the character's psychology and its musical expression in this scene is taken from Xun Huisheng and Cheng Yanqiu, as quoted in unpublished manuscripts of Wu Junda. The scene is available in English as scene 2 of "The Faithful Harlot" in Josephine Hung Huang, *Classical Chinese Plays,* 51–74.

4. Yao Mingde and Yao Tongsheng.

5. Pian, "Aria Structural Patterns," 72.

6. Bell Yung, "The Role of Speech Tones in the Creative Process of Cantonese Opera," 164. Yung is of course referring to the techniques and patterns of Cantonese opera *(yueju),* a major southern form of *xiqu* popular in Guangdong (Canton) Province, the Guangxi Zhuang Autonomous Region, and overseas Chinese communities. It uses music from all four principal musical systems, including *pihuang,* and therefore both *banqiang*-form and joined-song-form musical structure (see chapter 3, note 55). In terms of composition, the primary difference between Cantonese and Beijing opera is that, according to Yung, Cantonese opera performers frequently compose on stage in performance; Beijing opera performers compose primarily in rehearsal. Additionally, Beijing opera may have a larger body of standard, traditional pieces that serve as models for composition.

7. Zhongguo Xiqu Yanjiu Yuan, *Yu Tangchun: Cheng Yanqiu changqiang xuanji zhi er.*

8. Hu Qiaomu, *Zhongguo da baike quanshu: Xiqu quyi,* 552–553; and Scott, *Traditional Chinese Plays,* 3:65–66.

9. Cheng Yanqiu, as quoted in the personal notes of Wu Junda and translated by the author.

10. From Zhongguo Xiqu Yanjiu Yuan, *Yu Tangchun,* 35 and 46–47, with corrections by Wu Junda. Translations are by the author, as are those in all succeeding examples.

11. The emotional connotations of pitch, melodic-phrase length, and the use of coloration tones in these two passages were analyzed with the assistance of Wu Junda.

12. The quote is from the notes of Wu Junda, recorded at the 1957 Forum on *Xiqu* Music (Xiqu Yinyue Zuotanhui) in Beijing; it was translated by the author.

13. The Mei Lanfang passage was transcribed by Wu Junda from a record produced by the Bai Dai Company, title and year unknown. The Cheng Yanqiu version is from Zhongguo Xiqu Yanjiu Yuan, *Yu Tangchun,* 7–9, with corrections by Wu Junda. The Xun Huisheng version was transcribed by Wang Qiu and published in *Xiju yuekan,* date of publication unknown, from which it was copied by Wu Junda.

14. Wu Junda.

15. The emotional connotations of pitch, melodic-phrase length, and the use of coloration tones and standard interpretive techniques in these three passages were analyzed with the assistance of Wu Junda.

16. Wu Junda.

17. The other is Shang Xiaoyun; because I have been unable to locate a recording or transcription of *Yu Tangchun* as performed by Shang Xiaoyun, his interpretation of this play and character has not been included in this comparison.

18. Huang Kexiao of the Jiangsu Province Beijing Opera Company, recorded spring 1980.

19. The published notation is from Zhongguo Xiqu Yanjiu Yuan, *Yu Tangchun,*

7–9, with corrections by Wu Junda. Notation for the 1957 performance was transcribed by Wu Junda.

20. Yung, "Role of Speech Tones," 164–165.

CHAPTER V: THE VOICE

1. Hwang Mei-shu, "Peking Opera," 219. The quote is a translation and summation of the discussions in Qi Rushan, *Qi Rushan quan ji,* 1:1–20; and Qi Rushan, *Guoju yishu huikao,* 115–146.

2. Hwang Mei-shu, "Peking Opera," 220.

3. The description of vocal production is based primarily on information provided by Shen Xiaomei and Wu Junda, and by other performers including Gong Suping, Huang Kailiang, Liu Debao, Lu Genzhang, Sha Yu, Wu Xingyue, and Zhu Ya; and on Hu Qiaomu, *Zhongguo da baike quanshu: Xiqu quyi,* 419; Sun Rongbai, *Jingju changshi jianghua,* 49–59; Yang Mao, *Jingju changshi,* 14–23; Zhou Yibai, *Xiqu yanchang lunzhu jishi,* 196–197; and analysis of live and recorded performances and interviews.

4. Sun Rongbai, *Jingju changshi jianghua,* 53.

5. From Zhongguo Xiqu Yanjiu Yuan, *Mei Lanfang yanchu juben xuanji qupu,* 11; translation by the author.

6. Shen Xiaomei.

7. Sun Rongbai, *Jingju changshi jianghua,* 54.

8. A. C. Scott, "The Performance of Classical Theatre," 128–129.

9. The description of Beijing opera song is based primarily on information provided by Shen Xiaomei and Wu Junda, and by other performers including Gong Suping, Huang Kailiang, Jiang Yan, Liu Debao, Lu Genzhang, Wu Xingyue, and Zhu Ya of the Jiangsu Province Beijing Opera Company; and on Hu Qiaomu, *Zhongguo da baike quanshu,* 472; Sun Rongbai, *Jingju changshi jianghua,* 51–53; and analysis of live and recorded performances and interviews.

10. Many contemporary Beijing opera performers use Western key designations, such as C, D, E, F, etc. However, many others still use traditional key designations. According to Wu Junda, these designations are based on the *gongchepu* (lit. "*gong che* scores") traditional Chinese musical notation system, and correspond to the Western designations as follows:

shangzidiao	is the key of B^b $(1 = B^b)$
chezidiao	is the key of C $(1 = C)$
(sometimes pronounced *chizidiao*)	
xiaogongdiao	is the key of D $(1 = D)$
fanzidiao	is the key of E^b $(1 = E^b)$
fanbandiao	is the key of E $(1 = E)$
liuzidiao	is the key of F $(1 = F)$

| *zhenggongdiao* | is the key of G (1 = G) |
| *yizidiao* | is the key of A (1 = A) |

Fanbandiao (the key of E) is perhaps the most frequently used key in Beijing opera.

11. Delza, "Classical Theatre of China," 226.

12. Notation in this example is from Zhongguo Xiqu Yanjiu Yuan, *Mei Lanfang yanchu juben xuanji qupu,* 10, with corrections by Wu Junda.

13. Notation in this example is by the author.

14. The description of Beijing opera speech is based primarily on information provided by Wu Junda, Shen Xiaomei, and Huang Yuqi; by other performers including Gong Suping, Liu Debao, Lu Genzhang, and Zhu Ya; and on Sun Rongbai, *Jingju changshi jianghua,* 50; Yang Mao, *Jingju changshi,* 14–18; and analysis of live and recorded performances and interviews.

15. Hwang Mei-shu, "Peking Opera," 220.

16. Ci Hai Bianji Weiyuanhui, *Ci hai,* 3227; hereafter cited as *Ci hai.*

17. In standard Mandarin, *yi* is read with a level-tone when not followed by another word, with a rising-tone when followed by a falling-tone word, and with a falling-tone when followed by a level-tone, rising-tone, or turning-tone; *qi* and *ba* are read with level-tones unless followed by falling-tone words, in which case they are given rising-tone pronunciations; *bu* is read with a falling-tone except when followed by a falling-tone, when it is given a rising-tone reading.

18. Figures 21 and 22 were provided by Wu Junda.

19. The graphs of Mandarin and heightened speech intonations, provided by Wu Junda, are conceptual; in all heightened speech examples, the central pitch of each written-character's pronunciation is indicated by a dot.

20. Scott, "Performance of Classical Theatre," 129.

21. Yang Mao, *Jingju changshi,* 18.

22. It may not be technically accurate to say that women who perform these roles use a falsetto voice—some performers and scholars believe that falsetto vocal production is physiologically possible for men only. However, when young *dan* roles are spoken and sung well, it is virtually impossible to distinguish the voices of female performers from those of male performers. The same can be said of young *sheng* roles. For convenience and consistency, as well as to reflect standard Beijing opera terminology, I shall therefore use the term "falsetto" to characterize the timbre of the small-voice in Beijing opera.

23. The description of role-specific vocal characteristics is based primarily on information provided by Shen Xiaomei and Wu Junda; by other performers including Gui Weizhen, Jiang Yan, Lu Genzhang, and Zhong Rong of the Jiangsu Province Beijing Opera Company; and on Hu Qiaomu, *Zhongguo da baike quanshu,* 471–472; Yang Mao, *Jingju changshi,* 19–22; and analysis of live and recorded performances and interviews.

24. Scott, *Classical Theatre of China,* 72.

25. Hu Qiaomu, *Zhongguo da baike quanshu,* 471.

26. Ibid., 472.

27. Ibid.

28. Scott, "Performance of Classical Theatre," 129.

29. Hu Qiaomu, *Zhongguo da baike quanshu,* 471.

30. Scott, *Classical Theatre of China,* 68.

31. Ibid., 74.

32. Hu Qiaomu, *Zhongguo da baike quanshu,* 471.

33. Ibid., 472.

34. Scott, *Classical Theatre of China,* 75.

35. Hu Qiaomu, *Zhongguo da baike quanshu,* 472.

36. From the field notes of John Rosenhow, Professor of Chinese Linguistics, University of Illinois at Chicago Circle; notes taken in China (predominantly in Hangzhou and Nanjing), September 1979 through August 1981.

37. Hu Qiaomu, *Zhongguo da baike quanshu,* 472.

38. This characterization was made by Wei Chengwu, a *chou* performer at the Jiangsu Province Beijing Opera Company.

CHAPTER VI: THE ORCHESTRA

1. The descriptions of the instruments and functions of the Beijing opera orchestra are based primarily on information provided by Wu Junda and Ye Hexiang; by Yao Mingde and Yao Tongsheng; and on analysis of live and recorded performances, available notation, and interviews. In describing the instruments, *Ci hai* and Scott, *Classical Theatre of China,* were also important sources.

2. *Ci hai,* 3444.

3. "Red-wood" is a literal translation of the Chinese term *hongmu;* this wood comes from any of several trees of the genus *Pterocarpus,* known in English by its Burmese name, *padauk.* The wood is reddish in color, resembling mahogany; it is not the same wood as that of the California redwood, nor is it rosewood.

4. *Ci hai,* 4299, states that these last two holes are "for expelling air." Professor Emeritus Barbara Smith of the Department of Music at the University of Hawaii points out that they determine the pitch when all finger holes are closed. In some instances, especially when these two holes are on the lower side of the flute, they are strung with decorative tassles.

5. The written-character *ban* is used in three separate but related ways in the *pihuang* musical system. It refers to accented beats; to metrical types, which are characterized by a pattern of accented and unaccented beats; and to the clapper, which is used to mark accented beats.

6. Technically, the sound produced is concussive rather than percussive; the latter word is used for consistency throughout.

7. It is also called the *sukun;* Suzhou is the home of *kunqu,* Beijing opera's predecessor as the nationally dominant form of *xiqu.*

8. The instruments examined are those in the collection of the Department of Theatre and Dance at the University of Hawaii. Their sounds were analyzed with the assistance of Professor Emeritus Barbara Smith of the Department of Music.

9. Scott, *Classical Theatre of China,* 47.

10. Collections of "percussive classics" are compiled by percussive orchestras and schools, and frequently by amateur performers as well—for example, Xiaweiyi Zhongguo Xiju Yanjiu She, *Luogu jing.*

11. The listing of percussive strikes is based primarily on information provided by Wu Junda and Ye Hexiang, and on Hao et al., *Xu Ce pao cheng,* 2–3; Xiaweiyi Zhongguo Xiju Yanjiu She, *Luogu jing;* and Daniel Shih-p'eng Yang, "Percussion Instruments and Important Percussion Scores." Although the use of roman letters to represent strikes is not uncommon, the specific choice of letters here is in large part the author's own.

12. Xiaweiyi Zhongguo Xiju Yanjiu She, *Luogu jing,* an incomplete listing, names and describes 101 percussive passages.

13. The diagram is based on observation, and on consultation with Wu Junda, Ye Hexiang, and Bian Shuangxi, the instructor of conducting at the Jiangsu Province School of *Xiqu.*

14. See John Hazedel Levis, *Foundations of Chinese Musical Art.*

15. From Zhongguo Xiqu Yanjiu Yuan, *Mei Lanfang yanchu juben xuanji qupu,* 10–11.

16. Although the first text (Zhongguo Xiqu Yanjiu Yuan, *Yu Tangchun,* 7–9) does not give the specific date of the performance transcribed, it also occurred in the late 1950s according to Wu Junda.

17. Scott, *Classical Theatre of China,* 42–43.

18. This term is the author's own. Beijing opera practitioners and scholars refer to this characteristic of instrumental connectives more generally and indirectly by saying that accompaniment for song is "governed" *(guanli)* by the "authority of the melodic-passages" *(changqiang de quanli),* whereas instrumental connectives are governed only by modal identity and metrical type.

19. The description of action-strings and fixed-melodies is based primarily on Hu Qiaomu, *Zhongguo da baike quanshu: Xiqu quyi,* 27–28, 285–286, and 515–516; on information provided by Wu Junda and Ye Hexiang; and on analysis of live and recorded performances and available notation.

20. Yan Songzhou, *Jinghu yanzou fa,* 53.

21. See notes 42 and 55 in chapter 3.

22. Zhongguo Xiqu Yanjiu Yuan, *Mei Lanfang yanchu juben xuanji qupu,* 14–15.

23. Hao et al., *Xu Ce pao cheng,* 5.

24. Yang, "Percussion Instruments."

25. Hao et al., *Xu Ce pao cheng,* 5.

26. Yang, "Percussion Instruments."

27. Hao et al., *Xu Ce pao cheng,* 4.

28. Ibid., 5.

29. Zhongguo Xiqu Yanjiu Yuan, *Yu Tangchun,* 7.

30. Wu Junda.

31. Ye Hexiang.

32. Ye Hexiang.

33. Zhongguo Xiqu Yanjiu Yuan, *Yu Tangchun,* 10.

34. Wu Junda.

35. Scott, *Traditional Chinese Plays,* 1:34.

36. Ye Hexiang and Liu Debao, in conversation, spring 1980.

37. Zhongguo Xiqu Yanjiu Yuan, *Yu Tangchun,* 13–14.

38. All examples of movement punctuation are from Yang, "Percussion Instruments."

39. Ye Hexiang.

40. Ye Hexiang.

LIST OF WRITTEN CHARACTERS

This list includes Chinese names and theatrical terms that appear in the text. Excluded are names of characters in plays, place names, and names of Chinese dynasties. Bibliographic items are listed in Sources.

a 啊
ai 嗳
an qi 按气

ba 八 or 巴
bada 八大 or 八答
Bai Dai 百代
baihua 白话
Bai she zhuan 白蛇传
ban 板
bangu 板鼓
bangzi 梆子
bangziqiang 梆子腔
banju guomen 半句过门
banqiangti 板腔体
banshi 板式
Bawang bie ji 霸王别姬
beigong 背供
beng 八 or 巴
bi 鼻
Bian Shuangxi 卞双喜
bidou 鼻窦
bie qi 憋气
bodi xue 薄底靴
bohu 拨胡
bolangyin 波浪音
buju 布局
bu shi li 不使力

cai 采
caidan 彩旦
cang 仓
caozong qi 操纵气
cei 采

cengcixing buju 层次性布局
chang 唱
changbai 唱白
changci 唱词
changduan 唱段
changger 唱歌
changjing yinyue 场景音乐
changkao 长靠
changmian 场面
changqiang 唱腔
changqiang de quanli 唱腔的权力
changqiang jianzhu 唱腔建筑
chang sanle 唱散了
changxi 唱戏
chanyin 颤音
che 撤
"Che luo" 撤锣
Chengpai xi 程派戏
chengshi 程式
chengshi nianbai 程式念白
Cheng Yanqiu 程砚秋
chenju 衬句
chenzi 衬字
chezidiao 尺字调
chi 齿
chizidiao 尺字调
"Chong tou" 冲头
chou 丑
choudan 丑旦
choupozi 丑婆子
chuanqi 传奇
chuantongju 传统剧
chuantongxi 传统戏
chuchang shi 出场诗

chui　吹

chuida qupai　吹打曲牌

chuiqiang　吹腔

chun　唇

Chun deng mi　春灯谜

chu zi　出字

ci　词

Ci Tang ([*Shen tou*] *Ci Tang*)
　[审头] 刺汤

cuchui　粗吹

cun qi　存气

cunzi　存字

cuochun　撮唇

da 打 (combat)

da 大 or 答 (one firm beat of the right
　stick of the clapper-drum)

dabo　大铙

daduan　大段

da guomen　大过门

dahu　大胡

dahualian　大花脸

daji yuedui　打击乐队

"Da kai men"　大开门

daluo　大锣

"Daluo da shang"　大锣打上

"Daluo yi ji"　大锣一击

damian　大面

dan　旦

danpigu　单皮鼓

dantian　丹田

daoban 导板 or 倒板

"Daoban tou"　导板头

daomadan　刀马旦

Dao zong juan　盗宗卷

Da pi guan　大劈棺

dasangzi　大嗓子

dashailuo　大筛锣

datanggu　大堂鼓

da wayaya　打哇呀呀

daxi　大戏

da yinzi　大引子

Dayu sha jia　打渔杀家

dei　台

Deyi yuan　得意缘

di　低

diao　调

diaochang　吊场

diaoshi　调式

diaoshi jiezou　调式节奏

diaoshixing　调式性

digu　底鼓

dihu　低胡

dingchang bai　定场白

dingchang shi　定场诗

Dingjun shan　定军山

dizi　笛子

dou 逗 or 读

duanda　短打

duer　嘟儿

duibixing buju　对比性布局

duiju qushi de jiegou　对句曲式的结构

duizhang　对仗

dumuxi　独幕戏

duo　哆

duoban　垛板

duochangxi　多场戏

duoluo　哆啰

duozi　垛字

e　嚬

edou　额窦

erhu　二胡

erhualian　二花脸

erhuang　二黄

Er jin gong　二进宫

erliuban 二六板 (two-six-meter)

erliuban 二流板 (two-flowing-meter)

fa hua　发花

Fa men si　法门寺

fan　反

fanbandiao　凡半调

fanerhuang　反二黄

Fang Jinsen 方锦森
fangyanbai 方言白
Fan ma ji 贩马记
fanmian renwu 反面人物
fanqie 反切
fanxipi 反西皮
fanzidiao 凡字调
fasheng 发声
fayin 发音
Feng huan chao 凤还巢
fu 赋 (Han dynasty poetic form)
fu 腹 (belly)
fujing 副净
fu qi 浮气

gan 干
gannian 干念
Gansu bangzi 甘肃梆子
gao 高
gaobozi 高拨子
gaoqiang 高腔
ge 个
gong 功 (skill)
gong 宫 (first tone in the Chinese
     pentatonic scale)
gongchepu 工尺谱
gongming dian 共鸣点
gongnü 宫女
Gong Suping 龚苏萍
guaizhang 拐杖
guan 管
guanli 管理
guanxian yuedui 管弦乐队
guan xue 官靴
guban 鼓板
Guifei zui jiu 贵妃醉酒
guilü 规律
guimendan 闺门旦
Gui Weizhen 桂卫桢
gui yun 归韵
guoju 国剧
guomen 过门

gushi 古诗
gu su 姑苏

hanju 汉剧
He hou ma dian 贺后骂殿
heitou 黑头
hekou 合口
heng qi 横气
hongmu 红木
hou 喉
houdi xue 厚底靴
houtou 喉头
hou xiang 后响
huadan 花旦
huai lai 怀来
huaju 话剧
hualian 花脸
Huang Kailiang 黄凯良
Huang Kexiao 黄克孝
Huang Yuqi 黄玉琪
huan qi 换气
huanweishi 换尾式
huaqiang 花腔
huashan 花衫
Huatian cuo 花田错
huayin 滑音
Hudie meng 蝴蝶梦
Hu Dongsheng 胡冬生
hui dui 灰堆
huiju 徽剧
huilong 回龙
huokou 合口
huqin 胡琴
hutou yinzi 虎头引子
huyin 虎音
Hu Zhongwu 胡忠武

ji 急 or 疾
jiamao 加帽
jian 尖
Jiangsu Sheng Jingju Yuan
     江苏省京剧院

Jiangsu Sheng Xiqu Xuexiao
  江苏省戏曲学校
Jiang xiang he 将相和
Jiang Yan 江燕
jiang yang 江阳
jianman 渐慢
jianpu 简谱
jiao 角
"Jiao tou" 叫头
jiaqiang 加腔 (adding/additional
  melodic-passages)
jiaqiang 加强 (strengthening)
jiasangzi 假嗓子
jiawei 加尾
jiazhong 加重
jiazi hualian 架子花脸
jichu changqiang 基础唱腔
Jie dong feng 借东风
jieshu 结束
Ji jiang 祭江
jin 劲
jin da man chang 紧打慢唱
jin da san chang 紧打散唱
jing 净
jingbai 京白
jinghu 京胡
jingju 京剧
Jingju jumu chu tan 京剧剧目初探
jingluo 京锣
jingxi 京戏
ji qie fa 急切法
"Jiu chui ban" 九锤半
jiu qi 就气
Jiu qu qiao 九曲桥
jiuyinluo 九音锣
ju 句
juben changdu 剧本长度
Ju ding guan hua 举鼎观画
jue 角
juqing shijian de kuandu 剧情时间的宽度

kaichang 开场
kaida 开打

kaikou 开口
Kaishan fu 开山府
kaitou 开头
kang 亢
Kan yu chuan 勘玉钏
kao 靠
kong 空 (empty; one light beat of the
  large gong)
Kong cheng ji 空城计
kou 口
kuai 快
kuaiban 快板
"Kuai chang chui" 快长锤
kuai erliu 快二六
kuaisanyan 快三眼
kuan 宽
kuang 亢
Kuang Yaming 匡亚明
kunju 昆剧
kunqu 昆曲
kunshanqiang 昆山腔
kunyiqiang 昆弋腔
kuoqiang 扩腔
ku xiangsi 哭相思

la 拉
laodan 老旦
laosheng 老生
la yin da qiang 6 音大腔
"Leng luo" 冷锣
lian 联
Liang Huichao 梁慧超
liangong 练功
Lian Jinfeng 廉锦枫
lianpu 脸谱
lianquti 联曲体
ling 令
lingzi 翎子
Liu Debao 刘德宝
Liu Jingjie 刘静杰
liupai 流派
"Liu qing niang" 柳青娘
liushuiban 流水板

qinqiang　秦腔
Qi shuang hui　奇双会
qiyue qupai　器乐曲牌
qu　曲
quanbenxi　全本戏
quan yuedui　全乐队
qudiao　曲调
qupai　曲牌
qu qi　取气
qusheng　去声
qushi　曲式

rankou　髯口
ren chen　人臣
ruan　阮
rusheng　入声

sanban　散板
san da jian　三大件
sangyin　嗓音
sangzi　嗓子
san qi　散气
"San tang hui shen"　三堂会审
sanxian　三弦
san zhe bing ju　三者并举
saotou　扫头
"Sao tou"　扫头
secaiyin　色彩音
"Shan chui"　内锤
shang　商
shangban de banshi　上板的板式
shangchang　上场
shangchang bai　上场白
shangchang dui　上场对
shangchang shi　上场诗
shang ju　上句
shangkouzi　上口字
shangsheng　上声
Shang tian tai　上天台
Shang Xiaoyun　尚小云
shangzidiao　上字调
Sha Yu　沙钰

she　舌
sheng　生 (role type of standard male
　characters)
sheng　笙 (a multiple reed-pipe
　instrument)
shengmu　声母
shengqiang xitong　声腔系统
shengyue　声乐
Shen tou ci Tang　审头刺汤
Shen Xiaomei　沈小梅
Shen Xiaowei　沈小卫
shi　诗
shijian de gainian　时间的概念
shijie　世界
shiqiang　使腔
Shi yu zhuo　拾玉镯
shou　收
shou sheng　收声
shoushi　手势
shuban　数板
"Shui di yu"　水底鱼
shuixiu　水袖
shuqing　抒情
si　死
si ban wu yan　四板无眼
si da jian　四大件
si da ming dan　四大名旦
sigu　司鼓
sihu　四呼
Silang tan mu　四郎探母
sipingdiao　四平调
si ren bang zhihou　四人帮之后
sixian qupai　丝弦曲牌
souyin　擞音
sukun　苏昆
suluo　苏锣
suo buo　梭波
suona　唢呐

taici　台词
tan　弹
tanggu　堂鼓

tangyin 膛音
Tan Muping 谭慕平
Tan Xinpei 谭鑫培
Tao Junqi 陶君起
Tao yu shui 讨鱼税
tei 台
Tiao huache 挑滑车
tiao qi 调气
tilian 提炼
tiluo 提锣
tingxi 听戏
tong chuang yi meng 同床异梦
tongchui 铜锤
tongming 通名
tou 头
tou qi 偷气
tuan 团
tuanyuan 团圆
tuo qi 托气
tu zi 吐字

wa 哇
waixian 外弦
Wang Qinsheng 王琴生
Wang Qiu 王球
Wang Xiurong 王秀荣
Wang Yaoqing 王瑶卿
"Wan nian huan" 万年欢
wanzheng changqiang 完整唱腔
wanzheng yishu 完整艺术
wawadiao 娃娃调
wei 尾
Wei Chengwu 魏承武
weisheng 尾声
wei zhongxin 为中心
wen 文
wenchang 文场
wenchou 文丑
wenxi 文戏
wenxiaosheng 文小生
wenyan wen 文言文
wu 武

wuchang 武场
wuchou 武丑
wudan 武旦
wujing 武净
Wu Junda 武俊达
wulaosheng 武老生
Wu long yuan 乌龙院
wuqiang 五腔
wusheng 武生
wutai shijian 舞台时间
wuxi 武戏
wuxiaosheng 武小生
Wu Xingyue 吴星月
wuyin 五音
Wuzhao guan 武昭关

xi 细
xia 狭
xiachang 下场
xiachang bai 下场白
xiachang dui 下场对
xiachang shi 下场诗
xia ju 下句
xiandaiju 现代剧
xiandaixi 现代戏
"xian ding zi, hou xing qiang" 先定字, 后行腔
"xian ding zi, hou yun qiang" 先定字, 后运腔
xiangsheng 相声
xiao 箫
xiaoduan 小段
xiaogongdiao 小工调
xiao guomen 小过门
xiaohualian 小花脸
"Xiao kai men" 小开门
xiaoluo 小锣
"Xiaoluo dan shangchang" 小锣单上场
　　("Solitary Small Gong Entrance")
"Xiaoluo dan shangchang" 小锣旦上场
　　("*Dan* Small Gong Entrance")
xiaosangzi 小嗓子
xiaosheng 小生
xiaoxi 小戏

xichui　细吹
xie qi　泄气 (releasing the breath)
xie qi　歇气 (resting the breath)
xie shi　写实
xie yi　写意
xiguanyin　习惯音
xiju　戏剧
Xiju yuekan　戏剧月刊
xinbian de gudaiju　新编的古代剧
xinbian de gudaixi　新编的古代戏
xinbian de guzhuangju　新编的古装剧
xinbian de guzhuangxi　新编的古装戏
xinbian de lishiju　新编的历史剧
xinbian de lishixi　新编的历史戏
xingqiang　行腔
xingrong　形容
xingxian　行弦
xiong　胸
xipi　西皮
xiqu　戏曲
Xiqu Yinyue Zuotanhui
　戏曲音乐座谈会
xu　徐
Xu Ce pao cheng　徐策跑城
Xu Manhua　徐曼华
Xu Meiyun　徐美云
Xun Huisheng　荀慧生
Xunpai xi　荀派戏
xu qi　蓄气
xushu　叙述
Xu Xiaotao　徐小涛
Xu Yifang　许义芳
xuzi　虚字

ya　牙 (front teeth)
ya　呀 (an empty-word)
yabo　哑钹
yan　眼
yanchu shijian　演出时间
Yandang shan　雁荡山
yang　阳
Yang men nü jiang　杨门女将

yangpingsheng　阳平声
Yang Shengming　杨盛鸣
Yang Yimei　杨逸梅
yangzhe　阳辙
yan qian　言前
yanshenxing　延伸型
yanyin　延音
yaoban　摇板
Yao Mingde　姚明德
yao tiao　摇条
Yao Tongsheng　姚桐生
yao zi　咬字
ya qi　压气
yatou　丫头
Ye Hexiang　叶和祥
yi　衣 (one light beat of the clapper)
yi　乙 (a rest in which no instrument is
　played)
yi ban san yan　一板三眼
yi ban yi yan　一板一眼
yin　阴
yin duan qiang bu duan　音断腔不断
yin duan qi bu duan　音断气不断
Ying Yicheng　应宜诚
yinpingsheng　阴平声
yinzhe　阴辙
yinzi　引子
yi qi　一七
yitao dongxi　一套东西
yiyangqiang　弋阳腔
yizidiao　乙字调
yongqi　用气
you ban wu yan　有板无眼
you qiu　由求
yu　羽
yuanban　原板
yuanxing　圆性
yuedui　乐队
yueju　粤剧
yueqin　月琴
yun　韵
yunbai　韵白

yunbu 韵部

yunfu 韵腹

yunluo 云锣

yunmu 韵母

yun qiang 运腔

yuntou 韵头

yunwei 韵尾

yunzheyue 云遮月

yuqi 语气

Yu Tangchun 玉堂春

Yuzhou feng 宇宙锋

za 匝

zaju 杂剧

za qi 砸气

za yin 砸音

ze 仄

zha 扎

zhai 窄

zhang kou 张口

Zhan jing tang 斩经堂

Zhan Ma Chao 战马超

Zhan Shouzhou 战寿州

Zhan Taiping 战太平

Zhao Yuan 赵沅

zhayin 炸音

zhe 辙

zhengbian 争辩

zheng diaoshi 正调式

zhengerhuang 正二黄

zhenggongdiao 正工调

zhengmian renwu 正面人物

zhengxipi 正西皮

zhensangzi 真嗓子

zhezixi 折子戏

zhi 徵

zhinian 直念

zhiwei 雉尾

zhize 指责

zhong 重

zhongdian tuchuxing buju 重点突出型布局

zhong dong 中东

zhonghu 中胡

zhong qi xing qiang 中气行腔

Zhong Rong 钟荣

zhong xiang 中响

zhongzhiyin 终止音

Zhongzhou yun 中洲韵

Zhou Enlai 周恩来

Zhou Liping 周立平

Zhou Lixia 周丽霞

zhuanchang 转场

zhuandiao 转调

zhuangshiyin 装饰音

Zhuangyuan pu 状元谱

Zhuangzi shan fen 庄子扇坟

Zhui Han Xin 追韩信

Zhuo fang Cao 捉放曹

zhuoyin 浊音

Zhu Ya 朱雅

zi 字

zi bao jiamen 自报家门

ziran 自然

ziyou banshi 自由板式

zi zheng qiang yuan 字正腔圆

zonghexing 综合性

zuo 做

zuochang shi 坐场诗

zuogong 做功

SOURCES

SOURCES IN ENGLISH AND EUROPEAN LANGUAGES

Chang, Donald, and William Packard, trans. *The White Snake,* by Tian Han. In *The Red Pear Garden,* ed. John D. Mitchell, 49–120. Boston: David R. Godine, 1973.

Crump, J. I., and William P. Malm, eds. *Chinese and Japanese Music Dramas.* Ann Arbor: Center for Chinese Studies, University of Michigan, 1975.

Delza, Sophia. "The Classical Theatre of China." In *Total Theatre: A Critical Anthology,* ed. E. T. Kirby, 224–242. New York: E. P. Dutton, 1969.

Dolby, William. *A History of Chinese Drama.* New York: Barnes and Noble, 1976.

Halson, Elizabeth. *Peking Opera: A Short Guide.* Hong Kong: Oxford University Press, 1966.

Hsu, Dolores Menstell. "Musical Elements of Chinese Opera." *The Musical Quarterly* 50, no. 4 (Oct. 1964): 439–451.

Huang, C. C. *A Modern Chinese-English Dictionary for Students.* Reference Publication, no. 1. Lawrence, Kansas: Center for East Asian Studies, University of Kansas, 1968.

Hung, Josephine Huang, ed. and trans. *Classical Chinese Plays.* Taipei: Mei Ya Publications, 1971.

Hwang Mei-shu. "Peking Opera: A Study of the Art of Translating the Scripts with Special Reference to Structure and Conventions." Ph.D. diss., Florida State University, 1976.

Kirby, E. T. "Introduction." In *Total Theatre: A Critical Anthology,* ed. E. T. Kirby, xiii–xxxi. New York: E. P. Dutton, 1969.

Levis, John Hazedel. *Foundations of Chinese Musical Art.* Peiping [Beijing]: Henri Vetch, 1936.

Lieberman, Fredric. *Chinese Music: An Annotated Bibliography.* New York: Society for Asian Music, 1970.

———. "Some Contributions of Ethnomusicology to the Study of Oral Literature." *CHINOPERL News,* no. 5 (1975): 126–153.

Liu Wu-ch'i. *An Introduction to Chinese Literature.* Bloomington: Indiana University Press, 1966.

Mackerras, Colin P., ed. *Chinese Theatre: From Its Origins to the Present Day.* Honolulu: University of Hawaii Press, 1983.

———. *The Rise of the Peking Opera, 1770–1870: Social Aspects of the Theatre in Manchu China.* Oxford: Clarendon Press, 1972.

Mei Lanfang. "Old Art with a New Future." *China Reconstructs,* no. 4 (Sept.–Oct. 1952): 21–24.

Pian, Rulan Chao. "Aria Structural Patterns in the Peking Opera." In *Chinese and Japanese Music Dramas,* ed. J. I. Crump and William P. Malm, 65–97. Ann Arbor: Center for Chinese Studies, University of Michigan, 1975.

———. "The Functions of Rhythm in the Peking Opera." In *The Musics of Asia,* ed. Jose Maceda, 114–131. Manila: National Music Council of the Philippines, 1971.

Schonfelder, Gerd. *Die Musik der Peking-Oper.* Leipzig: Deutscher Verlag fur Musik, 1972.

Scott, A. C. *The Classical Theatre of China.* London: Allen and Unwin, 1957.

———. "The Performance of Classical Theatre." In *Chinese Theatre: From Its Origins to the Present Day,* ed. Colin P. Mackerras. Honolulu: University of Hawaii Press, 1983.

———. *Traditional Chinese Plays.* Vols. 1 and 3. Madison: University of Wisconsin Press, 1967 and 1975.

Wu Zuguang, Huang Zuolin, and Mei Shaowu. *Peking Opera and Mei Lanfang: A Guide to China's Traditional Theatre and the Art of Its Great Master.* Beijing: New World Press, 1981.

Yang, Daniel Shih-p'eng. *An Annotated Bibliography of Materials for the Study of the Peking Theatre.* Wisconsin China Series, no. 2. Madison: University of Wisconsin, 1967.

———, trans. "Black Dragon Residence." Unpublished performance script, University of Hawaii, Honolulu, 1971.

———. "Percussion Instruments and Important Percussion Scores." Unpublished listing, University of Hawaii, Honolulu, 1971.

Yung, Bell. "The Role of Speech Tones in the Creative Process of Cantonese Opera." *CHINOPERL News,* no. 5 (1975): 157–167.

SOURCES IN CHINESE

PRINTED AND WRITTEN MATERIALS

Ah Jia (阿甲). 戏曲表演论集 (*Xiqu biaoyan lunji*) (A collection of essays on the performance of *xiqu*). Shanghai: Shanghai Wenyi Chubanshe, 1962, 1979.

Beijing Waiguoyu Xueyuan Yingyu Xi Han Ying Cidian Bianxie Zu (北京外国语学院英语系汉英词典编写组) (The Chinese-English Dictionary Editorial Committee of the English Language Department of the Beijing Foreign Languages Institute), eds. 汉英词典 *Han Ying cidian* (The Chinese-English dictionary). Hong Kong: Shangwu Yinshuguan, The Commercial Press, Ltd., 1979.

Chen Weilun (陈维苍), ed. 京胡学习法 (*Jinghu xuexi fa*) (Methods of studying the *jinghu*). Shanghai: Xixue Shuchu, n.d.

Ci Hai Bianji Weiyuanhui (辞海编辑委员会) (The Ci Hai Editorial Committee), eds.

辞海 (*Ci hai*) (lit., "Sea of words/phraseology"; an encyclopedia). 3 vols. Shanghai: Shanghai Ci Shu Chubanshe, 1979.

Hao Dequan (郝德泉), Li Buhai (厉不害), Lo Xuanbing (罗选斌), eds. 徐策跑城: 周信芳演出本 (*Xu Ce pao cheng: Zhou Xinfang yanchu ben*) (Xu Ce runs on the city wall: The performance script of Zhou Xinfang). Shanghai: Shanghai Wenyi Chubanshe, 1963, 1981.

Hu Qiaomu (胡乔木), chief ed. 中国大百科全书: 戏曲曲艺 (*Zhongguo da baike quanshu: Xiqu quyi*) (Encyclopedia of China: *Xiqu* and story-telling). Beijing and Shanghai: Zhongguo Da Baike Quanshu Chubanshe, 1983.

京剧传统唱腔选集 (*Jingju chuantong changqiang xuanji*) (A selection of traditional Beijing opera melodic-passages). Beijing: Renmin Yinyue Chubanshe, 1981.

Li Jiazai (李家载) and Fan Shiren (范石人), eds. 贺后骂殿 (*He hou ma dian*) (The dowager empress He curses the throne). Shanghai: Shanghai Wenyi Chubanshe, 1963.

Li Pinrong (李品荣). 唢呐吹奏法 (*Suona chuizou fa*) (Methods of playing the *suona*). Beijing: Yinyue Chubanshe, 1957.

Li Qingsen (李庆森). 为什么男怕西皮女怕二黄? ("Weishenma nan pa xipi nü pa erhuang?") (Why are men afraid of *xipi* and women afraid of *erhuang*?). 北京艺术 (*Beijing yishu*) (Beijing art), no. 2 (1981):24.

Liu Jidian (刘吉典). 京剧音乐概论 (*Jingju yinyue gailun*) (An outline of the music of Beijing opera). Beijing: Renmin Yinyue Chubanshe, 1981.

———. 京剧音乐介绍 (*Jingju yinyue jieshao*) (An introduction to the music of Beijing opera). Beijing: Beijing Yinyue Chubanshe, 1960, 1962.

Liu Min (刘敏), ed. 怎样学二胡 (*Zenyang xue erhu*) (How to study the *erhu*). Hong Kong: Jinxiu Chubanshe, 1977.

Lo Chin-t'ang (罗锦堂). 中国戏曲总目汇编 (*Zhongguo xiqu zongmu huibian*) (A comprehensive bibliography of China's *xiqu*). Hong Kong: Wanyou Tushu Gongsi, 1966.

Lu Mai (鲁麦), ed. 怎样打锣鼓 (*Zenyang da luogu*) (How to play the percussive instruments). Hong Kong: Jinxiu Chubanshe, 1973.

Mei Lanfang (梅兰芳) (in dictation to Xu Jichuan [徐姬传]). 舞台生活四十年 (*Wutai shenghuo sishi nian*) (Forty years of life on the stage). 2 vols. Beijing: Zhongguo Xiju Chubanshe, 1961, 1980.

———. 中国戏曲艺术的新方向 ("Zhongguo xiqu yishu de xin fangxiang") (The new direction of China's *xiqu*). 文艺报 (*Wenyi bao*) (Journal of literature and art), no. 16 (1952):10–14.

Ouyang Yuqian (欧阳予倩). 我怎样学会了演京戏 (*Wo zenyang xuehuile yan jingxi*) (How I learned to perform Beijing opera). Beijing: Beijing Baowentang Shudian, 1959.

Qi Rushan (齐如山). 国剧艺术汇考 (*Guoju yishu huikao*) (A collection of studies of Beijing opera art). Taibei: Zhongguang Wenyi Chubanshe, 1962.

———. 齐如山全集 (*Qi Rushan quan ji*) (The complete works of Qi Rushan), ed.

Chen Jiying (陈纪滢) and Zhang Daxia (张大夏). 9 vols. Taibei: Qi Rushan Xiansheng Yizhu Bianyin Weiyuanhui, 1964.

Qiu Wen (秋文). 京剧流派欣赏 (*Jingju liupai xinshang*) (An appreciation of the schools of Beijing opera). Shanghai: Shanghai Wenyi Chubanshe, 1962.

Shanghai Yishu Yanjiu Suo (上海艺术研究所) (Shanghai Institute of Art Research) and Zhongguo Xijujia Xiehui Shanghai Fenhui (中国戏剧家协会上海分会) (Association of Chinese Theatre Artists, Shanghai Branch), eds. 中国戏曲曲艺词典 (*Zhongguo xiqu quyi cidian*) (Dictionary of China's *xiqu* and story-telling). Shanghai: Shanghai Cishu Chubanshe, 1981.

Sun Kaidi (孙楷弟). 傀儡戏考原 (*Kuilei xi kao yuan*) (An examination of origins in puppet theatre). Shanghai: Shangza Chubanshe, 1953.

Sun Rongbai (孙荣柏). 京剧常识讲话 (*Jingju changshi jianghua*) (A guide to general knowledge of Beijing opera). Beijing: Zhongguo Xiju Chubanshe, 1959.

Tao Junqi (陶君起). 京剧剧目初探 (*Jingju jumu chu tan*) (An initial exploration of the Beijing opera repertoire). Beijing: Zhongguo Xiju Chubanshe, 1957, 1964, 1980.

Xia Ye (夏野). 戏曲音乐研究 (*Xiqu yinyue yanjiu*) (A study of *xiqu* music). Shanghai: Shanghai Wenyi Chubanshe, 1959.

Xiao Qing (肖晴). 戏曲唱工讲话 (*Xiqu changgong jianghua*) (General knowledge of singing skill in *xiqu*). Beijing: Zhongguo Xiju Chubanshe, 1960.

Xiaweiyi Zhongguo Xiju Yanjiu She (夏威夷中国戏剧研究社) (The Chinese Theatre Research Society of Hawaii), eds. 锣鼓经 (*Luogu jing*) (Percussive classics). Honolulu: Xiaweiyi Zhongguo Xiju Yanjiu She, n.d.

Xu Fuming (徐扶明). 元代杂剧艺术 (*Yuandai zaju yishu*) (The art of Yuan dynasty *zaju*). Shanghai: Shanghai Wenyi Chubanshe, 1981.

Xu Lanyuan (徐兰源). 徐兰源操琴生活 (*Xu Lanyuan caoqin shenghuo*) (Xu Lanyuan's life as a *huqin* player). 4 vols. Beijing (?): hand-copied version, n.p., n.d.

Xun Huisheng (荀慧生). 荀慧生演剧散论 (*Xun Huisheng yanju sanlun*) (Xun Huisheng's random essays on theatrical performance). Shanghai: Shanghai Wenyi Chubanshe, 1963, 1980.

Yan Songzhou (晏诵周). 京胡演奏法 (*Jinghu yanzou fa*) (Methods of playing the *jinghu*). Beijing: Yinyue Chubanshe, 1956.

Yang Mao (扬貌). 京剧常识 (*Jingju changshi*) (General knowledge of Beijing opera). Shanghai: Shanghai Wenyi Chubanshe, n.d.

Yu Binsheng (余滨生). 国剧音韵及唱念法研究 (*Guoju yin yun ji chang nian fa yanjiu*) (A study of rhyme schemes and the techniques of song and speech in Beijing opera). Taibei: Zhonghua Shuju, 1972.

Yu Dagang (俞大纲). 国剧简介 (*Guoju jianjie*) (A brief introduction to Beijing opera). Taibei: Jiaoyubu Shehui Jiaoyusi Bianyin, n.d.

Yuan Yong (元泳) and Liu Shui (流水). 京剧的曲调与板式 ("Jingju de qudiao yu banshi") (The tunes and metrical types of Beijing opera). 辽宁戏剧 (*Liaoning xiju*) (Liaoning theatre), no. 6 (1980):10–11.

在中国戏剧家协会第三次会员代表大会上赵寻同志作剧协工作报告 ("Zai Zhong-guo Xijujia Xiehui disanci huiyuan daibiao dahui shang, Zhao Xun tongzhi zuo Ju Xie gongzuo baogao") (At the third general meeting of member delegates of the Association of Chinese Theatre Artists, comrade Zhao Xun reports on the work of the Association). 人民戏剧 (*Renmin xiju*) (People's theatre), no. 12 (1979):8–16.

Zhang Geng (张庚). 戏曲艺术论 (*Xiqu yishu lun*) (On *xiqu* art). Beijing: Zhongguo Xiju Chubanshe, 1980.

Zhang Yuci (张宇慈) and Wu Chunli (吴春礼), comps. and eds. 京剧唱腔 (*Jingju changqiang*) (Beijing opera melodic-passages). Vol. 1, parts 1 and 2. Beijing: Yinyue Chubanshe, 1959.

———, eds. 京剧曲牌简编 (*Jingju qupai jianbian*) (A concise edition of Beijing opera fixed-melodies). Beijing: Zhongguo Xiju Chubanshe, 1960.

Zhongguo Jingju Yuan Zong Daoyan Shi Yinyue Zu (中国京剧院总导演室音乐组) (The Music Group of the Chief Director's Office of the China Beijing Opera Company), eds. 京剧唱腔选集 (*Jingju changqiang xuanji*) (A selection of Beijing opera melodic-passages). Vol. 1. Beijing: Yinyue Chubanshe, 1958, 1959.

Zhongguo Xijujia Xiehui (中国戏剧家协会) (The Association of Chinese Theatre Artists), eds. 梅兰芳演出剧本选集 (*Mei Lanfang yanchu juben xuanji*) (A selection of Mei Lanfang's performance scripts). Beijing: Zhongguo Xiju Chubanshe, 1961, 1980.

Zhongguo Xiqu Xueyuan (中国戏曲学院) (The China *Xiqu* Academy), eds. 京剧选编 (*Jingju xuanbian*) (Selected Beijing operas). Vols. 3–5. Beijing: Zhongguo Xiju Chubanshe, 1980.

Zhongguo Xiqu Yanjiu Yuan (中国戏曲研究院) (The China Academy of *Xiqu* Research), eds. 京剧唱腔, 第一集, 下编 (老生, 小生) (*Jingju changqiang, di yi ji, xia bian: laosheng, xiaosheng*) (Beijing opera melodic-passages, volume one, last part: older *sheng*, young *sheng*). Beijing: Yinyue Chubanshe, 1959.

———, eds. 梅兰芳演出剧本选集曲谱 (*Mei Lanfang yanchu juben xuanji qupu*) (Selected scores from the performance scripts of Mei Lanfang). Beijing: Yinyue Chubanshe, 1959.

———, eds. 玉堂春: 程砚秋唱腔选集之二 (*Yu Tangchun: Cheng Yanqiu changqiang xuanji zhi er*) (Yu Tangchun: Selections from the melodic-passages of Cheng Yanqiu, the second selection). Beijing: Yinyue Chubanshe, 1960.

Zhongguo Yishu Yanjiu Yuan Yinyue Yanjiu Suo, Zhongguo Yinyue Cidian Bianji Bu (中国艺术研究院音乐研究所, 中国音乐词典编辑部) (The Music Research Institute of the China Academy of Art Research, Dictionary of Chinese Music Editorial Department), eds. 中国音乐词典 (*Zhongguo yinyue cidian*) (Dictionary of Chinese music). Beijing: Renmin Yinyue Chubanshe, 1984.

Zhou Xiyuan (周羲园) and Ni Qiuping (倪秋平), eds. 审头刺汤 (*Shen tou ci Tang*)

(Investigating the head and executing Tang). Shanghai: Shanghai Wenyi Chubanshe, 1962.

Zhou Yibai (周贻白), ed. 戏曲演唱论著辑释 (*Xiqu yanchang lunzhu jishi*) (An edited and interpreted treatise on the performance of song in *xiqu*). Beijing: Zhongguo Xiju Chubanshe, 1962, 1980.

———. 中国戏剧史 (*Zhongguo xiju shi*) (History of Chinese theatre). 3 vols. Shanghai: Zhonghua Shuju, 1953.

———. 中国戏曲发展史纲要 (*Zhongguo xiqu fazhan shi gangyao*) (An outline history of the development of China's *xiqu*). Shanghai: Shanghai Guji Chubanshe, 1979.

PLAYS ATTENDED IN LIVE PERFORMANCE

[In many instances I attended more than one performance of a single production; the date listed here indicates the first performance attended for a given production. Successive dates indicate my initial attendance at different productions of the same play by the same company. The designation RP means that I also attended the entire rehearsal process for the production; CR indicates that I have made a complete audio recording of the production. The majority of productions attended were those of the Jiangsu Province Beijing Opera Company (Jiangsu Sheng Jingju Yuan 江苏省京剧院); for brevity's sake, the name of that company is abbreviated as JPBOC in this listing. The names of all other companies are given in full.]

The Battle of Shouzhou (*Zhan Shouzhou* 战寿州). JPBOC, Nanjing. Dir. Liang Huichao (梁慧超). With Dong Jinfeng (董金凤) and Zhan Guozhi (詹国治). Nov. 23, 1979. RP, CR.

Borrowing the Fan (*Jie shan* 借扇). JPBOC, Nanjing. With Chen Baoqin (陈宝琴) and Luo Liankun (罗连坤). Dec. 8, 1979. RP.

The Butterfly Cup (*Hudie bei* 蝴蝶杯). JPBOC, Nanjing. Dir. Shi Yukun (石玉昆). With Shen Xiaomei (沈小梅) and Yang Xiaoqing (扬小卿). July 22, 1980.

The Case of the Murder of Mei (*Zha Mei an* 铡美案). 上海京剧一团 (Shanghai Jingju Yi Tuan) (The First Troupe of the Shanghai Beijing Opera Company), Shanghai. March 28, 1980.

Chen Sanliang (*Chen Sanliang* 陈三两). JPBOC, Nanjing. With Zhong Rong (钟荣) and Zhan Guozhi (詹国治). Dec. 16, 1979. RP, CR.

Chun Cao Braves the Court (*Chun Cao chuang tang* 春草闯堂). JPBOC, Nanjing. With Huang Xiaoci (黄孝慈). Oct. 31, 1979; Feb. 26, 1980.

The Cosmic Blade (*Yuzhou feng* 宇宙锋). JPBOC, Nanjing. With Shen Xiaomei (沈小梅), Fu Guansong (付关松), and Zong Yunlan (宗云兰). March 28, 1980. RP.

Destiny in the Cabinet (*Gui zhong yuan* 柜中缘). JPBOC, Nanjing. With Zhang Ling (张玲), Zhu Hongfa (朱鸿发), and Ji Huimin (季慧敏). May 1, 1980.

Dragon Palace Borrows a Treasure (*Long gong jie bao* 龙宫借宝). JPBOC, Nanjing. May 28, 1980.

Ehu Village (*Ehu cun* 恶虎村). JPBOC, Nanjing. Dec. 6, 1979. CR.

Eight Immortals Float on the Sea (*Ba xian piao hai* 八仙飘海). JPBOC, Nanjing. With Xu Meiyun (徐美云), Wang Pengyun (汪朋云), Sha Yu (沙钰), and Zhang Licai (张立才). Nov. 11, 1979; Jan. 1, 1979; May 20, 1980.

Eighteen Lohans Struggle with Wukong (*Shiba lohan dou Wukong* 十八罗汉斗悟空). JPBOC, Nanjing. Dir. Ma Miaofang (马妙芳). With Zhou Yunliang (周云亮). Jan. 16, 1981.

An Entrancing Woman Separates from Her Soul (*Qian nü li hun* 倩女离魂). JPBOC, Nanjing. With Shen Xiaomei (沈小梅) and Yang Xiaoqing (扬小卿). May 10, 1980. RP, CR.

The Favorite Concubine Becomes Intoxicated (*Guifei zui jiu* 贵妃醉酒). JPBOC, Nanjing. With Shen Xiaomei (沈小梅). April 30, 1980. RP, CR.

Fighting Jiao Zan (*Da Jiao Zan* 打焦赞). 苏州市京剧团 (Suzhou Shi Jingju Tuan) (Suzhou City Beijing Opera Troupe), Suzhou. With Zhang Lizhu (张丽珠) and Xiao Zhang Yipeng (小张翼鹏). Nov. 6, 1979.

Hong Niang (*Hong Niang* 红娘). JPBOC, Nanjing. With Gong Suping (龚素萍), Chen Baoqin (陈宝琴), and Zhan Guozhi (詹国治). Jan. 16, 1981. CR.

Hongyang Cave (*Hongyang dong* 洪羊洞). 苏州市京剧团 (Suzhou Shi Jingju Tuan) (Suzhou City Beijing Opera Troupe), Suzhou. With Yu Shaoquan (俞少荃), Liu Chuanhai (刘传海), and Xu Hongliang (许洪良). Nov. 6, 1979.

Investigating the Jade Bracelets (*Kan yu chuan* 勘玉钏). JPBOC, Nanjing. With Huang Xiaoci (黄孝慈). May 28, 1980. Also, 北京京剧二团 (Beijing Jingju Er Tuan) (The Second Troupe of the Beijing Opera Company of Beijing), Beijing. With Xun Linglai (荀令莱). Aug. 15, 1980.

Jing De Feigns Madness (*Jing De zhuang feng* 敬德装疯). JPBOC, Nanjing. With Li Zhiyu (李植玉) and Chen Baoqin (陈宝琴). May 11, 1980. CR.

Li Huiniang (*Li Huiniang* 李慧娘). 苏州市京剧团 (Suzhou Shi Jingju Tuan) (Suzhou City Beijing Opera Troupe), Suzhou. Script by Pang Genhui (庞根会). Dir. Lu Yongchang (陆永昌). With Hu Zhifeng (胡芝凤), Chen Shaohua (陈少华), Xu Hongliang (许鸿良), and Liu Chuanhai (刘传海). Nov. 3, 1979.

The Locked Bag (*Suo lin nang* 锁麟囊). JPBOC, Nanjing. With Zhong Rong (钟荣). May 20, 1980. RP.

Lü Bu and Diao Chan (*Lü Bu yu Diao Chan* 吕布与貂蝉). JPBOC, Nanjing. With Yang Xiaoqing (扬小卿) and Huang Xiaoci (黄孝慈). Jan. 15, 1980; May 14, 1980. CR.

Meeting in the Mulberry Field (*Sang yuan hui* 桑园会). 上海京剧一团 (Shanghai Jingju Yi Tuan) (The First Troupe of the Shanghai Beijing Opera Company), Shanghai. March 28, 1980.

Memorial for Judge Bao (*Ji Bao gong* 祭包公). JPBOC, Nanjing. Script by Huang Yuqi (黄玉琪) and Pan Heyun (潘鹤云). Dir. Pan Heyun (潘鹤云). With Huang Xiaoping (黄晓萍) and Li Zhiyu (李植玉). Jan. 9, 1980. RP, CR.

The Mu Family Axhandle Stockade (*Mu ke zhai* 穆柯寨). 江苏省戏曲学校试验京剧团 (Jiangsu Sheng Xiqu Xuexiao Shiyan Jingju Tuan) (Jiangsu Province School of Xiqu, Experimental Beijing Opera Troupe), Nanjing. Feb. 16, 1980.

Obstructing the Horse (*Dang ma* 挡马). 苏州市京剧团 (Suzhou Shi Jingju Tuan) (Suzhou City Beijing Opera Troupe), Suzhou. With Shen Xiajuan (沈霞娟) and Zhang Lingde (张令德). Nov. 6, 1979. Also, 上海京剧一团 (Shanghai Jingju Yi Tuan) (The First Troupe of the Shanghai Beijing Opera Company), Shanghai. March 28, 1980.

Orphan of the Zhao Family (*Zhao shi guer* 赵氏孤儿). 南京市京剧团 (Nanjing Shi Jingju Tuan) (Nanjing City Beijing Opera Troupe), Nanjing. Sept. 20, 1979. Also, 上海京剧一团 (Shanghai Jingju Yi Tuan) (The First Troupe of the Shanghai Beijing Opera Company), Shanghai. Script revised by Wang Yan (王雁). Dir. Wang Yan (王雁). With Zhang Xuejin (张学津). March 27, 1980.

Overturning the War Machine (*Tiao huache* 挑滑车). JPBOC, Nanjing. Nov. 11, 1979; Jan. 5, 1980.

Picking Up the Jade Bracelet (*Shi yu zhuo* 拾玉镯). JPBOC, Nanjing. With Zhang Ling (张玲), Zhu Hongfa (朱鸿发), and Wang Pengyun (汪朋云). Nov. 11, 1979. Also, 北京试验京剧团 (Beijing Shiyan Jingju Tuan) (Beijing Experimental Beijing Opera Troupe), Beijing. With Li Yuxiu (李宇秀), Zhang Xueji (张学济), and Wang Xiaolin (王晓临). Aug. 19, 1981.

A Pig Butcher Places First in the Imperial Examinations (*Tufu zhuangyuan* 屠夫状元). JPBOC, Nanjing. Dir. Shi Yukun (石玉昆). With Jiang Yan (江燕), Wang Changhai (王长海), Zhan Guozhi (詹国治), Zhao Liyong (赵立庸), and Chen Junling (陈君玲). March 30, 1980. RP.

Record of Bloody Injustice (*Xue yuan ji* 血冤记). 苏州市京剧团 (Suzhou Shi Jingju Tuan) (Suzhou City Beijing Opera Troupe), Suzhou. Script by Wu Shijian (吴石坚), Bai Dongwu (白东吾), Jin Xun (金煦), and Li Chunting (李春亭). Dir. Li Chunting (李春亭) and Zhang Shanhong (张善鸿). With Fu Yiqun (傅艺群) and Hu Zhifeng (胡芝凤). Nov. 8, 1979.

Seven Warriors and Five Righteous Men (*Qi xia wu yi* 七侠五义). 上海京剧三团 (Shanghai Jingju San Tuan) (The Third Troupe of the Shanghai Beijing Opera Company), Shanghai. Script by Xu Siyan (许思言). Dir. Li Zhonglin (李仲林). With Qi Shufang (齐淑芳). April 13, 1980.

Silang Visits His Mother (*Silang tan mu* 四郎探母). JPBOC, Nanjing. With Wang Qinsheng (王琴生). Nov. 11, 1979. With Liang Huichao (梁慧超). Dec. 8, 1979. CR. With Lu Genzhang (陆根章). March 15, 1980. RP. Also, 上海京剧一团 (Shanghai Jingju Yi Tuan) (The First Troupe of the Shanghai Beijing Opera Company), Shanghai. With Zhang Xuejin (张学津). March 31, 1980. CR.

Stealing the Mushroom of Immortality (*Dao xian cao* 盗仙草). JPBOC, Nanjing. With Ai Jinmei (艾金梅), Wu Xingyue (吴星月), and Yang Yunkun (扬云坤). May 11, 1980. RP.

Strike of the Gold Brick (*Da jin zhuan* 打金砖). 北京试验京剧团 (Beijing Shiyan Jingju Tuan) (Beijing Experimental Beijing Opera Troupe), Beijing. With Li Haotian (李浩天), Liu Yonggui (刘永贵), and Xu Xiuqin (徐秀琴). Aug. 19, 1981.

Sun Wukong Stirs Up Trouble in Heaven (*Sun Wukong da nao tiangong* 孙悟空大闹天宫). JPBOC, Nanjing. With Zhou Yunliang (周云亮). Dec. 12, 1979; May 1, 1980.

Tears of the Pipa (*Pipa lei* 琵琶泪). JPBOC, Nanjing. Script by Feng Yucheng (冯玉玶) and Jin Enqu (金恩渠). Dir. Feng Yucheng (冯玉玶) and You Chengren (尤诚仁). With Wang Qinsheng (王琴生), Huang Xiaoping (黄晓萍), Lu Genzhang (陆根章), Huang Kailiang (黄凯良), and Gong Suping (龚苏萍). Oct. 28, 1979.

Tablets of Life and Death (*Sheng si pai* 生死牌). JPBOC, Nanjing. Dir. You Chengren (尤诚仁). With Lu Genzhang (陆根章), Huang Kailiang (黄凯良), Zhong Rong (钟荣), and Sha Yu (沙钰). Nov. 4, 1979.

Three Attacks on Zhu Village (*San da Zhujiazhuang* 三打祝家庄). 旅大市京剧团 (Lüda Shi Jingju Tuan) (Lüda City Beijing Opera Troupe), Dalian. Script by Wei Chenxu (魏晨旭), Li Lun (李纶), and Ren Guilin (任桂林). July 12, 1978.

The True and the False Sun Wukong (*Zhen jia Sun Wukong* 真假孙悟空). JPBOC, Nanjing. With Zhou Yunliang (周云亮) and Zhu Hongfa (朱鸿发). Feb. 5, 1980. RP, CR.

Wang Xifeng Disrupts Ningguo Prefecture (*Wang Xifeng da nao Ningguo fu* 王熙凤大闹宁国府). JPBOC, Nanjing. Script by Chen Xiting (陈西汀). Dir. Shi Yukun (石玉昆). With Zhao Daoying (赵道英) and Jiang Yan (江燕). Nov. 19, 1980; Jan. 14, 1981.

Where Three Roads Meet (*San cha kou* 三岔口). JPBOC, Nanjing. Dec. 12, 1979. Also, 上海京剧一团 (Shanghai Jingju Yi Tuan) (The First Troupe of the Shanghai Beijing Opera Company), Shanghai. March 31, 1980.

The White Haired Girl (*Bai mao nü* 白毛女). 江苏省戏曲学校青年试验京剧团 (Jiangsu Sheng Xiqu Xuexiao Qingnian Shiyan Jingju Tuan) (Jiangsu Province School of Xiqu, Young People's Experimental Beijing Opera Troupe), Nanjing. Dir. Yang Shengming (扬盛鸣). Feb. 19, 1981. RP.

The White Snake (*Bai she zhuan* 白蛇传). JPBOC, Nanjing. With Huang Xiaoping (黄晓萍) and Xu Meiyun (徐美云). June 24, 1980.

Wu Song (*Wu Song* 武松). 苏州市京剧团 (Suzhou Shi Jingju Tuan) (Suzhou City Beijing Opera Troupe), Suzhou. With Xiao Zhang Yiping (小张翼鹏) and Feng Younian (冯友年). Nov. 9, 1979.

Yandang Mountain (*Yandang shan* 雁荡山). JPBOC, Nanjing. With Ji Penglin
  (稽朋林) and Wang Xingkang (王兴康). May 11, 1980.
Yu Tangchun (*Yu Tangchun* 玉堂春). JPBOC, Nanjing. With Huang Xiaoping
  (黄晓萍) and Zhang Shilan (张世兰). Nov. 1, 1979. With Zhong Rong
  (钟荣) and Zhang Shilan (张世兰), Nov. 20, 1979. With Jiang Yan (江燕),
  Huang Kailiang (黄凯良), Wang Pengyun (汪朋云), and Zhan Guozhi
  (詹国治). May 22, 1980. RP, CR.

PLAYS ATTENDED IN FILMED VERSION

The Broken Bridge (*Duan qiao* 断桥). With Mei Lanfang (梅兰芳). Part 1 of
  纪念梅兰芳舞台艺术五十年 (*Jinian Mei Lanfang wutai yishu wushi nian*)
  (Commemorating the fiftieth year of Mei Lanfang's stage art). Beijing, 1955.
The Cosmic Blade (*Yuzhou feng* 宇宙锋). With Mei Lanfang (梅兰芳). Part 2 of
  纪念梅兰芳舞台艺术五十年 (*Jinian Mei Lanfang wutai yishu wushi nian*)
  (Commemorating the fiftieth year of Mei Lanfang's stage art). Beijing, 1955.
The Favorite Concubine Becomes Intoxicated (*Guifei zui jiu* 贵妃醉酒). With Mei
  Lanfang (梅兰芳). Part 4 of 纪念梅兰芳舞台艺术五十年 (*Jinian Mei Lan-
  fang wutai yishu wushi nian*) (Commemorating the fiftieth year of Mei Lan-
  fang's stage art). Beijing, 1955.
Four Successful Examinees: Song Shijie (*Si jin shi: Song Shijie* 四进士: 宋士杰). With
  Zhou Xinfang (周信芳). Shanghai (?), 195?.
The Hegemon King Parts with His Favorite (*Bawang bie ji* 霸王别姬). With Mei
  Lanfang (梅兰芳). Part 3 of 纪念梅兰芳舞台艺术五十年 (*Jinian Mei Lan-
  fang wutai yishu wushi nian*) (Commemorating the fiftieth year of Mei Lan-
  fang's stage art). Beijing, 1955.
The Pursuit of Han Xin (*Zhui Han Xin* 追韩信). With Zhou Xinfang (周信芳).
  Shanghai (?), 195?.
The White Snake (*Bai she zhuan* 白蛇传). Shanghai, 1980.
Wild Boar Forest (*Ye zhu lin* 野猪林). With Li Shaochun (李少春) and Du Jinfang
  (杜近芳). Shanghai (?), 195?.

PLAYS BROADCAST ON RADIO AND RECORDED

[All plays and play excerpts recorded were broadcast by the Jiangsu Guangbo Di-
antai (Jiangsu Broadcasting Company) between February and July 1981; specific
dates of broadcast and other pertinent bibliographic material were not noted and
therefore cannot be listed here.]

Beating the Drum and Cursing Cao Cao (*Ji gu ma Cao* 击鼓骂曹).
The Capture of Five Dragons (*Suo wu long* 锁五龙).
Catching and Releasing Cao Cao (*Zhuo fang Cao* 捉放曹).
The Dowager Empress He Curses the Throne (*He hou ma dian* 贺后骂殿).

Exchange on the Execution Ground (*Fachang huan zi* 法场换子).
The Fisherman's Revenge (*Dayu sha jia* 打渔杀家).
Flag of the Blazing Pearl (*Zhenzhu liehuo qi* 珍珠烈火旗).
Killing Bao Mian (*Zha Bao Mian* 铡包勉).
The Love of the Butterfly and the Flower (*Die lian hua* 蝶恋花).
The Peacock Flies to the Southeast (*Kongque dong nan fei* 孔雀东南飞).
The Ruse of the Empty City (*Kong cheng ji* 空城计).
Tears of the Desolate Mountain (*Huang shan lei* 荒山泪).
Third Sister You (*You Sanjie* 尤三姐).
Yingtai Resists Marriage (*Yingtai kang hun* 英台抗婚).
Zhan Tianyou (*Zhan Tianyou* 詹天佑).

PERSONAL INTERVIEWS AND CONVERSATIONS

[Most of the individuals listed are members of the Jiangsu Province Beijing Opera Company (Jiangsu Sheng Jingju Yuan 江苏省京剧院) in Nanjing. I was at the Company daily from November 1979 to June 1980, and frequently from September 1980 to July 1981; all company members listed were formally interviewed several times each, in addition to innumerable informal conversations. The following list therefore does not reiterate the period of our contact for members of that company.]

Performers

Chen Baoqin (陈宝琴).
Chen Junling (陈君玲).
Dong Jinfeng (董金凤).
Fu Guansong (傅关松).
Ge Dexiang (葛德祥).
Gong Suping (龚苏萍).
Gui Weizhen (桂卫桢).
Guo Haiting (郭海亭).
Han Junkui (韩俊奎).
Han Junming (韩俊鸣).
Huang Kailiang (黄凯良).
Huang Kexiao (黄克孝).
Huang Xiaoping (黄晓萍).
Jiang Yan (江燕).
Li Fuzhong (李福忠).
Li Yongcai (李永才).
Li Zhiyu (李植玉).
Liu Changyu (刘长瑜). Beijing. Aug. 15, 1980.
Liu Debao (刘德宝).
Liu Ranhua (刘然华).

Liu Zhixiang (刘志翔).
Lu Genzhang (陆根章).
Luo Liankun (罗连坤).
Qi Shufang (齐淑芳). Shanghai. April 1980.
Qu Shousen (曲守森).
Sha Yu (沙钰).
Shen Xiaomei (沈小梅).
Tao Meijuan (陶美娟).
Wang Changhai (王长海).
Wang Pengyun (汪朋云).
Wang Qinsheng (王琴生).
Wei Chengwu (魏承武).
Wu Xingyue (吴星月).
Xu Meiyun (徐美云).
Xu Xiaotao (徐小涛). Nanjing. Oct. 1980–Jan. 1981.
Xun Linglai (荀令莱). Beijing. Aug. 15, 1980.
Yan Shaokui (颜少奎).
Yang Xiaoqing (扬小卿).
Yu Shouqi (于守启).
Zhan Guozhi (詹国治).
Zhang Licai (张立才).
Zhang Shilan (张世兰).
Zhang Xuejin (张学津). Shanghai. April 1980.
Zhao Liyong (赵立庸).
Zhong Rong (钟荣).
Zhou Yunliang (周云亮).
Zhu Hongfa (朱鸿发).
Zhu Ya (朱雅).
Zong Yunlan (宗云兰).

Musicians

Bian Shuangxi (卞双喜). Nanjing. Jan.–March 1980.
Fang Jinsen (方锦森).
Hu Zhongwu (胡忠武). Nanjing. Jan.–May 1980.
Shen Yang (沈阳).
Xu Yifang (许义芳). Nanjing. Jan.–March 1980.
Yao Mingde (姚明德).
Yao Tongsheng (姚桐生).
Ye Hexiang (叶和祥).

Directors

Liang Huichao (梁慧超).
Liu Jingjie (刘静杰). Nanjing. Dec. 1980–Jan. 1981.

Pan Heyun (潘鹤云).
Shi Yukun (石玉昆).
Yang Shengming (扬盛鸣). Nanjing. Oct.–Nov. 1980.
You Chengren (尤诚仁).

Playwrights and Research Fellows

Huang Yuqi (黄玉琪).
Wu Junda (武俊达). Nanjing. Oct. 1980–July 1981.

INDEX